Lecture Notes in Computer Science 7374

Commenced Publication in 1973
Founding and Former Series Editors:
Gerhard Goos, Juris Hartmanis, and Jan van Leeuwen

Aikaterini Mitrokotsa Serge Vaudenay (Eds.)

Progress in Cryptology - AFRICACRYPT 2012

5th International Conference on Cryptology in Africa
Ifrane, Morocco, July 10-12, 2012
Proceedings

 Springer

Volume Editors

Aikaterini Mitrokotsa
Serge Vaudenay
École Polytechnique Fédérale de Lausanne, IC LASEC
Bâtiment INF, Station 14, 1015 Lausanne, Switzerland
E-mail: {katerina.mitrokotsa, serge.vaudenay}@epfl.ch

ISSN 0302-9743   e-ISSN 1611-3349
ISBN 978-3-642-31409-4   e-ISBN 978-3-642-31410-0
DOI 10.1007/978-3-642-31410-0
Springer Heidelberg Dordrecht London New York

Library of Congress Control Number: 2012940535

CR Subject Classification (1998): E.3, K.6.5, C.2.0, C.2, E.4, K.4.4, H.4, J.1, F.2

LNCS Sublibrary: SL 4 – Security and Cryptology

Typesetting: Camera-ready by author, data conversion by Scientific Publishing Services, Chennai, India

Printed on acid-free paper

Springer is part of Springer Science+Business Media (www.springer.com)

Preface

The 5th Africacrypt conference was held July 10–12, 2012 in Ifrane, Morocco. It followed previous editions in Casablanca, Morocco (2008), Gammarth, Tunisia (2009), Stellenbosch, South Africa (2010), and Dakar, Senegal (2011).

The goal of the conference is to present research advances in the area of cryptography. It aims at bringing together in a friendly atmosphere researchers from all countries, beyond borders and political issues.

The conference received 56 submissions. They went through a doubly anonymous review process aided by 42 Program Committee members and 54 external reviewers. Our submission software invited authors to indicate from which continent they were. We counted 12 papers with at least one co-author from Africa.

Our invited talks were given by:

- Willi Meier (University of Applied Sciences and Arts Northwestern Switzerland) - *Stream Ciphers, A Perspective*
- Craig Gentry (IBM) - *Fully Homomorphic Encryption: Current State of the Art*
- Marc Fischlin (The Darmstadt University of Technology, Germany) - *Black-Box Reductions and Separations in Cryptography*

This volume represents the revised version of the 24 accepted contributed papers which were presented at the conference along with abstracts of invited speakers.

The Program Committee selected a paper to award. Committee members were invited to oppose to nominated papers and to vote on remaining ones. After this selection, the Program Committee decided to give the Africacrypt 2012 Best Paper Award to Elena Andreeva, Bart Mennink, Bart Preneel, and Marjan Skrobot for their paper:

"Security Analysis and Comparison of the SHA-3 Finalists BLAKE, Groestl, JH, Keccak, and Skein"

The submission and review process was done using the *iChair* Web-based software system developed by Thomas Baignères and Matthieu Finiasz.

We would like to thank the authors of all submitted papers. Moreover, we are indebted to the members of the Program Committee and the external subreviewers for their diligent work. We would also like to acknowledge the conference organizers and the Steering Committee for supporting us and for the excellent collaboration we had.

Finally, we heartily thank the sponsors of Africacrypt 2012 for their generous support.

Aikaterini Mitrokotsa
Serge Vaudenay

Organization

Conference Chairs

General Chairs

Abdelhak Azhari   Ecole Normale Supérieure de Casablanca, Morocco

Tajjeeddine Rachidi   Al Akhawayn University in Ifrane, Morocco

Program Chair

Serge Vaudenay   EPFL, Switzerland

Publication Chair

Aikaterini Mitrokotsa   EPFL, Switzerland

Program Committee

Hatem M. Bahig	Ain Shams University, Egypt
Hussain Ben-Azza	Ensam-Meknès, Moulay Ismail University, Morocco
Alex Biryukov	University of Luxembourg, Luxembourg
Ivan Bjerre Damgård	University of Aarhus, Denmark
Riaal Domingues	South African Communications Security Agency, South Africa
Orr Dunkelman	University of Haifa and Weizmann Institute, Israel
Georg Fuchsbauer	University of Bristol, UK
Mustapha Hedabou	ENSA of Safi, Morocco
Antoine Joux	University of Versailles, France
Mike Just	Glasgow Caledonian University, UK
Seny Kamara	Microsoft Research, USA
Aggelos Kiayias	University of Athens, Greece
Evangelos Kranakis	Carleton University, Canada
Pascal Lafourcade	Verimag, University of Grenoble, France
Pil Joong Lee	Pohang University of Science and Technology (POSTECH), Korea
Reynald Lercier	DGA & University of Rennes, France
Helger Lipmaa	University of Tartu, Estonia
Javier Lopez	University of Malaga, Spain
Bruno Martin	University of Nice-Sophia Antipolis, France
Barbara Masucci	University of Salerno, Italy
Kanta Matsuura	The University of Tokyo, Japan

Aikaterini Mitrokotsa   EPFL, Switzerland
David Naccache   Ecole Normale Supérieure, France
Phong Nguyen   INRIA, France, and Tsinghua University, China
Abderrahmane Nitaj   University of Caen, France
Kaisa Nyberg   Aalto University, Finland
Ayoub Otmani   University of Caen and ENSICAEN, France
Khaled Ouafi   EPFL, Switzerland
Kenny Paterson   Royal Holloway University of London, UK
Goutam Paul   Jadavpur University, India
Christian Rechberger   DTU, Denmark
Magdy Saeb   Arab Academy of Science and Technology,
                             Egypt
Rei Safavi-Naini   University of Calgary, Canada
Taizo Shirai   Sony Corporation, Japan
Djiby Sow   Cheikh Anta Diop University, Senegal
Martijn Stam   University of Bristol, UK
Ron Steinfeld   Macquarie University, Australia
Christine Swart   University of Cape Town, South Africa
Serge Vaudenay   EPFL, Switzerland
Ingrid Verbauwhede   K.U. Leuven, Belgium
Christopher Wolf   Ruhr University Bochum, Germany
Amr Youssef   Concordia University, Canada

External Reviewers

Ahmad Ahmadi   Pooya Farshim   Miodrag Mihaljevic
Hadi Ahmadi   Anna Lisa Ferrara   Shiho Moriai
Toru Akishita   Martin Gagné   Kris Narayan
Mohsen Alimomeni   David Galindo   Svetla Nikova
Tomoyuki Asano   Sourav Sen Gupta   Onur Özen
Josep Balasch   Anthony Van Herrewege   Sumit Kumar Pandey
Rishiraj Bhattacharyya   M. Jason Hinek   Ludovic Perret
Olivier Blazy   Sebastiaan Indesteege   Rodrigo Roman
Julia Borghoff   Kimmo Järvinen   Vladimir Rudskoy
Ioana Boureanu   Saqib A. Kakvi   Katerina Samari
Billy Brumley   Nikos Karvelas   Kyoji Shibutani
Pierre-Louis Cayrel   Geonwoo Kim   Rosemberg Silva
Rafik Chaabouni   Aleksandar Kircanski   Petr Sušil
Ashish Choudhury   Gregor Leander   Bogdan Warinschi
Marion Daubignard   Eun Sung Lee   Bingsheng Zhang
Jean Paul Degabriele   Jin-woo Lee   Wei Zhang
Vivien Dubois   Vadim Lyubashevsky
Nadia El Mrabet   Roel Maes
Mohamed Elkadi   Nele Mentens

Table of Contents

Network Security Protocols

Public-Key Cryptography

Cryptanalysis of Hash Functions

Hash Functions: Design and Implementation

Algorithms for Public-Key Cryptography

Cryptographic Protocols

Invited Talks

Batch Verification of ECDSA Signatures

Sabyasachi Karati[1], Abhijit Das[1], Dipanwita Roychowdhury[1],
Bhargav Bellur[2], Debojyoti Bhattacharya[2], and Aravind Iyer[2]

[1] Department of Computer Science and Engineering
Indian Institute of Technology Kharagpur, India
{skarati,abhij,drc}@cse.iitkgp.ernet.in
[2] General Motors Technical Centre India
India Science Lab, Bangalore, India
bhargav_bellur@yahoo.com,
Debojyoti.bhattacharya@gmail.com,
aravind.iyer@gm.com

Abstract. In this paper, we study several algorithms for batch verification of ECDSA signatures. The first of these algorithms is based upon the naive idea of taking square roots in the underlying field. We also propose two new and efficient algorithms which replace square-root computations by symbolic manipulations. Experiments carried out on NIST prime curves demonstrate a maximum speedup of above six over individual verification if all the signatures in the batch belong to the same signer, and a maximum speedup of about two if the signatures in the batch belong to different signers, both achieved by a fast variant of our second symbolic-manipulation algorithm. In terms of security, all the studied algorithms are equivalent to standard ECDSA* batch verification. These algorithms are practical only for small ($\leqslant 8$) batch sizes. To the best of our knowledge, this is the first reported study on the batch verification of *original* ECDSA signatures.

Keywords: Digital Signatures, Elliptic Curves, ECDSA, ECDSA*, Batch Verification, Modular Square Root, Symbolic Computation, Linearization.

1 Introduction

Batch verification is used to verify multiple digital signatures in time less than total individual verification time. The concept of batch verification is introduced by Naccache et al [7] in EuroCrypt'94. They propose an interactive batch-verification protocol for DSA [8]. In this protocol, the signer generates t signatures through interaction with the verifier, and then the verifier validates all these t signatures simultaneously.

Harn, in 1998, proposes an efficient scheme [4,5] for the batch verification of RSA signatures [12], where multiple signatures signed by the same private key can be verified simultaneously. Harn's scheme uses only one exponentiation for batches of any size t. There are some weaknesses in this scheme. For example, if batch verification fails, we cannot identify the faulty signature(s) without making individual verification. Moreover, Harn's scheme does not adapt to the case of signatures from multiple signers.

These protocols are not straightaway applicable to ECDSA signatures [2,6]. Since ECDSA requires smaller key and signature sizes than DSA and RSA, there has been a

A. Mitrokotsa and S. Vaudenay (Eds.): AFRICACRYPT 2012, LNCS 7374, pp. 1–18, 2012.

growing interest in ECDSA. ECDSA* [1], a modification of ECDSA, permits an easy adaptation of Naccache et al's batch-verification protocol for DSA. Cheon and Yi [3] study batch verification of ECDSA* signatures, and report speedup factors of up to 7 for same signer and 4 for different signers. However, ECDSA* is not a standard, and is thus unacceptable, particularly in applications where interoperability is of concern. More importantly, ECDSA* increases the signature size compared to ECDSA without any increase in the security. Consequently, batch verification of original ECDSA signatures turns out to be a practically important open research problem. To the best of our knowledge, no significant result in this area has ever been reported in the literature.

In this paper, we propose three algorithms to verify *original* ECDSA signatures in batches. Our algorithms apply to all cases of ECDSA signatures sharing the same curve parameters, although we obtain good speedup figures when all the signatures in the batch come from the same signer. Our algorithms are effective only for small batch sizes (like $t \leqslant 8$). The first algorithm we introduce (henceforth denoted as Algorithm N) is based upon a naive approach of taking square roots in the underlying field. As the field size increases, square-root computations become quite costly. We modify Algorithm N by replacing square-root calculations by symbolic manipulations. We propose two ECDSA batch-verification algorithms, called S1 and S2, using symbolic manipulations. Algorithm S1 is not very practical, but is discussed in this paper, for it provides the theoretical and practical foundations for arriving at Algorithm S2. For a wide range of field and batch sizes, Algorithm S2 convincingly outperforms the naive Algorithm N. Both S1 and S2 are probabilistic algorithms in the Monte Carlo sense, that is, they may occasionally fail to verify correct signatures. We analytically establish that for randomly generated signatures, the failure probability is extremely low.

The rest of this paper is organized as follows. In Section 2, we identify the problems associated with ECDSA batch verification. In this process, we introduce the ECDSA signature scheme, and set up the notations which we use throughout the rest of the paper. In Section 3, we introduce a naive batch-verification algorithm N and its variant N'. Section 4 elaborates our new algorithm S1 based upon symbolic manipulations. Section 5 presents an analytic study of Algorithm S1. We furnish details about the running time, the cases of failure, and the security of Algorithm S1. The running time estimates for Algorithm S1 indicate that this algorithm is expected to perform poorly unless the batch size t is very small. In Section 6, we improve upon this algorithm to arrive at Algorithm S2. Analytic results for Algorithm S2 are provided in Section 7. A heuristic capable of significantly speeding up Algorithms S1 and S2 is presented in Section 8. In Section 9, we list our experimental results, and compare the performances of the three algorithms N, S1 and S2. We also study the performances of three faster variants N', S1' and S2' of these algorithms. Although we have concentrated only upon the curves over prime fields, supplied in the NIST standard [9], our algorithms readily apply to other curves with cofactor 1. As mentioned in [1], cofactor values larger than 1 can be easily handled by appending only a few bits of extra information to standard ECDSA signatures. The concluding Section 10 highlights some future research directions.

2   Notations

The elliptic-curve digital signature algorithm (ECDSA) is based upon some parameters common to all entities participating in a network.

q = Order of the prime field $\mathbb{F}_q$.

E = An elliptic curve $y^2 = x^3 + ax + b$ defined over the prime field $\mathbb{F}_q$.

P = A random non-zero base point in $E(\mathbb{F}_q)$.

n = The order of P, typically a prime.

h = The cofactor $\dfrac{|E(\mathbb{F}_q)|}{n}$.

For the time being, we assume that $h = 1$, that is, $E(\mathbb{F}_q)$ is a cyclic group, and P is a generator of $E(\mathbb{F}_q)$. This is indeed the case for certain elliptic curves standardized by NIST. By Hasse's theorem, we have $|n - q - 1| \leqslant 2\sqrt{q}$. If $n \geqslant q$, an element of $\mathbb{Z}_n$ has a unique representation in $\mathbb{Z}_q$. On the other hand, if $n < q$, an element of $\mathbb{Z}_n$ has at most two representations in $\mathbb{Z}_q$. The density of elements of $\mathbb{Z}_n$ having two representations in $\mathbb{Z}_q$ is $\leqslant 2/\sqrt{q}$ which is close to zero for large values of q.

In an ECDSA signature (M, r, s), the values r and s are known modulo n. However, r corresponds to an elliptic-curve point and should be known modulo q. If r corresponds to a random point on E, it uniquely identifies an element of $\mathbb{F}_q$ with probability close to 1. In view of this, we will ignore the effect of issues associated with the ambiguous representation stated above, in the rest of this article.

Note that the ambiguities arising out of $h > 1$ and/or $q > n$ can be practically solved by appending only a few extra bits to standard ECDSA signatures [1,3]. Consequently, our assumptions are neither too restrictive nor too impractical.

An ECDSA key pair consists of the public key Q and the private key d satisfying $Q = dP$. The steps for generating the ECDSA signature (r, s) on a message M follow.

1. k = A randomly chosen element in the range $[1, n - 1]$ (the session key).
2. $R = kP$.
3. $r = x(R)$ (the x-coordinate of R) reduced modulo n.
4. $s = k^{-1}(H(M) + dr)(\mathrm{mod}\ n)$ (where H is a cryptographic hash function like SHA-1 [10]).

The following steps verify the ECDSA signature (r, s) on a message M.

1. $w = s^{-1}\ (\mathrm{mod}\ n)$.
2. $u = H(M)w\ (\mathrm{mod}\ n)$.
3. $v = rw\ (\mathrm{mod}\ n)$.
4. $R = uP + vQ \in E(\mathbb{F}_q)$. \hfill (1)
5. Accept the signature if and only if $x(R) = r\ (\mathrm{mod}\ n)$.

3   Naive Batch Verification Algorithms N and N′ for ECDSA

Throughout the rest of this paper, we plan to simultaneously verify t ECDSA signatures $(r_1, s_1), (r_2, s_2), \ldots, (r_t, s_t)$ on messages $M_1, M_2, \ldots, M_t$. By m, we will denote 2^t.
For t signed messages (M_i, r_i, s_i), $i = 1, 2, \ldots, t$, we have

$$\sum_{i=1}^{t} R_i = \left(\sum_{i=1}^{t} u_i \right) P + \sum_{i=1}^{t} v_i Q_i. \tag{2}$$

If all the signatures belong to the same signer, we have $Q_1 = Q_2 = \cdots = Q_t = Q$ (say), and the last equation simplifies to:

$$\sum_{i=1}^{t} R_i = \left(\sum_{i=1}^{t} u_i \right) P + \left(\sum_{i=1}^{t} v_i \right) Q. \tag{3}$$

The basic idea is to compute the two sides of Eqn (2) or Eqn (3), and check for the equality. Use of these equations reduces the number of scalar multiplications from $2t$ to $[2, t + 1]$, where 2 corresponds to the case where all the signatures belong to same signer, and $t + 1$ corresponds to the case where the t signers are distinct from one another. However, only the x-coordinates of R_i are known from the signatures. In general, there are two y-coordinates corresponding to a given x-coordinate, but computing these y-coordinates requires taking square roots modulo q, a time-consuming operation. Moreover, there is nothing immediately available in the signatures to remove the ambiguity in these two values of y. Finally, computing all R_i using Eqn (1) misses the basic idea of batch verification, since after this expensive computation, there is only an insignificant amount of effort left to complete individual verifications of the t signatures.

ECDSA* [1], a modification of ECDSA where the entire point R is included in the signature instead of r, adapts readily to the above batch-verification idea. Nonetheless, a naive algorithm (to be denoted as Algorithm N) for the batch verification of original ECDSA signatures can be conceived of. For each i, we compute the square roots y_i of $r_i^3 + ar_i + b$ modulo q. There are (usually) 2^t choices of the square roots y_i for all $i = 1, 2, \ldots, t$. If any of these combinations of square roots satisfies Eqn (2), we accept the batch of signatures. This is definitely an obvious way of solving the ECDSA batch-verification problem, but we have not found any previous mention of this algorithm in the literature. Modular square-root computation turns out to be a costly operation. Moreover, we need to check (at most) $m = 2^t$ possible conditions for batch verification—a step that is also quite costly unless t is small.

Using a single extra bit of information in an ECDSA signature, one can unambiguously identify the *correct* square root of $r_i^3 + ar_i + b$, and thereby avoid the $\Theta(2^t)$ overhead associated with Algorithm N. This updated (and efficient) version of the naive algorithm will henceforth be denoted by Algorithm N′. Despite this updating, there is apparently nothing present in ECDSA signatures, that provides a support for quickly *computing* the correct square root. The basic aim of this paper is to develop algorithms to reduce the overhead associated with square-root calculations. In effect, we are converting ECDSA signatures to ECDSA* signatures. In that sense, this paper is not competing with but complementary to the earlier works [1,3] on ECDSA*.

4   A New Batch-Verification Algorithm for ECDSA (Algorithm S1)

In this section, we present a new algorithm to convert Eqn (2) or Eqn (3) to a form which eliminates the problems associated with the lack of knowledge of the y-coordinates of R_i. We compute the right side of Eqn (2) or Eqn (3) as efficiently as possible. The left side is not computed explicitly, but symbolically in the unknown values $y_1, y_2, \ldots, y_t$ (the y-coordinates of $R_1, R_2, \ldots, R_t$). By solving a system of linear equations over $\mathbb{F}_q$, we obtain enough information to verify the t signatures simultaneously. This new algorithm, called Algorithm S1, turns out to be faster than Algorithm N for small batch sizes (typically for $t \leqslant 4$) and for large underlying fields.

4.1   Symbolic Computation of $R = \displaystyle\sum_{i=1}^{t} R_i$

Let $R_i = (x_i, y_i)$. The x-coordinates $x_i = x(R_i)$ are available from the signatures, namely, $x_i = r_i$ or $x_i = r_i + n$. The second case pertains to the condition $n < q$ and has a very low probability. So we plan to ignore this case, and take $x_i = x(R_i) = r_i$. It is indeed easy to detect when the reduced x-coordinate r_i has two representatives in $\mathbb{F}_q$, and if so, we repeat Algorithm S1 for both these values.

Although the y-coordinate $y_i = y(R_i)$ is unknown to us, we know the values of

$$y_i^2 = r_i^3 + ar_i + b \pmod{q} \tag{4}$$

for all $i = 1, 2, \ldots, t$, since $R_i = (r_i, y_i)$ is a point on the curve E.

Applying the elliptic-curve point-addition formula repeatedly gives the following representation of the point $R = \sum_{i=1}^{t} R_i$:

$$R = \left(\frac{g_x(y_1, y_2, \ldots, y_t)}{h_x(y_1, y_2, \ldots, y_t)}, \frac{g_y(y_1, y_2, \ldots, y_t)}{h_y(y_1, y_2, \ldots, y_t)} \right), \tag{5}$$

where g_x, g_y, h_x, h_y are polynomials in $\mathbb{F}_q[y_1, y_2, \ldots, y_t]$. In view of Eqn (4), we may assume that these polynomials have y_i-degrees $\leqslant 1$ for all $i = 1, 2, \ldots, t$. This implies that the denominator $h_x(y)$ is of the form $u(y_2, y_3, \ldots, y_t)y_1 + v(y_2, y_3, \ldots, y_t)$. Multiplying both g_x and h_x by $u(y_2, y_3, \ldots, y_t)y_1 - v(y_2, y_3, \ldots, y_t)$ and using Eqn (4), we can eliminate y_1 from the denominator. Repeating this successively for $y_2, y_3, \ldots, y_t$ allows us to represent the point R as a pair of polynomial expressions:

$$R = (R_x(y_1, y_2, \ldots, y_t), R_y(y_1, y_2, \ldots, y_t)) \tag{6}$$

with the polynomials R_x and R_y linear individually with respect to all y_i. It is useful to clear the denominator after every symbolic addition instead of only once after the entire sum $R = \sum_{i=1}^{t} R_i$ is computed symbolically. It is easy to establish that R_x is a polynomial with each non-zero term having even total degree, whereas R_y is a polynomial with each non-zero term having odd total degree (See Appendix A).

From the right side of Eqn (2) or Eqn (3), we compute the x- and y-coordinates of R as $R = (\alpha, \beta)$ for some $\alpha, \beta \in \mathbb{F}_q$. This gives us two initial multivariate equations:

$$R_x(y_1, y_2, \ldots, y_t) = \alpha, \tag{7}$$
$$R_y(y_1, y_2, \ldots, y_t) = \beta. \tag{8}$$

4.2 Solving the Multivariate Equations

We treat Eqns (7) and (8) as linear equations in the square-free monomials y_i, $y_i y_j$, $y_i y_j y_k$, and so on. R_x contains non-zero terms involving only the even-degree monomials, that is, $y_i y_j$, $y_i y_j y_k y_l$, and so on. There are exactly $\mu = 2^{t-1} - 1 = \frac{m}{2} - 1$ such monomials, where $m = 2^t$. We name these monomials as $z_1, z_2, \ldots, z_\mu$, and take out the constant term from R_x to rewrite Eqn (7) as

$$\rho_{1,1} z_1 + \rho_{1,2} z_2 + \cdots + \rho_{1,\mu} z_\mu = \alpha_1. \tag{9}$$

If we square both sides of this equation, and use Eqn (4) to eliminate all squares of variables, we obtain another linear equation:

$$\rho_{2,1} z_1 + \rho_{2,2} z_2 + \cdots + \rho_{2,\mu} z_\mu = \alpha_2. \tag{10}$$

By repeated squaring, we generate a total of μ linear equations in $z_1, z_2, \ldots, z_\mu$. We then solve the resulting system and obtain the values of $z_1, z_2, \ldots, z_\mu$.

If the system is not of full rank, we make use of Eqn (8) as follows. Each non-zero term in R_y has odd degree. However, the equation $R_y^2 = \beta^2$ (along with the substitution given by Eqn (4)) leads to a linear equation in the even-degree monomials $z_1, z_2, \ldots, z_\mu$ only. Repeated squaring of this equation continues to generate a second sequence of linear equations in $z_1, z_2, \ldots, z_\mu$.

We expect to obtain μ linearly independent equations from these two sequences.

4.3 A Strategy for Faster Equation Generation

There are indeed other ways of generating new linear equations in $z_1, z_2, \ldots, z_\mu$. Let

$$\rho_1 z_1 + \rho_2 z_2 + \cdots + \rho_\mu z_\mu = \gamma \tag{11}$$

be an equation already generated, and let $f(z_1, z_2, \ldots, z_\mu)$ be any $\mathbb{F}_q$-linear combination of the monomials $z_1, z_2, \ldots, z_\mu$. Simplification of the equation

$$(\rho_1 z_1 + \rho_2 z_2 + \cdots + \rho_\mu z_\mu) f(z_1, z_2, \ldots, z_\mu) = \gamma f(z_1, z_2, \ldots, z_\mu)$$

using Eqn (4) again yields a linear equation in $z_1, z_2, \ldots, z_\mu$. In particular, the choice $f(z_1, z_2, \ldots, z_\mu) = z_i$ with a small degree of z_i typically leads to a faster generation of a new equation than squaring Eqn (11). Our experiments indicate that we can generate a full-rank system by monomial multiplications and a few squaring operations. Moreover, only Eqn (7) suffices to generate a uniquely solvable linearized system.

4.4 Retrieving the Unknown y-Coordinates

The final step in Algorithm S1 involves the determination of the y-coordinates y_i of the points R_i. Multiplying both sides of Eqn (8) by y_1 gives an equation of the form

$$\beta y_1 = \epsilon_0 + \epsilon_1 z_1 + \epsilon_2 z_2 + \cdots + \epsilon_\mu z_\mu.$$

Substitution of the values of z_i available from the previous stage gives y_1 (provided that $\beta \neq 0$). Subsequently, the values y_i for $i = 2, 3, \ldots, t$ can be obtained by dividing the known value of $y_1 y_j$ by y_1 provided that $y_1 \neq 0$. Even if $y_1 = 0$, we can multiply Eqn (8) by y_2 to solve for y_2. If $y_2 \neq 0$, we are allowed to compute $y_i = (y_2 y_i)/y_2$ for $i \geqslant 3$. If $y_2 = 0$ too, we compute y_3 by directly using Eqn (8), and so on. The only condition that is necessary to solve for all y_i values uniquely is $\beta \neq 0$, where β is the y-coordinate of the point on the right side of Eqn (2) (or Eqn (3)).

We finally check whether Eqn (4) is valid for all $i = 1, 2, \ldots, t$. If so, all the signatures are verified simultaneously. If one or more of these equations fail(s) to hold, batch verification fails.

In short, Algorithm S1 uniquely reconstructs the points R_i with $x(R_i) = r_i$. The computations do not involve taking modular square roots in $\mathbb{F}_q$. We also avoid computing the points $R'_i = u_i P + v_i Q_i$ needed in individual verification. The final check $(y_i^2 = r_i^3 + a r_i + b)$ guarantees that the reconstructed points really lie on the curve. In the next section, we prove that the reconstruction process succeeds with very high probability. Moreover, for small batch sizes, the reconstruction process is efficient.

5   Analysis of Algorithm S1

5.1   Running Time

The count of monomials handled during the equation-generation and equation-solving stages is $\mu = 2^{t-1} - 1 = \frac{m}{2} - 1$ which grows exponentially with t. Determination of the Eqns (7) and (8) needs $t - 1$ symbolic additions involving rational functions with at most $\Theta(m)$ non-zero terms. Each symbolic addition is followed by at most t uses of Eqn (4). Therefore, the symbolic derivation of R requires $O(mt^2)$ operations in $\mathbb{F}_q$. The subsequent generation of the $\mu \times \mu$ linearized system requires $O(m^2 t)$ field operations. Finally, Gaussian elimination on an $\mu \times \mu$ system demands $\Theta(m^3)$ field operations. Retrieving individual y_i values calls for $O(mt^2)$ (usually $O(mt)$) field operations. The running time of Algorithm S1 is dominated by the linear system-solving stage. Evidently, Algorithm S1 becomes impractical except only for small values of t.

It is worthwhile to investigate the running time of the naive Algorithm N. First, this algorithm needs to compute t modular square roots in the field $\mathbb{F}_q$. Each such square-root computation (for example, by the Tonelli-Shanks algorithm [13]) involves an exponentiation in $\mathbb{F}_q$. Subsequently, one needs to check at most $m = 2^t = 2(\mu + 1)$ conditions, with each check involving the computation of the sum of t points on the curve. Therefore, the total running time of Algorithm N is $O((\sigma + m)t)$, where σ is the time for computing one square root in $\mathbb{F}_q$. Thus, Algorithm S1 outperforms Algorithm N only in situations where σ is rather large compared to m. This happens typically when the batch size t is small and the field size q is large.

5.2   Unique Solvability of the Linearized System

In Algorithm S1, we solve a linearized $\mu \times \mu$ system to obtain the values of the even-degree monomials $z_1, z_2, \ldots, z_\mu$ in the unknown y-coordinates $y_1, y_2, \ldots, y_t$. Let us call the coefficient matrix M. In order that the linearized system is uniquely solvable, we require $\det M \neq 0$. We now investigate how often this condition is satisfied, and also how we can force this condition to hold in most cases.

For a moment, let us treat the x-coordinates $r_1, r_2, \ldots, r_t$ as symbols. But then the failure condition $\det M = 0$ can be rephrased in terms of a multivariate polynomial equation in $r_1, r_2, \ldots, r_t$. Let us denote this equation as $D(r_1, r_2, \ldots, r_t) = 0$. If D is identically zero, then any values of $r_1, r_2, \ldots, r_t$ constitute a root of D. We explain shortly how this situation can be avoided.

Assume that D is not identically zero. Let δ be the maximum degree of each individual r_i in D. One can derive that $\delta \leqslant \left(2^{2t+3\lceil \log_2 t \rceil +2} + 3\right)\left(2^{2^{t-1}-1} - 1\right) \approx 2^{2^{t-1}+2t+3\lceil \log_2 t \rceil +1}$ (See Appendix B). If we restrict our attention to the values $t \leqslant 6$, we have $\delta \leqslant 2^{54}$. The maximum number of roots of D is bounded below $t\delta q^{t-1}$ (See Appendix C). The total number of t-tuples $(r_1, r_2, \ldots, r_t)$ over $\mathbb{F}_q$ is q^t. Therefore, a randomly chosen tuple $(r_1, r_2, \ldots, r_t)$ is a root of D with probability $\leqslant t\delta q^{t-1}/q^t = t\delta/q$. If we use the inequalities $t \leqslant 6$, $\delta \leqslant 2^{54}$ and $q \geqslant 2^{160}$, we conclude that this probability is less than 2^{-103}. Therefore, if D is not the zero polynomial, we can solve for $z_1, z_2, \ldots, z_\mu$ uniquely with very high probability.

What remains is to propose a way to avoid the condition $D = 0$. We start with any t randomly chosen ECDSA signatures with r-values $r_1, r_2, \ldots, r_t$. We then choose any sequence of squaring and multiplication by z_i in order to arrive at a linear system in $z_1, z_2, \ldots, z_\mu$. If the corresponding coefficient matrix M is not invertible, we discard the chosen sequence of squaring and multiplication. This is because $\det M = 0$ implies that either D is the zero polynomial or the chosen $r_1, r_2, \ldots, r_t$ constitute a root of a non-zero D. The second case is extremely unlikely. With high probability, we, therefore, conclude that the chosen sequence of squaring and multiplication gives $D = 0$ identically. We change the sequence, and repeat the above process until we come across the situation where $r_1, r_2, \ldots, r_t$ do not constitute a root of the non-zero polynomial equation $D(r_1, r_2, \ldots, r_t) = 0$. This implies that D is not identically zero, and randomly chosen $r_1, r_2, \ldots, r_t$ satisfy $D(r_1, r_2, \ldots, r_t) = 0$ with very low probability. We keep this sequence for all future invocations of our batch-verification algorithm.

Table 1 lists some sequences of squaring and multiplication, that work for NIST prime curves. Here, S stands for a squaring step, whereas a monomial (like y_2y_4) stands for multiplication by that monomial. In all these cases, we use only Eqn (7), whereas Eqn (8) is used only for the unique determination of individual y_i values. These sequences depend upon t alone, but not on the NIST curves. For other curves, this method is expected to work equally well. Indeed, we may consider $D(r_1, r_2, \ldots, r_t)$ as a polynomial in $\mathbb{Z}[r_1, r_2, \ldots, r_t]$. If D is not identically zero, then it is identically zero modulo only a finite number of primes (the common prime divisors of the coefficients of D).

Table 1. Sequences to generate linearized systems for NIST prime curves

t	Sequence in the linearization phase
2	No squaring or multiplication needed
3	y_1y_2, y_1y_3
4	$y_1y_2, y_1y_3, y_1y_4, y_2y_3, y_3y_4, y_1y_4$
5	$y_1y_2, y_1y_3, y_1y_4, y_1y_5, y_2y_3, y_2y_4, y_4y_5, y_1y_2, y_1y_3, y_1y_4, y_1y_5, y_1y_2, y_2y_4, y_2y_3$
6	$y_1y_2, y_1y_3, y_1y_4, y_1y_5, y_1y_6, y_2y_3, y_2y_4, y_2y_5, y_1y_2, y_3y_4, y_3y_5, y_1y_5, y_1y_6, y_1y_2y_3y_6, y_1y_5,$ $y_1y_4, y_1y_3, y_1y_2y_3y_6, y_1y_2, y_1y_3, y_1y_4, y_1y_5, y_2y_5, y_2y_3, S, y_2y_6, y_4y_6, y_3y_6, y_5y_6, y_1y_5$

5.3   Security Analysis

In Algorithm S1, we reconstruct the points R_i with x-coordinates $x(R_i) = r_i$ by forcing the condition $R = \sum_{i=1}^{t} R_i = \sum_{i=1}^{t} R_i' = R'$, where $R_i' = u_i P + v_i Q_i$. Suppose that an adversary too can force the condition $R = R'$. The adversary must also reveal the x-coordinates $r_1, r_2, \ldots, r_t$ as parts of ECDSA signatures. Given these x-coordinates and the condition $R = R'$, there exists (with high probability) a unique solution for the corresponding y-coordinates $y_1, y_2, \ldots, y_t$ of $R_1, R_2, \ldots, R_t$. This solution can be computed by the adversary, for example, using Algorithm S1 (or by taking modular square roots in $\mathbb{F}_q$ as in Algorithm N). So long as t is restricted to small constant values (like $t \leqslant 6$), the adversary requires only moderate computing resources for determining $y_1, y_2, \ldots, y_t$ uniquely. This implies that although the adversary needs to reveal only the x-coordinates r_i, (s)he essentially *knows* the full points R_i. But these points $R_1, R_2, \ldots, R_t$ satisfy the standard batch-verification condition for ECDSA*. That is, if the adversary can fool Algorithm S1, (s)he can fool the standard ECDSA* batch-verification algorithm too. It follows that Algorithm S1 is no less secure than the standard batch-verification algorithm for ECDSA*. Conversely, if an adversary can fool any ECDSA* batch-verification algorithm, (s)he can always fool any ECDSA batch-verification algorithm, since ECDSA signatures are only parts of ECDSA* signatures. To sum up, Algorithm S1 is as secure as standard ECDSA* batch verification [7].

   An analysis of the security of Algorithm N is also worth including here. Suppose that an adversary can pass one of the $m = 2^t$ checks in Algorithm N along with disclosing $r_1, r_2, \ldots, r_t$. The correct choices y_i of the square roots of $r_i^3 + ar_i + b$ (that is, those choices corresponding to the successful check) constitute a case of fulfillment of the ECDSA* batch-verification criterion. Consequently, Algorithm N too is as secure as standard ECDSA* batch verification.

5.4   Cases of Failure for Algorithm S1

Our Monte Carlo batch-verification Algorithm S1 may fail for a few reasons. We now argue that these cases of failure are probabilistically very rare.

1. Taking $x_i = r_i$ blindly is a possible cause of failure for Algorithm S1. As discussed earlier, this situation has a very low probability. Furthermore, it is easy to identify when this situation occurs. In case of ambiguity in the values of x_i, we can repeat Algorithm S1 for all possible candidate tuples $(x_1, x_2, \ldots, x_t)$. If the points R_i are randomly chosen in $E(\mathbb{F}_q)$, most of these x_i values are unambiguously available to us, and there should not be many repeated runs (if any) of Algorithm S1. Repeated runs, if necessary, may be avoided, because doing so goes against the expected benefits achievable by batch verification.

2. Although we are able to identify good sequences of squaring and multiplication in order to force the determinant polynomial $D(r_1, r_2, \ldots, r_t)$ to be not identically zero, roots of this polynomial may appear in some cases of ECDSA signatures. We have seen that if $r_1, r_2, \ldots, r_t$ are randomly chosen, the probability of this situation is no more than 2^{-103} (for $t \leqslant 6$).

3. Eqn (5) is derived using the point-addition formula on the curve E, which is different from the doubling formula. So long as we work symbolically using the unknown
quantities $y_1, y_2, \ldots, y_t$, it is impossible to predict when the two points being added
turn out to be equal. If $R_1, R_2, \ldots, R_t$ are randomly chosen from $E(\mathbb{F}_q)$, the probability of this occurrence is extremely low.
4. Algorithm S1 fails if R' is the point at infinity or lies on the x-axis ($\beta = 0$). In
that case, one should resort to individual verification. For randomly chosen session
keys, this case occurs with a very small probability (nearly $4/q$).

6   A More Efficient Batch-Verification Algorithm (Algorithm S2)

The linearization stage in Algorithm S1 (requiring $O(m^2 t)$ field operations) and the
subsequent Gaussian-elimination stage ($O(m^3)$ field operations) are rather costly, m
being an exponential function of the batch size t. Our second symbolic-manipulation
algorithm S2 avoids these two stages altogether.

Algorithm S1 uniquely solves for the monomials $z_1, z_2, \ldots, z_\mu$ using the equation
$R_x = \alpha$ only. At this point, there are only two possible solutions for the y_i values:
$(y_1, y_2, \ldots, y_t)$ and $(-y_1, -y_2, \ldots, -y_t)$. This *sign* ambiguity is eliminated by using
the other equation $R_y = \beta$. As mentioned in connection with the security analysis of
Algorithm N, the exact determination of these signs is not important. In other words,
we would be happy even if we can determine each y_i correctly up to multiplication by
± 1. This, in turn, implies that if we have any multivariate equation (linear in y_i) of the
form $u y_i + v = 0$ (where u, v are polynomials in $y_1, \ldots, y_{i-1}, y_{i+1}, \ldots, y_t$), we do
not mind multiplying this equation by $u y_i - v$ so that $\pm y_i$ satisfy $u^2 y_i^2 - v^2 = 0$. But
$y_i^2 = r_i^3 + a r_i + b$, so we have $u_i^2(r_i^3 + a r_i + b) - v_i^2 = 0$, an equation in which y_i is
eliminated. This observation leads to Algorithm S2.

Like Algorithm S1, we first symbolically compute $R = \sum_{i=1}^{t} R_i$, and arrive at
Eqns (7) and (8). Then, we consider only the multivariate equation $R_x - \alpha = 0$ linear
individually in each y_i. We first eliminate y_1, and with substitutions given by Eqn (4)
for $i = 2, 3, \ldots, t$, we arrive at a multivariate equation in $y_2, y_3, \ldots, y_t$, again linear in
each of these variables. We eliminate y_2 from this equation, and arrive at a multivariate
equation in $y_3, y_4, \ldots, y_t$. We repeat this process until all variables $y_1, y_2, \ldots, y_t$ are
eliminated. If the polynomial after all these eliminations reduces to zero, the original
equation $R_x = \alpha$ is consistent with respect to $y_i^2 = r_i^3 + a r_i + b$ for all $i = 1, 2, \ldots, t$.

We may likewise eliminate $y_1, y_2, \ldots, y_t$ from $R_y - \beta = 0$ too, but this is not
necessary, because it suffices to know y_i uniquely up to multiplication by ± 1.

Some comments on efficient implementations of the elimination stage are now in
order. First, we are not using Eqn (8) at all in Algorithm S2. Consequently, it is not
necessary to compute the polynomial R_y. However, in the symbolic-computation stage,
we need to compute all intermediate y-coordinates, since they are needed in the final
value of R_x. The computation of only the last y-coordinate R_y may be avoided. Still,
this saves quite some amount of effort ($O(mt)$ field operations, to be precise). This
saving does not affect the theoretical complexity of the algorithm in the big-Oh notation,
but its practical effects are noticeable.

The second issue is that the polynomials u and v in each elimination step have some
nice properties. Throughout this step, $\phi = u y_i + v$ and v are polynomials with each

non-zero term having even degree, whereas u is a polynomial with each non-zero term having odd degree. In particular, when the first $t - 2$ y-coordinates are eliminated, we have $\phi = uy_{t-1}y_t + v$ with $u, v \in \mathbb{F}_q$. Elimination of y_{t-1} eliminates y_t too, so an explicit elimination of y_t is not necessary.

The y-coordinates $y_1, y_2, \ldots, y_t$ are not explicitly reconstructed in Algorithm S2. However, if necessary, we can compute two sets of solutions $y_1, y_2, \ldots, y_t$ and $-y_1$, $-y_2, \ldots, -y_t$ by using the values of $\phi = uy_i + v$ for $i = t - 1, t - 2, \ldots, 2, 1$. The sign ambiguity can be removed by using $R_y = \beta$. Algorithm S2 does not include this reconstruction phase, since this is cryptographically unimportant. However, we use this result in the security proof for S2.

It is also important to note that the determination of individual y_i values is cryptographically unimportant for Algorithm S1 too, since $R_x = \alpha$ already identi-fies exactly two solutions for the reconstructed points. If these steps are omitted, the batch-acceptance criterion would match z_i^2 against appropriate products of $r_j^3 + ar_j + b$ for all $i = 1, 2, \ldots, \mu$. In fact, it suffices to consider only the monomials z_i of degree 2. However, the unique determination of y_i values takes only an insignificant fraction of time in Algorithm S1, so it does not practically matter to make a choice between whether we carry out these steps or not.

7   Analysis of Algorithm S2

7.1   Running Time

The symbolic computation of (R_x, R_y) involves $O(mt^2)$ field operations (as in Al-gorithm S1). Subsequently, we start with the polynomial $\phi = R_x - \alpha$ with at most $\mu + 1 = \frac{m}{2} + 1$ non-zero terms. Elimination of y_i requires computing the squares u^2 and v^2, carrying out the polynomial arithmetic $u^2(r_i^3 + ar_i + b) - v^2$, and $t - i$ sub-stitutions of y_j^2 by $r_j^3 + ar_j + b$. Therefore, the reduction of ϕ too requires $O(mt^2)$ field operations. This is significantly better than the $O(m^3)$ operations needed by Al-gorithm S1. Moreover, Algorithm S2 outperforms Algorithm N for a wide range of t and q, since the condition $(\sigma + m)t \gg mt^2$ is more often satisfied than the condition $(\sigma + m)t \gg m^3$.

7.2   Security Analysis

We establish the equivalence between the security of Algorithm S2 and the security of standard ECDSA* batch verification, as we have done for the earlier algorithms (N and S1). Suppose that an adversary reveals the x-coordinates $r_1, r_2, \ldots, r_t$ in ECDSA signatures which pass the batch-verification procedure of Algorithm S2. We mentioned above that there are exactly two solutions $(y_1, y_2, \ldots, y_t)$ and $(-y_1, -y_2, \ldots, -y_t)$ consistent with $R_x - \alpha = 0$ and $y_i^2 = r_i^3 + ar_i + b$ for $i = 1, 2, \ldots, t$. One of these solutions corresponds to the ECDSA* signatures based upon the disclosed values $r_1, r_2, \ldots, r_t$. It is that solution that would pass $R_y = \beta$. To sum up, the adversary can forge the standard ECDSA* batch-verification algorithm. Moreover, this forging pro-cedure which essentially involves the unique reconstruction of the points $R_i = (r_i, y_i)$ is practical for any adversary with only a moderate amount of computing resources, so long as t is restricted only to small values (the only cases where we can apply S2).

8   Efficient Variants of S1 and S2

In Algorithm S1, we generate a system of linearized equations in $\frac{m}{2} - 1 = 2^{t-1} - 1$ monomials. Solving the resulting equation turns out to be the costliest step of Algorithm S1, demanding $\Theta(m^3)$ field operations. In Algorithm S2, the symbolic computation of $R = (R_x, R_y)$ turns out to be the most time-consuming step. This step calls for $\Theta(mt^2)$ field operations. The elimination phase too calls for $\Theta(mt^2)$ operations.

In this section, we explain a strategy to reduce the number of monomials in Algorithms S1 and S2. So far, we have been symbolically computing the point $R = \sum_{i=1}^{t} R_i$, and equating the symbolic sum to $R' = (\alpha, \beta)$. This results in polynomial expressions with $\Theta(2^{t-1})$ (that is, $\Theta(m)$) non-zero terms.

Now, let $\tau = \lceil t/2 \rceil$. We symbolically compute the two sums:

$$R^{(1)} = \sum_{i=1}^{\tau} R_i \text{ and } R^{(2)} = R' - \sum_{i=\tau+1}^{t} R_i. \tag{12}$$

The polynomial expressions involved in $R^{(1)}$ and $R^{(2)}$ contain only $\Theta(2^\tau)$, that is, $\Theta(\sqrt{m})$ non-zero terms. So computing these two symbolic sums needs $\Theta(2^\tau \tau^2)$, that is, $\Theta(\sqrt{m}t^2)$ field operations which is significantly smaller than the $\Theta(mt^2)$ operations associated with the symbolic computation of the complete sum $\sum_{i=1}^{t} R_i$. The condition $R = R'$ is equivalent to the condition $R^{(1)} = R^{(2)}$. Using this new condition helps us in speeding up the subsequent steps too.

8.1   Algorithm S1′

The symbolic computation of R in Algorithm S1 can be replaced by the two symbolic computations given by Eqn (12). In that case, we replace the initial equations $R_x = \alpha$ and $R_y = \beta$ by the two equations $x(R^{(1)}) = x(R^{(2)})$ and $y(R^{(1)}) = y(R^{(2)})$. It is easy to argue that $x(R^{(1)})$ is a polynomial in $y_1, y_2, \ldots, y_\tau$ with each non-zero term having even degree, whereas $y(R^{(1)})$ is a polynomial in $y_1, y_2, \ldots, y_\tau$ with each non-zero term having odd degree. That is, the number of non-zero terms in these two expressions is $2^{\tau-1} = \frac{\sqrt{m}}{2}$. However, the presence of $R' = (\alpha, \beta)$ on the right side of the expression for $R^{(2)}$ (Eqn 12) lets both $x(R^{(2)})$ and $y(R^{(2)})$ contain all (square-free) monomials in $y_{\tau+1}, y_{\tau+2}, \ldots, y_t$ (both even and odd degrees). There are exactly $2^{\lfloor t/2 \rfloor} - 1 \leqslant \sqrt{m} - 1$ monomials in these two expressions. In the linearized system that we subsequently generate, we consider, as variables, only the even-degree monomials in $y_1, y_2, \ldots, y_\tau$ and all monomials in $y_{\tau+1}, y_{\tau+2}, \ldots, y_t$.

We start with the equation $x(R^{(1)}) = x(R^{(2)})$. Subsequently, we keep on squaring the equation $x(R^{(1)}) = x(R^{(2)})$ (and substituting values of y_i^2 wherever necessary). This sequence does not increase the number of monomials in the linearized equations. More precisely, for any $j \geqslant 0$, the equation $x(R^{(1)})^{2^j} = x(R^{(2)})^{2^j}$ contains only the $\Theta(\sqrt{m})$ monomials with which we start. If we fail to obtain a linearized system of full rank, we start squaring the other initial equation $y(R^{(1)}) = y(R^{(2)})$. For any $j \geqslant 1$, the equation $y(R^{(1)})^{2^j} = y(R^{(2)})^{2^j}$ again contains only the monomials with which we start. In all the cases studied, we have been able to obtain a full-rank linearized system by squaring the two initial equations. Since the number of linearized variables is $\Theta(\sqrt{m})$, the linearization step of Algorithm S1 now reduces to $O(mt)$ field operations. Finally, we solve a system with $\Theta(\sqrt{m})$ variables using $\Theta(m^{3/2})$ field operations.

To sum up, using the trick introduced in this section decreases the number of field operations from $\Theta(m^3)$ to $\Theta(m^{3/2})$. Let us plan to call this efficient variant of S1 as S1$'$. Fundamentally, S1$'$ is not a different algorithm from S1. In particular, the security of S1$'$ is the same as the security of S1 (in fact, little better, because fewer linearized equations are involved). However, the reduction in the running time is very significant, both theoretically and practically.

8.2   Algorithm S2$'$

Instead of starting with $\phi = R_x - \alpha$, Algorithm S2$'$ starts with the initial expression

$$\phi = x(R^{(1)}) - x(R^{(2)}). \tag{13}$$

We then repeatedly eliminate $y_1, y_2, \ldots, y_t$. Although the initial expression of ϕ contains much less number of monomials than in the original Algorithm S2, elimination of y_1 itself introduces many new monomials in ϕ, that is, soon ϕ becomes almost *full*. Consequently, the elimination phase continues to make $\Theta(mt^2)$ field operations as before, that is, the theoretical running time of S2$'$ is the same as that of S2. Still, the effects of our heuristic are clearly noticeable in practical implementations.

As described in Section 6, the y-coordinates $y(R^{(1)})$ and $y(R^{(2)})$ need not be computed. It is, however, necessary to symbolically compute the y-coordinates of all intermediate sums.

9   Experimental Results

Our batch-verification algorithms are implemented using the GP/PARI calculator [11] (version 2.3.5). Our choice of this implementation platform is dictated by the symbolic-computation facilities and an easy user interface provided by the calculator. All experiments are carried out in a 2.33 MHz Xeon server running Mandriva Linux Version 2010.1. The GNU C compiler 4.4.3 is used for compiling the GP/PARI calculator.

In Table 2, we list the average times for carrying out single scalar multiplications in the NIST prime curves. This table also lists the times for single square-root calculations in the underlying fields. Table 3 lists the overheads associated with the three algorithms N, S1 and S2, and their variants N$'$, S1$'$ and S2$'$. These overhead figures do not include the scalar-multiplication times. The algorithms S1, S1$'$ and S2 become impractical for batch sizes $t > 6$, so these algorithms are not implemented for $t = 7$ and $t = 8$.

Table 2. Timings (ms) for NIST prime curves

	P-192	P-224	P-256	P-384	P-521
Time for Scalar Multiplication (in $E(\mathbb{F}_q)$)	1.82	2.50	3.14	7.33	14.38
Time for Square-root (in $\mathbb{F}_q$)	0.06	0.35	0.09	0.26	0.67

Table 3. Overheads (ms) for different batch-verification algorithms

| | Naive (N) | | | | | | | Naive (N′) | | | | | | |
| | t | | | | | | | t | | | | | | |
Curve	2	3	4	5	6	7	8	2	3	4	5	6	7	8
P-192	0.18	0.39	0.76	1.57	3.40	7.71	17.00	0.13	0.19	0.26	0.33	0.39	0.46	0.52
P-224	0.81	1.34	2.04	3.29	5.63	10.60	21.50	0.71	1.06	1.42	1.78	2.14	2.49	2.85
P-256	0.24	0.49	0.97	1.95	4.18	9.27	20.85	0.19	0.29	0.38	0.48	0.58	0.68	0.78
P-384	0.66	1.15	1.95	3.51	6.76	13.80	29.90	0.53	0.81	1.08	1.35	1.62	1.90	2.17
P-521	1.66	2.70	4.21	6.73	11.63	21.00	43.10	1.36	2.05	2.74	3.42	4.11	4.80	5.49

| | Symbolic (S1) | | | | | Symbolic (S1′) | | | | |
| | t | | | | | t | | | | |
Curve	2	3	4	5	6	2	3	4	5	6
P-192	0.14	0.57	2.01	8.66	40.50	0.07	0.20	0.70	1.60	4.40
P-224	0.15	0.60	2.10	9.50	45.60	0.07	0.20	0.80	1.80	4.70
P-256	0.16	0.61	2.17	9.78	46.30	0.08	0.21	0.82	1.90	4.90
P-384	0.18	0.74	2.71	12.56	62.10	0.08	0.30	0.90	2.20	6.10
P-521	0.22	0.90	3.45	16.80	88.40	0.12	0.40	1.30	2.90	8.00

| | Symbolic (S2) | | | | | Symbolic (S2′) | | | | | | |
| | t | | | | | t | | | | | | |
Curve	2	3	4	5	6	2	3	4	5	6	7	8
P-192	0.07	0.30	0.76	2.39	6.65	0.07	0.11	0.32	0.61	1.14	2.36	5.46
P-224	0.07	0.32	0.84	2.53	7.11	0.07	0.12	0.33	0.64	1.21	2.51	5.91
P-256	0.08	0.32	0.80	2.51	7.08	0.08	0.12	0.33	0.64	1.22	2.52	5.88
P-384	0.09	0.37	0.91	2.85	8.15	0.09	0.14	0.38	0.72	1.41	2.95	7.12
P-521	0.11	0.44	1.07	3.45	10.02	0.11	0.18	0.42	0.95	1.76	3.72	9.26

Table 4 records the speedup values achieved by the six algorithms N, N′, S1, S1′, S2 and S2′. Here, the speedup is computed with respect to individual verification, and incorporates both scalar-multiplication times and batch-verification overheads. The maximum achievable speedup values (t in the case of same signer, and $2t/(t+1)$ in the case of different signers) are also listed in Table 4, to indicate how our batch-verification algorithms compare with the ideal cases. The maximum speedup obtained by our fully ECDSA-compliant algorithms is 6.20 in the case of same signer, and 1.70 in the case of different signers, both achieved by Algorithm S2′ for the curve P-521 and for $t = 7$.

From Table 4, it is evident that one should use Algorithm S2′ if extra information (a bit identifying the correct square root of each $r_i^3 + ar_i + b$) is not available. In this case, the optimal batch size is $t = 7$ (or $t = 6$ if the underlying field is small). If, on the other hand, disambiguating extra bits are appended to ECDSA signatures, one should use S2′ for $t \leqslant 4$ for (curves over) small fields and for $t \leqslant 6$ (or $t \leqslant 7$) for large fields. If the batch size increases beyond these bounds, it is preferable to use Algorithm N′.

Table 4. Speedup obtained by different batch-verification algorithms

Curve	t	\multicolumn{6}{c}{Same signer}	\multicolumn{6}{c}{Different signers}
		Ideal	N	N'	S1	S1'	S2	S2'	Ideal	N	N'	S1	S1'	S2	S2'
P-192	2	2.00	1.91	1.94	1.93	1.96	1.96	1.96	1.33	1.29	1.30	1.30	1.32	1.32	1.32
	3	3.00	2.71	2.86	2.59	2.84	2.77	2.91	1.50	1.42	1.46	1.39	1.46	1.44	1.48
	4	4.00	3.31	3.75	2.58	3.35	3.31	3.68	1.60	1.48	1.56	1.31	1.49	1.48	1.55
	5	5.00	3.49	4.62	1.48	3.47	3.02	4.28	1.67	1.46	1.62	0.93	1.45	1.37	1.58
	6	6.00	3.10	5.46	0.49	2.72	2.12	4.57	1.71	1.35	1.67	0.41	1.27	1.13	1.57
	7	7.00	2.24	6.28	–	–	–	4.25	1.75	1.14	1.70	–	–	–	1.51
	8	8.00	1.41	7.07	–	–	–	3.20	1.78	0.87	1.73	–	–	–	1.33
P-224	2	2.00	1.72	1.75	1.94	1.97	1.97	1.97	1.33	1.20	1.22	1.31	1.32	1.32	1.32
	3	3.00	2.37	2.48	2.68	2.88	2.82	2.93	1.50	1.32	1.36	1.42	1.47	1.45	1.48
	4	4.00	2.84	3.12	2.82	3.45	3.42	3.75	1.60	1.38	1.44	1.37	1.50	1.50	1.56
	5	5.00	3.02	3.70	1.72	3.68	3.32	4.43	1.67	1.37	1.49	1.02	1.49	1.43	1.60
	6	6.00	2.82	4.23	0.59	3.09	2.48	4.83	1.71	1.30	1.53	0.48	1.35	1.22	1.60
	7	7.00	2.24	4.70	–	–	–	4.66	1.75	1.14	1.56	–	–	–	1.55
	8	8.00	1.51	5.13	–	–	–	3.67	1.78	0.91	1.58	–	–	–	1.41
P-256	2	2.00	1.93	1.94	1.95	1.97	1.97	1.97	1.33	1.30	1.31	1.31	1.32	1.32	1.32
	3	3.00	2.78	2.88	2.73	2.90	2.85	2.94	1.50	1.44	1.47	1.43	1.48	1.46	1.49
	4	4.00	3.46	3.78	2.97	3.54	3.55	3.80	1.60	1.51	1.56	1.41	1.52	1.52	1.57
	5	5.00	3.82	4.67	1.96	3.84	3.57	4.54	1.67	1.51	1.63	1.10	1.51	1.47	1.61
	6	6.00	3.60	5.52	0.72	3.37	2.82	5.02	1.71	1.44	1.67	0.55	1.40	1.30	1.62
	7	7.00	2.83	6.36	–	–	–	5.00	1.75	1.28	1.71	–	–	–	1.59
	8	8.00	1.85	7.18	–	–	–	4.13	1.78	1.02	1.73	–	–	–	1.47
P-384	2	2.00	1.91	1.93	1.98	1.99	1.99	1.99	1.33	1.29	1.30	1.32	1.33	1.33	1.33
	3	3.00	2.78	2.85	2.86	2.94	2.93	2.97	1.50	1.44	1.46	1.46	1.48	1.48	1.49
	4	4.00	3.53	3.74	3.38	3.77	3.77	3.90	1.60	1.52	1.56	1.49	1.56	1.56	1.58
	5	5.00	4.03	4.59	2.69	4.35	4.19	4.77	1.67	1.54	1.62	1.30	1.59	1.57	1.64
	6	6.00	4.11	5.42	1.15	4.24	3.86	5.47	1.71	1.51	1.66	0.78	1.53	1.48	1.67
	7	7.00	3.61	6.23	–	–	–	5.83	1.75	1.42	1.70	–	–	–	1.67
	8	8.00	2.63	7.01	–	–	–	5.38	1.78	1.22	1.72	–	–	–	1.60
P-521	2	2.00	1.89	1.91	1.98	1.99	1.99	1.99	1.33	1.28	1.29	1.33	1.33	1.33	1.33
	3	3.00	2.74	2.80	2.91	2.96	2.95	2.98	1.50	1.43	1.45	1.48	1.49	1.49	1.50
	4	4.00	3.49	3.66	3.57	3.83	3.86	3.94	1.60	1.51	1.54	1.53	1.57	1.58	1.59
	5	5.00	4.05	4.48	3.16	4.54	4.46	4.84	1.67	1.55	1.60	1.40	1.61	1.60	1.65
	6	6.00	4.27	5.26	1.47	4.69	4.45	5.65	1.71	1.54	1.65	0.91	1.59	1.56	1.68
	7	7.00	4.05	6.02	–	–	–	6.20	1.75	1.48	1.68	–	–	–	1.70
	8	8.00	3.20	6.74	–	–	–	6.05	1.78	1.33	1.71	–	–	–	1.66

10   Conclusion

In this paper, we have proposed six algorithms for the batch verification of ECDSA signatures. To the best of our knowledge, these are the first batch-verification algorithms ever proposed for ECDSA. In particular, development of algorithms based upon symbolic manipulations appears to be a novel approach in the history of batch-verification algorithms. There are several ways to extend our study, some of which are listed below.

- Section 8 describes a way to reduce the running time of the symbolic-addition phase of Algorithm S2 from $O(mt^2)$ to $O(\sqrt{m}t^2)$. An analogous speedup for the elimination phase would be very useful.
- Our best symbolic-computation algorithm runs in $O(mt^2)$ time. Removal of a factor of t (that is, designing an $O(mt)$-time algorithm) would be useful to achieve higher speedup values.
- It is of interest to study our algorithms in conjunction with the earlier works [1,3] on ECDSA*.
- Our batch verification algorithms can be easily ported to other curves (like the Koblitz and Pseudorandom families recommended by NIST). Solving quadratic equations in binary fields is somewhat more involved than modular square-root computations in prime fields, so our symbolic-manipulation algorithms are expected to be rather effective for binary fields.

References

1. Antipa, A., Brown, D., Gallant, R., Lambert, R., Struik, R., Vanstone, S.: Accelerated Verification of ECDSA Signatures. In: Preneel, B., Tavares, S. (eds.) SAC 2005. LNCS, vol. 3897, pp. 307–318. Springer, Heidelberg (2006)
2. ANSI, Public Key Cryptography for the Financial Services Industry: The Elliptic Curve Digital Signature Algorithm (ECDSA), ANSI X9.62, approved January 7 (1999)
3. Cheon, J.H., Yi, J.H.: Fast Batch Verification of Multiple Signatures. In: Okamoto, T., Wang, X. (eds.) PKC 2007. LNCS, vol. 4450, pp. 442–457. Springer, Heidelberg (2007)
4. Harn, L.: Batch verifying multiple RSA digital signatures. Electronics Letters 34(12), 1219–1220 (1998)
5. Hwang, M.-S., Lin, I.-C., Hwang, K.-F.: Cryptanalysis of the Batch Verifying Multiple RSA Digital Signatures. Informatica 11(1), 15–19 (2000)
6. Johnson, D., Menezes, A.: The Elliptic Curve Digital Signature Algorithm (ECDSA). International Journal on Information Security 1, 36–63 (2001)
7. Naccache, D., M'Raïhi, D., Vaudenay, S., Raphaeli, D.: Can D.S.A. be Improved: Complexity Trade-Offs with the Digital Signature Standard. In: De Santis, A. (ed.) EUROCRYPT 1994. LNCS, vol. 950, pp. 77–85. Springer, Heidelberg (1995)
8. NIST, Digital Signature Standard (DSS) (2006),
   http://csrc.nist.gov/publications/drafts/fips_186-3/Draft-FIPS-186-3%20_March2006.pdf
9. NIST, Recommended elliptic curves for federal government use (July 1999),
   http://csrc.nist.gov/groups/ST/toolkit/documents/dss/NISTReCur.pdf
10. NIST, Secure Hash Standard (SHS) (2007), http://csrc.nist.gov/publications/drafts/fips_180-3/draft_fips-180-3_June-08-2007.pdf
11. PARI Group, PARI/GP Development Headquarters (2003-2008),
    http://pari.math.u-bordeaux.fr/
12. Rivest, R.L., Shamir, A., Adleman, L.: A method for obtaining digital signatures and pubic-key cryptosystem. Communications of the ACM 2, 120–126 (1978)
13. Shanks, D.: Five number theoretic algorithms. In: Proceedings of the Second Manitoba Conference on Numerical Mathematics, pp. 51–70 (1973)

Appendix

A   Properties of R_x and R_y

Theorem 1. R_x *contains only even-degree monomials, and* R_y *contains only odd-degree monomials in the variables* $y_1, y_2, \ldots, y_t$.

Proof. We proceed by induction on the batch size $t \geqslant 1$. If $t = 1$ (case of individual verification), we have $R_x = r_1$ and $R_y = y_1$, for which the theorem evidently holds.

So assume that $t \geqslant 2$. We compute $R = \sum_{i=1}^{t} R_i$ as $R' + R''$ with $R' = \sum_{i=1}^{\tau} R_i$ and $R'' = \sum_{i=\tau+1}^{t} R_i$ for some τ in the range $1 \leqslant \tau \leqslant t - 1$. Let $R' = (R'_x, R'_y)$ and $R'' = (R''_x, R''_y)$. The inductive assumption is that all non-zero terms of R'_x and R''_x are of even degrees (in $y_1, \ldots, y_\tau$ and $y_{\tau+1}, \ldots, y_t$, respectively), and all non-zero terms of R'_y and R''_y are of odd degrees.

We first symbolically compute $\lambda = (R''_y - R'_y)/(R''_x - R'_x)$ as a rational function. Clearing the variables y_i from the denominator multiplies both the numerator and the denominator of λ by polynomials of non-zero terms having even degrees. Every substitution of y_i^2 by the field element $r_i^3 + ar_i + b$ reduces the y_i-degree of certain terms by 2, so the parity of the degrees in these terms is not altered. Finally, λ becomes a polynomial with each non-zero term having odd degree. But then, $R_x = \lambda^2 - R'_x - R''_x$ is a polynomial with each non-zero term having even degree, whereas $R_y = \lambda(R'_x - R_x) - R'_y$ is a polynomial with each non-zero term having odd degree. Further substitutions of y_i^2 by $r_i^3 + ar_i + b$ to simplify R_x and R_y preserve these degree properties.

B   Derivation of δ

For computing the number of roots $(r_1, r_2, \ldots, r_t)$ of $\det M = 0$, we treat $r_1, r_2, \ldots, r_t$ as symbols, and need to calculate an upper bound on the degree δ of each individual r_i. Without loss of generality, we compute an upper bound on the degree δ of r_1 in $\det M = 0$. To this effect, we first look at the expressions for R_x and R_y which are elements of $\mathbb{F}_q(r_1, r_2, \ldots, r_t)[y_1, y_2, \ldots, y_t]$. We can write $R_x = g_x/h$ and $R_y = g_y/h$, where g_x, g_y are polynomials in $\mathbb{F}_q[r_1, r_2, \ldots, r_t, y_1, y_2, \ldots, y_t]$, and the common denominator h is a polynomial in $\mathbb{F}_q[r_1, r_2, \ldots, r_t]$. Let η_t denote the maximum of the r_1-degrees in g_x, g_y and h. We first recursively derive an upper bound for η_t.

We compute $R = R' + R''$ with $R' = (R'_x, R'_y) = \sum_{i=1}^{\tau} R_i$ and $R'' = (R''_x, R''_y) = \sum_{i=\tau+1}^{t} R_i$, where $\tau = \lceil t/2 \rceil$. The r_1-degree of R' is η_τ, whereas the r_1-degree of R'' is 0. The initial r_1-degree of $\lambda = (R''_y - R'_y)/(R''_x - R'_x)$ is at most η_τ. Clearing y_1 from the denominator of λ changes the r_1-degree to $2\eta_\tau + 3$. Subsequent eliminations of $y_2, \ldots, y_t$ finally reduces λ with a y-free denominator. The maximum r_1-degree of this expression for λ is $2^{t-1}(2\eta_\tau + 3)$. Therefore, λ^2 has r_1-degree $\leqslant 2^t(2\eta_\tau + 3)$. Subsequent computations of $R_x = \lambda^2 - R'_x - R''_x$ and $R_y = \lambda(R'_x - R_x) - R'_y$ yield

$$\eta_t \leqslant (2^t + 2^{t-1})(2\eta_\tau + 3) + 2\eta_\tau \leqslant (2^t + 2^{t-1})(2\eta_\tau + 3) + 2\eta_\tau$$

with $\tau = \lceil t/2 \rceil$. Solving this recurrence gives the upper bound $\eta_t \leqslant 2^{2t+3\lceil \log_2 t \rceil + 2}$.

Now, we follow a sequence of squaring and monomial multiplication to convert $R_x = \alpha$ to a set of linear equations. If Δ_i is the r_1-degree of the i-th equation, we have

$$\Delta_1 = \eta_t,$$
$$\Delta_i \leqslant 2\Delta_{i-1} + 3 \text{ for } i \geqslant 2.$$

The recurrence relation pertains to the case of squaring. One easily checks that $\Delta_i \leqslant (\eta_t + 3)2^{i-1}$ for all $i \geqslant 1$. Finally, the r_1-degree of the equation $\det M = 0$ is

$$\delta \leqslant \Delta_1 + \Delta_2 + \cdots + \Delta_\mu \leqslant (\eta_t + 3)(2^\mu - 1) \leqslant \left(2^{2t+3\lceil \log_2 t\rceil + 2} + 3\right)\left(2^{2^{t-1}-1} - 1\right).$$

Notice that this is potentially a very loose upper bound for δ. In general, we avoid squaring. Multiplication by a monomial can increase the r_1-degree by 3 if the monomial contains y_1. If the monomial does not contain y_1, the r_1-degree does not increase at all. Nevertheless, this loose upper bound is good enough in the present context.

C   Number of Roots of $\det M = 0$

Let us write the equation $\det M = 0$ as $D(r_1, r_2, \ldots, r_t) = 0$, where the r_i-degree of the multivariate polynomial D is $\leqslant \delta$ for each i. We assume that D is not identically zero. We plan to show that the maximum number $B^{(t)}$ of roots of D is $\leqslant t\delta q^{t-1}$. To that effect, we first write D as a polynomial in r_t:

$$D(r_1, r_2, \ldots, r_t) = D_\delta(r_1, r_2, \ldots, r_{t-1})r_t^\delta + D_{\delta-1}(r_1, r_2, \ldots, r_{t-1})r_t^{\delta-1} + \cdots +$$
$$D_1(r_1, r_2, \ldots, r_{t-1})r_t + D_0(r_1, r_2, \ldots, r_{t-1}).$$

If D is not identically zero, at least one D_i is not identically zero. If $(r_1, r_2, \ldots, r_{t-1})$ is a common root of each D_i, appending any value of r_t gives a root of D. The maximum number of common roots of $D_0, D_1, \ldots, D_\delta$ is $B^{(t-1)}$. On the other hand, if $(r_1, r_2, \ldots, r_{t-1})$ is not a common root of all D_i, there are at most δ values of r_t satisfying $D(r_1, r_2, \ldots, r_t) = 0$. We, therefore, have

$$B^{(t)} \leqslant B^{(t-1)}q + (q^{t-1} - B^{(t-1)})\delta = (q - \delta)B^{(t-1)} + \delta q^{t-1}. \tag{14}$$

Moreover, we have

$$B^{(1)} \leqslant \delta. \tag{15}$$

By induction on t, one can show that $B^{(t)} \leqslant t\delta q^{t-1}$. This bound is rather tight, particularly for $\delta \ll q$ (as it happens in our cases of interest). A polynomial D satisfying equalities in (14) and (15) can be constructed as $D(r_1, r_2, \ldots, r_t) = \Delta(r_1)\Delta(r_2) \cdots \Delta(r_t)$, where Δ is a square-free univariate polynomial of degree δ, that splits over $\mathbb{F}_q$. By the principle of inclusion and exclusion (or by explicitly solving the recurrence (14)), we obtain the total number of roots of this D as

$$\delta t q^{t-1} - \binom{t}{2}\delta^2 q^{t-1} + \binom{t}{3}\delta^3 q^{t-3} - \cdots + (-1)^{t-1}\delta^t$$
$$= q^t - (q - \delta)^t = \delta(q^{t-1} + (q - \delta)q^{t-2} + (q - \delta)^2 q^{t-3} + \cdots + (q - \delta)^{t-1}).$$

If $\delta \ll q$, this count is very close to $t\delta q^{t-1}$. It remains questionable whether our equation $\det M = 0$ actually encounters this worst-case situation, but this does not matter, at least in a probabilistic sense.

Extended Security Arguments
for Signature Schemes

Sidi Mohamed El Yousfi Alaoui[1], Özgür Dagdelen[1], Pascal Véron[2],
David Galindo[3], and Pierre-Louis Cayrel[4]

[1] Darmstadt University of Technology, Germany
[2] IML/IMATH Université du Sud Toulon-Var, France
[3] University of Luxembourg, Luxembourg
[4] Laboratoire Hubert Curien Université de Saint-Etienne, France

Abstract. The well-known forking lemma by Pointcheval and Stern has
been used to prove the security of the so-called generic signature schemes.
These signature schemes are obtained via the Fiat-Shamir transform
from three-pass identification schemes. A number of five-pass identification protocols have been proposed in the last few years. Extending
the forking lemma and the Fiat-Shamir transform would allow to obtain new signature schemes since, unfortunately, these newly proposed
schemes fall outside the original framework. In this paper, we provide an
extension of the forking lemma in order to assess the security of what we
call n-generic signature schemes. These include signature schemes that
are derived from certain $(2n + 1)$-pass identification schemes. We thus
obtain a generic methodology for proving the security of a number of
signature schemes derived from recently published five-pass identification protocols, and potentially for $(2n + 1)$-pass identification schemes
to come.

Keywords: signature schemes, forking lemma, identification schemes.

1 Introduction

The focus of this work is on methodologies to prove the security of digital signature schemes. Thus, instead of providing security reductions from scratch, the
goal is to provide security arguments for a class of signature schemes, as previously done in [12,13,9,1,19]. In particular, we aim at extending a pioneering work
by Pointcheval and Stern [12] where a reduction technique was introduced to obtain security arguments for the so-called generic signature schemes. These security
arguments allow for simple proofs and for efficient signature schemes. Moreover,
this type of signature schemes can be derived from identification schemes if the
latter satisfy certain requirements.

Generic Signature Schemes. Pointcheval and Stern call generic signature schemes
those whose signatures are of the form $\sigma = (\sigma_0, h_1, \sigma_1)$, where σ_0 is uniformly

A. Mitrokotsa and S. Vaudenay (Eds.): AFRICACRYPT 2012, LNCS 7374, pp. 19–34, 2012.

distributed over a large set, $h_1 = H(m, \sigma_0)$ with H being a hash function modeled as a random oracle, m is the message to be signed and σ_1 depends just on σ_0 and h_1.

The works [12,13] provide security arguments for generic signature schemes thanks to the use of the forking lemma. This lemma states that a successful forger can be restarted with a different random oracle in order to get two distinct but related forgeries. If the generic signature schemes additionally enjoy the existence of a polynomial-time algorithm, called extractor, that recovers the signing key from two signatures $\sigma = (\sigma_0, h_1, \sigma_1)$ and $\sigma' = (\sigma_0, h_1', \sigma_1')$ with $h_1 \neq h_1'$, then unforgeability is guaranteed under a supposedly intractable problem.

Unfortunately, the forking lemma is restricted to 3-tupled signatures. One would like to obtain an unbounded version of this lemma for signatures of the form $(\sigma_0, h_1, \sigma_1, \ldots, h_n, \sigma_n)$ where $h_i = H_i(m, \sigma_0, h_1, \sigma_1, \ldots, h_{i-1}, \sigma_{i-1})$ for $n \in \mathbb{N}$. This would allow to address a greater class of signatures. In this work, we provide such an extension and apply it to assess the security of n-generic signature schemes. Roughly speaking, n-generic signature schemes are built as generic signature schemes but are not restricted in the number of tuple entries as mentioned above.

From Identification Schemes to Signature Schemes. One of the ways to build a signature scheme is to depart from an existing identification protocol and convert it into a signature scheme using the well-known Fiat-Shamir (FS) paradigm [5]. In an identification protocol a series of messages are exchanged between two parties, called prover and verifier, in order to enable a prover to convince a verifier that it knows a given secret. Zero-knowledge identification protocols [7] convince a verifier without revealing any other information whatsoever about the secret itself. Informally, the FS paradigm builds a signature scheme as the transcript of one execution of the identification scheme, where the challenges sent by the verifier are replaced by the output of a secure hash function having as input the message and the current transcript.

In [12] the signatures obtained by applying the FS transform to canonical identification schemes were generalized to the concept of generic signatures schemes. Schematically, in a canonical identification scheme a prover sends first a commitment Com, then receives a challenge Ch drawn from a uniform distribution, and finishes the interaction with a message, called response Rsp. Finally, the verifier applies a verifying algorithm to the prover's public key, determining acceptance or rejection. In addition, the identification protocol needs to satisfy special-soundness. Roughly, special-soundness means there exists a polynomial-time algorithm which is able to extract the witness of the prover, given two correlated transcripts $(\mathsf{Com}, \mathsf{Ch}, \mathsf{Rsp}), (\mathsf{Com}', \mathsf{Ch}', \mathsf{Rsp}')$ with $\mathsf{Com} = \mathsf{Com}'$ and $\mathsf{Ch} \neq \mathsf{Ch}'$.

Many zero-knowledge identification schemes have been proposed whose conversion to signature schemes lead to generic signature schemes like [5,6,17]. However, several signature schemes which are derived from 5-pass identification protocols are not covered by the abstraction above. Thus, we are obliged to prove their security from scratch. Examples of schemes falling outside the

Pointcheval-Stern framework can be found in [3,16,17,4,10,11,15,8,18]. The authors must provide direct proofs for the signature schemes in these works deriving from 5-pass identification. These proofs often appear quite complex. Moreover, the authors of [14] recently left open to find a security reduction for signatures derived from a 5-pass identification protocol. We show that all aforementioned 5-pass identification schemes give raise to 2-generic signature schemes. We isolate a property, called n-soundness, that implies unforgeability of all the schemes satisfying it. Informally, n-soundness means that the signing key can be extracted from two correlated valid signatures $\sigma = (\sigma_0, h_1, \ldots, \sigma_{n-1}, h_n, \sigma_n)$ and $\sigma' = (\sigma_0, h_1, \ldots, \sigma_{n-1}, h'_n, \sigma'_n)$ with $h_n \neq h'_n$. In particular, we prove in Section 4 the security of the resulting signature scheme from [14], which was missing in the original paper.

Related Work. Pointcheval and Stern [12,13] provided security arguments for generic signature schemes. However, these generic signature schemes are restrictive in the sense that (a) they allow transformations only based on canonical identification schemes, and (b) there exists an extractor for these schemes. The work of Abdalla *et al.* [1] introduced a new transformation from identification schemes (IS) to signature schemes (SS) without insisting on the existence of such an extractor. Nonetheless, they require again canonical IS. Ohta and Okamoto [9] assume that the IS is honest-verifier (perfect) zero-knowledge and that it is computationally infeasible for a cheating prover to convince the verifier to accept. Again, this result is valid only for three-pass IS.

Very recently, Yao and Zhao [19] presented what they call challenge-divided Fiat-Shamir paradigm. Here, security results are set for three-pass IS with divided random challenges. Even though they consider more challenges, still identification schemes with more than three interactions are not captured by their paradigm. In this work, we consider an unlimited number of challenges as long as they are randomly chosen from large enough sets. To the best of our knowledge this is the first transformation which gives generic security statements for SS derived from $(2n + 1)$-pass IS.

Organization. We introduce in Section 2 the necessary background to understand the paper. In Section 3 we present the notion of n-generic signature schemes and provide an extended forking lemma that applies to this new signature type. We exemplify in Section 4 our paradigm and derive a provably secure 2-generic signature scheme based on multivariate polynomials.

2   Preliminaries

We begin by introducing some notations and briefly reviewing some definitions. A function $\mu(\cdot)$ is *negligible in n*, or just *negligible*, if for every positive polynomial $p(\cdot)$ and all sufficiently large n it holds that $\mu(n) < 1/p(n)$. Otherwise, we call $\mu(\cdot)$ *non-negligible*. Note that the sum of two negligible functions (resp. non-negligible) is again negligible (resp. non-negligible) whereas the sum of one non-negligible function $\pi(\cdot)$ and one negligible function $\mu(\cdot)$ is non-negligible, i.e. there exists a positive polynomial $p(\cdot)$ such that for infinitely many n's it holds that $\pi(n) + \mu(n) > 1/p(n)$.

Two distributions ensembles $\{X_n\}_{n\in\mathbb{N}}$ and $\{Y_n\}_{n\in\mathbb{N}}$ are said to be *(computationally) indistinguishable*, if for every non-uniform polynomial-time algorithm D, there exists a negligible function $\mu(\cdot)$ such that

$$|\Pr[D(X_n) = 1] - \Pr[D(Y_n) = 1]| \leq \mu(n).$$

We write $s \xleftarrow{\$} \mathcal{A}^{\mathcal{O}}(x)$ to denote the output s by a probabilistic algorithm $\mathcal{A}$ with input x having black-box access to an oracle $\mathcal{O}$. In particular, this means, that $\mathcal{A}$ may query oracle $\mathcal{O}$ in order to derive s from its answers.

Digital Signatures. In the following we give the definition of a signature scheme together with the corresponding standard security level.

Definition 1 (Signature scheme). *A signature scheme is a collection of the following algorithms* S = (KGen, Sign, Vf) *defined as follows.*

KGen(1^κ) *is a probabilistic algorithm which, on input a security parameter* 1^κ, *outputs a secret and a public key* (sk, pk).

Sign(sk, m) *is a probabilistic algorithm which, on input a secret key* sk *and a message* m, *outputs a signature* σ.

Vf(pk, m, σ) *is a deterministic algorithm which, on input a public key* pk, *a message* m *and a signature* σ, *outputs either* 1 (= *valid*) *or* 0 (= *invalid*).

We require correctness of the verification, i.e., the verifier will always accept genuine signatures. More formally, for all (sk, pk) $\leftarrow$ KGen(1^κ), any message m, any $\sigma \leftarrow$ Sign(sk, m), we always have Vf(pk, m, σ) = 1.

From signature schemes we require that no outsider should be able to forge a signer's signature. The following definition captures this property formally.

Definition 2 (Unforgeability of a Signature Scheme). *A signature scheme* S = (KGen, Sign, Vf) *is existentially unforgeable under (adaptively) chosen-message attacks if for any efficient algorithm* $\mathcal{A}$ *making at most* q_s *oracle queries, the probability that the following experiment returns* 1 *is negligible:*

Experiment Unforgeability$_{\mathcal{A}}^{\mathrm{S}}(\kappa)$

    (sk, pk) $\xleftarrow{\$}$ KGen(1^κ)

    (σ^*, m^*) $\xleftarrow{\$}$ $\mathcal{A}^{\mathsf{Sign}'(\cdot)}$(pk)

        Sign$'(\cdot)$ *on input* m *outputs* $\sigma \xleftarrow{\$}$ Sign(sk, m)

    Return 1 *iff*

        Vf(pk, m^*, σ^*) = 1 *and* m^* *was not queried to* Sign$'(\cdot)$ *by* $\mathcal{A}$

The probability is taken over all coin tosses of KGen, Sign, *and* $\mathcal{A}$.

Note that q_s is bounded by a polynomial in the security parameter κ. Definition 2 captures unforgeability against adaptively chosen-message attacks for signature schemes. Unforgeability against no-message attacks is defined analogously but q_s must be 0.

Splitting Lemma. The following lemma is extensively used in the forking lemma proofs. It states that one can split a given set X into two subsets, (a) a non-negligible subset Ω consisting of "good" x's which provides a non-negligible probability of success over y, and (b) its complement, consisting of "bad" x's.

Lemma 1 (Splitting Lemma [12, Lemma 3]). *Let A be a subset of $X \times Y$ such that $Pr[A(x,y)] \geq \epsilon$, then there exist $\Omega \subset X$ such that*

1. $Pr[x \in \Omega] \geq \epsilon/2$
2. *If $a \in \Omega$, then $Pr[A(a,y)] \geq \epsilon/2$.*

See [12, Lemma 3] for the proof.

3 Extended Security Arguments for Digital Signatures

In this section we give the formal definition of an n-generic signature scheme and extend the forking lemma accordingly. This allows us to prove that any n-generic signature scheme satisfying what we call n-soundness is existentially unforgeable in the random oracle model.

3.1 n-Generic Signature Schemes

Let H_i denote a hash function with output of cardinality 2^{κ_i} (derived from the security parameter κ).

Definition 3 (n-Generic Signature Scheme). *An n-generic signature scheme is a digital signature scheme $S = (\mathsf{KGen}, \mathsf{Sign}, \mathsf{Vf})$ with the following properties:*

Structure *A signature σ for a message m is of the form $(\sigma_0, h_1, \ldots, \sigma_{n-1}, h_n, \sigma_n)$ where $h_1 = H_1(m, \sigma_0)$ and $h_i = H_i(m, \sigma_0, \ldots, h_{i-1}, \sigma_{i-1})$ for $i = 2, \ldots, n$ with H_i being modeled as a random oracle. σ_i depends on previous $\sigma_0, \ldots, \sigma_{i-1}$ and hash values $h_1, \ldots, h_i$ for $i = 1, \ldots, n$.*

Honest-Verifier Zero-Knowledge (HVZK) *Assume the hash functions H_i are modeled by publicly accessible random oracles. There exists a PPT algorithm Z, the zero-knowledge simulator, controlling the random oracles, such that for any pair of PPT algorithms $D = (D_0, D_1)$ the following distributions are computationally indistinguishable:*

– *Let $(\mathsf{pk}, \mathsf{sk}, m, state) \leftarrow D_0(1^\kappa)$. If pk belongs to sk, then set $\sigma = (\sigma_0, h_1, \ldots, \sigma_{n-1}, h_n, \sigma_n) \leftarrow \mathsf{Sign}(\mathsf{sk}, m)$, else $\sigma \leftarrow \perp$. Output $D_1(\sigma, state)$.*

– *Let $(\mathsf{pk}, \mathsf{sk}, m, state) \leftarrow D_0(1^\kappa)$. If pk belongs to sk, then set $\sigma = (\sigma_0, h_1, \ldots, \sigma_{n-1}, h_n, \sigma_n) \leftarrow Z(\mathsf{pk}, m, 1)$, else $\sigma \leftarrow Z(\mathsf{pk}, m, 0)$. Output $D_1(\sigma, state)$.*

Notice that the structure of a generic signature as originally proposed in [12] matches that of a 1-generic signature. For the sake of simplicity we occasionally write $\sigma = (\sigma_0, \ldots, \sigma_n, h_1 \ldots, h_n)$ instead of $(\sigma_0, h_1, \ldots, \sigma_{n-1}, h_n, \sigma_n)$.

3.2   An Extended Forking Lemma

Pointcheval and Stern introduced in [12] the forking lemma as a technique to prove the security of some families of signature schemes, namely generic signature schemes with special-soundness. This well-known lemma is applied to get two forgeries for the same message using a replay attack, after that, one can use the two obtained forgeries to recover the secret key. They also show that a successful forger in the adaptive chosen-message attack model implies a successful forger in the no-message attack model, as long as the honest-verifier zero-knowledge property holds. In the following we propose an extension of the original forking lemma that applies to n-generic signature schemes. We first provide the Extended Forking Lemma in the no-message attack model.

No-Message Attack Model

Lemma 2. *Let* S *be an n-generic signature scheme with security parameter κ. Let $\mathcal{A}$ be a PPT Turing machine given only the public data as input. If $\mathcal{A}$ can find a valid signature $(\sigma_0, \ldots, \sigma_n, h_1, \ldots, h_n)$ for a message m with a non-negligible probability, after asking the n random oracles $\mathcal{O}_1, \ldots, \mathcal{O}_n$ polynomially often (in κ), then, a replay of this machine with the same random tape, the same first oracles $\mathcal{O}_1, \ldots, \mathcal{O}_{n-1}$ and a different last oracle $\mathcal{O}_n$, outputs two valid signatures $(\sigma_0, \ldots, \sigma_n, h_1, \ldots, h_n)$ and $(\sigma_0, \ldots, \sigma'_n, h_1, \ldots, h'_n)$ for the same message m with a non-negligible probability such that $h_n \neq h'_n$.*

Proof. We are given a no-message adversary $\mathcal{A}$, which is a PPT Turing machine with a random tape ω taken from a set R_ω. During the attack, $\mathcal{A}$ may ask $q_1, \ldots, q_n$ (polynomially bounded in κ) queries to random oracles $\mathcal{O}_1, \ldots, \mathcal{O}_n$ with $q_j^{(i)}$ denoting the j-query to oracle $\mathcal{O}_i$. We denote by $q_1^{(i)}, \ldots, q_{q_i}^{(i)}$ the q_i distinct queries to the random oracles $\mathcal{O}_i$ and let $r^{(i)} = (r_1^{(i)}, \ldots, r_{q_i}^{(i)})$ be the answers of $\mathcal{O}_i$, for $1 \leq i \leq n$. Let $S_i^{q_i}$ denote the set of all possible answers from $\mathcal{O}_i$, i.e., $\{r_1^{(i)}, \ldots, r_{q_i}^{(i)}\} \in S_i^{q_i}$. Furthermore, we denote by

$\mathcal{E}$ the event that $\mathcal{A}$ can produce a valid signature $(\sigma_0, \ldots, \sigma_n, h_1, \ldots, h_n)$ for message m by using random tape ω and the answers $r_1^{(i)}, \ldots, r_{q_i}^{(i)}$ for $i \leq n$. Note that a valid signature implies $h_i = \mathcal{O}_i(m, \sigma_0, h_1, \ldots, h_{i-1}, \sigma_{i-1})$.

$\mathcal{F}$ the event that $\mathcal{A}$ has queried the oracle $\mathcal{O}_n$ with input $(m, \sigma_0, h_1, \ldots, h_{n-1}, \sigma_{n-1})$, i.e.,

$$\exists j \leq q_n : q_j^{(n)} = (m, \sigma_0, h_1, \ldots, h_{n-1}, \sigma_{n-1}).$$

Accordingly, its complement $\neg\mathcal{F}$ denotes

$$\forall j \leq q_n : q_j^{(n)} \neq (m, \sigma_0, h_1, \ldots, h_{n-1}, \sigma_{n-1}).$$

By hypothesis of the lemma, the probability that event $\mathcal{E}$ occurs ($\Pr[\mathcal{E}]$), is non-negligible, i.e., there exists a polynomial function $T(\cdot)$ such that $\Pr[\mathcal{E}] \geq \frac{1}{T(\kappa)}$. We know that

$$\Pr[\mathcal{E}] = \Pr[\mathcal{E} \wedge \mathcal{F}] + \Pr[\mathcal{E} \wedge \neg\mathcal{F}]. \tag{1}$$

Furthermore, we get

$$
\begin{aligned}
\Pr\left[h_n = \mathcal{O}_n(m, \sigma_0, h_1, \ldots, h_{n-1}, \sigma_{n-1}) \wedge \neg \mathcal{F}\right] \\
= \Pr\left[h_n = \mathcal{O}_n(m, \sigma_0, h_1, \ldots, h_{n-1}, \sigma_{n-1}) \mid \neg \mathcal{F}\right] \cdot \Pr[\neg \mathcal{F}] \\
\leq \Pr\left[h_n = \mathcal{O}_n(m, \sigma_0, h_1, \ldots, h_{n-1}, \sigma_{n-1}) \mid \neg \mathcal{F}\right] \\
\leq \frac{1}{2^{k_n}},
\end{aligned}
$$

because the output of $\mathcal{O}_n$ is unpredictable. The event $\mathcal{E}$ implies that $h_n = \mathcal{O}_n(m, \sigma_0, h_1, \ldots, h_{n-1}, \sigma_{n-1})$, and thus we get

$$
\Pr[\mathcal{E} \wedge \neg \mathcal{F}] \leq \Pr\left[h_n = \mathcal{O}_n(m, \sigma_0, h_1, \ldots, h_{n-1}, \sigma_{n-1}) \wedge \neg \mathcal{F}\right] \leq \frac{1}{2^{k_n}} \tag{2}
$$

Relations (1) and (2) lead to

$$
\Pr[\mathcal{E} \wedge \mathcal{F}] \geq \frac{1}{T(\kappa)} - \frac{1}{2^{k_n}} \geq \frac{1}{T'(\kappa)} \tag{3}
$$

Note that a polynomial $T'(\cdot)$ must exist since the difference between a non-negligible and negligible term is non-negligible. Therefore, $\exists l \leq q_n$ so that

$$
\Pr\left[\mathcal{E} \wedge q_l^{(n)} = (m, \sigma_0, h_1, \ldots, h_{n-1}, \sigma_{n-1})\right] \geq \frac{1}{q_n T'(\kappa)}.
$$

Indeed, if we suppose that, $\forall l \in \{1, \ldots, q_n\}$,

$$
\Pr\left[\mathcal{E} \wedge q_l^{(n)} = (m, \sigma_0, h_1, \ldots, h_{n-1}, \sigma_{n-1})\right] < \frac{1}{q_n T'(\kappa)}
$$

then,

$$
\begin{aligned}
\Pr[\mathcal{E} \wedge \mathcal{F}] &= \Pr\left[\mathcal{E} \wedge (\exists j \leq q_n, q_j^{(n)} = (m, \sigma_0, h_1, \ldots, h_{n-1}, \sigma_{n-1}))\right] \\
&\leq \sum_{j=1}^{q_n} \Pr\left[\mathcal{E} \wedge q_j^{(n)} = (m, \sigma_0, h_1, \ldots, h_{n-1}, \sigma_{n-1})\right] \\
&< \frac{q_n}{q_n T'(\kappa)} = \frac{1}{T'(\kappa)}
\end{aligned}
$$

This leads to a contradiction with (3). Further, we define

$$
B = \{(\omega, r^{(1)}, \ldots, r^{(n)}) \text{ s.t. } \mathcal{E} \wedge q_l^{(n)} = (m, \sigma_0, h_1, \ldots, h_{n-1}, \sigma_{n-1})\}.
$$

Since, $B \subset R_\omega \times S_1^{q_1} \times \ldots \times S_n^{q_n}$ and $\Pr[B] \geq \frac{1}{q_n T'(\kappa)}$, by using the splitting lemma we have:

- $\exists \Omega \subset R_\omega$ such that $\Pr[\omega \in \Omega] \geq \frac{1}{2q_n T'(\kappa)}$.
- $\forall \omega \in \Omega$, $\Pr\left[(\omega, r^{(1)}, \ldots, r^{(n)}) \in B\right] \geq \frac{1}{2q_n T'(\kappa)}$, where the probability is taken over $S_1^{q_1} \times \ldots \times S_n^{q_n}$.

We define

$$B' = \{(\omega, r^{(1)}, \ldots, r^{(n)}) \text{ s.t. } (\omega, r^{(1)}, \ldots, r^{(n)}) \in B \wedge \omega \in \Omega\}.$$

Recall that $r^{(i)} = (r_1^{(i)}, \ldots, r_{q_i}^{(i)})$ where $r_j^{(i)} \in S_i$ for $1 \leq j \leq q_i$. Since,

$$B' \subset (R_\omega \times S_1^{q_1} \times \ldots \times S_n^{l-1}) \times S_n^{q_n - l + 1},$$

by using the splitting lemma again we get

- $\exists \Omega' \subset R_\omega \times S_1^{q_1} \times \ldots \times S_n^{l-1}$ such that
$$\Pr\left[(\omega, r^{(1)}, \ldots, r^{(n-1)}, (r_1^{(n)}, \ldots, r_{l-1}^{(n)})) \in \Omega' \right] \geq \frac{1}{4q_n T'(\kappa)}.$$
- $\forall (\omega, r^{(1)}, \ldots, r^{(n-1)}, (r_1^{(n)}, \ldots, r_{l-1}^{(n)})) \in \Omega'$,
$$\Pr\left[(\omega, r^{(1)}, \ldots, r^{(n-1)}, (r_1^{(n)}, \ldots, r_{l-1}^{(n)}, r_l^{(n)}, \ldots, r_{q_n}^{(n)})) \in B' \right] \geq \frac{1}{4q_n T'(\kappa)},$$
where the probability is taken over $S_n^{q_n - l + 1}$.

As a result, if we choose l, ω, $(r^{(1)}, \ldots, r^{(n-1)}, (r_1^{(n)}, \ldots, r_{l-1}^{(n)})), (r_l^{(n)}, \ldots, r_{q_n}^{(n)})$, and $(r_l'^{(n)}, \ldots, r_{q_n}'^{(n)})$ randomly, then we obtain two valid signatures $(\sigma_0, \ldots, \sigma_n, h_1, \ldots, h_n)$ and $(\sigma_0, \ldots, \sigma_n', h_1, \ldots, h_n')$ for message m with a non-negligible probability such that $h_n \neq h_n'$.[1]

□

Chosen-Message Attack Model

We now provide the Extended Forking Lemma in the adaptively chosen-message attack model. In this model, an adversary may adaptively invoke a signing oracle and is successful if it manages to compute a signature on a new message. If the signing oracle outputs signatures which are indistinguishable from a genuine signer without knowing the signing key, then using the simulator one can obtain two distinct signatures with a suitable relation from a single signature, similarly to the no-message scenario.

Theorem 1 (The Chosen-Message Extended Forking Lemma). *Let* S *be an n-generic signature scheme with security parameter κ. Let $\mathcal{A}$ be a PPT algorithm given only the public data as input. We assume that $\mathcal{A}$ can find a valid signature $(\sigma_0, \ldots, \sigma_n, h_1, \ldots, h_n)$ for message m with a non-negligible probability, after asking the n random oracles $\mathcal{O}_1, \ldots, \mathcal{O}_n$, and the signer polynomially often (in κ). Then, there exists another PPT algorithm $\mathcal{B}$ which has control over $\mathcal{A}$ by replacing interactions with the real signer by a simulation, and which provides with a non-negligible probability two valid signatures $(\sigma_0, \ldots, \sigma_n, h_1, \ldots, h_n)$ and $(\sigma_0, \ldots, \sigma_n', h_1, \ldots, h_n')$ for the same message m such that $h_n \neq h_n'$.*

---

[1] Since l is the index of $\mathcal{A}$'s query and there are only polynomially number of queries made by $\mathcal{A}$, our success probability remains non-negligible when picking l randomly.

Proof. We consider a PPT algorithm $\mathcal{B}$ that executes $\mathcal{A}$ in such a way that $\mathcal{B}$ simulates the environment of $\mathcal{A}$. Therefore, $\mathcal{B}$ must simulate the interactions of $\mathcal{A}$ with random oracles $\mathcal{O}_1, \ldots, \mathcal{O}_n$ and with the real signer. Then, we could see $\mathcal{B}$ as an algorithm performing a no-message attack against the signature scheme S.

Let Sim denote the zero-knowledge simulator of S that can simulate the answers of the real signer without knowledge of the secret key and has access to the random oracles $\mathcal{O}_i$ ($1 \le i \le n$). Let $\mathcal{A}$ be an adaptively chosen-message adversary, which is a probabilistic polynomial time Turing machine with a random tape ω taken from a set R_ω. During the attack, $\mathcal{A}$ may ask $q_1, \ldots, q_n$ queries to random oracles $\mathcal{O}_1, \ldots, \mathcal{O}_n$, and q_s queries (possibly repeated) to Sim. The values $q_1, \ldots, q_n$ and q_s are polynomially bounded in κ. We denote by $q_1^{(i)}, \ldots, q_{q_i}^{(i)}$ the q_i distinct queries to the random oracles $\mathcal{O}_i$, and by $m^{(1)}, \ldots, m^{(q_s)}$ the q_s queries to the simulator Sim.

The simulator Sim answers a tuple $(\sigma_0^{(j)}, \ldots, \sigma_n^{(j)}, h_1^{(j)}, \ldots, h_n^{(j)})$ as a signature for a message $m^{(j)}$, for each integer j with $1 \le j \le q_s$. Then, the adversary $\mathcal{A}$ assumes that $h_i^{(j)} = \mathcal{O}_i(m^{(j)}, \sigma_0^{(j)}, h_1^{(j)}, \ldots, h_{i-1}^{(j)}, \sigma_{i-1}^{(j)})$ holds for all $1 \le i \le n$ and $1 \le j \le q_s$, and stores all these relations.

Now we need to consider potential "collisions" of queries in the random oracles. There are two kind of collisions that can appear. That is, (a) the simulator Sim queries the random oracle with the same input the adversary has asked before (let us denote this event by $\mathcal{E}_1$), and (b) Sim asks the same question repeatedly (let us denote this event by $\mathcal{E}_2$).

We show that the probabilities of such events are negligible.

$$\Pr[\mathcal{E}_1] = \Pr[\exists i \in \{1, \ldots, n\}; \exists j \in \{1, \ldots, q_s\}; \exists t \in \{1, \ldots, q_n\}|$$
$$(m^{(j)}, \sigma_0^{(j)}, h_1^{(j)}, \ldots, h_{i-1}^{(j)}, \sigma_{i-1}^{(j)}) = q_t^{(i)}]$$

$$\le \sum_{i=1}^{n} \sum_{j=1}^{q_s} \sum_{t=1}^{q_n} \Pr[(m^{(j)}, \sigma_0^{(j)}, h_1^{(j)}, \ldots, h_{i-1}^{(j)}, \sigma_{i-1}^{(j)}) = q_t^{(i)}] \le \frac{n q_s q_n}{2^\kappa},$$

which is negligible, assuming that the σ_i's are random values drawn from a large set with cardinality greater than 2^κ.
Moreover, we have

$$\Pr[\mathcal{E}_2] = \Pr[\exists i \in \{1, \ldots, n\}; \exists j, j' \in \{1, \ldots, q_s\} : j \ne j'|$$
$$(m^{(j)}, \sigma_0^{(j)}, h_1^{(j)}, \ldots, h_{i-1}^{(j)}, \sigma_{i-1}^{(j)}) = (m^{(j')}, \sigma_0^{(j')}, h_1^{(j')}, \ldots, h_{i-1}^{(j')}, \sigma_{i-1}^{(j')})]$$

$$\le \sum_{i=1}^{n} \sum_{j=1}^{q_s} \sum_{j'=1}^{j} \Pr[(m^{(j)}, \sigma_0^{(j)}, h_1^{(j)}, \ldots, h_{i-1}^{(j)}, \sigma_{i-1}^{(j)}) =$$
$$(m^{(j')}, \sigma_0^{(j')}, h_1^{(j')}, \ldots, h_{i-1}^{(j')}, \sigma_{i-1}^{(j')})] \le \frac{n q_s^2}{2^\kappa},$$

which is also negligible.

Algorithm $\mathcal{B}$ succeeds whenever the machine $\mathcal{A}$ produces a valid signature without any collisions. Hence, we have

$$\Pr[\mathcal{B} \text{ succeeds }] = \Pr[\mathcal{A} \text{ succeeds }] - \Pr[\mathcal{E}_1] - \Pr[\mathcal{E}_2] \geq \frac{1}{T(\kappa)} - \frac{nq_s q_n}{2^\kappa} - \frac{nq_s^2}{2^\kappa},$$

which is non-negligible.

Summing up, we have an algorithm $\mathcal{B}$ that performs a no-message attack against the signature scheme S in polynomial time with non-negligible probability of success. So we can use Lemma 2 applied to algorithm $\mathcal{B}$, and we will obtain two valid signatures for the same message, such that $h_n \neq h'_n$ again in polynomial time.

$\square$

3.3   Security of n-Generic Signature Schemes

Similar to generic signature schemes defined by Pointcheval and Stern [12], for security under chosen-message attacks we require from n-generic signature schemes a property which we call n-soundness. Informally, n-soundness means that the secret key can be extracted from two correlated valid signatures $\sigma = (\sigma_0, h_1, \ldots, \sigma_{n-1}, h_n, \sigma_n)$ and $\sigma' = (\sigma_0, h_1, \ldots, \sigma_{n-1}, h'_n, \sigma'_n)$ with $h_n \neq h'_n$ in polynomial-time and with a non-negligible probability. The notion of special-soundness[2] and n-soundness coincide if $n = 1$.

Definition 4 (n-Soundness). *Let* S $=$ (KGen, Sign, Vf) *be an n-generic signature scheme. We call* S *n-sound if there exists a PPT algorithm K, the knowledge extractor, such that for any κ and m, any* (sk, pk) $\leftarrow$ KGen(1^κ)*, any* $\sigma = (\sigma_0, h_1, \ldots, \sigma_{n-1}, h_n, \sigma_n)$ *and* $\sigma' = (\sigma_0, h_1, \ldots, \sigma_{n-1}, h'_n, \sigma'_n)$ *with* Vf(pk, m, σ) = Vf(pk, m, σ') = 1 *and* $h'_n \neq h_n$*, we have* sk $\leftarrow K$(pk, σ, σ') *with non-negligible probability.*

The following theorem states that all n-generic signature schemes satisfying n-soundness are existentially unforgeable under adaptively chosen-message attacks in the random oracle model.

Theorem 2 (Security of n-Generic Signature Schemes). *Let* S *be an n-generic signature scheme satisfying n-soundness with underlying hard problem* **P***. Let κ be the security parameter. Then,* S *is existentially unforgeable under adaptively chosen-message attacks.*

Proof. We assume that the underlying hardness **P** of the n-generic signature scheme is hard, i.e., for all PPT algorithms $\mathcal{A}$ the probability to solve a hard instance of **P** is negligible. The key generation algorithm KGen of S outputs a secret and public key pair (sk, pk) derived by a hard instance and its corresponding solution of the problem **P**.

---

[2] Actually, special-soundness is a notion belonging to identification schemes. However, since this property is quite similar to the required property of generic signature schemes, this concept is used for both cases in the literature.

Now, assume by contradiction, that S is *not* existentially unforgeable under chosen-message attacks. That is, there exists a PPT algorithm $\mathcal{B}_1$ such that $\mathcal{B}_1$ is able to output a signature $\sigma^* = (\sigma_0, h_1, \ldots, \sigma_{n-1}, h_n, \sigma_n)$ for a fresh message m^* with non-negligible probability. Then, due to the Extended Forking Lemma, one can construct a PPT algorithm $\mathcal{B}_2$ which outputs two correlated signatures $\sigma^* = (\sigma_0, h_1, \ldots, \sigma_{n-1}, h_n, \sigma_n)$ and $\sigma^{**} = (\sigma_0, h_1, \ldots, \sigma_{n-1}, h'_n, \sigma'_n)$ with non-negligible probability such that $h_n \neq h'_n$.

Due to the n-soundness of S, we know that there exists an "extractor" which extracts the secret key given the two signatures above. This contradicts with the assumption that the underlying problem $\mathbf{P}$ is hard, and by implication, we learn that there cannot exist such a successful forger $\mathcal{B}_1$.

4 Applications

In this section we first discuss a transformation from $(2n + 1)$-pass identification protocols with a special structure to signature schemes that in many cases yields n-generic signature schemes. This is essentially an extended Fiat-Shamir transform. Then we go on with a specific instance of the aforementioned transformation. We obtain a new signature scheme based on multivariate polynomials by applying our method to a five-pass identification scheme recently introduced in [14].

4.1 n-Generic Signature Schemes Derived from Identification Schemes

Our goal is to enlarge the class of identification protocols to which the Fiat-Shamir transformation can be applied. We identify a potential set of candidates that we name *n-canonical identification schemes*. By n-canonical identification we mean schemes secure with respect to impersonation against passive attacks, where the challenges are drawn from an uniform distribution and have $2n + 1$ moves.

Definition 5 (n-canonical Identification Protocol). *An n-canonical identification scheme* IS $= (\mathcal{K}, \mathcal{P}, \mathcal{V})$ *is a $(2n + 1)$-pass interactive protocol. $\mathcal{K}$ and $\mathcal{P} = (\mathsf{P}_1, \ldots, \mathsf{P}_{n+1})$ are PPT algorithms whereas $\mathcal{V} = (\mathsf{ChSet}, \mathsf{Vf})$ with ChSet being a PPT algorithm and Vf a deterministic boolean algorithm. These algorithms are defined as follows:*

$\mathcal{K}(1^\kappa)$ *upon input a security parameter 1^κ, outputs a secret and public key $(\mathsf{sk}, \mathsf{pk})$ and challenge spaces $G_1, \ldots, G_n$ with $1/|G_i|$ negligible in 1^κ.*

$\mathsf{P}_1(\mathsf{sk})$ *upon input a secret key sk outputs the commitment R_1.*

$\mathsf{P}_i(\mathsf{sk}, R_1, C_1, \ldots, R_{i-1}, C_{i-1})$ *for $i = 2, \ldots, n$, upon input a secret key sk and the current transcript $R_1, C_1, \ldots, R_{i-1}, C_{i-1}$, outputs the i-th commitment R_i.*

$\mathsf{P}_{n+1}(\mathsf{sk}, R_1, C_1, \ldots, R_n, C_n)$ *upon input a secret key sk and the current transcript $R_1, C_1, \ldots, R_n, C_n$, outputs a response Rsp.*

ChSet(pk, i) *upon input a public key* pk *and round number* i, *outputs a challenge* $C_i \in G_i$.

Vf(pk, $R_1, C_1, \ldots, R_n, C_n, Rsp$) *upon input a public key* pk, *and the current transcript* $R_1, C_1, \ldots, R_n, C_n, Rsp$, *outputs either* 1 (= *valid*) *or* 0 (= *invalid*).

An n-canonical identification scheme IS *has the following properties.*

Public-Coin. *For any index* $i \in \{1, \ldots, n\}$ *and any* (sk, pk, $G_1, \ldots, G_n$) $\leftarrow$ $\mathcal{K}(1^\kappa)$ *the challenge* $C_i \leftarrow$ ChSet(pk, i) *is uniform in* G_i.

Honest-Verifier Zero-Knowledge. *There exists a PPT algorithm* Z, *the zero-knowledge simulator, such that for any pair of PPT algorithms* $D = (D_0, D_1)$ *the following distributions are computationally indistinguishable:*

  – *Let* (pk, sk, *state*) $\leftarrow D_0(1^\kappa)$, *and trans* = $(R_1, C_1, \ldots, R_n, C_n, Rsp)$ $\leftarrow$ $\langle \mathcal{P}(\mathsf{sk}, \mathsf{pk}), \mathcal{V}(\mathsf{pk}) \rangle$ *if* pk *belongs to* sk, *and otherwise trans* $\leftarrow \perp$. *Output* $D_1(trans, state)$.

  – *Let* (pk, sk, *state*) $\leftarrow D_0(1^\kappa)$, *and trans* = $(R_1, C_1, \ldots, R_n, C_n, Rsp)$ $\leftarrow$ $Z(\mathsf{pk}, 1)$ *if* pk *belongs to* sk, *and otherwise trans* $\leftarrow Z(\mathsf{pk}, 0)$. *Output* $D_1(trans, state)$.

Note that the definition of 1-canonical identification schemes is identical to that of canonical identification schemes [1]. An extended Fiat-Shamir transform is applied to an n-canonical identification scheme and yields an n-generic signature scheme, just as the original Fiat-Shamir transform yields a generic signature scheme in [12]. The idea of this transformation consists on replacing the uniformly random challenges of the verifier as set by ChSet in the identification scheme by the outputs of some secure hash functions $H_i : \{0,1\}^* \to G_i$ modeled as random oracles. More precisely, let IS = $(\mathcal{K}, \mathcal{P}, \mathcal{V})$ be an n-canonical identification scheme. The joint execution of $\mathcal{P}(\mathsf{sk}, \mathsf{pk})$ and $\mathcal{V}(\mathsf{pk})$ then defines an interactive protocol between the prover $\mathcal{P}$ and the verifier $\mathcal{V}$. At the end of the protocol $\mathcal{V}$ outputs a decision bit $b \in \{0, 1\}$. An n-generic signature scheme S = (KGen, Sign, Vf) is derived as follows:

KGen(1^κ) takes as input security parameter 1^κ and returns $\mathcal{K}(1^\kappa)$.

Sign(sk, m) takes as input a secret key sk and a message m and returns the transcript $\langle \mathcal{P}(\mathsf{sk}, \mathsf{pk}), \mathcal{V}(\mathsf{pk}) \rangle$ as the signature σ, i.e.,

$$\sigma = (\sigma_0, h_1, \ldots, h_n, \sigma_n) = (R_1, C_1, \ldots, R_n, C_n, Rsp)$$

or simply $\sigma = (\sigma_0, \ldots, \sigma_n, h_1 \ldots, h_n) = (R_1, \ldots, R_n, Rsp, C_1, \ldots, C_n)$. Here, C_i is defined by the equation $C_i := H_i(m, R_1, \ldots, R_i, C_1, \ldots, C_{i-1})$.

Vf(pk, m, σ) takes as input a public key pk, a message m and a signature σ and returns $\mathcal{V}.\mathsf{Vf}(\mathsf{pk}, m, \sigma)^3$ as the decision bit.

---

[3] By $\mathcal{V}.\mathsf{Vf}(\mathsf{pk}, m, \sigma)$ we mean the verification algorithm performed by the verifier from the underlying identification scheme IS.

The resulting scheme S is an n-generic signature scheme. Indeed, the obtained scheme S has the right structure and the honest-verifier zero-knowledge property is guaranteed by (the similar property of) the identification scheme.

However, it is still not guaranteed that S is existentially unforgeable. It lacks then to check/prove that the resulting scheme S is n-sound. If this is the case then one can apply Theorem 2 and S is guaranteed to have security against adaptive chosen-message attacks.

Let us point out that the plain version of most identification protocols does not directly satisfy the required security level by their choice of challenges spaces $G_1, \ldots, G_n$. In particular, it might be the case that $1/|G_i|$ is not negligible in the security parameter 1^κ. For that reason, one should typically repeat the ID protocol several (say δ) times until the desired security level is reached. In that case the concatenation of δ transcripts $\langle \mathcal{P}(\mathsf{sk}, \mathsf{pk}), \mathcal{V}(\mathsf{pk}) \rangle$ builds the signature (instead of a single execution of the ID scheme). Moreover, for our security analysis, we consider that the commitments R_i in all contain more entropy than k_n, the output size of the last hash function. This condition can be achieved by choosing their domain as large as necessary. Note that in [12] it is assumed that R_1 is uniformly distributed over its corresponding set.

4.2 Examples

Many zero-knowledge identification schemes have been proposed, whose conversion to signature schemes does not lead to generic signature schemes according to the definition of Pointcheval and Stern [12]. Examples of such schemes are those based on the Permuted Kernel Problem [15,8], the Permuted Perceptron Problem [10,11], the Constrained Linear Equations [18], the five-pass variant of SD problem [17,2], the q-SD problem [4], the SIS problem [3,16] and the MQ-problem [14]. Fortunately, their conversion to signature schemes belong to the class of n-generic signature schemes. Unlike [10,11], they even satisfy n-soundness. Consequently, our result for security of n-generic signature schemes satisfying n-soundness carries over to the resulting signature schemes derived from all these aforementioned identification schemes in the random oracle model.

We provide next the security argument for the resulting signature scheme derived from the MQ-based identification scheme [14]. The conversion of all aforementioned identification schemes to n-generic signature schemes and its security can be formulated in a very similar fashion. For this reason, we omit these proofs here.

The (Five-Pass) MQ Identification Scheme [14] and Its Signature. Recently at Crypto 2011, Sakumoto et al. presented a five-pass public-key identification scheme based on multivariate quadratic polynomials [14]. Assuming the existence of a non-interactive commitment scheme Com which should be statistically hiding and computationally binding, the authors of [14] showed that their scheme is an honest-verifier zero-knowledge identification scheme whereas the n-soundness property is also verified as we will later see in the security analysis.

We first briefly describe the identification scheme [14], following the procedure to convert it into a signature scheme using Section 4.1. Finally, we analyze the security of the obtained signature scheme using the Extended Forking Lemma discussed in Section 3.2.

Let n, m and q be positive integers. We denote by $\mathcal{MQ}(n, m, \mathbb{F}_q)$ a family of functions

$$\{F(x) = (f_1(x), \cdots, f_m(x)) \mid$$
$$f_l(x) = \sum_{i,j} a_{l,i,j} x_i x_j + \sum_i b_{l,i} x_i, \quad a_{l,i,j}, b_{l,i} \in \mathbb{F}_q \text{ for } l = 1, \cdots, m\},$$

where $x = (x_1, \cdots, x_n)$. An element F of $\mathcal{MQ}(n, m, \mathbb{F}_q)$ is called an MQ function and a function $G(x, y) = F(x + y) - F(x) - F(y)$ is called the polar form of F.

Let κ be a security parameter. Let $n = n(\kappa), m = m(\kappa)$ and $q = q(\kappa)$ be polynomially bounded functions. The key-generation algorithm $\mathcal{K}$ of this identification scheme can be described as follows. It takes 1^κ as input and creates a system parameter $F \in \mathcal{MQ}(n, m, \mathbb{F}_q)$ which consists of an m-tuple of random multivariate quadratic polynomials. Then, it randomly chooses a vector $s \in \mathbb{F}_q^n$ (secret key), and computes the corresponding public key $v := F(s)$. Finally, it returns the key pair $(\mathsf{pk}, \mathsf{sk}) = (v, s)$. Figure 1 illustrates the interaction protocol between the prover and the verifier.

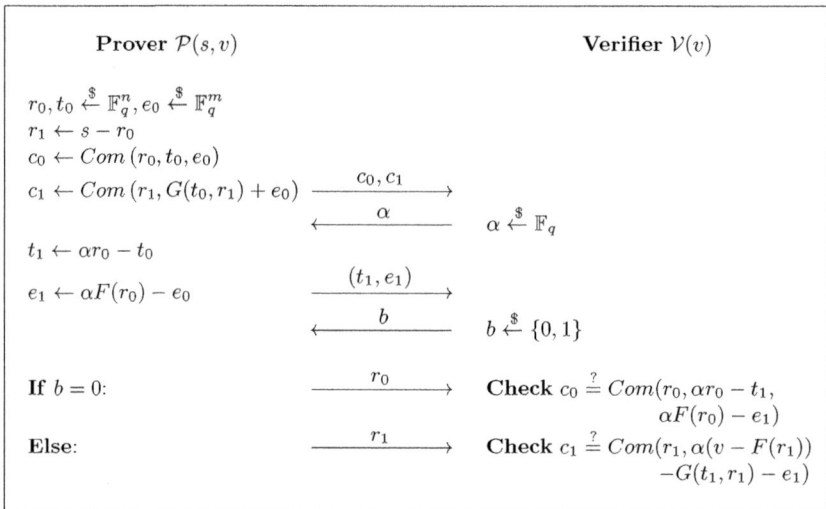

Fig. 1. The five-pass MQ identification scheme

The resulting Signature Scheme and its Security. According to Section 4.1, the MQ-based identification scheme described above can be turned to an n-generic signature scheme $\mathsf{S} = (\mathsf{KGen}, \mathsf{Sign}, \mathsf{Vf})$ as follows. Let δ be the number of rounds needed to achieve the required impersonation resistance.

$\mathsf{KGen}(1^\kappa)$ takes as input a security parameter 1^κ and outputs $\mathcal{K}(1^\kappa)$. The random oracles $\mathcal{O}_1$ and $\mathcal{O}_2$ output elements of $\mathbb{F}_q$ and $\{0,1\}$, respectively.

$\mathsf{Sign}(\mathsf{sk}, m)$ takes as input sk and a message m, and computes for all $1 \le i \le \delta$,

- $r_{1,i} = s - r_{0,i}$ where $r_{0,i} \xleftarrow{\$} \mathbb{F}_q^n$,
- $c_{0,i} = Com\,(r_{0,i}, t_{0,i}, e_{0,i})$, $c_{1,i} = Com\,(r_{1,i}, G(t_{0,i}, r_{1,i}) + e_{0,i})$, and sets $\sigma_{0,i} = (c_{0,i}, c_{1,i})$, where $t_{0,i} \xleftarrow{\$} \mathbb{F}_q^n$ and $e_{0,i} \xleftarrow{\$} \mathbb{F}_q^m$,
- $h_{1,i} \in \mathbb{F}_q$ such that $h_{1,i} = \mathcal{O}_1(m, \sigma_{0,i})$,
- $(t_{1,i}, e_{1,i}) = (h_{1,i} r_{0,i} - t_{0,i}, h_{1,i} F(r_{0,i}) - e_{0,i})$ and sets $\sigma_{1,i} = (t_{1,i}, e_{1,i})$,
- $h_{2,i}$ such that $h_{2,i} = \mathcal{O}_2(m, \sigma_{0,i}, h_{1,i}, \sigma_{1,i})$,
- $(\sigma_{0,i}, h_{1,i}, \sigma_{1,i}, h_{2,i}, \sigma_{2,i})$, where $\sigma_{2,i} := r_{0,i}$ if $h_{2,i} = 0$ and, otherwise, $\sigma_{2,i} := r_{1,i}$,
- and finally, returns the signature σ for the message m as $(\sigma_0, h_1, \sigma_1, h_2, \sigma_2)$, where $\sigma_j = (\sigma_{j,1}, \ldots, \sigma_{j,\delta})$ and $h_k = (h_{k,1}, \ldots, h_{k,\delta})$ with $0 \le j \le 2$ and $1 \le k \le 2$.

$\mathsf{Vf}(\mathsf{pk}, m, \sigma)$ takes as input a public key pk, a message m and a signature σ, outputs 1 iff $(\sigma_{0,1}, \ldots, \sigma_{0,\delta})$ is well calculated as in the identification protocol, i.e., the following respective equation is valid for all $1 \le i \le \delta$:

$$\text{If } h_{2,i} = 0 : \ c_{0,i} = Com\,(r_{0,i}, h_{1,i} r_{0,i} - t_{1,i}, h_{1,i} F(r_{0,i}) - e_{1,i})$$

$$\text{If } h_{2,i} = 1 : \ c_{1,i} = Com\,(r_{1,i}, h_{1,i}(v - F(r_{1,i})) - G(t_{1,i}, r_{1,i}) - e_{1,i})$$

Security Argument. Using the Extended Forking Lemma, we prove in the following that the signature scheme derived from the MQ-based zero-knowledge identification scheme is secure against adaptively chosen message attacks. We assume that an adversary produces a valid signature $(\sigma_0, h_1, \sigma_1, h_2, \sigma_2)$ for a message m. By applying Theorem 1 we can find a second forgery $(\sigma_0, h_1, \sigma_1, h_2', \sigma_2')$ with a non-negligible probability, such that $h_2 \ne h_2'$. That leads to the existence of an index i with $1 \le i \le \delta$, such that $h_{2,i} \ne h_{2,i}'$. W.l.o.g. assume $h_{2,i} = 0$ and $h_{2,i}' = 1$. Now, the adversary gets the answers for two distinct challenges, namely $r_{0,i}$ and $r_{1,i}$. Finally, by adding the last two values, the secret key can be disclosed. This contradicts the intractability of the MQ problem.

References

1. Abdalla, M., An, J.H., Bellare, M., Namprempre, C.: From Identification to Signatures via the Fiat-Shamir Transform: Minimizing Assumptions for Security and Forward-Security. In: Knudsen, L.R. (ed.) EUROCRYPT 2002. LNCS, vol. 2332, pp. 418–433. Springer, Heidelberg (2002)
2. Aguilar Melchor, C., Gaborit, P., Schrek, J.: A new zero-knowledge code based identification scheme with reduced communication. CoRR, abs/1111.1644 (2011)
3. Cayrel, P.-L., Lindner, R., Rückert, M., Silva, R.: Improved Zero-Knowledge Identification with Lattices. In: Heng, S.-H., Kurosawa, K. (eds.) ProvSec 2010. LNCS, vol. 6402, pp. 1–17. Springer, Heidelberg (2010)
4. Cayrel, P.-L., Véron, P., El Yousfi Alaoui, S.M.: A Zero-Knowledge Identification Scheme Based on the q-ary Syndrome Decoding Problem. In: Biryukov, A., Gong, G., Stinson, D.R. (eds.) SAC 2010. LNCS, vol. 6544, pp. 171–186. Springer, Heidelberg (2011)

5. Fiat, A., Shamir, A.: How to Prove Yourself: Practical Solutions to Identification and Signature Problems. In: Odlyzko, A.M. (ed.) CRYPTO 1986. LNCS, vol. 263, pp. 186–194. Springer, Heidelberg (1987)
6. El Gamal, T.: A Public Key Cryptosystem and a Signature Scheme Based on Discrete Logarithms. In: Blakely, G.R., Chaum, D. (eds.) CRYPTO 1984. LNCS, vol. 196, pp. 10–18. Springer, Heidelberg (1985)
7. Goldwasser, S., Micali, S., Rackoff, C.: The knowledge complexity of interactive proof-systems. In: STOC 1985, pp. 291–304. ACM (1985)
8. Lampe, R., Patarin, J.: Analysis of some natural variants of the PKP algorithm. Cryptology ePrint Archive, Report 2011/686 (2011), http://eprint.iacr.org/
9. Ohta, K., Okamoto, T.: On Concrete Security Treatment of Signatures Derived from Identification. In: Krawczyk, H. (ed.) CRYPTO 1998. LNCS, vol. 1462, pp. 354–369. Springer, Heidelberg (1998)
10. Pointcheval, D.: A New Identification Scheme Based on the Perceptrons Problem. In: Guillou, L.C., Quisquater, J.-J. (eds.) EUROCRYPT 1995. LNCS, vol. 921, pp. 319–328. Springer, Heidelberg (1995)
11. Pointcheval, D., Poupard, G.: A new NP-complete problem and public-key identification. Des. Codes Cryptography 28, 5–31 (2003)
12. Pointcheval, D., Stern, J.: Security Proofs for Signature Schemes. In: Maurer, U.M. (ed.) EUROCRYPT 1996. LNCS, vol. 1070, pp. 387–398. Springer, Heidelberg (1996)
13. Pointcheval, D., Stern, J.: Security arguments for digital signatures and blind signatures. J. Cryptology 13(3), 361–396 (2000)
14. Sakumoto, K., Shirai, T., Hiwatari, H.: Public-Key Identification Schemes Based on Multivariate Quadratic Polynomials. In: Rogaway, P. (ed.) CRYPTO 2011. LNCS, vol. 6841, pp. 706–723. Springer, Heidelberg (2011)
15. Shamir, A.: An Efficient Identification Scheme Based on Permuted Kernels (Extended Abstract). In: Brassard, G. (ed.) CRYPTO 1989. LNCS, vol. 435, pp. 606–609. Springer, Heidelberg (1990)
16. Silva, R., Cayrel, P.-L., Lindner, R.: Zero-knowledge identification based on lattices with low communication costs. XI Simpósio Brasileiro de Segurança da Informação e de Sistemas Computacionais 8, 95–107 (2011)
17. Stern, J.: A New Identification Scheme Based on Syndrome Decoding. In: Stinson, D.R. (ed.) CRYPTO 1993. LNCS, vol. 773, pp. 13–21. Springer, Heidelberg (1994)
18. Stern, J.: Designing Identification Schemes with Keys of Short Size. In: Desmedt, Y.G. (ed.) CRYPTO 1994. LNCS, vol. 839, pp. 164–173. Springer, Heidelberg (1994)
19. Yao, A.C., Zhao, Y.: Digital signatures from challenge-divided sigma-protocols. Cryptology ePrint Archive, Report 2012/001 (2012), http://eprint.iacr.org/

Sanitizable Signatures
with Several Signers and Sanitizers

Sébastien Canard[1], Amandine Jambert[2], and Roch Lescuyer[1,3]

[1] Orange Labs, Applied Crypto Group, Caen, France
[2] CNIL, Paris, France
[3] ENS, Paris, France

Abstract. Sanitizable signatures allow a signer of a message to give one specific receiver, called a sanitizer, the power to modify some designated parts of the signed message. Most of the existing constructions consider one single signer giving such a possibility to one single sanitizer. In this paper, we formalize the concept with n signers and m sanitizers, taking into account recent models (for 1 signer and 1 sanitizer) on the subject. We next give a generic construction based on the use of both group signatures and a new cryptographic building block, called a trapdoor or proof, that may be of independent interest.

Keywords: Sanitizable signatures, anonymity, trapdoor or proof.

1 Introduction

Cryptographic research provides today a large choice of tools to secure our networks and services. Besides authentication and encryption, it exists several ways to lighten or slightly modify the main cryptographic tools. Regarding signature schemes, it is for example possible to blind the identity of the signer (using e.g. group signatures) or to add properties on the resulting message-signature pair.

Among those variants, the idea of a signature on a document which can be further modified by a designated "sanitizer", without interaction with the signer, has been introduced in [19]. The current definition, introduced in [1] under the named of sanitizable signatures, allows the signer to control which parts of the message can be modified by the chosen sanitizer. The security properties sketched in [1] have been formalized in [7] for the case of one single signer giving the modification power to one single sanitizer[1]: such a scheme should be *transparent* (only the signer and the sanitizer are able to distinguish an original signature from a sanitized one), *immutable* (the sanitizer is unable to modify non admissible blocks of a signed message), *signer-accountable* (a signer can not force a judge to accuse a sanitizer) and *sanitizer-accountable* (a sanitizer can not force a judge to accuse a signer). The notion of *unlinkability* (infeasibility to identify message-signature pairs from the same source) has later been proposed in [8]. Some extensions [18,9] have also been described, allowing the signer to better control the modifications the sanitizer can do.

---

[1] Even if several sanitizers could exist in the system.

A. Mitrokotsa and S. Vaudenay (Eds.): AFRICACRYPT 2012, LNCS 7374, pp. 35–52, 2012.

It currently exists several sanitizable signature constructions in the literature [1,10,7,9,8,17] which consider *one single* signer allowing *one single* sanitizer to sanitize a given message-signature pair. But nobody has really taken into account the case of multiple signers and sanitizers in a unique system. The closest solutions are either trapdoor solutions [10,21] which allows signer to chose afterwards one sanitizer in a group or the recent work in [8] about unlinkable schemes which can be extended to the case of "one signer and m sanitizers".

Regarding concrete applications, sanitizable signatures with one signer and one sanitizer may be useful in the context of Digital Right Management [10] (signer of a license vs. modifier of a given license), database applications [1] (commercial vendor vs. database administrator) or medical ones [1] but the one-one case does not cover all use cases. The secure routing application proposed in [1] should *e.g.* use a group of n entities acting as both signers and sanitizers. Sanitizable signatures can also be used *e.g.* to protect the privacy of customers in a billing system where the service provider does not obtain the identity of the customer and the billing provider does not know the provided service.

In this paper, we propose the first complete model for sanitizable signatures with n signers and m sanitizers. Our model includes the Brzuska *et al.* [7,8] for 1 signer and 1 sanitizer and considers collusion of adversary.

IDEAS BEHIND OUR MODEL. A signer can choose several designated sanitizers for a given message and each of them is able to modify the resulting message/signature pair. We thus redefine accordingly the notions of accountability and immutability and introduce several notions of transparency: the *no-transparency* where anybody can distinguish a signed message from a sanitized one, the *group transparency* where only signers can make such a distinction and the *full transparency* where this can only be done by the true signer, the true sanitizer and a designated authority.

As there are several signers and sanitizers, we study the case where the signer (resp. the sanitizer) is anonymous within the group of signers (resp. sanitizers). Similarly to the transparency, we also introduce the concept of *group anonymity* where a signer (resp. sanitizer) is anonymous for people who are not in the group of signers (resp. sanitizers). To be complete, we also treat the anonymity revocation by some designated authorities and study the notion of traceability and non-frameability from the group signature world [3,4].

IDEA OF OUR CONSTRUCTION. Our main (n, m) multi-players sanitizable signature construction is based on the work of Brzuska *et al.* [8], using group signatures [3,5,4,13]. More precisely, we base our new solution on a new cryptographic building block that may be of independent interest: *trapdoor or proof.* Zero-knowledge proofs of knowledge allow one prover to prove to one verifier that she knows some secrets verifying some public relations. An *or proof* enables to prove *e.g.* that the known secret is the discrete logarithm of either y in base g *or* of z in base h. We introduce the concept, and give a practical construction, for a *trapdoor or proof* where a given authority can reveal which discrete logarithm is known. Independently, this tool can be used to design electronic voting systems.

The paper is organized as follows. Our model for multi-players sanitizable signature is described in Section 2 (for procedures) and in Section 3 (for security). Section 4 is dedicated to useful tools and Section 5 to our new *trapdoor or proof*. Our main multi-players sanitizable signature scheme is described in Section 6.

2   Multi-players Sanitizable Signatures

Our aim is to propose a model where one signer (among n) can choose a set of sanitizers (among m) such that any sanitizer of the chosen subset is able to sanitize the output message-signature pair. Moreover we want to be consistent with the initial model from Brzuska *et al.* where one signer chooses one sanitizer [7]. We thus keep traditional procedures (SIGN, SANITIZE, VERIFY, SIGOPEN and JUDGE) and security properties: *immutability, signer and sanitizer accountabilities* and *transparency* (see below). We also add the *unlinkability* property [8].

ADDING ANONYMITY. As we now have a group of signers and sanitizers, we can handle these groups in different ways. One possibility is to publicly know who is the initial signer (resp. sanitizer) of a given message-signature pair (*no-anonymity*). We can also take the example of group signatures by considering that the signer (resp. sanitizer) can be *anonymous*, except for a designated authority (*full anonymity*). In some cases, the other signers (resp. sanitizers) may need to identify the signer (resp. the sanitizer) of a given message, while this is still not feasible for other parties (*group-anonymity*).

We thus add a full opener $\mathcal{O}_{\text{FULL}}$ who is able to determine (during the FULLOPEN procedure) the real producer of a given message-signature pair. Similarly, the origin opener $\mathcal{O}_{\text{ORI}}$ is able to retrieve (during the FINDORI algorithm) the signer who is at the origin of a given message-signature pair.

The notion of anonymity and the possibility to revoke this property necessary lead to the notion of *traceability* (the identity of an anonymous signer or an anonymous sanitizer can always be retrieved if needed) and *non-frameability* (the infeasibility to produce a wrong opening).

THE CASE OF THE TRANSPARENCY. The notion of *transparency* says [7] that only the signer and the sanitizer are able to distinguish an original signature from a sanitized one. For this purpose, the signer in [7] has access to a SIGOPEN procedure which permits her to prove that a given message/signature pair is an original or a sanitized one.

As we consider the case of a group, we introduce, as for anonymity, the notion of *group anonymity* where the the SIGOPEN procedure is extended to any signer in the group (not only the real signer).

We also keep the traditional notion (called *full transparency*) where only the true original signer, the true sanitizer (if relevant), and a new introduced authority called the algorithm opener $\mathcal{O}_{\text{ALG}}$, are able to prove that one message-signature pair is an original or not. For the latter, we introduce the ALGOPEN procedure which can be executed by $\mathcal{O}_{\text{ALG}}$. Note that the true signer is always able to make such distinction but she is not necessarily able to prove it.

Remark 1. We do not need to add an unforgeability property since it is implied by the accountability, traceability and non-frameability. In fact, from Proposition 4.2 of [7], we obtain that accountabilities imply unforgeability and the given proof still work in our case. Moreover (cf. Appendix A of [4]), the group signature's unforgeability follows from traceability plus non-frameability.

GENERAL DEFINITION. A multi-players sanitizable signature scheme involves a set of signers, a set of sanitizers, an issuer $\mathcal{I}$ that may be divided into $\mathcal{I}_{\text{SIG}}$ and $\mathcal{I}_{\text{SAN}}$ and an opener $\mathcal{O}$ that may be divided into $\mathcal{O}_{\text{FULL}}$, $\mathcal{O}_{\text{ALG}}$, and $\mathcal{O}_{\text{ORI}}$.

Given a message m of length ℓ and divided into t blocks, ADM is defined by the signer as (i) the length ℓ_i of each block m_i (such that $\ell = \sum_{i=1}^{t} \ell_i$) and (ii) the index of the block which will be modifiable by the sanitizer, i.e. the subset $\mathcal{T}$ of $[1, t]$ such that for all $i \in \mathcal{T}$, m_i is modifiable. By misuse of notation, we say that $i \in$ ADM if $i \in \mathcal{T}$. If two messages m_0 and m_1 are defined as having the same admissible parts ADM, we note that $\text{ADM}(m_0, m_1) = 1$. On input a message m and the variable ADM, the sanitizer define the modifications MOD as the set of all the (i, m_i') such that she is able to replace the i-th block of m by m_i'. We say that MOD matches ADM if $\forall i \in$ MOD, $i \in$ ADM.

Definition 1 (Multi-players sanitizable signature scheme). *Let λ be a security parameter. A (n, m)-multi-players sanitizable signature scheme Π is composed of the following eleven algorithms.*

SETUP(1^λ) *outputs the public key* gpk *of the system, the secret key* isk := $(\text{isk}_{\text{SIG}}, \text{isk}_{\text{SAN}})$ *of some issuers and, in some cases, an additional opening secret key denoted by* osk := $(\text{osk}_{\text{FULL}}, \text{osk}_{\text{ALG}}, \text{osk}_{\text{ORI}})$.

SIGKG($1^n, 1^\lambda, \text{isk}_{\text{SIG}}$) *and* SANKG($1^m, 1^\lambda, \text{isk}_{\text{SAN}}$) *take as input the issuer key* isk_{SIG} *(resp.* isk_{SAN}*), the number n (resp. m) of signers (resp. of sanitizers) and λ. They output two vectors of keys* $(\boldsymbol{sk}_{\text{SIG}}, \boldsymbol{pk}_{\text{SIG}})$ *(resp.* $(\boldsymbol{sk}_{\text{SAN}}, \boldsymbol{pk}_{\text{SAN}})$*). From now on, the whole public key* (gpk, $\boldsymbol{pk}_{\text{SIG}}, \boldsymbol{pk}_{\text{SAN}}$) *is denoted* PK.

SIGN($m, \boldsymbol{sk}_{\text{SIG}}[i], \widetilde{\boldsymbol{pk}}_{\text{SAN}}, \text{ADM}, \text{PK}$) *enables the signer i to sign a message m for authorized sanitizers* $\widetilde{\boldsymbol{pk}}_{\text{SAN}} \subseteq \boldsymbol{pk}_{\text{SAN}}$ *according to* ADM *as defined above. It outputs a signature σ on m. By convention σ contains* ADM *and* $\widetilde{\boldsymbol{pk}}_{\text{SAN}}$. *Note that σ also contains the way for authorized sanitizers to sanitize m.*

SANITIZE($m, \sigma, \boldsymbol{sk}_{\text{SAN}}[j], \text{MOD}, \text{PK}$) *is carried out by the sanitizer j to sanitize a message-signature pair (m, σ). The modifications* MOD *describe the new message m' as defined above. This algorithm outputs a new signature σ' and the modified message m' or $\perp$ in case of error (for example, j is not able to sanitize this message).*

VERIFY(m, σ, PK) *allows to verify the signature σ (sanitized or not) on the message m. It outputs 1 if the signature is correct and 0 if it is not.*

FULLOPEN($\mathsf{m}, \sigma, \mathsf{osk}_{\text{FULL}}, \mathsf{PK}$) *enables the opener* $\mathcal{O}_{\text{FULL}}$ *to find the identity of the producer of the given message. It outputs the string* FULL, *an identity* I_{FULL} *which is either* ($\mathsf{sig}, i_{\text{FULL}}$) *or* ($\mathsf{san}, j_{\text{FULL}}$), *and a proof* τ_{FULL} *of this claim. In case* $I_{\text{FULL}} = 0$, *it is claiming that no one produced* σ.

ALGOPEN($\mathsf{m}, \sigma, \mathsf{osk}_{\text{ALG}}, \mathsf{PK}$) *enables the opener* $\mathcal{O}_{\text{ALG}}$ *to find whether the couple* (m, σ) *is an original or a sanitized couple. It outputs the string* ALG, *next either* $I_{\text{ALG}} = \mathsf{sig}$ *(original signature) or* $I_{\text{ALG}} = \mathsf{san}$ *(sanitized signature), and a proof* τ_{ALG} *of this claim. In case* $I_{\text{ALG}} = 0$, *the result is that the opener* $\mathcal{O}_{\text{ALG}}$ *cannot conclude.*

FINDORI($\mathsf{m}, \sigma, \mathsf{osk}_{\text{ORI}}, \mathsf{PK}$) *enables the opener* $\mathcal{O}_{\text{ORI}}$ *to find the original signer of the given message. It outputs the string* ORI, *the identity* $I_{\text{ORI}} = (\mathsf{sig}, i_{\text{ORI}})$ *of the original signer and a proof* τ_{ORI} *of this claim. In case* $I_{\text{ORI}} = 0$, *it is claiming that no signer is at the origin of* σ. *Note that* i_{ORI} *is not necessarily the identity of the actor having produced the signature* σ, *since this one may have been sanitized after the original signature from* i_{ORI}.

SIGOPEN($\mathsf{m}, \sigma, (\text{ORI}, I_{\text{ORI}}, \tau_{\text{ORI}}), \boldsymbol{sk}_{\text{SIG}}[\tilde{i}], \mathsf{PK}, \mathsf{DB}$) *enables the signer* $\tilde{i}$ *to be convinced, using an entry* (ORI, $I_{\text{ORI}}, \tau_{\text{ORI}}$) *(with* $I_{\text{ORI}} := (\mathsf{sig}, i_{\text{ORI}})$) *which could have been produced by the* FINDORI *algorithm, that the signer* i_{ORI} *is the originator of the given message. The signer* $\tilde{i}$ *may use a set* DB *of couples* (m_k, σ_k) *and proves that the given message-signature pair* (m, σ) *is or is not a sanitized pair. It outputs a triple containing the string* SIG, *either* $I_{\text{SIG}} = I_{\text{ORI}}$ *if* (m, σ) *a true signature or* ($\mathsf{san}, 0$) *if* (m, σ) *was sanitized, and a proof* τ_{SIG} *(including* τ_{ORI}). *It outputs* $I_{\text{SIG}} = 0$ *if the signer* $\tilde{i}$ *can not conclude.*

JUDGE($\mathsf{m}, \sigma, \mathsf{gpk}, (s, I_s, \tau_s), \mathsf{PK}$) *is a public algorithm which aims at deciding the origin of a given message-signature pair* (m, σ). *According to the string* $s \in \{\text{FULL}, \text{ALG}, \text{ORI}, \text{SIG}\}$, *it outputs 1 if the predicate guessed in* τ_s *is exact and 0 otherwise.*

The correctness property states that all of them should be correct, from the verification to the different opening algorithms.

3   Security Requirements

We now give the security definitions a multi-players sanitizable signature scheme should satisfy. Our work is based on those from [7] and [3].

ORACLES. The security properties will be displayed using experiments in which the adversary's attacks are modelled by having access to some oracles. In the following, $\mathcal{CU}$ denotes the set of corrupted users (as a signer or a sanitizer).

- setup($\cdot, \cdot, \cdot$): this oracle corresponds to the generation of the different keys and parameters. It takes as input the parameters $\lambda, n, m \in \mathbb{N}$ and executes the procedures SETUP($\cdot$), SIGKG($\cdot, \cdot, \cdot$) and SANKG($\cdot, \cdot, \cdot$) and the set PK is given on output, while SK = $\{\mathsf{isk}, \mathsf{osk}, \boldsymbol{sk}_{\text{SIG}}, \boldsymbol{sk}_{\text{SAN}}\}$ is kept secret (for now).

- corrupt$(\cdot, \cdot, \cdot)$: the adversary can corrupts a signer or a sanitizer. This oracle takes as input three elements: the first one $a \in \{\mathsf{sig}, \mathsf{san}\}$ says whether the corrupted player is a signer or a sanitizer, the second argument $k \in \mathbb{N}$ gives the identity of the corresponding signer ($k \in [1, n]$) or sanitizer ($k \in [1, m]$) and the third one corresponds to a public key pk. The couple (a, k) is added to the set $\mathcal{CU}$ and the oracle sets $(\mathsf{pk}_{\mathrm{SIG}}[k], \mathsf{sk}_{\mathrm{SIG}}[k]) = (\mathsf{pk}, \perp)$ if $a = \mathsf{sig}$ (or $(\mathsf{pk}_{\mathrm{SAN}}[k], \mathsf{sk}_{\mathrm{SAN}}[k]) = (\mathsf{pk}, \perp)$ if $a = \mathsf{san}$). An adversary having access to no corruption oracle is denoted $\mathcal{A}^{(0)}$, an adversary only having access to corrupt$(\mathsf{sig}, \cdot, \cdot)$ (resp. corrupt$(\mathsf{san}, \cdot, \cdot)$) is denoted $\mathcal{A}^{(\mathsf{si})}$ (resp. $\mathcal{A}^{(\mathsf{sa})}$), while an adversary having access to both is denoted by $\mathcal{A}^{(*)}$.
- sign$(\cdot, \cdot, \cdot)$, sanitize$(\cdot, \cdot, \cdot, \cdot)$, fullopen$(\cdot, \cdot)$, algopen$(\cdot, \cdot)$, findorigin$(\cdot, \cdot)$ and finally sigopen$(\cdot, \cdot, \cdot, \cdot)$: these oracles are related to the procedures given in Definition 1 (without the non necessary public parameters). The set of queries and answers to and from the sign (resp. the sanitize) oracle is denoted Σ_{sig} (resp. Σ_{san}) and is composed of elements of the form $(\mathsf{m}_k, i_k, \widetilde{\mathsf{pk}}_{\mathrm{SAN},k}, \mathsf{ADM}_k, \sigma_k)$ (resp. $(\mathsf{m}_k, \sigma_k, j_k, \mathsf{MOD}_k, \mathsf{m}'_k, \sigma'_k)$).

ADVERSARIES. For each property, there are two types of adversary.

1. A generator adversary $\mathcal{A}_{\mathsf{gen}}$ outputs something that will pass some given criteria. The experiment outputs 1 if all criteria on the adversary's output are verified. For any adversary $\mathcal{A}_{\mathsf{gen}}$ against a property prop and any parameters $\lambda, n, m \in \mathbb{N}$, the success probability of $\mathcal{A}_{\mathsf{gen}}$ is the probability that the experiment outputs 1. We say that the scheme verifies prop if this success is negligible (as a function of λ, n, m) for any polynomial-time $\mathcal{A}_{\mathsf{gen}}$.
2. A choose-then-guess adversary $\mathcal{A} = (\mathcal{A}_{\mathsf{ch}}, \mathcal{A}_{\mathsf{gu}})$ is divided into two phases: $\mathcal{A}_{\mathsf{ch}}$ for the "choose" phase or $\mathcal{A}_{\mathsf{gu}}$ for the "guess" one. For the experiments, a challenge bit $b \in \{0, 1\}$ is set and for any adversary $\mathcal{A}$ against a property prop and any parameters $\lambda, n, m \in \mathbb{N}$, the advantage of $\mathcal{A}$ is $\Pr\left[\mathbf{Exp}_{\Pi,\mathcal{A}}^{\mathsf{prop}\text{-}1} = 1\right] - \Pr\left[\mathbf{Exp}_{\Pi,\mathcal{A}}^{\mathsf{prop}\text{-}0} = 1\right]$. We next say that the whole scheme verifies the property prop if this advantage is negligible for any polynomial-time $\mathcal{A}$.

IMMUTABILITY. The immutability says that it is not feasible, for an adversary controlling all the sanitizers, to make a modification on a signed message by a non-authorized sanitizer, to modify a signed message in a non admissible part, or to modify ADM (see [17]). We allow the adversary to corrupt signers, but the output pair should not originally come from a corrupted signer.

$\mathbf{Exp}_{\Pi,\mathcal{A}}^{\mathsf{imm}}(\lambda, n, m)$:

- $(\mathsf{PK}, \mathsf{SK}) \leftarrow \mathsf{setup}(1^\lambda)$;
- $(\mathsf{m}^*, \sigma^*) \leftarrow \mathcal{A}_{\mathsf{gen}}^{(*)}(\mathsf{PK}, \mathsf{isk}_{\mathrm{SAN}})$; // let $(\widetilde{\mathsf{pk}}_{\mathrm{SAN}}^*, \mathsf{ADM}^*) \in \sigma^*$
- $(\mathrm{ORI}, I_{\mathrm{ORI}}, \tau_{\mathrm{ORI}}) \leftarrow \mathrm{FINDORI}(\mathsf{m}^*, \sigma^*, \mathsf{osk}_{\mathrm{ORI}}, \mathsf{PK})$
- if $\big[\mathrm{VERIFY}(\mathsf{m}^*, \sigma^*, \mathsf{PK}) = 0\big]$ or $\big[I_{\mathrm{ORI}} = (\mathsf{sig}, i_{\mathrm{ORI}}) \in \mathcal{CU}\big]$, return 0;
- if $\forall (\mathsf{m}_k, i_{\mathrm{ORI}}, \widetilde{\mathsf{pk}}_{\mathrm{SAN},k}, \mathsf{ADM}_k, \cdot) \in \Sigma_{\mathsf{sig}}$, $\big[\widetilde{\mathsf{pk}}_{\mathrm{SAN},k} \neq \widetilde{\mathsf{pk}}_{\mathrm{SAN}}^*\big]$ or $\big[\mathsf{ADM}_k \neq \mathsf{ADM}^*\big]$ or $\big[\exists \ell \in [1, t_k] \text{ s.t. } \mathsf{m}_k[\ell] \neq \mathsf{m}^*[\ell] \text{ and } \ell \notin \mathsf{ADM}_k\big]$, then return 1.

SANITIZER ACCOUNTABILITY. The adversary controls all the sanitizers and outputs a (m^*, σ^*) pair which will be attributed to a signer, while this is not the case. The first possibility for the adversary is to output a valid tuple (ALG, sig, τ_{ALG}) accepted by the judge. The second possibility is to make use of an honest signer i^* of its choice, such that when i^* executes the SIGOPEN algorithm, the output is (SIG, I_{sig}) with I_{sig} being an honest signer. Since the adversary is given the ability to corrupt signers, we should be convinced that σ^* neither comes from a corrupted signer nor from the sign oracle.

$\boxed{\begin{array}{l}
\mathbf{Exp}_{\Pi,\mathcal{A}}^{\text{san-acc}}(\lambda, n, m)\text{:} \\
\hline
- \ (\mathsf{PK}, \mathsf{SK}) \leftarrow \mathsf{setup}(1^\lambda, n, m); \\
- \ (\mathsf{m}^*, \sigma^*, (I_{\text{ALG}}^*, \tau_{\text{ALG}}^*), I^* := (\text{sig}, i^*)) \leftarrow \mathcal{A}_{\text{gen}}^{(*)}(\mathsf{PK}, \mathsf{osk}, \mathsf{isk}_{\text{SAN}}); \ // \ \textit{let } \widetilde{\textbf{pk}}_{\text{SAN}}^* \in \sigma^* \\
- \ (\text{ORI}, I_{\text{ORI}}, \tau_{\text{ORI}}) \leftarrow \text{FINDORI}(\mathsf{m}^*, \sigma^*, \mathsf{osk}_{\text{ORI}}, \mathsf{PK}); \\
- \ \text{if} \ \big[\text{VERIFY}(\mathsf{m}^*, \sigma^*, \mathsf{PK}) = 0\big] \ \text{or} \ \big[I^* \in \mathcal{CU}\big] \ \text{or} \ \big[I_{\text{ORI}} = (\text{sig}, i_{\text{ORI}}) \in \mathcal{CU}\big] \ \text{or} \\
\big[\exists(\mathsf{m}_k, i_k, \widetilde{\textbf{pk}}_{\text{SAN},k}, \cdot, \sigma_k) \in \Sigma_{\text{sig}} \ \text{s.t.} \ (i_k, \mathsf{m}_k, \widetilde{\textbf{pk}}_{\text{SAN},k}) = (i_{\text{ORI}}, \mathsf{m}^*, \widetilde{\textbf{pk}}_{\text{SAN}}^*)\big], \ \text{return} \\
0; \\
- \ (\text{SIG}, I_{\text{SIG}}, \tau_{\text{SIG}}) \leftarrow \text{SIGOPEN}(\mathsf{m}^*, \sigma^*, (\text{ORI}, I_{\text{ORI}}, \tau_{\text{ORI}}), \mathsf{sk}_{\text{SIG}}[i^*], \mathsf{PK}, \mathsf{DB}); \ \text{where} \\
\mathsf{DB} := \{(\mathsf{m}_k, \sigma_k) \mid \forall(\mathsf{m}_k, i_k, \cdot, \cdot, \sigma_k) \in \Sigma_{\text{sig}} \ \text{s.t.} \ i_k = i_{\text{ORI}}\} \\
- \ \text{if} \ \big[(I_{\text{ALG}}^* = \text{sig} \wedge \text{JUDGE}(\mathsf{m}^*, \sigma^*, (\text{ALG}, I_{\text{ALG}}^*, \tau_{\text{ALG}}^*), \mathsf{PK}) = 1) \ \text{or} \ (I^* \notin \mathcal{CU} \wedge I_{\text{ORI}} = \\
I_{\text{SIG}} \wedge \text{JUDGE}(\mathsf{m}^*, \sigma^*, (\text{SIG}, I_{\text{SIG}}, \tau_{\text{SIG}}), \mathsf{PK}) = 1)\big], \ \text{then return } 1.
\end{array}}$

SIGNER ACCOUNTABILITY. The adversary controls all the signers and outputs a (m^*, σ^*) pair which will be attributed to a sanitizer, while this is not the case. The first possibility is to output a judge-accepted tuple (ALG, san, τ_{ALG}). The second possibility is to produce a judge-accepted proof (SIG, (san, 0), τ_{SIG}), which may be output by the SIGOPEN procedure. Again, we should be convinced that σ^* neither comes from a corrupted sanitizer/signer nor from the sanitize oracle.

$\boxed{\begin{array}{l}
\mathbf{Exp}_{\Pi,\mathcal{A}}^{\text{sig-acc}}(\lambda, n, m)\text{:} \\
\hline
- \ (\mathsf{PK}, \mathsf{SK}) \leftarrow \mathsf{setup}(1^\lambda, n, m); \\
- \ (\mathsf{m}^*, \sigma^*, (I^*BOn, \tau^*)) \leftarrow \mathcal{A}_{\text{gen}}^{(*)}(\mathsf{PK}, \mathsf{osk}, \mathsf{isk}_{\text{SIG}}); \\
- \ (\text{FULL}, I_{\text{FULL}}, \tau_{\text{FULL}}) \leftarrow \text{FULLOPEN}(\mathsf{m}^*, \sigma^*, \mathsf{osk}_{\text{FULL}}, \mathsf{PK}); \\
- \ \text{if} \ \big[\text{VERIFY}(\mathsf{m}^*, \sigma^*, \mathsf{PK}) = 0\big] \ \text{or} \ \big[I_{\text{FULL}} = (\text{san}, j^*) \in \mathcal{CU}\big] \ \text{or} \\
\big[\exists(\cdot, \sigma_k, \cdot, \cdot, m_k', \cdot) \in \Sigma_{\text{san}} \ \text{s.t.} \ (\textbf{pk}_{\text{SAN}}[j^*] \in \widetilde{\textbf{pk}}_{\text{SAN},k} \ \text{or} \ m_k' = \mathsf{m}^*)\big], \ \text{return } 0; \\
- \ \text{if} \ \big[(I^* = \text{san} \wedge \text{JUDGE}(\mathsf{m}^*, \sigma^*, (\text{ALG}, I^*, \tau^*), \mathsf{PK}) = 1) \ \text{or} \\
((I^* = (\text{san}, 0) \wedge \text{JUDGE}(\mathsf{m}^*, \sigma^*, (\text{SIG}, I^*, \tau^*), \mathsf{PK}) = 1)\big], \ \text{then return } 1.
\end{array}}$

TRANSPARENCY. The aim of the adversary is here to decide whether a given message-signature is a sanitized one or not. In the *full transparency* case, she has access to the signer corruption oracle, while she does not in the *group transparency* case. The existence of SIGOPEN obviously implies that the full transparency can not be reached. Therefore, to design a fully transparent multi-players sanitizable signature scheme, the SigOpen procedure must be restricted to the case $\tilde{i} = i_{\text{ORI}}$.

$\mathbf{Exp}_{\Pi,\mathcal{A}}^{\text{tran-}b}(\lambda, n, m) \text{ // } b \in \{0,1\} \text{ ; } \mathcal{A} = \mathcal{A}^{(*)} \text{ if full and } \mathcal{A} = \mathcal{A}^{(sa)} \text{ if group:}$

– $(\mathsf{PK}, \mathsf{SK}) \leftarrow \mathsf{setup}(1^\lambda, n, m);$
– $(\mathsf{m}^*, \mathsf{ADM}^*, \mathsf{MOD}^*, i^*, j^*, \widetilde{\mathbf{pk}}_{\text{SAN}}^*, st) \leftarrow \mathcal{A}_{\text{ch}}^{(*)}(\mathsf{PK});$
– if $i^* \in \mathcal{CU}$ or $j^* \in \mathcal{CU}$, return $\bot$;
– $\sigma^* \leftarrow \mathrm{SIGN}(\mathsf{m}^*, \mathbf{sk}_{\text{SIG}}[i^*], \widetilde{\mathbf{pk}}_{\text{SAN}}^*, \mathsf{ADM}^*, \mathsf{PK});$
– $(\mathsf{m}'^*, \sigma_0'^*) \leftarrow \mathrm{SANITIZE}(\mathsf{m}^*, \sigma^*, \mathbf{sk}_{\text{SAN}}[j^*], \mathsf{MOD}^*, \mathsf{PK});$
– if $b = 1$, then $\sigma_1'^* \leftarrow \mathrm{SIGN}(\mathsf{m}'^*, \mathbf{sk}_{\text{SIG}}[i^*], \widetilde{\mathbf{pk}}_{\text{SAN}}^*, \mathsf{ADM}^*, \mathsf{PK});$
– $b^* \leftarrow \mathcal{A}_{\text{gu}}^{(*)}(\mathsf{m}'^*, \sigma_b'^*, st)$
– if $(\mathsf{m}'^*, \sigma_b'^*)$ was queried to sigopen, return $\bot$, else return b^*.

UNLINKABILITY. The aim of the adversary is here to choose two messages that become identical once sanitized and decide which one has been sanitized. The adversary has access to a left-or-right oracle which executes the sanitization according to a random bit the adversary must guess.

$\mathbf{Exp}_{\Pi,\mathcal{A}}^{\text{unlink-}b}(\lambda, n, m) \text{ // } b \in \{0,1\}:$

– $(\mathsf{PK}, \mathsf{SK}) \leftarrow \mathsf{setup}(1^\lambda, n, m);$
– $(\mathsf{m}_0^*, \mathsf{m}_1^*, \sigma_0^*, \sigma_1^*, \mathsf{MOD}_0^*, \mathsf{MOD}_1^*, j_0^*, j_1^*, st) \leftarrow \mathcal{A}_{\text{ch}}^{(*)}(\mathsf{PK});$
– $(\mathsf{m}'^*, \sigma'^*) \leftarrow \mathrm{SANITIZE}(\mathsf{m}_b^*, \sigma_b^*, \mathbf{sk}_{\text{SAN}}[j_b^*], \mathsf{MOD}_b^*, \mathsf{PK});$
– $(\mathrm{ORI}, I_{\text{ORI}}, \tau_{\text{ORI}}) \leftarrow \mathrm{FINDORI}(\mathsf{m}'^*, \sigma'^*, \mathsf{osk}_{\text{ORI}}, \mathsf{PK});$
– if $[I_{\text{ORI}} = 0]$ or $[I_{\text{ORI}} = (\mathsf{sig}, i_{\text{ORI}})$ and $i_{\text{ORI}} \in \mathcal{CU}]$ or $[j_0 \in \mathcal{CU}]$ or $[j_1 \in \mathcal{CU}]$
or $[\mathrm{JUDGE}(\mathsf{m}'^*, \sigma_b'^*, (\mathrm{ORI}, I_{\text{ORI}}, \tau_{\text{ORI}}), \mathsf{PK}) = 0]$, return $\bot$;
– $b^* \leftarrow \mathcal{A}_{\text{gu}}^{(*)}(\mathsf{m}'^*, \sigma_b'^*, st)$
– if $(\mathsf{m}'^*, \sigma'^*)$ was queried to sigopen, return $\bot$, else return b^*.

TRACEABILITY. The traceability says that the opening should always conclude. The adversary wins if she is able to output a message-signature pair such that the opener $(\mathcal{O}_{\text{FULL}}, \mathcal{O}_{\text{ORI}})$ outputs $\bot$ or is unable to produce a correct proof τ of its claim.

$\mathbf{Exp}_{\Pi,\mathcal{A}}^{\text{trac}}(\lambda, n, m):$

– $(\mathsf{PK}, \mathsf{SK}) \leftarrow \mathsf{setup}(1^\lambda, n, m);$
– $(\mathsf{m}^*, \sigma^*) \leftarrow \mathcal{A}_{\text{gen}}^{(*)}(\mathsf{PK}, \mathsf{osk});$
– $(\mathrm{FULL}, I_{\text{FULL}}, \tau_{\text{FULL}}) \leftarrow \mathrm{FULLOPEN}(\mathsf{m}^*, \sigma^*, \mathsf{osk}_{\text{FULL}}, \mathsf{PK});$
– $(\mathrm{ORI}, I_{\text{ORI}}, \tau_{\text{ORI}}) \leftarrow \mathrm{FINDORI}(\mathsf{m}^*, \sigma^*, \mathsf{osk}_{\text{ORI}}, \mathsf{PK});$
– if $\mathrm{VERIFY}(\mathsf{m}^*, \sigma^*, \mathsf{PK}) = 0$, return 0;
– if $[\mathrm{JUDGE}(\mathsf{m}^*, \sigma^*, (s, I_s, \tau_s), \mathsf{PK}) = 0]$ or $[I_s = 0]$, with $s \in \{\mathrm{FULL}, \mathrm{ORI}\}$,
then return 1.

SANITIZER ANONYMITY. The adversary here controls all the signers, chooses two sanitizers (j_0^*, j_1^*), a pair (m^*, σ^*) and some MOD^* of her choice. Then the j_b^*-th sanitizer sanitizes the signature (for a uniformly chosen bit b) and the adversary aims at guessing b. In the *full anonymity* case, she has access to the sanitizer corruption oracle, while this is not the case in the *group anonymity*. Note that the "no-" and "group-" anonymity can only be defined if the signer is also viewed as a sanitizer (the contrary not being true) because of the transparency property.

$\mathbf{Exp}_{\Pi,\mathcal{A}}^{\mathsf{san\text{-}ano\text{-}}b}(\lambda, n, m)$ // $b \in \{0,1\}$; $\mathcal{A} = \mathcal{A}^{(*)}$ *if full and* $\mathcal{A} = \mathcal{A}^{(sa)}$ *if group*:

- $(\mathsf{PK}, \mathsf{SK}) \leftarrow \mathsf{setup}(1^\lambda, n, m)$;
- $(j_0^*, j_1^*, \mathsf{m}^*, \sigma^*, \mathsf{MOD}^*, st^*) \leftarrow \mathcal{A}_{\mathsf{ch}}^{(\mathsf{si})}(\mathsf{PK}, \mathsf{isk}_{\mathsf{SIG}})$;
- $(m'^*, \sigma'^*) \leftarrow \mathsf{SANITIZE}(m^*, \sigma^*, \mathbf{sk}_{\mathsf{SAN}}[j_b^*], \mathsf{MOD}^*, \mathsf{PK})$;
- if $\big[\mathrm{VERIFY}(m^*, \sigma^*, \mathsf{PK}) = 0\big]$ or $\big[j_0^* \in \mathcal{CU}\big]$ or $\big[j_1^* \in \mathcal{CU}\big]$, return $\perp$;
- $b^* \leftarrow \mathcal{A}_{\mathsf{gu}}^{(\mathsf{si})}(m'^*, \sigma'^*, st)\big]$;
- if (m'^*, σ'^*) was queried to fullopen, return $\perp$, else return b^*.

SIGNER ANONYMITY. The adversary now controls all the sanitizers and aims at distinguish between two signers (i_0^*, i_1^*) of her choice, which one has signed a message m^* according to a chosen ADM^*. We next make the same division as for the sanitizer anonymity part, regarding the corruption possibility for the adversary.

$\mathbf{Exp}_{\Pi,\mathcal{A}}^{\mathsf{sig\text{-}ano\text{-}}b}(\lambda, n, m)$ // $b \in \{0,1\}$; $\mathcal{A} = \mathcal{A}^{(*)}$ *if full and* $\mathcal{A} = \mathcal{A}^{(sa)}$ *if group*:

- $(\mathsf{PK}, \mathsf{SK}) \leftarrow \mathsf{setup}(1^\lambda, n, m)$;
- $(i_0^*, i_1^*, \mathsf{m}^*, \widetilde{\mathbf{pk}}_{\mathsf{SAN}}^*, \mathsf{ADM}^*, st) \leftarrow \mathcal{A}_{\mathsf{ch}}^{(\mathsf{sa})}(\mathsf{PK}, \mathsf{isk}_{\mathsf{SAN}})$;
- if $\big[i_0^* \in \mathcal{CU}\big]$ or $\big[i_1^* \in \mathcal{CU}\big]$, return $\perp$;
- $\sigma^* \leftarrow \mathrm{SIGN}(m^*, \mathbf{sk}_{\mathsf{SIG}}[i_b^*], \widetilde{\mathbf{pk}}_{\mathsf{SAN}}^*, \mathsf{ADM}^*, \mathsf{PK})$;
- $b^* \leftarrow \mathcal{A}_{\mathsf{gu}}^{(\mathsf{sa})}(m^*, \sigma^*, st)$;
- if (m^*, σ^*) was queried to fullopen, return $\perp$, else return b^*.

NON-FRAMEABILITY. The non-frameability property argues that it is not possible for an adversary, even being the openers, to falsely accuse an honest user (signer or sanitizer) from having produced a valid signature. This property is different from the accountability ones since it takes into account the case where some corrupted signers (resp. sanitizers) try to accuse an honest signer (resp. sanitizer). Moreover, we study the case of a false accusation during the FULLOPEN and FINDORI procedures. The adversary does not control all users but can corrupt them, as it wants. It finally outputs a valid (m^*, σ^*) pair and a (i^*, τ^*) pair which could have been output by the FULLOPEN (resp. FINDORI) procedure. She wins if the judge outputs that i^* has truly produced σ^*, while this is not the case.

$\mathbf{Exp}_{\Pi,\mathcal{A}}^{\mathsf{nf}}(\lambda, n, m)$:

– $(\mathsf{PK}, \mathsf{SK}) \leftarrow \mathsf{setup}(1^\lambda, n, m)$;
– $(\mathsf{m}^*, \sigma^*, i^*, \tau^*) \leftarrow \mathcal{A}_{\mathsf{gen}}^{(*)}(\mathsf{PK}, \mathsf{isk}, \mathsf{osk})$;
– If $\big[\text{VERIFY}(\mathsf{m}^*, \sigma^*, \mathsf{PK}) = 0\big]$ or $\big[I^* \in \mathcal{CU}\big]$ or $\big[(I^* = (\mathsf{sig}, i^*) \text{ and } \exists(\mathsf{m}_k, i_k, \cdot, \cdot, \cdot) \in \Sigma_{\mathsf{sig}} \text{ s.t. } (i_k, \mathsf{m}_k) = (i^*, \mathsf{m}^*))\big]$ or $\big[(I^* = (\mathsf{san}, j^*) \text{ and } \exists(\cdot, \cdot, j_k, \cdot, \mathsf{m}'_k, \cdot) \in \Sigma_{\mathsf{san}} \text{ s.t. } (j_k, \mathsf{m}'_k) = (j^*, \mathsf{m}^*))\big]$, then return 0.
– If $\exists s \in \{\text{FULL}, \text{ORI}\}$ s.t. $\text{JUDGE}(\mathsf{m}^*, \sigma^*, (s, I^*, \tau^*)) = 1$, then return 1.

Remark 2. Even if relations exist between security properties, no implication remains. This is less obvious in the relationship between non frameability and accountability but (i) an adversary against accountability and using the ALGOPEN procedure to win the experiment is unable to win against the non frameability experiment ; (ii) an adversary against the non-frameability is stronger (as he controls all the issuing keys isk) than an adversary against the accountabilities (who only controls $\mathsf{isk}_{\mathsf{SAN}}$ or $\mathsf{isk}_{\mathsf{SIG}}$).

The suitability with simple sanitizable signature schemes [7] and the way to add extensions [9] are given in the full version of the paper.

4   Primitives

Before giving a construction, let us begin by describing some cryptographic primitives we will use. Let λ be a security parameter.

DIGITAL SIGNATURE SCHEMES. We will need a standard signature scheme $\mathcal{S} = (\text{KGN}, \text{SIGN}, \text{VERIF})$ specified by algorithms for key generation, signing and verifying. It should satisfy the standard notion of unforgeability under chosen message attack [16]. In a nutshell, the adversary is given the public key and can interact with a signing oracle. Finally, the adversary outputs an attempted forgery (m, σ) and wins if σ is valid, and m was never queried to the signing oracle. We denote by $\mathbf{Succ}_{\mathcal{S},\mathcal{A}}^{\mathsf{unf}}(\lambda)$ the success probability of the adversary $\mathcal{A}$ against $\mathcal{S}$.

PSEUDO-RANDOM FUNCTIONS. Let $\mathcal{PRF} = (\text{FKGN}, \text{PRF})$ be a pseudo-random function, which is defined by the generation algorithm and the pseudo-random function itself. An adversary $\mathcal{A}$ against such scheme is given access to a random function oracle and outputs a value x_0. After that, a bit b is secretly and randomly chosen. If $b = 0$, the adversary receives the output of the $\mathcal{PRF}$ on x_0. If $b = 1$, the adversary receives a random value. The adversary finally outputs a bit b'. The advantage $\mathbf{Adv}_{\mathcal{PRF},\mathcal{A}}^{\mathsf{prf}}(\lambda)$ of $\mathcal{A}$ is the difference between $1/2$ and the probability that $b' = b$.

GROUP SIGNATURES. In the following, we will need two different types of group signature schemes. First, a BSZ type group signature scheme [4] and second, a similar concept where we do not want an interactive join protocol between the group manager and a group member, but the non-frameability property. This is an hybrid model between the BMW model [3] for static groups and the BSZ [4] one for dynamic groups. The non-frameability property is needed to ensure accountability, since the signer needs to produce a signature without the presence of the sanitizers [8].

A group signature scheme $\mathcal{GS}$ is composed of an issuer, an opener and members and is given by a tuple (GKGN, UKGN, JOIN, [NI-JOIN, GSKGN,] GSIGN, GVERIF, OPEN, JUDGE) described as follows. The join protocol is denoted NI-JOIN in case of a non-interactive procedure and it is next necessary for each user to execute the GSKGN procedure. If JOIN is interactive, the latter is not necessary.

GKGN is a probabilistic algorithm which on input 1^λ outputs the key pair $(\mathsf{ik}, \mathsf{gpk}_i)$ of the issuer (sub-procedure called IGKGN), the key pair $(\mathsf{ok}, \mathsf{gpk}_o)$ of the opener (sub-procedure called OGKGN) and the group public key $\mathsf{gpk} = (\mathsf{gpk}_i, \mathsf{gpk}_o)$.

UKGN is a probabilistic algorithm executed by each user i and which on input 1^λ outputs her key pair $(\mathbf{upk}[i], \mathbf{usk}[i])$.

JOIN is an interactive protocol between the issuer taking on input ik and $\mathbf{upk}[i]$ and user i taking on input $\mathbf{usk}[i]$. The issuer makes a new entry $\mathbf{reg}[i]$ in its registration table $\mathbf{reg}$. The new group member i obtains $\mathbf{msk}[i]$.

$\Big[$NI-JOIN is an algorithm executed by the issuer taking on input ik and $\mathbf{mpk} \subseteq \mathbf{upk}$. The issuer outputs its registration table $\mathbf{reg}$.

GSKGN is an algorithm executed by a group member i that on input $\mathbf{usk}[i]$ and $\mathbf{reg}[i]$ outputs a private signing key denoted $\mathbf{msk}[i]$.$\Big]$

GSIGN is a probabilistic algorithm that takes on input a message m and a private signing key $\mathbf{msk}[i]$ and outputs a group signature σ on m.

GVERIF is an algorithm that on input a message m, a group signature σ and gpk outputs 1 if the signature is valid, and 0 otherwise.

OPEN is an algorithm which on input a message m, a group signature σ and the opener key ok outputs (in a deterministic way) an integer $i \geq 0$ and (in a probabilistic way) a proof τ that i has produced the signature σ on m. If $i = 0$, then no group member produced σ.

JUDGE is a deterministic algorithm taking on input a message m, a group signature σ, an integer i, the public key $\mathbf{upk}[i]$ of the entity with identity i and a proof-string τ. It outputs 1 if the proof τ is valid and 0 otherwise.

– **Anonymity.** The anonymity property says that the adversary, given signatures produced by a user (among two of his choice) is not able to guess which users provided the signatures. During the related experiment, $\mathcal{A}$ is given access to ik, can corrupt user, obtain their keys, ask for the opening of group signatures and has access to a challenge oracle which takes as input two non-corrupted member i_0 and i_1 and a message m and outputs the group signature of user i_b, for a bit b set by the experiment. Eventually, $\mathcal{A}$ outputs a bit b'. Next, the advantage $\mathbf{Adv}^{\mathrm{ano}}_{\mathcal{GS},\mathcal{A}}(\lambda)$ of $\mathcal{A}$ is the difference between $1/2$ and the probability that $b' = b$.

– **Traceability.** This property says that the adversary is not able to output a valid group signature such that the opening and judge procedures do not occur properly. $\mathcal{A}$ is given access to ok and outputs a valid (m, σ) which is accepted by the experiment if either the opening procedure outputs $i = 0$ or the JUDGE procedure cannot succeed. The success probability $\mathbf{Succ}_{\mathcal{GS},\mathcal{A}}^{\mathsf{trac}}(\lambda)$ the adversary $\mathcal{A}$ is next the probability that the experiment accepts.

– **Non-frameability.** An adversary $\mathcal{A}$ is not able to falsely accuse an honest user from having produced a valid group signature. $\mathcal{A}$ is given access to $(\mathsf{ik}, \mathsf{ok})$ and outputs a valid $(\mathsf{m}, \sigma, i, \tau)$ which is accepted by the experiment if i is not corrupted (and her keys are unknown) and the judge accepts the proof τ that i has produced σ while this is not the case. The success probability $\mathbf{Succ}_{\mathcal{GS},\mathcal{A}}^{\mathsf{nf}}(\lambda)$ the adversary $\mathcal{A}$ is next the probability that the experiment accepts.

5   A New Tool: Trapdoor "or" Proof

A Zero Knowledge Proof of Knowledge (ZKPK) is an interactive protocol during which a prover proves to a verifier that he knows a set $(\alpha_1, \ldots, \alpha_q)$ of secret values verifying a given relation R without revealing any information about the known secrets. We denote by $\mathrm{POK}(\alpha_1, \ldots, \alpha_q : \mathsf{R}(\alpha_1, \ldots, \alpha_q))$ such proof of knowledge.

INTRODUCTION. Let $\mathrm{REL} = \{(x, w)\}$ be a binary relation. We first consider the protocol, corresponding to a proof of knowledge for REL, which is played by a prover, taking on input x and a witness w, and a verifier taking on input x. In fact, following [12,20], we consider a set $\mathcal{X} = (x_1, \cdots, x_\ell)$ and a proof of knowledge of the "or" statement where both the prover and the verifier take the common input $\mathcal{X}$, while the prover is also given a private input w_i such that $\exists x_i \in \mathcal{X}$ such that $(x_i, w_i) \in \mathrm{REL}$. Additionally to the witness itself, the verifier should not be able to obtain the index i related to x_i.

In our construction, a designated entity should be able to know which index i is really used by the witness of a user to verify REL, while it is still infeasible for every other actors. To the best of our knowledge, this notion of *trapdoor or proof* does not exist in the literature. However, it can be very useful, as we will see later for our main construction of an (n, m)-sanitizable signature scheme, but also *e.g.* for e-voting where the result of the vote (candidate A "or" candidate B) should not be known, except by authorized scrutineers.

DEFINITIONS. In the following, the above or proof is next denoted $\mathrm{TPOK}(w_i : \exists i \in [1, \ell] | (x_i, w_i) \in \mathrm{REL})$ and the whole system, including the key generation TKGN for the trap, and the "opening" procedure TOPEN, is denoted $\mathcal{TOP} = (\mathrm{TKGN}, \mathrm{TPOK}, \mathrm{TOPEN})$.

As usual, such a proof of knowledge should verify the completeness (a valid prover knowing one such w_i is accepted with overwhelming probability), the soundness (a false prover who does not know any such w_i should be rejected with overwhelming probability) and the honest-verifier zero-knowledge properties (the proof does not reveal any information about the witness).

CIPHER COMMUTING RELATIONS. In the following, we will describe a way to generically design a trapdoor or proof for any relation REL. For this purpose, we need to commute the relation and the encryption procedure of a public key encryption scheme and we thus need to restrict the relations where such commuting operation is possible, which gives us the following definition.

Definition 2 (Cipher commuting relation). *Let λ be a security parameter. Let $\mathcal{E}$ = (EKG, ENC, DEC) be a secure probabilistic encryption scheme. Let REL be a binary relation. We say that REL is a cipher commuting relation if for all x, w, for all (epk, esk) $\longleftarrow$ EKG(1^λ),*

$$(x, w) \in \text{REL} \iff (\text{ENC}(x, \text{epk}), w) \in \text{REL}.$$

OUR GENERIC CONSTRUCTION. Let λ be a security parameter, $\mathcal{E}$ = (EKG, ENC, DEC) be a secure probabilistic encryption scheme and REL be a cipher commuting relation. We want to design the proof $\text{TPOK}(w_i : \exists i \in [1, \ell] | (x_i, w_i) \in \text{REL})$ where the prover knows w_i such that $(x_i, w_i) \in \text{REL}$.

In a nutshell, we encrypt x_i and use a traditional or proof that the encrypted value is one element related to REL, without revealing which one. We next use the cipher commuting property of REL to prove that the knowledge of a witness which verifies REL with the cipher c_i related to x_i.

Let us first consider that the trap has been generated by executing (epk, esk) $\leftarrow$ EKG(1^λ). The proof next works as follows.

1. Computes $c_i = \text{ENC}(x_i, \text{epk})$.
2. Generates the standard honest-verifier zero-knowledge proof with both relations:
   (a) $\text{POK}(x_i : \exists i \in [1, \ell] | c_i = \text{ENC}(x_i, \text{epk}))$ and
   (b) $\text{POK}(w_i, x_i : (\text{ENC}(x_i, \text{epk}), w_i) \in \text{REL})$.

As they are connected with an "and", these two proofs of knowledge can be composed together, using standard techniques [11]. The verifier, knowing the relation REL, the ciphertext c_i and epk, can easily verify the two above POK, using standard techniques. Finally, the owner of esk can easily decrypt c_i to retrieve x_i.

A CONCRETE CONSTRUCTION. Let $\mathbb{G}$ be a group of prime order p. Let u, h be random generators of $\mathbb{G}$ and let v and z be two elements of $\mathbb{G}$. We want to design the trapdoor or proof denoted $\text{TPOK}(\alpha : \exists (b, f)\{(u, v), (h, z)\} | f = b^\alpha)$.

Our solution makes use of a homomorphic encryption scheme π = (KEYGEN, ENC, DEC) such that the trapdoor of our construction is the decryption key dk. The encryption public key is ek = a and the corresponding secret key is $\alpha \in \mathbb{Z}_p^*$ such that $a = d^\alpha$ where $d \in \mathbb{G}$. A prover having access to e.g. the discrete logarithm $x \in \mathbb{Z}_p^*$ of v in base u, that is $v = u^x$, can produce a *trapdoor or proof* as follows, with the ElGamal encryption scheme as an concrete instantiation (see [15]).

1. Encrypt v and u as $c_v = (t_1 = va^w, t_2 = d^w)$ and $c_u = (t_3 = ua^r, t_4 = d^r)$ where $w, r \in \mathbb{Z}_p^*$.
2. Produce a (traditional) proof of knowledge on x, r and w such that:
   (a) the pair of encrypted values corresponds to either (v, u) or (z, h), using a set membership proof: $(t_1/v = a^w \wedge t_3/u = a^r)$ or $(t_1/z = a^w \wedge t_3/h = a^r)$ (together with the proof that $t_2 = d^w$ and that $t_4 = d^r$.

(b) using the encrypted value (which satisfies the relation $v = u^x$) and the homomorphic property of the encryption scheme, it is done by producing the proof of knowledge of x such that $c_v = c_u^x$. For this purpose, we use that $t_3^x = u^x a^{rx} = v a^{rx} = t_1 a^{rx-w}$.

The final *trapdoor or proof* is composed of (t_1, t_2, t_3, t_4) and the following proof of knowledge:

$$V = \text{POK}\big(w, r, x, \bar{r} : \big((\tfrac{t_1}{v} = a^w \wedge \tfrac{t_3}{u} = a^r) \vee (\tfrac{t_1}{z} = a^w \wedge \tfrac{t_3}{h} = a^r)\big)$$
$$\wedge t_2 = d^w \wedge t_4 = d^r \wedge t_1 = t_3^x a^{-\bar{r}} a^w \wedge 1 = t_4^x d^{-\bar{r}}\big)$$

Anyone in possession of α can retrieve the encrypted pair (v, u) and obtain the known discrete logarithm. We here present the more general case where we need to encrypt both u and v. As in [12,20], the (trapdoor) or proof for a representation can also be treated similarly. We do not detailed the case of a representation but we will use it in the following section.

6   Full Transparent and Fully Anonymous Multi-players Sanitizable Signature

We now describe our *fully transparent* and *fully anonymous* sanitizable signature scheme for several signers and sanitizers.

Following the idea from [8], one user is able to sanitize a message/signature pair if she belongs to a group created by the initial signer and related to this message/signature pair. Next, the principle of our signature is to associate (i) a signature of the signer, as member of a group of signers, on the fixed parts of the message with (ii) a group signature on the admissible parts of the message, on behalf of the new group generated by the signer and (iii) a trapdoor or proof of knowledge of either a certified signer key or a certified sanitizer key. The latter is added to prevent everybody to distinguish a signed message from a sanitized one, except by $\mathcal{O}_{alg}$.

Our scheme is composed of openers $\mathcal{O}_{\text{FULL}}$, $\mathcal{O}_{\text{ALG}}$, $\mathcal{O}_{\text{ORI}}$, a group manager $\mathcal{GM}$ for a group signature scheme and a certification authority denoted $\mathcal{CA}$.

GENERATION PHASES. Let μ be a security parameter. We note $\mathcal{GS}_1$ (resp. $\mathcal{GS}_2$) an interactive-join (resp. non-interactive) group signature scheme, $\mathcal{S}$ a standard signature scheme, $\mathcal{TOP}$ a trapdoor or proof system (cf. Section 5) and $\mathcal{PRF}$ a pseudo-random function.

Setup Phase. The certification authority $\mathcal{CA}$ executes twice the key generation $\mathcal{S}.\text{KGN}$ for the standard signature scheme $\mathcal{S}$ to obtain two different keys pairs denoted $(\text{cask}_{\text{si}}, \text{capk}_{\text{si}})$ and $(\text{cask}_{\text{sa}}, \text{capk}_{\text{sa}})$. The group manager $\mathcal{GM}$ executes $\mathcal{GS}_1.\text{IGKGN}$, which gives isk and gpk_i. The opener $\mathcal{O}_{\text{FULL}}$ executes $\mathcal{GS}_2.\text{OGKGN}$, which gives osk_{FULL} and gpk_{FULL}. The opener $\mathcal{O}_{\text{ALG}}$ executes the $\mathcal{TOP}.\text{TKGN}$ algorithm, which gives osk_{ALG} and gpk_{ALG}. The opener $\mathcal{O}_{\text{ORI}}$ executes $\mathcal{GS}_1.\text{OGKGN}$, which gives osk_{ORI} and gpk_o. In the following, we denote $\text{gpk}_{\text{si}} = (\text{gpk}_i, \text{gpk}_o)$.

To sum up, we have $\mathsf{isk}_{\text{SIG}} = (\mathsf{isk}, \mathsf{cask}_{\mathsf{si}})$, $\mathsf{isk}_{\text{SAN}} = (\mathsf{cask}_{\mathsf{sa}})$ and the general public key $\mathsf{gpk} = (\mathsf{capk}_{\mathsf{si}}, \mathsf{capk}_{\mathsf{sa}}\ \mathsf{gpk}_{\mathsf{si}}, \mathsf{gpk}_{\text{FULL}}, \mathsf{gpk}_{\text{ALG}})$.

Signer Key Generation. Each signer i executes the following. She uses the JOIN interactive protocol with $\mathcal{GM}$ to get her private signing key $\mathbf{msk}[i]$. Next, she executes the key generation for the pseudo-random function to obtain $\mathsf{uk}[i] = \mathcal{PRF}.\text{FKGEN}(1^\mu)$. Then, she uses the user key generation $\mathcal{GS}_2.\text{UKGN}$ for $\mathcal{GS}_2$ to obtain both $\mathbf{upk}_{si}[i]$ and $\mathbf{usk}_{si}[i]$. Finally, she sends $\mathbf{upk}_{si}[i]$ to $\mathcal{CA}$ with a non-interactive proof of knowledge of the related $\mathbf{usk}_{si}[i]$ and $\mathcal{CA}$ generates $\mathbf{uc}_{si}[i] = \mathcal{S}.\text{SIGN}(\mathbf{upk}_{si}[i], \mathsf{cask}_{\mathsf{si}})$.

Sanitizer Key Generation. Each sanitizer j uses $\mathcal{GS}_2.\text{UKGN}$ to get $(\mathbf{usk}_{sa}[j], \mathbf{upk}_{sa}[j])$ and sends $\mathbf{upk}_{sa}[j]$ to $\mathcal{CA}$ with a non-interactive proof of knowledge of the related $\mathbf{usk}_{sa}[j]$. Then, $\mathcal{CA}$ generates $\mathbf{uc}_{sa}[j] = \mathcal{S}.\text{SIGN}(\mathbf{upk}_{sa}[j], \mathsf{cask}_{\mathsf{sa}})$.

SIGNATURE PROCEDURE. During this procedure, the signer first generates the keys of a new group signature scheme (for herself and the chosen sanitizers). She next produces two different group signatures, the first as a member of the group of signers and the second as a member of the new formed group. Let us consider the i-th signer, $i \in [1, n]$ and let m be the message, divided into t parts, she wants to sign. Following ADM given on input, let m_{FIX} be the part of m which will not be sanitizable by the sanitizers. The SIGN procedure is described as follows.

Choice of Sanitizers. The signer chooses a subset $J \subseteq [1, m]$ of sanitizers allowed to modify her message with $\widetilde{\mathbf{pk}}_{\text{SAN}}$ the set of their public keys.

Generation of a Group. The signer creates a group for herself and the chosen sanitizers. For this purpose, she uses the group signature scheme $\mathcal{GS}_2$ with a non-interactive join. More precisely, she computes $rd = \text{PRF}(\mathsf{uk}[i], id_{\mathsf{m}})$ where $id_{\mathsf{m}} = \mathsf{m}_{\text{FIX}} \| \text{ADM}$ is the identifier of the initial message.

She next carries out the key generation algorithm IGKGN of the group signature scheme $\mathcal{GS}_2$, using rd as a random (see also [8]). It gives $\mathsf{isk}[i, id_{\mathsf{m}}]$ and $\mathsf{gpk}_i[i, id_{\mathsf{m}}]$. We note $\mathsf{gpk}[i, id_{\mathsf{m}}] = (\mathsf{gpk}_i[i, id_{\mathsf{m}}], \mathsf{gpk}_{\text{FULL}})$. Then, she uses the non-interactive join procedure NI-JOIN of $\mathcal{GS}_2$ to generate the private signing key for each group members, using rd as a random. We denote it $\mathbf{reg}[i, id_{\mathsf{m}}]$ for the signer and $\mathbf{reg}_{sa}[j, id_{\mathsf{m}}]$ for each sanitizer $j \in J$.

She finally obtains her own membership secret key for this group $\mathbf{msk}[i, id_{\mathsf{m}}]$ thanks to the GSKGN procedure on input $\mathbf{upk}_{si}[i]$ and $\mathbf{reg}[i, id_{\mathsf{m}}]$.

Group Signatures Generation. She computes two group signatures, the first as a signer $\sigma_{\mathtt{fix}} = \mathcal{GS}_1.\text{GSIGN}(\mathbf{msk}[i], \mathsf{m}_{\text{SIG}})$ with $\mathsf{m}_{\text{SIG}} = id_{\mathsf{m}} \| \widetilde{\mathbf{pk}}_{\text{SAN}} \| \mathbf{reg}_{sa}$, the second as a member of the new group $\sigma_{\mathtt{full}} = \mathcal{GS}_2.\text{GSIGN}(\mathbf{msk}[i, id_{\mathsf{m}}], \mathsf{m})$.

Proof of Validity. The signer finally proves, thanks to the non-interactive zero-knowledge proofs of knowledge π, that (i) the above is correctly done and (ii) she is either a signer or a sanitizer.

- $\text{POK}(\mathbf{msk}[i, id_{\mathsf{m}}], \mathbf{upk}_{si}[i], \mathbf{reg}[i, id_{\mathsf{m}}]) : \mathbf{msk}[i, id_{\mathsf{m}}] = \mathcal{GS}_2.\text{GSKGN}(\mathbf{upk}_{si}[i], \mathbf{reg}[i, id_{\mathsf{m}}]))$; and

- $\text{POK}(\mathbf{msk}[i, id_\mathsf{m}] : \sigma_\mathtt{full} = \mathcal{GS}_2.\text{GSIGN}(\mathbf{msk}[i, id_\mathsf{m}], \mathsf{m}));$ and
- $\text{TPOK}(\mathbf{upk}_{si}[i], \mathbf{uc}_{si}[i] : \exists \mathbf{sk} \in \{\mathsf{cask}_{\mathsf{si}}, \mathsf{cask}_{\mathsf{sa}}\} | \mathbf{uc}_{si}[i] = \mathcal{S}.\text{SIGN}(\mathbf{upk}_{si}[i], \mathbf{sk})).$

As the proofs are connected with an "and" (which is the case for the trapdoor or proof), these relations can be composed together [11].

The resulting signature is $\sigma = (\pi, \sigma_\text{FIX}, \sigma_\text{FULL}, \text{ADM}, \widetilde{\mathbf{pk}}_\text{SAN}, \mathsf{w}_i, \mathbf{reg}_{sa})$ where $\mathbf{reg}_{sa}$ allows sanitizers to obtain their group member keys afterwards.

SANITIZATION PROCEDURE. The sanitization algorithm consists, for the sanitizer, in (i) the creation of a new σ'_FULL, according to her own keys and the modified message, and (ii) the construction of the corresponding modified proof π'. Let us consider the j-th sanitizer, $j \in [1, m]$, let m be the initial message, with fixed part m_FIX, and let $\sigma = (\pi, \sigma_\text{FIX}, \sigma_\text{FULL}, \text{ADM}, \widetilde{\mathbf{pk}}_\text{SAN}, \mathsf{w}_i, \mathbf{reg}_{sa})$ be a signature on m and MOD be instructions for a new message m'. First of all, if $\mathbf{pk}_\mathsf{san}[j] \notin \widetilde{\mathbf{pk}}_\text{SAN}$, then the algorithm returns $\perp$. Otherwise, she executes the following steps.

Proof of Group Membership. The sanitizer retrieves its value $\mathbf{reg}_{sa}[j, id_\mathsf{m}]$ in $\mathbf{reg}_{sa}$. She executes the GSKGN procedure on input $\mathbf{upk}_{sa}[j]$ and $\mathbf{reg}_{sa}[j, id_\mathsf{m}]$ to compute $\mathbf{msk}[j, id_\mathsf{m}]$. Then, she produces a new group signature $\sigma'_\mathtt{full} = \mathcal{GS}_2.\text{GSIGN}(\mathbf{msk}[j, id_\mathsf{m}], \mathsf{m}')$ as a member of the authorized modifier.

Proof of validity. She next produces a proof π' as a sanitizer :

- $\text{POK}(\mathbf{msk}[j, id_\mathsf{m}], \mathbf{upk}_{sa}[i], \mathbf{reg}_{sa}[j, id_\mathsf{m}]) :$
    $\mathbf{msk}[j, id_\mathsf{m}] = \mathcal{GS}_2.\text{GSKGN}(\mathbf{upk}_{sa}[j], \mathbf{reg}_{sa}[j, id_\mathsf{m}]));$ and
- $\text{POK}(\mathbf{msk}[j, id_\mathsf{m}] : \sigma_\mathtt{full} = \mathcal{GS}_2.\text{GSIGN}(\mathbf{msk}[j, id_\mathsf{m}], \mathsf{m}'));$ and
- $\text{TPOK}(\mathbf{upk}_{sa}[j], \mathbf{uc}_{sa}[j] : \exists \mathbf{sk} \in \{\mathsf{cask}_{\mathsf{si}}, \mathsf{cask}_{\mathsf{sa}}\} | \mathbf{uc}_{sa}[j] = \mathcal{S}.\text{SIGN}(\mathbf{upk}_{sa}[j], \mathbf{sk})).$

The resulting signature is $\sigma' = (\pi', \sigma_\text{FIX}, \sigma'_\text{FULL}, \text{ADM}, \widetilde{\mathbf{pk}}_\text{SAN}, \mathsf{w}_i, \mathbf{reg}_{sa})$.

VERIFICATION AND OPENING PROCEDURES. VERIFICATION. On input a signature $\sigma = (\pi, \sigma_\text{FIX}, \sigma_\text{FULL}, \text{ADM}, \widetilde{\mathbf{pk}}_\text{SAN}, \mathsf{w}_i, \mathbf{reg}_{sa})$ on a message m, the verification procedure simply checks both signatures σ_FIX and σ_FULL and the whole proof π. If all is correct, she outputs 1, otherwise 0.

Opening. We finally describe the different opening procedures for a signature σ as defined above. The ALGOPEN procedure is simply executed by using the trap of the trapdoor or proof as shown in Section 5 with the key osk_ALG. The FINDORI procedure is the execution of the $\mathcal{GS}_1.\text{OPEN}$ algorithm related to the group signature scheme for signers. Next, the SIGOPEN is executed as described in [8], by using the pseudo-random function and the opening algorithm of the group signature scheme. The FULLOPEN algorithm corresponds to $\mathcal{GS}_2.\text{OPEN}$.

SECURITY THEOREM. We finally give the following security theorem.

Theorem 1. *Our full transparent and fully anonymous multi-players sanitizable signature verifies all the required security properties, assuming that the used group signature, the pseudo-random function, the signature scheme (underlying the trapdoor or proof) and the trapdoor or proof are secure.*

Proof (sketch, see full paper for the full proof). Several parts of the proof (immutability, unlinkability and accountabilities) are similar to the the the one given in [8], except that we have to replace the unforgeability of the used signature scheme by the traceability and non-frameability of the group signature scheme $\mathcal{GS}_2$. The anonymity properties are given by the anonymity of the group signature scheme, together with the zero-knowledge property of our trapdoor or proof. The non-frameability and traceability properties are related to the ones related to the used group signature schemes, together with the unforgeability of $\mathcal{CA}$'s signature scheme. The full transparency is obtained according to the anonymity of the group signature scheme and the zero-knowledge property of the trapdoor or proof. □

DEALING WITH THE GROUP ANONYMITY. The group anonymity states that the anonymity of sanitizers (resp. signers) is preserved, except for the sanitizers (resp. signers). In this case and regarding the above construction, each sanitizer (resp. signer) should be able to independently decrypt the same message, corresponding to the one related to the full opener or the origin opener: we need a *multi receiver encryption scheme.*

In such a scheme, a designated authority having a master key generates all the "receivers" (sanitizers or signers) secret keys. Such concept already exists, it is named broadcast encryption [14] when it includes a revocation mechanism, traitor tracing [6] when it treats the case of fraudulent receivers or multi-recipient encryption [2] when several messages are encrypted for several recipients. Our need is close to public key traitor tracing scheme, except we do not necessarily need a tracing procedure. Thus a practical construction can be obtained with [6].

Acknowledgments. This work has been supported by the European Commission under Contract ICT-2007-216676 ECRYPT II. We are grateful to the anonymous referees for their valuable comments.

References

1. Ateniese, G., Chou, D.H., de Medeiros, B., Tsudik, G.: Sanitizable Signatures. In: di Vimercati, S.d.C., Syverson, P.F., Gollmann, D. (eds.) ESORICS 2005. LNCS, vol. 3679, pp. 159–177. Springer, Heidelberg (2005)
2. Bellare, M., Boldyreva, A., Staddon, J.: Randomness Re-use in Multi-recipient Encryption Schemeas. In: Desmedt, Y.G. (ed.) PKC 2003. LNCS, vol. 2567, pp. 85–99. Springer, Heidelberg (2002)
3. Bellare, M., Micciancio, D., Warinschi, B.: Foundations of Group Signatures: Formal Definitions, Simplified Requirements, and a Construction Based on General Assumptions. In: Biham, E. (ed.) EUROCRYPT 2003. LNCS, vol. 2656, pp. 614–629. Springer, Heidelberg (2003)

4. Bellare, M., Shi, H., Zhang, C.: Foundations of Group Signatures: The Case of Dynamic Groups. In: Menezes, A. (ed.) CT-RSA 2005. LNCS, vol. 3376, pp. 136–153. Springer, Heidelberg (2005)
5. Boneh, D., Boyen, X., Shacham, H.: Short Group Signatures. In: Franklin, M. (ed.) CRYPTO 2004. LNCS, vol. 3152, pp. 41–55. Springer, Heidelberg (2004)
6. Boneh, D., Franklin, M.: An Efficient Public Key Traitor Scheme (Extended Abstract). In: Wiener, M. (ed.) CRYPTO 1999. LNCS, vol. 1666, pp. 338–353. Springer, Heidelberg (1999)
7. Brzuska, C., Fischlin, M., Freudenreich, T., Lehmann, A., Page, M., Schelbert, J., Schröder, D., Volk, F.: Security of Sanitizable Signatures Revisited. In: Jarecki, S., Tsudik, G. (eds.) PKC 2009. LNCS, vol. 5443, pp. 317–336. Springer, Heidelberg (2009)
8. Brzuska, C., Fischlin, M., Lehmann, A., Schröder, D.: Unlinkability of Sanitizable Signatures. In: Nguyen, P.Q., Pointcheval, D. (eds.) PKC 2010. LNCS, vol. 6056, pp. 444–461. Springer, Heidelberg (2010)
9. Canard, S., Jambert, A.: On Extended Sanitizable Signature Schemes. In: Pieprzyk, J. (ed.) CT-RSA 2010. LNCS, vol. 5985, pp. 179–194. Springer, Heidelberg (2010)
10. Canard, S., Laguillaumie, F., Milhau, M.: *Trapdoor* Sanitizable Signatures and Their Application to Content Protection. In: Bellovin, S.M., Gennaro, R., Keromytis, A.D., Yung, M. (eds.) ACNS 2008. LNCS, vol. 5037, pp. 258–276. Springer, Heidelberg (2008)
11. Chaum, D., Pedersen, T.P.: Transferred Cash Grows in Size. In: Rueppel, R.A. (ed.) EUROCRYPT 1992. LNCS, vol. 658, pp. 390–407. Springer, Heidelberg (1993)
12. Cramer, R., Damgrard, I., Schoenmakers, B.: Proof of Partial Knowledge and Simplified Design of Witness Hiding Protocols. In: Desmedt, Y.G. (ed.) CRYPTO 1994. LNCS, vol. 839, pp. 174–187. Springer, Heidelberg (1994)
13. Delerablée, C., Pointcheval, D.: Dynamic Fully Anonymous Short Group Signatures. In: Nguyên, P.Q. (ed.) VIETCRYPT 2006. LNCS, vol. 4341, pp. 193–210. Springer, Heidelberg (2006)
14. Fiat, A., Naor, M.: Broadcast Encryption. In: Stinson, D.R. (ed.) CRYPTO 1993. LNCS, vol. 773, pp. 480–491. Springer, Heidelberg (1994)
15. El Gamal, T.: A Public Key Cryptosystem and a Signature Scheme Based on Discrete Logarithms. In: Blakely, G.R., Chaum, D. (eds.) CRYPTO 1984. LNCS, vol. 196, pp. 10–18. Springer, Heidelberg (1985)
16. Goldwasser, S., Micali, S., Rivest, R.L.: A digital signature scheme secure against adaptive chosen-message attacks. SIAM J. Comput. 17(2), 281–308 (1988)
17. Gong, J., Qian, H., Zhou, Y.: Fully-Secure and Practical Sanitizable Signatures. In: Lai, X., Yung, M., Lin, D. (eds.) Inscrypt 2010. LNCS, vol. 6584, pp. 300–317. Springer, Heidelberg (2011)
18. Klonowski, M., Lauks, A.: Extended Sanitizable Signatures. In: Rhee, M.S., Lee, B. (eds.) ICISC 2006. LNCS, vol. 4296, pp. 343–355. Springer, Heidelberg (2006)
19. Krawczyk, H., Rabin, T.: Chameleon signatures. In: NDSS 2000. The Internet Society (2000)
20. De Santis, A., Di Crescenzo, G., Persiano, G., Yung, M.: On monotone formula closure of SZK. In: FOCS 1994, pp. 454–465. IEEE (1994)
21. Yum, D.H., Seo, J.W., Lee, P.J.: Trapdoor Sanitizable Signatures Made Easy. In: Zhou, J., Yung, M. (eds.) ACNS 2010. LNCS, vol. 6123, pp. 53–68. Springer, Heidelberg (2010)

Attack Based on Direct Sum Decomposition against the Nonlinear Filter Generator

Jingjing Wang[1], Xiangxue Li[2,⋆], Kefei Chen[1,⋆⋆], and Wenzheng Zhang[3]

[1] Department of Computer Science and Engineering,
Shanghai Jiaotong University, Shanghai, China
{wangjingjing,kfchen}@sjtu.edu.cn
[2] Department of Computer Science and Technology,
East China Normal University, Shanghai, China
[3] National Laboratory of Modern Communications, Chengdu, China

Abstract. The nonlinear filter generator (NLFG) is a powerful building block commonly used in stream ciphers. In this paper, we present the direct sum decomposition of the NLFG output sequence that leads to a system of linear equations in the initial state of the NLFG and further to an efficient algebraic attack. The coefficients of the equation system rely only on the NLFG structure. The attack is operated in an online/offline manner, doing most of the work (determining the coefficients of the equation system) in the offline phase. Thus the online phase is very fast, requiring only four multiplications and one diagonalization of $n \times n$ matrices.

Compared with related works, our attack has the advantages in both online computation cost and success probability. On the one hand, far fewer output bits and significantly less matrix computation are required in our attack, although the online computation complexity $O(LC)$ (LC is the linear complexity of the output sequence) is the same as in the known Rønjom-Helleseth attack. On the other hand, the success probability of the attack is analyzed in this paper, different from most prior work. The success probability of this algebraic attack is $1 - 2^{-\phi(2^n-1)}$ ($\phi(\cdot)$ is the Euler function), which is much greater than $1 - 2^{-n}$, the success probability of the Rønjom-Helleseth attack.

Keywords: nonlinear filter generator, algebraic attack, direct sum decomposition, characteristic polynomial, success probability.

1 Introduction

The nonlinear filter generator (NLFG) consists of an n-bit linear feedback shift register (LFSR) and a Boolean function $g : GF(2)^n \rightarrow GF(2)$, called filter

⋆ The author is supported by the National Natural Science Foundation of China (60703031). Corresponding author.
⋆⋆ The author is supported by the National Natural Science Foundation of China (61133014, 60970111) and NLMC (9140C110201110C1102), kfchen@sjtu.edu.cn.

A. Mitrokotsa and S. Vaudenay (Eds.): AFRICACRYPT 2012, LNCS 7374, pp. 53–66, 2012.
© Springer-Verlag Berlin Heidelberg 2012

function, whose n inputs are taken from some shift register stages, called taps, to produce the $GF(2)$ keystream sequence $z = z_0, z_1, z_2, \ldots$. It can either be used to produce the key stream itself [8] or as a building block in a more complex stream cipher system [23]. In this paper, all sequence elements are considered over the field $GF(2)$ which consists of the two elements $\{0, 1\}$.

It is known that any encryption map between finite dimensional vector spaces over a finite field is polynomial [22]. Thus one may represent the task of breaking a cryptosystem by the problem of solving a multivariate polynomial system of equations over a finite field. Such techniques are usually called algebraic attacks [9, 11, 15] and have been a powerful tool to cryptanalyze many stream ciphers previously believed secure [1, 6–8].

A major parameter which influences the complexity of the algebraic attack is the degree of the underlying equation system [9]. It is known for a long time that those nonlinear functions involved in stream ciphers which implement the encryption map should have high degrees [12, 20]. One interesting line in the cryptography community recently is to find efficient methods of decreasing the degree of the final equation system to be solved, especially in the literature about the attacks against the NLFG [2, 3, 9–11, 21].

PRIOR WORK. For an NLFG, the encryption map consists of the feedback function of the LFSR and the nonlinear filter function[20]. The degree of this encryption map degree is equal to the degree of the nonlinear filter function and the latter is usually high. An equation system constructed directly from that map is hard to solve [21].

Traditional algebraic attack methods overcome this by constructing low-degree equations from low-degree multiples of the Boolean function [9], whereas *fast algebraic attacks* reduce unknowns of original equations by combining them linearly [11]. Both attacks treat equations as random and include the computation of the coefficients of final low-degree equations in their online phases.[15]. *Rønjom-Helleseth attacks* (RH) overcome that problem by analyzing the output sequence of the NLFG [21]. Given the low-degree equations generated via the fast algebraic attack method in [11], Rønjom and Helleseth show that the coefficients of these low-degree equations can be computed in an offline manner by using $LC \times n$ output bits of the NLFG, where LC is the linear complexity of the output sequence. With the pre-computation, RH attacks are more efficient than the traditional algebraic attack and fast algebraic attack [14]. And as a consequence, to resist RH attacks the Boolean function should have a much higher algebraic degree than they have before[5].

MOTIVATION. This paper focuses on more efficient methods of computing the coefficients of those low-degree equations. To fulfill this purpose, the pre-computation technique is employed.

The NLFG keystream is produced by filtering the LFSR stages; the initial state of the NLFG is that of the LFSR. Our motivation is to view the keystream as a direct sum of some particular sequences in such a way that the initial state of the LFSR can be recovered easily. This can be further explained in these three steps:

- firstly, we will build a relationship between a component sequence of the direct sum decomposition of the NLFG keystream and the output sequence of the LFSR;
- secondly, we recover the current state of the component sequence;
- and lastly, we determine the initial state of the LFSR from that current state.

The first step above will construct some low-degree equations and pre-compute their coefficients efficiently. More details may be found in Section 4.1.

OUR CONTRIBUTIONS. We notice an interesting property of the NLFG keystream:

one component sequence of the direct sum is a shifted sequence of the LFSR output sequence, and the shift value is independent of the initial state.

By a pre-determination of the shift value and a direct sum decomposition algorithm, we recover the current state of the LFSR. After that a linear equation system is used to deduce the initial state from the current state. The pre-determination of the shift value and the subsequent pre-computation of the coefficients of the linear equation system require only LC offline output bits of the NLFG; they take far less matrix computation than that of the RH attack. In addition, the linear equation system is exactly the one generated via the pre-computation of the *fast algebraic attack* and also the one constructed in the RH attack. It can be solved as efficiently as it is in the RH attack. Concrete comparison with known prior work shows that our attack is amongst the most efficient algebraic methods applicable to NLFG. Refer to Table 1 and Table 2 in Section 4 for more details.

Different from most previous work [3, 9–11] that estimate via experiment simulations the probability of successful recovery of the LFSR initial state, we analyze the probability from a theoretical point of view. By employing our attack against any nonlinear filter generator, one can succeed in recovering the LFSR initial state with probability $1 - 2^{-\phi(2^n - 1)}$ ($\phi(\cdot)$ is the Euler function), which is significantly greater than the success probability $1 - 2^{-n}$ of the Rønjom-Helleseth attack [21].

ROADMAP. This paper is organized as follows. Section 2 gives some necessary definitions and notations for the paper. In Section 3 we use direct sum decomposition to distinguish the shifted sequence of the LFSR in the NLFG. Section 4 presents an efficient algebraic attack against the NLFG and discusses its success probability and time/space complexity. Section 5 concludes the paper.

2   Preliminaries

In this section we give some necessary definitions and notations about linear recurring sequences and sequence spaces. While this paper considers the binary case, the results can be extended to other finite fields. See [17] for a thorough discussion.

Let $\underline{s} = s_0, s_1, \ldots$ be a binary sequence. Let $\mathbb{F}_2$ denote the binary field. If the sequence $\underline{s}$ satisfies the following relation, for any positive integer t,

$$s_{t+n} = a_{n-1}s_{t+n-1} + a_{n-2}s_{t+n-2} + \ldots + a_0 s_t$$

with $a_0, a_1, \ldots, a_{n-1} \in \mathbb{F}_2$, then $\underline{s}$ is called a linear recurring sequence. The polynomial $f(x) = x^n + a_{n-1}x^{n-1} + a_{n-2}x^{n-2} + \ldots + a_0 \in \mathbb{F}_2[x]$ is called a characteristic polynomial of $\underline{s}$. The companion matrix of the polynomial is defined as

$$A = \begin{pmatrix} 0 & 0 & 0 & \cdots & 0 & a_0 \\ 1 & 0 & 0 & \cdots & 0 & a_1 \\ 0 & 1 & 0 & \cdots & 0 & a_2 \\ \vdots & \vdots & \vdots & & \vdots & \vdots \\ 0 & 0 & 0 & \cdots & 1 & a_{n-1} \end{pmatrix}$$

For any state vector $\boldsymbol{s_t} \overset{\triangle}{=} (s_t, s_{t+1}, \ldots, s_{t+n-1})$, we have $\boldsymbol{s_t} = \boldsymbol{s_0}A^t$.

Let $\mathrm{Tr}_1^n(x) : \mathbb{F}_{2^n} \to \mathbb{F}_2$ be the trace function. If the characteristic polynomial $f(x)$ is irreducible and α is one of its root over the extension field $\mathbb{F}_{2^n}$, then we have

$$s_t = \mathrm{Tr}_1^n(\beta \alpha^t), \text{for some } \beta \in \mathbb{F}_{2^n}.$$

Moreover if $f(x)$ is primitive, then $\underline{s}$ is an m-sequence.

If $g(x)$ is a multiple of $f(x)$, i.e., $f(x)|g(x)$, then a sequence s with characteristic polynomial $g(x)$ is also with characteristic polynomial $f(x)$. If all characteristic polynomials of $\underline{s}$ can be divided by $f(x)$, then $f(x)$ is the minimal polynomial of $\underline{s}$.

Let $S(f(x))$ be the set of sequences with characteristic polynomial $f(x)$. It follows that $S(f(x)) \subseteq S(g(x))$ if $f(x)|g(x)$. $\forall b \in \mathbb{F}_2$ and the sequences $\underline{v} = v_0, v_1, \ldots \in S(f(x))$ and $\underline{w} = w_0, w_1, \ldots \in S(f(x))$, we define in the set $S(f(x))$

$$\underline{v} + \underline{w} = v_0 + w_0, v_1 + w_1, \ldots$$

and

$$b \cdot \underline{v} = bv_0, bv_1, \ldots$$

Thus, $S(f(x))$ is a vector space over $\mathbb{F}_2$ with zero element $\underline{0} = 0, 0, \ldots$.

If the polynomial $f(x)$ is reducible, i.e., $f(x) = \prod_{i=0}^{d} f_i(x)$, where $f_i(x), i = 0, 1, \ldots, d$ are co-prime to each other, then $S(f(x))$ is a direct sum of vector spaces $S(f_0(x)), S(f_1(x)), \ldots, S(f_d(x))$, i.e., a sequence $\underline{s}$ with characteristic polynomial $f(x)$ is a direct sum of sequences $\underline{u_i}, i = 0, 1, \ldots, d$ with $\underline{u_i}$ with characteristic polynomial $f_i(x)$, $i = 0, 1, \ldots, d$ respectively.

3 Using Direct Sum Decomposition to Distinguish the Shifted Sequence

In this section, we first express one characteristic polynomial of the NLFG keystream as the product of some particular co-primes polynomials. Then we identify the direct sum decomposition of the NLFG keystream corresponding to that particular couple of co-prime polynomials. This direct sum decomposition is of special interest for us as it gives the shifted sequence of the LFSR output sequence.

An NLFG consists of an n-bit LFSR and a Boolean function g to produce its keystream $\underline{z} = z_0, z_1, \ldots$. Let $u_t, u_{t+1}, \ldots, u_{t+n-1}$ be the n LFSR stages, and g be an n-variable Boolean function. We have $z_t = g(u_t, u_{t+1}, \ldots, u_{t+n-1}), t = 0, 1, \ldots$. The keystream $\underline{z}$ can thus be viewed as a sum of e-th order product sequences of the LFSR output sequence $\underline{u}$, $0 \le e \le d$ where d is the maximum order of product sequences and it is also the degree of the Boolean function g. The LFSR of the NLFG has a primitive feedback polynomial and as a result, the LFSR output sequence $\underline{u}$ is an maximal sequence. Let α be one of the roots of the primitive characteristic polynomial of $\underline{u}$. [16] shows that an e-th order product sequence has characteristic polynomial $\prod\limits_{i=0}^{e} \prod\limits_{wt(\ell)=i} (x + \alpha^\ell)$, where $wt(\ell)$ is the binary Hamming weight of the integer ℓ. It follows that all the e-thorder product sequences, $e = 0, 1, \ldots, d$ are with characteristic polynomial $\prod\limits_{i=0}^{d} \prod\limits_{wt(\ell)=i} (x + \alpha^\ell) \overset{\Delta}{=} f(x)$. The keystream $\underline{z}$, a sum of some of them, is thus also with characteristic polynomial $f(x)$.

Let $f_1(x)$ be the primitive characteristic polynomial of the LFSR output sequence $\underline{u}$. The root α of the polynomial $f_1(x)$ is primitive over $\mathbb{F}_{2^n}$. Set $f_i(x), 0 \le i \le d$ as the following:

$$f_i(x) = \prod_{wt(\ell)=i} (x + \alpha^\ell).$$

The polynomials $f_i(x), i = 0, 1, \ldots, d$ are co-prime factors of the characteristic polynomial $f(x) = \prod\limits_{i=0}^{d} \prod\limits_{wt(\ell)=i} (x + \alpha^\ell)$ of $\underline{z}$, and the sequence $\underline{z}$ decomposed as below has the special shifted sequence as its component.

Lemma 1. *The output sequence $\underline{z}$ is a direct sum of sequences $\underline{u_i} \in S(f_i(x)), i = 0, 1, \ldots, d$.*

Let us now assume that $\underline{u_1} \ne \underline{0}$. We then consider the sequence vector space $S(f_1(x))$. The polynomial $f_1(x)$ is a primitive polynomial and thus the vector space contains exactly those m-sequences with the same characteristic polynomial $f_1(x)$. Then $\underline{u_1} = u_{1,0}, u_{1,1}, \ldots \in S(f_1(x))$ is an m-sequence. If we denote the state of the LFSR at any time instant t by $(u_t, u_{t+1}, \ldots, u_{t+n-1})$, then the sequence $\underline{u} = u_0, u_1, \ldots$ is also an m-sequence in $S(f_1(x))$. Therefore, there exists an integer $c, 0 \le c \le 2^n - 2$ such that

$$u_{1,t} = u_{t+c}, \quad t = 0, 1, \ldots. \tag{1}$$

Suppose that e is an integer, $0 \le e \le n - 1$. We denote by $i_0, i_1, \ldots, i_{e-1}$ some e integers in $R_n = \{0, 1, \ldots, n-1\}$ and by $j_0, j_1, \ldots, j_{e-1}$ some e different integers in R_n. Then for the integers $i_0, i_1, \ldots, i_{e-1}$ and the integers $j_0, j_1, \ldots, j_{e-1}$, set $I = 2^{i_0} + 2^{i_1} + \ldots + 2^{i_{e-1}}$, and

$$\mu_{j_0, j_1, \ldots, j_{e-1}} = \sum_{i_0, i_1, \ldots, i_{e-1}, \text{s.t.} I = 1} \alpha^{2^{i_0} j_0} \alpha^{2^{i_1} j_1} \cdots \alpha^{2^{i_{e-1}} j_{e-1}}.$$

For brevity, we omit hereafter $i_0, i_1, \ldots, i_{e-1}$ in the summation index "$i_0, i_1, \ldots, i_{e-1}$, s.t. $I = a$" for some positive integer a. The following theorem presents the significant property of the shift value c in the equation (1).

Theorem 1. *Let the filter function g be of the form:*

$$\begin{aligned}
g(x_0, x_1, \ldots, x_{n-1}) = {} & b + b_0 x_0 + \ldots + b_{n-1} x_{n-1} \\
& + b_{01} x_0 x_1 + \ldots + b_{n-2,n-1} x_{n-2} x_{n-1} \\
& + \cdots + \\
& + b_{01 \cdots n-1} x_0 x_1 \cdots x_{n-1}
\end{aligned} \tag{2}$$

for some $b, b_0, \ldots, b_{01 \cdots n-1} \in \mathbb{F}_2$.
    Then we have

$$\alpha^c = \mu,$$

where

$$\begin{aligned}
\mu = {} & b_0 \mu_0 + \ldots + b_{n-1} \mu_{n-1} \\
& + b_{01} \mu_{0,1} + \ldots + b_{n-2,n-1} \mu_{n-2,n-1} \\
& + \cdots + \\
& + b_{01 \cdots n-1} \mu_{0,1,\ldots,n-1}.
\end{aligned}$$

Proof. It suffices to prove this for the case that $g(x_0, x_1, \ldots, x_{n-1}) = x_{j_0} x_{j_1} \cdots x_{j_{e-1}}$. Now the output bit is $z_t = g(u_t, u_{t+1}, \ldots, u_{t+n-1}) = u_{t+j_0} u_{t+j_1} \cdots u_{t+j_{e-1}}$, where $u_t = \mathrm{Tr}_1^n(\beta \alpha^t)$ for some $\beta \in \mathbb{F}_{2^n}$. Then we have

$$\begin{aligned}
z_t &= \mathrm{Tr}_1^n(\beta \alpha^{t+j_0}) \mathrm{Tr}_1^n(\beta \alpha^{t+j_1}) \cdots \mathrm{Tr}_1^n(\beta \alpha^{t+j_{e-1}}) \\
&= \sum_{k=0}^{n-1} (\beta \alpha^{t+j_0})^{2^k} \cdot \sum_{k=0}^{n-1} (\beta \alpha^{t+j_1})^{2^k} \cdots \sum_{k=0}^{n-1} (\beta \alpha^{t+j_{e-1}})^{2^k} \\
&= \sum_{i=1}^{d} \sum_{wt(I)=i} (\beta^I \alpha^{It} \cdot (\alpha^{2^{i_0} j_0} \alpha^{2^{i_1} j_1} \cdots \alpha^{2^{i_{e-1}} j_{e-1}})).
\end{aligned} \tag{3}$$

Define $u_{i,t} = \sum_{wt(I)=i} (\beta^I \alpha^{It} \cdot (\alpha^{2^{i_0} j_0} \alpha^{2^{i_1} j_1} \cdots \alpha^{2^{i_{e-1}} j_{e-1}}))$. One can see that the sequence formed by $u_{i,t}, t = 0, 1, \ldots$ is with the characteristic polynomial $f_i(x)$. Therefore, those $u_{i,t}, t = 0, 1, \ldots$ are exactly the terms of the sequence $\underline{u_i}$ defined in Lemma 1.

Now consider the sequence $\underline{u_1}$. For $m = 0, 1, \ldots, n - 1$, set

$$\lambda_m = \sum_{I=2^m} \alpha^{2^{i_0} j_0} \alpha^{2^{i_1} j_1} \cdots \alpha^{2^{i_{e-1}} j_{e-1}}. \tag{4}$$

Especially, we have $\lambda_1 = \mu_{j_0, j_1, \ldots, j_{e-1}}$. An immediate consequence of (4) is that $\lambda_{m+1} = (\lambda_m)^2$. Then following the definition of $u_{i,t}$, the term of $\underline{u_1}$ at time t is

$$
\begin{aligned}
u_{1,t} &= \sum_{m=0}^{n-1} \beta^{2^m} \alpha^{t 2^m} \lambda_m \\
&= \sum_{m=0}^{n-1} \beta^{2^m} \alpha^{t 2^m} (\lambda_1)^{2^m} \\
&= \mathrm{Tr}_1^n (\beta \alpha^t \mu_{j_0, j_1, \ldots, j_{e-1}}).
\end{aligned}
\tag{5}
$$

Comparing this with $u_t = \mathrm{Tr}_1^n(\beta \alpha^t)$, one can conclude that the integer c in the equation (1) satisfies $\alpha^c = \mu_{j_0, j_1, \ldots, j_{e-1}} = \mu$. This ends the proof.   □

Theorem 1 implies that the sequence $\underline{u_1}$ is a shifted one of $\underline{u}$, where the shift value c relies only on α (or, the feedback function of the LFSR) and the filter function g if $\underline{u_1} \neq \underline{0}$. For simplicity, we view hereafter the zero sequence as a kind of shifted sequence; namely the zero sequence is the shifted sequence for any one by infinite positions.

Corollary 1. *Let Γ_i be the set of (cyclotomic) coset leaders of binary Hamming weight i modulo $2^n - 1$. For positive integer a, we denote by $\underline{u^a}$ the decimated sequence $u_0, u_a, u_{2a}, \ldots$. Then for $2 \leq i \leq d$,*

1) the direct sum decomposition of the sequence $\underline{u_i}$ gives the shifted sequences of $\underline{u^a}, a \in \Gamma_i, (a, 2^n - 1) = 1$;

2) the shift values also rely only on α and the filter function g.

Proof. The proof is similar to that of Theorem 1. Thus we here give only a sketch of the proof.

First, it is easy to see that the sequences $\underline{u_i}$ is with characteristic polynomial $f_i(x)$ and that $\underline{u_i}$ can be seen as a direct sum including the shifted sequences of $\underline{u^a}, a \in \Gamma_i, (a, 2^n - 1) = 1$ as its component (consider the factorization of $f_i(x)$).

Second, it is still sufficient to prove the case that $g(x_0, x_1, \ldots, x_{n-1}) = x_{j_0} x_{j_1} \cdots x_{j_{e-1}}$. The corresponding shift value c_a of sequence $\underline{u^a}$ satisfies $\alpha^{c_a} = \sum_{I=a} \alpha^{2^{i_0} j_0} \alpha^{2^{i_1} j_1} \cdots \alpha^{2^{i_{e-1}} j_{e-1}}, a \in \Gamma_i$. Thus like the value c in Theorem 1, the shift values mentioned in the Corollary 1 also rely only on α and the filter function g.   □

4   Attack Based on Direct Sum Decomposition against the NLFG

Now we describe how to use Theorem 1 to design an algebraic attack against the NLFG. Suppose that the attacker has somehow known the shift value c. Then with the linear recurrence relation of both the sequences $\underline{u}$ and $\underline{u_1}$, he knows how to convert the $(t + c)$th state of $\underline{u_1}$ to the initial state of $\underline{u}$ which is exactly the initial state of the NLFG. This is illustrated in matrix operations as follows.

4.1   Main Idea

We represent those states by vectors. Let $\boldsymbol{u_0}$ be the initial state vector $(u_0, u_1, \ldots, u_{n-1})$, $\boldsymbol{u_{1,t}}$ the state vector $(u_{1,t}, u_{1,t+1}, \ldots, u_{1,t+n-1})$ of the sequence $\underline{u_1}$, and A the companion matrix of the polynomial $f_1(x)$. Therefore, we have

$$\boldsymbol{u_{1,t}} = \boldsymbol{u_0} A^{t+c}. \tag{6}$$

Assume that $f(x)$ of degree $deg(f) = LC$ is the minimal polynomial of $\underline{z}$. And we have $LC \leq \sum_{i=0}^{d} \binom{n}{i}$ as the degree of the minimal polynomial is no greater than that of any characteristic polynomial of $\underline{z}$. Assume that $h(x) = h_0 x^0 + h_1 x^1 + \ldots + h_N x^N$ for some degree N is a multiple of the polynomial $f(x)/f_1(x)$ that satisfies $(h(x), f_1(x)) = 1$. Let $\boldsymbol{h}$ be the vector $(h_0, h_1, \ldots, h_N)$ and Z be the matrix $(\boldsymbol{z_t}^T, \boldsymbol{z_{t+1}}^T, \ldots, \boldsymbol{z_{t+n-1}}^T)$ with $\boldsymbol{z_t} = (z_t, z_{t+1}, \ldots, z_{t+N})$. It is easy to show that

$$\boldsymbol{u_{1,t}} = \boldsymbol{h} Z. \tag{7}$$

Combining the equation (6) with the equation (7), we obtain a linear equation system between the output bits and the initial state

$$\boldsymbol{u_0} A^{t+c} = \boldsymbol{h} Z, \tag{8}$$

with coefficient matrix A^{t+c} and the variables $u_0, u_1, \ldots, u_{n-1}$. An immediate consequence of (8) is that the initial state vector can be computed by

$$\boldsymbol{u_0} = \boldsymbol{h} Z A^{-(t+c)}. \tag{9}$$

Namely, if we can compute the matrix A^{t+c} and the vector $\boldsymbol{h}Z$, then we can recover the initial state $\boldsymbol{u_0}$. The coming sections show the details.

Remarks. Note that if the polynomial $h(x)$ is only a multiple of $f(x)/f_1(x)$, then $\boldsymbol{h}Z$ gives a shifted vector of $\boldsymbol{u_{1,t}}$ with some constant shift value c' and the coefficient matrix to be computed should be $A^{t+c-c'}$. However, as we care little about the specific value c, we can set $h(x) = f(x)/f_1(x)$, substitute c for $c - c'$ and still get equation (9). In this way we can reduce the number of keystream bits required by computing $\boldsymbol{h}Z$ to only $LC - n$.

4.2   Computing the Coefficient Matrix A^{t+c}

To compute the coefficient matrix, one can calculate the element μ through its explicit expression in Theorem 1, deduce the value c from μ, and do the matrix multiplications. But through the linear equation system (8), one can see that the only use of the shift value c is to compute the coefficient matrix. In other words, the deduction of the value c is unnecessary if we have an alternative to fulfill the computation.

In fact, such an alternative does exist by diagonalizing the companion matrix A. The trick can also be used to determine the element μ. Here we use this alternative to compute the coefficient matrix A^{t+c}.

Let D be the diagonal matrix $\mathrm{diag}(\alpha, \alpha^2, \ldots, \alpha^{2^{n-1}})$. The elements $\alpha, \alpha^2, \ldots, \alpha^{2^{n-1}}$ are roots of the polynomial $f_1(x)$ and thus are the eigenvalues of A. By diagonalizing the matrix A, one can find a nonsingular matrix P over $\mathbb{F}_{2^n}$ such that

$$A = PDP^{-1}. \tag{10}$$

Combining the equation (7) and the equation (10), we have

$$\boldsymbol{u_0} A^t P \cdot D^c = \boldsymbol{h} Z P. \tag{11}$$

Suppose γ_1 and γ_2 are the first elements of the row vectors $\boldsymbol{u_0} A^t P$, $\boldsymbol{h} Z P$ respectively. Then we have $\mu = \gamma_1 / \gamma_2$, as D^c is the diagonal matrix $\mathrm{diag}(\mu, \mu^2, \ldots, \mu^{2^{n-1}})$.

As shown in Theorem 1, the element μ is a constant independent of the initial state vector $\boldsymbol{u_0}$, which implies that μ can be computed from any initial state $\boldsymbol{u_0}^{(1)}$ and its corresponding output $Z^{(1)}$. Therefore, to compute μ, we can just feed into the NLFG some selected initial state, obtain the corresponding output bits, and do the calculations above.

Despite that the element μ has been known already, we can not calculate the coefficient matrix A^{t+c} from the $(t + c)$th power of A because it is infeasible to deduce c from $\mu = \alpha^c$ due to the hardness of discrete logarithm problem. But the diagonalization of A enables its $(t + c)$ times multiplication from the $(t + c)$ times multiplication, or the c times multiplication of its eigenvalue α which is just the element μ. More precisely, from the diagonalization equation (10), we have

$$A^{t+c} = A^t \cdot PD^c P^{-1} = A^t \cdot P \, \mathrm{diag}(\mu, \mu^2, \ldots, \mu^{2^{n-1}}) P^{-1}. \tag{12}$$

Moreover, we can just replace for the element μ its inverse if we want to compute directly the matrix $A^{-(t+c)}$ for the initial state recovery equation (9).

The following algorithm 1 presents the concrete steps of computing A^{t+c}. Note that all the steps can be performed in an offline manner (i.e., without the knowledge of the output bits to be attacked), and that the coefficient matrix needs only to be computed once for any output sequence of the same NLFG. Thus Algorithm 1 can be seen as the precomputation phase of the algebraic attack described in the next section.

Algorithm 1. Pre-calculation of Coefficient Matrix

Inputs: the time instant t; the companion matrix A and the roots $\alpha, \alpha^2, \ldots, \alpha^{2^{n-1}}$ of the polynomial $f_1(x)$.
Outputs: the coefficient matrix A^{t+c}.

1. Calculate the minimal polynomial $f(x)$ and $h(x) = f(x)/f_1(x)$. Suppose $h(x) = h_0 x^0 + h_1 x^1 + \ldots h_{LC-n} x^{LC-n}$, set $\boldsymbol{h} = (h_0, h_1, \ldots, h_{LC-n})$.
2. Select a initial state $u_0^{(1)}, u_1^{(1)}, \ldots, u_{n-1}^{(1)}$ and generate LC bits $z_0, z_1, \ldots, z_{LC-1}$ by the NLFG. Set them into the vector $\boldsymbol{u}_0^{(1)}$ and the matrix $Z^{(1)}$ respectively.
3. Calculate the first element $\gamma_1^{(1)}$ of the vector $\boldsymbol{u}_0 A^t P$ and the first element $\gamma_2^{(1)}$ of hZP.
4. Compute $\mu = \gamma_1^{(1)}/\gamma_2^{(1)}$.
5. Diagonalize A to find a nonsingular P such that $A = P \operatorname{diag}(\alpha, \alpha^2, \ldots, \alpha^{2^{n-1}}) P^{-1}$.
6. Calculate the coefficient matrix $A^{t+c} = P \operatorname{diag}(\mu\alpha^t, \mu^2\alpha^{2t}, \ldots, \mu^{2^{n-1}}\alpha^{2^{n-1}t}) P^{-1}$ and output it.

In Algorithm 1, calculating the minimal polynomial $f_0(x)$ is the most dominant operation and takes the complexity of $O(LC(n(\log n)^2 + (\log(LC))^3))$, according to [15]. Therefore, the time complexity of Algorithm 1 is $O(LC(n(\log n)^2 + (\log(LC))^3))$. For the data complexity, we need only LC offline bits to fulfill the algorithm.

4.3   Attack against the NLFG

After obtaining the coefficient matrix A^{t+c}, we are close to the attack against the NLFG. In fact, what's remaining is to solve a linear equation system. We summarize the whole algebraic attack in Algorithm 2.

Algorithm 2. Algebraic Attack on the NLFG

Inputs: the output sequence $\underline{z} = z_0, z_1, \ldots$; the feedback polynomial of the LFSR $f_1(x)$; the Boolean function $g(x_0, x_1, \ldots, x_{n-1})$.
Outputs: the initial state $u_0, u_1, \ldots, u_{n-1}$.

1. Pre-compute the coefficient matrix by Alg. 1 and store the vector $\boldsymbol{h}$.
2. Set consecutive LC bits of $\underline{z}$ in to Z and calculate hZ.
3. Solve the equations $\boldsymbol{u_0} A^{t+c} = \boldsymbol{h}Z$ and output the result.

We assume that $\boldsymbol{h}Z = \boldsymbol{u_{1,0}} \neq \boldsymbol{0}$ in previous sections to launch the attack. If it is not the case we may pick an integer $a \neq 1$ such that $(a, 2^n - 1) = 1$. Then the initial state of $\underline{u}^a$ can be converted into the initial state of $\underline{u}$ by the discrete fourier transform [13]. By Corollary 1 the shifted sequence of $\underline{u}^a$ falls into the direct sum decomposition of $\underline{z}$ and the shift value can be pre-determined in a similar way. Therefore we can still recover the initial state $\boldsymbol{u_0}$ even if $\underline{u_1} = \underline{0}$.

4.4   Results

To see how efficient our attack against the NLFG is, we analyze the success probability of our attack in recovering the initial state and the time and space complexities of the attack.

Success Probability

Now we analyze the success probability of recovering the initial state by using the proposed attack against the NLFG. Suppose that with probability $1/2$, that shifted sequence of $\underline{u}^a$, $(a, 2^n - 1) = 1$ in the direct sum decomposition is not the zero sequence. Then one can succeed in recovering the initial state with a probability at most

$$1 - \frac{1}{2^{\phi(2^n-1)}}, \tag{13}$$

which is sufficiently high for the attacker. Herein, $\phi(\cdot)$ is the Euler function. The coefficient matrix of the underlying algebraic system is the power of a state transition matrix for some LFSR and is thus non-singular. As long as there exists an integer a such that $(a, 2^n - 1) = 1$ and the shifted sequence of $\underline{u}^a$ is not $\underline{0}$, the initial state is exactly the unique solution of the algebraic system.

Therefore, the probability in (13) is the exact value of the success probability of recovering the initial state. We are inclined to address here that most of the existing algebraic attacks only estimate via experiment simulations the probability of successful recovery of the LFSR initial state. Although Rønjom and Helleseth also analyzed the probability of successful attack in [21] from a theoretical point of view, one can employ our method to recover the LFSR initial state with a probability significantly greater than the success probability

$$1 - \frac{1}{2^n} \tag{14}$$

in the Rønjom-Helleseth attack.

Complexity Comparison

Consider the performance of the Algorithm 2. The space complexity of Algorithm 2 is $O(n^2 + LC)$. The time complexity and the data complexity are $O(LC)$ and $O(LC)$ respectively. Table 1 compares the known algebraic attacks applicable to the NLFGs in the literature.

Table 1. Comparison among Known Algebraic Attacks on NLFG

	Data	Space	Time	
			Precomputation	Computation
AA[9]	$O(D_1)$	$O((D_1)^2)$	uncertain	$O((D_1)^\omega)^b$
FAA[11][15]^a	$O(LC)$	$O(n^2)$	$O((LC)^2)$	$O(n^2 LC)$
Improved FAA for the NLFG[15]	$O(D_2)$	$O(n^2 + LC)$	$O(D_2(n(\log n)^2 + (\log D_2)^3))$	$O(n \log n D_2)$
RH[21]	$O(LC)$	$O(n^2 + LC)$	$O(LC(n(\log n)^2 + (\log(LC))^3))$	$O(LC)$
Alg.2	$O(LC)$	$O(n^2 + LC)$	$O(LC(n(\log n)^2 + (\log(LC))^3))$	$O(LC)$

^{a} Part of the complexity result in [11] is corrected by [15].
^{b} $\omega \approx 2.807$.

In the table, we denote by D_1 the sum $\sum_{i=0}^{d/2} \binom{n}{i}$ and by D_2 the sum $\sum_{i=2}^{d} \binom{n}{i}$. W.l.o.g., $LC \leq D_2$. For the time complexity comparison, both pre-computation and on-line computation are concerned. Note that the pre-computation stage of the *algebraic attack* (AA) in [9] relies heavily on the complexity of finding low-degree multiples of the filter function of the NLFG and thus is uncertain to be measured [4]. Table 1 shows that from the complexity perspective, our proposed attack is as efficient as the RH algebraic attack and is more efficient than the *fast algebraic attack* (FAA) and the improved fast algebraic attack on the NLFG.

Comparisons between Our Attack and the RH Attack

As the RH attack in [21] is amongst the most efficient methods sofar, we compare it with the method proposed in this paper step by step as shown in Table 2. Both methods use pre-computation to improve the performance of the attacks. But

Table 2. Comparison between RH Algebraic Attack and Algorithm 2

	Precomputation				Computation	
	Calculate $f_0(x)$	Generate D_0 bits ^{a}	Calculate hZ	Diagonalize and multiply $n \times n$ matrices	Calculate hZ	Solve n linear equations
RH[21]	once	n times	n times	-	once	once
Alg.2	once	once	once	C times ^{b}	once	once

^{a} $D_0 = D_2 + n$.
^{b} C is a constant.

we observe that the output sequence of the NLFG has the very special property that one direct sum decomposition of the sequence includes the shifted LFSR sequence of the NLFG and that shift value is not affected by the initial state of the NLFG. This motivates our attack to gain two advantages over the RH attack: far fewer output bits and significantly less matrix computation. Moreover, the success probability of the proposed method is much greater than that in the RH attack, as shown in the equations (13) and (14).

5 Conclusion

Based on direct sum decomposition, a special property of the NLFG output sequence has been explored and exploited to provide new methods of decreasing the degree of the algebraic equation system for the algebraic attack. We show that the output sequence can be decomposed in a direct sum of a series of sequences, one of which is a shifted one of the LFSR sequence. The shift value is a constant independent of the NLFG initial state and thus can be pre-determined. The resulting equation system is linear and thus easy to be solved. Moreover, the coefficient matrix of the algebraic system, which depends just on the shift value, needs only to be calculated once for the NLFG. The total complexity of our algebraic attack based on that equation system is the same as that of the RH algebraic attack, one of the most efficient algebraic methods applicable to the NLFG sofar. Theoretical analysis shows that our attack requires fewer operations and achieves higher success probability than the RH algebraic attack.

References

1. Al-Hinai, S., Dawson, E., Henricksen, M., Simpson, L.: On the Security of the LILI Family of Stream Ciphers against Algebraic Attacks. In: Pieprzyk, J., Ghodosi, H., Dawson, E. (eds.) ACISP 2007. LNCS, vol. 4586, pp. 11–28. Springer, Heidelberg (2007)
2. Armknecht, F., Krause, M.: Algebraic Attacks on Combiners with Memory. In: Boneh, D. (ed.) CRYPTO 2003. LNCS, vol. 2729, pp. 162–175. Springer, Heidelberg (2003)
3. Armknecht, F., Ars, G.: Introducing a New Variant of Fast Algebraic Attacks and Minimizing Their Successive Data Complexity. In: Dawson, E., Vaudenay, S. (eds.) Mycrypt 2005. LNCS, vol. 3715, pp. 16–32. Springer, Heidelberg (2005)
4. Canteaut, A.: Open Problems Related to Algebraic Attacks on Stream Ciphers. In: Ytrehus, Ø. (ed.) WCC 2005. LNCS, vol. 3969, pp. 120–134. Springer, Heidelberg (2006)
5. Carlet, C., Feng, K.: An Infinite Class of Balanced Functions with Optimal Algebraic Immunity, Good Immunity to Fast Algebraic Attacks and Good Nonlinearity. In: Pieprzyk, J. (ed.) ASIACRYPT 2008. LNCS, vol. 5350, pp. 425–440. Springer, Heidelberg (2008)
6. Billet, O., Gilbert, H.: Resistance of SNOW 2.0 Against Algebraic Attacks. In: Menezes, A. (ed.) CT-RSA 2005. LNCS, vol. 3376, pp. 19–28. Springer, Heidelberg (2005)

7. Cho, J.Y., Pieprzyk, J.: Algebraic Attacks on SOBER-t32 and SOBER-t16 without Stuttering. In: Roy, B., Meier, W. (eds.) FSE 2004. LNCS, vol. 3017, pp. 49–64. Springer, Heidelberg (2004)

8. Courtois, N.T.: Higher Order Correlation Attacks,XL Algorithm and Cryptanalysis of Toyocrypt. In: Lee, P.J., Lim, C.H. (eds.) ICISC 2002. LNCS, vol. 2587, pp. 182–199. Springer, Heidelberg (2003)

9. Courtois, N.T., Meier, W.: Algebraic Attacks on Stream Ciphers with Linear Feedback. In: Biham, E. (ed.) EUROCRYPT 2003. LNCS, vol. 2656, pp. 345–359. Springer, Heidelberg (2003)

10. Courtois, N.: Cryptanalysis of SFINKS. In: ICISC 2005, Cryptology ePrint Archive Report 2005/243 (2005), http://eprint.iacr.org/

11. Courtois, N.T.: Fast Algebraic Attacks on Stream Ciphers with Linear Feedback. In: Boneh, D. (ed.) CRYPTO 2003. LNCS, vol. 2729, pp. 176–194. Springer, Heidelberg (2003)

12. Ding, C., Shan, W., Xiao, G.: The Stability Theory of Stream Ciphers. LNCS, vol. 561. Springer, Heidelberg (1991)

13. Golomb, S.W., Gong, G.: Signal Design for Good Correlation: For Wireless Communication, Cryptography and Radar. Cambridge University Press, Cambridge (2005)

14. Gong, G., Ronjom, S., Helleseth, T., Hu, H.: Fast Discrete Fourier Spectra Attacks on Stream Ciphers. IEEE Trans. Inform. Theory 57(8), 5555–5565 (2011)

15. Hawkes, P., Rose, G.: Rewriting Variables: The Complexity of Fast Algebraic Attacks on Stream Ciphers. In: Franklin, M. (ed.) CRYPTO 2004. LNCS, vol. 3152, pp. 390–406. Springer, Heidelberg (2004)

16. Key, E.L.: An Analysis of the Structure and Complexity of Nonlinear Binary Sequence Generators. IEEE Trans. Inform. Theory 22(6) (1976)

17. Lidl, R., Niederreiter, H.: Finite Fields, Encyclopedia of Mathematics and its Applications, 2nd edn., vol. 20. Cambridge University Press, Cambridge (1997)

18. Meier, W., Pasalic, E., Carlet, C.: Algebraic Attacks and Decomposition of Boolean Functions. In: Cachin, C., Camenisch, J.L. (eds.) EUROCRYPT 2004. LNCS, vol. 3027, pp. 474–491. Springer, Heidelberg (2004)

19. Menezes, A.J., van Oorschot, P.C., Vanstone, S.A.: Handbook of Applied Cryptography. CRC Press, Boca Raton (1996)

20. Rueppel, R.A.: Analysis and Design of Stream Ciphers. Springer, Heidelberg (1986)

21. Rønjom, S., Helleseth, T.: A New Attack on the Filter Generator. IEEE Trans. Inform. Theory 53(5), 1752–1758 (2007)

22. Shannon, C.E.: Communication theory of secrecy systems. Bell Syst. Tech. J. 28, 656–715 (1949)

23. Simpson, L.R., Dawson, E., Golić, J.D., Millan, W.L.: LILI Keystream Generator. In: Stinson, D.R., Tavares, S. (eds.) SAC 2000. LNCS, vol. 2012, pp. 248–261. Springer, Heidelberg (2001)

Fuzzy Vault for Multiple Users*

Julien Bringer[1], Hervé Chabanne[1,2], and Mélanie Favre[1]

[1] Morpho
[2] Télécom ParisTech

Abstract. We introduce an extension of the Fuzzy Vault scheme to support multiple users. Namely, different participants might share the same vault to store their secret. In the classical Fuzzy Vault, a user locks a secret using a set A and one can unlock it by providing another set B which overlaps substantially with A. In our extension, our Extended Fuzzy Vault is locked thanks to different sets A^j, $j = 1, \ldots, l$ and can be unlocked with a set B with enough common elements with one of these A^j. Our results are based on Folded Reed-Solomon Codes and their recent list recovery algorithm. This way, our idea can be interpreted as a natural extension of the list decoding of the Reed-Solomon Codes to list recovery. We give a security analysis of our proposal relying on Secure Sketches security properties to gauge our results. Finally, we provide details on an implementation to support our ideas.

Keywords: Fuzzy Vault, Folded Reed-Solomon Codes, list recovery algorithm.

1 Introduction

Since its introduction in 2002 by Juels and Sudan [7, 8], the Fuzzy Vault (FV) scheme has attracted a lot of attention; in particular in the biometric community [1,2,9–13,16–19,23]. This Fuzzy Vault scheme relies on the Reed-Solomon codes and their decoding capacity. More precisely, to contrust a FV scheme, each information symbol x_i – considered as element of a finite field – is accompanied by its evaluation by a given polynomial p to form a pair $(x_i, y_i = p(x_i))$. Moreover, some chaff points are added to thwart an adversary who should not be able to differentiate genuine pairs from fake ones. Whenever a user comes back to recover data from a FV, he has to produce a sufficient number of genuine pairs; this way, the errors decoding capacity of the Reed-Solomon code enables to recover the underlying polynomial p.

In this paper, we introduce the idea of an Extended Fuzzy Vault (EFV) scheme for multiple users. This means that following the idea of FV, different users can now share the same EFV. From a technical point of view, an immediate difficulty comes from the fact that different users can have the same information symbol x_i. To deal with this problem, we replace the underlying list decoding of Reed-Solomon codes suggested by FV scheme [8] by a more advanced technique

---

* This work has been partially funded by the French ANR project BMOS.

A. Mitrokotsa and S. Vaudenay (Eds.): AFRICACRYPT 2012, LNCS 7374, pp. 67–81, 2012.

called list recovery. Indeed, this is the needed method to handle multiplicities we can now encounter for each x_i. Doing so, we also switch from Reed-Solomon codes to a variant called folded Reed-Solomon codes. Folded Reed-Solomon codes are an explicit family of codes that achieve the optimal trade-off between rate and error-correction capability. Moreover, recently [4] introduces effective list decoding algorithms for this family of codes which can be easily extended to list recovery algorithms [5].

The origin of the motivation for our extension can be found in [8] where the case of encoding multiple sets in the same fuzzy vault is briefly mentioned. For instance, the idea of replacing part of, or all, chaff points by points corresponding to other polynomials is introduced. However, [8] does not try to deal with potential collisions between the different sets to be encoded. Another solution would be to use several fuzzy vaults for single sets in parallel but then one has to execute as many decoding algorithms to test if a set can open one of the vaults. Our contribution is to show how to generally encode multiple sets in the same vault with only one associated unlocking algorithm to be executed.

On an applicative side, and in particular in the biometric domain, the demand of encoding multiple sets is natural [15]. Today, the FV scheme permits to users to authenticate themselves through their biometric data. For an identification scenario, where a comparison with a database of several users is needed, [15] studies the way to reduce the number of comparisons to run among the several vaults – each corresponding only to one set – by filtering techniques. Going further, our proposal can directly address identification protocols, which is the largest application of biometric recognition process, by seeing the whole database as a single vault.

2 Fuzzy Vault (FV) Scheme

Let $\mathcal{F}$ stand for a finite field of cardinality q ($\mathcal{F} = GF(q)$). We have a secret value $\kappa \in \mathcal{F}^k$ to be protected and a secret set $A = \{a_i \in \mathcal{F}, i = 1, \dots, t\}$. Let r, a parameter of the scheme, be an integer greater than t.

The associated Fuzzy Vault (FV) $V_A \in \mathcal{F}^{2r}$, as introduced by Juels and Sudan in [7,8], is computed thanks to the LOCK algorithm that takes as inputs the set A and a vector κ. This algorithm transforms κ into a polynomial p. Moreover, to each value in A, its evaluation by the polynomial p is made to form a pair. Finally, some chaff points, i.e. points taken at random are chosen. This gives:

> $LOCK(A, \kappa) = V_A = \{(x_i, y_i) \in \mathcal{F} \times \mathcal{F}, i = 1, \dots, r\}$ with
> **for** $i = 1$ **to** t **do**
> $\quad | \quad x_i = a_i, \, y_i = p(x_i)$
> **end**
> **for** $i = t + 1$ **to** r **do**
> $\quad | \quad x_i \in \mathcal{F} \setminus A, \, y_i \in \mathcal{F} \setminus \{p(x_i)\}$ (both taken randomly)
> **end**

Whenever one gets a set B with many common elements with the secret set A, he should be able to recover the secret κ from V_A. To this end, an algorithm UNLOCK is provided. This gives:

Definition 1 ([8]). *A locking/unlocking pair (*LOCK; UNLOCK*) with parameter set $(k; t; r)$ is complete with ϵ-fuzziness if the following holds. For $\kappa \in \mathcal{F}^k$, for 2 sets $A, B \in \mathcal{F}^t$ such that $\|A - B\| \leq \epsilon$, we have* UNLOCK$(B; $LOCK$(A; \kappa)) = \kappa$ *with overwhelming probability.*

In [8], the UNLOCK algorithm relies on the error correction capacity of the Reed-Solomon codes.

A Reed-Solomon code over the finite field $\mathcal{F}$, of length t, and dimension k, is made by the evaluations of polynomials of $\mathcal{F}[X]$ of degree strictly less than k for t elements of $\mathcal{F}$. Each polynomial p is associated with the codeword $(p(a_1), \ldots, p(a_t))$ where the a_i's stand for elements in $\mathcal{F}$. Reed-Solomon codes can be decoded up to $\frac{t-k}{2}$ errors by the Peterson-Berlekamp-Massey algorithm [14]. List decoding algorithms [22], such as the one introduced by Guruswami and Sudan in [6], enable to correct even more errors. We denote by RSDECODE such a decoding algorithm which takes as input a set of t points of $\mathcal{F}^2$ and returns either a polynomial of degree k or null.

To achieve complete $\frac{t-k}{2}$-fuzziness for the (LOCK; UNLOCK) pair with $k \leq t \leq r \leq q$, one has to simply take in the Fuzzy-Vault V_A, the points with an abscissa in B and recover the underlying polynomial using the RSDECODE Peterson-Berlekamp-Massey decoding algorithm.

In [8] the security analysis is formalized through an attack model that captures the possibility for an attacker to have prior knowledge of a part of the set A when trying to find out the value of κ from LOCK$(A; \kappa)$: Given an uniformly random subset A' of A of a given bounded size, the probability for the adversary to guess the right value κ (given A' and LOCK$(A; \kappa)$) should remain small.

The security is directly depending on the number $r - t$ of chaff points that are added. In fact, the more chaff points they are, the more possible polynomials of degree less than k are encoded in the vault, thus leading to higher conditional entropy of κ knowing the vault V_A. The authors quantify this by showing that for any $\mu > 0$ there is, with probability at least $1 - \mu$, at least $\frac{\mu}{3} q^{k-t} (\frac{r}{t})^t$ possible polynomials. This enables to prove the security for uniformly drawn set A. The case of non-uniform distribution is also analyzed when $r = q - 1$.

Another security model to analyze the Fuzzy Vault scheme is to see it in the secure sketch [3] framework. Let $\mathcal{H}$ be a metric space with distance function d. The formal definition of secure sketches functions is the following.

Definition 2. *A $(\mathcal{H}, m, m', t)$-secure sketch is a pair of functions $(\mathsf{SS}, \mathsf{Rec})$ where the sketching function SS takes $w \in \mathcal{H}$ as input, and outputs a sketch in $\{0, 1\}^*$, such that for all random variables W over $\mathcal{H}$ with min-entropy $\mathbf{H}_\infty(W) \geq m$, we have the conditional min-entropy $\overline{\mathbf{H}}_\infty(W \mid \mathsf{SS}(W)) \geq m'$.*

The recovery function Rec takes a sketch P and a vector $w' \in \mathcal{H}$ as inputs, and outputs a word $w'' \in \mathcal{H}$, such that for any $P = \mathsf{SS}(w)$ and $\mathrm{d}(w, w') \leq t$, it holds that $w'' = w$.

Where $\mathbf{H}_\infty(X) = -\log_2 \max_x \mathbb{P}(X = x)$ _stands for the **min-entropy** and_ $\overline{\mathbf{H}}_\infty(X \mid Y) = -\log_2 \mathbf{E}_{y \leftarrow Y}(2^{-\mathbf{H}_\infty(X|Y=y)})$ _for the **conditional min-entropy**._

The difference between m and m' gives the entropy loss of the scheme. In [21], it is shown that the entropy loss of the fuzzy vault scheme is at most

$$(t - k)\log_2 q + \log_2 \binom{q}{r} - \log_2 \binom{q - t}{r - t}.$$

This leads to the lower bound

$$\log_2 \binom{r}{t} - (t - k)\log_2 q \qquad (1)$$

on the remaining entropy $\overline{\mathbf{H}}_\infty(A \mid \mathrm{LOCK}(A; \kappa))$.

One advantage of this measure compared to the original security analysis from [7,8] is that it is independent on the distribution assumption of the encoded set A (in particular this handles non-uniformity for all $r \leq q - 1$).

Example 1. _The movie lover's problem is introduced in [8] as an example of application of the FV scheme. In this problem, Alice – a movie lover – has to choose among 10^4 movies her 22 favorites. She is looking for someone with similar affinities. She does not want to reveal her preferences to other people. She uses the FV scheme to encrypt her phone number as whenever someone unlocks her vault, he demonstrates that he shares her film taste and this enables him to call her._

3   Folded Reed-Solomon Codes

After recalling some definitions from [5], we present the list decoding algorithm taken from [4] used in our scheme.

3.1   A Few Definitions

Definition 3 (Folded Reed-Solomon Code). _Given γ a generator of $\mathcal{F}$, the m-folded version of the Reed Solomon code $C[n, k]$, denoted $FRS_{\mathcal{F}, \gamma, m, N, k}$, is a code of block length $N = n/m$ over $\mathcal{F}^m$ where $n = q - 1$ is divisible by m. The encoding of a message $p \in \mathcal{F}[X]$ of degree at most $k - 1$ is given by_

$$p(X) = \left(\begin{bmatrix} p(1) \\ p(\gamma) \\ \vdots \\ p(\gamma^{m-1}) \end{bmatrix}, \begin{bmatrix} p(\gamma^m) \\ p(\gamma^{m+1}) \\ \vdots \\ p(\gamma^{2m-1}) \end{bmatrix}, \dots, \begin{bmatrix} p(\gamma^{n-m}) \\ p(\gamma^{n-m+1}) \\ \vdots \\ p(\gamma^{n-1}) \end{bmatrix} \right)$$

The m-tuple $(p(\gamma^{jm}), p(\gamma^{jm+1}), \dots, p(\gamma^{jm+m-1}))$ is the j'th symbol of the encoding of p for $0 \leq j < n/m$.

More generally any restriction of $p(X)$ on part of its columns will form a codeword of a folded Reed Solomon code $FRS_{\mathcal{F},\gamma,m,N,k}$ of shorter length $N = n/m$ with $n < q - 1$. In the paper, we consider this general case where n can be either equal to $q - 1$ or lower than $q - 1$.

Definition 4 (List decodable code). *Let C be a code of block length N, let $\sigma \geq 1$ be an integer and $0 < \rho < 1$ be a real. C is called (ρ, σ)-list decodable if every Hamming ball of radius ρN has at most σ codewords in it.*

List decoding is a relaxation of unique decoding. Instead of outputting a single codeword, given an error bound e, the decoding algorithm gives the list of all polynomials $p \in \mathcal{F}[X]$ of degree at most $k - 1$ whose encoding differs with the received word in at most e symbols.

List recovery is an extension of list decoding where for each position i of the received message the input is of the form of a set T_i of possible values.

Definition 5 (List recoverable code). *Let C be a code of block length N, let $\ell, \sigma \geq 1$ be integers and $0 < \rho < 1$ be a real. C is called (ρ, ℓ, σ)-list recoverable if for all sequences of sets $T_0, \ldots, T_{N-1}$ where $|T_i| \leq \ell$, for every $0 \leq i \leq N - 1$, there are at most σ codewords $\mathbf{c} = \langle c_0, \ldots, c_{N-1} \rangle$ such that $c_i \in T_i$ for at least $(1 - \rho)N$ positions i.*

For $\ell = 1$, a $(\rho, 1, \sigma)$-list recoverable code C is (ρ, σ)-list decodable.

3.2   List Decoding of Folded Reed-Solomon Codes

We chose to use Guruswami's list decoding algorithm [4] from which we give here a brief overview. Decoding of FRS codes is a two-step process: first interpolate a multivariate polynomial $Q \in \mathcal{F}[X, Y_1, \ldots, Y_s]$, where s is a chosen a parameter lower than m, and secondly find all candidate polynomials p of degree $k - 1$ satisfying $Q(X, p(X), \ldots, p(\gamma^{s-1}X)) = 0$. Both steps can be reduced to the solving of linear systems over $\mathcal{F}$.

Interpolation. Starting from a received word $\mathbf{y} \in (\mathcal{F}^m)^N$ of the form $\langle y_0, \ldots, y_N \rangle = \langle [y_0, \ldots, y_{m-1}], \ldots, [y_{n-m}, \ldots, y_{n-1}] \rangle$, we are looking for a nonzero polynomial

$$Q(X, Y_1, Y_2, \ldots, Y_s) = A_0(X) + A_1(X)Y_1 + A_2(X)Y_2 + \ldots + A_s(X)Y_s \quad (2)$$

over $\mathcal{F}$ where $deg(A_i) \leq D$ for $i = 1, \ldots, s$ and $deg(A_0) \leq D + k - 1$ and D is chosen as

$$D = \left\lfloor \frac{N(m - s + 1) - k + 1}{s + 1} \right\rfloor \quad (3)$$

For $i = 0, .., N - 1, j = 0, .., m - s$, Q has to satisfy

$$Q(\gamma^{im+j}, y_{im+j}, y_{im+j+1}, \ldots, y_{im+j+s-1}) = 0 \quad (4)$$

The number $N(m - s + 1)$ of these interpolation conditions are smaller than the number $(D + 1)s + D + k$ of monomials in Q, which guarantees the existence of such a polynomial. Note that we can choose *any* polynomial Q satisfying the conditions (4).

From the choice of D (3), we can deduce that the fractional agreement needed to decode a received word $\mathbf{y}$ is $\tau > \frac{1}{s+1} + \frac{s}{s+1}\frac{mR}{m-s+1}$ where $R = k/n$ is the rate of the code. This is equivalent to say that we can tolerate up to $e = \frac{s}{s+1}(N - \frac{k}{m-s+1})$ erroneous symbols in $\mathbf{y}$.

Root Finding. We need now to find all polynomials $p \in \mathcal{F}[X]$ satisfying

$$A_0(X) + A_1(X)p(X) + A_2(X)p(\gamma X) + \ldots + A_s(X)p(\gamma^{s-1}X) = 0 \quad (5)$$

This equation can be seen as a linear system in the coefficients $p_0, \ldots, p_{k-1}$ of p. Let us define $B(X) = a_{1,0} + a_{2,0}X + \ldots + a_{s,0}X^{s-1}$ and we denote $A_i(X) = \sum_{j=0}^{D+k-1} a_{i,j}X^j$ for $0 \le i \le s$. Then for $r = 0, \ldots, k - 1$ we can deduce from equation (5) that

$$a_{0,r} + p_r(a_{1,0} + a_{2,0}\gamma^r + \ldots + a_{s,0}\gamma^{(s-1)r}) + p_{r-1}(a_{1,1} + a_{2,1}\gamma^{r-1} + \ldots + a_{s,1}\gamma^{(s-1)(r-1)})$$
$$+ \ldots + p_1(a_{1,r-1} + a_{2,r-1}\gamma + \ldots + a_{s,r-1}\gamma^{s-1}) + p_0(a_{1,r} + \ldots + a_{s,r}) = 0 \quad (6)$$

which is equivalent to

$$B(\gamma^r)p_r + \left(\sum_{i=0}^{r-1} b_i^{(r)}p_i\right) + a_{0,r} = 0 \quad (7)$$

This leads to a lower-triangular linear system with on its diagonal the $B(\gamma^r)$'s. If $B(\gamma^r) \ne 0$, p_r is an affine combination of $p_0, \ldots, p_{r-1}$. The dimension of the space of solutions is thus limited by the amount of $B(\gamma^r) = 0$. As γ is a generator of $\mathcal{F}$, all γ^r values for $0 \le r < k$ are different. Moreover B is a $s - 1$ degree polynomial, thus $B(\gamma^r)$ vanishes for at most $s - 1$ values of r.

The whole decoding procedure can be summed up as follows

Theorem 1 ([4]). *Given a received word* $\mathbf{y} \in (\mathcal{F}^m)^N$, *for any integer* s, $1 \le s \le m$, *one can find a subspace of dimension at most* $s - 1$ *containing all polynomials* $p \in \mathcal{F}[X]$ *of degree less than* k *whose FRS encoding agrees with* $\mathbf{y}$ *in at least a fraction* $\frac{1}{s+1} + \frac{s}{s+1}\frac{mR}{m-s+1}$ *of the* N *codeword symbols.*

According to Definition 4, for any integer $1 \le s \le m$, an $FRS_{\mathcal{F},\gamma,m,N,k}$ code is an (ρ, q^{s-1})-list decodable code with $\rho = 1 - (\frac{1}{s+1} + \frac{s}{s+1}\frac{mR}{m-s+1})$. The algorithm described previously gives the corresponding list decoding procedure.

Remark 1. *The fuzzy vault construction from Section 2 can be adapted to the folded Reed-Solomon codes. The y-axis points of the vault will still be associated to one coordinate of a codeword associated to a random polynomial; but with a coordinate that corresponds here to several evaluations (one column of $p(X)$ in Definition 3). Based on the list decoding property – here applied with a folded*

*Reed-Solomon code of length t with t the size of the locked set as in Section 2 –
this would lead to a fuzzy vault scheme ensuring $\frac{s}{s+1}(t - \frac{k}{m-s+1})$-fuzziness.*

3.3   Generalization to List Recovery

Suppose now that for each position $i = 0, \ldots, N - 1$ of a received message we
have a set T_i of possible values $y_{i,1}, \ldots, y_{i,\#T_i}$ with $y_{i,j} = [y_{im,j}, \ldots, y_{im+m-1,j}] \in
\mathcal{F}^m$ and $1 \leq j \leq \#T_i \leq \ell$. Fortunately, list recovering is also possible with
Guruswami's algorithm [4] but with some slight modifications. As we have now
up to ℓ values for each symbol, we need to expand the $N(m-s+1)$ interpolation
conditions to $\ell N(m - s + 1)$ to take all symbols into account. For $i = 0, .., N -
1, j = 0, .., m - s$, Q has now to satisfy

$$Q(\gamma^{im+j}, y_{im+j,1}, y_{im+j+1,1}, \cdots, y_{im+j+s-1,1}) = 0$$
$$Q(\gamma^{im+j}, y_{im+j,2}, y_{im+j+1,2}, \cdots, y_{im+j+s-1,2}) = 0$$

$$\vdots$$

$$Q(\gamma^{im+j}, y_{im+j,\#T_i}, y_{im+j+1,\#T_i}, \cdots, y_{im+j+s-1,\#T_i}) = 0$$

The same way, D becomes

$$D = \left\lfloor \frac{\ell N(m - s + 1) - k + 1}{s + 1} \right\rfloor \tag{8}$$

The interpolation step works just as before but with a bigger linear system to
solve and root finding is exactly the same. Finally, we have the new agreement
fraction $\tau > \frac{\ell}{s+1} + \frac{s}{s+1}\frac{mR}{m-s+1}$.

This means that an $FRS_{\mathcal{F},\gamma,m,N,k}$ code is an (ρ, ℓ, q^{s-1})-list recoverable code
with $\rho = 1 - (\frac{\ell}{s+1} + \frac{s}{s+1}\frac{mR}{m-s+1})$.

Remark 2. *Following the preceding facts, one has to note that there are some
restrictions on the values of parameters m, s and ℓ, indeed we need to have
$1 \leq \ell \leq s \leq m$.*

4   Extended Fuzzy Vault (EFV) Scheme

In this section, we show how to extend the FV scheme to the case where the
vault is made thanks to different secret sets A^j, $j = 1, \ldots, l$. As before for the
FV scheme, we want to unlock the vault from a set B which contains enough
common elements with one of these A^j's.

Let $\mathcal{E}$ be an alphabet containing N symbols denoted by $x_1, \ldots, x_N$. Each A^j
possesses t of these symbols.

We will rely on the list recovery capacity of the Folded Reed-Solomon Codes
as described in the previous section to build our EFV scheme. We take back the
notations of Section 3, $N = n/m$ is the length of the underlying Folded Reed-
Solomon Code in the finite field $\mathcal{F}$. As before γ is a generator of its multiplicative
group. Let $F_1, \ldots, F_l$ be l evaluation functions according to Definition 3. More
precisely, each set A^j is associated to a function F_j. Let p_j a random polynomial

of degree $k-1$ in $\mathcal{F}[X]$. The value $F_j(x_i)$ is defined as the $i-1$'th symbol of the encoding of p_j for $0 \leq i-1 < N$, $(p_j(\gamma^{(i-1)m}), p_j(\gamma^{(i-1)m+1}), \ldots, p_j(\gamma^{(i-1)m+m-1}))$.

4.1   LOCK

We take back the idea of the Fuzzy Vault scheme that is made with genuine polynomial evaluations hidden within a cloud of chaff points.

The extended vault $V = \text{LOCK}(A^1, \ldots, A^l; \kappa)$ corresponding to the secret sets A^j is made as follows (κ represents here the randomness used to generate the l evaluation functions $F_1, \ldots, F_l$). Consider N sets $S_1, \ldots, S_N$ that will be related to the N symbols in $\mathcal{E}$. Let r, ℓ be two integers corresponding to parameters for the addition of chaff points.

Initialize a counter $cpt \leftarrow 0$ and the sets $S_1, \ldots, S_N$ to the empty set:
$S_i \leftarrow \emptyset$, $i = 1, \ldots, N$
for $i = 1$ **to** N **do**
    for $j = 1$ **to** l **do**
        if $x_i \in A^j$ **then**
            $S_i \leftarrow S_i \cup \{F_j(x_i)\}$
        end
    end
    set $l_i \leftarrow \#S_i$
    if $l_i \neq 0$ **then**
        $cpt \leftarrow cpt + 1$
        for $j = l_i + 1$ **to** ℓ **do**
            let y_i^j randomly chosen in $\mathcal{F}^m \setminus \{F_d(x_i)\}_{d=1,\ldots,l}$
            let $S_i \leftarrow S_i \cup \{y_i^j\}$
        end
    end
end
randomly choose $i_{cpt+1}, \ldots, i_r$ such that $\#S_{i_e} = 0$ for $e \in \{cpt + 1, \ldots, r\}$
for $e = cpt + 1$ **to** r **do**
    for $j = 1$ **to** ℓ **do**
        let $y_{i_e}^j$ randomly chosen in $\mathcal{F}^m \setminus \{F_d(x_{i_e})\}_{d=1,\ldots,l}$
        let $S_{i_e} \leftarrow S_{i_e} \cup \{y_{i_e}^j\}$
    end
end
Finally, every set S_i for $i = 1, \ldots, N$ is shuffled

At the end, the locked vault is $V = \text{LOCK}(A^1, \ldots, A^l) = \{(x_i, S_i), i = 1, \ldots, N\}$.

To simplify the description and the security analysis, the same number of points is associated to each set S_i. Note that this constraint could be relaxed.

Remark 3. *In other words, we construct a collection of sets* $S_1, \ldots, S_N$ *where*

- *there are $N - r$ empty sets*
- *and r indices $i_1, \ldots, i_r$ such that for $e \in \{1, \ldots, r\}$, S_{i_e} is constituted with the union of the sets*

$$S_{i_e}^{(1)} = \{F_j(x_{i_e}) | x_{i_e} \in A^j, \, j = 1, \ldots, l\}$$

with some chaff points

$$S_{i_e}^{(2)} = \{y_{i_e}^j \in \mathcal{F}^m \setminus \{F_d(x_{i_e})\}_{d=1,\ldots,l} \, | \, j = 1, \ldots, \rho\}$$

such that $\#S_{i_e}^{(1)} + \#S_{i_e}^{(2)} = \ell$.

As for the original fuzzy vault scheme, we have a number of chaff points that hide the genuine positions that correspond to polynomial values. Moreover we now have another dimension where at one given position, a genuine polynomial value is mixed among other polynomial values and additional chaff points. And even the genuine sets (the A^j's) can be seen as chaff with respect to one given set A^i.

4.2   UNLOCK

Let $A^1, \ldots, A^l$ be l sets of size t. The unlocking procedure of a vault

$$\text{LOCK}(A^1, \ldots, A^l) = \{(x_i, S_i), i = 1, \ldots, N\}$$

is as follows.

When receiving a new set $B = \{b_1, \ldots, b_t\}$, take the subcollection $S_{i_1}, \ldots, S_{i_t}$ where the i_e's are such that $x_{i_e} = b_e$ and run the list recovery decoding algorithm with input $((x_{i_1}, S_{i_1}), \ldots, (x_{i_t}, S_{i_t}))$. More precisely, here the list recovery decoding algorithm is executed by restricting the folded RS code to a folded RS code $FRS_{\mathcal{F},\gamma,m,t,k}$ of length t that is constituted with codewords

$$\left(\begin{bmatrix} p(\gamma^{(i_1-1)m}) \\ \vdots \\ p(\gamma^{(i_1-1)m+m-1}) \end{bmatrix}, \ldots, \begin{bmatrix} p(\gamma^{(i_t-1)m}) \\ \vdots \\ p(\gamma^{(i_t-1)m+m-1}) \end{bmatrix} \right)$$

for any $p \in \mathcal{F}[X]$ of degree at most $k-1$.

We thus apply the list recovery algorithm within this code with the sets $S_{i_1}, \ldots, S_{i_t}$ corresponding to the set of possible received message values (the T_i's in Definition 5) at each position $i_1, \ldots, i_t$. Thanks to the list recoverable property of the Folded Reed-Solomon codes (cf. Section 3.3), the algorithm will output all the codewords $\mathbf{c} = \langle c_{i_1}, \ldots, c_{i_t} \rangle$ such that $c_{i_e} \in S_{i_e}$ for at least $(1-\rho)t$ positions i_e with $\rho = 1 - (\frac{\ell}{s+1} + \frac{s}{s+1}\frac{mR}{m-s+1})$.

Consequently, as soon an A^j is sufficiently close to B, the output list will contain the codeword associated to the evaluation function F_j. From F_j, this leads to retrieving the content of A^j. Based on the parameters of the list recovery decoding algorithm, for any s such that $\ell \leq s \leq m$, we can hence retrieve the A^j's such that $\|A^j - B\| \leq \epsilon$ with $\epsilon = \frac{1}{s+1}((s+1-\ell)t - \frac{sk}{m-s+1})$.

Lemma 1. *Following a straightforward extension of Definition 1, our Extended Fuzzy Vault scheme based on a $FRS_{\mathcal{F},\gamma,m,N,k}$ code is complete with ϵ-fuzziness where*

$$\epsilon = \frac{1}{s+1}((s+1-\ell)t - \frac{sk}{m-s+1})$$

Remark 4. *Although our EFV construction is described in the folded Reed-Solomon context, it can also be applied to other codes for which a list recovery algorithm exists. This is for instance the case for classical Reed-Solomon codes. So the EFV scheme can be instantiated for RS codes but then the list recovery decoding will be suboptimal [20].*

5   Security Properties of the EFV Scheme

5.1   Uniform Case

As in [8], we can estimate the difficulty for an attacker to retrieve a genuine polynomial among the different possible combinations of points in the vault by approximating the number of polynomials. As explained in Section 2, for the Reed-Solomon fuzzy vault of dimension k over $\mathcal{F}$ with t genuine points and $r - t$ chaff points, for any $\mu > 0$ there is at least $\frac{\mu}{3} q^{k-t} (\frac{r}{t})^t$ possible polynomials, with probability at least $1 - \mu$.

Similarly to [8], we can use this number of possible polynomials as an estimation of the security when the sets are uniformly random (ideal case): In the case of the application of the EFV scheme to RS codes, following the fact that one can extract ℓ^r different possible combinations of r pairs (x_i, y_i) (with distinct abscissas) from a vault for multiple sets $\mathrm{LOCK}(A^1, \dots, A^l) = \{(x_i, S_i), i = 1, \dots, N\}$, this leads to the following security bound.

Lemma 2. *Assume that the sets $A^1, \dots, A^l$ are randomly and uniformly chosen into $\mathcal{F}^t$. Given a vault $\mathrm{LOCK}(A^1, \dots, A^l)$ with chaffing parameters ℓ, r, then for any $\mu > 0$, with probability at least $1 - \mu$, there exist at least $\frac{\mu}{3} \ell^r q^{k-t} (\frac{r}{t})^t$ polynomials p of degree lower than k such that the Reed-Solomon codeword generated by p has t coordinates that are included in the vault.*

We remark an important difference compared with the use of l independent vaults (one for each A^j): instead of multiplying the number of possible polynomials by l, it is increased by a multiplicative factor ℓ^r (with $l \leq \ell$). This underlines the interest of using our extended fuzzy vault scheme instead of l parallel independent fuzzy vaults. Other advantages are explained in next subsection and Section 6.

5.2   General Case

The assumption of uniform distribution is often not practical (in particular for application to biometrics). Moreover, when using folded RS codes, the result does not hold at all. The analysis to estimate the number of polynomials is more complex as one should take in account the information given by the correlations within one column of evaluations. In order to obtain a generic security bound that is valid for folded Reed-Solomon codes with any kind of distribution for the A^j's, we estimate the entropy loss as for a secure sketch scheme:

Lemma 3. *The entropy loss of our Extended Fuzzy Vault scheme based on a* $FRS_{\mathcal{F},\gamma,m,N,k}$ *code is at most*

$$(mt - k)l \times \log_2 q - \log_2 \binom{r}{\lambda} + \log_2 \binom{N}{\lambda}$$

with $t \leq \lambda \leq lt$ *is the number of indexing sets (the* S_i's*) covered by the genuine points.*

Proof. Choosing the l evaluation functions corresponds to $l \times k \times \log_2 q$ bits of entropy (the choice of l polynomials). Let l_i be the size of each indexing set S_i after filling the vault only with genuine points (from the A^j's). Let λ the number of l_i strictly greater than 0. The choice of additional chaff positions requires $\log_2 \binom{N-\lambda}{r-\lambda}$ bits of randomness. The choice of the chaff values requires about $((r - \lambda) \times \ell + \sum_{i=1..N|l_i \neq 0}(\ell - l_i)) \log_2 q^m = m \times (r\ell - lt) \log_2 q$ (we assume here that ℓ is sufficiently small to neglect the difference between $\mathcal{F}^m$ and $\mathcal{F}^m \setminus \{F_d(x_i)\}_{d=1,...,l}$).

Thus, we have approximately $\mathbf{H}_\infty(A^1, \ldots, A^l, R) = \mathbf{H}_\infty(A^1, \ldots, A^l) + \log_2 q \times (lk + m(r\ell - lt)) + \log_2 \binom{N-\lambda}{r-\lambda}$ where R denote the random bits that are used to lock the vault $\text{LOCK}(A^1, \ldots, A^l)$.

Note that R is entirely determined by $A^1, \ldots, A^l$ and $\text{LOCK}(A^1, \ldots, A^l)$, so $\overline{\mathbf{H}}_\infty(A^1, \ldots, A^l, R \mid \text{LOCK}(A^1, \ldots, A^l)) = \overline{\mathbf{H}}_\infty(A^1, \ldots, A^l \mid \text{LOCK}(A^1, \ldots, A^l))$. We know also that the output can be encoded with $\log_2 \binom{N}{r} + mr\ell \log_2 q$.

This leads to $\overline{\mathbf{H}}_\infty(A^1, \ldots, A^l \mid \text{LOCK}(A^1, \ldots, A^l)) \geq \mathbf{H}_\infty(A^1, \ldots, A^l) - (mt - k)l \times \log_2 q + \log_2 \binom{N-\lambda}{r-\lambda} - \log_2 \binom{N}{r}$.

We conclude from $\binom{N-\lambda}{r-\lambda}\binom{N}{\lambda} = \binom{N}{r}\binom{r}{\lambda}$. $\qquad\square$

Note that we have at most $\mathbf{H}_\infty(A^1, \ldots, A^l) = l \log_2 \binom{N}{t}$. Assuming that the sets are independent, this would give us a remaining entropy $\overline{\mathbf{H}}_\infty(A^1, \ldots, A^l \mid \text{LOCK}(A^1, \ldots, A^l))$ greater than

$$\left(l \log_2 \binom{N}{t} - \log_2 \binom{N}{\lambda}\right) + \log_2 \binom{r}{\lambda} - ((mt - k)l \times \log_2 q)$$

This is somehow comparable with the remaining entropy when using l independent fuzzy vaults that can be approximated from Equation (1) as

$$l \left(\log_2 \binom{r}{t} - (t - k) \log_2 q\right)$$

With t and λ small in front of N and r, the first equation can be approximated as $lN^t - N^\lambda + r^\lambda - (mt - k)l \times \log_2 q$ and the second equation is approximated as $lr^t - (t - k)l \times \log_2 q$. In both situation, r needs in general to be large to ensure that the entropy is large. Note that despite this possibility to achieve similar security levels in term of entropy loss between our construction and the use of l parallel independent fuzzy vaults, this leads to different costs. In particular:

- For l independent fuzzy vaults, additional noise is needed for each vault. For one A^j, the number of chaff points is then $r - \#A^j$; that would be large if $\#A^j$ is small. Globally, this requires $rl - lt$ chaff points.
- Whereas in the case of our extended fuzzy vault, the amount of additional noise to be added is mainly determined by ℓ, λ and $r - \lambda$ where λ is equal to the number of indexing sets (the S_i's) that are filled with one of the genuine points (from the sets $A^1, \dots A^l$). More precisely, the number of chaff points is $r\ell - lt$. This means that when l is large and when the genuine points are quite well distributed (which implies that we can choose $\ell << l$), then that number can be very small compared with the trivial construction.

6   Implementation Aspects

Based on our experiments, we discuss in this section some practical aspects of the Extended Fuzzy Vault scheme (based on folded Reed-Solomon codes), especially those that are related to the number of sets or the number of collisions (and thus ℓ).

We also emphasize the difference between the classical fuzzy vault scheme and our scheme to explain several advantages of our scheme compared to the use of several independent and parallel fuzzy vaults.

6.1   Noise

In [8], Juels and Sudan provide an example of their Fuzzy Vault scheme where the number of chaff points, to hide a given set, equals $q - t$. Transposed to our case, this would mean to have $N - t$ chaff points for each set (with N that can be up to q^m due to the folded Reed-Solomon framework). But precisely as we deal with multiple sets encoded in the same vault, we can decrease the amount of chaff points needed: we can see this as a kind of upper bound on the number of chaff points we add for each set. Nevertheless, we could fill the space of possible symbols with noise up to ℓ for each of the N symbols (see one example in Table 1).

Table 1. An example of noise filling for $\ell = 3$

x_1	x_2	x_3	x_4	x_5	x_6	$\dots$	x_{N-1}	x_{N-2}
$y_{1,1}$	$y_{2,1}$	$\times$	$y_{4,1}$	$y_{5,1}$	$y_{6,1}$		$y_{N-1,1}$	$y_{N,1}$
$y_{1,2}$	$y_{2,2}$	$\times$	$y_{4,2}$	$y_{5,2}$	$\times$	$\dots$	$\times$	$y_{N,2}$
$\times$	$y_{3,3}$	$\times$	$\times$	$\times$	$\times$		$\times$	$\times$

The lower amount of random chaff points per encoded set in the EFV scheme is compensated by the multiple sets themselves. The more there are sets, the more it is difficult for an attacker to find a specific set's attributes.

6.2   Complexity

List Size. Parameter s gives an upper bound on the size of the output list of algorithm from Section 3.3: recalling that the cardinality of $\mathcal{F}$ is q, output list is smaller than q^{s-1}. This was already stressed in [4] that this can be very large. In the EFV scheme, this is in particular dependent on the amount $l_i \leq \ell$ of users sharing a same information symbol x_i which can be quite large. As s has to be bigger than ℓ, we could have to deal with potentially very big output lists. Note that in practice, our experiments have resulted into much smaller output lists.

Example 2. *Suppose the amount of referenced movies is $N = 10^4$, Alice has a list $(x_1, \ldots, x_{22})$ of her $t = 22$ favorites. Among the other users, we can easily imagine that two people love one common movie x_i with Alice ($l_i = 3$). Let us fix $\ell = 3$, $s = 4$ and $m = 5$ to tolerate up to $e = 3$ errors and $q > mN$. When Bob tries to learn who gets the same tastes as him, giving another set of 22 titles including the above movie x_i, the EFV scheme could be faced with a large output list (q^3).*

Although we did not encounter this situation in our experiments, the theoretical large size of the list could be a limitation for increasing the number of sets in the vault.

Memory Space and Execution Time. Another point is that s and ℓ give a lower bound on m and determine the parameter D (cf. Equation (8)). The code size is directly impacted by these parameters, which leads to the memory space needed and the execution time. In particular, the size of the first linear system to solve – that is a critical element in the algorithm implementation – grows fast.

Table 2. Some execution timings for EFV scheme with 100 users on $\mathcal{F} = \mathbb{F}_{2053}$

t	m	s	ℓ	k	System size	Execution time
22	5	4	3	14	132*133	125 ms
50	10	8	6	15	900*905	14.5 sec
73	14	11	8	16	2336*2343	6 min 44 sec

Table 2 gives an overview of the size of the systems one have to solve while decoding. Implementation has been done using PARI/GP on a common desktop computer. Although the size is growing quickly, the execution time remains quite reasonable for these parameters.

Vault Size. A vault obtained from locking multiple sets can be represented with $\log_2 \binom{N}{r} + mr\ell \log_2 q$ bits. As explained in Section 5, r needs in general to be large for security. This has an impact on the size of the vault representation.

It is important to remark that it is also the case for the original FV scheme (for which a vault can be represented with $\log_2 \binom{N}{r} + r \log_2 N$ bits).

Consequently, we underline another advantage of using our EFV scheme instead of l independent FV vaults (one for each A^j): If the number of collisions between the l sets $A^1, \dots, A^l$ is small, then ℓ can be chosen small. The overall size of our EFV vault will be then about $\log_2 \binom{N}{r} + mr\ell(\log_2 N + \log_2 m)$ bits while the l vaults will need $l \times (\log_2 \binom{N}{r} + r \log_2 N)$ bits. For instance, if $N = r$, as soon $m\ell$ is much smaller than l, then the EFV vault size will become much smaller. In fact, this is due to the randomness that needs to be renewed for l independent vaults whereas we use the same for all sets in our EFV scheme.

7   Conclusion

In this paper, we extend the Fuzzy Vault scheme to handle multiple users at the same time, leading to several benefits compared to the trivial solution of using several single fuzzy vaults in parallel. Our extension follows the quite recent improvements of the decoding properties of Reed Solomon codes as we are using list recovery methods for which effective algorithms have been discovered last year. From our first experiments, we think that, today, direct applications of our proposal can be attempted. One of the next step is to apply our Extended Fuzzy Vault scheme to biometric identification (in particular, for fingerprint modality). As for application of fuzzy vault, due to the level of errors to handle, a specific and concrete fine tuning will be required to reach a good trade-off between biometric error rates and the level of security. Moreover, the current decoding techniques would also need further improvements, specifically for decoding complexity and list size, to be practically able to embed a large number of sets in the same vault.

Acknowledgments. The authors thank Daniel Augot for his valuable comments on list decoding algorithms and the reviewers for their comments.

References

1. Chae, S.H., Lim, S.J., Bae, S.H., Chung, Y., Pan, S.B.: Parallel processing of the fuzzy fingerprint vault based on geometric hashing. TIIS 4(6), 1294–1310 (2010)
2. Chung, Y., Moon, D., Lee, S., Jung, S., Kim, T., Ahn, D.: Automatic Alignment of Fingerprint Features for Fuzzy Fingerprint Vault. In: Feng, D., Lin, D., Yung, M. (eds.) CISC 2005. LNCS, vol. 3822, pp. 358–369. Springer, Heidelberg (2005)
3. Dodis, Y., Reyzin, L., Smith, A.: Fuzzy Extractors: How to Generate Strong Keys from Biometrics and Other Noisy Data. In: Cachin, C., Camenisch, J.L. (eds.) EUROCRYPT 2004. LNCS, vol. 3027, pp. 523–540. Springer, Heidelberg (2004)
4. Guruswami, V.: Linear-algebraic list decoding of folded Reed Solomon codes. In: IEEE Conference on Computational Complexity, pp. 77–85. IEEE Computer Society (2011)
5. Guruswami, V., Rudra, A.: Explicit codes achieving list decoding capacity: Error-correction with optimal redundancy. IEEE Transactions on Information Theory 54(1), 135–150 (2008)
6. Guruswami, V., Sudan, M.: Improved decoding of Reed Solomon and algebraic-geometric codes. In: FOCS, pp. 28–39. IEEE Computer Society (1998)

7. Juels, A., Sudan, M.: A fuzzy vault scheme. In: Proceedings of IEEE International Symposium on Information Theory, ISIT. LNCS, p. 408 (2002)
8. Juels, A., Sudan, M.: A fuzzy vault scheme. Des. Codes Cryptography 38(2), 237–257 (2006)
9. Lee, S., Moon, D., Jung, S., Chung, Y.: Protecting Secret Keys with Fuzzy Fingerprint Vault Based on a 3D Geometric Hash Table. In: Beliczynski, B., Dzielinski, A., Iwanowski, M., Ribeiro, B. (eds.) ICANNGA 2007, Part II. LNCS, vol. 4432, pp. 432–439. Springer, Heidelberg (2007)
10. Li, J., Yang, X., Tian, J., Shi, P., Li, P.: Topological structure-based alignment for fingerprint fuzzy vault. In: 19th International Conference on Pattern Recognition (ICPR 2008), Tampa, Florida, USA, December 8-11, pp. 1–4 (2008)
11. Li, P., Yang, X., Cao, K., Shi, P., Tian, J.: Security-Enhanced Fuzzy Fingerprint Vault Based on Minutiae's Local Ridge Information. In: Tistarelli, M., Nixon, M.S. (eds.) ICB 2009. LNCS, vol. 5558, pp. 930–939. Springer, Heidelberg (2009)
12. Li, P., Yang, X., Cao, K., Tao, X., Wang, R., Tian, J.: An alignment-free fingerprint cryptosystem based on fuzzy vault scheme. J. Network and Computer Applications 33(3), 207–220 (2010)
13. Lim, S.J., Chae, S.-H., Pan, S.B.: VLSI Architecture of the Fuzzy Fingerprint Vault System. In: Schwenker, F., El Gayar, N. (eds.) ANNPR 2010. LNCS, vol. 5998, pp. 252–258. Springer, Heidelberg (2010)
14. MacWilliams, F.J., Sloane, N.J.A.: The theory of error correcting codes. North-Holland Pub. Co. (1977)
15. Merkle, J., Niesing, M., Schwaiger, M., Ihmor, H., Korte, U.: Performance of the fuzzy vault for multiple fingerprints. In: Brömme, A., Busch, C. (eds.) BIOSIG. LNI, vol. 164, pp. 57–72. GI (2010)
16. Moon, D., Lee, S., Jung, S., Chung, Y., Park, M., Yi, O.: Fingerprint Template Protection Using Fuzzy Vault. In: Gervasi, O., Gavrilova, M.L. (eds.) ICCSA 2007, Part III. LNCS, vol. 4707, pp. 1141–1151. Springer, Heidelberg (2007)
17. Nagar, A., Nandakumar, K., Jain, A.K.: Securing fingerprint template: Fuzzy vault with minutiae descriptors. In: 19th International Conference on Pattern Recognition (ICPR 2008), Tampa, Florida, USA, December 8-11, pp. 1–4 (2008)
18. Nandakumar, K., Jain, A.K., Pankanti, S.: Fingerprint-based fuzzy vault: Implementation and performance. IEEE Transactions on Information Forensics and Security 2(4), 744–757 (2007)
19. Nandakumar, K., Nagar, A., Jain, A.K.: Hardening Fingerprint Fuzzy Vault Using Password. In: Lee, S.-W., Li, S.Z. (eds.) ICB 2007. LNCS, vol. 4642, pp. 927–937. Springer, Heidelberg (2007)
20. Rudra, A.: List Decoding and Property Testing of Error Correcting Codes. Ph.D. thesis, University of Washington (2007)
21. Smith, A.D.: Maintaining secrecy when information leakage is unavoidable. Ph.D. thesis, Cambridge, MA, USA (2004), aAI0807529
22. Sudan, M.: Decoding of Reed Solomon codes beyond the error-correction bound. J. Complexity 13(1), 180–193 (1997)
23. Uludag, U., Pankanti, S., Jain, A.K.: Fuzzy Vault for Fingerprints. In: Kanade, T., Jain, A., Ratha, N.K. (eds.) AVBPA 2005. LNCS, vol. 3546, pp. 310–319. Springer, Heidelberg (2005)

Bounds and Constructions for 1-Round $(0, \delta)$-Secure Message Transmission against Generalized Adversary

Reihaneh Safavi-Naini and Mohammed Ashraful Alam Tuhin

Department of Computer Science, University of Calgary
{rei,maatuhin}@ucalgary.ca

Abstract. In the Secure Message Transmission (SMT) problem, a sender S is connected to a receiver R through n node-disjoint paths in the network, a subset of which are controlled by an adversary with *unlimited computational power*. S wants to send a message m to R in a *private* and *reliable* way. Constructing secure and efficient SMT protocols against a threshold adversary who can corrupt at most t out of n wires, has been extensively researched. However less is known about SMT problem for a generalized adversary who can corrupt one out of a set of possible subsets.

In this paper we focus on 1-round $(0, \delta)$-SMT protocols where privacy is perfect and the chance of protocol failure (receiver outputting **NULL**) is bounded by δ. These protocols are especially attractive because of their possible practical applications.

We first show an equivalence between secret sharing with cheating and canonical 1-round $(0, \delta)$-SMT against a generalized adversary. This generalizes a similar result known for threshold adversaries. We use this equivalence to obtain a lower bound on the communication complexity of canonical 1-round $(0, \delta)$-SMT against a generalized adversary. We also derive a lower bound on the communication complexity of a general 1-round $(0, 0)$-SMT against a generalized adversary.

We finally give a construction using a linear secret sharing scheme and a special type of hash function. The protocol has almost optimal communication complexity and achieves this efficiency for a single message (does not require block of message to be sent).

1 Introduction

The **S**ecure **M**essage **T**ransmission (**SMT**) problem was introduced by Dolev, Dwork, Waarts and Yung [6] to address the problem of secure communication between two nodes in an incomplete network. In the SMT problem, the sender S and the receiver R do not share a key but are connected by n 'wires', a subset of which are controlled by an adversary A with unlimited computational power. Wires are abstractions of node-disjoint paths between S and R. The sender S wants to send a message m to a receiver R in a 'private' and 'reliable' way. 'Private' means that the adversary should not learn any information about

A. Mitrokotsa and S. Vaudenay (Eds.): AFRICACRYPT 2012, LNCS 7374, pp. 82–98, 2012.

m and 'reliable' means that $\mathcal{R}$ will receive the same message m that $\mathcal{S}$ has sent. Security of an SMT protocol means achieving both privacy and reliability. A *perfectly secure message transmission (PSMT)* guarantees that $\mathcal{R}$ always receives the sent message and the adversary never learns anything about the message.

One of the main motivations of studying SMT has been to reduce connectivity requirements in secure multi-party protocols in unconditional setting [1,2,17]. These protocols assume reliable and secure channels between every two nodes. This assumption cannot be satisfied in many real life scenarios and so, SMT is used to simulate a secure channel between nodes using redundant paths in the network. Algorithms and techniques developed in the study of SMT, and in particular one round protocols, have found other applications including in key distribution and in particular strengthening keys shared between nodes in sensor networks [19,20].

Franklin and Wright relaxed the original definition of PSMT and proposed (ε, δ)-SMT $(0 \leq \varepsilon, \delta \leq 1)$ [9] where privacy and reliability losses are bounded by ϵ and δ respectively. Relaxing security and reliability reduces connectivity requirement and results in more efficient protocols.

Motivation of This Work

Secure message transmission problem against a threshold adversary has been extensively researched in the literature. [6,9,11]. Generalized adversaries provide a flexible way of modelling real life adversaries and so it is important to develop the SMT theory in the case of generalized adversaries. This is the main motivation of this work.

Our Results. We present a number of results.

- We first show an equivalence between secret sharing with cheating and a 1-round $(0, \delta)$-SMT against generalized adversary, assuming SMT and the adevrsary structure satisfy certain conditions. In particular, the decoding function of SMT must be of a special form which is called *canonical*. This result generalizes a similar result for threshold adversaries due to Kurosawa and Suzuki [11]. Using this equivalence we will derive a lower bound on the communication complexity of a canonical 1-round $(0, \delta)$-SMT against a generalized adversary.
- We derive a lower bound on the communication complexity of a 1-round $(0, 0)$-SMT against a generalized adversary. The bound is the first of this kind for generalized adversary case. A similar bound on the communication complexity was known for the case of threshold adversary.
- We finally give the construction of a 1-round $(0, \delta)$-SMT protocol with security against a generalized adversary. The protocol is simpler than the only other known protocol with the same property [5], and can be used for transmission of a single message, while the protocol of [5] requires a block of messages to be sent. Both protocols have the same efficiency (polynomial in the size of the adversary structure).

Organization of the paper

We recall the basic definitions of secure message transmission, secret sharing, secret sharing with cheating, and linear secret sharing in Section 2. In Section 3 we show the equivalence between 1-round $(0, \delta)$-SMT and secret sharing with cheating against a generalized adversary under some assumptions. In Section 4 we derive the lower bound on the communication complexity of 1-round $(0, \delta)$-SMT from the shown equivalence. We also show the lower bound on the communication complexity of 1-round $(0, 0)$-SMT in Section 4. Finally in Section 5, we design a 1-round $(0, \delta)$-SMT protocol using a secret sharing with cheating scheme.

2   Preliminaries

Communication Model. We consider a *synchronous, incomplete* network. The sender $\mathcal{S}$ and the receiver $\mathcal{R}$ are connected by n node-disjoint paths, also known as wires or channels. Both $\mathcal{S}$ and $\mathcal{R}$ are honest. The goal is for $\mathcal{S}$ to send a message m, drawn from the message space $\mathcal{M}$, to $\mathcal{R}$ such that $\mathcal{R}$ receives it correctly and privately.

The network is undirected and wires are two-way. SMT protocols proceeds in one or more rounds. In a round, a message is sent by either $\mathcal{S}$ or $\mathcal{R}$ to the other party over the wires. Messages are received by the recipient of the round before the next round starts. We consider only 1-round in this work, where the sender sends the message to the receiver.

Adversary Model. We consider an adversary $\mathcal{A}$ having *unlimited* computational power who can corrupt a subset of nodes in the network. Honest nodes forward the received messages to the next nodes on the path. A path (wire) that includes a corrupted node is controlled by the adversary. Corrupted nodes can fully control the corrupted wires and arbitrarily eavesdrop, modify or block messages sent over them. $\mathcal{A}$ is *adaptive* and can corrupt wires any time during the protocol execution and after observing communications over the wires that she has corrupted so far. $\mathcal{A}$ is also *rushing*, i.e., in each round it sees the messages sent by $\mathcal{S}$ and $\mathcal{R}$ over the corrupted wires before deciding on the messages to be sent over those wires in that round. $\mathcal{S}$ and $\mathcal{R}$ *do not know which wires are corrupted.*

Notation. $\mathcal{M}$ be the message space from which messages are chosen according to a probability distribution $\Pr(m)$. Let $m_{\mathcal{S}}$ be the message randomly selected by $\mathcal{S}$. We assume $\mathcal{M}$ and $\Pr(m)$ are known in advance to all parties including the adversary. Let $R_{\mathcal{A}}$ be the random coins used by $\mathcal{A}$ to choose one set of wires in the adversary structure Γ to corrupt.

In an execution of an SMT protocol Π, $\mathcal{S}$ draws $M_{\mathcal{S}}$ from $\mathcal{M}$ using the distribution $\Pr(m)$, and aims to send it to $\mathcal{R}$ privately and reliably. We assume that by the end of the protocol, $\mathcal{R}$ outputs a message $M_{\mathcal{R}} \in \mathcal{M}$ or **NULL** and so, an execution is completely determined by the random coins selected by all parties and the messages selected by the sender.

2.1 Secure Message Transmission

Let the sender $\mathcal{S}$ and the receiver $\mathcal{R}$ are connected by a set of n wires $\mathcal{W} = \{w_1, w_2, ..., w_n\}$. $\mathcal{S}$ wants to send a message m to a receiver in private and reliable way. A computationally unbounded byzantine adversary $\mathcal{A}$ can control a subset of wires. The set of possible subsets of wires that the adversary can control forms the adversary structure Γ defined as,

$$\Gamma = \{B \subset \mathcal{W} : \mathcal{A} \text{ can corrupt } B\}.$$

We assume the adversary structure is monotone. This means that, if $C \in \Gamma$ and $C' \subset C \subset \mathcal{W}$, then $C' \in \Gamma$. A threshold adversary is a special case of an adversary structure where Γ includes all subsets of $\mathcal{W}$ with size at most t.

The receiver, on the other hand, can reconstruct the secret message using the values sent on specific subsets of wires, defined by the *access structure*, Σ defined as follows:

$$\Sigma = \{C \subset \mathcal{W} : \text{ values sent on wires in } C \text{ uniquely determine the message}\}.$$

We assume Σ is monotone, that is, if $B \in \Sigma$ and $B \subset B' \subset \mathcal{W}$, then $B' \in \Sigma$. We assume any subset in $2^{\mathcal{W}}$ is either an adversary set or an access set. That is,

$$\Gamma = 2^{\mathcal{W}} \setminus \Sigma.$$

Definition 1. *(Q^k condition [10]) An adversary structure Γ satisfies Q^k condition with respect to the wire set $\mathcal{W}$ if there are no k sets in Γ, which cover the full $\mathcal{W}$. Mathematically,*

$$\Gamma \text{ satisfies } Q^k \Leftrightarrow \forall B_1, ..., B_k \in \Gamma : B_1 \cup ... \cup B_k \neq \mathcal{W}.$$

An SMT protocol tolerating a generalized adversary consists of a pair of algorithms (**Enc, Dec**) defined as follows.

- **Enc** is a probabilistic encoding algorithm which takes a secret $m \in \mathcal{M}$ as input and outputs an encoding $(x_1, ..., x_n)$, of the message. x_i is transmitted through the ith wire. **Enc** is called by the sender $\mathcal{S}$.
- **Dec** is a deterministic decoding algorithm which takes $(x'_1, ..., x'_n)$, a corrupted version of the encoded message, and outputs $m' \in \mathcal{M}$ or **NULL** (denoting failure). **Dec** is called by the receiver $\mathcal{R}$.

$(x_1, ..., x_n)$ is corrupted to $(x'_1, ..., x'_n)$ by the adversary who controls wires corresponding to an adversary set. It is required that **Dec**(**Enc**(m))=m, for any $m \in \mathcal{M}$. Let X_i denote the random variable representing value x_i, and $\mathcal{X}_i$ denote the set of possible values $x_i, 1 \leq i \leq n$.

Definition 2. *An SMT protocol is called an $(0, \delta)$-Secure Message Transmission ($(0, \delta)$-SMT) protocol if the following conditions are satisfied:*

- **Privacy:** $\mathcal{A}$ *learns no information about the secret* m. *More precisely, if* $\{w_{i_1}, ..., w_{i_k}\} \in \Gamma$ *then for any* $m \in \mathcal{M}$,

$$\Pr(\mathcal{M} = m | X_{i_1} = x_{i_1}, ..., X_{i_k} = x_{i_k}) = \Pr(\mathcal{M} = m).$$

- **General Reliability:** *The receiver* $\mathcal{R}$ *always outputs* $\hat{m} = m$ *or* **NULL**. He never outputs an incorrect secret.
- **Trivial Reliability:** If the adversary blocks the transmissions on the wires he corrupts (*i.e.*, the received transmissions on those wires are all null strings) then the receiver $\mathcal{R}$ outputs $\hat{m} = m$.
- **Failure:** $\mathcal{R}$ *receives the message* m *with probability* $\geq 1 - \delta$. *That is, if* $\{w_{i_1}, ..., w_{i_k}\} \in \Sigma$ *then,*

$$\Pr(\mathcal{R} \text{ outputs } \textbf{NULL}) \leq \delta.$$

When $\delta = 0$, we call it a **Perfectly Secure Message Transmission** (**PSMT**, for short) or $(0, 0)$-SMT.

Remark: An alternative definition of general reliability used in the literature [9] allows the receiver to reconstruct a message $m' \neq m$. The trivial reliability requirement was first assumed in [11]. The requirement although natural, is not required in general.

It has been shown that 1-round $(0, 0)$-SMT and 1-round $(0, \delta)$-SMT is possible if and only if the adversary structure Γ satisfies the Q^3 [7] and Q^2 [15] conditions, respectively.

The number of **rounds** of a protocol is the number of interactions between $\mathcal{S}$ and $\mathcal{R}$. We consider synchronous network where time is divided into clock ticks and in each clock tick the sender or the receiver sends a message and the message is received by the other party before the next clock tick.

Communication complexity is the total number of bits transmitted (b) between $\mathcal{S}$ and $\mathcal{R}$ for communicating the message(s). Communication efficiency is often measured in terms of *transmission rate*, which is the ratio of the communication complexity to the length of the message $M_{\mathcal{S}}$. That is,

$$Transmission \ Rate = \frac{\text{total number of field elements transmitted}(b)}{\text{size of the secrets}(|M_{\mathcal{S}}|)}.$$

The message $M_{\mathcal{S}}$ is either one element or a sequence of elements from an alphabet.

Computation complexity is the amount of computation performed by $\mathcal{S}$ and $\mathcal{R}$ throughout the protocol. A protocol which needs *exponential* (in the size of the adversary structure) computation is called *inefficient*. Efficient protocols need *polynomial* (in the size of the adversary structure) computation. We note here that if the size of the adversary structure is exponential (in n), then the protocol will have inefficient computation.

Related Work. Chowdury, Kurosawa, and Patra gave an efficient 1-round $(0, \delta)$-SMT protocol for against a generalized adversary satisfying the Q^2 condition [5].

2.2 Secret Sharing

A secret sharing scheme is a cryptographic primitive that distributes a secret s among n participants such that only qualified subsets of participants can reconstruct the secret, while non-qualified subsets get no information about the secret. In a secret sharing scheme, there are n participants $P = \{P_1, ..., P_n\}$ and a trusted dealer D. The set of participants who are qualified to reconstruct the secret is specified by an access structure $\Sigma \subseteq 2^P$. We consider monotone access structures in which any subset that contains a qualified subset is also a qualified set. In this case the access structure Σ is uniquely determined by the family of minimal qualified subsets, Σ_0, known as the basis of Σ. The set of participants who are not allowed to learn any information about the secret is specified by the adversary structure Γ, which is defined as $\Gamma = 2^P \setminus \Sigma$. For monotone access structures, the adversary structure is also monotone. In a monotone adversary structure if $B \in \Gamma$ and $B' \subset B \subset P$, then $B' \in \Gamma$.

A secret sharing scheme with a monotone access structure Σ must satisfy the following conditions:

- **SS1:** A set of participants $P_{i_1}, ..., P_{i_k}$ can reconstruct the secret if and only if $\{P_{i_1}, ..., P_{i_k}\} \in \Sigma$.
- **SS2:** Any set of participants $P \notin \Sigma$ must have no information about the secret.

A secret sharing model consists of two algorithms: **ShareGen** and **Reconst**. The share generation algorithm **ShareGen** takes a secret $s \in S$ as input and outputs a list $(v_1, v_2, ..., v_n)$. Each v_i is called a share and is given to participant P_i. The **ShareGen** algorithm is invoked by the dealer D. The secret reconstruction algorithm **Reconst** takes a list of shares and outputs a secret $s \in S$.

Let V_i denotes the random variable that represents the share values v_i and denote, $\mathcal{V}_i = \{v_i | \Pr[V_i = v_i] > 0\}$, the set of possible shares held by participant P_i.

The efficiency of a secret sharing scheme is measured by the *information rate* which is the ratio of the size of the secret to the size of the largest share given to any participant. The maximum possible rate is 1 and such schemes are called *ideal*.

2.3 Linear Secret Sharing Scheme

A secret sharing scheme for a monotone access structure Σ can be realized by a linear secret sharing scheme (LSSS). Let M be a $d \times e$ matrix over a finite field S and $\psi : \{1, ..., d\} \rightarrow \{1, ..., n\}$ be a labelling function, where $d \geq e$ and $d \geq n$. The share generation algorithm **ShareGen** is as follows.

ShareGen

1. To share a secret $s \in S$, the dealer D first chooses a random vector $\mathbf{r} \in S^{e-1}$ and computes a vector,

$$\mathbf{v} = (v_1, ..., v_d)^T = M \times \begin{pmatrix} s \\ \mathbf{r} \end{pmatrix}.$$

2. Let LSSS$(s, \mathbf{r}) = (share_1, ..., share_n)$, here $share_i = \{v_j : \psi(j) = i\}$. P_i will receive $share_i$ as its share, $i = 1, ..., n$.

The reconstruction algorithm **Reconst** is as follows:

A set of participants $A \in \Sigma$ can reconstruct the secret s if and only if $(1, 0, ..., 0)$ is in the linear span of,

$$M_A = \{m_j : \psi(j) \in A\},$$

here m_j is the jth row of M.

3   Secret Sharing Scheme with Cheaters

Tompa and Woll first considered the problem of secret sharing with cheaters [18] who submit wrong shares with the aim of learning the secret while preventing an honest member of a qualified set to do so. That is, given a qualified set $\{P_{i_1}, ..., P_{i_{k+1}}\} \in \Gamma$, the adversary can corrupt $P_{i_1}, ..., P_{i_k}$ (this is a non-qualified set) who will submit incorrect shares to cheat the $(k + 1)^{st}$ participant. The cheaters (i.e., the adversary) succeed if the shares presented by $P_{i_1}, ..., P_{i_{k+1}}$ construct a secret $s' \neq s$. Secret sharing schemes that detect cheating has been studied by a number of authors using slightly different models. In [3], authors assumed that the cheaters know the secret when cheating, while some other [13] assumed the cheaters do not know the secret. Also in some cases it is assumed that the secret is uniformly distributed, while in other arbitrary distribution is assumed [12]. In nearly all cases the access structure is assumed threshold. Secret sharing schemes with cheating for a special type of access structure has been considered in [16,14,4]. To the best of our knowledge, only [12] considers non-threshold adversary for any monotone access structure.

In a secret sharing scheme with cheaters, the reconstruction algorithm is modified to as follows. The secret reconstruction algorithm Reconst takes a list of shares corresponding to an access set and outputs either a secret $s \in S$, or a special symbol $\perp, \perp \notin S$. Here $\perp$ is a special symbol indicating the event that a cheating has been detected. The success probability of the adversary in cheating is defined as $\Pr[s' \in S \wedge s' \neq s]$.

4   Relations between Secret Sharing with Cheating and 1-Round $(0, \delta)$-SMT against a Generalized Adversary

The relationship between 1-round $(0, \delta)$-SMT with a threshold adversary structure, and threshold secret sharing scheme with cheating probability λ, has been considered in [11] where authors showed equivalence of the two under certain restrictions on the two. In this paper we revisit the same problem, assuming general adversary structure and derive restrictions under which the two are equivalent.

4.1 From Secret Sharing to Secure Message Transmission Tolerating a Generalized Adversary

Theorem 1. *If there exists a secure secret sharing scheme with cheating probability $\leq \lambda$ for the secret space S against a generalized adversary, then there exists a 1-round $(0, \delta)$-SMT protocol against the same adversary satisfying the Q^2 condition for the message space $\mathcal{M} = S$ such that $\delta = \lambda(|\Sigma| - 1)$. Further it holds that $\mathcal{V}_i = \mathcal{X}_i$, for $1 \leq i \leq n$.*

Proof

We show a construction of SMT from secret sharing with cheating detection such that δ for the SMT is bounded by a function of λ in the secret sharing with cheating detection.

For a *maximal* adversary set $B = \{P_{i_1}, ..., P_{i_k}\} \in \Gamma$, the chance of cheating a target participant $P_{i_{k+1}}$ such that $C = \{P_{i_1}, ..., P_{i_k}, P_{i_{k+1}}\} \in \Sigma$ is at most λ, where cheating means that the reconstruction algorithm of secret sharing outputs a different secret s', than the original secret s.

Enc and **Dec** for SMT are generated from **ShareGen** and **Reconst** of secure secret sharing with cheating as follows. **Enc** is just the same as **ShareGen**. That is, on input of the secret message $m \in \mathcal{M}$, **Enc** runs **ShareGen** to generate $(x_1, ..., x_n) = (v_1, ..., v_n)$. Then $\mathcal{S}$ sends the shares over the wires, one share per wire.

Dec works as follows. Note that an adversary set can intersect with a number of access sets and so access sets will include corrupted members (cheaters). **Dec** invokes **Reconst** for every access set $a \in \Sigma$. The result will be a set $\{m, m_1, ..., m_i, \perp\}$ where $m_i \neq m$ corresponds to the output of **Reconst** when an access set includes cheaters and cheater detection algorithm has failed to detect the cheating. **Dec** algorithm outputs m if the output set is $\{m, \perp\}$, and **NULL** indicating failure, otherwise.

We have to show that all the conditions of a SMT are satisfied. The privacy of SMT follows from the corresponding property **SS2** of secret sharing with cheating. This is true as the participants corresponding to an adversary set in secret sharing with cheating learn no information about the secret.

Trivial reliability follows from the Q^2 property of the adversary structure. If the adversary blocks the transmission on the wires corresponding to an adversary set $\gamma \in \Gamma$, the remaining wires in $\sigma = \mathcal{W} \setminus \Gamma$, constitutes an access set with no cheating participant. The **Dec** algorithm uses **Reconst** on all the access sets. **Reconst** will output the correct m for σ. For all other access sets that are disjoint with γ, the same m will be output. For the access sets that have nonempty intersection with γ, there will not be sufficient shares and so **Reconst** will output $\perp$. So the set of messages that are output from **Reconst** will include only m and $\perp$ and so **Dec** will output m.

The message recovery algorithm **Dec** of SMT will output **NULL**, or the message m and will never output an incorrect message. This is because if the adversary corrupts an adversary set γ, its complement will be an access set and so **Reconst**, when applied to this access set, will result in m. According to the description of **Dec**, if the set of messages that are obtained from applying **Reconst** to all access sets include only this message (other than $\perp$) then this message will be output; otherwise **Dec** outputs **NULL**. Suppose the adversary corrupts an adversary set γ. All the access sets that have non-empty intersection with this set will include cheaters and so the **Reconst** algorithm applied to such sets can potentially output a message $m' \neq m$. The adversary will maximize his success chance in causing **Dec** to fail, by choosing an adversary set that intersects with the most number of access sets. Note that since the complement of an adversary set is an access set, the maximum number of access sets that have nonempty intersection with γ is $|\Sigma| - 1$. For each such access sets the cheaters succeed in cheating with probability at most λ and so with probability at least $1 - \lambda$ the cheating will be detected. **Dec** outputs the correct m if all cheatings are detected. This will happen with probability at least $(1 - \lambda)^{|\Sigma| - 1} = 1 - (|\Sigma| - 1)\lambda$. That is $1 - \delta \geq 1 - (|\Sigma| - 1)\lambda$ or $\delta \leq (|\Sigma| - 1)\lambda$. $\square$

4.2   From Secure Message Transmission to Secret Sharing Tolerating a Generalized Adversary

First consider the followings which hold if Q^2 holds.

1. The complement of an adversary set γ is an access set.
   This is true because a subset in 2^P is either an access set or an adversary set. Let $\bar{\gamma} = \mathcal{W} \setminus \gamma$. Then if $\bar{\gamma}$ is not an access set, it will be an adversary set which cannot be the case because of Q^2.
2. Complement of an access set σ is not necessarily an adversary set. It may be another access set.

In the following we assume that:

R1. The adversary structure satisfies Q^2.
R2. Complement of a minimal access set is a maximal adversary set.

Note that these requirements imply the following.
R3 The complement of a maximal adversary set is a minimal access set.
    This is true because of the following. Suppose γ is a maximal adversary set. Then, because of Q^2 its complement is not an adversary set and so is an access set σ. Note that σ must be minimal. If not, then $\sigma' \subset \sigma$ is a minimal access set and by the above assumption $(R2)$ $\gamma' = \mathcal{W} \setminus \sigma'$ is a maximal adversary set. We have $\gamma \subset \gamma'$ which contradicts with γ being maximal. With the above assumptions, we denote the access structures as $\hat{Q}^2$.
    For a maximal adversary set γ, we use σ to represent the set $\bar{\gamma} = \mathcal{W} \setminus \gamma$ as defined above, i.e., $\bar{\gamma} = \sigma \in \Sigma$. Note that σ is a minimal access set. For $\sigma = \{i_1, \cdots i_k\}$, define the function $F_\sigma(x'_{i_1}, ..., x'_{i_k})$ as follows:

$$F_\sigma(x'_{i_1}, ..., x'_{i_k}) = m_\sigma \text{ or } \perp, \quad (w_{i_1}, ..., w_{i_k}) \in \Sigma,$$

were, m_σ is defined as follows:

$m_\sigma =$ the unique message that because of trivial reliability, is the output of the decoding algorithm when wires in γ are blocked,

$=$ for other (not blocking) corruptions, either (i) a message m' if this is the unique message that has $x'_{i_1}, ..., x'_{i_k}$ on these wires, or

(ii) $\perp$ if more than one message has $x'_{i_1}, ..., x'_{i_k}$ on these wires.

Note that the above function *is defined for all minimal access sets* because from the assumption on the adversary set, any minimal access set is the complement of a maximal adversary set.

We say that a 1-round $(0, \delta)$-SMT protocol is *canonical* if, for all corrupted transcripts $(x'_1, x'_2, \cdots x'_n)$ of a message m (from the original transcript $(x_1, x_2, \cdots, x_n)$ corrupted by an adversary set) we have:

$$\mathbf{Dec}(x'_1, ..., x'_n) = m, \text{ if } F_\sigma(x'_{i_1}, ..., x'_{i_k}) = m, \text{ or } \perp \text{ for all minimal access sets } \sigma \in \Sigma,$$
$$= \mathbf{NULL}, otherwise, \tag{1}$$

where $m \in \mathcal{M}$.

That is decoding function of a canonical SMT can be written in terms of $F_\sigma()$ for all minimal access sets $\sigma \in \Sigma$.

Theorem 2. *If there exists a canonical 1-round $(0, \delta)$-SMT protocol for the message space $\mathcal{M}$, then there exits a secure secret sharing scheme with cheating probability $\leq \lambda$ where $\lambda \leq \delta$, for the secret space $S = \mathcal{M}$. Further it holds that $\mathcal{X}_i = \mathcal{V}_i$, for $1 \leq i \leq n$.*

Proof

The share generation algorithm **ShareGen** works by invoking **Enc** of SMT as follows. On input a secret $s \in S$, **ShareGen** calls **Enc**(s) and generates $(v_1, ..., v_n) = (x_1, ..., x_n)$. The Dealer D gives the share x_i to the participant $P_i, 1 \leq i \leq n$.

We have to show that the conditions **SS1** and **SS2** of secret sharing with cheating are satisfied. **SS1** requires that for any access set there is a unique message that can be constructed from the set of participants' shares. An access set contains a minimal access set which because of trivial reliability, uniquely determines the secret. **SS2** follows from the privacy condition of SMT. This is true because in SMT the shares corresponding to an adversary set, reveal no information about the secret.

To show that success probability of cheaters in the secret sharing scheme is less than δ, we assume this is not true. That is, there is a *maximal* adversary set $\gamma = \{w_{i_1}, \cdots, w_{i_k}\}$, such that cheaters using the shares on $\{w_{i_1}, \cdots, w_{i_k}\}$ can cheat $P_{i_{k+1}}$ with probability higher than δ.

Now suppose in the SMT the adversary corrupts wires $\{w_{i_1}, \cdots, w_{i_k}\}$. The SMT decoding algorithm is canonical and so uses $F_\sigma()$ for all minimal access sets as defined in decoding function definition in (1). Note that the set

$\{w_{i_1}, \cdots, w_{i_k}, w_{i_{k+1}}\}$ is a minimal access set (this is true because $\{w_{i_1}, \cdots, w_{i_k}\}$ is a maximal adversary set and so adding $w_{i_{k+1}}$ will make it an access set. This access set is minimal also- because if it is not, then a subset of it is a minimal access set which implies that γ is not maximal) and $F_\sigma()$ will output $m' \neq m$ with probability higher than δ. On the other hand, secret reconstruction algorithm applied to the complement of γ which is a minimal access set results in a message m and so $Dec(x'_1, \cdots, x'_n)$ will output $\perp$ with probability higher than δ.   □

5   Lower Bound on Communication Complexity of 1-Round (0, 0)-SMT and (0, δ)-SMT against Generalized Adversaries

Using the equivalence between canonical (0, δ)-SMT and secret sharing with cheating against a generalized adversary, and the known bounds on share size of the latter, we can derive lower bound on the communication complexity of canonical (0, δ)-SMT against a generalized adversary (using our definition of reliability).

Proposition 1. *The lower bound on the communication complexity of a canonical 1-round (0, δ)-SMT tolerating a generalized adversary with adversary structure Γ and satisfying the condition Q^2 is $n \log(\frac{|\mathcal{M}|-1}{\delta} + 1)$, where δ is the cheating probability and $\mathcal{M}$ is the message space.*

Proof: A lower bound on the share size of secret sharing scheme with cheating probability δ is $\log(\frac{|\mathcal{M}|-1}{\delta} + 1)$, derived in [13]. The result follows by noting that the secret sharing scheme can be used to construct a canonical (0, δ)-SMT (See proof of Theorem 1).

In the following we will derive a lower bound on the communication complexity of 1-round (0, 0)-SMT tolerating a generalized adversary,

We will first state the following lemma.

Lemma 1. *In a 1-round (0, δ)-SMT tolerating a generalized adversary with $\delta < 1/2$, for any pair of adversary sets B_i and B_j, the information transmitted on the wires in the set $C_{ij} = [n] - (B_i \cup B_j)$ will uniquely determine the message. Here C_{ij} is the set of all wires minus the wires in B_i and B_j.*

This is true because otherwise, we have two different messages m and m' such that:

$-XYZ$ is the transmission over the wires in C, B_i, B_j, respectively when message m is sent;

$-XY'Z'$ is the transmission over the wires in C, B_i, B_j, respectively when message m' is sent.

Now the transcript $XY'Z$ corresponds to message m with adversary set B_i and m' with adversary set B_j, respectively. So the success chance of the receiver in correctly outputting the message is $1/2$.

Theorem 3. *A 1-round PSMT protocol tolerating a generalized adversary with the adversary structure Γ satisfying Q^3, has communication complexity lower bounded by $\geq \frac{\gamma}{\gamma-3}\ell$, where $\ell = \log|\mathcal{M}|$ is the size of the message in bits and $\gamma = |\Gamma|$.*

Proof. The proof of the theorem is inspired by the proof in [8] for threshold adversary.

Let T_i^m denote the set of all possible transmissions that can occur on wire $w_i \in \mathcal{W}$ when the sender $\mathcal{S}$ transmits message m. Suppose for $j \geq i$, $M_C^m \subseteq \times_{w_i \in C} T_i^m$ denote the set of all possible transmissions (as vectors) that can occur on the set of wires in the set C when $\mathcal{S}$ transmits message m. Let the set of all transmission (for all messages) on wire w_i given by, $T_i = \bigcup_{m \in M} T_i^m$ be the capacity of the wire w_i. The capacity of the set C of wires is $M_C = \bigcup_{m \in M} M_C^m$.

Perfect reliability of a SMT protocol implies that the (uncorrupted) transmissions on the wires in any set C_{ij}, uniquely determines the secret (Lemma 1) and so:

$$M_{C_{ij}}^{m_1} \cap M_{C_{ij}}^{m_2} = \emptyset. \tag{2}$$

On the other hand, perfect privacy means that if the adversary $\mathcal{A}$ corrupts any set in Γ, they should get no information about the message m. This implies the transmission vector corresponding to the adversary set corrupted by the adversary, should reveal no information about the message and so is a possible transmission for any message. Thus for any two messages $m_1, m_2 \in M$ and any adversary set $B \in \Gamma$, it must be true that,

$$M_B^{m_1} = M_B^{m_2}. \tag{3}$$

We know that for a 1-round $(0,0)$-SMT, Γ satisfies Q^3.

Let $|\Gamma| = \gamma$ and define $C_{ijk} = [n] - (B_i \cup B_j \cup B_k)$. We know that the wires in C_{ij} uniquely determine the secret. Also that for any $B_i \cup B_j \cup B_k$, transmission on $B_i \cup B_j \cup B_k \setminus B_i \cup B_j$ will be common to all messages (it is a subset of transmission in M_{B_k}), and so transmission on wires in C_{ijk} will satisfy, $|C_{ijk}| \geq |M|$.

And so,

$$\prod_{a \in C_{ijk}} |T_a| > |M_{C_{ijk}}| > |M|. \tag{4}$$

Now consider the following product:

$$\prod_{B_i, B_j, B_k \in \Gamma} \prod_{a \in C_{ijk}} |T_a| > \prod_{B_i, B_j, B_k \in \Gamma} M_{C_{ijk}} > |M|^{\frac{\gamma(\gamma-1)(\gamma-2)}{6}}, \tag{5}$$

where $\binom{\gamma}{3} = \frac{\gamma(\gamma-1)(\gamma-2)}{6}$ is the number of C_{ijk}.

We would like to find the maximum number of times that a wire can appear in $\prod_{B_i, B_j, B_k \in \Gamma} \prod_{a \in C_{ijk}} |T_a|$.

Note that a wire x must appear in *at least* one adversary set (otherwise that wire is secure and can be used for secure transmission). This means that at most $\binom{\gamma-1}{3} = \frac{(\gamma-1)(\gamma-2)(\gamma-3)}{6}$ sets of the form C_{ijk} will include the wire x.

This means that we can always (for any Γ) write,

$$(\prod_{a=1}^{n} |T_a|)^{\frac{(\gamma-1)(\gamma-2)(\gamma-3)}{6}} \geq \prod_{B_i,B_j,B_k \in \Gamma} \prod_{a \in C_{ijk}} |T_a| > \prod_{B_i,B_j,B_k \in \Gamma} M_{C_{ijk}} > |M|^{\frac{\gamma(\gamma-1)(\gamma-2)}{6}} \quad (6)$$

That is,

$$(\gamma - 3) \log \Sigma_{a=1}^{n} |T_a|) \geq \gamma \log |M|,$$

and,

$$\frac{\Sigma_{a=1}^{n} \log |T_a|)}{\log |M|} \geq \frac{\gamma}{\gamma - 3}.$$

Therefore, the lower bound on the transmission rate of a 1-round $(0, 0)$-SMT against a generalized adversary is $\frac{\gamma}{\gamma-3}$.

Thus the lower bound on the communication complexity is $\geq \frac{\ell\gamma}{\gamma-3}$. □

Remark. The lower bound above is for any generalized adversary and so will not in general be tight for a given adversary structure. That is, one can derive better (higher) lower bound if the adversary structure satisfies certain properties. For example, for threshold adversaries, the above lower bound when specialized to threshold case will give a weaker bound than what is directly derived in [8].

6   An Efficient 1-Round $(0, \delta)$-SMT Protocol against a Generalized Adversary

In this section we construct an efficient 1-round $(0, \delta)$-SMT protocol against a generalized adversary inspired by a construction of cheater detecting ε-secure secret sharing schemes [12]. The construction uses linear secret sharing scheme (LSSS) and a special class of hash functions.

The basic idea of the protocol is to generate a key-dependent hash value for the message, and then send the shares of the message and the key of the hash function, generated using two LSSSs, over the wires. The hash value of the message is broadcasted to the receiver. The receiver will be able to recover the message with small failure probability, from the received shares and hash value.

The hash functions required for this construction are called, *strongly key-differential universal hash function*, introduced in [12].

Definition 3. *A family of hash function $H : \mathcal{A} \rightarrow \mathcal{B}$ is called a strongly key-differential universal ε-SKDU$_2$ if there exists $\hat{b} \in \mathcal{B}$ such that for two distinct $a, a' \in \mathcal{A}$ and for any $c \in \mathcal{E}$, where $\mathcal{E}$ is the key space,*

$$\frac{|\{h_e | e \in \mathcal{E}, h_e(a) = \hat{b}, h_{e+c}(a') = \hat{b}\}|}{|\{h_e | e \in \mathcal{E}, h_e(a) = \hat{b}\}|} \leq \varepsilon,$$

such that for any $a \in \mathcal{A}$ and $b \in \mathcal{B}$, $|\{h_e \in H | h_e(a) = b\}| = \frac{|H|}{|\mathcal{B}|}$.

Construction. Let H be a family of ε-SKDU$_2$ that maps the set $A = \mathcal{M}$ to B.

Let SS$_1 = (ShareGen_1, Reconst_1)$, and SS$_2 = (ShareGen_2, Reconst_2)$, are two linear secret sharing schemes for adversary set Γ, for the message set $\mathcal{M}$ and key set $\mathcal{E}$, respectively. and assume Γ satisfies Q^2. Let $\Sigma = 2^P \setminus \Gamma$.

The SMT protocol Π is described below.

- **Message Transmission:**
  Suppose the sender $\mathcal{S}$ wants to send a secret $m \in \mathcal{M}$ to the receiver $\mathcal{R}$. $\mathcal{S}$ does the following.
  Step 1 Randomly select $e \in \mathcal{E}$ and find $h_e(m) = \hat{b}$.
  Step 2 Call **ShareGen**$_i$ of SS$_i$, $i = 1, 2$, to generate two sets of shares for m and e respectively: $(s_1^m, ..., s_n^m) \leftarrow$ SS$_1(m)$, and $(s_1^e, ..., s_n^e) \leftarrow$ SS$_2(e)$.
  Step 3 send $s_i = (s_i^m, s_i^e), \hat{b}$ through wire $i, 1 \le i \le n$.

- **Message Recovery:**
  The receiver $\mathcal{R}$ receives the shares $s_i' = (s_i'^m, s_i'^e)$ through wire $i, 1 \le i \le n$ and does the following.
  Step 1 Set $\mathcal{L} = \emptyset$. For each minimal access set $a \in \Sigma$ do:
  1. Call the reconstruction algorithms **Reconst**$_i$, $i = 1, 2$, on the shares $\{s_i'^m | i \in a\}$ and recover $\hat{m}$ and $\hat{e}$.
  2. If $h_{\hat{e}}(\hat{m}) \ne \hat{b}$, output **NULL**. Otherwise add $\hat{m}$ to $\mathcal{L}$.
  Step 2 If $\mathcal{L}$ contains more than one distinct value, output **NULL**.
  Otherwise output the unique element in $\mathcal{L}$, as the protocol output.

Let k denote the number of minimal access sets in Σ.

Theorem 4. Π *is a 1-round $(0, \delta)$-SMT protocol, $\delta = (k - 1)\epsilon$ tolerating the generalized adversary with the adversary structure Γ satisfying Q^2. The protocol sends a message that is one field element, by transmitting $O(n)$ field elements.*

Proof (sketch)

Perfect privacy

Suppose the adversary corrupts a maximal adversary set B and accesses the values sent over the associated wires. Let $B = \{w_{i_1} \cdots, w_{i_{t-1}}\}$ with message and key shares, $s_{i_j} = (s_{i_j}^m, s_{i_j}^e), j = 1, \cdots, t - 1$. We need to show that $\Pr(m | s_{i_j}, j = 1, \cdots, t - 1, h_e(m) = \hat{b}) = \Pr(m)$. Note that because of perfect privacy of SS$_i$, $i = 1, 2$, and independent choice of m and e, we have $\Pr(m | s_{i_j}, j = 1, \cdots, t - 1) = \Pr(m)$ (also $\Pr(e | s_{i_j}, j = 1, \cdots, t - 1) = \Pr(e)$). For any $\hat{b}$, we have $\Pr(m, e | h_e(m) = \hat{b})$ is the number of pairs e, m where $h_e(m) = \hat{b}$ divided by $|\mathcal{M}| \times |\mathcal{E}|$ which because of the property of hash function, is constant and so $\hat{b}$ does not leak any information about the pair.

δ-reliability

Receiver attempts to recover the message for all minimal access sets. Note that because of the Q^2 property, for any maximal adversary set B that is corrupted by the adversary, the set $\mathcal{W} \setminus B$ is an access set (otherwise it is an adversary set which contradicts Q^2) and contains a minimal access set. So the correct message will be reconstructed for this access set and so $\mathcal{L}$, will always contain the correct message.

Note that the adversary may succeed in constructing a pair of message and key, m', e', such that $h_{e'}(m') = \hat{b}$. The following argument shows that this probability is at most ϵ.

This is true because of the following. Let $B = \{w_{i_1}, \cdots, w_{i_{t-1}}\}$ with message and key shares, $s_{i_j} = (s^m_{i_j}, s^e_{i_j}), j = 1, \cdots, t-1$. Note that due to linear property of secret sharing schemes there are recombination constants $c^M_{A,j}, j = 1, \cdots, t-1, x$, and $c^E_{A,j}, j = 1, \cdots, t_1, x$, that depend on the access set $A = B \cup \{x\}$ such that,

$$m = c^M_{A,x} s^m_x + \sum_{i=1}^{t-1} c^M_{A,j} s^m_{i_j},$$

$$e = c^E_{A,x} s^e_x + \sum_{i=1}^{t-1} c^E_{A,j} s^e_{i_j}.$$

Now e' and m' are constructed using the same constants, but forged values of shares for B and so,

$$m' = c^M_{A,x} s^m_x + \sum_{i=1}^{t-1} c^M_{A,j} s'^m_{i_j},$$

$$e' = c^E_{A,x} s^e_x + \sum_{i=1}^{t-1} c^E_{A,j} s'^e_{i_j} \Rightarrow e' = e + \sum_{i=1}^{t-1} (c^E_{A,j} s'^e_{i_j} - c^E_{A,j} s^e_{i_j}) = e + C.$$

The success probability of the adversary is, $\Pr(m' \in \mathcal{M}, m' \neq m, h_{e'}(m') = \hat{b})$ which is bounded as,

$$\Pr(m' \in \mathcal{M}, m' \neq m, h_{e'}(m') = \hat{b}|h_e(m) = \hat{b})$$
$$= \frac{\Pr(h_e(m) = \hat{b}, h_{e+C}(m') = \hat{b})}{\Pr(h_e(m) = \hat{b})} = \frac{|\{h_e : h_e(m) = \hat{b}, h_{e+C}(m') = \hat{b}\}|}{|\{h_e : h_e(m) = \hat{b}\}|} \leq \epsilon.$$

Note that according to the SMT reconstruction algorithm, adversary's success in this case result in the SMT protocol to output **NULL**. Then, at most $k-1$ can be influenced by the adversary. Probability of protocol not outputting **NULL** is at least $(1-\epsilon)^{k-1} \approx 1 - (k-1)\epsilon$. That is $\delta = (k-1)\epsilon$.

6.1   Comparison with the Protocol in [5]

Chowdhury, Kurosawa, and Patra designed an efficient 1-round $(0, \delta)$-SMT protocol tolerating a generalized adversary [5]. But their protocol needs to send $\ell = n$ messages. On the other hand, our protocol can work for a single message.

In many scenarios we may need to send just one message, for example a key in sensor network. In those scenarios our protocol is better than their protocol. It is to be noted here that both the protocols need computation which is polynomial in the size of the adversary structure Γ and the underlying LSSS.

References

1. Ben-Or, M., Goldwasser, S., Wigderson, A.: Completeness Theorems for Non-cryptographic Fault-tolerant Distributed Computation (extended abstract). In: Proceedings of the Twentieth Annual ACM Symposium on Theory of Computing (STOC 1988), pp. 1–10. ACM, New York (1988)
2. Chaum, D., Crépeau, C., Damgard, I.: Multiparty Unconditionally Secure Protocols (extended abstract). In: Proceedings of the Twentieth Annual ACM Symposium on Theory of Computing (STOC 1988), pp. 11–19. ACM, New York (1988)
3. Carpentieri, M., De Santis, A., Vaccaro, U.: Size of Shares and Probability of Cheating in Threshold Schemes. In: Helleseth, T. (ed.) EUROCRYPT 1993. LNCS, vol. 765, pp. 118–125. Springer, Heidelberg (1994)
4. Cabello, S., Padró, C., Sáez, G.: Secret Sharing Schemes with Detection of Cheaters for a General Access Structure. Des. Codes Cryptography 25(2), 175–188 (2002)
5. Choudhury, A., Kurosawa, K., Patra, A.: Simple and Efficient Single Round almost Perfectly Secure Message Transmission Tolerating Generalized Adversary. In: Lopez, J., Tsudik, G. (eds.) ACNS 2011. LNCS, vol. 6715, pp. 292–308. Springer, Heidelberg (2011)
6. Dolev, D., Dwork, C., Waarts, O., Yung, M.: Perfectly Secure Message Transmission. Journal of the ACM 40(1), 17–47 (1993)
7. Desmedt, Y., Wang, Y., Burmester, M.: A Complete Characterization of Tolerable Adversary Structures for Secure Point-to-Point Transmissions Without Feedback. In: Deng, X., Du, D.-Z. (eds.) ISAAC 2005. LNCS, vol. 3827, pp. 277–287. Springer, Heidelberg (2005)
8. Fitzi, M., Franklin, M., Garay, J., Vardhan, S.H.: Towards Optimal and Efficient Perfectly Secure Message Transmission. In: Vadhan, S.P. (ed.) TCC 2007. LNCS, vol. 4392, pp. 311–322. Springer, Heidelberg (2007)
9. Franklin, M.K., Wright, R.N.: Secure Communication in Minimal Connectivity Models. Journal of Cryptology 13(1), 9–30 (2000)
10. Hirt, M., Maurer, U.: Player Simulation and General Adversary Structures in Perfect Multiparty Computation. Journal of Cryptology 13(1), 31–60 (2000)
11. Kurosawa, K., Suzuki, K.: Almost Secure (1-Round, n-Channel) Message Transmission Scheme. In: Desmedt, Y. (ed.) ICITS 2007. LNCS, vol. 4883, pp. 99–112. Springer, Heidelberg (2009)
12. Obana, S., Araki, T.: Almost Optimum Secret Sharing Schemes Secure Against Cheating for Arbitrary Secret Distribution. In: Lai, X., Chen, K. (eds.) ASIACRYPT 2006. LNCS, vol. 4284, pp. 364–379. Springer, Heidelberg (2006)
13. Ogata, W., Kurosawa, K., Stinson, D.R.: Optimum Secret Sharing Scheme Secure against Cheating. SIAM J. Discrete Math. 20(1), 79–95 (2006)
14. Padro, C.: Robust Vector Space Secret Sharing Schemes. Inf. Process. Lett. 68(3), 107–111 (1998)
15. Patra, A., Choudhary, A., Srinathan, K., Rangan, C.P.: Unconditionally Reliable and Secure Message Transmission in Undirected Synchronous Networks: Possibility, Feasibility and Optimality. Int. J. Appl. Cryptol. 2(2), 159–197 (2010)

16. Padró, C., Sáez, G., Villar, J.: Detection of Cheaters in Vector Space Secret Sharing Schemes. Des. Codes Cryptography 16(1), 75–85 (1999)
17. Rabin, T., Ben-Or, M.: Verifiable Secret Sharing and Multiparty Protocols with Honest Majority (extended abstract). In: Johnson, D.S. (ed.) Proceedings of the Twenty-First Annual ACM Symposium on Theory of Computing (STOC 1989), pp. 73–85. ACM, New York (1989)
18. Tompa, M., Woll, H.: How to Share a Secret with Cheaters. Journal of Cryptology 1(2), 133–138 (1988)
19. Wang, Y.: Robust Key Establishment in Sensor Networks. SIGMOD Record 33(1), 14–19 (2004)
20. Wu, J., Stinson, D.R.: Three Improved Algorithms for Multi-path Key Establishment in Sensor Networks Using Protocols for Secure Message Transmission, http://eprint.iacr.org/2009/413.pdf

Improving the Performance
of the SYND Stream Cipher

Mohammed Meziani[1], Gerhard Hoffmann[2], and Pierre-Louis Cayrel[3]

[1] CASED – Center for Advanced Security Research Darmstadt,
Mornewegstrasse 32, 64293 Darmstadt, Germany
mohammed.meziani@cased.de
[2] Technische Universität Darmstadt
Fachbereich Informatik
Kryptographie und Computeralgebra,
Hochschulstraße 10
64289 Darmstadt, Germany
hoffmann@mathematik.tu-darmstadt.de
[3] Laboratoire Hubert Curien, UMR CNRS 5516,
Bâtiment F 18 rue du professeur Benoît Lauras,
42000 Saint-Etienne, France
pierre.louis.cayrel@univ-st-etienne.fr

Abstract. In 2007, Gaborit et al. proposed the stream cipher SYND as
an improvement of the pseudo random number generator due to Fischer
and Stern. This work shows how to improve considerably the efficiency
the SYND cipher without using the so-called regular encoding and without compromising the security of the modified SYND stream cipher.
Our proposal, called XSYND, uses a generic state transformation which
is reducible to the Regular Syndrome Decoding problem (RSD), but has
better computational characteristics than the regular encoding. A first
implementation shows that XSYND runs much faster than SYND for
a comparative security level (being more than three times faster for a
security level of 128 bits, and more than 6 times faster for 400-bit security), though it is still only half as fast as AES in counter mode. Parallel
computation may yet improve the speed of our proposal, and we leave it
as future research to improve the efficiency of our implementation.

Keywords: Stream ciphers, Provable security, Syndrome Decoding.

1 Introduction

A stream cipher is a secret key cryptosystem that employs a symmetric secret key
for producing an arbitrary long pseudo random sequence, called keystream. This
keystream is then combined with the plaintext, typically by means of the bitwise
XOR, to produce the ciphertext. Stream ciphers are necessary in many real-
life applications, especially the wireless communication standards such as IEEE
802.11b [2] and Bluetooth [3]. Therefore, stream ciphers are usually required to
be fast and implementable on constrained hardware.

A. Mitrokotsa and S. Vaudenay (Eds.): AFRICACRYPT 2012, LNCS 7374, pp. 99–116, 2012.

It is easy to design a stream cipher. The challenge here is to make it theoretically secure and at the same time very efficient. A variety of efficient stream ciphers have been proposed, but most of them were proven to be insecure as reported during the eSTREAM project [1]. It is thus desirable to have provably secure stream ciphers, whose security is grounded on hard problems. The first constructions in this direction are [14,13] whose security is based on the hardness of factoring problem. Another proposal was developed by Kaliski [24], its security relies on the intractability of the discrete logarithm problem. Assuming the hardness of solving RSA problem, Alexi et al. [4] proposed a pseudo-random number generator (PRNG). The one-way function hard-core bit construction by Goldreich et al. [19] has also led to the construction of the efficient PRNG, called BMGL [32], which was developed by Håstad and Näslund using Rijndael.

Although proving the hardness of all mentioned problems is an important open problem, they are all known to be easy on quantum attacks as shown in [31]. It is therefore advantageous to design stream ciphers whose security relies on other assumptions, and which are more promising even in the age of quantum computers. The first construction addressing this challenge is due to Impagliazzo et al. [23], based on the subset sum problem. Later, Fisher and Stern [16] proposed a PRNG whose security relies on the syndrome decoding (SD) problem [10]. Recently, further provably secure constructions have been proposed. The first one, called QUAD, due to Berbain et al. [9] under assumption that solving a multivariate quadratic system is hard (MQ-problem). The second one, named SYND, proposed by Gaborit et al. [18], is an improved variant of [16]. The security of SYND is also reducible to the SD problem. Recently, Meziani et al. [27] proposed the 2SC stream cipher based on the same problem, following the sponge construction. This cipher is much more efficient than SYND [18] in terms of performance and has small key/IV size, but it suffers from the drawback of having big matrices.

Our contribution. In this paper we propose an efficient variant of the SYND stream cipher [18], called XSYND, this new construction is reducible to the SD problem. This cipher is faster than all existing code-based stream ciphers [18,27] and requires comparatively little storage capacity, making it attractive for practical implementations. We also propose parameters for fast keystream generation for different security levels.

Outline of the paper. Section 2 provides a background of coding theory. Section 3 describes the SYND stream cipher. A detailed description of the XSYND stream cipher is presented in Section 4, its security is discussed in Section 5. In Section 6 secure parameters and experimental results for XSYND are presented. Section 7 concludes this paper.

2   Coding Theory Background

This section provides a short introduction to error-correcting codes and recall some hard problems in this area.

In general, a linear code $\mathcal{C}$ is a k-dimensional subspace of an n-dimensional vector space over a finite field $\mathbb{F}_q$, where k and n are positive integers with $k < n$ and q a prime power. Elements of $\mathbb{F}_q^n$ are called *words* and elements of $\mathcal{C}$ are called *codewords*. The integer $r = n - k$ is called the co-dimension of $\mathcal{C}$. The *weight* of a word x, denoted by $w = wt(x)$, is the number of non-zero entries in x, and the *Hamming distance* between two words x and y is $wt(x - y)$. The minimum distance d of a code is the smallest distance between any two distinct codewords. A generator matrix G of $\mathcal{C}$ is a matrix whose rows form a basis of $\mathcal{C}$, .i.e., $\mathcal{C} = \{x \cdot G : x \in \mathbb{F}_q^k\}$. A parity check matrix H of $\mathcal{C}$ is defined by $\mathcal{C} = \{x \in \mathbb{F}_q^n : H \cdot x^T = 0\}$ and generates the dual space of the code $\mathcal{C}$.

A linear code $\mathcal{C}$ is called a cyclic code if any cyclic shift of a codeword is another codeword. That is, $x_0, \cdots, x_n \in \mathcal{C}$ implies $x_n, x_0, \cdots, x_{n-1} \in \mathcal{C}$. In this case, the parity check matrix of $\mathcal{C}$ can be only described by its first row. Furthermore, $\mathcal{C}$ is called a quasi cyclic code if its parity check matrix is composed of a number of cyclic submatrices. In practice, such codes are very good from the decoding capacity point of view and behave like random codes with small requirement on the length as shown in [17].Throughout this paper we consider $q = 2$.

Definition 1 (Regular word). *A regular word of length n and weight w is a word consisting of w blocks of length n/w, each with a single non-zero entry.*

In code-based cryptography, the security of most of the cryptographic primitives is related to the hardness of the following problems.

Definition 2 (Binary Syndrome Decoding (SD) problem). *Given a binary $r \times n$ matrix H, a binary vector $y \in \mathbb{F}_2^r$, and an integer $w > 0$, find a word $x \in \mathbb{F}_2^n$ of weight $wt(x) = w$, such that $H \cdot x^T = y$.*

This problem is proven NP-complete in [10]. A particular case of this problem is the Regular Syndrome Decoding (RSD) problem, which has been proved to be NP-complete in [5]. It can be stated as follows.

Definition 3 (Regular Syndrome Decoding (RSD) Problem). *Given a binary $r \times n$ matrix H, a binary vector $y \in \mathbb{F}_2^r$,and an integer $w > 0$, find a regular word $x \in \mathbb{F}_2^n$ of weight $wt(x) = w$, such that $H \cdot x^T = y$.*

Through this paper, we will denote $\mathrm{RSD}(n, r, w)$ to indicate an instance of RSD problem with parameters (n, r, w). Before ending this section, we recall the definition of a hardcore bit (or hardcore predicate).

Definition 4 (Hardcore bit). *Let f be a one-way function. Let $h : \{0,1\}^* \to \{0,1\}$ be a polynomial-time computable function. We say that h is a hardcore bit for f if for all PPT adversary $\mathcal{A}$ there exists one negligible function ϵ, such that*

$$\Pr[A(f(x)) = h(x)] \le \frac{1}{2} + \epsilon(n), \quad \forall n$$

where the probability is over x chosen randomly and the coin tosses of $\mathcal{A}$.

3   The SYND Stream Cipher

This section gives a short description of the original SYND design. SYND is a synchronous stream cipher with security reduction proposed in 2007 by Gaborit et. al [18]. SYND is a improved variant of Fisher-Stern's PRNG [16] with two improvements: the use of quasi-cyclic codes, which reduces the storage capacity and the introduction of regular words used in [5], which speeds up the keystream generation of the system. This PRNG can be seen as a finite automaton, S, determined by a set of inner states with lengths ranging from 256 to 1024 bits. SYND accepts keys of length 128 to 512 bits and produces a keystream twice as large as the key size in each round.

More precisely, let n, w, and r be three positive integers such that the ratio n/w is a power of two and $r = w \log_2(n/w)$. The key stream generation of SYND works in three steps using three different one-to-one functions called Ini, Upd, and Out, respectively (See Figure 1). The Ini function takes a secret key K concatenated with an initial vector IV, both of length $r/2$ bits, and returns an initial state $e_0 = \mathtt{Ini}(K|IV)$, which starts the key stream generation process, where $(a|b)$ denotes the concatenation of bit strings a and b. The Ini function is a three-Feistel transformation based on Upd and Out, and given by:

$$\mathtt{Ini}(x) = y \oplus \mathtt{Out}(x \oplus \mathtt{Upd}(y)); \quad y = x \oplus \mathtt{Upd}(y), \quad \forall x = (\mathtt{K}, \mathtt{IV}) \in \mathbb{F}_2^{r/2} \times \mathbb{F}_2^{r/2},$$

where Upd and Out functions are defined by

$$\mathtt{Upd}(x) = A \cdot \theta(x); \quad \mathtt{Out}(x) = B \cdot \theta(x), \quad \forall x \in \mathbb{F}_2^r.$$

Here, A and B are random binary matrices which describe the same binary quasi-cyclic (QC) code of length n, correcting up to w errors. The mapping $x \mapsto \theta(x)$ is an encoding algorithm which transforms an r-bit string into a regular word of length n and weight w. Starting from e_0, in each time unit i, S outputs a key bit $z_i = \mathtt{Out}(e_i)$ and changes the inner state as follows: $e_{i+1} = \mathtt{Upd}(e_i)$.

After generating the key bit stream $z_0, z_1, \cdots$, a cleartext bit stream $m_0, m_1, \cdots$ is encrypted into a cyphertext stream $c_0, c_1, \cdots$ by the bitwise XOR operator as $c_i = z_i \oplus m_i$. Knowing the secret state e_0 the receiver can generate the keystream $z_0, z_1, \cdots$ and therefore recover the cleartext bitstream by $m_i = z_i \oplus c_i$.

Thus, the evaluation of Upd and Out for state x is done by first encoding x into a regular word $\theta(x)$ of length n and weight w, and then multiplying the resulting word by a random $r \times n$ binary matrix. This process can be regarded as XORing w columns from the underlying random matrix with one another (these r-bit long columns correspond to the non-zero positions of the regular word $\theta(x)$). This idea was first introduced in the FSB hash family [5] in order to speed up the hashing process. In the next section, we show how to speed up SYND by eliminating the encoding $x \mapsto \theta(x)$, while at the same time preserving the security properties of the underlying scheme.

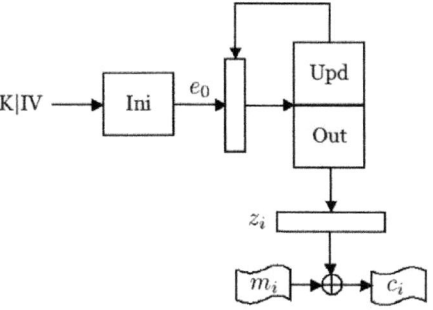

Fig. 1. A graphical illustration of the SYND stream cipher

4 Our Proposal: XSYND

This section describes an eXtended SYND algorithm (XSYND), which adds two main features to the original SYND structure. In what follows, we use the notations of the previous section.

Firstly, we modify the Ini function such that it requires only two, rather than three function evaluations, without loss of security. We denote the new function by XIni and depict it in Fig. 2. Note that this modification does not affect the recovery of the secret K or the initial vector IV. In fact, it is straightforward to prove that, given an initial state e_0 output by XIni, if an adversary can extract K and IV from e_0, it can also easily solve an instance $RSD(n, r, w)$. The new function XIni function is defined by:

$$\texttt{XIni}(x) = y \oplus \texttt{Out}(y); \quad y = x \oplus \texttt{Upd}(x); \quad \forall x = (\texttt{K}, \texttt{IV}) \in \mathbb{F}_2^{r/2} \times \mathbb{F}_2^{r/2}.$$

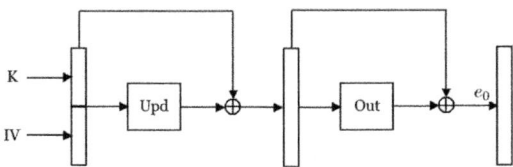

Fig. 2. The XIni function of XSYND

The second modification in XSYND is to avoid the regular encoding $x \mapsto \theta(x)$ in Upd and Out by using the randomize-then-combine paradigm due to Bellare et al. [6,7,8] as depicted in Figure 3. More precisely, given an input x consisting of w blocks $x_1, \ldots, x_w$, each block being b bits (where b is chosen at will), we first feed each block through a random function f, obtaining an output y_i. The values $y_1, y_2, \cdots, y_w$ are combined by bitwise XOR to generate the final output. In XSYND, we use the following function f: let H be a random binary matrix of size $wb \times w \cdot 2^b$, consisting of w submatrices $H_1 \ldots H_w$ of size $wb \times 2^b$ (we write $H = H_1| \ldots |H_w$). If we write the submatrices as $H_i = (h_i^{(0)}, h_i^{(1)}, \ldots, h_i^{(2^b-1)})$, where $h_i^{(j)} \in \mathbb{F}^{wb}$ for $j \in \{0, 1, \ldots, 2^b - 1\}$, then we can define f by $y_i = h_i^{(j)}$ if and only if the decimal value of x_i is equal to j. We have 2^b possible value for each y_i, depending on the decimal value of the block x_i. In this way, we redefine the functions Upd and Out as follows (see also Fig. 4):

$$\mathtt{Upd}(x) = a_1^{(x_1)} \oplus a_2^{(x_2)} \oplus \cdots \oplus a_w^{(x_w)}; \quad \mathtt{Out}(x) = b_1^{(x_1)} \oplus b_2^{(x_2)} \oplus \cdots \oplus b_w^{(x_w)}; \quad \forall x \in \mathbb{F}_2^{wb}.$$

Here, $a_i^{(j)}$ (resp. $b_i^{(j)}$) is the jth column of the ith submatrix A_i (resp. B_i) of a random binary matrix A (resp. B), both of size $wb \times w2^b$.

Remark 1. It is worth noting that the same technique has been recently used by Berstein et al. [12] to improve the efficiency of the FSB hash family [5].

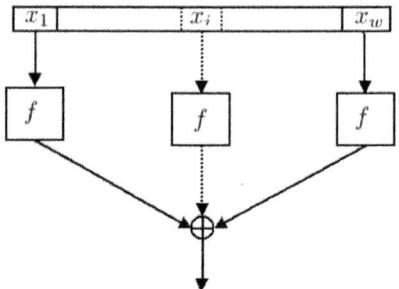

Fig. 3. Randomize-then-combine paradigm

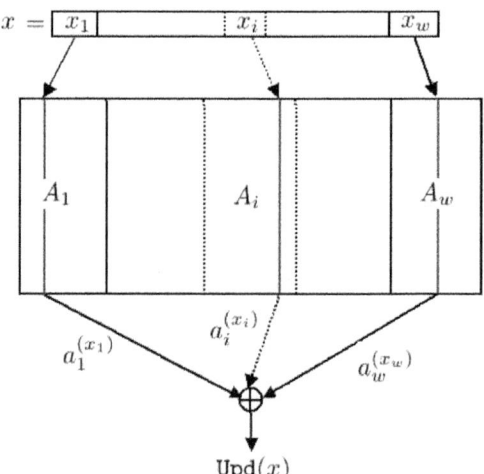

Fig. 4. The Update Function Upd of XSYND

5   Security of XSYND

5.1   Theoretical Security

In this section we present the theoretical security of our construction. The presentation is done in two steps. In the first step, we show that it is hard to find the secret state x given $\mathtt{Upd}(x)$ and $\mathtt{Out}(x)$ as described in section 4. More precisely, we show that inverting $\mathtt{Upd}(x)$ and $\mathtt{Out}(x)$ is reducible to the RSD problem. In the second step, we prove that XSYND is a pseudo-random generator, meaning that the key stream produced by XSYND is indistinguishable from truly random sequences.

Step 1: We consider general transformations g defined as:

$$g(x) = a_1^{(x_1)} \oplus a_2^{(x_2)} \oplus \cdots \oplus a_w^{(x_w)}, \ \forall x = (x_1, \ldots, x_w) \in \mathbb{F}_2^{wb}.$$

In this transformation, $a_i^{(j)}$ for $j = 0, \ldots, 2^b$ is the $(j+1)^{th}$ column of the ith submatrix A_i of a random binary matrix A of size $wb \times w2^b$. Note that both $\mathtt{Upd}(x)$ and $\mathtt{Out}(x)$ are particular instantiations of g, for random matrices A and B (see previous section). Our argument in this section is as follows: we first show that (1) for each x there exists a regular word z such that $g(x) = A \cdot z^T$, then prove that (2) learning x from $y = g(x)$ is equivalent to finding a regular word z such that $A \cdot z^T = y$ (this is an instantiation of $\mathrm{RSD}(n, r, w)$ for $r = wb$ and $n = w2^b$). Thus, under the RSD assumption, the modified XSYND protocol security can be reduced to the hardness of RSD.

First consider (1). We write $A = A_1 | \ldots | A_w$ as in section 4, for $wb \times 2^b$ submatrices A_i. Each submatrix has columns $a_i^{(0)}, \ldots, a_i^{(2^b-1)}$. We note that any regular word z is in fact a word of length $n = w2^b$ and weight w, whose decimal entries $z_1, \ldots, z_w$ indicate the positions of its non-zero entries (and each z_i is a unique value between $(i-1)2^b + 1$ and $i2^b$ since the word is regular). Let $x = (x_1, \ldots, x_w)$ be a state in decimal notation. We associate each x with a value z whose decimal notation is $(z_1, \ldots, z_w)$ for $z_i = (x_i + 1) + (i-1)2^b$. The reverse transformation of z to x is obtained as follows:

$$\begin{cases} x_1 \equiv z_1 - 1 \pmod{2^b} \\ x_2 \equiv z_2 - 1 \pmod{2^b} \\ \cdots \quad \cdots \quad \cdots \quad \cdots \\ x_w \equiv z_w - 1 \pmod{2^b} \end{cases}$$

It is easy to check that:

$$A \cdot z^T = a_1^{(x_1)} \oplus a_2^{(x_2)} \oplus \cdots \oplus a_w^{(x_w)}.$$

Toy Example. Let us consider $w = 3$ and $b = 2$. Then the matrix A should be $(3 \cdot 2) \times (3 \cdot 2^2) = 6 \times 12$ and binary. Consider in this example the following matrix A:

$$A = \begin{bmatrix} a_1^{(0)} & a_1^{(1)} & a_1^{(2)} & a_1^{(3)} & a_2^{(0)} & a_2^{(1)} & a_2^{(2)} & a_2^{(3)} & a_3^{(0)} & a_3^{(1)} & a_3^{(2)} & a_3^{(3)} \\ \hline 1 & 0 & 1 & 0 & 1 & 0 & 1 & 0 & 1 & 0 & 0 & 1 \\ 0 & 1 & 1 & 0 & 0 & 0 & 1 & 0 & 1 & 1 & 1 & 0 \\ 1 & 0 & 0 & 0 & 0 & 1 & 0 & 1 & 0 & 1 & 0 & 0 \\ 0 & 1 & 0 & 1 & 0 & 1 & 0 & 1 & 0 & 1 & 1 & 1 \\ 0 & 0 & 1 & 1 & 0 & 1 & 1 & 0 & 1 & 1 & 1 & 0 \\ 1 & 0 & 0 & 0 & 0 & 1 & 0 & 1 & 0 & 1 & 0 & 0 \end{bmatrix}$$

Let us consider a state x in decimal form, with $x = (2, 1, 0)$. Compute z in decimal form according to the formula $z_i = (x_i + 1) + (i - 1)2^b$. Thus $z_1 = 3$, $z_2 = 6$, and $z_3 = 9$. In binary notation, z_i denotes the positions of z's non-zero entries, i.e. $z = [0010|0100|1000]$. We can now verify that for this z we have

$$g(x) = a_1^{(2)} \oplus a_2^{(1)} \oplus a_3^{(0)} = [001111] = A \cdot z^T.$$

Now let us consider the security reduction of general transformations g to the RSD problem, i.e. step (2) outlined above. We have shown that for each input value x we can find a regular word z of weight w such that $A \cdot z^T = g(x)$. Assume that there exists an adversary that can invert $g(x)$, i.e. given $y = g(x)$, the adversary outputs x. Then the same adversary computes z as above and can thus, given a matrix A, and a value $y = g(x) = A \cdot z^T$, this adversary can output the regular word z. This is exactly an instantiation of $\mathrm{RSD}(n, r, w)$ for $r = wb$ and $n = w2^b$. In conclusion, we can reduce the security of XSYND to the hardness of the RSD problem.

Step 2: In this step, we prove that XSYND is a pseudo-random generator. Our proof is an adaption of that given for the Fischer-Stern's PRNG [16]. We will show that if there exists an algorithm that is able of distinguishing a random bit string from the output of the mapping $x \rightarrow (\mathtt{Out}(x), \mathtt{Upd}(x))$, then this algorithm can be converted into a predicator that can predicts the inner product of an input x and a random bit string chosen at random. Before doing so, we state the following assumptions.

1. *Indistinguishability:* The binary matrices A and B (both of size $r \times n$) are computationally indistinguishable from uniform matrices of the same dimensions.
2. *Regular syndrome decoding (RSD):* The family of mappings defined as $g_M(z) = M \cdot z^T$ for an uniform $2r \times n$ binary matrix M is one-way on the set of all regular words of length n and weight w.

As shown in the last subsection, the mapping $x \rightarrow \mathtt{Upd}(x)$ (resp. $x \rightarrow \mathtt{Out}(x)$) can be regarded as $f_u(z) = A \cdot z^T$ (resp. $f_o(z) = B \cdot z^T$), where A and B are binary matrices, both of size $r \times n$, and z is taken from the set of regular words. Therefore, from now on, we will use f_u (resp. f_o) instead of Upd (resp. Out).

From A and B we build a $2r \times n$ block matrix M by stacking them vertically, i.e.

$$M = \left(\frac{A}{B} \right)$$

In this case, we can write the mapping $x \to (\text{Out}(x), \text{Upd}(x))$ as $g_M(z) = M \cdot z^T = (f_u(z), f_o(z))$. Consequently, in order to prove that XSYND is a pseudo-random generator, it is sufficient to prove that the output of $z \to g_M(z)$ is pseudo random as proved in [16]. Our proof is based on the Goldreich-Levin Theorem [19], which says that, for any one-way function, the inner product of its argument and a randomly chosen bit string is a hardcore bit (or hardcore predicate). Recall that the inner product of two bit strings a and b (of the same size) is defined by

$$\langle a, b \rangle = \sum_i a_i b_i \quad \text{mod } 2.$$

Theorem 1. *(Goldreich-Levin theorem) Let $f : \mathbb{F}_2^{\lambda(n)} \to \mathbb{F}_2^{\mu(n)}$ be a one-way function. For every PPT algorithm $\mathcal{A}$, for all polynomials p and all but finitely many n's,*

$$\Pr[\mathcal{A}(f(x), \nu) = \langle x, \nu \rangle] \leq \frac{1}{2} + \frac{1}{p(n)}$$

where the probability is taken over x uniformly chosen x and $\nu \in \mathbb{F}_2^{\lambda(n)}$.

The theorem proving that XSYND is a pseudo-random generator is stated as follows.

Theorem 2. *Suppose n, r, and w are chosen such that the indistinguishability and the regular syndrome decoding assumptions hold. Then the output distribution of XSYND is computationally indistinguishable from a truly random distribution. That is, XSYND is a pseudo-random generator.*

Proof. (by contradiction). Let us assume that an $2r$-bit output of the mapping $g_M(z) = M \cdot z^T$ is not pseudo-random, and there exists a distinguisher $\mathcal{D}$, which is capable to differentiate this output of from a $2r$-bit random string v. More precisely, $\mathcal{D}$ takes as input $2r \times n$ binary random matrix M and a random $v \in \{0, 1\}^{2r}$ as a candidate being equal to $M \cdot z^T$ for some unknown regular word z. In the event that $M \cdot z^T = v$, $\mathcal{D}$ outputs 1 with probability above $\frac{1}{2} + \frac{1}{p(n)}$, for every polynomial $p(n)$. Otherwise, when v is chosen uniformly from $\{0, 1\}^{2r}$, $\mathcal{D}$ outputs 1 with probability at most $\frac{1}{2}$. Formally, the distinguisher $\mathcal{D}$ behaves as follows:

$$\begin{cases} \Pr[\mathcal{D}(M, v) = 1] \geq \frac{1}{2} + \frac{1}{p(n)}, & \text{if } v = M \cdot z^T, \text{ for some regular word } z \\ \Pr[\mathcal{D}(M, v) = 1] < \frac{1}{2}, & \text{if } v \text{ is taken uniformly from } \{0, 1\}^{2r} \end{cases}$$

As next step, we will build an algorithm $\mathcal{P}$, which uses the distinguisher $\mathcal{D}$ as subroutine. This algorithm will predicts the inner product $\langle z, \nu \rangle$ with probability at least $\frac{1}{2} + \frac{1}{2p(n)}$, where z is an unknown regular word (an input of g_M) and ν a randomly chosen n-bit string. To this end, let write $\nu = (\nu_1, \cdots, \nu_n)$. In addition, let σ be the number of the positions j such that where $z_i = \nu_j = 1$, i.e. the size of the intersection $z \cap \nu$ and ρ its parity, i.e. the inner product $\langle z, \nu \rangle$. Then the algorithm $\mathcal{P}$ takes as input $g_M(z)$ and ν and executes the following steps:

- Select a random $\rho' \in \{0, 1\}$ as candidate to ρ
- Choose randomly $\xi \in \{0, 1\}^{2r}$
- Build a new $2r \times n$ binary matrix $\widehat{M} = (\widehat{m}_1, \cdots, \widehat{m}_n)$ such that for every $j \in \{1, \cdots, n\}$ it holds

$$\widehat{m}_j = \begin{cases} m_j + \xi & \text{if } \nu_j = 1, \\ m_j & \text{if } \nu_j = 0 \end{cases}$$

- Feed the distinguisher with $\widehat{M}$ and $g_M(z) + \rho' \cdot \xi$
- If the distinguisher outputs 1, then output $\rho' = \rho$. Otherwise, output the opposite of ρ'.

Now, we show next that $\mathcal{P}$ predicts the inner product $\langle z, \nu \rangle$ with probability above $\frac{1}{2} + \frac{1}{2p(n)}$. We have to consider two events:

(1) $\mathbf{E_1}$:"ρ is guessed correctly". Then the prognosticated value for the inner product $\langle z, \nu \rangle$ is correct if the distinguisher outputs 1. The distribution seen by the distinguisher on $(\widehat{M}, g_M(z) + \rho' \cdot \xi)$ is identical to the distribution on input $(M, g_M(z))$. By construction, this is the case with probability at least $\frac{1}{2} + \frac{1}{p(n)}$.

(2) $\mathbf{E_2}$:"ρ is not guessed correctly". The distinguisher receives uniformly distributed inputs because of the randomness of ξ. It then returns 1 with probability $\frac{1}{2}$.

Since $\Pr[\mathbf{E_1}] = \Pr[\mathbf{E_2}] = \frac{1}{2}$, we conclude that the overall probability of correctly predicting the inner product $\langle z, \nu \rangle$ is at least $\frac{1}{2} + \frac{1}{2p(n)}$. This contradicts the Theorem 1 because of the RSD assumption. ∎

5.2 Practical Security

This section presents what are provably the most generic attacks against XSYND. We will only address the hardness of inverting the mapping g defined in the previous section, since this is the main building block of XSYND design. If an attacker can invert g, then she can recover the secret key and recover inner states.

In what follows, we denote by $\text{WF}_Y(n, w, r)$ the work factor (i.e. number of binary operations) required to solve the instance $\text{RSD}(n, w, r)$ by using an algorithm Y. Furthermore, in estimating the complexity of each attack against XSYND we use $r = wb$ with $b = \log_2 \left(\frac{n}{w} \right)$.

There are essentially three types of known attacks that are applicable to XSYND:

1. **Linearization Attacks.** There are two types of linearization attacks that are relevant for XSYND, namely the Bellare-Micciancio (BM) attack [8] against the XHASH function [8], and the attack due to Saarinen [30]. We discuss these attacks below.

   (a) The Bellare-Micciancio's attack. This is a preimage attack proposed by Bellare and Micciancio [8] against the so-called XHASH mapping. This attack relies on finding a linear dependency among w r-bit vectors, where w is the number of vectors XORred together and r, the length (in bits) of the target value. This is likely to succeed if the value w is close to r. More precisely, let l and k be two positive integers. Let f be a random function with $f : \mathbb{F}_2^l \mapsto \mathbb{F}_2^r$. Let $[i]$ denote the binary representation of an integer i. Based on f, the XHASH is defined as

$$\text{XHASH}(x) = f([1]|x_1) \oplus \cdots \oplus f([w]|x_w), \quad \text{with } x = (x_1, x_2, \ldots, x_w).$$

   The BM attack finds a preimage x of a given $z = \text{XHASH}(x) \in F_2^r$ as follows. First, one finds w-bit string $y = (y_1, \ldots, y_w)$, with $y_i \in \mathbb{F}_2$, such that $\text{XHASH}(x^y) = z$, where $x^y = x_1^{y_1} \ldots x_w^{y_w}$. To achieve this, one first computes $2w$ values $\beta_i^k = f([i]|x_i^j)$ for $k \in \{0, 1\}$ and $i \in \{1, \ldots, w\}$; the next step is to try to solve the following system of equations over $\mathbb{F}_2$ using linear algebra:

$$\begin{cases} y_i \oplus \bar{y}_i = 1, & i \in \{1, \ldots, w\}, \\ \oplus_{i=1}^w \beta_i^0(j)y_i \oplus \beta_i^1(j)\bar{y}_i = z(i), & j \in \{1, \ldots, r\}. \end{cases}$$

   Here, $\beta_i^0(j)$ (resp. $\beta_i^1(j)$) denotes the j^{-th} bit of β_i^0 (resp. β_i^1) and $\bar{y}_i = 1 - y_i$ are the unknowns. This system has $r + w$ equations in $2w$ unknowns and is easy to solve when $w = r + 1$. More generally, it was shown in [8] (Appendix A, Lemma A.1) that for all $y \in \mathbb{F}_2^w$ the probability to have $\text{XHASH}(x^y) \neq z$ is at most 2^{r-w}. That is, the complexity of inverting XHASH is at least 2^{r-w}; in our notation,

$$\text{WF}_{\text{BM}}(n, w, r) \geq 2^{r-w} = 2^{(b-1)w}.$$

   (b) The Saarinen's attack. This attack is due to Saarinen [30] and it was proposed against the FSB [5] hash function. The main idea behind this attack is reducing the problem of finding collisions or preimages to that of solving systems of equations. This attack is very efficient when $r < 2w$. We briefly show how this attack works in our setting, where we must invert the map g.

   As shown in section 5.1, $g(x) = A \cdot z^T$, where A is the random binary matrix of size $r \times n$, whose entries define g, and z is a regular word of length n and weight w. We can in turn write $A \cdot z^T$ out as follows:

$$y = \oplus_{i=1}^w a_{(i-1)\frac{n}{w}+x_i+1}, \ 0 \leq x_i \leq \frac{n}{w}, \tag{1}$$

where $x = (x_1, \ldots, x_w)$ and a_j denotes the j^{-th} column of A. For simplicity, assume that $x_i \in \{0, 1\}$. In this case, we define a constant r-bit vector c and an additional $r \times w$ binary matrix B as follows.

$$c = \oplus_{i=1}^{w} a_{(i-1)\frac{n}{w}+1}, \quad B = [b_1 \cdots b_w] \text{ with } b_i = a_{(i-1)\frac{n}{w}+1} \oplus a_{(i-1)\frac{n}{w}+2}. \quad (2)$$

It is easy to check that $y = B \cdot x + c$. As a consequence if $r = w$, then B is square and we can find the preimage x from y as:

$$x = B^{-1} \cdot (y \oplus c), \quad (3)$$

where B^{-1} denotes the inverse of B. Note that this inverse exists with probability without proof of $\prod_{i=1}^{r}(1 - 1/2^i) \approx 0.29$ for r moderately large. The expected complexity of this attack is the the workload of inverting B, which is al most $0.29 \cdot r^3$. It has been proved in [30] that the same complexity is obtained even if $r \leq 2w$.

In the opposite direction, Saarinen also extended his attack for the case when $w \leq r/\alpha$ for $\alpha > 1$ and $x_i \notin \{0, 1\}$. In this case, the complexity is about $2^r/(\alpha + 1)^w$. Moreover, the recent result[12] shows that if $\alpha = 2\beta$, for $\beta > 1$, this complexity becomes $2^r/(\beta + 1)^{2w}$. As consequence we obtain:

$$\text{WF}_{\text{Saarinen}}(n, w, r) \geq \begin{cases} 2^r/(\alpha + 1)^w & \text{if } w \leq r/\alpha \\ 2^r/(\alpha + 1)^{2w} & \text{if } w \leq r/2\alpha \end{cases}$$

which can be rewritten in our setting as:

$$\text{WF}_{\text{Saarinen}}(n, w, r) \geq \begin{cases} (\frac{2^b}{\alpha+1})^w & \text{if } \alpha \leq b \\ (\frac{2^b}{(\alpha+1)^2})^w & \text{if } \alpha \leq b/2 \end{cases}$$

2. **Generalized Birthday Attacks (GBA).** This class of attacks attempt to solve the following, so-called k-sum problem: given k random lists $L_1, L_2, \ldots,$ L_k of r-bit strings selected uniformly and independently at random, find $x_1 \in L_1, x_2 \in L_2, \ldots, x_k \in L_k$ such that $\oplus_{i=1}^{k} x_i = 0$. For $k = 2$, a solution can be found in time $2^{r/2}$ using the standard birthday paradox. For $k > 2$ Wagner's algorithm [33] and its extended variants [5,11,28,15] can be applied. When $k = 2^{j-1}$ and $|L_i| > 2^{r/j}$, Wagner's algorithm can find at least one solution in time $2^{r/j}$.

The main idea behind a GBA algorithm is depicted Fig. 5. We consider the case $k = 4$. Let $L_1, \ldots, L_4$ be four lists, each of length $2^{r/3}$. The algorithm proceeds in two iterations. In the first iteration, we build two new lists $L_{1,2}$ and $L_{3,4}$. The list $L_{1,2}$ contains all sums $x_1 \oplus x_2$ with $x_1 \in L_1$ and $x_2 \in L_2$ such that the first $r/3$ bits of the sum are zero. Similarly, $L_{3,4}$ contains all sums $x_3 \oplus x_4$ with $x_3 \in L_3$ and $x_4 \in L_4$ such that the first $r/3$ bits of the sum are zero. So the expected length of $L_{1,2}$ is equal to $2^{-r/3} \cdot |L_1| \cdot |L_2| = 2^{r/3}$. Similarly, the expected length of $L_{3,4}$ is also $2^{r/3}$. In the second iteration of the algorithm, we construct a new list L_1' containing all pairs $(x_1', x_2') \in L_{1,2} \times L_{3,4}$ such that the first $r/3$ bits of the sum $x_1' \oplus x_2'$ are zero. Then the probability that $x'_1 \oplus x'_2$ equals zero is $2^{-2r/3}$. Therefore, the expected number of matching sums is $2^{-2r/3} \cdot |L_{1,2}| \cdot |L_{3,4}| = 1$. So we expected to find a solution. This idea can be generalized for $k = 2^{j-1}$ by repeating the same procedure $j - 2$ times. In each iteration a, we construct lists, each containing $2^{r/j}$ elements that are zero on their first ar/j bits, until obtaining, on average, one r-bit element with all entries equal to 0.

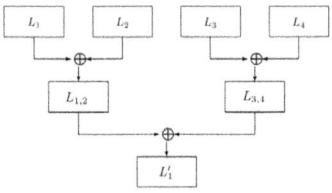

Fig. 5. The GBA idea for $k = 4$

We estimate the security of XSYND against GBA attacks by using the GBA algorithm from [15]. This algorithm attempts to find a set of indices $I = \{1, 2, \cdots, 2^\gamma\}$ satisfying $\oplus_{i \in I} H_i = 0$, where H_i are columns of the matrix H. As shown in [15], the algorithm is applicable when $\binom{2^b w}{2^{(1-\gamma)}w} \geq 2^{bw+\gamma(\gamma-1)}$. Under this condition, the cost of solving an instance RSD problem with parameters (n, r, w) is given by:

$$\mathsf{WF}_{\mathsf{GBA}}(n, w, r) \geq \left(\frac{wb}{\gamma} - 1\right) 2^{\frac{wb}{\gamma} - 1}.$$

Note that the recent result in [29] shows that the time and memory efficiency of GBA attacks can be improved, but only by a small factor. In Section 6 we take this improvement into account when proposing parameters for XSYND.

3. **Information Set Decoding (ISD).** ISD is one of the most important generic algorithm for decoding errors in an arbitrary linear code. An ISD algorithm consists (in its simplest form) in finding a valid, so-called information set, which is a subset of k error-free positions amongst the n positions of each codeword. Here, k is the dimension and n the length of the code. The validity of this set is checked by using Gaussian elimination on the $r \times n$ parity check matrix H. If we denote by $p(n, r, w)$ the probability of finding a valid information set and by $c(r)$ the cost of Gaussian elimination, then the overall cost of ISD algorithms equals the ratio $c(r)/p(n, r, w)$.

In the following, we estimate the cost of finding a solution to the regular syndrome decoding (RSD) problem, i.e. we wish to invert the map g. Let $n_s(n, r, w)$ be the expected number of solutions of RSD instance. This quantity is:

$$n_s(n, r, w) = \frac{\left(\frac{n}{w}\right)^w}{2^r} = 1,$$

because $r = w \log_2(\frac{n}{w})$. In addition, let $p_v(n, r, w)$ be the probability that a given information set is valid for one given solution of RSD. As shown in [5], $p(n, r, w)$ can be approximated by: $p(n, r, w) \approx p_v(n, r, w) \cdot n_s(n, r, w)$. Furthermore, as shown in [5], $p_v(n, r, w)$ is given by:

$$p_v(n, r, w) = \left(\frac{r}{n}\right)^w = \left(\frac{\log_2(n/w)}{n/w}\right)^w$$

We thus conclude that the probability of selecting a valid set to invert RSD is equal to: $p(n, r, w) = \left(\frac{b}{2^b}\right)^w$.

Hence, the cost $\mathtt{WF}_{\mathtt{ISD}}(n, w, r)$ of solving an instance of RSD with parameters (n, r, w) is approximately:

$$\mathtt{WF}_{\mathtt{ISD}}(n, w, r) \approx c(r) \cdot \left(\frac{2^b}{b}\right)^w . \tag{4}$$

If we assume that the complexity of Gaussian elimination is r^3, then $\mathtt{WF}_{\mathtt{ISD}}(n, w, r)$ becomes:

$$\mathtt{WF}_{\mathtt{ISD}}(n, w, r) \approx (wb)^3 \cdot \left(\frac{2^b}{b}\right)^w . \tag{5}$$

In practice, we use the lower bound for ISD algorithms presented in [26] to estimate the security of XSYND against ISD attacks and show our results in Table 1 .

Remark 2. One could also use Time Memory trade-off attacks against stream ciphers. This attack was first introduced in [21] as a generic method of attacking block ciphers. To make this attack unfeasible, one must adjust the cipher parameters as shown in [20,22], i.e., the initial vector should be at least as large as the key, and the state should be at least twice the key.

Table 1 briefly summarizes the expected complexity of the previous attacks against XSYND.

Table 1. The estimated complexities of possible attacks against XSYND

Attack	The binary logarithm of the complexity: $\log_2(\mathtt{WF}_{(.)}(n, w, r))$
BM	$w(b - 1)$
Sarinnen	$\begin{cases} w(b - \log_2(\alpha + 1)), & \text{if } \alpha \leq b \\ w(b - 2\log_2(\alpha + 1)), & \text{if } \alpha \leq b/2 \end{cases}$
GBA	$wb/\gamma + \log_2(wb/\gamma - 1) - 1$ for $\gamma \in \mathbb{N}$
ISD	$w(b - \log_2(b)) + 3\log_2(wb)$

6   Parameters and Experimental Results

Suitable parameters (n, r, w) for XSYND must provide both efficiency and high security against all known attacks. Firstly, we account for Time Memory Trade-Off attacks (see section 5.2) and choose (n, r, w) such that:

$$r = w \log_2(n/w) \geq 2|\text{IV}| \quad \text{and} \quad |\text{IV}| \geq |\text{K}|.$$

For XSYND we choose $r = w \log_2(n/w) = 2|\text{IV}| = 2|\text{K}|$. We then fix $b = \log_2(n/w) = 8$ and for each security level λ we vary w to obtain both high performance and a complexity of solving the RSD problem of at least 2^λ.

We have tested a large set of potential parameters for a number of security levels. Table 2 presents the optimal parameter sets (n, w, r) resulted from running our implementation for several security levels. Note that in our implementation, we only use random binary codes without any particular structure. But it is possible to find parameters providing the same security levels when the parity check matrix is quasi-cyclic as in [18]. In this case, r has to be a prime and 2 is primitive root of the finite field $\mathbb{F}_r^*$ in order to guarantee the randomness property of QC-codes as demonstrated in [17].

Table 2. Proposed parameters for XSYND

Security Level	n	r	w	Key/IV size [bits]	Speed of XSYND [cpb]
80	8192	256	32	128	14.92
120	12288	384	48	192	16.98
160	16384	512	64	256	35.40
200	20480	640	80	320	43.68
240	24576	768	96	384	55.42
280	28672	896	112	448	77.09

The results shown in Table 2 are for a pure C/C++ implementation with additional use of C/C++-Intrinsics). The operating system was Debian 6.0.3, the source has been compiled with gcc (Debian 4.4.5-8) 4.4.5. All results have been gained on an AMD Phenom(tm) 9950 Quad-Core Processor, running at a clock rate of 1300 MHz. Due to the row-major convention of C/C++, the two matrices H_1 resp. H_2 have been used and stored in transposed form. In order to compare the speed of XSYND with the claimed speed of SYND [18] and 2SC [27] (Table 4), we have tested our implementation using the parameter sets suggested in [18]. Our results presented in Table 3 show that, for comparable security levels, XSYND runs faster than SYND [18] and 2SC cipher [27]. It is worth to stress that the authors of 2SC [27] compared the performance of 2SC [27] to that of SYND [18] based on their own implementations (of both schemes), because no freely-available implementation of SYND exists.

Table 3. Performance of XSYND vs. SYND using parameter sets proposed in [18]

Security Level	n	r	w	key/IV size [bits]	speed of SYND [cpb]	speed of XSYND [cpb]
80	8192	256	32	128	27	14.92
128	8192	384	48	192	47	16.86
180	8192	512	64	256	53	35.18
400	8192	1024	128	512	83	55.69

Compared to the (bitsliced and parallel) fastest software implementation of AES in CTR mode proposed by Käsper et al. [25], XSYND runs about two times slower. Indeed, this implementation is written in assembly using 128-bit XMM registers and runs at 7.59 cycles/byte on a Intel Core 2 Q9550 and 6.92 cycles/byte on Core i7 920. Note that our implementation could be sped up by using parallel computations achieving much better results than what Tables 2 and 3 show. It is therefore interesting to implement this to see how much further XSYND can be improved.

Table 4. Parameters and performance of 2SC cipher given in [27]

Security Level	n	r	w	key/IV size [bits]	speed of 2SC [cpb]
100	1572864	384	24	144	37
160	2228224	544	34	208	47
250	3801088	928	58	352	72

7   Conclusion

In this paper we presented XSYND, an improved variant of SYND stream cipher, without compromising its security. Our proposal uses a generic state transformation which is directly reducible to the regular syndrome decoding problem (RSD), but has better computational characteristics than the regular encoding introduced in the SYND system. A software implementation shows that our proposal runs much faster than all code-based stream ciphers for different security levels, but it is only half as fast as AES in counter mode without making any parallel computation. Moreover, unlike to SYND, we show how the security reduction of our proposal works.

References

1. http://www.ecrytp.eu.org/stream
2. Overview of IEEE 802.11b Security. Intel Technology Journal Q2 (2000)
3. Specification of the Bluetooth system, vol. 1.1 (February 2001),
   http://www.bluetooth.org/spec/
4. Alexi, W., Chor, B., Goldreich, O., Schnorr, C.P.: RSA and Rabin functions: certain parts are as hard as the whole. SIAM J. Comput. 17(2), 194–209 (1988)
5. Augot, D., Finiasz, M., Sendrier, N.: A Family of Fast Syndrome Based Cryptographic Hash Functions. In: Dawson, E., Vaudenay, S. (eds.) Mycrypt 2005. LNCS, vol. 3715, pp. 64–83. Springer, Heidelberg (2005)
6. Bellare, M., Goldreich, O., Goldwasser, S.: Incremental Cryptography: The Case of Hashing and Signing. In: Desmedt, Y.G. (ed.) CRYPTO 1994. LNCS, vol. 839, pp. 216–233. Springer, Heidelberg (1994)
7. Bellare, M., Goldreich, O., Goldwasser, S.: Incremental cryptography and application to virus protection. In: Proceedings of the Twenty-Seventh Annual ACM Symposium on Theory of Computing, STOC 1995, pp. 45–56. ACM (1995)
8. Bellare, M., Micciancio, D.: A New Paradigm for Collision-Free Hashing: Incrementality at Reduced Cost. In: Fumy, W. (ed.) EUROCRYPT 1997. LNCS, vol. 1233, pp. 163–192. Springer, Heidelberg (1997)
9. Berbain, C., Gilbert, H., Patarin, J.: QUAD: A multivariate stream cipher with provable security. J. Symb. Comput. 44(12), 1703–1723 (2009)
10. Berlekamp, E., McEliece, R., van Tilborg, H.: On the inherent intractability of certain coding problems. IEEE Transactions on Information Theory 24(2), 384–386 (1978)
11. Bernstein, D.J.: Better price-performance ratios for generalized birthday attacks. In: Workshop Record of SHARCS 2007: Special-purpose Hardware for Attacking Cryptographic Systems (2007)
12. Bernstein, D.J., Lange, T., Peters, C., Schwabe, P.: Really Fast Syndrome-Based Hashing. In: Nitaj, A., Pointcheval, D. (eds.) AFRICACRYPT 2011. LNCS, vol. 6737, pp. 134–152. Springer, Heidelberg (2011)
13. Blum, L., Blum, M., Shub, M.: A simple unpredictable pseudo random number generator. SIAM J. Comput. 15(2), 364–383 (1986)
14. Blum, M., Micali, S.: How to generate cryptographically strong sequences of pseudo-random bits. SIAM J. Comput. 13(4), 850–864 (1984)
15. Finiasz, M., Sendrier, N.: Security Bounds for the Design of Code-Based Cryptosystems. In: Matsui, M. (ed.) ASIACRYPT 2009. LNCS, vol. 5912, pp. 88–105. Springer, Heidelberg (2009)
16. Fischer, J.-B., Stern, J.: An Efficient Pseudo-random Generator Provably as Secure as Syndrome Decoding. In: Maurer, U.M. (ed.) EUROCRYPT 1996. LNCS, vol. 1070, pp. 245–255. Springer, Heidelberg (1996)
17. Gaborit, P., Zémor, G.: Asymptotic improvement of the Gilbert-Varshamov bound for linear codes, vol. abs/0708.4164 (2007)
18. Gaborit, P., Laudaroux, C., Sendrier, N.: SYND: a very fast code-based cipher stream with a security reduction. In: IEEE Conference, ISIT 2007, Nice, France, pp. 186–190 (July 2007)
19. Goldreich, O., Levin, L.A.: A hard-core predicate for all one-way functions. In: STOC 1989: Proc. of the Twenty-First Annual ACM Symposium on Theory of Computing, pp. 25–32. ACM (1989)

20. Golić, J.D.: Cryptanalysis of Alleged A5 Stream Cipher. In: Fumy, W. (ed.) EUROCRYPT 1997. LNCS, vol. 1233, pp. 239–255. Springer, Heidelberg (1997)
21. Hellman, M.: A cryptanalytic time-memory trade-off. IEEE Transactions on Information Theory 26, 401–406 (1980)
22. Hong, J., Sarkar, P.: Rediscovery of time memory tradeoffs. Cryptology ePrint Archive, Report 2005/090 (2005), http://eprint.iacr.org/
23. Impagliazzo, R., Naor, M.: Efficient cryptographic schemes provably as secure as subset sum. J. Cryptology 9(4), 199–216 (1996)
24. Kaliski, B.S.: Elliptic Curves and Cryptography: A Pseudorandom Bit Generator and Other Tools. Phd thesis. MIT, Cambridge, MA, USA (1988)
25. Käsper, E., Schwabe, P.: Faster and Timing-Attack Resistant AES-GCM. In: Clavier, C., Gaj, K. (eds.) CHES 2009. LNCS, vol. 5747, pp. 1–17. Springer, Heidelberg (2009)
26. May, A., Meurer, A., Thomae, E.: Decoding Random Linear Codes in $\tilde{\mathcal{O}}(2^{0.054n})$. In: Lee, D.H. (ed.) ASIACRYPT 2011. LNCS, vol. 7073, pp. 107–124. Springer, Heidelberg (2011)
27. Meziani, M., Cayrel, P.-L., El Yousfi Alaoui, S.M.: 2SC: An Efficient Code-Based Stream Cipher. In: Kim, T.-H., Adeli, H., Robles, R.J., Balitanas, M. (eds.) ISA 2011. CCIS, vol. 200, pp. 111–122. Springer, Heidelberg (2011)
28. Minder, L., Sinclair, A.: The extended k-tree algorithm. In: Proc. of the Twentieth Annual ACM-SIAM Symposium on Discrete Algorithms, SODA 2009, pp. 586–595 (2009)
29. Niebuhr, R., Cayrel, P.-L., Buchmann, J.: Improving the Efficiency of Generalized Birthday Attacks Against Certain Structured Cryptosystems. In: WCC 2011. LNCS, pp. 163–172. Springer, Heidelberg (2011)
30. Saarinen, M.-J.O.: Linearization Attacks Against Syndrome Based Hashes. In: Srinathan, K., Rangan, C.P., Yung, M. (eds.) INDOCRYPT 2007. LNCS, vol. 4859, pp. 1–9. Springer, Heidelberg (2007)
31. Shor, P.W.: Algorithms for Quantum Computation: Discrete Logarithms and Factoring. In: SFCS 1994: Proc. of the 35th Annual Symposium on Foundations of Computer Science, pp. 124–134. IEEE Computer Society (1994)
32. Håstad, J., Näslund, M.: BMGL: Synchronous key-stream generator with provable security (2001)
33. Wagner, D.: A Generalized Birthday Problem (Extended Abstract). In: Yung, M. (ed.) CRYPTO 2002. LNCS, vol. 2442, pp. 288–304. Springer, Heidelberg (2002)

Impossible Differential Cryptanalysis of the Lightweight Block Ciphers TEA, XTEA and HIGHT

Jiazhe Chen[1,2,*], Meiqin Wang[1,2,**], and Bart Preneel[2]

[1] Key Laboratory of Cryptologic Technology and Information Security,
Ministry of Education, School of Mathematics,
Shandong University, Jinan 250100, China
[2] KU Leuven, ESAT/COSIC and IBBT, Belgium
mqwang@sdu.edu.cn

Abstract. TEA, XTEA and HIGHT are lightweight block ciphers with 64-bit block sizes and 128-bit keys. The round functions of the three ciphers are based on the simple operations XOR, modular addition and shift/rotation. TEA and XTEA are Feistel ciphers with 64 rounds designed by Needham and Wheeler, where XTEA is a successor of TEA, which was proposed by the same authors as an enhanced version of TEA. HIGHT, which is designed by Hong et al., is a generalized Feistel cipher with 32 rounds. These block ciphers are simple and easy to implement but their diffusion is slow, which allows us to find some impossible properties.

This paper proposes a method to identify the impossible differentials for TEA and XTEA by using the weak diffusion, where the impossible differential comes from a bit contradiction. Our method finds a 14-round impossible differential of XTEA and a 13-round impossible differential of TEA, which result in impossible differential attacks on 23-round XTEA and 17-round TEA, respectively. These attacks significantly improve the previous impossible differential attacks on 14-round XTEA and 11-round TEA given by Moon et al. from FSE 2002. For HIGHT, we improve the 26-round impossible differential attack proposed by Özen et al.; an impossible differential attack on 27-round HIGHT that is slightly faster than the exhaustive search is also given.

1 Introduction

TEA [22], XTEA [19] and HIGHT [6] are lightweight block ciphers suitable for low resource devices such as RFID tags and sensor nodes. TEA was proposed by Needham and Wheeler in 1994; it is a simple design that is easy to understand and implement. By exploiting its too simple key schedule, Kelsey et al.

---

* This author is supported by Graduate Independent Innovation Foundation of Shandong University (No. 11140070613183).
** This author is supported by NSFC Projects (No.61133013, No.61070244, No. 61103237 and No.60931160442), Outstanding Young Scientists Foundation Grant of Shandong Province (No.BS2009DX030).

A. Mitrokotsa and S. Vaudenay (Eds.): AFRICACRYPT 2012, LNCS 7374, pp. 117–137, 2012.

proposed a related-key attack on full TEA [10]. In order to preclude the attack, the authors enhanced the cipher with an improved key schedule and a different round function by rearranging the operations; the new version is called XTEA. Both TEA and XTEA are implemented in the Linux kernel; they use modular addition (modulo 2^{32}), shift (left and right) and XOR in their round functions. Several cryptanalytic results on TEA and XTEA have been published. In the single-key setting, Moon et al. gave impossible differential attacks on 11-round TEA and 14-round XTEA [18] based on 10-round and 12-round impossible differentials, respectively. Hong et al. [7] proposed truncated differential attacks that can break TEA reduced to 17 rounds with $2^{123.73}$ encryptions and XTEA reduced to 23 rounds with $2^{120.65}$ encryptions. Later, Sekar et al. presented a meet-in-the-middle attack on 23-round XTEA with complexity 2^{117} [21]. Very recently, Bogdanov and Wang proposed attacks on TEA and XTEA [3] with a new technique named zero correlation linear cryptanalysis [2]; these attacks are best attacks on TEA and XTEA in terms of the number of rounds to date, which can break 21 rounds of TEA and 25 rounds of XTEA. If the full codebook is available, their attacks are improved to 23/27 rounds for TEA/XTEA. There are also attacks on XTEA in the related-key setting, which are given in [4][13][15][17].

HIGHT, designed by Hong et al. [6], was standardized by the Telecommunications Technology Association (TTA) of Korea. Recently, it was adopted as an International Standard by ISO/IEC 18033-3 [8]. It is an 8-branch generalized Feistel with initial and final whitening layers; its round function uses addition modulo 2^8, rotation and XOR. The best related-key attack on HIGHT is a full-round rectangle attack with complexity $2^{125.83}$ [14]. The best single-key attack is a 26-round impossible differential cryptanalysis proposed by [20], which does not take the initial whitening layer into account and needs $2^{119.53}$ encryptions.

The impossible differential attack, which was independently proposed by Biham et al. [1] and Knudsen [12], is a widely used cryptanalytic method. The attack starts with finding an input difference that can never result in an output difference, which makes up an impossible differential. By adding rounds before and/or after the impossible differential, one can collect pairs with certain plaintext and ciphertext differences. If there exists a pair that meets the input and output values of the impossible differential under some subkey bits, these bits must be wrong. In this way, we discard as many wrong keys as possible and exhaustively search the rest of the keys, this phase is called *key recovery phase*. The early abort technique is usually used during the key recovery phase, that is, one does not guess all the subkey bits at once, but guess some subkey bits instead to discard some pairs that do not satisfy certain conditions step by step. In this case, we can discard the unwished pairs as soon as possible to reduce the time complexity.

Our Contribution. This paper presents a novel method to derive impossible differentials for TEA and XTEA. Due to the one-directional diffusion property of TEA and XTEA, one can determine a one-bit difference after a chosen difference propagates several steps forward/backward, which might lead to a one-bit contradiction in certain rounds if we choose two differences and make them propagate towards each other. Based on this technique we identify 13-round and 14-round impossible differentials for TEA and XTEA respectively. These impossible differentials are significantly better than the 10-round impossible differential of TEA and 12-round impossible differential of XTEA in [18], and result in improved impossible differential attacks on 17-round TEA and 23-round XTEA. Our attack on 17-round TEA needs 2^{57} chosen plaintexts and $2^{106.6}$ encryptions. If we use $2^{62.3}$ chosen plaintexts, we can attack 23-round XTEA with $2^{114.9}$ encryptions; if we increase the data complexity to 2^{63}, the complexity of the attack will become 2^{106} memory accesses and $2^{105.6}$ encryptions. 15-round impossible differentials can also be found for both TEA and XTEA, however, we should use the full codebook to carry out the attacks. In this case, 19 rounds of TEA and 26 rounds of XTEA can be attacked. Although the attacks on TEA and XTEA are not as good as those in [3], they greatly improve the corresponding impossible differential attacks in [18].

Table 1. Summary of Single-Key Attacks on TEA, XTEA and HIGHT

Attack	#Rounds	Data	Time	Ref.
TEA				
Impossible Differential	11	$2^{52.5}$ CP	2^{84}EN	[18]
Truncated Differential	17	1920 CP	$2^{123.37}$EN	[7]
Impossible Differential	**17**	2^{57} **CP**	$2^{106.6}$**EN**	**this paper**
Zero Correlation Linear	21	$2^{62.62}$KP	$2^{121.52}$EN	[3]
Zero Correlation Linear	23	2^{64}	$2^{119.64}$EN	[3]
XTEA				
Impossible Differential	14	$2^{62.5}$ CP	2^{85}EN	[18]
Truncated Differential	23	$2^{20.55}$ CP	$2^{120.65}$EN	[7]
Meet-in-the-Middle	23	18 KP	2^{117}EN	[21]
Impossible Differential	**23**	$2^{62.3}$ **CP**	$2^{114.9}$**EN**	**this paper**
Impossible Differential	**23**	2^{63} **CP**	2^{101}**MA**+$2^{105.6}$**EN**	**this paper**
Zero Correlation Linear	25	$2^{62.62}$KP	$2^{124.53}$EN	[3]
Zero Correlation Linear	27	2^{64}	$2^{120.71}$EN	[3]
HIGHT				
Saturation	22	$2^{62.04}$ CP	$2^{118.71}$EN	[23]
Impossible Differential	25	2^{60} CP	$2^{126.78}$EN	[16]
Impossible Differential	26	2^{61} CP	$2^{119.53}$EN	[20]
Impossible Differential	**26**	$2^{61.6}$ **CP**	$2^{114.35}$**EN**	**this paper**
Impossible Differential	**27**	2^{58} **CP**	2^{120} **MA**+$2^{126.6}$**EN**	**this paper**

CP: Chosen Plaintext; KP: Known Plaintext;
EN: Encryptions; MA: Memory Accesses.

Furthermore, we present impossible differential attacks on HIGHT reduced to 26 and 27 rounds that improve the result of [20]. Like the attack in [20], our 26-round attack also does not take the initial whitening layer into account; the complexity of our attack is $2^{61.6}$ chosen plaintexts and $2^{114.35}$ encryptions. While the 27-round attack includes both the initial and final whitening layers; it needs 2^{58} chosen plaintexts, $2^{126.6}$ 27-round encryptions and 2^{120} memory accesses. We summarize our results of TEA, XTEA and HIGHT, as well as the major previous results in Table 1.

The rest of the paper is organized as follows. We give some notations and brief descriptions of TEA, XTEA and HIGHT in Sect. 2. Some properties of TEA, XTEA and HIGHT are described in Sect. 3. Section 4 gives the impossible differentials and our attacks on reduced TEA and XTEA. The impossible differential cryptanalysis of HIGHT is presented in Sect. 5. Finally, Section 6 concludes the paper.

2   Preliminary

2.1   Notations

- $\boxplus$: addition modular 2^{32} or 2^8
- $\oplus$: exclusive-OR (XOR)
- MSB: most significant bit, which is the left-most bit
- LSB: least significant bit, which is the right-most bit
- ?: an indeterminate difference
- $||$: concatenation of bits
- ΔA: the XOR difference of a pair (A, A'), where A and A' are values of arbitrary length
- A_i: the i-th bit of A, where the 1st bit is the LSB
- $A_{i \sim j}$: the i-th to j-th bits of A
- $(\cdot)_2$: the binary representation a byte, where the left-most bit is the MSB
- e_0: $(???????0)_2$, e_1: $(???????1)_2$, e_4: $(?????100)_2$
- $D[i]$: a 32-bit difference where the i-th bit is 1, the first to the $(i-1)$-th bits are 0, and the $(i+1)$-th to 32-th bits are indeterminate. For $i < 0$, $D[i]$ means that all the 32 bits of the difference are indeterminate.

2.2   Brief Description of TEA and XTEA

TEA and XTEA are 64-bit block ciphers with 128-bit key-length. The key K can be described as follows: $K = (K_0, K_1, K_2, K_3)$, where K_i ($i = 0, ..., 3$) are 32-bit words. Denote the plaintext by (P_L, P_R), the ciphertext by (C_L, C_R), and the input of the i-th round by (L_{i-1}, R_{i-1}), so $(L_0 = P_L, R_0 = P_R)$. Then we can briefly describe the encryption procedure of TEA.

For $i = 1$ to 64, if $i \mod 2 = 1$,
$L_i = R_{i-1}$,
$R_i = L_{i-1} + (((R_{i-1} \ll 4) + K_0) \oplus (R_{i-1} + (i+1)/2 \times \delta) \oplus ((R_{i-1} \gg 5) + K_1))$.
If $i \mod 2 = 0$,
$L_i = R_{i-1}$,
$R_i = L_{i-1} + (((R_{i-1} \ll 4) + K_2) \oplus (R_{i-1} + (i+1)/2 \times \delta) \oplus ((R_{i-1} \gg 5) + K_3))$.

Finally, $(C_L = L_{64}, C_R = R_{64})$. Note that the constant $\delta = $ 0x9e3779b9. XTEA is also very simple, it has similar structure and round function as TEA. To make the cipher resist against related-key attack, XTEA has a key schedule which is more complicated. By using the same notion, the encryption procedure of XTEA is depicted as follows.

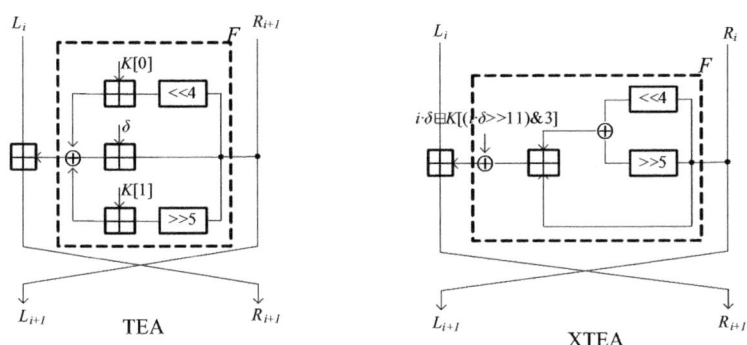

Fig. 1. Round Functions of TEA and XTEA

For $i = 1$ to 64,
$L_i = R_{i-1}$,
$R_i = L_{i-1} + (((R_{i-1} \ll 4 \oplus R_{i-1} \gg 5) + R_{i-1}) \oplus (i/2 \times \delta + K_{((i-1)/2 \times \delta \gg 11) \cap 3}))$.

The round functions of TEA and XTEA are illustrated in Fig. 1. The sequence K_i that is used in each round of XTEA can be found in Table 2.

Table 2. Subkey Used in Each Round of XTEA

K_0	K_3	K_1	K_2	K_2	K_1	K_3	K_0	K_0	K_0	K_1	K_3	K_2	K_2	K_3	K_1
K_0	K_0	K_1	K_0	K_2	K_3	K_3	K_2	K_0	K_1	K_1	K_1	K_2	K_0	K_3	K_3
K_0	K_2	K_1	K_1	K_2	K_1	K_3	K_0	K_0	K_3	K_1	K_2	K_2	K_1	K_3	K_1
K_0	K_0	K_1	K_3	K_2	K_2	K_3	K_2	K_0	K_1	K_1	K_0	K_2	K_3	K_3	K_2

2.3 Brief Description of HIGHT

HIGHT is a lightweight block cipher with a 64-bit block size and a 128-bit key. The cipher consists of 32 rounds with four parallel Feistel functions in each round; whitening keys are applied before the first round and after the last round. The master key of HIGHT is composed of 16 bytes $MK=(MK_{15}, MK_{14}, MK_{13}, MK_{12}, MK_{11}, MK_{10}, MK_9, MK_8, MK_7, MK_6, MK_5, MK_4, MK_3, MK_2, MK_1, MK_0)$; the whitening keys ($WK_0, WK_1, WK_2, WK_3, WK_4, WK_5, WK_6, WK_7$) and round subkeys ($SK_0, ..., SK_{127}$) are generated from the master key by the key schedule algorithm. The schedule of whitening keys is relatively simple and results in $WK_0 = MK_{12}$, $WK_1 = MK_{13}$, $WK_2 = MK_{14}$, $WK_3 = MK_{15}$, $WK_4 = MK_0$, $WK_5 = MK_1$, $WK_6 = MK_2$, $WK_7 = MK_8$. The 128 7-bit constants $\delta_0, ..., \delta_{127}$ have to be generated before generating the round subkeys; the algorithm is described in Fig. 2. Let the plaintext and ciphertext

Set $s_0 \leftarrow 0$, $s_1 \leftarrow 1$, $s_2 \leftarrow 0$, $s_3 \leftarrow 1$, $s_4 \leftarrow 1$, $s_5 \leftarrow 0$ and $s_6 \leftarrow 1$.
$\delta_0 = s_6||s_5||s_4||s_3||s_2||s_1||s_0$.
For $i = 1$ to 127,
$\quad s_{i+6} = s_{i+2} \oplus s_{i-1}$,
$\quad \delta_i = s_{i+6}||s_{i+5}||s_{i+4}||s_{i+3}||s_{i+2}||s_{i+1}||s_i$.

For $i = 0$ to 7,
$\quad$ for $j = 0$ to 7,
$\quad\quad SK_{16i+j} = MK_{(j-i) \mod 8} \boxplus \delta_{16i+j}$.
$\quad$ for $j = 0$ to 7,
$\quad\quad SK_{16i+j+8} = MK_{((j-i) \mod 8)+8} \boxplus \delta_{16i+j+8}$.

Fig. 2. Subkey Generation of HIGHT

be $P = (P_7, P_6, P_5, P_4, P_3, P_2, P_1, P_0)$ and $C = (C_7, C_6, C_5, C_4, C_3, C_2, C_1, C_0)$, where P_j, C_j $(j = 0, ..., 7)$ are 8-bit values. If we denote the input of the $(i+1)$-round be $X^i = (X_7^i, X_6^i, X_5^i, X_4^i, X_3^i, X_2^i, X_1^i, X_0^i)$, then an initial transformation is first applied to P by setting $X_0^0 \leftarrow P_0 \boxplus WK_0$, $X_1^0 \leftarrow P_1$, $X_2^0 \leftarrow P_2 \oplus WK_1$, $X_3^0 \leftarrow P_3$, $X_4^0 \leftarrow P_4 \boxplus WK_2$, $X_5^0 \leftarrow P_5$, $X_6^0 \leftarrow P_6 \oplus WK_3$ and $X_7^0 \leftarrow P_7$. After this, the round transformation iterates for 32 times:

For $i = 0$ to 32,
$$X_1^{i+1} = X_0^i, \ X_3^{i+1} = X_2^i, \ X_5^{i+1} = X_4^i, \ X_7^{i+1} = X_6^i,$$
$$X_0^{i+1} = X_7^i \oplus (F_0(X_6^i) \boxplus SK_{4i+3}),$$
$$X_2^{i+1} = X_1^i \boxplus (F_1(X_0^i) \oplus SK_{4i+2}),$$
$$X_4^{i+1} = X_3^i \oplus (F_0(X_2^i) \boxplus SK_{4i+1}),$$
$$X_6^{i+1} = X_5^i \boxplus (F_1(X_4^i) \oplus SK_{4i}).$$

Here $F_0(x) = (x \lll 1) \oplus (x \lll 2) \oplus (x \lll 7)$, and $F_1(x) = (x \lll 3) \oplus (x \lll 4) \oplus (x \lll 6)$. One round of HIGHT is illustrated in Fig. 3.

A final transformation is used to obtain the ciphertext C, where $C_0 = X_1^{32} \boxplus WK_4$, $C_1 = X_2^{32}$, $C_2 = X_3^{32} \oplus WK_5$, $C_3 = X_4^{32}$, $C_4 = X_5^{32} \boxplus WK_6$, $C_5 = X_6^{32}$, $C_6 = X_7^{32} \oplus WK_7$ and $C_7 = X_0^{32}$.

3   Diffusion Properties of TEA, XTEA and HIGHT

For XTEA and TEA, instead of rotations, shifts (left and right) are used, hence the differences that are shifted beyond MSB/LSB will be absorbed, which results

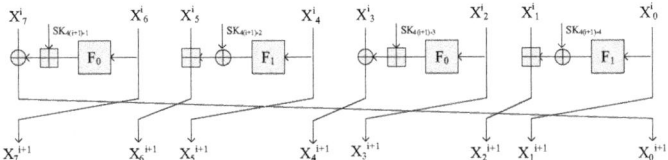

Fig. 3. One Round of HIGHT

in a slower diffusion than for rotations. In other words, the difference in the most significant bits can only influence the least significant bits after several rounds. This is the starting point of our attacks, which allows us to construct impossible differentials. The derivation of the impossible differentials will be elaborated in Sect. 4.1.

There is also a common property in the block ciphers TEA, XTEA and HIGHT, that is, the round subkeys are added (or XORed) to the intermediate values after the diffusion operations. Furthermore, the operations used in all the three ciphers are modular addition, XOR and shift (rotation), which may allow us to guess the subkey bit by bit from the LSB to the MSB to abort the wrong pairs as soon as possible to reduce the time complexity.

In the rest of this section, we will first give the definition of the T-function [11], then give Theorem 1 and Property 1 that are useful for attacks on TEA and XTEA.

Definition 1. *(From [11]) A function ϕ from $\mathbb{B}^{m \times n}$ to $\mathbb{B}^{l \times n}$ is called a T-function if the k-th column of the output $[\phi(x)]_{*,k-1}$ depends only on the first k columns of the input: $[x]_{*,0}, ..., [x]_{*,k-1}$, where $\mathbb{B}$ is the set $\{0,1\}$ and $[x]_{*,i}$ is the i-th column of x.*

From the definition we know that modular addition is a T-function, more specifically, we have the following Theorem.

Theorem 1. *(From [5]). Let $[x+y]$ be $(x+y) \mod 2^n$, then $[x+y]_i = x_i \oplus y_i \oplus c_i$ $(i = 1, ..., n)$, where $c_1 = 0$ and $c_i = x_{i-1}y_{i-1} \oplus x_{i-1}c_{i-1} \oplus y_{i-1}c_{i-1}$, for $i = 2, ..., n$.*

From Theorem 1, Property 1 can be deduced:

Property 1. Given x, x', y, y' be n-bit values, and $z = (x + y) \mod 2^n$, $z' = (x' + y') \mod 2^n$. If the i-th (counting from 1) to j-th bits of x, x', y, y' and the i-th carry c_i, c_i' of $x + y$, $x' + y'$ are known, then the i-th to j-th $(i < j \le n)$ bits of Δz can be obtained, regardless of the values of least significant $i - 1$ bits of x (or x'), y (or y'). Note that if there are no differences in the the least significant $i - 1$ bits of $x + y$ and $x' + y'$, then $c_i = c_i'$.

4   Impossible Differential Attacks on Reduced XTEA and TEA

In this section, we first explain how to obtain the impossible differentials for TEA and XTEA. Then a 13-round impossible differential for TEA and a 14-round impossible differential for XTEA are given, which are used to attack 17-round TEA and 23-round XTEA .

4.1   Impossible Differentials of TEA and XTEA

As mentioned in Sect. 3, we know that the differences in the most significant bits propagate only in one direction. Since both TEA and XTEA use operations that shift to the left for 4 bits and shift to the right for 5 bits, they share the following properties.

Property 2. If the input difference of the i-th round of XTEA (TEA) is $(0, D[n])$, then the output difference is $(D[n], D[n-5])$. Vice versa, if the output difference of the j-th round of XTEA (TEA) is $(D[p], 0)$, then the input difference is $(D[p-5], D[p])$.

Property 3. If the input difference of the i-th round of XTEA (TEA) is $(D[m], D[n])$, where $(m > n - 5)$, then the output difference is $(D[n], D[n-5])$. Vice versa, if the output difference of the j-th round of XTEA (TEA) is $(D[p], D[q])$, where $(q > p - 5)$, then the input difference is $(D[p-5], D[p])$.

From Property 2 and Property 3, we propose a method to construct impossible differentials for TEA and XTEA. If we choose the input difference to be $(0, D[n])$ (or $(D[m], D[n])$ $(m > n - 5)$), then after i rounds, the difference should be of the form $(D[n-5(i-1)], D[n-5i])$. Similarly, if we choose the output difference $(D[p], 0)$ (or $(D[p], D[q])$ $(q > p - 5)$), then after propagating backwards for j rounds, the difference should be of the form $(D[p-5j], D[p-5(j-1)])$. Then at least one bit contradiction will appear if

$$n - 5(i - 1) > 0, p - 5j > 0, n - 5(i - 1) \neq p - 5j.$$

With this method, we can derived a 14-round impossible differential for XTEA and a 13-round impossible differential for TEA (see Fig. 4), where the left-most bit is the MSB, each small rectangle stands for one bit: blank rectangles mean that there are no differences in these bits, while black ones mean the differences are equal to 1, and gray ones mean that the differences are indeterminate. As mentioned, we can even derive 15-round impossible differentials for both XTEA and TEA, resulting in attacks that work for more rounds of TEA and XTEA. However, the resulting attacks require the full codebook and very high complexities, so we decided not to describe them in detail.

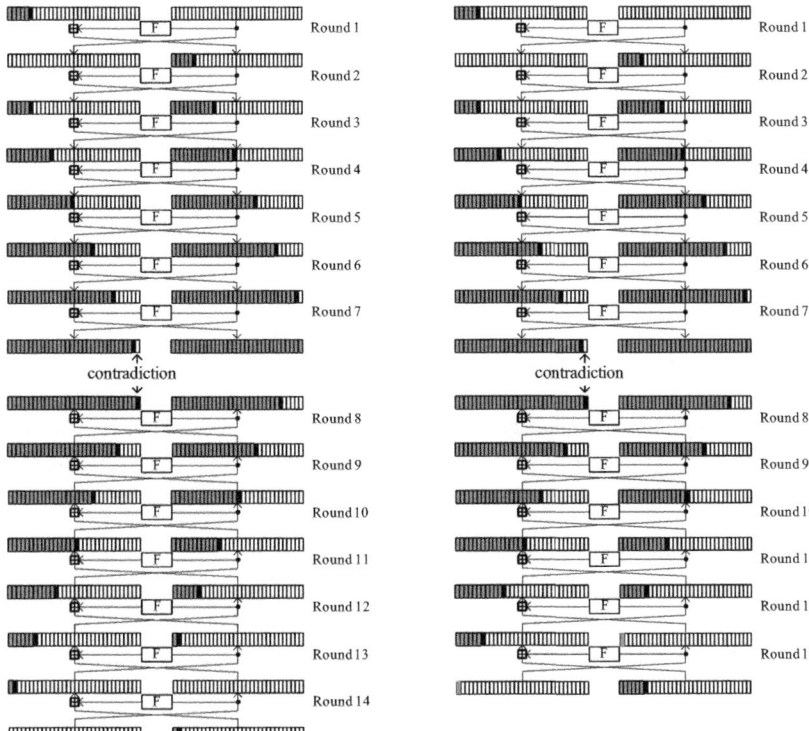

Fig. 4. Impossible Differentials of XTEA (left) and TEA (right)

4.2   Impossible Differential Attack of 23-Round XTEA

By placing the 14-round impossible differential on rounds $11 \sim 24$, we can attack XTEA from round 6 to round 28. This is clarified in Fig. 5.

Data Collection. We first construct $2^{5.3}$ structures of plaintexts, where in each structure the LSB of P_L and the 6 least significant bits of P_R are fixed, whereas the other bits take all values. For each structure, ask for the encryption of the plaintexts to get the corresponding ciphertexts. By the birthday paradox, we can get $2^{57 \times 2 - 1} \times 2^{-29} = 2^{84}$ pairs that satisfy $(\Delta P_L)_1 = 1$, $(\Delta P_R)_6 = 1$, $(\Delta C_L)_{15} = 1$, $(\Delta C_R)_{10} = 1$, the 15 least significant bits of ΔC_L are 0, and the 10 least significant bits of ΔC_R are 0 in each structure. As a result, $2^{89.3}$ pairs are obtained since we have $2^{5.3}$ structures; the number of chosen plaintexts is $2^{62.3}$.

Key Recovery. In order to find if there are pairs obtained from the data collection phase that may follow the differential in Fig. 5, we need to guess the key bits and sieve the pairs in rounds $6 \sim 10$ and $25 \sim 28$. From Table 2 we know the subkey used in each round (namely K_1, K_3, K_0, K_0, K_0; and K_0, K_1, K_1, K_1), hence we know the key bits we have to guess in each step.

As mentioned above, for XTEA the round subkeys intervene in the round functions after the diffusion, hence from Property 1 one can deduce that the attacker does not always have to guess all the 32 bits of the subkey to sieve the pairs with the required differences.

The key recovery process is described in Table 3, where the second column stands for the bits that have to be guessed in each step. Note that in Step 6, guessing bits $1 \sim 6$ of K_3 only takes 2^5 times, since one-bit information is known from c_2. Similarly, it takes 2^{10} and 2^{12} guesses for bits $1 \sim 11$ and $23 \sim 25$ of K_0, respectively. The fifth and fourth columns of Table 3 are the rounds where the sieving is launched and the conditions that can be used to sieve; the last column shows the number of remaining pairs after each step (for each key guess). Consequently, we can get the time complexity (measured by the number of 23-round encryptions) of each step, which is given in column 3 of the table.

In Step 7, if there is a pair kept, then we discard the key guess and try another one. Otherwise, for this key guess we exhaustively search the remaining 2^{32} keys by trial encryptions, and then either output the correct key or try another 96-bit key guess.

Analysis of the Attack. From the data collection phase we know that the data complexity, i.e., the number of plaintexts we need is equal to $2^{62.3}$. In Step 7 of the key recovery phase, about $2^{96} \times (1 - 2^{-20})^{2^{23.3}} \approx 2^{82.2}$ 96-bit values (K_0, K_1, K_3) will remain. Since the trial encryptions need two plaintext-ciphertext pairs, the cost of the trial encryptions is about $2^{32} \times 2^{82.2} + 2^{50.2} = 2^{114.2}$ 23-round XTEA encryptions. The complexity of this step is about $2 \times 2^{96} \times (1 + (1 - 2^{-20}) + ... + (1 - 2^{-20})^{2^{23.3}-1}) \times 2/23 + 2^{114.2} \approx 2^{113.5} + 2^{114.2} \approx 2^{114.9}$ encryptions, which is also the dominating time complexity of the attack. The memory complexity to store the pairs is $2^{94.3}$ bytes.

Reducing the Time Complexity. If we prepare the pairs that satisfy the conditions of rounds 8, 9 and 10 by precomputation, we can avoid guessing bits $1 \sim 25$ of K_0 by doing some table look-ups and memory accesses. If the same data complexity is used, the time complexity will be dominated by the trial encryptions used to discard the remaining keys. Hence we also increase the data complexity to 2^{63} by choosing 2^6 structures. First we illustrate the procedure of precomputation: we choose $\Delta L_{10} = D[27]$ and $\Delta R_{10} = 0$, for each K_0, L_{10} and R_{10}, decrypt all $(L_{10}, L_{10} \oplus \Delta L_{10})$ and $(R_{10}, R_{10} \oplus \Delta R_{10})$ to get $(L_7, L_7 \oplus \Delta L_7)$ and $(R_7, R_7 \oplus \Delta R_7)$ (the subkey used in round 8, 9 and 10 is K_0); then insert bits $1 \sim 25$ of K_0 into a hash table T indexed by $(L_7, R_7, \Delta L_7, \Delta R_7, (K_0)_{26 \sim 32})$. There are $2^{64} \times 2^{35} \times 2^7 = 2^{106}$ $(L_7, R_7, \Delta L_7, \Delta R_7, (K_0)_{26 \sim 32})$s since $\Delta L_7 = D[12]$ and $\Delta R_7 = D[17]$; however, only $2^{64} \times 2^5 \times 2^{32} = 2^{101}$ $(L_{10}, R_{10}, \Delta L_{10}, \Delta R_{10}, K_0)$s can be chosen, which means that only a fraction 2^{-5} of the rows in Table T are not empty, and each non-empty row contains one $(K_0)_{1 \sim 25}$ on average. The complexity of precomputation is $2 \times 2^{101} = 2^{102}$ 3-round encryptions.

Table 3. Attack on 23-Round XTEA

Step	Guess Bits	Complexity	Sieve on	Conds	Pairs Kept
1	$K_1 : 1 \sim 12$	$2^{97.8}$	round 6	10	$2^{79.3}$
2	$K_1 : 13 \sim 22$	$2^{97.8}$	round 28	10	$2^{69.3}$
3	$K_1 : 23 \sim 32$	$2^{98.8}$	round 26,27	20	$2^{49.3}$
4	$K_0 : 26 \sim 32, c_1*$	$2^{85.8}$	round 25	6	$2^{43.3}$
5	$K_3 : 7 \sim 17, c_2\dagger$	$2^{90.8}$	round 7	10	$2^{33.3}$
6	$K_3 : 1 \sim 6, 18 \sim 32, K_0 : 12 \sim 22, c_3\ddagger$	$2^{103.8}$	round 8	10	$2^{23.3}$
7	$K_0 : 1 \sim 11, 23 \sim 25$	$2^{114.9}$	round 9,10	20	–

$*c_1$ is the 26th carry in the left modular addition of the 25th round
$\dagger$ c_2 is the 7th carry in the left modular addition of the 7th round
$\ddagger$ c_3 is the 12th carry in the left modular addition of the 8th round

With Table T, we can replace Step 6 and Step 7 of the key recovery procedure as follows: we construct another table Γ that contains all values of bits $1 \sim 25$ of K_0. In Step 6, after guessing bits $1 \sim 6, 18 \sim 32$ of K_3, we calculate $(L_7, R_7, \Delta L_7, \Delta R_7)$ and access the value from the corresponding row of Table T. If there is a value in the row, we delete this $(K_0)_{1 \sim 25}$ from Table Γ. For each guess of K_1, K_3 and bits $26 \sim 32$ of K_0, we get 2^{34} pairs before accessing Table T; a fraction 2^{-5} of the 2^{34} pairs will access Table T to get a $(K_0)_{1 \sim 25}$, which will be then deleted from Γ. Consequently, $2^{64} \times 2^7 \times 2^{25} \times (1 - 2^{-25})^{2^{29}} \approx 2^{73.6}$ (K_0, K_1, K_3) will remain, which have to be further tested by trial encryptions with each K_2. The complexity of this procedure is 2^{107} one-round encryptions, 2^{101} memory accesses to Table T, 2^{101} memory accesses to Table Γ and $2^{105.6}$ trial encryptions. If we assume that one memory access to Table Γ is equivalent to one one-round encryption, then the dominating complexity is 2^{101} memory accesses to Table T and $2^{105.6}$ trial encryptions, which is also the dominating complexity of the whole attack. The memory complexity of the attack is about 2^{103} bytes required for Table T.

4.3   Impossible Differential Attack of 17-Round TEA

Using the 13-round impossible differential, we can attack the first 17 rounds of TEA by extending the impossible differential forward and backward for two rounds (see Fig. 5).

Note from [9] one can deduce that the effective key size of TEA is only 126 bits: if the MSBs of K_0 and K_1 flip simultaneously, the output value of the round will be the same; actually, the same phenomenon happens for K_2 and K_3. As a result, every key value has three equivalent keys, which allows us to guess only one of the 4 equivalent keys when we mount an impossible differential attack on TEA. At the end of the attack, if we output one correct key, there are three other keys that are also correct.

In the data collection phase, we construct 2^{30} structures of plaintexts with the least 16 bits of P_L and the least 21 bits of P_R fixed, while the other bits take

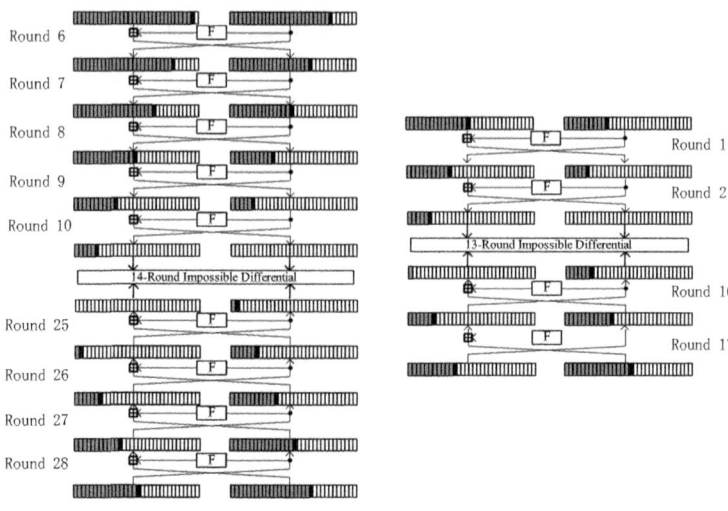

Fig. 5. 23-Round Attack on XTEA (left) and 17-Round Attack on TEA (right)

all values. Ask for the encryptions to get the ciphertexts; for each structure we can get $2^{53-39} = 2^{14}$ pairs that satisfy the required differences of the plaintext and ciphertext by the birthday paradox. Then the total number of pairs kept after the data collecting phase is 2^{44}.

Observe that K_0 and K_1 are used in the first and the 17th round, and K_2 and K_3 are used in the second and the 16th round. Hence for the remaining pairs, we first guess K_0 and K_1, partially encrypt the first round and discard the pairs that do not meet the condition of ΔR_1; then decrypt the 17th round and discard the pairs whose ΔL_{16} do not satisfy the required form. The number of pairs that meet the conditions should be 2^{24}; and the complexity of this step is about $2 \times 2^{107} + 2 \times 2^{97} = 2^{108}$ one-round encryptions, equivalent to 2^{104} 17-round encryptions.

Then we guess bits $21 \sim 32$ of K_2 and K_3, the 22th carry of the left modular addition in round 2, and the 26th carry of the left modular addition in round 16. For the remaining pairs, we partially encrypt round 2 and round 16, and keep only the pairs that satisfy the required differences. If there is a pair kept, then we discard the key guess and try another one. Otherwise, for this key guess we exhaustively search the remaining key values by trial encryption, and then either output the correct key or try another guess. Considering the equivalent keys, the key values we guessed are 88 bits (including the guessed carries); the expected number of remaining 88-bit key guesses is about $2^{88} \times (1 - 2^{-20})^{2^{24}} \approx 2^{65.6}$. Since each of the remaining key guesses has to be exhaustively searched with the other 2^{38} key values, so the time complexity of this step is about $2 \times 2^{88} \times (1 + (1 - 2^{-20}) + (1 - 2^{-20})^2 + ... + (1 - 2^{-20})^{2^{24}}) \times 2/17 + 2^{65.6+38} \approx 2^{106.3}$ encryptions; thus the time complexity of the attack is about $2^{106.3} + 2^{104} \approx 2^{106.6}$. The data complexity is 2^{57} and the memory complexity is 2^{49} bytes.

5 Impossible Differential Cryptanalysis of Reduced HIGHT

In this section, we improve the 26-round impossible differential attack on HIGHT in [20] by using a 16-round impossible differential that is similar to that of [20] (see Fig. 6a). In order to take advantage of the redundancy in the key schedule, we carefully choose the beginning and ending rounds of the impossible differential, which are round 10 and round 25, respectively. The attack excludes the initial whitening layer (as in [20]), and works for round 5 to round 30 (see Fig. 6b). In addition, a 27-round impossible differential attack with both the initial and final whitening layers, which is slightly better than exhaustive search, is also proposed based on the 16-round impossible differential in [20] (see Fig. 7a).

i	ΔX_7^i	ΔX_6^i	ΔX_5^i	ΔX_4^i	ΔX_3^i	ΔX_2^i	ΔX_1^i	ΔX_0^i
9	0	0	0	0	e_1	0	0	0
10	0	0	0	e_1	0	0	0	0
11	0	?	e_1	0	0	0	0	0
12	?	e_1	0	0	0	0	0	?
13	e_1	0	0	0	0	?	?	?
14	0	0	0	?	?	?	?	e_1
15	0	?	?	?	?	?	e_1	0
16	?	?	?	?	?	e_1	0	?
17	?	?	?	?	e_1	?	?	?
17	?	?	?	?	e_0	$0x80$	?	?
18	?	?	?	e_1	$0x80$	0	?	?
19	?	?	e_1	$0x80$	0	0	?	?
20	?	e_1	$0x80$	0	0	0	?	?
21	e_1	$0x80$	0	0	0	0	?	?
22	$0x80$	0	0	0	0	0	?	e_4
23	0	0	0	0	0	0	e_4	$0x80$
24	0	0	0	0	0	0	$0x80$	0
25	0	0	0	0	0	$0x80$	0	0

(a) The 16-Round Impossible Differential

i	ΔX_7^i	ΔX_6^i	ΔX_5^i	ΔX_4^i	ΔX_3^i	ΔX_2^i	ΔX_1^i	ΔX_0^i
P	?	e_1	0	0	?	?	?	?
4	?	e_1	0	0	?	?	?	?
5	e_1	0	0	0	?	?	?	?
6	0	0	0	0	?	?	?	e_1
7	0	0	0	0	?	?	e_1	0
8	0	0	0	0	?	e_1	0	0
9	0	0	0	0	e_1	0	0	0
Impossible Differential								
25	0	0	0	0	0	$0x80$	0	0
26	0	0	0	e_1	$0x80$	0	0	0
27	0	?	e_1	$0x80$	0	0	0	0
28	?	e_1	$0x80$	0	0	0	0	?
29	e_1	0	0	0	0	?	?	?
30	$0x80$	0	0	?	?	?	?	e_0
C	e_0	$0x80$	0	0	?	?	?	?

(b) Impossible Differential Attack on 26-Round HIGHT

Fig. 6.

5.1 Improved Impossible Differential Attack on 26-Round HIGHT

In order to reduce the time complexity of the 26-round attack in [20], we choose a similar impossible differential and a different beginning round; the data complexity is slightly higher because we want to reduce the complexity of the final trial encryptions that would otherwise dominate the complexity. Precomputation is also used to reduce the time complexity.

Data Collection. Construct $2^{13.6}$ structures with P_4, P_5 fixed and for which $P_0, ..., P_3, P_6, P_7$ take all values. Ask for the encryptions of all the plaintexts to get the corresponding ciphertexts. Since the ciphertext pairs with the difference

$((???????0)_2, 0x80, 0, 0, ?, ?, ?, ?)$ are required, and there is one more condition in the plaintext difference, which is $\Delta P_{6,0} = 1$; by the birthday paradox, there are $2^{82.6}$ pairs left.

Precomputation. Three pre-computed tables α, β and ϵ will be set up for the sake of reducing the complexity in the key recovery phase. The purpose of setting up α is finding all the $(X_2^6, \Delta X_2^6)$, $(X_1^6, \Delta X_1^6)$, $(X_0^6, \Delta X_0^6)$, MK_{12} and MK_{15} which satisfy $\Delta X_4^8 = 0$. Hence we choose all values of X_4^8, X_3^8, ΔX_3^8, X_1^7, ΔX_1^7, MK_{12} and MK_{15}, calculate $(X_2^6, \Delta X_2^6)$, $(X_1^6, \Delta X_1^6)$, and $(X_0^6, \Delta X_0^6)$ by $1/2$ round decryptions and insert MK_{15} to the row of α indexed by $(X_2^6, \Delta X_2^6, X_1^6, \Delta X_1^6, X_0^6, \Delta X_0^6, MK_{12})$. Hence there is one MK_{15} in each row on average; the size of α is 2^{55} bytes as there are only 2^7 ΔX_0^6s. When constructing Table β, all values of X_2^{25}, X_3^{25}, X_2^{26}, MK_7 and MK_{11} are chosen, then we compute X_3^{27}, X_4^{27} and $(X_5^{27}, \Delta X_5^{27})$, and insert MK_{11} to the row indexed by $(X_3^{27}, X_4^{27}, X_5^{27}, \Delta X_5^{27}, MK_7)$. Since there are 2^{40} tuples $(X_2^{25}, X_3^{25}, X_2^{26}, MK_7, MK_{11})$, but only 2^{39} tuples $(X_3^{27}, X_4^{27}, X_5^{27}, \Delta X_5^{27}, MK_7)$ are possible $(\Delta X_5^{27} = (???????1)_2)$, we have 2^{39} rows in β with 2 MK_{11} values in each row on average. The setting of Table ϵ is also similar: we choose all values of X_4^9, X_3^9, ΔX_3^9, X_1^8, MK_7 and MK_{11}, and calculate X_0^7, $(X_1^7, \Delta X_1^7)$, $(X_2^7, \Delta X_2^7)$; then insert X_0^7 to the row indexed by $(X_1^7, \Delta X_1^7, X_2^7, \Delta X_2^7, MK_7, MK_{11})$. There is one X_0^7 in each row on average. The sizes of β and ϵ are 2^{40} bytes and 2^{48} bytes, respectively. Constructing Table α dominates the time complexity of the precomputation, which is about 2^{56} $1/2$-round encryptions. To better illustrate the precomputation, we depict it in Fig. 8a;

Key Recovery. The key recovery phase is described in Table 4, where the second column contains the key bytes/bits which are guessed in the step, the third column indicates the whitening keys/subkeys used in the step to calculate the values that are needed, the fourth column gives the intermediate values that can be calculated in the step, the fifth column stands for the time complexity of each step, the sixth column gives the number of bit conditions which can be used, the seventh column indicates the number of the pairs that are kept after each step and the last column gives the position of Feistel branches where the sieving occurs ((x, y) means the y-th branch of the x-th round, where the rightmost branch is the 0th one). To better illustrate the procedure, we also give the subkeys used, as well as the corresponding master key bytes, in Table 5 in the Appendix; the subkeys that have to be guessed in the attack are in bold.

In Step 1, for each remaining pair from the data collection phase, we guess MK_0 and discard the pairs that do not satisfy $\Delta X_4^5 = 0$ by $1/4$-round encryptions. So the number of pairs kept after this step is $2^{82.6-8} = 2^{74.6}$ and the complexity of this step is about $2 \times 2^{82.6} \times 2^8 \times 1/4 \times 1/26 \approx 2^{84.9}$ 26-round encryptions. Steps $2 \sim 7$ are similar; we guess the subkey bytes, calculate the intermediate value and discard the pairs that do not meet the conditions. In Step 8, we do not guess all 8 bits of MK_8 at once, but guess them bit by bit from the LSB to the MSB by using the diffusion property mentioned in Sect. 3. Once we guess one bit of MK_8, we can compute the corresponding bit of ΔX_4^7 and discard the pairs that do not meet the condition. Since 8 bits of MK_8 should be guessed in 8 times, the complexity of this step is $2 \times 8 \times 2^{72} \times 2^{42.6} \times 1/4 \times 1/26 \approx 2^{111.9}$. Step 9 is similar to Step 8, except that we have to carry out $1/2$-round decryption for each pair other than $1/4$-round in Step 8.

In Step 11, for each pair obtained from Step 10 we first access Table α to get a value of MK_{15}, then we calculate X_3^{27} to access Table β. Two MK_{11} can be obtained on average, for each of the values, we access Table ϵ to get X_0^7 and calculate MK_{10} as X_6^6, X_7^6 are already known. The corresponding $(MK_{15}, MK_{11}, MK_{10})$ should be discarded. After processing all the pairs, if any tuples $(MK_{15}, MK_{11}, MK_{10})$ remain, we output them with the guessed $(MK_0, MK_1, MK_2, MK_3, MK_4, MK_5, MK_6, MK_7, MK_8, MK_9, MK_{12})$, and exhaustively search them with the remaining 16-bit key. Otherwise, we try another guess for $(MK_0, MK_1, MK_2, MK_3, MK_4, MK_5, MK_6, MK_7, MK_8, MK_9, MK_{12})$. In this step, $2^{88} \times 2^{26.6} = 2^{114.6}$ $1/4$-round decryptions (equivalent to $2^{107.9}$ encryptions) should be performed to compute X_3^{27}; $2 \times 2^{88} \times 2^{26.6} = 2^{115.6}$ $1/4$-round decryptions (equivalent to $2^{108.9}$ encryptions) should be performed to calculate MK_{10}. We also need $2^{88} \times 2^{26.6} = 2^{114.6}$ memory accesses to Table α, $2^{115.6}$ memory accesses to Table β and $2^{115.6}$ memory accesses to Table ϵ. After analyzing all the pairs, we expect $2^{112} \times (1 - 2/2^{24})^{2^{26.6}} \approx 2^{95}$ 112-bit key $(MK_0, MK_1, MK_2, MK_3, MK_4, MK_5, MK_6, MK_7, MK_8, MK_9, MK_{10}, MK_{11} MK_{12}, MK_{15})$ will remain. So the complexity of the exhaustive search is about $2^{111} + 2^{47} \approx 2^{111}$.

If we count one memory access to tables α, β and ϵ as one-round encryption, then the complexity of Step 11 will be about $2^{116.6} \times 1/26 + 2^{111} \approx 2^{112.5}$. From Table 4, we can deduce the time complexity, which is about $2^{110.8} + 2^{109.9} + 2^{109.9} + 2^{111.9} + 2^{112.9} + 2^{112.5} \approx 2^{114.35}$ encryptions. The data complexity of the attack is $2^{61.6}$ and the memory complexity is $2^{87.6}$ bytes.

5.2 Impossible Differential Attack on 27-Round HIGHT

Placing the impossible differential of [20] on round 10 to round 25, an attack on 27-round HIGHT can be mounted by discarding some of the wrong subkeys in rounds $4 \sim 9$ and $26 \sim 30$, see Fig. 7b in the Appendix. Note that for the 27-round attack, we take both the initial and final whitening layers into account.

Data Collection. Construct 2^2 structures with P_0 fixed and for which $P_1, ..., P_7$ take all values. Ask for the encryptions of all the plaintexts to get the corresponding ciphertexts. Since the ciphertext pairs with the difference $(?, ?, ?, ?, (???????0)_2, 0x80, 0, 0)$ are required, and there is one more condition in the plaintext difference, which is $\Delta P_{1,0} = 1$; by the birthday paradox, there are 2^{87} pairs left. Since the whitening keys are considered in our attack, we have:

$$X_0^3 = P_0 \boxplus WK_0, X_1^3 = P_1, X_2^3 = P_2 \oplus WK_1, X_3^3 = P_3,$$
$$X_4^3 = P_4 \boxplus WK_2, X_5^3 = P_5, X_6^3 = P_6 \oplus WK_3, X_7^3 = P_7.$$
$$C_7 = X_0^{30}, C_0 = X_1^{30} \boxplus WK_4, C_1 = X_2^{30}, C_2 = X_3^{30} \oplus WK_5,$$
$$C_3 = X_4^{30}, C_4 = X_5^{30} \boxplus WK_6, C_5 = X_6^{30}, C_6 = X_7^{30} \oplus WK_7.$$

Precomputation. Before the key recovery procedure, a precomputation is carried out for the sake of reducing the time complexity. We first choose all values of MK_1, MK_8, MK_9, MK_{13}, MK_{14}, X_0^9, X_7^9, ΔX_7^9, X_0^8, X_5^8, X_3^7, X_6^{25}, X_7^{25}, X_6^{26} and X_6^{27}, calculate $(X_6^6, X_6^{'6})$, $(X_5^6, X_5^{'6})$, $(X_4^6, X_4^{'6})$, X_3^6 and X_2^6 by 3-round decryption; and X_1^{29}, $(X_3^{29}, \Delta X_3^{29})$, X_7^{28} and X_3^{30} by 5-round encryption (see Fig. 8b in the Appendix). Then insert (MK_8, MK_9) to a hash table H indexed by $(MK_1,$ MK_{13}, MK_{14}, $(X_6^6, X_6^{'6})$, $(X_5^6, X_5^{'6})$, $(X_4^6, \Delta X_4^6)$, X_3^6, X_2^6, X_1^{29}, $(X_3^{29}, \Delta X_3^{29})$, X_7^{28}, $X_3^{30})$. There are 2^7 ΔX_7^9s, 2^7 ΔX_4^6s and 2^7 ΔX_3^{29}s, hence on average only a fraction 2^{-7} of the rows are not empty; and each non-empty row consists of one value (MK_8, MK_9). The complexity of the precomputation is less than 2^{89} three-round encryptions.

Key Recovery. The key recovery procedure is demonstrated in Table 7 in the Appendix; Table 7 has the same meaning as Table 4. Table 6 is also given in the Appendix to illustrate the subkeys that have to be guessed.

Table 4. Key Recovery Procedure of the Attack on 26-Round HIGHT

Step	Guess Bits	Known Keys	Known Values	Complexity	Conds	Pairs Kept	Sieve on
1	MK_0	SK_{17}	X_4^5	$2^{84.9}$ EN	8	$2^{74.6}$	$(5,1)$
2	MK_1, MK_6	WK_5, SK_{117}	X_3^{29}	$2^{92.9}$ EN	8	$2^{66.6}$	$(30,1)$
3	MK_5	WK_4, SK_{116}, SK_{112}	$X_1^{29}, \Delta X_1^{29}, X_1^{28}$	$2^{93.9}$ EN	8	$2^{58.6}$	$(29,0)$
4	MK_4, MK_7	SK_{16}, SK_{21}	$X_2^5, \Delta X_2^5, X_4^6$	$2^{101.9}$ EN	8	$2^{50.6}$	$(6, 1)$
5	MK_3, MK_9	WK_7, SK_{119}, SK_{115}, SK_{111}	$X_7^{29}, \Delta X_7^{29}, X_7^{28}$, $\Delta X_7^{28}, X_7^{27}$	$2^{110.8}$ EN	8	$2^{42.6}$	$(28,3)$
6	MK_2	SK_{19}, SK_{20}	$X_0^5, X_2^6, \Delta X_2^6$	$2^{109.9}$ EN	–	$2^{42.6}$	–
7	–	SK_{118}, SK_{114}, WK_6	X_5^{29}, X_5^{28}	$2^{109.9}$ EN	–	$2^{42.6}$	–
8	MK_8†	SK_{25}	X_4^7	$2^{111.9}$ EN	8	$2^{34.6}$	$(7,1)$
9	MK_{12}†	SK_{110}, SK_{106}	$X_5^{27}, \Delta X_5^{27}, X_5^{26}$	$2^{112.9}$ EN	8	$2^{26.6}$	$(27,2)$
10	–	SK_{18}, SK_{19}, SK_{22}, SK_{23}	X_0^6, X_7^6, X_0^6, $\Delta X_0^6, X_1^6, \Delta X_1^6$	$2^{109.9}$ EN	–	$2^{26.6}$	–
11	(accessing the pre-computed tables) Complexity: $2^{116.6}$ MA + 2^{111} EN						

MA: memory accesses; EN: 26-round HIGHT encryptions.
† The key byte is guessed bit by bit from the LSB to the MSB.

Step 1 and Step 2 are trivial: we guess the key bytes and test whether a 0 difference can be obtained. In Step 3 we guess MK_1 and MK_6 to calculate $(X_3^{29}, X_3^{'29})$; in Step 4, MK_{14} is guessed to calculate $(X_6^4, X_6^{'4})$ without discarding any pairs. In order to reduce the time complexity of Step 5, we guess MK_2 bit by bit, instead of guessing the whole byte at once. We guess the bits from the LSB to the MSB, so once we guess one bit of MK_2, we can compute the corresponding bit of ΔX_0^6 and discard the pairs that do not meet the condition. In Step 6, we do not guess any key byte, but calculate ΔX_4^{28} which can be used to sieve the pairs in Step 7. The other steps are similar except Step 13, to which have to be paid more attention. In Step 13, we first construct a small table γ which consists all values of (MK_8, MK_9); then guess MK_4 to look up table H. If the corresponding row is not empty, then access the value (MK_8, MK_9) and delete the value from γ. After analyzing all the pairs, if any values (MK_8, MK_9) remain, we output them with the guessed $(MK_0, MK_1, MK_2, MK_3, MK_4, MK_5, MK_6, MK_7, MK_{10}, MK_{12}, MK_{13}, MK_{14}, MK_{15})$, and exhaustively search them with the remaining 8-bit key. Otherwise, we try another guess for $(MK_0, MK_1, MK_2, MK_3, MK_4, MK_5, MK_6, MK_7, MK_{10}, MK_{12}, MK_{13}, MK_{14}, MK_{15})$.

We can see from Table 7 that all the values required to access table H can be calculated in Step 13 after guessing MK_4, since the only unknown values are X_4^6, ΔX_4^6 and X_7^{28}. The complexity to compute the values is less than 2^{128} one round encryptions, equivalent to $2^{123.25}$ 27-round encryptions. Since for each pair, Table H will be accessed with probability 2^{-7}, it will be accessed 2^{16} times for each key guess; hence the number of memory accesses is about $2^{104} \times 2^{16} = 2^{120}$. As each memory access discards one value (MK_8, MK_9) on average, about $2^{120} \times (1 - 2^{-16})^{2^{16}} = 2^{118.6}$ 120-bit keys will remain after processing all the pairs. For these remaining keys, we also need to guess the remaining 8 bits of the main key and test the $2^{118.6} \times 2^8 = 2^{126.6}$ keys by trial encryptions. As trial encryption needs 2 plaintext-ciphertext pairs, the complexity of the trial encryptions is about $2^{126.6} + 2^{62.6} \approx 2^{126.6}$ encryptions. Step 13 dominates the time complexity of the attack, which is $2^{126.6}$ encryptions and 2^{120} memory accesses. The data complexity is 2^{58} and the memory complexity is 2^{120} bytes for storing Table H.

6 Conclusion

This paper introduces impossible differential attacks on the lightweight block ciphers TEA, XTEA and HIGHT which are based on simple operations like modular addition, XOR, shift and rotation. We first propose a method to derive impossible differentials for TEA and XTEA, which improves the previous 10-round and 12-round impossible differentials up to 15 rounds. With the 13-round and 14-round impossible differentials, attacks on 17-round TEA and 23-round XTEA can be achieved. If the full codebook is available to the adversary, attacks on 19-round TEA and 26-round XTEA can be mounted based on 15-round impossible differentials. By using some carefully constructed pre-computed tables, we also give improved impossible differential attacks on HIGHT reduced to 26 and 27 rounds. The method for finding impossible differentials can also be applied to the other ciphers with similar operations as TEA and XTEA.

Acknowledgement. We are grateful to the anonymous reviewers for their valuable comments on this paper. This work was supported in part by the Research Council K.U.Leuven: GOA TENSE, the IAP Program P6/26 BCRYPT of the Belgian State (Belgian Science Policy), and in part by the European Commission through the ICT program under contract ICT-2007-216676 ECRYPT II.

References

1. Biham, E., Biryukov, A., Shamir, A.: Cryptanalysis of Skipjack Reduced to 31 Rounds Using Impossible Differentials. In: Stern, J. (ed.) EUROCRYPT 1999. LNCS, vol. 1592, pp. 12–23. Springer, Heidelberg (1999)
2. Bogdanov, A., Rijmen, V.: Zero-Correlation Linear Cryptanalysis of Block Ciphers. IACR Cryptology ePrint Archive 2011, 123 (2011)
3. Bogdanov, A., Wang, M.: Zero Correlation Linear Cryptanalysis with Reduced Data Complexity. Pre-proceedings of FSE 2012 (2012)
4. Bouillaguet, C., Dunkelman, O., Leurent, G., Fouque, P.A.: Another Look at Complementation Properties. In: Hong, S., Iwata, T. (eds.) FSE 2010. LNCS, vol. 6147, pp. 347–364. Springer, Heidelberg (2010)
5. Daum, M.: Cryptanalysis of Hash Functions of the MD4-Family. PhD thesis, http://www.cits.rub.de/imperia/md/content/magnus/idissmd4.pdf
6. Hong, D., Sung, J., Hong, S., Lim, J., Lee, S., Koo, B., Lee, C., Chang, D., Lee, J., Jeong, K., Kim, H., Kim, J., Chee, S.: HIGHT: A New Block Cipher Suitable for Low-Resource Device. In: Goubin, L., Matsui, M. (eds.) CHES 2006. LNCS, vol. 4249, pp. 46–59. Springer, Heidelberg (2006)
7. Hong, S., Hong, D., Ko, Y., Chang, D., Lee, W., Lee, S.: Differential Cryptanalysis of TEA and XTEA. In: Lim, J.-I., Lee, D.-H. (eds.) ICISC 2003. LNCS, vol. 2971, pp. 402–417. Springer, Heidelberg (2004)
8. International Standardization of Organization (ISO): International Standard-ISO/IEC 18033-3, Information technology-Security techniques-Encryption algorithms -Part 3: Block ciphers (2010)
9. Kelsey, J., Schneier, B., Wagner, D.: Key-Schedule Cryptanalysis of IDEA, G-DES, GOST, SAFER, and Triple-DES. In: Koblitz, N. (ed.) CRYPTO 1996. LNCS, vol. 1109, pp. 237–251. Springer, Heidelberg (1996)
10. Kelsey, J., Schneier, B., Wagner, D.: Related-key Cryptanalysis of 3-WAY, Biham-DES, CAST, DES-X, NewDES, RC2, and TEA. In: Han, Y., Okamoto, T., Qing, S. (eds.) ICICS 1997. LNCS, vol. 1334, pp. 233–246. Springer, Heidelberg (1997)
11. Klimov, A., Shamir, A.: A New Class of Invertible Mappings. In: Kaliski Jr., B.S., Koç, Ç.K., Paar, C. (eds.) CHES 2002. LNCS, vol. 2523, pp. 470–483. Springer, Heidelberg (2003)
12. Knudsen, L.: DEAL - A 128-bit Block Cipher. In: NIST AES Proposal (1998)
13. Ko, Y., Hong, S., Lee, W., Lee, S., Kang, J.S.: Related Key Differential Attacks on 27 Rounds of XTEA and Full-Round GOST. In: Roy, B., Meier, W. (eds.) FSE 2004. LNCS, vol. 3017, pp. 299–316. Springer, Heidelberg (2004)
14. Koo, B., Hong, D., Kwon, D.: Related-Key Attack on the Full HIGHT. In: Rhee, K.-H., Nyang, D. (eds.) ICISC 2010. LNCS, vol. 6829, pp. 49–67. Springer, Heidelberg (2011)
15. Lee, E., Hong, D., Chang, D., Hong, S., Lim, J.: A Weak Key Class of XTEA for a Related-Key Rectangle Attack. In: Nguyên, P.Q. (ed.) VIETCRYPT 2006. LNCS, vol. 4341, pp. 286–297. Springer, Heidelberg (2006)
16. Lu, J.: Cryptanalysis of Reduced Versions of the HIGHT Block Cipher from CHES 2006. In: Nam, K.-H., Rhee, G. (eds.) ICISC 2007. LNCS, vol. 4817, pp. 11–26. Springer, Heidelberg (2007)
17. Lu, J.: Related-key Rectangle Attack on 36 Rounds of the XTEA Block Cipher. Int. J. Inf. Sec. 8(1), 1–11 (2009)
18. Moon, D., Hwang, K., Lee, W., Lee, S., Lim, J.: Impossible Differential Cryptanalysis of Reduced Round XTEA and TEA. In: Daemen, J., Rijmen, V. (eds.) FSE 2002. LNCS, vol. 2365, pp. 49–60. Springer, Heidelberg (2002)

19. Needham, R.M., Wheeler, D.J.: TEA Extensions. Tech. rep., University of Cambridge (October 1997)
20. Özen, O., Varıcı, K., Tezcan, C., Kocair, Ç.: Lightweight Block Ciphers Revisited: Cryptanalysis of Reduced Round PRESENT and HIGHT. In: Boyd, C., Nieto, J.G. (eds.) ACISP 2009. LNCS, vol. 5594, pp. 90–107. Springer, Heidelberg (2009)
21. Sekar, G., Mouha, N., Velichkov, V., Preneel, B.: Meet-in-the-Middle Attacks on Reduced-Round XTEA. In: Kiayias, A. (ed.) CT-RSA 2011. LNCS, vol. 6558, pp. 250–267. Springer, Heidelberg (2011)
22. Wheeler, D.J., Needham, R.M.: TEA, a Tiny Encryption Algorithm. In: Preneel, B. (ed.) FSE 1994. LNCS, vol. 1008, pp. 363–366. Springer, Heidelberg (1995)
23. Zhang, P., Sun, B., Li, C.: Saturation Attack on the Block Cipher HIGHT. In: Garay, J.A., Miyaji, A., Otsuka, A. (eds.) CANS 2009. LNCS, vol. 5888, pp. 76–86. Springer, Heidelberg (2009)

Appendix

Table 5. Subkeys Used in the Attack on 26-Round HIGHT

#Round	Subkey Used			
5	$SK_{19}(MK_2)$	$SK_{18}(MK_1)$	$SK_{17}(MK_0)$	$SK_{16}(MK_7)$
6	$SK_{23}(MK_6)$	$SK_{22}(MK_5)$	$SK_{21}(MK_4)$	$SK_{20}(MK_3)$
7	$SK_{27}(MK_{10})$	$SK_{26}(MK_9)$	$SK_{25}(MK_8)$	$SK_{24}(MK_{15})$
8	$SK_{31}(MK_{14})$	$SK_{30}(MK_{13})$	$SK_{29}(MK_{12})$	$SK_{28}(MK_{11})$
9	$SK_{35}(MK_1)$	$SK_{34}(MK_0)$	$SK_{33}(MK_7)$	$SK_{32}(MK_6)$
...	...	...		
26	$SK_{103}(MK_1)$	$SK_{102}(MK_0)$	$SK_{101}(MK_7)$	$SK_{100}(MK_6)$
27	$SK_{107}(MK_{13})$	$SK_{106}(MK_{12})$	$SK_{105}(MK_{11})$	$SK_{104}(MK_{10})$
28	$SK_{111}(MK_9)$	$SK_{110}(MK_8)$	$SK_{109}(MK_{15})$	$SK_{108}(MK_{14})$
29	$SK_{115}(MK_4)$	$SK_{114}(MK_3)$	$SK_{113}(MK_2)$	$SK_{112}(MK_1)$
30	$SK_{119}(MK_0)$	$SK_{118}(MK_7)$	$SK_{117}(MK_6)$	$SK_{116}(MK_5)$
Post-Whitening	$WK_7(MK_3)$	$WK_6(MK_2)$	$WK_5(MK_1)$	$WK_4(MK_0)$

i	ΔX_7^i	ΔX_6^i	ΔX_5^i	ΔX_4^i	ΔX_3^i	ΔX_2^i	ΔX_1^i	ΔX_0^i
9	e_1	0	0	0	0	0	0	0
10	0	0	0	0	0	0	0	e_1
11	0	0	0	0	0	?	e_1	0
12	0	0	0	?	?	e_1	0	0
13	0	?	?	?	e_1	0	0	0
14	?	?	?	e_1	0	0	0	?
15	?	?	e_1	0	0	?	?	?
16	?	e_1	0	?	?	?	?	?
17	e_1	?	?	?	?	?	?	?
17	e_0	0x80	?	?	?	?	?	?
18	0x80	0	?	?	?	?	?	e_1
19	0	0	?	?	?	?	e_1	0x80
20	0	0	?	?	?	e_1	0x80	0
21	0	0	?	?	e_1	0x80	0	0
22	0	0	?	e_4	0x80	0	0	0
23	0	0	e_4	0x80	0	0	0	0
24	0	0	0x80	0	0	0	0	0
25	0	0x80	0	0	0	0	0	0

(a) 16-Round Impossible Differential from [20]

i	ΔX_7^i	ΔX_6^i	ΔX_5^i	ΔX_4^i	ΔX_3^i	ΔX_2^i	ΔX_1^i	ΔX_0^i
P	?	?	?	?	?	?	e_1	0
3	?	?	?	?	?	?	e_1	0
4	?	?	?	?	?	e_1	0	0
5	?	?	?	?	e_1	0	0	0
6	?	?	?	e_1	0	0	0	0
7	?	?	e_1	0	0	0	0	0
8	?	e_1	0	0	0	0	0	0
9	e_1	0	0	0	0	0	0	0
	Impossible Differential							
25	0	0x80	0	0	0	0	0	0
26	0x80	0	0	0	0	0	0	e_1
27	0	0	0	0	0	?	e_1	0x80
28	0	0	0	?	?	e_1	0x80	0
29	0	?	?	?	e_1	0x80	0	0
30	?	?	?	e_0	0x80	0	0	?
C	?	?	?	?	e_0	0x80	0	0

(b) Impossible Differential Attack on 27-Round HIGHT

Fig. 7.

Table 6. Subkeys Used in the Attack on 27-Round HIGHT

#Round	Subkey Used			
Pre-Whitening	$WK_3(MK_{15})$	$WK_2(MK_{14})$	$WK_1(MK_{13})$	$WK_0(MK_{12})$
4	$SK_{15}(MK_{15})$	$SK_{14}(MK_{14})$	$SK_{13}(MK_{13})$	$SK_{12}(MK_{12})$
5	$SK_{19}(MK_2)$	$SK_{18}(MK_1)$	$SK_{17}(MK_0)$	$SK_{16}(MK_7)$
6	$SK_{23}(MK_6)$	$SK_{22}(MK_5)$	$SK_{21}(MK_4)$	$SK_{20}(MK_3)$
7	$SK_{27}(MK_{10})$	$SK_{26}(MK_9)$	$SK_{25}(MK_8)$	$SK_{24}(MK_{15})$
8	$SK_{31}(MK_{14})$	$SK_{30}(MK_{13})$	$SK_{29}(MK_{12})$	$SK_{28}(MK_{11})$
9	$SK_{35}(MK_1)$	$SK_{34}(MK_0)$	$SK_{33}(MK_7)$	$SK_{32}(MK_6)$
...	...	...	...	...
26	$SK_{103}(MK_1)$	$SK_{102}(MK_0)$	$SK_{101}(MK_7)$	$SK_{100}(MK_6)$
27	$SK_{107}(MK_{13})$	$SK_{106}(MK_{12})$	$SK_{105}(MK_{11})$	$SK_{104}(MK_{10})$
28	$SK_{111}(MK_9)$	$SK_{110}(MK_8)$	$SK_{109}(MK_{15})$	$SK_{108}(MK_{14})$
29	$SK_{115}(MK_4)$	$SK_{114}(MK_3)$	$SK_{113}(MK_2)$	$SK_{112}(MK_1)$
30	$SK_{119}(MK_0)$	$SK_{118}(MK_7)$	$SK_{117}(MK_6)$	$SK_{116}(MK_5)$
Post-Whitening	$WK_7(MK_3)$	$WK_6(MK_2)$	$WK_5(MK_1)$	$WK_4(MK_0)$

Table 7. Key Recovery Procedure of the Attack on 27-Round HIGHT

Step	Guess Bits	Known Keys	Known Values	Complexity	Conds	Pairs Left	Sieve on
1	MK_{15}	WK_3, SK_{15}	X_0^4	$2^{91.2}$ EN	8	2^{79}	(4,3)
2	MK_0, MK_3	WK_7, SK_{119}	X_7^{29}	$2^{99.2}$ EN	8	2^{71}	(30,3)
3	MK_6, MK_1	SK_{117}, WK_5	$X_3^{29}, \Delta X_3^{29}$	$2^{107.2}$ EN	–	2^{71}	–
4	MK_{14}	WK_1, SK_{14}	$X_6^4, \Delta X_6^4$	$2^{115.2}$ EN	–	2^{71}	–
5	MK_2 †	SK_{19}	X_0^5, X_2^6	$2^{118.2}$ EN	8	2^{63}	(5,3)
6	–	SK_{113}, SK_{109}	$X_3^{28}, \Delta X_3^{28}$	$2^{115.2}$ EN	–	2^{63}	–‡
7	MK_7 †	WK_6, SK_{118}	$X_5^{29}, \Delta X_5^{29}$	$2^{118.2}$ EN	8	2^{55}	(30,2)
8	–	SK_{114}	X_5^{28}	$2^{115.2}$ EN	8	2^{47}	(29,2)
9	MK_{13}	$SK_{13}, SK_{18}, SK_{23},$ WK_2	$X_4^4, \Delta X_4^4, X_6^5,$ $\Delta X_6^5, X_0^6$	$2^{115.2}$ EN	8	2^{39}	(6,3)
10	MK_5	WK_4, SK_{116}, SK_{108}	$X_1^{29}, X_1^{28}, X_1^{27}, \Delta X_1^{27}$	$2^{115.2}$ EN	–	2^{39}	–
11	MK_{10} †	SK_{104}	X_1^{26}	$2^{118.2}$ EN	8	2^{31}	(27,0)
12	MK_{12}	$WK_0, SK_{12}, SK_{17},$ SK_{22}, SK_{27}	$X_2^4, \Delta X_2^4, X_4^5,$ $\Delta X_4^5, X_6^6, \Delta X_6^6, X_0^7$	$2^{123.2}$ EN	8	2^{23}	(7,3)
13	MK_4	$SK_{16}, SK_{21}, SK_{26},$ SK_{107}, SK_{31} SK_{111}, SK_{115}	$X_4^6, \Delta X_4^6, X_7^{28}$	2^{120} MA + $2^{126.6}$ EN			*

MA: memory accesses; EN: 27-round HIGHT encryptions
† The key byte is guessed bit by bit from the LSB to the MSB.
‡ calculate ΔX_4^{28}
* the sieving is already done by precomputation

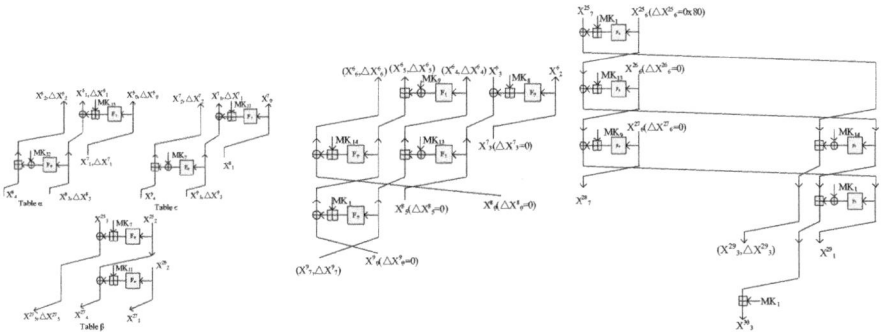

(a) The Construction of Tables α, β and ϵ in the Attack on 26-Round HIGHT

(b) Precomputation for Rounds 7 ~ 9 (top) and Rounds 26 ~ 30 (bottom) in the Attack on 27-Round HIGHT

Fig. 8.

Three-Subset Meet-in-the-Middle Attack on Reduced XTEA

Yu Sasaki[1], Lei Wang[2], Yasuhide Sakai[2], Kazuo Sakiyama[2], and Kazuo Ohta[2]

[1] NTT Secure Platform Laboratories, NTT Corporation
3-9-11 Midori-cho, Musashino-shi, Tokyo 180-8585 Japan
sasaki.yu@lab.ntt.co.jp
[2] The University of Electro-Communications
1-5-1 Choufugaoka, Choufu-shi, Tokyo, 182-8585 Japan
{lei.wang,s-yasu,sakiyama,kazuo.ota}@uec.ac.jp

Abstract. This paper presents an improved single-key attack on a block-cipher XTEA by using the three-subset meet-in-the-middle (MitM) attack. Firstly, a technique on a generic block-cipher is discussed. It points out that the previous work applying the splice-and-cut technique to the three-subset MitM attack contains incomplete arguments, and thus it requires a very large data complexity, which is close to the code book. This paper gives a corrected procedure to keep the data complexity small. Secondly, the three-subset MitM attack is applied for reduced-round XTEA, which is a 64-bit block-cipher with 64-round Feistel network and a 128-bit key. 25 rounds are attacked with 9 known plaintexts and $2^{120.40}$ XTEA computations, while the previous best single-key attack only reaches 23 rounds. In the chosen-plaintext model, the attack is extended to 28 rounds with 2^{37} chosen-plaintexts and $2^{120.38}$ computations.

Keywords: XTEA, 3-subset meet-in-the-middle, splice-and-cut, multi-pair match.

1 Introduction

Block-ciphers are one of the most fundamental symmetric-key primitives. In recent years, block-ciphers are required to be implemented in the resource-restricted environment such as an RFID tag. Due to this, the design and security of light-weight block-ciphers are receiving great attentions.

At FSE 1994, the block-cipher TEA was proposed by Wheeler and Needham [1]. Then, a series of block-ciphers called the TEA-family have been proposed.

- TEA was adopted in the Microsoft's Xbox gaming console for providing the hash function facility. However, an attack was proposed by Steil [2], which was based on a pioneering work by Kelsey, Schneier, and Wagner [3]. They also proposed a related-key attack [4].
- As a stronger version of TEA, Needham and Wheeler designed XTEA and Block TEA [5]. TEA and XTEA are implemented in the Linux kernel.

A. Mitrokotsa and S. Vaudenay (Eds.): AFRICACRYPT 2012, LNCS 7374, pp. 138–154, 2012.

– To correct the weaknesses of Block TEA, Needham and Wheeler designed Corrected Block TEA, which is called XXTEA [6]. However, an attack on full Block TEA and several weaknesses of XXTEA were pointed out by Saarinen [7]. Full XXTEA was also attacked by Yarrkov [8].

The full XTEA has not been attacked yet. In addition, XTEA is known to be suitable for the resource-restricted environment [9]. Hence, investigating the security of XTEA seems interesting and useful.

Several attacks on round-reduced XTEA are known. Related-key attacks and weak-key attacks can work on many rounds of XTEA [10–13]. On the other hand, single-key attacks without the weak-key assumption are more important in terms of the impact in practice. After the work by Moon et al. in 2002 [14] and Hong et al. in 2003 [15], the research on the single-key attack was stopped for a while. In 2011, Sekar et al. presented an attack on 23 rounds out of 64 rounds of XTEA with the MitM attack [16]. Recently, Chen et al. have presented another attack on 23 rounds with the impossible differential approach [17].

The MitM attack was introduced by Diffie and Hellman in 1977 [18]. Then, Chaum and Evertse applied it to reduced-round DES in 1985 [19] by exploiting the low diffusion of the key schedule to select subsets of key bits for the MitM guess. The basic idea is separating the block-cipher E_K into two sub-parts $E1_{k1}$ and $E2_{k2}$, where $k1$ and $k2$ are independent subkeys and $E_K = E2_{k2} \circ E1_{k1}$. For a pair of plaintext P and ciphertext C, an attacker independently computes $E1_{k1}(P)$ and $E2_{k2}^{-1}(C)$ for all possible $k1$ and $k2$, respectively. By checking the match of two results, wrong key candidates can be eliminated efficiently. The MitM attack is now widely applied to various block-ciphers. Note that several attacks that are a little bit different from the basic MitM attack are also called MitM attack. The attacks on AES [20] and XTEA [16] are such examples.

In recent years, the MitM attack was applied to various hash functions e.g. MD5 [21, 22], SHA-1 [23], SHA-2 [24], and many techniques were developed for the MitM attack on hash functions. In 2010, Bogdanov and Rechberger revisited the MitM attack on block-ciphers and proposed a framework called three-subset MitM attack [25]. It works efficiently against block-ciphers with a weak key schedule. This matches the property of light-weight ciphers on which a heavy key schedule cannot be implemented. Hence, the three-subset MitM attack is actively discussed presently. In addition, several researchers rearranged the techniques which were originally developed for hash functions, and applied them to block-ciphers [26–30].

Our Contributions

In this paper, we firstly point out the incomplete argument of the previous work [29], which applies the splice-and-cut technique [21] for the three-subset MitM attack. We show that its simple application will lead to a very large data complexity. We then propose a corrected procedure to keep the data complexity small. This procedure can be used for any block-cipher in generic. The optimization may be done depending on the detailed structure of the attack target.

Table 1. Comparison of key recovery attacks on reduced XTEA

	Single-key Attacks				Related-key Attacks				
Approach	Rounds	Time	Data	Ref.	Weak-key	Rounds	Time	Data	Ref.
Imp. Diff.	14	2^{85}	$2^{62.5}$ CPs	[14]		27	$2^{115.15}$	$2^{20.5}$ CPs	[11]
Trunc. Diff.	23	$2^{120.65}$	$2^{20.55}$ CPs	[15]	Yes	34	$2^{31.94}$	2^{62} CPs	[12]
MitM	23	$2^{117.00}$	18 KPs	[16]		36	$2^{126.44}$	$2^{64.98}$ CPs	[13]
Imp. Diff.	23	$2^{116.9}$	2^{62} CPs	[17]	Yes	36	$2^{104.33}$	$2^{63.83}$ CPs	[13]
3-Sub. MitM	25	$2^{120.40}$	9 KPs	**Ours**		37	2^{125}	2^{63} CPs	[10]
3-Sub. MitM	28	$2^{120.38}$	2^{37} CPs	**Ours**	Yes	51	2^{123}	2^{63} CPs	[10]

Secondly, by using this technique, the three-subset MitM attack is applied for reduced-round XTEA. The attack reaches 25 rounds in the known-plaintext model and 28 rounds in the chosen-plaintext model. The complexity of the attack is summarized in Table 1. As far as we know, our attack is the best in terms of the number of attacked rounds in a single-key setting.

Paper Outline

Section 2 describes the specification of XTEA. Section 3 summarizes the previous work. Section 4 explains the incompleteness of the previous attack procedure and describes a new generic technique for the three subset MitM attack on block-ciphers. Section 5 shows attacks on XTEA. Finally, we conclude the paper in Sect. 6.

2   Specification of XTEA

XTEA [5] has the block size of 64 bits and key size of 128 bits. It uses a 64-round Feistel network. The F-function of the Feistel network takes a 32-bit input x and produces a 32-bit output as:

$$F(x) = ((x \ll 4) \oplus (x \gg 5)) \boxplus x, \tag{1}$$

where '$\ll$' and '$\gg$' represent the left and right shifts (not rotations) respectively, '$\oplus$' represents the XOR, and '$\boxplus$' represents the modular addition over 2^{32}. The round function is described in Fig. 1

The 128-bit key K is separated into four 32-bit subkeys K_0, K_1, K_2, and K_3. The 64-bit input to round i consists of two 32-bit values L_{i-1} and R_{i-1}. First, the plaintext P is loaded into the state, namely $L_0 \| R_0 \leftarrow P$. Then, the following is computed recursively for $i = 0, 1, \ldots, 63$;

$$L_{i+1} \leftarrow R_i, \tag{2}$$

$$R_{i+1} \leftarrow L_i \boxplus ((\delta_i \boxplus K_{\pi(i)}) \oplus F(R_i)), \tag{3}$$

where δ_i is a pre-defined constant and $\pi(i) \in \{0, 1, 2, 3\}$ is a pre-defined subkey index in round i. The list of index $\pi(i)$ is shown in Table 2. Finally, $L_{64} \| R_{64}$ are produced as the ciphertext of P.

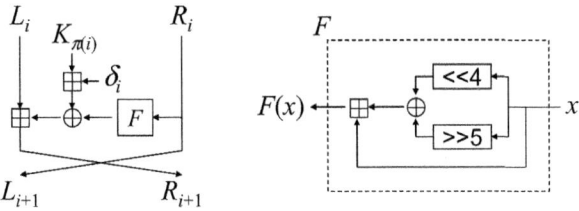

Fig. 1. Round function of XTEA

Table 2. Subkey index for each round

Round i	0	1	2	3	4	5	6	7	8	9	10	11	12	13	14	15
Index $\pi(i)$	0	3	1	2	2	1	3	0	0	0	1	3	2	2	3	1
Round i	16	17	18	19	20	21	22	23	24	25	26	27	28	29	30	31
Index $\pi(i)$	0	0	1	0	2	3	3	2	0	1	1	1	2	0	3	3
Round i	32	33	34	35	36	37	38	39	40	41	42	43	44	45	46	47
Index $\pi(i)$	0	2	1	1	2	1	3	0	0	3	1	2	2	1	3	1
Round i	48	49	50	51	52	53	54	55	56	57	58	59	60	61	62	63
Index $\pi(i)$	0	0	1	3	2	2	3	2	0	1	1	0	2	3	3	2

3   Previous Work

3.1   Previous Meet-in-the-Middle Attack on XTEA

At CT-RSA 2011, Sekar *et al.* presented a meet-in-the-middle attack on several intermediate 23 rounds of XTEA [16], e.g. from round 16 to 38, in total 23 rounds. Let E_{23} be the data processing transformation for 23 rounds. The main idea of this attack is separating E_{23} into an inner round I and outer rounds O_1 and O_2, namely $E_{23}(\cdot) = O_2 \circ I \circ O_1(\cdot)$, where one of the subkeys never appears in the outer rounds. Because all subkeys in the outer rounds are also used in an inner round, it is impossible to compute the inner and outer rounds independently. Hence this attack is a little bit different from the classical meet-in-the-middle attack, and we do not discuss it in this paper.

3.2   Three-Subset Meet-in-the-Middle Attack

The three-subset meet-in-the-middle attack is an approach of cryptanalysis on block-ciphers proposed by Bogdanov and Rechberger at SAC 2010 [25]. The framework is well summarized in [28] by Isobe. This attack essentially examines all possible key candidates. Because wrong keys can be filtered out efficiently by using the meet-in-the-middle technique, the attack can be faster than the exhaustive search.

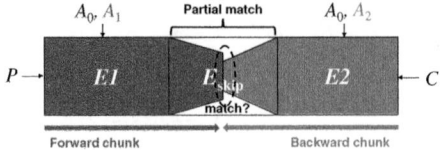

Fig. 2. Basic framework of 3-subset MitM attack with the partial match

Basic Framework. A block-cipher E_K with the block size of b bits is divided into two parts $E1_{K1}$ and $E2_{K2}$ so that $E_K(x) = E2_{K2} \circ E1_{K1}(x), x \in \{0, 1\}^b$, where $K1$ and $K2$ are sets of key bits involved in the computations of $E1$ and $E2$, respectively. $E1_{K1}$ is called the *forward chunk* and $E2_{K2}$ is called the *backward chunk*. $A_0 = K1 \cap K2$ is a common set of key bits used in both of $E1$ and $E2$. $A_1 = K1 \setminus K1 \cap K2$ and $A_2 = K2 \setminus K1 \cap K2$ are sets of key bits used in only $E1$ and only $E2$, respectively. The attack first prepares a pair of plaintext and ciphertext denoted by (P, C). The attack procedure is as follows.

MitM Phase

1. For all candidates of A_0, do as follows;
2. Compute $E1_{K1}(P)$ for all candidates of A_1, and store them in a table T.
3. For each value in A_2, compute $E2_{K2}^{-1}(C)$, and check whether or not the same value is in T. If the value exists, the key is stored as a valid key candidate.

Exhaustive Search Phase

4. Obtain another pair of plaintext and ciphertext denoted by (P', C'). For all valid key candidates, exhaustively check whether $E_K(P') = C'$ holds. If the equation holds, the key is stored as a valid key candidate.
5. Repeat Step 4 until the key space is reduced to 1.

Let ℓ be the size of the secret key. After the MitM phase, the key candidate space is reduced to $2^{\ell-b}$. With each iteration of the exhaustive search phase, the key candidate space is reduced by a factor of b bits. In step 2, $2^{|A_1|}$ values are stored, where $|A_1|$ is the number of elements in A_1. Therefore, the attack requires a memory to store $2^{|A_1|}$ values. The computational complexity for the MitM phase is $2^{|A_0|}(2^{|A_1|} + 2^{|A_2|})$ and the computational complexity for the exhaustive search phase is $2^{\ell-b} + 2^{\ell-2b} + \cdots$. Most of the case, the dominant complexity is $2^{|A_0|}(2^{|A_1|} + 2^{|A_2|})$. When $|A_1| = |A_2|$, the attack can be faster than the brute force attack by a factor of $2^{|A_1|}$. Therefore, finding two chunks with large $|A_1|$ and $|A_2|$ is important for the attacker.

Note that, E_K is often separated into three parts so that $E_K(\cdot) = E2_{K2} \circ E_{skip} \circ E1_{K1}(\cdot)$. This is illustrated in Fig. 2. In this case, the direct comparison of $E1_{K1}(P)$ and $E2_{K2}^{-1}(C)$ becomes impossible due to the existence of E_{skip}. However, the internal state inside E_{skip} often can be computed partially without the knowledge of subkeys. This is called *partial match*. As a result, by reducing the number of matched bits, the number of attacked rounds can be increased.

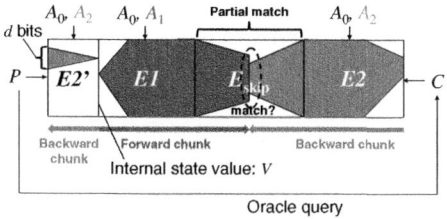

Fig. 3. Splice-and-cut technique for 3-subset MitM attack

Let m be the number of matched bits. As long as $m \geq |A_1| + |A_2|$, the attack is faster than the brute force attack by a factor of $2^{|A_1|}$. However, if $m < |A_1| + |A_2|$, the improved factor is reduced to 2^m. Hence, keeping m big is also important to mount an efficient MitM attack.

Recent Progress. Before Bogdanov and Rechberger presented the 3-subset meet-in-the-middle attack, the meet-in-the-middle attack was applied to various hash functions, e.g. MD5 [21, 22], HAVAL [31], SHA-1 [23], and SHA-2 [24]. Through these attacks, a lot of techniques for the meet-in-the-middle attack were proposed such as *splice-and-cut* [21] and *initial-structure* [22]. These techniques were developed in order to attack hash functions, and thus they cannot be directly applied to the 3-subset meet-in-the-middle attack whose targets are block-ciphers. However, several researchers reconstructed the techniques and successfully applied them to block-ciphers.

Wei *et al.* [29] applied the splice-and-cut technique [21] to the block-cipher KTANTAN. This is illustrated in Fig. 3. This enables the attacker to divide the target cipher E_K into $E2_{K2} \circ E_{\text{skip}} \circ E1_{K1} \circ E2'_{K2}$ instead of $E2_{K2} \circ E_{\text{skip}} \circ E1_{K1}$. Obviously, the search space of the chunk separation increases. The attack first fixes the value of the internal state between $E1_{K1}$ and $E2'_{K2}$, which is denoted by V. In the backward chunk, the attacker computes $P = E2'^{-1}_{K2}(V)$ for all possible values of A_2, and query P to the encryption oracle to obtain the corresponding ciphertext C. Then, $E2^{-1}_{K2}(C)$ is computed. Assume that the change of A_2 in the backward chunk only propagates to the partial bits (say d bits) in P. If the attacker has 2^d data (chosen plaintexts) for all possible such P in advance, the corresponding C can be queried. The data complexity increases depending on d, namely how the change of A_2 propagates to P. As [29] noted, we should avoid that the change of A_2 propagates to all bits in P. Otherwise, the attack requires the full code book. However, in Sect. 4, we will show that the discussion in [29] is not enough to perform the attack only with 2^d chosen plaintexts.

Bogdanov *et al.* [27] proposed a useful form of the initial-structure and applied it to full-round AES-128. The technique is called *biclique*. Because we do not discuss the application of the biclique for XTEA, we do not discuss its details.

4   Maintaining Small Data Complexity in Three-Subset MitM Attack with Splice-and-Cut Technique

In this section, we show that the discussion in [29] is not enough to perform the attack only with 2^d chosen plaintexts. We then propose the corrected procedure to keep the small data complexity even if the splice-and-cut technique is applied.

Let us use Fig. 3 to discuss the problem. The estimation of the data complexity by [29] can be summarized as follows.

> *Suppose that changing the value of A_2 only gives impact to d bits of the plaintext after computing $P = E2'^{-1}_{K2}(V)$. Then, the attack can be performed with 2^d chosen plaintexts.*

This argument is surely true as long as the value of A_0 is fixed. However, the meet-in-the-middle attack is repeated many times with changing the value of A_0, and the simple application of the procedure requires the data complexity of $2^{|A_0|+d}$. In many block-ciphers including KTANTAN and XTEA, the key size is bigger than the block size b. This means that the value of $|A_0|$ will be much bigger than the block size, and thus the data complexity becomes the same as the entire code book. Wei *et al.* [29] did not discuss the case where A_0 is changed[1].

The solution of this problem is that every time we change the value of A_0, we also change the internal state value V so that $b - d$ bits in the plaintext, which are not affected by A_2, always take the same value. However, achieving this is sometimes hard especially if the target cipher uses the Feistel network.

Let us discuss the case that $E2'^{-1}_{K2}$ covers 2 rounds of the Feistel ciphers whose round function consists of the key addition and a certain transformation F. This is depicted in Fig. 4. We assume that only a part of bits in $K_{\pi(i)}$ belong to A_2 and the other bits of $K_{\pi(i)}$ and all bits of $K_{\pi(i-1)}$ belong to A_0.

The impacts of changing A_2 is marked with blue lines, and we assume that only a limited number of bits in blue lines are influenced by changing A_2. We now consider the impact of changing the value of A_0. If we change the bits of $K_{\pi(i)}$ belonging to A_0 into various values, the value of $F(L_{i+1} \oplus K_{\pi(i)})$ takes various values. If the value of L_{i+1} is fixed in advance, we can compute $F(L_{i+1} \oplus K_{\pi(i)})$ and thus can modify R_{i+1} so that $b - d$ bits of R_{i-1} are always the fixed value. Then, in round $i - 1$, we also need to absorb the change of $F(L_i \oplus K_{\pi(i-1)})$ by modifying R_i. However, this is the contradiction in round i, where the value of $L_{i+1}(= R_i)$ needs to be fixed in advance. Consequently, fixing the $b - d$ bits of the plaintext for any A_0 cannot be done trivially.

We finally show that this problem can be solved, that is to say, the attack can work only with 2^d chosen plaintexts regardless of the cipher's structure. We stress that the value of d in this procedure is the number of bit positions in the plaintext which can be influenced by the change of neutral key bits. The worst-case configuration for the attacker is used to estimate the value of d. In other words, for any case, the change of the neutral key bits can impact to at most d bits. The procedure is depicted in Fig. 5. Assume that during the computation in

---

[1]   Bogdanov *et al.* [27] solved this problem in their analysis on AES.

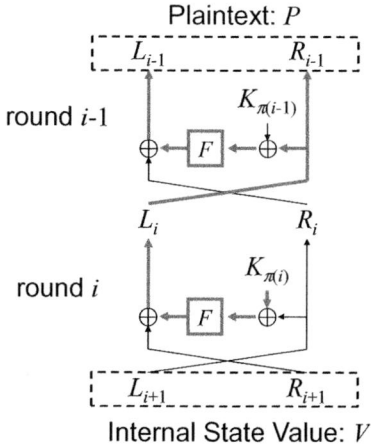

Plaintext: P

round i-1

$K_{\pi(i-1)}$

round i

$K_{\pi(i)}$

Internal State Value: V

Fig. 4. A problem of the splice-and-cut technique for block-ciphers. First, $L_{i+1}(= R_i)$ is fixed. Second, R_{i+1} is modified in round i. Third, R_i is modified in round $i-1$, but this is the contradiction against the first step.

Plaintext: P

fixed to 0 $P_{[0,d-1]}$ $P_{[d,b-1]}$ fixed to *fix*

$A0$, $A2$ → $E2_{K2}'$
fixed to 0

Internal State Value: V

Fig. 5. Computation of V which avoids increasing the data complexity

$E2_{K2}'^{-1}$, changing bits in A_2 only gives influence to at most d bits of the plaintext P. Without losing the generality, we assume that the left d bits are influenced. We denote the left d bits of P by $P_{0,d-1}$, and thus P is denoted by $P_{0,d-1} \| P_{d,b-1}$. At first, we choose a unique value for $b-d$ bits of $P_{d,b-1}$. We denote this value by *fix*. The goal is choosing the internal state value V so that *fix* can always be achieved for A_0.

1. Every time the bits in A_0 are chosen, do as follows;
2. Temporarily fix the value of d bits of $P_{0,d-1}$ and all bits in A_2, say 0.
3. Compute $V = E2'_{K2}(P_{0,d-1} \| P_{d,b-1})$ with chosen A_0 and fixed A_2.

When the attacker performs the meet-in-the-middle attack with the configuration of chosen A_0, she uses V as the internal state value. Then, $P_{d,b-1} = \textit{fix}$ is always satisfied and the attack can be performed with only 2^d chosen plaintexts.

Optimization of Our Procedure Depending on the Attack Target

In the previous section, the value of d was evaluated with the worst-case configuration. In this section, we explain that the worst-case-based evaluation may be improved by considering the details of the attack target.

Let us consider the structure of SHACAL-1 [32] as an example and apply the splice-and-cut technique for 2 rounds. The analysis is described in Fig. 6. $F(B, C, D)$ is a bitwise Boolean function which returns $(B \wedge C) \vee (\neg B \wedge D)$. Please refer to [32] for the detailed specification.

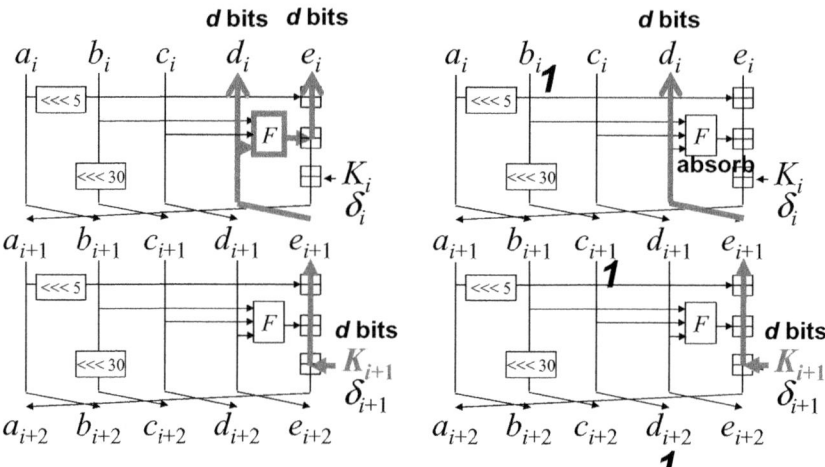

Fig. 6. Example of optimization for 2-round SHACAL-1. (Left) generic method requiring 2^{2d} chosen-plaintexts. (Right) optimization requiring 2^d chosen-plaintexts.

Assume that the most significant d bits are free bits for the backward chunk. In the worst case, changing d bits results in changing $2d$ bits of the plaintext. Hence, our generic method achieves the attack with 2^{2d} chosen-plaintexts. However, if inside of the F function is considered, the impact can be reduced to d bits by setting the value of d_{i+2} to 0xffffffff. In Fig. 6, we denote the values set to 0xffffffff by **1**. This illustrates the possibility of improving the generic method by considering the details of the attack target. Note that in some cases including our analysis on XTEA in the next section, the optimization is not necessary. The simple application of the generic method is already optimal.

5   Attacks on XTEA

5.1   Known Plaintext Attack on 25-Round XTEA

In this section, we propose a known plaintext attack on 25 rounds of XTEA with the single-key setting. Although the attack cost is a little bit worse than the previous best attack [16], the number of attacked rounds is extended. Note that the splice-and-cut technique is not used for this attack.

Chunk Separation. The chunk separation is shown in Table 3. The attacked rounds are from round 5 to 29, in total 25 rounds. The forward chunk covers the first 7 rounds, in which K_2 is not used in these rounds. The backward chunk covers the last 7 rounds, in which K_3 is not used in these rounds. Rounds 12 to 22, in total 11 rounds are skipped. In order to perform the match over skipped 11 rounds, we fix the least significant 21 bits of K_3 and K_2, and use the

Table 3. Chunk separation for known plaintext attack on 25-round XTEA

Round i	5	6	7	8	9	10	11	12	13	14	15	16	17	18	19	20	21	22	23	24	25	26	27	28	29
Index $\pi(i)$	1	3	0	0	0	1	3	2	2	3	1	0	0	1	0	2	3	3	2	0	1	1	1	2	0
	\multicolumn{7}{c}{forward chunk}							E_{skip}								backward chunk						

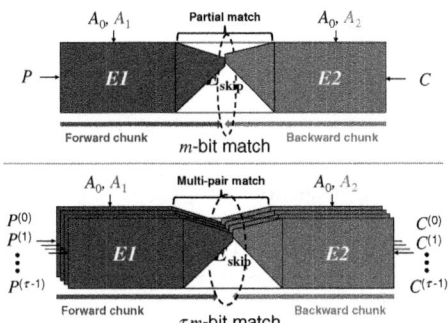

Fig. 7. (Top) match with one pair, (Bottom) multi-pair match

most significant 11 bits as the free bits for each chunk. Namely, $|A_1| = |A_2| = 11$. Inside E_{skip}, we only check the match of 1 bit for a pair of plaintext and ciphertext, namely $m = 1$. As explained in Sect. 3.2, because $m < |A_1| = |A_2|$, the simple application of the basic framework improves the complexity only by a factor of 2^1. In order to improve the attack efficiency, we use multi-pairs of plaintext/ciphertext $(P^{(j)}, C^{(j)})$ to check the match of two chunks.

Multi-pair Match. Assume $m = 1$ like our attack. Therefore, each plaintext/ciphertext pair produces 1-bit filtering condition. To filter out wrong key candidates more efficiently, we use multi-pairs rather than a single pair. This is illustrated in Fig. 7. As a result, with τ plaintext/ciphertext pairs, the 1-bit filtering condition is amplified into a τ-bit filtering function. The time complexity for each chunk becomes τ times (linear increase) to analyze τ pairs, instead 2^τ wrong key candidates can be filtered out (exponential increase). Hence, the efficiency of the entire attack increases.

In the following, we explain how to compute 1 matching bit during skipped 11 rounds in our attack. In the forward chunk, until the output of round 11 (L_{12}, R_{12}) can be computed in all bits. For round 12, in the computation of

$$R_{13} = L_{12} \boxplus ((\delta_{12} \boxplus K_2) \oplus F(R_{12})), \tag{4}$$

we do not know the value of the bit positions 21 to 31 of K_2, but we know the bit positions 0 to 20 of K_2. Hence, we cannot compute the bit positions 21 to 31 of R_{13} but can compute the bit positions 0 to 20 of R_{13}.

Table 4. Partial-match for 25-round XTEA. Each entry shows the known bit positions.

Forward chunk			Backward chunk		
j	L_j	R_j	j	L_j	R_j
12	31–0	31–0	23	31–0	31–0
13	31–0	20–0	22	20–0	31–0
14	20–0	15–0	21	15–0	20–0
15	15–0	10–0	20	10–0	15–0
16	10–0	5–0	19	5–0	10–0
17	5–0	0	18	0	5–0
18	0	?			

For round 13, R_{14} is computed as follows.

$$R_{14} = L_{13} \boxplus ((\delta_{13} \boxplus K_2) \oplus F(R_{13})), \tag{5}$$

$$F(R_{13}) = ((R_{13} \ll 4) \oplus (R_{13} \gg 5)) \boxplus R_{13}. \tag{6}$$

Because only the bit positions 0 to 20 of R_{13} are known, we can only compute the bit positions 0 to 15 of $F(R_{13})$. Hence, we can compute the bit positions 0 to 15 of R_{14}.

Similarly, we can trace the bit positions that can be computed. The result is shown in Table 4. As we process one round, the number of known bits decreases by 5 bits. Hence, we can compute the bit position 0 of L_{18}. The result for the backward chunk can be obtained in the same way, which is also shown in Table 4. We can compute the bit position 0 of L_{18}. Finally, we can check the match for 1 bit (bit position 0) of L_{18}.

To perform the multi-pair match, we use $\tau = 9$ pairs of known plaintext/ciphertext and apply the same matching method for 9 pairs simultaneously. Hence, we can check the match of 9 bits in total.

Attack Procedure. At first, the attacker prepares $\tau = 9$ pairs of known plaintexts and ciphertexts denoted by $(P^{(0)}, C^{(0)}), (P^{(1)}, C^{(1)}), \ldots, (P^{(8)}, C^{(8)})$.

1. Guess the value of A_0, namely the value of K_0, K_1, bit positions 0–20 of K_2, and bit positions 0–20 of K_3.
2. For all possible candidates of A_1, namely for the bit positions 21 to 31 in total 11 bits of K_2, compute the round function from round 5 to 11 for $P^{(j)}$, where $0 \leq j \leq 8$, and store the value of $(L_{12}^{(j)}, R_{12}^{(j)})$ and corresponding K_2. Then partially compute the round function from round 12 to 17 and store the value of $L_{18}^{(j)}$ in bit position 0.
3. For all possible candidates of A_2, namely for the bit positions 21 to 31 in total 11 bits of K_3, compute the round function from round 29 to 23 for $C^{(j)}$, $0 \leq j \leq 8$, and store the value of $(L_{23}^{(j)}, R_{23}^{(j)})$ and corresponding K_3. Then partially compute the round function from round 22 to 18 and check whether or not the value of $L_{18}^{(j)}$ in bit position 0 matches the value from the forward chunk.

4. If they match for all j, compute the round function from round 12 to 17 and 23 to 18 in all bits for the pair $(P^{(0)}, C^{(0)})$, and check whether or not the remaining 63 bits of $(L_{18}^{(0)}, R_{18}^{(0)})$ match.
5. If all bits match, examine $E_K(P^{(j)})$ equals to $C^{(j)}$ for all j. If they match for all j, the key candidate is the correct key. Otherwise, the key is wrong, and repeat the attack from Step 1 with a different guess of A_0.

Complexity Evaluation. Let us assume that 1 round operation is $\frac{1}{25}$ XTEA computation. Step 2 requires $9 \times 2^{11} \times \frac{12}{25}$ XTEA computations and Step 3 requires $9 \times 2^{11} \times \frac{12}{25}$ XTEA computations. After the 9-bit match at Step 3, $2^{11+11-9} = 2^{13}$ pairs will survive. Step 4 requires $2^{13} \times \frac{12}{25}$ XTEA computations. The complexity for Step 5 is negligible because the number of right key candidates are already reduced at Step 4. Finally, these procedures are iterated for $2^{|A_0|} = 2^{128-11-11} = 2^{106}$ times due to the recursion at Step 1. Hence, the total computational cost is

$$2^{106}(9 \times 2^{11} \times \frac{12}{25} + 9 \times 2^{11} \times \frac{12}{25} + 2^{13} \times \frac{12}{25}), \tag{7}$$

which is approximately $2^{120.40}$ XTEA computations. The attack requires to store $(2^{11} \times 4)$ 32-bit values at Step 2 and Step 3. Hence, the total required memory is 2^{14} 32-bit values, which correspond to 2^{13} XTEA state.

Remarks for the Choice of τ. The number of known plaintext/ciphertext pairs τ is chosen to optimize the time complexity. With τ pairs, the time complexity of the attack in Eq. (7) can be written as follows.

$$\text{Time} = 2^{106}(\tau \times 2^{11} \times \frac{12}{25} + \tau \times 2^{11} \times \frac{12}{25} + 2^{22-\tau} \times \frac{12}{25}), \tag{8}$$

$$= \frac{12}{25} \times 2^{106}(\tau \times 2^{12} + 2^{22-\tau}), \tag{9}$$

$$= \frac{12}{25} \times 2^{118}(\tau + 2^{10-\tau}). \tag{10}$$

When τ is an integer, $\tau = 9$ or 10 minimizes the equation. Hence, we chose $\tau = 9$. As is indicated above, a trade-off exists in this attack. The attack, with some increase of the time complexity, still can work even if only τ pairs where $\tau < 9$ is available.

Partial Experimental Verification. In the 25-round known-plaintext attack, the core part, which is a search of 2^{22} key space with the meet-in-the-middle approach, is iterated 2^{106} times. The complexity of the entire attack is obviously too expensive to be implemented, however only implementing the core part is feasible. In the following, we explain the experimental results of the single run of the core part.

At first, the key is set to the following value. Note that the data is described in the hexadecimal form.

$$(K_0, K_1, K_2, K_3) = (\texttt{01234567}, \texttt{89abcdef}, \texttt{76543210}, \texttt{fedcba98})$$

Table 5. Data set used in the partial experiment

i	$P^{(i)}$	$C^{(i)}$
0	(00000000,00000000)	(a3a559ab,f5c0a730)
1	(00001111,11110000)	(ca20b404,8726fe59)
2	(22220000,00002222)	(b1b1b57c,902f500a)
3	(03030303,30303030)	(e1dd4344,d6c0c7ce)
4	(40044004,04400440)	(006ca23f,c6f09208)
5	(ffff5555,5555ffff)	(cb50fab8,495d2a96)
6	(6666ffff,ffff6666)	(cf57dc3d,05db1f4f)
7	(f7f7f7f7,7f7f7f7f)	(0f54aa91,90b8f106)
8	(8ff88ff8,f88ff88f)	(76049dd8,a460d1b2)

Then, we prepare nine plaintexts and compute the corresponding ciphertexts. The data we used is listed in Table 5.

In the experiment, the value of A_0 is given to the attacker in Step 1 of the attack procedure. Hence, the remaining task is searching for bit positions 31–21 of K_2 and K_3. According to the theoretical evaluation, $2^{11+11-9} = 2^{13}$ pairs will survive after the 9-bit match at Step 3. In the experiment, 8,205 ($= 2^{13.002}$) pairs survived, which well-matched the theoretical evaluation. Then, at Step 5, only the valid key guess survived. The entire attack is a simple iteration of the core part. Therefore, we believe that the entire attack will work as it is estimated.

We also report the mean value and standard deviation when the above experiment is performed 100 times with randomly choosing the key value. Let x_i be the number of remaining pairs after the 9-bit match at Step 3 for i-th trial. The mean value $\overline{x}$: $\overline{x} = \Sigma_{i=1}^{100} x_i/100$ is 8185.4. The standard deviation $\sqrt{((\Sigma_{i=1}^{100}(x_i - \overline{x})^2)/100)}$ is 94.1.

5.2   Chosen Plaintext Attack on 28-Round XTEA

In the chosen plaintext scenario, the attack can be extended up to 28 rounds. We add three rounds to the beginning of the 25-round attack in Sect. 5.1 by using the splice-and-cut technique.

Chunk Separation. The chunk separation is shown in Table 6. The attacked rounds are from round 2 to 29, in total 28 rounds. Compared to Table 3, 3 rounds are added as a part of backward chunk before round 5. In fact, K_3 is not used in these rounds. Therefore, the attack is the same as 25-round known-plaintext attack except for the application of the splice-and-cut technique. In the following part, we explain how the splice-and-cut technique works in this attack.

1-Round Splice-and-Cut. For simplicity, we firstly explain the splice-and-cut technique for 1-round, namely the attack on 26 rounds (from round 4 to 29). The computation in the backward chunk in round 4 is depicted in Fig. 8. *fixed* represents the values which are fixed throughout the attack. *temporarily*

Table 6. Chunk separation for chosen plaintext attack on 28-round XTEA

Round i	2	3	4	5	6	7	8	9	10	11	12	13	14	15	16	17	18	19	20	21	22	23	24	25	26	27	28	29
Index $\pi(i)$	1	2	2	1	3	0	0	0	1	3	2	2	3	1	0	0	1	0	2	3	3	2	0	1	1	1	2	0
	backward chunk			forward chunk							E_{skip}											backward chunk						

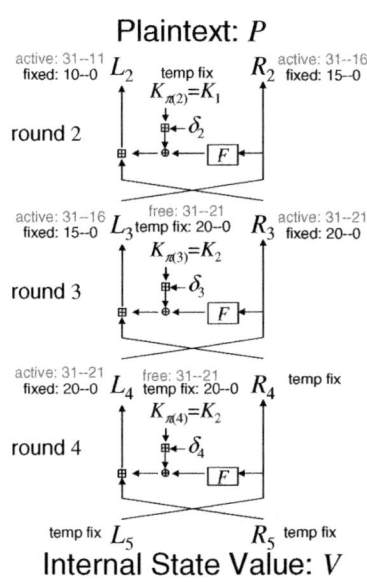

Plaintext: P

Fig. 9. Splice-and-cut for 3 rounds

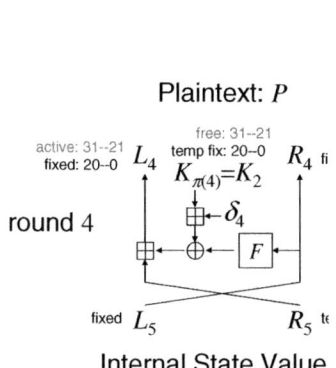

Plaintext: P

Fig. 8. Splice-and-cut for 1 round

fixed represents the values which are fixed during the meet-in-the-middle phase but are changed to repeat the meet-in-the-middle phase. *free* represents the free bits in the meet-in-the-middle phase. *active* represents the values which are influenced by free bits.

The free bits are bit positions 21 to 31 of K_2. Changing the free bits will impact to the bit positions 21 to 31 of the left-half of the plaintext (L_4). Therefore, in this attack, we firstly prepare 2^{11} chosen plaintexts where the bit positions 0 to 20 of L_4 and all bits of R_4 are fixed to a pre-chosen constant (any value is acceptable, say 0) and the bit positions 21 to 31 of L_4 take all possibilities. In the end, the data complexity is 2^{11} chosen plaintexts.

As pointed out in Sect. 4, it must be ensured that for any value of the bit positions 0 to 20 of K_2, we choose appropriate value of L_5 so that the fixed value (the bit positions 0 to 20) of L_4 can be realized. This is possible by using the procedure in Sect. 4. In details, we set the values labelled as *fixed* to pre-chosen values, and fix the values labelled as *active* in L_4 and *free* in K_2 to any value, say 0. Because L_4, R_4, and K_2 are fixed now, we can compute temporarily fixed values L_5 and R_5 by simply computing the round function. The resulting V

ensures that for any value of free bits in K_2, fixed values in the plaintext (L_4 and R_4) are always achieved.

Combination of the Splice-and-Cut and Multi-pair Match. These two techniques can be used at the same time. Let us firstly consider the simple method. When the interstate value V is computed, we prepare $\tau = 9$ patterns, say 0 to 8, for the *fixed values* of the plaintext, and compute the corresponding 9 patterns of V. This method requires 2^{11} chosen plaintexts for each pattern of the *fixed values* of the plaintext, thus $\tau \cdot 2^d = 9 \cdot 2^{11}$ chosen plaintexts in total.

By carefully choosing V, we can reduce the data complexity to $2^d = 2^{11}$. The idea is using the bit positions in V which the change of their bits only gives influence to the active bits of the plaintext. In the case of Fig. 8, the bit positions 21 to 31 of R_5 only gives influence to the active bits in the plaintext. In the end, the procedure to obtain τ intermediate states V is as follows.

1. Obtain one $V^{(0)}$ with the same manner as the case for the single pair.
2. Modify V^0 in bit positions discussed above to $\tau - 1$ patterns to obtain $V^{(1)}, V^{(2)}, \ldots, V^{(\tau-1)}$.

These τ intermediate values ensure that for any free bits in K_2, the fixed bits in L_4 can be achieved. Hence, the multi-pair match can be performed only with 2^d chosen plaintexts.

3-Round Splice-and-Cut. We show the 3-round backward computation for the attack on 28 rounds. See Fig. 9 for its illustration. After 2-rounds, the number of influenced bits becomes 27 and after 3-rounds, it becomes 37. In the end, 3-rounds are appended with the splice-and-cut technique by using 2^{37} chosen plaintexts.

Brief Description of the Attack

1. Prepare 2^{37} chosen plaintexts and obtain their corresponding ciphertexts.
2. For each candidate of A_0, do as follows.
3. Compute $V^{(j)}$, where $0 \le j \le 8$.
4. For all candidates of A_1, compute the forward chunk starting from $V^{(j)}$.
5. For all candidates of A_2, compute rounds 4 to 2 starting from $V^{(j)}$ to obtain $P^{(j)}$. By using the oracle query, obtain the corresponding ciphertext $C^{(j)}$ and compute the backward chunk.

The rest of the procedure is exactly the same as the 25-round known-plaintext attack. The computational cost slightly decreases because the ratio of the independently computed part becomes bigger, which is $2^{120.38}$ XTEA computations.

6   Concluding Remarks

We presented the 3-subset meet-in-the-middle attack on XTEA. We firstly corrected the procedure for using the splice-and-cut technique to keep the data complexity small. We then attacked reduced-round XTEA by using this technique. 25 rounds were attacked with 9 known plaintexts and 28 rounds were attacked 2^{37} chosen plaintexts. As far as we know, our attacks are best in terms of the number of attacked rounds as a single-key attack.

Acknowledgements. We would like to thank anonymous referees of Africacrypt 2012 for their helpful comments. Lei Wang was supported by Grant-in-Aid for JSPS Fellows (23001043).

References

1. Wheeler, D.J., Needham, R.M.: TEA, a Tiny Encryption Algorithm. In: Preneel, B. (ed.) FSE 1994. LNCS, vol. 1008, pp. 363–366. Springer, Heidelberg (1995)
2. Steil, M.: 17 mistakes microsoft made in the Xbox security system. In: 22nd Chaos Communication Congress (2005),
   http://events.ccc.de/congress/2005/fahrplan/events/559.en.html
3. Kelsey, J., Schneier, B., Wagner, D.: Key-Schedule Cryptanalysis of IDEA, G-DES, GOST, SAFER, and Triple-DES. In: Koblitz, N. (ed.) CRYPTO 1996. LNCS, vol. 1109, pp. 237–251. Springer, Heidelberg (1996)
4. Kelsey, J., Schneier, B., Wagner, D.: Related-key Cryptanalysis of 3-WAY, Biham-DES, CAST, DES-X, NewDES, RC2, and TEA. In: Han, Y., Okamoto, T., Qing, S. (eds.) ICICS 1997. LNCS, vol. 1334, pp. 233–246. Springer, Heidelberg (1997)
5. Needham, R.M., Wheeler, D.J.: TEA extensions. Technical report, Computer Laboratory, University of Cambridge (1997)
6. Needham, R.M., Wheeler, D.J.: Correction to xtea. Technical report, Computer Laboratory, University of Cambridge (1998),
   http://www.movable-type.co.uk/scripts/xxtea.pdf
7. Saarinen, M.J.O.: Cryptanalysis of Block-TEA (1998) (unpublished manuscript),
   http://groups.google.com/group/sci.crypt.research/msg/f52a533d1e2fa15e
8. Yarrkov, E.: Cryptanalysis of XXTEA. Cryptology ePrint Archive, Report 2010/254 (2010), http://eprint.iacr.org/2010/254
9. Kaps, J.-P.: Chai-Tea, Cryptographic Hardware Implementations of xTEA. In: Chowdhury, D.R., Rijmen, V., Das, A. (eds.) INDOCRYPT 2008. LNCS, vol. 5365, pp. 363–375. Springer, Heidelberg (2008)
10. Bouillaguet, C., Dunkelman, O., Leurent, G., Fouque, P.-A.: Another Look at Complementation Properties. In: Hong, S., Iwata, T. (eds.) FSE 2010. LNCS, vol. 6147, pp. 347–364. Springer, Heidelberg (2010)
11. Ko, Y., Hong, S., Lee, W., Lee, S., Kang, J.-S.: Related Key Differential Attacks on 27 Rounds of XTEA and Full-Round GOST. In: Roy, B., Meier, W. (eds.) FSE 2004. LNCS, vol. 3017, pp. 299–316. Springer, Heidelberg (2004)
12. Lee, E., Hong, D., Chang, D., Hong, S., Lim, J.: A Weak Key Class of XTEA for a Related-Key Rectangle Attack. In: Nguyên, P.Q. (ed.) VIETCRYPT 2006. LNCS, vol. 4341, pp. 286–297. Springer, Heidelberg (2006)
13. Lu, J.: Related-key rectangle attack on 36 rounds of the XTEA block cipher. Int. J. Inf. Sec. 8(1), 1–11 (2009)
14. Moon, D., Hwang, K., Lee, W., Lee, S., Lim, J.: Impossible Differential Cryptanalysis of Reduced Round XTEA and TEA. In: Daemen, J., Rijmen, V. (eds.) FSE 2002. LNCS, vol. 2365, pp. 49–60. Springer, Heidelberg (2002)

15. Hong, S., Hong, D., Ko, Y., Chang, D., Lee, W., Lee, S.: Differential Cryptanalysis of TEA and XTEA. In: Lim, J.-I., Lee, D.-H. (eds.) ICISC 2003. LNCS, vol. 2971, pp. 402–417. Springer, Heidelberg (2004)

16. Sekar, G., Mouha, N., Velichkov, V., Preneel, B.: Meet-in-the-Middle Attacks on Reduced-Round XTEA. In: Kiayias, A. (ed.) CT-RSA 2011. LNCS, vol. 6558, pp. 250–267. Springer, Heidelberg (2011)

17. Chen, J., Wang, M., Preneel, B.: Impossible differential cryptanalysis of the lightweight block ciphers TEA, XTEA and HIGHT. Cryptology ePrint Archive, Report 2011/616 (2011), http://eprint.iacr.org/2011/616

18. Diffie, W., Hellman, M.E.: Exhaustive cryptanalysis of the NBS Data Encryption Standard. Computer 6(10) (1977)

19. Chaum, D., Evertse, J.-H.: Cryptanalysis of DES with a Reduced Number of Rounds. In: Williams, H.C. (ed.) CRYPTO 1985. LNCS, vol. 218, pp. 192–211. Springer, Heidelberg (1986)

20. Demirci, H., Selçuk, A.A.: A Meet-in-the-Middle Attack on 8-Round AES. In: Nyberg, K. (ed.) FSE 2008. LNCS, vol. 5086, pp. 116–126. Springer, Heidelberg (2008)

21. Aoki, K., Sasaki, Y.: Preimage Attacks on One-Block MD4, 63-Step MD5 and More. In: Avanzi, R.M., Keliher, L., Sica, F. (eds.) SAC 2008. LNCS, vol. 5381, pp. 103–119. Springer, Heidelberg (2009)

22. Sasaki, Y., Aoki, K.: Finding Preimages in Full MD5 Faster Than Exhaustive Search. In: Joux, A. (ed.) EUROCRYPT 2009. LNCS, vol. 5479, pp. 134–152. Springer, Heidelberg (2009)

23. Aoki, K., Sasaki, Y.: Meet-in-the-Middle Preimage Attacks Against Reduced SHA-0 and SHA-1. In: Halevi, S. (ed.) CRYPTO 2009. LNCS, vol. 5677, pp. 70–89. Springer, Heidelberg (2009)

24. Aoki, K., Guo, J., Matusiewicz, K., Sasaki, Y., Wang, L.: Preimages for Step-Reduced SHA-2. In: Matsui, M. (ed.) ASIACRYPT 2009. LNCS, vol. 5912, pp. 578–597. Springer, Heidelberg (2009)

25. Bogdanov, A., Rechberger, C.: A 3-Subset Meet-in-the-Middle Attack: Cryptanalysis of the Lightweight Block Cipher KTANTAN. In: Biryukov, A., Gong, G., Stinson, D.R. (eds.) SAC 2010. LNCS, vol. 6544, pp. 229–240. Springer, Heidelberg (2011)

26. Biham, E., Dunkelman, O., Keller, N., Shamir, A.: New data-efficient attacks on reduced-round IDEA. Cryptology ePrint Archive, Report 2011/417 (2011), http://eprint.iacr.org/2011/417

27. Bogdanov, A., Khovratovich, D., Rechberger, C.: Biclique Cryptanalysis of the Full AES. In: Lee, D.H., Wang, X. (eds.) ASIACRYPT 2011. LNCS, vol. 7073, pp. 344–371. Springer, Heidelberg (2011)

28. Isobe, T.: A Single-Key Attack on the Full GOST Block Cipher. In: Joux, A. (ed.) FSE 2011. LNCS, vol. 6733, pp. 290–305. Springer, Heidelberg (2011)

29. Wei, L., Rechberger, C., Guo, J., Wu, H., Wang, H., Ling, S.: Improved meet-in-the-middle cryptanalysis of KTANTAN. Cryptology ePrint Archive, Report 2011/201 (2011), http://eprint.iacr.org/2011/201

30. Wei, L., Rechberger, C., Guo, J., Wu, H., Wang, H., Ling, S.: Improved Meet-in-the-Middle Cryptanalysis of KTANTAN (Poster). In: Parampalli, U., Hawkes, P. (eds.) ACISP 2011. LNCS, vol. 6812, pp. 433–438. Springer, Heidelberg (2011)

31. Sasaki, Y., Aoki, K.: Preimage Attacks on 3, 4, and 5-Pass HAVAL. In: Pieprzyk, J. (ed.) ASIACRYPT 2008. LNCS, vol. 5350, pp. 253–271. Springer, Heidelberg (2008)

32. Handschuh, H., Naccache, D.: SHACAL: A family of block ciphers. Submission to the NESSIE Project (2008)

Differential Cryptanalysis of Reduced-Round ICEBERG

Yue Sun[1], Meiqin Wang[2,*], Shujia Jiang[3], and Qiumei Sun[2]

[1] Institute for Advanced Study, Tsinghua University, Beijing, 100084, China
[2] Key Laboratory of Cryptologic Technology and Information Security,
Ministry of Education, Shandong University, Jinan 250100, China
[3] Venustech Incorporation, Beijing, 100193, China
yuesun@tsinghua.edu.cn, {mqwang,mei}@sdu.edu.cn,
jiang_shujia@venustech.com.cn

Abstract. ICEBERG is proposed by Standaert *et al.* in FSE 2004 for reconfigurable hardware implementations. It uses 64-bit block size and 128-bit key and the round number is 16. Specially, it is a SPN block cipher and all components are involutional and allow very efficient combinations of encryption/decryption. In this paper, we propose an elaborate method to identify the 6-round differentials and present the differential attack on 7-round ICEBERG with 2^{57} chosen plaintexts and $2^{90.28}$ 7-round encryptions. Then we use multiple differentials to attack 8-round ICEBERG with 2^{63} chosen plaintexts and 2^{96} 8-round encryptions. The previous linear cryptanalysis can only attack 7-round ICEBERG with the whole codebook. It means that ICEBERG is more resistant to linear cryptanalysis than differential cryptanalysis. Although our attack cannot threat ICEBERG, we give the best attack for ICEBERG published to date and our elaborate method to identify multiple differential can be used for other similar block ciphers.

Keywords: Differential Cryptanalysis, Light-Weight, Block Cipher, ICEBERG, Involutional.

1 Introduction

Along with the development of the internet of things, a variety of constraint equipments such as RFID devices, wireless sensor network etc have been pervasively used around us. Although they meet relative moderate security problem compared to Internet, only such a extremely resource constrained environment (weak computation ability, small storage space, strict power constraints and so on) is provided that it's hard to directly implement standard ciphers on it. So a requirement on low energy cost but efficient and secure cipher is rapidly developing. So the security primitives suitable for these light-weight environments must be designed. Recently, several light-weight block ciphers have been proposed such as PRESENT [1], mCRYPTON [2], HIGHT [3], SEA [4] and KTANTAN [5] etc.

---

* Corresponding author.

A. Mitrokotsa and S. Vaudenay (Eds.): AFRICACRYPT 2012, LNCS 7374, pp. 155–171, 2012.
© Springer-Verlag Berlin Heidelberg 2012

In general, a block cipher based on SP-network structure has the different encryption and decryption process like AES [6], which will increase the hardware costs. Although the block cipher based on the Feistel structure does not have such disadvantage, its slow avalanche effect requires the large round number to guarantee the security. In this way, how to design an involutional block cipher based on SP-network structure has become an important object in the field of light-weight block cipher.

At FSE 2004, Standaert *et al.* proposed a fast involutional block cipher with SP-network structure optimized for reconfigurable hardware implementations, named ICEBERG [7]. ICEBERG uses 64-bit text blocks and 128-bit keys and the round number is 16. Specially, all components are involutional and allow very efficient combinations of encryption/decryption. In practice, very low-cost hardware crypto-processors and high throughput data encryption are potential applications of ICEBERG. In [8], Sun *et al.* gave the linear cryptanalysis for 7-round ICEBERG with the whole codebook and $2^{91.19}$ 7-round encryptions, which is the first published attack for reduced-round ICEBERG.

Differential cryptanalysis, proposed by Biham and Shamir [9], has been one of the most classic cryptanalytic techniques for block ciphers. Later a variety of refinements to this attack has been suggested, such as differentials [10] and multiple differential attack [11] etc. Although the original ICEBERG proposal provided theoretical upper bounds of the probability for the differential characteristics of 16-round ICEBERG, the proposal did not give the concrete differential cryptanalysis. In this paper, we will give the concrete differential cryptanalysis for reduced-round ICEBERG. Specially, we will improve the differential cryptanalytic results for ICEBERG with multiple differential cryptanalysis, which has been put forward in [11].

In this paper, we make use of the property of the linear layer of ICEBERG and design an efficient searching algorithm to identify the differential characteristic for ICEBERG. As a result, we found that the highest probability of 6-round differential $2^{-60.53}$ is much greater than that of the 6-round differential characteristic $2^{-63.32}$, so we give two attacks with multiple differentials [12], the first one is the structure attack on 7-round ICEBERG with one output difference and multiple input differences and it requires that $2^{90.28}$ times of 7-round encryptions and 2^{57} chosen plaintexts; and the second one is the multiple differential attack on 8-round ICEBERG with multiple output differences. Although we cannot threat ICEBERG, the attack on 8-round ICEBERG we give is the best attack. Furthermore, our method to identify differentials can be used for other block ciphers.

The paper is organized as follows. Section 2 presents the description for ICEBERG block cipher. In Section 3, we identify the best 6-round differential characteristic and differentials based on the property of linear layer of ICEBERG. Section 4 presents the 7-round structure attack on ICEBERG and the 8-round multiple differential attack on ICEBERG, respectively. Section 5 concludes this paper.

2   Description of ICEBERG

ICEBERG is proposed by Standaert *et al.* on FSE 2004, and it is a fast involutional block cipher with SP-network structure optimized for reconfigurable hardware implementations [7]. Specially, all components are involutional and allow very efficient combinations of encryption/decryption. In practice, very low-cost hardware crypto-processors and high throughput data encryption are potential applications of ICEBERG. It operates on 64-bit block and uses a 128-bit key. The round number is 16. The round function ρ_K can be expressed as:

$$\rho_K : \mathbb{Z}_2^{64} \to \mathbb{Z}_2^{64} : \rho_K \equiv \epsilon_K \circ \gamma,$$

where γ is the non-linear layer and ϵ_K is the linear layer.

It is an involutional cipher since its encryption is only different from its decryption in the key schedule. Because the key schedule has little relationship with our analysis, we will not describe it here.

2.1   Non-linear Layer γ

Non-linear layer γ is composed of non-linear substitution layers $S0$ and $S1$ and bit permutation layer $P8$. Fig. 1 depicts the non-linear layer γ. Each substitution layer consists of 16 identical S-boxes in parallel. The bit permutation layer consists of eight identical bit permutations $P8$. The γ layer can be expressed as:

$$\gamma : \mathbb{Z}_2^{64} \to \mathbb{Z}_2^{64} : \gamma \equiv S0 \circ P8 \circ S1 \circ P8 \circ S0.$$

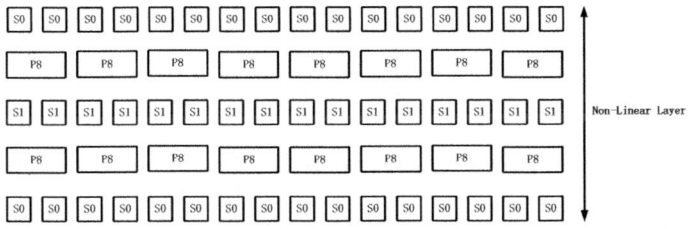

Fig. 1. The Non-Linear Layer γ

The γ layer can be viewed as one layer consisting of the application of eight identical 8×8 S-boxes listed in Table 1.

2.2   Linear Layer ϵ_K

Fig. 2 depicts the linear layer ϵ_K. The ϵ_K can be described as:

$$\epsilon_K : \mathbb{Z}_2^{64} \to \mathbb{Z}_2^{64} : \epsilon_K \equiv P64 \circ P4 \circ \sigma_K \circ M \circ P64.$$

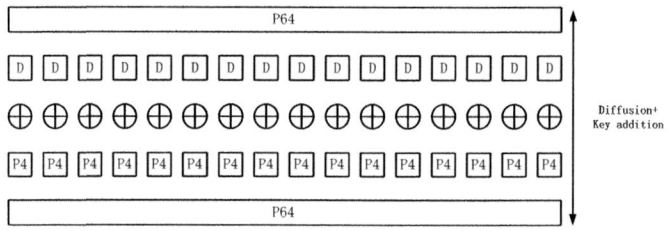

Fig. 2. The Linear Layer ϵ_K

Table 1. The 8×8 S-box

	00	01	02	03	04	05	06	07	08	09	0a	0b	0c	0d	0e	0f
00	24	c1	38	30	e7	57	df	20	3e	99	1a	34	ca	d6	52	fd
10	40	6c	d3	3d	4a	59	f8	77	fb	61	0a	56	b9	d2	fc	f1
20	07	f5	93	cd	00	b6	62	a7	63	fe	44	bd	5f	92	6b	68
30	03	4e	a2	97	0b	60	83	a3	02	e5	45	67	f4	13	08	8b
40	10	ce	be	b4	2a	3a	96	84	c8	9f	14	c0	c4	6f	31	d9
50	ab	ae	0e	64	7c	da	1b	05	a8	15	a5	90	94	85	71	2c
60	35	19	26	28	53	e2	7f	3b	2f	a9	cc	2e	11	76	ed	4d
70	87	5e	c2	c7	80	b0	6d	17	b2	ff	e4	b7	54	9d	b8	66
80	74	9c	db	36	47	5d	de	70	d5	91	aa	3f	c9	d8	f3	f2
90	5b	89	2d	22	5c	e1	46	33	e6	09	bc	e8	81	7d	e9	49
a0	e0	b1	32	37	ea	5a	f6	27	58	69	8a	50	ba	dd	51	f9
b0	75	a1	78	d0	43	f7	25	7b	7e	1c	ac	d4	9a	2b	42	e3
c0	4b	01	72	d7	4c	fa	eb	73	48	8c	0c	f0	6a	23	41	ec
d0	b3	ef	1d	12	bb	88	0d	c3	8d	4f	55	82	ee	ad	86	06
e0	a0	95	65	bf	7a	39	98	04	9b	9e	a4	c6	cf	6e	dc	d1
f0	cb	1f	8f	8e	3c	21	a6	b5	16	af	c5	18	1e	0f	29	79

It consists of the 64-bit permutation layer $P64$, the parallel binary matrix multiplications M, the key addition layer σ_K, the parallel 4-bit permutation layer and the identical 64-bit permutation as in Fig. 2. $P64$ and $P4$ are listed in Table 2 and Table 3, respectively. The matrix multiplication M is based on the parallel application of a simple involutional matrix multiplication. Let $V \in \mathbb{Z}_2^{4 \times 4}$ be a binary involutional matrix (i.e. such that $V^2 = I_n$):

$$V = \begin{bmatrix} 0 & 1 & 1 & 1 \\ 1 & 0 & 1 & 1 \\ 1 & 1 & 0 & 1 \\ 1 & 1 & 1 & 0 \end{bmatrix}.$$

M is then defined as:

$$M : \mathbb{Z}_{2^4}^{16} \to \mathbb{Z}_{2^4}^{16} : x \to y = M(x) \Leftrightarrow y_i = V \cdot x_i \qquad 0 \le i \le 15.$$

Then the diffusion box D is defined as performing multiplication by V.

Table 2. The $P64$ Permutation

0	1	2	3	4	5	6	7	8	9	10	11	12	13	14	15
0	12	23	25	38	42	53	59	22	9	26	32	1	47	51	61

16	17	18	19	20	21	22	23	24	25	26	27	28	29	30	31
24	37	18	41	55	58	8	2	16	3	10	27	33	46	48	62

32	33	34	35	36	37	38	39	40	41	42	43	44	45	46	47
11	28	60	49	36	17	4	43	50	19	5	39	56	45	29	13

48	49	50	51	52	53	54	55	56	57	58	59	60	61	62	63
30	35	40	14	57	6	54	20	44	52	21	7	34	15	31	63

Table 3. The $P4$ Permutation

0	1	2	3
1	0	3	2

The encryption process for R rounds is defined as follows:

$$\sigma_{RK_0^R} \circ \gamma \circ (\bigcirc_{r=1}^{R-1} \rho_{RK_1^r}) \circ \sigma_{RK_1^0}.$$

where σ_K is the key addition layer.

3   Differential Distinguishers of 6-Round ICEBERG

Differential cryptanalysis, introduced by Biham and Shamir in [9], is one of the most popular and important attack towards block ciphers. It uses the differential characteristic with high probability for inner rounds as a distinguisher to recover the subkey bits in fore or last few rounds. Then several works proposed that the effect of differential cryptanalysis can be strengthened with differentials [10] or multiple differential [12]. In this section, we will identify the differential characteristics of 6-round ICEBERG and the differentials of 6-round ICEBERG.

3.1   Differential Characteristic of 6-Round ICEBERG

The way to search the differential characteristic of an iterated SPN block cipher depends on two components. The differential distribution table of the active S-box in the non-linear layer determines the probability of the differential characteristic while the linear layer determines the least number of active S-boxes. So the higher probability of the active S-box and the fewer active S-boxes are there in one round, the better is the differential characteristic. According to the differential distribution table of 8×8 S-box for ICEBERG, we found that the probability ranges from 2^{-7} to 2^{-5}. The gap between them is so small that the number of active S-boxes in the differential characteristic is the determinant factor for its probability. Therefore, we will aim at finding the best one among differential characteristics with as few active S-boxes as possible which is determined by the linear layer of ICEBERG.

Property of Linear Layer $P64$-$DP4$-$P64$

The linear layer of ICEBERG includes three kinds of components, which are permutations, diffusion box and key addition. The permutation $P64$ mapping on 64 bit is respectively at the beginning and end of the linear layer of ICEBERG, while the 16 same permutations $P4$ are mapped on each 4 bit. The diffusion box D makes each output bit equal to the exclusive-or among the three input bits. The diffusion pattern of differential characteristic for 2-round is shown in Fig. 3. In view of differential cryptanalysis, $P4$ and D can be regarded as a whole, named $DP4$ depicted in Table 4.

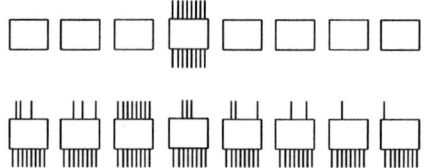

Fig. 3. Diffusion of Two Rounds ICEBERG

Table 4. $DP4$ Linear-Layer

0	1	2	3	4	5	6	7	8	9	10	11	12	13	14	15
0	13	14	3	7	10	9	4	11	6	5	8	12	1	2	15

Remind the observation on the linear layer of ICEBERG described in the linear cryptanalysis of ICEBERG [8], we learn that the property of $DP4$ remains the same. It means there are at least 4 active S-boxes for two rounds, so totally five patterns exist, which are three primary patterns $(1 \to 3, 2 \to 2, 3 \to 1)$ and two auxiliary patterns $(2 \to 3, 3 \to 2)$, where $m \to n$ means that there are m active S-boxes in the first round and n active S-boxes in the second round.

We obtained the similar analysis of the 5 patterns as the one we give in [8], so we take *Pattern* $(1 \to 3)$ as an example to explain.

☐ *Pattern* $(1 \to 3)$: It implies there should be m $(1 \leqslant m \leqslant 8)$ active $DP4(s)$ with $1 \to 3$ (1 nonzero input difference bit to 3 nonzero output difference bits). After the bottom $P64$, the $3m$ nonzero output difference bits of $DP4$s will input to three S-boxes, each of which has m nonzero input difference bits. Whilst the m non-zoro input difference bits will input to the same S-box before the top $P64$ in reverse order. To sustain this condition, we need to search m-$DP4$s whose three nonzero output difference bits will be located in the same three bytes after $P64$. Meanwhile, deduced by the reversed $P64$, the m nonzero input difference bits should be just right located in the same one byte. The pattern is depicted in Fig. 4(a).

To efficiently search all the possible combinations of m-$DP4$, we divide them into several sets by m and look into the relation of these sets during their generation, which has been given in proposition 1 in [8].

Proposition 1. *Assuming Γ_m is the set of all m-$DP4$ possible combinations. If $(\alpha_0, \alpha_1 \ldots \alpha_m) \in \Gamma_{m+1}(m \geqslant 1)$, then there should be $(\alpha_0, \alpha_1 \ldots \alpha_{m-1}) \in \Gamma_m$ and $(\alpha_0, \alpha_1 \ldots \alpha_{m-2}, \alpha_m) \in \Gamma_m$. So Γ_{m+1} can be generated from Γ_m. Vice versa, if $(\alpha_0, \alpha_1 \ldots \alpha_{m-1}) \in \Gamma_m$ and $(\alpha_0, \alpha_1 \ldots \alpha_{m-2}, \beta_{m-1}) \in \Gamma_m$, then $(\alpha_0, \alpha_1 \ldots \alpha_{m-1}, \beta_{m-1}) \in \Gamma_{m+1}$.*

We will produce each possible Γ_m from *Proposition* 1. Firstly, in order to generate Γ_1, we searched the combinations for 1-$DP4$s with only one active $DP4$ locating in 16 kinds of possible positions. Then we used the elements from Γ_1 to produce Γ_2, and then we produce Γ_3 from Γ_2. In the similar way, we will stop the process until there is no element in some Γ_m (As the data in Table 5 shows, the process stops at Γ_4). The sets of possible combinations for $Pattern(1 \rightarrow 3)$ are shown in the first row in Table 5. As we can see, $1 \leqslant m \leqslant 3$, and in each sub row we give an example in each Γ_m. For example, the first sub row means that there is a possible combination for Γ_1, in which the output difference of the active S-box S_0 in top round (we will name it as top output difference for short in following sections) is 1_x, the input difference and output difference on the 0-th $DP4$ are 1_x and d_x, and the input difference of the active S-boxes in the next round (for short we call bottom input difference) S_0 is 1_x, S_2 is 80_x, S_3 is 2_x.

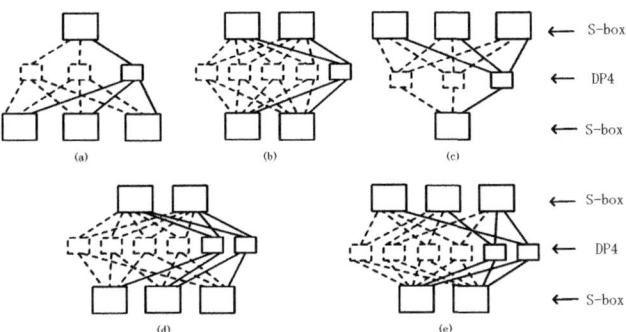

Fig. 4. Patterns for Linear Layer $P64$-$DP4$-$P64$

Table 5 gives the set $|\Gamma_m|$ and one example in Γ_m for each pattern. It should be noticed that the pattern is not an intact two-round differential characteristic, it begins with the output differences of the active S-boxes in the first round and ends at the input differences of the active S-boxes in the second round, as shown in Fig. 4. We name this semi-joint 2-round differential characteristic as a **node** for short in following sections which involves two members: top output difference and bottom input difference.

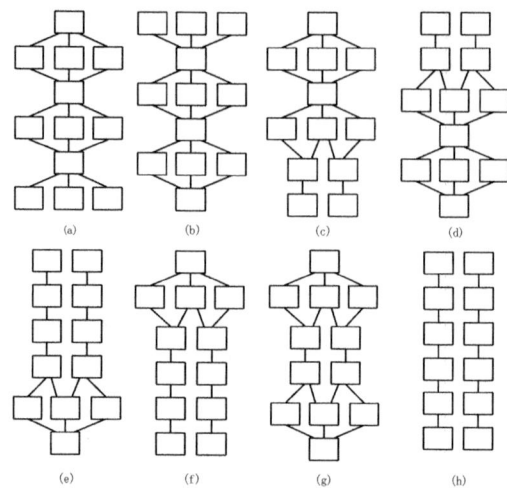

Fig. 5. 6-round Best Differential Characteristic Patterns

Search the 6-Round Differential Characteristics

According to the above five patterns, eight patterns for 6-round differential characteristics can be produced in Fig. 5.

Because $S(x) = S^{-1}(x)$, $P64(x) = P64^{-1}(x)$ and $DP4(x) = DP4^{-1}(x)$, each differential characteristic in Fig. 5(a) will generate a reversed differential characteristic in Fig. 5(b) by turning its input and output differences upside down in each round. The same scenario is for (Fig. 5(c), Fig. 5(d)) and (Fig. 5(e), Fig. 5(f)). In this way, in order to search the differential characteristic with highest probability among the 5 patterns, firstly, we can concatenate 2-round nodes in the five patterns depicted in Table 5 to the 6-round nodes. Two 2-round nodes can be linked with each other only if they are on same series of active S-boxes and the joint entries whose bottom input difference is from the above node and the top output difference comes from the node below have nonzero probability. For example, the bottom input difference of the 2-round node $\{(0, 5_x), (1, 11_x)\} \to \{(0, 5_x), (1, 11_x)\}$ and the top output difference of the 2-round node $\{(0, 4_x), (1, 1_x)\} \to \{(0, 4_x), (1, 1_x)\}$ are both on the active S-boxes S_0 and S_1, and from the difference distribution table of the S-box, $P_r\{5_x \to 4_x\} = 2^{-7}, P_r\{11_x \to 1_x\} = 2^{-5.42}$, so they can be concatenated to 3-round node $\{(0, 5_x), (1, 11_x)\} \to \{(0, 4_x), (1, 1_x)\}$ with probability $2^{-12.42}$. By concatenating 2-round nodes one by one or iterative concatenation (two 2-round nodes can concatenate to a 3-round node, then two 3-round nodes can concatenate to a 5-round node, go along with concatenating another 2-round node at end), we will get a 6-round node.

Table 6 gives examples for the best 6-round node for the eight patterns in Fig. 5. From the last column of Table 6, we can see the highest probability is $2^{-43.32}$. From column Δ_{out} and Δ_{in}, we see that there are 4 active S-boxes in

Table 5. Patterns for $DP4$

Pattern	m	$\|\Gamma_m\|$	Δ_{out} (pos, out)	Δ_{in} (pos, in)	$DP4$ (pos, in, out)
$1 \to 3$	1	64	$(0, 1_x)$	$(0, 1_x), (2, 80_x), (3, 2_x)$	$(0, 1_x, d_x)$
	2	13	$(5, 84_x)$	$(5, 84_x), (6, 28_x), (7, 28_x)$	$(1, 2_x, e_x), (3, 2_x, e_x)$
	3	1	$(5, c4_x)$	$(5, c4_x), (6, 29_x), (7, 68_x)$	$(1, 2_x, e_x), (3, 2_x, e_x), (7, 2_x, e_x)$
$2 \to 2$	1	96	$(0, 1_x), (1, 10_x)$	$(0, 1_x), (1, 10_x)$	$(0, 3_x, 3_x)$
	2	27	$(0, 5_x), (1, 11_x)$	$(0, 5_x), (1, 11_x)$	$(0, 3_x, 3_x), (5, c_x, c_x)$
	3	12	$(6, a8_x), (7, 2c_x)$	$(6, a8_x), (7, 2c_x)$	$(1, c_x, c_x), (3, c_x, c_x), (5, 3_x, 3_x)$
	4	5	$(6, a9_x), (7, 6c_x)$	$(6, a9_x), (7, 6c_x)$	$(1, c_x, c_x), (3, c_x, c_x),$
					$(5, 3_x, 3_x), (7, c_x, c_x)$
	5	1	$(6, ab_x), (7, 7c_x)$	$(6, ab_x), (7, 7c_x)$	$(1, c_x, c_x), (3, c_x, c_x),$
					$(5, 3_x, 3_x), (7, c_x, c_x), (8, c_x, c_x)$
$3 \to 1$	1	64	$(0, 1_x), (2, 80_x), (3, 2_x)$	$(0, 1_x)$	$(0, d_x, 1_x)$
	2	13	$(5, 84_x), (6, 28_x), (7, 28_x)$	$(5, 84_x)$	$(1, e_x, 2_x), (3, e_x, 2_x)$
	3	1	$(5, c4_x), (6, 29_x), (7, 68_x)$	$(5, c4_x)$	$(1, e_x, 2_x), (3, e_x, 2_x), (7, e_x, 2_x)$
$2 \to 3$	2	218	$(1, 12_x), (3, 6_x)$	$(0, 1_x), (2, c0_x), (4, 1_x)$	$(0, a_x, 5_x), (2, 6_x, 9_x)$
	3	119	$(2, c4_x), (3, 2_x)$	$(2, c4_x), (3, 7_x), (4, 21_x)$	$(0, c_x, c_x), (2, 1_x, d_x), (4, 4_x, 7_x)$
	4	51	$(1, 1c_x), (3, 1c_x)$	$(1, 1e_x), (2, c0_x), (3, 1e_x)$	$(0, 2_x, e_x), (2, 4_x, 7_x)$
					$(6, c_x, c_x), (8, 3_x, 3_x)$
	5	17	$(1, 3c_x), (3, 3c_x)$	$(1, 3e_x), (2, c0_x), (3, 3e_x)$	$(0, 2_x, e_x), (2, 4_x, 7_x)$
					$(6, c_x, c_x), (8, 3_x, 3_x), (11, c_x, c_x)$
	6	3	$(6, eb_x), (7, 7c_x)$	$(0, 40_x), (6, eb_x), (7, 7e_x)$	$(1, c_x, c_x), (3, c_x, c_x), (5, 3_x, 3_x)$
					$(7, c_x, c_x), (8, c_x, c_x), (13, 4_x, 7_x)$
$3 \to 2$	2	218	$(0, 1_x), (2, c0_x), (4, 1_x)$	$(1, 12_x), (3, 6_x)$	$(0, 5_x, a_x), (2, 9_x, 6_x)$
	3	119	$(2, c4_x), (3, 7_x), (4, 21_x)$	$(2, c4_x), (3, 2_x)$	$(0, c_x, c_x), (2, d_x, 1_x), (4, 7_x, 4_x)$
	4	51	$(1, 1e_x), (2, c0_x), (3, 1e_x)$	$(1, 1c_x), (3, 1c_x)$	$(0, e_x, 2_x), (2, 7_x, 4_x)$
					$(6, c_x, c_x), (8, 3_x, 3_x)$
	5	17	$(1, 3e_x), (2, c0_x), (3, 3e_x)$	$(1, 3c_x), (3, 3c_x)$	$(0, e_x, 2_x), (2, 7_x, 4_x)$
					$(6, c_x, c_x), (8, 3_x, 3_x), (11, c_x, c_x)$
	6	3	$(0, 40_x), (6, eb_x), (7, 7e_x)$	$(6, eb_x), (7, 7c_x)$	$(1, c_x, c_x), (3, c_x, c_x), (5, 3_x, 3_x)$
					$(7, c_x, c_x), (8, c_x, c_x), (13, 7_x, 4_x)$

Δ_{out} means the output difference of the active S-box in this round;
Δ_{in} means the input difference of the active S-box in the next round;
The tuple (a, b) means a is the index of S-box, and b is the output difference in Δ_{out} column or the input difference in Δ_{in} column;
The triple (a, b, c) means on the a-th $DP4$, the input difference is b and the output difference is c.

the first and the last round. According to the differential distribution table, the probability of one entry is at most 2^{-5}, so the probability of the best differential characteristic for the first node pattern depicted in Table 6 is at least $2^{-66.84}$

Table 6. Results of Eight 6-Round Nodes

Node pattern	Amount	Δ_{out}	Δ_{in}	Pr
$1 \to 3 \to 1 \to 3 \to 1 \to 3$	306	$(5, c0_x)$	$(5, c0_x), (6, 9_x), (7, 60_x)$	$2^{-46.84}$
$3 \to 1 \to 3 \to 1 \to 3 \to 1$	306	$(5, c0_x), (6, 9_x), (7, 60_x)$	$(5, c0_x)$	$2^{-46.84}$
$1 \to 3 \to 1 \to 3 \to 2 \to 2$	347	$(6, 10_x)$	$(6, 40_x), (7, 2_x)$	$2^{-59.42}$
$2 \to 2 \to 3 \to 1 \to 3 \to 1$	347	$(6, 40_x), (7, 2_x)$	$(6, 10_x)$	$2^{-59.42}$
$2 \to 2 \to 2 \to 2 \to 3 \to 1$	4606	$(6, b_x), (7, 70_x)$	$(7, 2_x)$	$2^{-56.66}$
$1 \to 3 \to 2 \to 2 \to 2 \to 2$	4606	$(7, 2_x)$	$(6, b_x), (7, 70_x)$	$2^{-56.66}$
$1 \to 3 \to 2 \to 2 \to 3 \to 1$	757	$(1, 4_x)$	$(1, 40_x)$	$2^{-63.66}$
$2 \to 2 \to 2 \to 2 \to 2 \to 2$	53846	$(6, ab_x), (7, 7c_x)$	$(6, ab_x), (7, 7c_x)$	$2^{-43.32}$
		$(6, b_x), (7, 70_x)$	$(6, b_x), (7, 70_x)$	$2^{-43.32}$

Amount: the total number of nodes.

$(\Delta_{out}, \Delta_{in}, Pr)$: the node with highest probability Pr, its top output difference is Δ_{out} and bottom input difference is Δ_{in}.

Pr: the probability of the 6-round nodes; it is exclusive of the probability of the active S-boxes in the first round and the last round.

less than 2^{-64}. So we only identify the 6-round differential characteristics with the probability greater than 2^{-64}. By computing all the eight node patterns, the 6-round differential characteristics with the probability greater than 2^{-64} have been identified from the last node pattern $2 \to 2 \to 2 \to 2 \to 2 \to 2$.

By further analysis on the 6-round nodes $\{(6, ab_x), (7, 7c_x) \to (6, ab_x), (7, 7c_x)\}$ and $\{(6, b_x), (7, 70_x) \to (6, b_x), (7, 70_x)\}$, we obtain four best 6-round differential characteristics with probability $2^{-63.32}$ as follows,

$$(93ab0000\ 00000000_x) \xrightarrow{6r} (93ab0000\ 00000000_x) \xrightarrow{LL} (93ebc446\ 2010a106_x),$$

$$(93ab0000\ 00000000_x) \xrightarrow{6r} (c7ab0000\ 00000000_x) \xrightarrow{LL} (c7eb8444\ 3010a802_x),$$

$$(c7ab0000\ 00000000_x) \xrightarrow{6r} (93ab0000\ 00000000_x) \xrightarrow{LL} (93ebc446\ 2010a106_x),$$

$$(c7ab0000\ 00000000_x) \xrightarrow{6r} (c7ab0000\ 00000000_x) \xrightarrow{LL} (c7eb8444\ 3010a802_x).$$

where "6r" stands for the 6-round node with input difference of the active S-boxes in the first round and output difference of the active S-boxes in the last round; the "LL" stands for the linear layer in the last round. Due to the limited space, we only list the details for the last 6-round differential characteristic in Table 7.

Table 7. 6-Round Differential Characteristic

Round		Output Difference	Probability P_r
		$S_6{=}ab_x$, $S_7{=}c7_x$	
R_1	S-box	$S_6{=}ab_x$, $S_7{=}7c_x$	2^{-10}
R_1	LT	$S_6{=}ab_x$, $S_7{=}7c_x$	1
R_2	S-box	$S_6{=}b_x$, $S_7{=}70_x$	$2^{-10.83}$
R_2	LT	$S_6{=}b_x$, $S_7{=}70_x$	1
R_3	S-box	$S_6{=}ab_x$, $S_7{=}7c_x$	$2^{-10.83}$
R_3	LT	$S_6{=}ab_x$, $S_7{=}7c_x$	1
R_4	S-box	$S_6{=}b_x$, $S_7{=}70_x$	$2^{-10.83}$
R_4	LT	$S_6{=}b_x$, $S_7{=}70_x$	1
R_5	S-box	$S_6{=}ab_x$, $S_7{=}7c_x$	$2^{-10.83}$
R_5	LT	$S_6{=}ab_x$, $S_7{=}7c_x$	1
R_6	S-box	$S_6{=}ab_x$, $S_7{=}c7_x$	2^{-10}
R_6	LT	$S_0{=}2_x$, $S_1{=}a8_x$, $S_2{=}10_x$, $S_3{=}30_x$, $S_4{=}44_x$, $S_5{=}84_x$, $S_6{=}eb_x$, $S_7{=}c7_x$	1

3.2 Differentials of 6-Round ICEBERG

From Table 6, there are 53846 6-round nodes in $2 \to 2 \to 2 \to 2 \to 2 \to 2$ pattern. Not only the active S-Boxes for the input difference and the output difference of the above four best 6-round nodes with highest probability are located in (S_6, S_7), but also other 52384 nodes are located in them. So we traverse 2^{32} different input differences and output differences to compute the probability of each differential on the given input and output difference value on the four fixed active S-boxes. As a result, we identify some differentials with higher probability in Table 8. The first column is the differential; the second column shows how many 6-round nodes contribute to the differential among all the 52384 6-round nodes; the third column is the corresponding probability of the differential.

Table 8. Differentials of 6-Round ICEBERG

Differential	Amount/52384	Pr
$(7c0b0000\ 00000000_x) \to (7c0b0440\ 00000104_x)$	1338	$2^{-60.53}$
$(7cab0000\ 00000000_x) \to (7c0b0440\ 00000104_x)$	2046	$2^{-60.59}$
$(7c0b0000\ 00000000_x) \to (7cab0000\ 00000000_x)$	2046	$2^{-60.59}$
$(c7ab0000\ 00000000_x) \to (7c0b0440\ 00000104_x)$	2242	$2^{-60.59}$
$(7c0b0000\ 00000000_x) \to (c7eb8444\ 3010a802_x)$	2242	$2^{-60.59}$

3.3 Structures of Differentials of 6-Round ICEBERG

Now we consider the effect of a set of differentials whose active S-boxes locate in S_6 and S_7. Firstly, we collected differentials with different input differences and fixed given output difference on active S-boxes S_6 and S_7 whose probabilities are greater than the average probability 2^{-64} as a set. Then we compared all the 2^{16} sets with different output differences to obtain the set of differentials with highest probability. Some of them with higher probability are shown in Table 9. Because the number of input differences is large, we have not listed the input differences in Table 9. The first column is the sets of the differentials with fixed output differences; the second column shows the amount of various of differentials' input differences; the third column is the sum of probabilities of all the differentials in the set.

Table 9. Sets of Differentials of 6-Round ICEBERG

Set of Differentials	Amount	Pr
$(\text{xxxx}0000\ 00000000_x) \rightarrow (7c0b0440\ 00000104_x)$	10981	$2^{-49.77}$
$(\text{xxxx}0000\ 00000000_x) \rightarrow (c7eb8444\ 3010a802_x)$	10784	$2^{-49.82}$
$(\text{xxxx}0000\ 00000000_x) \rightarrow (7cab0000\ 00000000_x)$	10501	$2^{-49.86}$
$(\text{xxxx}0000\ 00000000_x) \rightarrow (93ebc446\ 2010a106_x)$	10473	$2^{-49.87}$

Amount: the number of different input differences.

4   Attacks against Reduced-Round ICEBERG

4.1   Structure Attack to 7-Round ICEBERG

In this section, we will use the set with 10981 6-round differentials in the first row in Table 9 to proceed the structure attack on 7-round ICEBERG. Firstly, we construct 2^{41} structures, in each structure, the 16-bit plaintext input to S-boxes S_6 and S_7 traverses all possible values and other plaintext bits will take the fixed value. So our attack will use $2^{41} \cdot 2^{16} = 2^{57}$ chosen plaintexts. The sum of the probability for all differentials is $2^{-49.77}$. In each structure, there are $2^{15} \cdot 10981 \approx 2^{28.42}$ plaintext pairs satisfying any of the 10981 input differences. So the expected number of right pairs is $2^{41} \cdot 2^{15} \cdot 2^{-49.77} = 2^{6.23} \approx 75.06$. According to the input difference in round 7 $(7c0b0440\ 00000104_x)$, there are six active S-boxes, which results in 48 subkey bits to be guessed. Considering all the possible output differences of the six active S-boxes and the two non-active S-boxes, the filtering probability β and the average number of subkey values counted per pair α should be computed. We list the number of the output differences and the number of subkey values counted according to the different cases in Table 10, which can be obtained from the differential distribution table of S-box. As we see in each row of Table 10, the number of possible subkey values for the given input difference of the active S-box varies on 2, 4, 6 and 8. In column 3 of Table 10, we classify the number of the output differences by the number of candidate subkey values. Column 4 is the average number of subkeys suggested by the given input difference. As a result, the filtering ratio $\beta = \left(\frac{94}{256}\right)^2 \cdot \left(\frac{99}{256}\right)^3 \cdot \frac{102}{256} \cdot 2^{-16} \approx 2^{-24.33}$, the average increment on per counter for wrong pairs will be $2^{41} \cdot 2^{15} \cdot 10981 \cdot 2^{-24.33} \cdot 2^{8.34} \cdot 2^{-48} \approx 2^{5.43} \approx 43.11$.

Table 10. Number of Candidate Subkey Values

Input Difference	Number of Output Differences	Number of Candidate Subkeys				Average Number
		2	4	6	8	
1_x	94	65	25	3	1	$2^{1.45}$
4_x	99	75	20	3	1	$2^{1.37}$
40_x	102	80	18	4	0	$2^{1.33}$
b_x	94	70	15	8	1	$2^{1.45}$
$7c_x$	99	76	19	2	2	$2^{1.37}$
ab_x	99	76	18	4	1	$2^{1.37}$
70_x	105	84	19	2	0	$2^{1.29}$

Next, we will give the attacking procedure as follows:

- For each structure:
    a: Insert all the ciphertexts into the hash table according to the 16-bit ciphertext bits of the non-active S-boxes in the last round.
    b: For each entry with collision (a pair of ciphertext with equal 16-bit values) check whether the plaintexts difference (in round 1) is one of the 10981 differentials's input differences.
    c: Filter wrong pairs which satisfy none of 48-bit of the ciphertext differences on the six active S-boxes of the 10981 differentials.
    d: For each possible subkey in round 7, decrypt the last round to obtain the output difference of round 6, and check whether the difference equals to the output difference of the differentials. If a pair passes the above test, add one to the counter related to the subkey value. The average increment on per counter for wrong pairs will be 43.11.
- Collect all the subkeys whose counter has at least 75 hits. With the high probability the correct subkey is in this list.
- Exhaustively search the remaining 80-bit subkey key and we can obtain the whole 128-bit master key.

In step (a), the time complexity is 2^{16} memory accesses. In step (b), about 2^{15} pairs remain through the filter of step (a), so the time complexity is 2^{16} memory accesses. So for all structures, the two steps require 2^{58} memory accesses. For all structures, the time complexity of step (c) is negligible, and the time complexity of step (d) is about $2^{41} \cdot 2^{15} \cdot 10981 \cdot 2^{-24.33} \cdot 2^{48} \approx 2^{93.09}$ one-round decryptions, which equals to $2^{90.28}$ 7-round encryptions.

The signal to noise ratio is:

$$S/N = \frac{2^{-49.77} \cdot 2^{48}}{10981 \cdot 2^{-24.33} \cdot 2^{8.34}} \approx 1.74.$$

The success rate is computed with the method in [13] as follows,

$$Ps = \Phi(\frac{\sqrt{\mu S_N} - \Phi^{-1}(1 - 2^{-a})}{\sqrt{S_N + 1}})$$
$$= \Phi(\frac{\sqrt{75.06 \cdot 1.74} - \Phi^{-1}(1 - 2^{-48})}{\sqrt{1.74 + 1}}) = 98.65\%,$$

To recover the 48 subkey bits, the time complexity is about $2^{90.28}$ 7-round encryptions. The remaining 80-bit key can be exhaustively searched within 2^{80} 7-round encryptions.

In all, the data complexity is 2^{57} chosen plaintexts, and the time complexity is $2^{90.28}$ 7-round encryptions. The memory requirements are 2^{48} counters. The success rate is 98.65%.

4.2   Multiple Differential Attack against 8-Round ICEBERG

As we see in Table 7 and Table 8, the best differential characteristic or differential for 6-round has at least six active S-boxes for the output difference because of the fast diffusion of the linear layer of ICEBERG in the last round, which make it infeasible to produce 8-round differential with high probability. For example, the best 6-round differential $(7c0b0000\ 00000000_x) \rightarrow (7c0b0440\ 00000104_x)$ will result in six active S-boxes in the following round. But it should be noticed that the difference before the linear layer of the last round is $(7c0b0000\ 00000000_x)$, with only two active bytes.

If the number of active bytes passing through the linear layer remains two, it will be helpful to extend more rounds for the differential. So the differentials of 6-round ICEBERG which can be used to produce 8-round differentials should have two properties: higher probability and the two active bytes before linear layer in the last round should confirm to $Pattern(2 \rightarrow 2)$. Recall that all of the 6-round differentials of ICEBERG whose probabilities are greater than 2^{-64} confirm to $2 \rightarrow 2 \rightarrow 2 \rightarrow 2 \rightarrow 2 \rightarrow 2$. At last, we searched in this pattern and found 28 differentials satisfying the above properties, whose input difference or output difference doesn't change after passing the linear layer. We list the best four differentials in Table 11. The first column is the differential; the second column shows how many 6-round nodes contribute to the differential among all the 52384 6-round nodes; the third column is the corresponding probability of the differential.

Table 11. Differentials of 6-Round ICEBERG Whose Output Differences Confirm to $Pattern(2 \rightarrow 2)$

Differential	Amount/52384	Pr
$(7cab0000\ 00000000_x) \rightarrow (7cab0000\ 00000000_x)$	3382	$2^{-60.64}$
$(700b0000\ 00000000_x) \rightarrow (7cab0000\ 00000000_x)$	2761	$2^{-60.96}$
$(7cab0000\ 00000000_x) \rightarrow (700b0000\ 00000000_x)$	2761	$2^{-60.96}$
$(700b0000\ 00000000_x) \rightarrow (700b0000\ 00000000_x)$	2817	$2^{-61.26}$

We use the four differentials from round 2 to round 7 to recover total 32 subkey bits in round 0 and round 8, so the input difference of the 8-th round will be $(7cab0000\ 00000000_x)$ or $(700b0000\ 00000000_x)$. According to Table 10, we can see the size of the set of possible output differences of round 8 for $(7cab0000\ 00000000_x)$ will be $99 \cdot 99 \approx 2^{13.26}$, for $(700b0000\ 00000000_x)$ it will be $94 \cdot 105 \approx 2^{13.27}$. Because there are totally 42 shared output differences for (ab_x, b_x) and 40 ones for $(7c_x, 70_x)$, the size of the set of possible output differences in round 8 for the input differences set $\{(7cab0000\ 00000000_x),$ $(700b0000\ 00000000_x)\}$ is $99 \cdot 99 + 94 \cdot 105 - 42 \cdot 40 = 17991 \approx 2^{14.13}$. So we construct 2^{47} structures different on bits from 0 to 46. Since the linear layer is involutional, the set of input differences in round 1 is the same as the one in round 8, the size of the set of chosen plaintexts differences should be $2^{14.13}$. In each structure, there are $2^{15+14.13} = 2^{29.13}$ pairs.

The right pairs for each differential can be computed respectively. We take $(7cab0000\ 00000000_x) \to (7cab0000\ 00000000_x)$ as an example. In each structure, the expected number of pairs with input differences $\Delta S_6 = \Delta x_i$ and $\Delta S_7 = \Delta y_i$ in the first round should be $2^{15} \cdot p_i \cdot q_i$, and denote $p_i = P_r\{\Delta x_i \to ab_x\}$ and $q_i = P_r\{\Delta y_i \to 7c_x\}$. Since all the input differences are considered, $\sum_i p_i \cdot q_i = 1$. So the expected number of right pairs for $(7cab0000\ 00000000_x) \to$ $(7cab0000\ 00000000_x)$ should be $2^{47} \cdot 2^{15} \cdot 2^{-60.64} = 2^{1.36}$. So the total expected number of right pairs for the four differentials should be $2^{47} \cdot 2^{15} \cdot (2^{-60.64} + 2 \cdot 2^{-60.96} + 2^{-61.26}) \approx 2^{3.06} \approx 8.36$.

Since there are six non-active S-boxes in round 8, the filter ratio is $2^{-48} \cdot 2^{14.13} \cdot 2^{-16} = 2^{-49.87}$, there will be $2^{47} \cdot 2^{15+14.13} \cdot 2^{-49.87} = 2^{26.26}$ pairs remained after the ciphertext differences filter. Considering the 42 shared output differences for (ab_x, b_x) and 40 ones for $(7c_x, 70_x)$, the average number of counted subkey values for each pair is $\frac{23472+16800+17472+15264+14000+21600+21840}{17991} \approx 7.25$, which is computed out by a tiny programme we wrote. So the expected increment on each counter for wrong subkey values will be $2^{26.26} \cdot (7.25)^2 \cdot 2^{-32} \approx 2^{-0.02} \approx 0.98$, while the value of the counter corresponding to the right key is at least 8.36.

The signal noise $S/N = 8.36/0.98 = 8.51$. The success rate is computed as follows,

$$Ps = \Phi(\frac{\sqrt{\mu S_N} - \Phi^{-1}(1 - 2^{-a})}{\sqrt{S_N + 1}})$$
$$= \Phi(\frac{\sqrt{8.36 \cdot 8.51} - \Phi^{-1}(1 - 2^{-32})}{\sqrt{8.51 + 1}}) = 76.10\%.$$

After recovering the 32-bit subkey, we can exhaustively search the remaining 96-bit subkey to get 128-bit master key. In this attack, the data complexity is 2^{63} chosen plaintexts and the time complexity is about 2^{96} times of 8-round encryptions. The memory requirements are 2^{32} counters.

5 Summary

As a block cipher for reconfigurable hardware implementations, ICEBERG is a SP-network structure involutional block cipher, so the property with very low-cost hardware crypto-processors and high throughput data encryption will result in the potential applications of ICEBERG. In this paper, we elaborately analyze the property of the linear layer of ICEBERG and design an efficient searching algorithm to identify the 6-round differential characteristics. Then we present the first differential analysis of 7-round ICEBERG using structure attack. Our attack requires $2^{90.28}$ 7-round encryptions and 2^{57} chosen plaintexts. Then we give multiple differential attack against 8-round ICEBERG, which requires 2^{63} chosen plaintexts and 2^{96} 8-round encryptions. We have improved the previous linear cryptanalysis for 7-round ICEBERG and it shows that ICEBERG can resist linear cryptanalysis more than differential cryptanalysis.

Acknowledgments. We would like to thank anonymous reviewers for their very important comments. This work was supported by National Natural Science Foundation of China (No.61133013, No.61070244, No.61103237 and No.60931160442), Outstanding Young Scientists Foundation Grant of Shandong Province (No.BS2009DX030).

References

1. Bogdanov, A., Knudsen, L.R., Leander, G., Paar, C., Poschmann, A., Robshaw, M.J.B., Seurin, Y., Vikkelsoe, C.: PRESENT: An Ultra-Lightweight Block Cipher. In: Paillier, P., Verbauwhede, I. (eds.) CHES 2007. LNCS, vol. 4727, pp. 450–466. Springer, Heidelberg (2007)
2. Lim, C.H., Korkishko, T.: mCrypton – A Lightweight Block Cipher for Security of Low-Cost RFID Tags and Sensors. In: Song, J., Kwon, T., Yung, M. (eds.) WISA 2005. LNCS, vol. 3786, pp. 243–258. Springer, Heidelberg (2006)
3. Hong, D., Sung, J., Hong, S., Lim, J., Lee, S., Koo, B.-S., Lee, C., Chang, D., Lee, J., Jeong, K., Kim, H., Kim, J., Chee, S.: HIGHT: A New Block Cipher Suitable for Low-Resource Device. In: Goubin, L., Matsui, M. (eds.) CHES 2006. LNCS, vol. 4249, pp. 46–59. Springer, Heidelberg (2006)
4. Standaert, F., Piret, G., Gershenfeld, N., Quisquater, J.: SEA: a Scalable Encryption Algorithm for Small Embedded Applications. In: Domingo-Ferrer, J., Posegga, J., Schreckling, D. (eds.) CARDIS 2006. LNCS, vol. 3928, pp. 222–236. Springer, Heidelberg (2006)
5. De Cannière, C., Dunkelman, O., Knežević, M.: KATAN and KTANTAN — A Family of Small and Efficient Hardware-Oriented Block Ciphers. In: Clavier, C., Gaj, K. (eds.) CHES 2009. LNCS, vol. 5747, pp. 272–288. Springer, Heidelberg (2009)
6. Daemen, J., Rijmen, V.: The Design of Rijndael: AES - The Advanced Encryption Standard. Springer, Heidelberg (2002)
7. Standaert, F.-X., Piret, G., Rouvroy, G., Quisquater, J.-J., Legat, J.-D.: ICEBERG: An Involutional Cipher Efficient for Block Encryption in Reconfigurable Hardware. In: Roy, B., Meier, W. (eds.) FSE 2004. LNCS, vol. 3017, pp. 279–299. Springer, Heidelberg (2004)
8. Sun, Y., Wang, M.Q.: Linear Cryptanalysis of Reduced-Round ICEBERG. In: Ryan, M.D., Smyth, B., Wang, G. (eds.) ISPEC 2012. LNCS, vol. 7232, pp. 381–392. Springer, Heidelberg (2012)
9. Biham, E., Shamir, A.: Differential Cryptanalysis of DES-like Cryptosystems. Journal of Cryptology 4(1), 3–72 (1991)
10. Lai, X., Massey, J.L., Murphy, S.: Markov Ciphers and Differential Cryptanalysis. In: Davies, D.W. (ed.) EUROCRYPT 1991. LNCS, vol. 547, pp. 17–38. Springer, Heidelberg (1991)

11. Blondeau, C., Gérard, B.: Multiple Differential Cryptanalysis: Theory and Practice. In: Joux, A. (ed.) FSE 2011. LNCS, vol. 6733, pp. 35–54. Springer, Heidelberg (2011)
12. Wang, M., Sun, Y., Tischhauser, E., Preneel, B.: A Model for Structure Attacks, with Applications to PRESENT and Serpent. In: FSE 2012. LNCS. Springer, Heidelberg (2012)
13. Selçuk, A.A., Biçak, A.: On Probability of Success in Linear and Differential Cryptanalysis. In: Cimato, S., Galdi, C., Persiano, G. (eds.) SCN 2002. LNCS, vol. 2576, pp. 174–185. Springer, Heidelberg (2003)

Compact Implementation and Performance Evaluation of Block Ciphers in ATtiny Devices

Thomas Eisenbarth[1], Zheng Gong[2], Tim Güneysu[3], Stefan Heyse[3],
Sebastiaan Indesteege[4,5], Stéphanie Kerckhof[6], François Koeune[6],
Tomislav Nad[7], Thomas Plos[7], Francesco Regazzoni[6,8],
François-Xavier Standaert[6], and Loïc van Oldeneel tot Oldenzeel[6]

[1] Department of Mathematical Sciences, Florida Atlantic University, FL, USA
[2] School of Computer Science, South China Normal University
[3] Horst Görtz Institute for IT Security, Ruhr-Universität, Bochum, Germany
[4] Department of Electrical Engineering ESAT/COSIC, KULeuven, Belgium
[5] Interdisciplinary Institute for BroadBand Technology (IBBT), Ghent, Belgium
[6] UCL Crypto Group, Université catholique de Louvain, Belgium
[7] Institute for Applied Information Processing and Communications (IAIK),
Graz University of Technology, Austria
[8] ALaRI Institute, University of Lugano, Switzerland

Abstract. The design of lightweight block ciphers has been a very active
research topic over the last years. However, the lack of comparative source
codes generally makes it hard to evaluate the extent to which implementations of different ciphers actually reach their low-cost goals on various
platforms. This paper reports on an initiative aiming to relax this issue.
First, we provide implementations of 12 block ciphers on an ATMEL AVR
ATtiny45 8-bit microcontroller, and make the corresponding source code
available on a web page. All implementations are made public under an
open-source license. Common interfaces and design goals are followed by
all designers to achieve comparable implementation results. Second, we
evaluate performance figures of our implementations with respect to different metrics, including energy-consumption measurements and show our
improvements compared to existing implementations.

Keywords: Lightweight, Block Cipher, AVR ATtiny, Implementation,
Open Source.

1 Introduction

Small embedded devices including smart cards, RFIDs, and sensor nodes are
deployed in many applications today. They are usually characterized by strong
cost constraints. Yet, as they increasingly manipulate sensitive data, they require cryptographic protection. As a result, many lightweight ciphers have been
proposed in order to allow strong security guarantees at a lower cost than standard solutions. Quite naturally, the very idea of "low-cost" is highly dependent
on the target technology. Some operations that are extremely low-cost in hardware (e.g., wire crossings) turn out to be annoyingly expensive in software. Even

A. Mitrokotsa and S. Vaudenay (Eds.): AFRICACRYPT 2012, LNCS 7374, pp. 172–187, 2012.

within a class of similar targets, the presence or absence of some options such as hardware multipliers may cause strong variations in the performance analysis of different algorithms. As a result, it is difficult to have a good understanding of which algorithms are actually lightweight on which device. Also, the lack of comparative studies prevents a good understanding of the cost vs. performance trade-off for these algorithms.

In this paper, we provide performance evaluations for low-cost block ciphers, and investigate their implementation on an ATMEL AVR ATtiny45 device [2], i.e. a small 8-bit microcontroller with limited memory and limited instruction set. Despite the relatively frequent use of such devices in different applications, little work has been done in benchmarking cryptographic algorithms in this context. Notable exceptions include B. Poettering's open-source codes for AES [18], the XBX frameworks [20] and an interesting survey of lightweight cryptography implementations [9]. Unfortunately, these references are still limited by the number of ciphers under investigation and the fact that in some cases the source code is not available for evaluation.

The goal of our work is to extend the benchmarking of 12 lightweight and standard block ciphers, namely AES, DESXL, HIGHT, IDEA, KASUMI, KATAN, KLEIN, mCrypton, NOEKEON, PRESENT, SEA, TEA, and to make their implementation available under an open-source license. To the best of our knowledge, four of these algorithms (KASUMI, KLEIN, mCrypton, KATAN) are implemented for the first time on an 8-bit platform. We selected the ciphers according to three criteria: all selected candidates should (a) give no indication of flawed security, (b) be freely usable without patent restrictions, and (c) likely result in lightweight implementations with a footprint of less than 256 bytes of RAM and 4 KB of code size for a combined encryption and decryption function.

In order to make comparisons as meaningful as possible, we adapt the guidelines for evaluations of hardware implementations proposed in [10] to our software context. Yet, as the project involves 12 different designers, we also acknowledge that some biases can appear due to slightly different implementation choices. Hence, as usual for performance evaluations, looking at the source codes is essential in order to properly understand the reasons of different performance figures. Overall, we hope that this initiative can be used as a first step in better analyzing the performances of block ciphers in a specific but meaningful class of devices. We also hope that it can be used as a starting point to further develop cryptographic libraries for embedded platforms and, in the long run, add security against physical attacks (e.g., based on faults or side-channel leakage) as another evaluation criteria.

The remainder of this paper is structured as follows. Section 2 contains a brief overview of the implemented ciphers. Section 3 establishes our evaluation methodology and metrics, followed by Section 4 that gives details about the ATtiny45 microcontroller. Section 5 provides succinct descriptions and motivation of the implementation choices made by the designers. Finally, performance evaluations are given in Section 6 and conclusions are drawn in Section 7. The web page containing all our open-source codes is available at [8].

2   Investigated Ciphers

AES [6] is the new encryption standard selected in 2002 replacing the former DES. It supports key sizes of 128, 192 or 256 bits, and its block size is 128 bits. The encryption iterates a round function a number of times, depending on the key size. The round is composed of four transformations: SubBytes (that applies a non-linear S-box to the bytes of the states), ShiftRows (a wire crossing), MixColumns (a linear diffusion layer), and finally AddRoundKey (a bitwise XOR of the round key). The round keys are generated from the secret key by means of an expansion routine that re-uses the S-box used in SubBytes. For low-cost applications, the typical choice is to fix the key size to 128 bits.

DESL, DESX, and DESXL [14] are lightweight variants of the DES cipher with the main goal to minimize the gate count required in hardware implementations. In the L-variant, all eight DES S-boxes are replaced by a single S-Box with well chosen characteristics to resist known attacks against DES. Additionally, the initial permutation (IP) and its inverse (IP^{-1}) are omitted, because they do not provide additional cryptographic strength. The X-variant includes an additional key whitening of the form: $\text{DESX}_{k,k1,k2}(x) = k2 \oplus \text{DES}_k(k1 \oplus x)$. DESXL is the combination of both variants.

HIGHT [12] is a hardware-oriented block cipher designed for low-cost and low-power applications. It uses 64-bit blocks and 128-bit keys. HIGHT is a variant of the generalized Feistel network and is composed of simple operations: XOR, additions mod 2^8 and bitwise rotations. Its key schedule consists of two algorithms: one generating whitening key bytes for initial and final transformations; the other one generating subkeys for the 32 rounds. Each subkey byte is the result of an addition mod 2^8 between a master key byte and a constant generated using a linear feedback shift register.

IDEA [13] is a patented cipher whose patent expired in May 2011 (in all countries with a 20 year term of patent filing). Its underlying Lai-Massey construction does not involve an S-box or a permutation network such as in other Feistel or common SPN ciphers. Instead, it interleaves mathematical operations from three different groups to establish security, such as addition modulo 2^{16}, multiplication modulo $2^{16} + 1$ and addition in $\text{GF}(2^{16})$ (XOR). IDEA has a 128-bit key and 64-bit input and output. A major drawback of its construction is the inverse key schedule that requires the complex extended Euclidean algorithm during decryption. For efficient implementation, this complex key schedule needs to be precomputed and stored in memory.

KASUMI [1] is a block cipher derived from MISTY1 [17]. It is used as a keystream generator in UMTS, GSM, and GPRS mobile communication systems. KASUMI has a 128-bit key and 64-bit input and output. The core of KASUMI is an eight-round Feistel network. The round functions in the main Feistel network are irreversible Feistel-like network transformations. The key scheduling is done by bitwise rotating the 16-bit subkeys or XORing them with a constant. There are two S-boxes, one with 7 bit, the other with 9 bit input/output.

KATAN and KTANTAN [4] are two families of hardware-oriented block ciphers. They have 80-bit keys and a block size of either 32, 48 or 64 bits. The cipher structure resembles that of a stream cipher, consisting of shift registers and non-linear feedback functions. An LFSR counter is used to protect against slide attacks. The difference between KATAN and KTANTAN lies in the key schedule. KTANTAN is intended to be used with a single key per device, which can then be burnt into the device. This allows KTANTAN to achieve a smaller footprint in a hardware implementation. In our implementation, we consider KATAN with 64-bit block size.

KLEIN [11] is a family of lightweight software-oriented block ciphers with 64-bit plaintexts and variable key length (64, 80 or 96 bits - our performance evaluations focus on the 80-bit version). It is primarily designed for software implementations in resource-constrained devices such as wireless sensors and RFID tags, but its hardware implementation can be compact as well. The structure of KLEIN is a typical Substitution-Permutation Network (SPN) with 12/16/20 rounds for KLEIN-64/80/96, respectively. One round transformation consists of four operations AddRoundKey, SubNibbles (4-bit involutive S-box), RotateNibbles and MixNibbles (borrowed from AES MixColumns). The key schedule of KLEIN has a Feistel-like structure. It is agile even if keys are frequently changed and it is designed to avoid potential related-key attacks.

mCrypton [15] is a block cipher designed for resource-constrained devices such as RFID tags and sensors. It has a block length of 64 bits and a variable key length of 64, 96 or 128 bits. Here, we implement the variant with 96-bit key length. mCrypton consists of an AES-like round transformation (12 rounds) and a key schedule. The round transformation operates on a 4×4 nibble (4-bit) array and consists of a nibble-wise non-linear substitution, a column-wise bit permutation, a transposition and a key-addition step. The substitution step uses four 4-bit S-boxes. Encryption and decryption have almost the same form. The key scheduling algorithm generates round keys using non-linear S-box transformations, word-wise rotations, bit-wise rotations and a round constant. The same S-boxes are used for the round transformation and key scheduling.

NOEKEON [5] is a block cipher with a key length and a block size of 128 bits. The block cipher consists of a simple round function based only on bit-wise Boolean operations and cyclic shifts. The round function is iterated 16 times for both encryption and decryption. Within each round, a working key is XORed with the data. The working key is fixed during all rounds and is either the cipher key itself (direct mode) or the cipher key encrypted with a null string. The self-inverse structure of NOEKEON allows to efficiently combine the implementation of encryption and decryption operation with only little overhead.

PRESENT [3] is a hardware-oriented lightweight block cipher designed to meet tight area and power restrictions. It features a 64-bit block size and 80-bit or 128-bit key size (we focus on the 80-bit variant). PRESENT implements a substitution-permutation network and iterates 31 rounds. The permutation layer consists only of bit permutations (i.e. wire crossings). Together with the tiny

4-bit S-box, the design enables minimalistic hardware implementations. The key scheduling consists of a single S-box lookup, a counter addition and a rotation.

SEA [19] is a scalable family of encryption algorithms, defined for low-cost embedded devices, with variable bus sizes and block/key lengths. In this paper, we focus on $SEA_{96,8}$, i.e. a version of the cipher with 96-bit block and key size. SEA is a Feistel cipher that exploits rounds with 3-bit S-boxes, a diffusion layer made of bit and word rotations and a mod 2^n key addition. Its key scheduling is based on rounds similar to the encryption ones and is designed such that keys can be derived "on-the-fly" both in encryption and decryption.

TEA [21] is a 64-bit block cipher using 128-bit keys (although equivalent keys effectively reduce the key space to 2^{126}). TEA stands for Tiny Encryption Algorithm and, as the name says, this algorithm was built with simplicity and ease of implementation in mind. An implementation of the algorithm in C corresponds to about 20 lines of code, and does not involve a S-box. TEA has a 64-round Feistel structure, each round being based on XOR, 32-bit addition and rotation. The key schedule is also very simple, alternating the two halves of the key at each round. TEA is sensitive to related-key attacks using 2^{23} chosen plaintexts and one related-key query, with a time complexity of 2^{32}.

3   Methodology and Metrics

In order to be able to compare the performances of the different ciphers in terms of speed, memory space and energy, the developers were asked to respect a list of common constraints, detailed hereunder.

1. The code has to be written in assembly, in a single file. It has to be commented and easily readable, e.g., naming functions similar to their original specifications.
2. The cipher has to be implemented in a low-cost way, minimizing the code size and the use of data memory.
3. Both encryption and decryption routines have to be implemented.
4. Whenever possible, and in order to minimize the data-memory use, the key schedule has to be computed "on-the-fly". The computation of the key schedule is always included in the algorithm evaluations.
5. The encryption process should start with plaintext and key in data memory. The ciphertext should overwrite the plaintext at the end of this process (and vice versa for decryption).
6. The target device is the 8-bit microcontroller ATtiny45 from ATMEL's AVR device family. It has a reduced instruction set and does not provide a hardware multiplier.
7. The encryption and decryption routines have to be called by a common interface.

The SEA reference code was sent as an example to all designers, together with the common interface (also provided at [8]).

The basic metrics considered for evaluation are code size, RAM size, cycle count in en- and decryption, and energy consumption. From these basic metrics, a combined metric is extracted (see Section 6). For the energy-consumption evaluations, each cipher is programmed and executed on an ATtiny45 mounted on a power-measurement board. A 22 Ohm shunt resistor is inserted between the Vdd pin and the 5 V power supply, in order to measure the current consumed by the controller while encrypting. The common interface generates a trigger at the beginning and end of each encryption. The power traces are measured between those two triggers using an oscilloscope that is equipped with a differential probe. We average one hundred encryption traces for each energy evaluation using randomly generated plaintexts and keys for each encryption. The average energy consumed by an encryption is deduced by integrating the measured current.

Finally note that, as mentioned in the introduction, the 12 ciphers are implemented by 12 different designers, with slightly different interpretations of low-cost optimizations. As a result, some of the guidelines could not always be followed, because of the cipher specifications making them less relevant. In particular, the following exceptions deserve to be mentioned.

(1) The key scheduling of IDEA is not computed "on-the-fly" but precomputed (as explained in Section 2).
(2) The key in KATAN has to be restored externally for subsequent invocations.
(3) The 4-bit S-boxes of KLEIN, mCrypton, and PRESENT are implemented as 8-bit tables (because of a better time/memory trade-off).

4   Description of the ATtiny45 Microcontroller

The ATtiny45 is an 8-bit RISC microcontroller from ATMEL's AVR series. It uses a Harvard architecture with separate instruction and data memory. Instructions are stored in a 4 kB Flash memory (2048×16 bits). Data memory involves 256-byte of static RAM, a register file with 32 8-bit general-purpose registers, and special I/O memory for peripherals like timer, analog-to-digital converter or serial interface. Different direct and indirect addressing methods are available to access data in RAM. Especially indirect addressing allows accessing data in RAM with very compact code size. Moreover, the ATtiny45 features a 256-bytes EEPROM memory for non-volatile data storage.

The instruction set of the ATtiny45 consists of 120 instructions which are typically 16-bit wide. Instructions can be divided into arithmetic logic unit (ALU) operations (arithmetic, logical, and bit operations) and conditional and unconditional jump and call operations. The instructions are processed within a two-stage pipeline with a pre-fetch and an execute phase. Most instructions are executed within a single clock cycle, leading to a good instructions-per-cycle ratio. Compared to other microcontrollers from ATMEL's AVR series such as the ATmega or ATxmega devices, the ATtiny45 has a reduced instruction set (e.g., no multiply instruction), smaller memories (Flash, RAM, EEPROM), no in-system debug capabilities, and less peripherals. On the bright side, the ATtiny45 consumes less power and is cheaper in price.

5   Implementation Details

AES. The code is written following the specification for 128-bit key/block size and operates on a state matrix of 16 bytes. In order to improve performance, the state is stored in 16 registers, while the key is stored in RAM. In addition, five temporary registers are used to implement the MixColumn step. The S-box and the round constants are implemented as look-up tables. The multiplication operation needed for MixColumn is computed using shift and XOR instructions.

DESXL. In order to keep code size small, a function which can compute all permutations and expansions depending on the calling parameters is used. This function is also capable of generating 6-bit outputs for direct usage as S-box input. Because of the bit-oriented structure of the permutations which are slow in software, this function is the performance bottleneck of the implementation. The rest of the code is a straightforward application of the specification. Besides the memory requirements for plain-/ciphertext and the keys k, k_1, k_2, additional 16 bytes of RAM are required for the round key and the state. The S-box and all permutation and expansion tables are stored in Flash memory and are processed directly from there.

HIGHT. First, the intermediate states are stored in RAM at each round and two bytes of the plaintext and one byte of the key are loaded at a time. This way, it is possible to re-use the same code fragment four times per round. Next, the byte rotation at the output of the round function is integrated in the memory accesses of the surrounding functions, thus minimizing temporary storage and gaining cycles. Eight subkey bytes are generated once every two rounds and are stored in RAM. Finally, except for the additions mod 2^8 that are replaced by subtractions mod 2^8 and some other minor changes, the same functions as in encryption are used in decryption.

IDEA. This cipher is implemented including a precomputed key schedule performed by separate functions for encryption and decryption, prior to the actual cipher operation. During cipher execution the precomputed key (104 bytes) is then read byte by byte from RAM. The plaintext/ciphertext and the internal state are kept completely in 16 registers and 9 additional registers are used for temporary computations and counters. IDEA requires a 16-bit modular multiplication as basic operation. However, in the AVR device used in this work, no dedicated hardware multiplier unit is available. Multiplication is therefore implemented in software resulting in a data-dependent execution time of the cipher operation and an increased cycle count (about a factor of 4) compared to an implementation for a device with a hardware multiplier. Note that IDEA's multiplication is special and maps zero as any input to 2^{16} (which is equivalent to $-1 \mod 2^{16} + 1$). Therefore, whenever a zero is detected as input to the multiplication, our implementations returns the additive inverse of the other input, reduced modulo $2^{16} + 1$.

KASUMI. The code is written following the functions described in the cipher specifications. During the execution, the 16-byte key as well as the 8-byte running state remain stored in RAM. This allows using only 12 registers and 24 bytes of RAM. Some rearrangements are done to skip unnecessary moves between registers. The 9-bit S-box is implemented as 8-bit table, with the MSBs concatenated in a second 8-bit table. The 7-bit S-box is implemented as 8-bit table, leaving the MSBs unused in this table. The round keys are derived "on-the-fly". Decryption is very similar to encryption, as usual for a Feistel structure.

KATAN-64[1]. The main optimization goal is to limit the code size. The entire state of the cipher is kept in registers during operation. To avoid excessive register pressure, the in- and outputs are stored in RAM, and this RAM space is used to backup the register contents during operation. Only three additional registers need to be stored on the stack. The fact that three rounds of KATAN can be run in parallel is not used in this implementation. Doing so would require more complicated shifting and masking to extract bits from the state, and thus significantly increase the code size, for little or no performance gain. As the KATAN key schedule is computed "on-the-fly", the key in RAM is clobbered and needs to be restored externally for subsequent invocations. Keeping the master key in RAM would require 10 additional words (note that the KTANTAN key schedule does not modify the key, so it does not have this limitation). In order to implement the non-linear functions efficiently, addition instructions are used to compute several logical AND's and XOR's in parallel through carefully positioning the input bits and using masking to avoid undesired carry propagation.

KLEIN-80. Despite the goal of small memory footprint, the 4-bit involutive S-box is stored as an 8-bit table for saving clock cycles. As it can be used in both encryption and decryption, this corresponds to a natural trade-off between code size and processing speed (a similar choice is made for mCrypton and PRESENT, see the next paragraphs). In order to save memory usage during processing, the MixNibbles step (borrowed from AES MixColumns) is implemented by a single function without using lookup tables. Overall, 29 registers are used during the computations. Among them, 8 registers correspond to the intermediate state, 10 registers to the key scheduling, 9 registers are used for temporary storage and 2 registers for the round counter.

mCrypton. The reference code directly follows the cipher specification. The implementation aims for a limited code size. Therefore, as much code as possible is reused for decryption and encryption. In addition, up to 20 registers are used during the computations to reduce the cycle count. 12 registers are used to compute the intermediate state and the key scheduling, 6 registers for temporary storage, one for the current key scheduling constant and one for the round counter. After each round the modified state and key scheduling state are stored in RAM. The round key is derived from the key scheduling state and is temporarily stored in RAM. The four 4-bit S-boxes are stored in four 8-bit tables, wasting the 4 most significant bits of each entry, but saving cycle counts. The constants used in the key scheduling algorithm are stored in an 8-bit table.

---

[1] All six variants of the KATAN/KTANTAN family are supported via conditional assembly. Our performance evaluations focus on the 64-bit version of KATAN.

NOEKEON. The implementation aims to minimize the code size and the number of utilized registers. During execution of the block cipher, input data and cipher key are stored in the RAM (32 bytes are required). In that way, only 4 registers are used for the running state, one register for the round counter, and three registers for temporary computations. The X-register is used for indirect addressing of the data in the RAM. Similar to the implementation of SEA (detailed below), using more registers for the running state will decrease the cycle count, but will also increase the code size because of a less generic programming. For decrypting data, the execution sequence of the computation functions is changed, which leads to a very small increase in code size.

PRESENT. The implementation is optimized in order to limit the code size with throughput as secondary criteria. State and round key are stored in the registers to minimize accesses to RAM. The S-boxes are stored as two 256-byte tables, one for encryption and one for decryption. This allows for two S-box lookups in parallel. However, code size can easily be reduced if only encryption or decryption is performed. A single 16-byte table for the S-boxes could halve the overall code size, but would significantly impact encryption times. The code for permutation, which is the true performance bottleneck, can be used for both encryption and decryption.

SEA. The reference code is written directly following the cipher specifications. During its execution, plaintexts and keys are stored in RAM (accounting for a total of 24 bytes), limiting the register consumption to 6 registers for the running state, one register for the round counter and three registers of temporary storage. Note that higher register consumption would allow decreasing the cycle count at the cost of a less generic programming. The S-box is implemented using its bitsliced representation. Decryption uses exactly the same code as encryption, with "on-the-fly" key derivation in both cases.

TEA. Implementing TEA is almost straightforward due to the simplicity of the algorithm. The implementation is optimized to limit the RAM usage and code size. As far as RAM is concerned, we only use 24 bytes needed for plaintext and key storage, with the ciphertext overwriting the plaintext in RAM at the end of the process. The only notable issue regarding implementing TEA concerns rotations. TEA is optimized for a 32-bit architecture and the fact that only 1-position shift and rotations are available on the ATtiny, plus the need to propagate carries, make these operations slightly more complex. In particular, 5-position shifts are optimized by replacing them by a 3-position shift in the opposite direction and recovering boundary carries. Nonetheless, TEA proves to be very easy to implement, resulting in a compact code of 648 bytes.

6   Performance Evaluation

We consider 6 different metrics: code size (in bytes), RAM use (in bytes), cycle count in encryption and decryption, energy consumption (in μJ) and a combined metric, namely the code size $\times$ cycle count product, normalized by the block size. The results for our different implementations are given in Table 1 which are compared in Figures 1, 2, 3, 4, 5, 6 as shown in the appendix. We detail a few meaningful observations below.

Table 1. Performance evaluation of our implementations on the AVR ATtiny45 microcontroller. Results obtained in this work are given in **bold** face.

Cipher	Block Size [bits]	Key Size [bits]	Code Size [bytes]	RAM [bytes]	Cycles (enc+key)	Cycles (dec+key)	Energy [μJ]
AES	128	128	1659	33	4557	7015	19,2
AES[9]	128	128	2606	0	6637	7429	-
DESXL	64	184	820	48	84602	84602	348,9
DESXL[9]	64	184	3192	0	8531	7961	-
HIGHT	64	128	402	32	19503	20159	79,8
HIGHT[9]	64	128	5672	0	2964	2964	-
IDEA	64	128	836	232	∼8250	∼22729	34,3
IDEA[9]	64	128	596	0	2700	15393	-
KASUMI	64	128	1264	24	11939	11939	47,6
KATAN	64	80	338	18	72063	88525	289,2
KLEIN	64	80	1268	18	6095	7658	25,1
mCrypton	64	96	1076	28	16457	22656	68
NOEKEON	128	128	364	32	23517	23502	95,9
PRESENT	64	80	1000	18	11342	13599	45,3
PRESENT[9]	64	80	936	0	10723	11239	-
SEA	96	96	426	24	41604	40860	173,7
SEA[9]	96	96	2132	0	9654	9654	-
TEA	64	128	648	24	7408	7539	30,3
TEA[9]	64	128	1140	0	6271	6299	-

First, as our primary goal is to consider compact implementations, we compare our code sizes with the ones listed in [9]. Note, however, that secure implementation is not considered a goal of this work. As illustrated in Figure 1, we reduce the memory footprint for most investigated ciphers, with specially strong improvements for DESXL, HIGHT and SEA. The code sizes among our new implementations can also be compared using this figure. The frontrunners are HIGHT, NOEKEON, SEA and KATAN (all take less than 500 bytes of ROM). One can notice the relatively poor performances of mCrypton, PRESENT and KLEIN. This can in part be explained by the hardware-oriented flavor of these ciphers (e.g., the use of bit permutations or manipulation of 4-bit nibbles is not optimal when using 8-bit microcontrollers). As expected, standard ciphers such as AES and KASUMI are more expensive, but only up to a limited extent since both can be implemented using less than 2000 bytes of ROM.

The RAM usage in Figure 2 first exhibits the large needs of IDEA regarding this metric (232 words) that is essentially due to the need to store a precomputed key schedule for this cipher. Besides, and following our design guidelines, this metric essentially reflects the size of the intermediate state that has to be stored during the execution of the algorithms. Note that for AES, this is in contrast to the "Furious" implementation [18] that uses 192 bytes of RAM and explains our slightly reduced performance for this cipher.

The cycle count in Figure 3 clearly illustrates the performance loss that is implied by the use of simple round functions in most lightweight ciphers. This loss is critical for DESXL and KATAN where the large number of round iterations leads to cycle counts beyond 50,000 cycles. It is also large for SEA, NOEKEON and HIGHT. By contrast, these metrics show the excellent efficiency of AES. Cycle count for decryption (Figure 4) shows similar results, with some noticeable changes. Most visibly, IDEA decryption is much less efficient than its encryption. AES also shows an non-negligible overhead when decrypting. In contrast, a number of ciphers behave identically in encryption and decryption, e.g., SEA where the two routines perform almost identical.

As expected, the energy consumption of all the implemented ciphers (Figure 5) is strongly correlated with the cycle count, confirming the experimental results in [7]. However, slight code dependencies can be noticed. This raises an interesting question whether (and to what extend) different coding styles can further impact the energy consumption.

Lastly, the combined metric in Figure 6 first shows the excellent size vs. performance trade-off offered by AES. Among the low-cost ciphers, NOEKEON and TEA exhibit excellent figures as well, most likely due to their very simple key scheduling. This comes at the cost of possible security concerns regarding related-key attacks. HIGHT and KLEIN provide a good trade-off between code size and cycle count. A similar comment applies to SEA, where parts of the overhead comes from a complex key scheduling algorithm (key rounds are as complex as the rounds for this cipher). Despite their hardware-oriented nature, PRESENT and mCrypton offer decent performance on 8-bit devices as well. KATAN falls a bit behind, mainly because of its very large cycle count. Only DESXL appears not to be suitable in such an implementation context.

7   Conclusion

This paper reported on an initiative to evaluate the performance of different standard and lightweight block ciphers on a low cost microcontroller. In total, 12 different ciphers have been implemented with compactness as main optimization criteria. Their source code is available on a web page, under an open-source license. Our results improve most prior work obtained for similar devices. They highlight the different trade-offs between code size and cycle count that is offered by different algorithms. They also put forward the weaker performances of ciphers that were specifically designed with hardware performance in mind. Scopes for further research include the extension of this work towards more algorithms and the addition of countermeasures against physical attacks.

Acknowledgements. This work has been funded in part by the European Commission's ECRYPT-II NoE (ICT-2007-216676), by the Belgian State's IAP program P6/26 BCRYPT, by the ERC project 280141 (acronym CRASH), by the

7th framework European project TAMPRES, by the Walloon region's S@T Skywin, MIPSs and NANOTIC-COSMOS projects. This work has been also been supported in part by the Ministry of Economic Affairs and Energy of the State of North Rhine-Westphalia (Grant 315-43-02/2-005-WFBO-009). Stéphanie Kerckhof is a PhD student funded by a FRIA grant, Belgium. F.-X. Standaert is a Research Associate of the Belgian Fund for Scientific Research (FNRS-F.R.S). Zheng Gong is supported by NSFC (No. 61100201). The authors would like to thank Svetla Nikova for her help regarding the implementation of the block cipher KLEIN.

References

1. 3rd Generation Partnership Project. Technical Specification Group Services and System Aspects, 3G Security, Specification of the 3GPP Confidentiality and Integrity Algorithms, Document 2: KASUMI Specification (Release 10) (2011)
2. ATMEL. AVR 8-bit Microcontrollers, http://www.atmel.com/products/avr/
3. Bogdanov, A., Knudsen, L.R., Leander, G., Paar, C., Poschmann, A., Robshaw, M.J.B., Seurin, Y., Vikkelsoe, C.: PRESENT: An Ultra-Lightweight Block Cipher. In: Paillier, P., Verbauwhede, I. (eds.) CHES 2007. LNCS, vol. 4727, pp. 450–466. Springer, Heidelberg (2007)
4. De Cannière, C., Dunkelman, O., Knežević, M.: KATAN and KTANTAN — A Family of Small and Efficient Hardware-Oriented Block Ciphers. In: Clavier, C., Gaj, K. (eds.) CHES 2009. LNCS, vol. 5747, pp. 272–288. Springer, Heidelberg (2009)
5. Daemen, J., Peeters, M., Assche, G.V., Rijmen, V.: Nessie Proposal: NOEKEON (2000), http://gro.noekeon.org/Noekeon-spec.pdf
6. Daemen, J., Rijmen, V.: The Design of Rijndael: AES - The Advanced Encryption Standard. Springer (2002)
7. de Meulenaer, G., Gosset, F., Standaert, F.-X., Pereira, O.: On the Energy Cost of Communication and Cryptography in Wireless Sensor Networks. In: WiMob, pp. 580–585. IEEE (2008)
8. Eisenbarth, T., Gong, Z., Güneysu, T., Heyse, S., Indesteege, S., Kerckhof, S., Koeune, F., Nad, T., Plos, T., Regazzoni, F., Standaert, F.-X., van Oldeneel tot Oldenzeel, L.: Implementations of Low-Cost Block Ciphers in Atmel AVR Devices (2011), http://perso.uclouvain.be/fstandae/lightweight_ciphers/
9. Eisenbarth, T., Kumar, S.S., Paar, C., Poschmann, A., Uhsadel, L.: A Survey of Lightweight-Cryptography Implementations. IEEE Design & Test of Computers 24(6), 522–533 (2007)
10. Gaj, K., Homsirikamol, E., Rogawski, M.: Fair and Comprehensive Methodology for Comparing Hardware Performance of Fourteen Round Two SHA-3 Candidates Using FPGAs. In: Mangard, Standaert (eds.) [16], pp. 264–278
11. Gong, Z., Nikova, S., Law, Y.W.: KLEIN: A New Family of Lightweight Block Ciphers. In: Juels, A., Paar, C. (eds.) RFIDSec 2011. LNCS, vol. 7055, pp. 1–18. Springer, Heidelberg (2012)
12. Hong, D., Sung, J., Hong, S., Lim, J., Lee, S., Koo, B.-S., Lee, C., Chang, D., Lee, J., Jeong, K., Kim, H., Kim, J., Chee, S.: HIGHT: A New Block Cipher Suitable for Low-Resource Device. In: Goubin, L., Matsui, M. (eds.) CHES 2006. LNCS, vol. 4249, pp. 46–59. Springer, Heidelberg (2006)

13. Lai, X., Massey, J.L.: A Proposal for a New Block Encryption Standard. In: Damgård, I.B. (ed.) EUROCRYPT 1990. LNCS, vol. 473, pp. 389–404. Springer, Heidelberg (1991)
14. Leander, G., Paar, C., Poschmann, A., Schramm, K.: New Lightweight DES Variants. In: Biryukov, A. (ed.) FSE 2007. LNCS, vol. 4593, pp. 196–210. Springer, Heidelberg (2007)
15. Lim, C.H., Korkishko, T.: mCrypton – A Lightweight Block Cipher for Security of Low-Cost RFID Tags and Sensors. In: Song, J., Kwon, T., Yung, M. (eds.) WISA 2005. LNCS, vol. 3786, pp. 243–258. Springer, Heidelberg (2006)
16. Mangard, S., Standaert, F.-X. (eds.): CHES 2010. LNCS, vol. 6225. Springer, Heidelberg (2010)
17. Matsui, M.: New Block Encryption Algorithm MISTY. In: Biham, E. (ed.) FSE 1997. LNCS, vol. 1267, pp. 54–68. Springer, Heidelberg (1997)
18. Poettering, B.: RijndaelFurious AES-128 Implementation for AVR Devices (2007), http://point-at-infinity.org/avraes/
19. Standaert, F.-X., Piret, G., Gershenfeld, N., Quisquater, J.-J.: SEA: A Scalable Encryption Algorithm for Small Embedded Applications. In: Domingo-Ferrer, J., Posegga, J., Schreckling, D. (eds.) CARDIS 2006. LNCS, vol. 3928, pp. 222–236. Springer, Heidelberg (2006)
20. Wenzel-Benner, C., Gräf, J.: XBX: eXternal Benchmarking eXtension for the SUPERCOP Crypto Benchmarking Framework. In: Mangard, Standaert (eds.) [16], pp. 294–305
21. Wheeler, D.J., Needham, R.M.: TEA, a Tiny Encryption Algorithm. In: Preneel, B. (ed.) FSE 1994. LNCS, vol. 1008, pp. 363–366. Springer, Heidelberg (1995)

Appendix

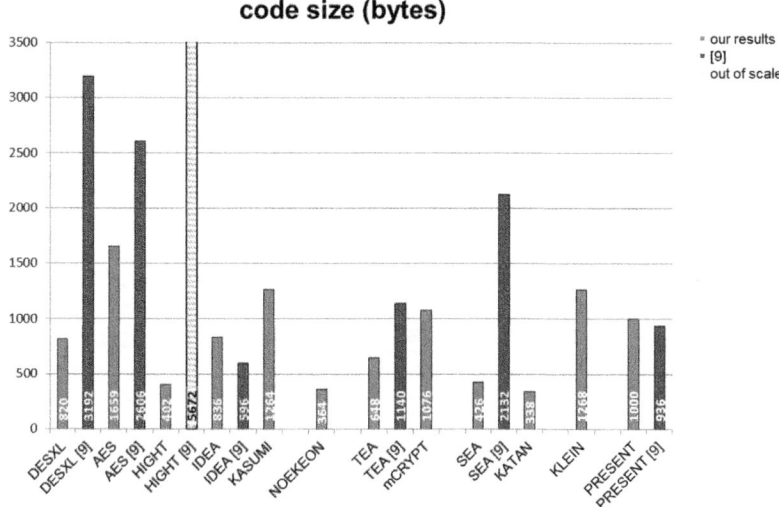

Fig. 1. Code size: comparison with previous work [9]

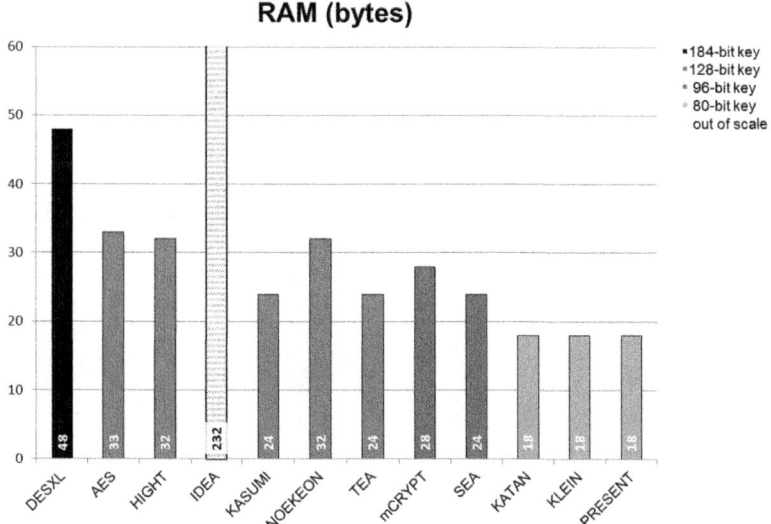

Fig. 2. Performance evaluation: RAM use

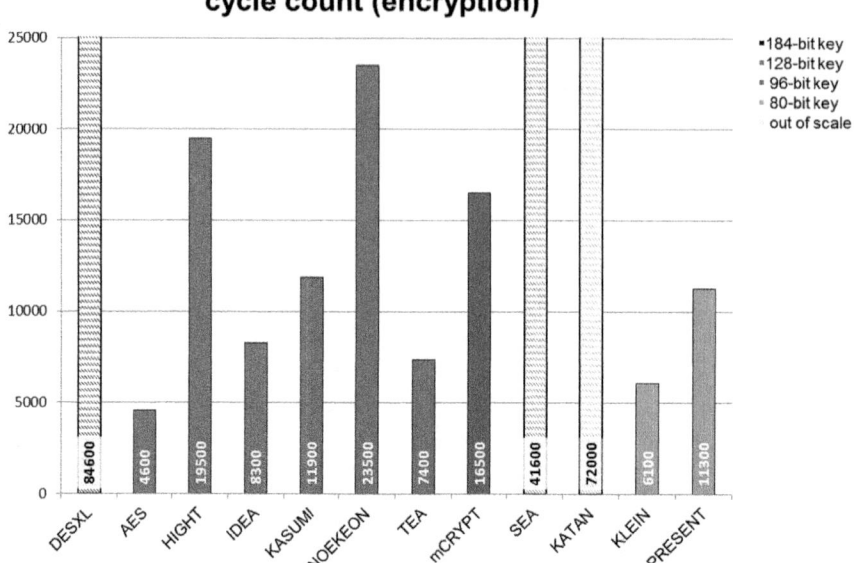

Fig. 3. Performance evaluation: cycle count (encryption)

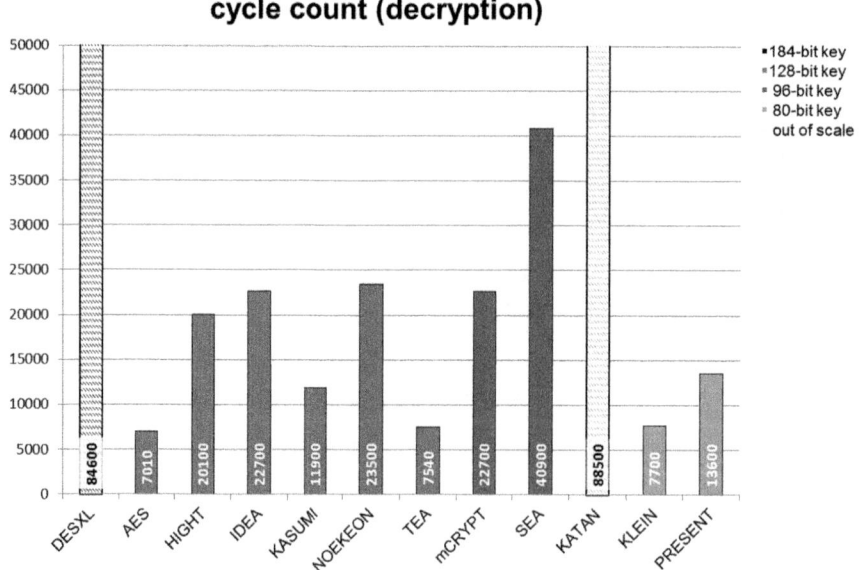

Fig. 4. Performance evaluation: cycle count (decryption)

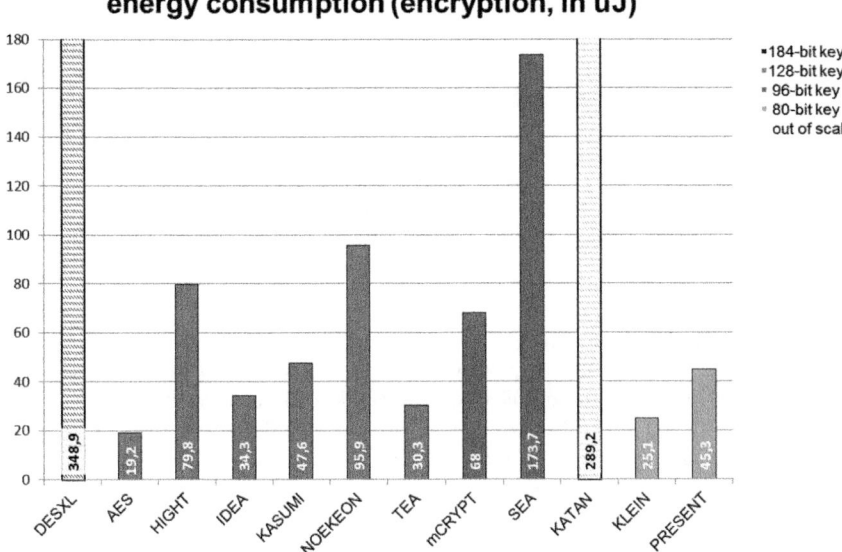

Fig. 5. Performance evaluation: energy consumption

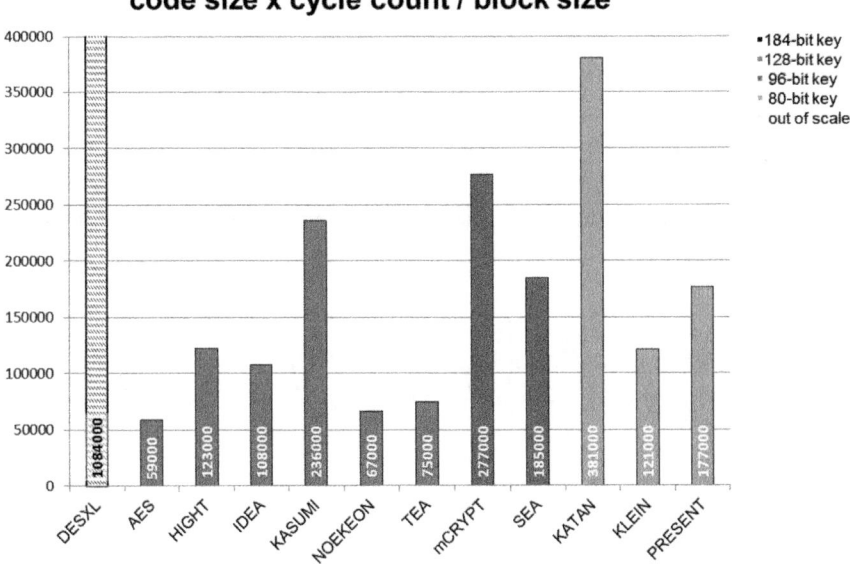

Fig. 6. Performance evaluation: combined metric

Cryptanalysis of Enhanced TTS, STS and All Its Variants, or: Why Cross-Terms Are Important

Enrico Thomae and Christopher Wolf

Horst Görtz Institute for IT-security
Faculty of Mathematics
Ruhr-University of Bochum, 44780 Bochum, Germany
enrico.thomae@rub.de, chris@Christopher-Wolf.de

Abstract. We show that the two multivariate signature schemes *Enhanced STS*, proposed at PQCrypto 2010, and *Enhanced TTS*, proposed at ACISP 2005, are vulnerable due to systematically missing cross-terms. To this aim, we generalize equivalent keys to so-called good keys for an improved algebraic key recovery attack. In particular, we demonstrate that it is impossible to choose both secure and efficient parameters for Enhanced STS and break all current parameters of both schemes.

Since 2010, many variants of Enhanced STS, such as Check Equations or Hidden Pair of Bijections were proposed. We break all these variants and show that making STS secure will either lead to a variant known as the Oil, Vinegar and Salt signature scheme or, if we also require the signing algorithm to be efficient, to the well-known Rainbow signature scheme. We show that our attack is more efficient than any previously known attack.

Keywords: Multivariate Cryptography, Algebraic Cryptanalysis, STS, TTS, Rank Attack, Key Recovery Attack, Equivalent Keys.

1 Introduction

All signature schemes discussed in this article use a public multivariate quadratic map $\mathcal{P} : \mathbb{F}_q^n \to \mathbb{F}_q^m$ with

$$
\mathcal{P} := \begin{pmatrix} p^{(1)}(x_1, \ldots, x_n) \\ \vdots \\ p^{(m)}(x_1, \ldots, x_n) \end{pmatrix}
$$

and

$$
p^{(k)}(x_1, \ldots, x_n) := \sum_{1 \leq i \leq j \leq n} \gamma_{ij}^{(k)} x_i x_j = x^\mathsf{T} \mathfrak{P}^{(k)} x, \text{ for } 1 \leq k \leq m, \gamma_{ij} \in \mathbb{F}_q
$$

where $\mathfrak{P}^{(k)}$ is the $(n \times n)$ matrix describing the quadratic form of $p^{(k)}$ and $x = (x_1, \ldots, x_n)^\mathsf{T}$. Note that we can neglect linear and constant terms for cryptanalytical purposes as they never mix with quadratic terms and thus have no

A. Mitrokotsa and S. Vaudenay (Eds.): AFRICACRYPT 2012, LNCS 7374, pp. 188–202, 2012.

positive effect on security. In the case of TTS those linear terms will even decrease security as we will see later. Inverting a system of *generic* multivariate quadratic ($\mathcal{MQ}$) polynomials $\mathcal{P}$ is known to be hard, as the corresponding $\mathcal{MQ}$-problem is proven to be $\mathcal{NP}$-complete [9]. However, the trapdoor is given by a structured central map $\mathcal{F} : \mathbb{F}_q^n \to \mathbb{F}_q^m$ with

$$\mathcal{F} := \begin{pmatrix} f^{(1)}(u_1, \ldots, u_n) \\ \vdots \\ f^{(m)}(u_1, \ldots, u_n) \end{pmatrix}$$

and

$$f^{(k)}(u_1, \ldots, u_n) := \sum_{1 \leq i \leq j \leq n} \gamma_{ij}^{(k)} u_i u_j = u^{\mathsf{T}} \mathfrak{F}^{(k)} u.$$

To hide the trapdoor we choose two secret linear transformations S, T and define $\mathcal{P} := T \circ \mathcal{F} \circ S$. See figure 1 for illustration.

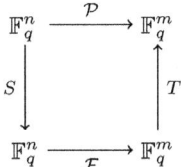

Fig. 1. $\mathcal{MQ}$-Scheme in general

One way to achieve a secret map $\mathcal{F} = (f_1, \ldots, f_m)^{\mathsf{T}}$ was given by the *Sequential Solution Method* of Tsujii [18,21]. The idea was somehow similar to the independently proposed schemes of Shamir [16] and Moh [14]. In 2004 Kasahara and Sakai extended this idea to the so-called RSE system [11], which later was generalized to the *Stepwise Triangular System* (STS) by Wolf et al. [22]. Here the central polynomials $f^{(k)}$ are some random quadratic polynomial in a restricted number of variables. See figure 2 for the stepped structure of the resulting $\mathcal{MQ}$-system. Inverting this map is possible as long as solving r quadratic equations in r variables is practical (cf. section 2 for the complexity of solving $\mathcal{MQ}$-systems). Consequently, we need to restrict r to rather small values, *e.g.* $r = 4 \ldots 9$.

In the same year Wolf et al. [22] showed how to efficiently break the proposed parameters of the STS schemes RSSE(2)PKC and RSE(2)PKC using a HighRank attack. At PQCrypto 2010 Tsujii et al. [20] tried to fix the scheme by proposing a new variant called *Enhanced STS*, which uses a complementary STS structure (cf. section 2). Only a few months later they noticed themselves that the scheme is obviously not immune to HighRank attacks, although this was originally a design goal. To fix this problem, they proposed several new variants [10,19]. In section 2 we will shortly repeat the HighRank Attack. We then give a more efficient algebraic key recovery attack which makes use of a generalization

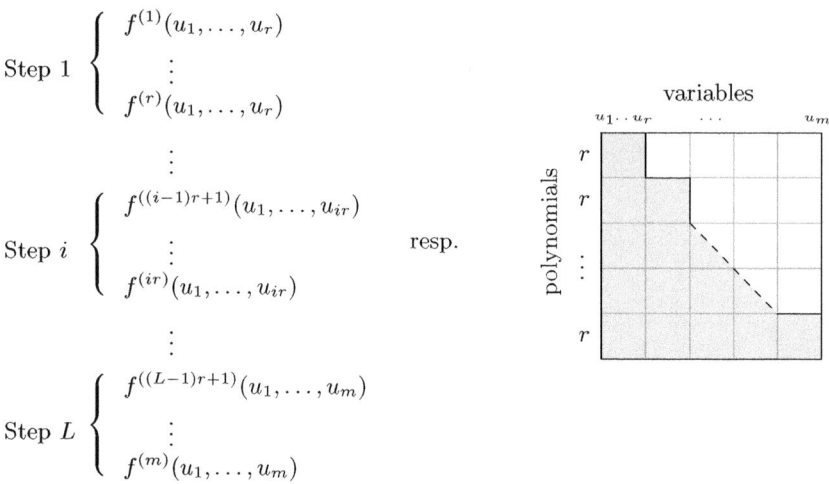

Fig. 2. Central map of STS based signature schemes like RSSE(2)PKC or RSE(2)PKC. The gray parts of the matrix indicate that those variables occur in the corresponding polynomial and white parts indicate that they do not.

of equivalent keys, which we call *good keys*, and missing cross-terms. The latter are quadratic monomials of two variables from different sets, which do not exist in the central map $\mathcal{F}$ by construction. We want to mention that our attack can be seen as a generalization of the Rainbow Band Separation attack [6]. Please refer to the full version of this article [17] for a comprehensive description of this connection.

Section 2 concludes with the statement that it is impossible to find a secure *and* efficient parameter set for Enhanced STS. In section 3 we will also break the new variants of STS. In section 4 we apply our attack to Enhanced TTS and break current sets of parameters. Note that we can repair Enhanced TTS by just raising parameters. In section 5 we discuss possible improvements and conclude our work.

2   Cryptanalysis of Enhanced STS

To exploit different ranks in plain STS, we use the quadratic form of the polynomials $f^{(k)}$, *i.e.* $f^{(k)} = u^{\mathsf{T}}\mathfrak{F}^{(i)}u$ for $u = (u_1, \ldots, u_m)^{\mathsf{T}}$ and some $(m \times m)$ matrix $\mathfrak{F}^{(i)}$. Note that we have $n = m = Lr$ here. Obviously the rank of these matrices in the i-th step is ir. Now we use that the rank is invariant under the bijective transformation $S^{-1}u = x$ of variables, *i.e.* $\text{rank}(S^{\mathsf{T}}\mathfrak{F}^{(i)}S) = \text{rank}(\mathfrak{F}^{(i)})$ for all i. In addition, the public polynomials $p^{(i)} = x^{\mathsf{T}}\mathfrak{P}^{(i)}x$ are given by some linear combination $\mathfrak{P}^{(i)} = \sum_{j=1}^{m} t_{ij}S^{\mathsf{T}}\mathfrak{F}^{(j)}S = S^{\mathsf{T}}\left(\sum_{j=1}^{m} t_{ij}\mathfrak{F}^{(j)}\right)S$. As the rank is changed by the transformation of equations T, we can use the rank property of the underlying central equations $f^{(k)}$ as a distinguisher to obtain the full transformation T.

Enhanced STS was thought to resist rank attacks. Tsujii *et al.* introduced two sets $U = \{u_1, \ldots, u_m\}$ and $V = \{v_1, \ldots, v_{m-r}\}$ of variables and constructed central polynomials $f^{(k)}$ which all have the *same* rank m. The construction is very similar to figure 2, but every polynomial $f^{(k)}$ depends on m variables. See figure 3 for details.

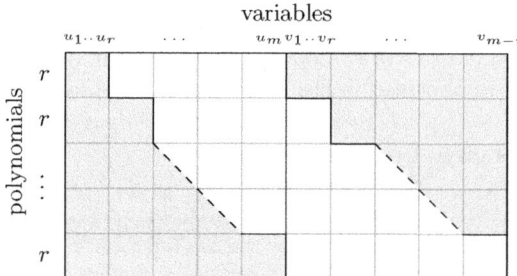

Fig. 3. Central map of Enhanced STS. The gray parts of the matrix indicate that those variables occur in the corresponding polynomial and white parts indicate that they do not.

As the corresponding $\mathcal{MQ}$-system $\mathcal{F}$ has m quadratic equations but $n = 2m - r$ variables, we could fix all variables of V to random values and obtain an $\mathcal{MQ}$-system of r equations and r variables in the first step. Solving this $\mathcal{MQ}$-system, substituting the solution in the next step and so on, allows for a reasonable efficient inversion of $\mathcal{F}$.

Tsujii *et al.* themselves noticed [19] that having the same rank m for the central polynomials $f^{(k)}$ does not prevent rank attacks in any way, as the rank of the public polynomials is $2m - r$. The following simple HighRank attack is still applicable. Note that due to the additional variables v_i the minimal rank of the central polynomials is m, for $m \geq 26$ in practice to prevent direct attacks. Thus Enhanced STS is at least secure against MinRank attacks [8,4].

HighRank Attack. In order to reconstruct T we have to search for linear combinations of the public polynomials $\mathfrak{P}^{(i)}$, such that the rank decrease from $2m - r$ to m. Let $\sigma \in S_m$ be a random permutation, which we need for randomization. Then there exist $\lambda_i \in \mathbb{F}_q$ such that the following linear combination has rank $2m - 2r$ and thus the rank drops by r.

$$\mathfrak{P}^{(\sigma(r+1))} + \sum_{i=1}^{r} \lambda_i \mathfrak{P}^{(\sigma(i))} =: \widetilde{\mathfrak{P}}$$

There are 2 different solutions, as we can eliminate the r matrices $\mathfrak{F}^{(1)}, \ldots, \mathfrak{F}^{(r)}$ or $\mathfrak{F}^{(m-r+1)}, \ldots, \mathfrak{F}^{(m)}$ such that $\widetilde{\mathfrak{P}}$ has rank $2m - 2r$. In the first case $\widetilde{\mathfrak{P}}$ is a linear combination of secret polynomials, who do not contain variables $v_1, \ldots, v_r$

respectively $u_{m-r+1}, \ldots, u_m$ in the latter case. Thus brute forcing all λ_i has complexity $q^r/2$. Once we have eliminated all the $\mathfrak{F}^{(i)}$ of one block (*e.g.* $1 \leq i \leq r$) in one polynomial $\widetilde{\mathfrak{P}}$ we easily eliminate those $\mathfrak{F}^{(i)}$ in all the other $m - r$ public polynomials by just determining $\ker(\widetilde{\mathfrak{P}})$. The linear system $\sum_{i=1}^{m} \lambda_i \mathfrak{P}^{(i)} \omega = 0$ with $\omega \in \ker(\widetilde{\mathfrak{P}})$ provides all $m - r$ polynomials of rank $2m - 2r$. The complexity of this step is $2(2m - r)^3$. Repeating this whole procedure L times yields r matrices $\widetilde{\mathfrak{P}}^{(i)}$ of rank m. At this point we know the kernel of one of the central blocks of $\mathcal{F}$ and could use this to separate the matrices in the steps before, which are still linear combinations of some $S^\top \mathfrak{F}^{(i)} S$. Choosing a vector that lies in the kernel of the matrices obtained in the i-th step, but not in the kernel of matrices recovered in step $i + 1, \ldots, L$ easily provides T. The overall complexity of this HighRank attack is given by

$$\frac{L}{2}q^r + 2L(2m - r)^3 + \sum_{i=1}^{L-1}(ir)^3 = \mathcal{O}(q^r).$$

Algebraic Key Recovery Attack. For readers not familiar with solving algorithms for multivariate non-linear systems of equations, we first briefly sketch how to determine the complexity of solving a $\mathcal{MQ}$-system using a Gröbner Basis algorithm like F_4 (cf. [2] for details). In a nutshell, we first have to calculate the degree of regularity d_{reg}. For semi-regular sequences, which generic systems are assumed to be, the degree of regularity is the index of the first non-positive coefficient in the Hilbert series $S_{m,n}$ with

$$S_{m,n} = \frac{\prod_{i=1}^{m}(1 - z^{d_i})}{(1 - z)^n},$$

where d_i is the degree of the i-th equation, m is the number of equations and n the number of variables. The complexity of solving a zero-dimensional (semi-regular) system using F_4 is

$$\mathcal{O}\left(\binom{n + d_{reg}}{d_{reg}}^\alpha\right),$$

with $2 \leq \alpha \leq 3$ the linear algebra constant. The internal equations used by F_4 are very sparse and thus $\alpha = 2$ is applied by cryptanalyst. Well, the constructors of schemes are often of a different opinion and use $\alpha = 3$. Note that generic $\mathcal{MQ}$-systems are assumed to have worst-case complexity. As soon as the equations contain some structure, *e.g.* they are bihomogeneous, the complexity of solving them decrease [7].

We saw that the complexity of the HighRank attack strongly depends on the field size q and the parameter r. Even if r is restricted to small values due to efficiency constraints, it is possible to choose q large enough to obtain a scheme secure against the previously mentioned attack. For example, let $r = 9$ and $q = 2^9$. Now we describe a new key recovery attack that is almost independent of the field size q and thus makes it impossible to find a parameter set that is both efficient and secure. To ease explanation we fix a parameter set of enhanced STS to illustrate the attack. As there are no parameters given in [19], which is by the way not very courteous to cryptanalyst, we choose $m = 27$, $r = 9$ and $q = 2^9$ as this prevents message recovery attacks via Gröbner Bases on the public key as well as HighRank attacks. The number of steps is given by $L = m/r = 3$. The number of variables is $n = 2m - r = |U| + |V| = 27 + 18 = 45$. Note that a legitimate user would need to solve three generic $\mathcal{MQ}$-system with 9 equations and variables over $\mathbb{F}_{2^9}$ to compute a signature. Using the fastest known method, i.e. the hybrid approach [3] by guessing one variable has theoretical complexity of $3q\binom{8+5}{5}^2 \approx 2^{31}$ with $d_{reg} = 5$. Using the very fast F_4 implementation of Magma V2.16-1 [5] on a Intel Xeon X33502.66GHz (Quadcore) with 4 GB of RAM using only one core, solving one system took us 0.3 seconds. Thus the worst case signing time is $3 \cdot 2^9 \cdot 0.3 \approx 461$ seconds. But despite of choosing such a large r, we now show that the resulting scheme still is not secure.

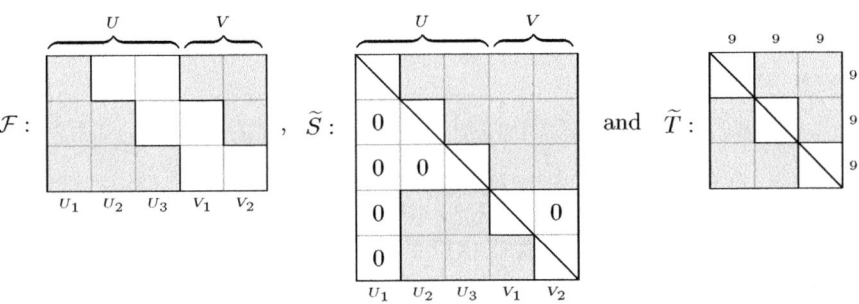

Fig. 4. Central map $\mathcal{F}$ of Enhanced STS and the minimal representative S and T of the class of equivalent keys

Figure 4 shows the structure of the central map $\mathcal{F}$. The picture describing $\mathcal{F}$ has to be read as figure 3. Every little square denotes a (9×9) array. Moreover, we give the structure of the secret key $\widetilde{S} := S^{-1}$, which is a (45×45) matrix with ones at the diagonal, zeros at the white parts and unknown values at the gray parts. Note that there are many different secret keys S respectively S^{-1} that preserve the structure of $\mathcal{F}$, i.e. preserve systematical zero coefficients in the polynomials $f^{(i)}$. We call all them *equivalent keys* and can assume that there is one representative with the structure given in figure 4 with overwhelming probability. The same holds for $\widetilde{T} := T^{-1}$. The notion of equivalent keys was introduced by Wolf et al. [23,24]. We skip the derivation of $\widetilde{S}$ and $\widetilde{T}$ given in figure 4 as it was already known and is very similar to the proof of lemma 1.

An algebraic key recovery attack uses the special structure of $\mathcal{F}$ to obtain equations in $\widetilde{S}$ and $\widetilde{T}$ through the following equality derived from $\mathcal{F} = T^{-1} \circ \mathcal{P} \circ S^{-1}$ with $\widetilde{T} := T^{-1} =: (\widetilde{t}_{ij})$ and $\widetilde{S} := S^{-1}$.

$$\mathfrak{F}^{(i)} = \widetilde{S}^{\mathsf{T}} \left(\sum_{j=1}^{m} \widetilde{t}_{ij} \mathfrak{P}^{(j)} \right) \widetilde{S} \tag{1}$$

As $\mathfrak{P}$ is publicly known and we further know that some of the entries of $\mathfrak{F}$ are systematically zero, we obtain cubic equations in the elements of $\widetilde{S}$ and $\widetilde{T}$. To ease notation in (2) we use $u_{j+m} := v_j$ for $j = 1, \ldots, m - r$. It is interesting to observe that the equations obtained from the coefficients $u_i u_j$ in f_k are of the form

$$0 = \sum_{x=1}^{n} \sum_{y=1}^{n} \sum_{z=1}^{n} \alpha_{xyz} \widetilde{t}_{kx} \widetilde{s}_{yi} \widetilde{s}_{zj} \tag{2}$$

for some coefficients $\alpha_{xyz} \in \mathbb{F}_q$ that depend on the public key matrices $\mathfrak{P}^{(j)}$ (cf. [15, Sec. 3] for an explicit formula). In particular every monomial contains one variable of the i-th column and one variable of the j-th column of $\widetilde{S}$. Due to the special form of $\widetilde{S}$ this immediately implies that all equations obtained by zero monomials $u_i u_j$ with $u_i \in U_1 := \{u_1, \ldots, u_9\}$ and $u_j \in U_2 \cup U_3 := \{u_{10}, \ldots, u_{18}\} \cup \{u_{19}, \ldots, u_{27}\}$, as well as $u_i v_j$ with $u_i \in U_1$ and $v_j \in V_1 \cup V_2 := \{v_1, \ldots, v_9\} \cup \{v_{10}, \ldots, v_{18}\}$ become quadratic instead of cubic. This change hence greatly improves the overall attack complexity. Defining $U \times V := \{\{u, v\} \mid u \in U, v \in V\}$ the total amount of equations obtained by systematical zeros in $\mathcal{F}$ is

$$9 \cdot (|(U_2 \cup U_3) \times (U_2 \cup U_3)| + |(U_2 \cup U_3) \times (V_1 \cup V_2)|)$$
$$+ 9 \cdot (|(U_3 \cup V_1) \times (U_3 \cup V_1)| + |(U_3 \cup V_1) \times (U_2 \cup V_2)|)$$
$$+ 9 \cdot (|(V_1 \cup V_2) \times (V_1 \cup V_2)| + |(V_1 \cup V_2) \times (U_2 \cup U_3)|)$$
$$= 9 \cdot 3 \cdot ((18 \cdot 19)/2 + 18 \cdot 18)$$
$$= 27 \cdot (171 + 324) = 13\,365 \text{ cubic equations and}$$

$$9 \cdot |(U_2 \cup U_3) \times U_1| + 9 \cdot |(U_3 \cup V_1) \times U_1| + 9 \cdot |(V_1 \cup V_2) \times U_1|$$
$$= 27 \cdot 162 = 4\,374 \text{ quadratic equations.}$$

Solving this system of equations in 486 variables $\widetilde{t}_{ij}$ and 1134 variables $\widetilde{s}_{ij}$ with a common Gröbner basis algorithm like F$_4$ has a total complexity of 2^{877} (cf. [1,2]). This huge complexity is due to the large number of variables and the fact that the complexity estimation assumes *generic equations* and thus does not take the structure of the equations into account. In order to decrease the complexity, we have to break down the problem into smaller pieces. This can be done if we further decrease the number of variables in $\widetilde{S}$ and $\widetilde{T}$. Therefore we generalize the notion of equivalent keys to keys that do not preserve the *whole* structure of $\mathcal{F}$ but just parts of it. We call these keys *good keys* if they also reveal some parts of the keys $\widetilde{S}$ respectively $\widetilde{T}$. At a first glance it is not clear that such good keys actually exists. The following lemma proves the existence of good keys and constructively give a special class of them.

Lemma 1. *Let $\widetilde{S}$ and $\widetilde{T}$ be equivalent keys for enhanced STS of the form given in figure 4. Then there exist good keys S' and T', of the following form. S' is all zero except the gray parts, which are equal to the corresponding values in $\widetilde{S}$ and the diagonal, which contains only ones. Similarly, the gray parts of T' equal the corresponding values in $\widetilde{T}$.*

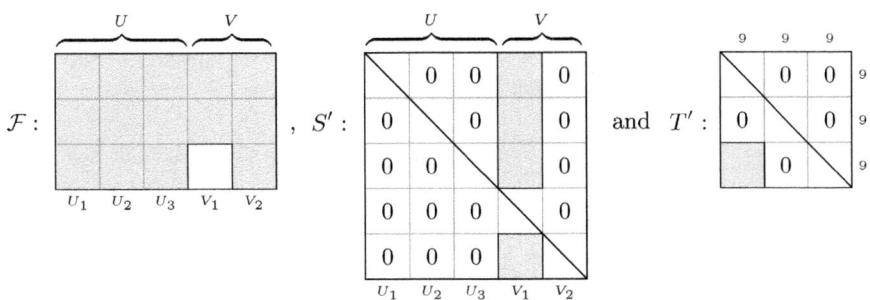

Proof. To preserve the structure of $\mathcal{F}$ given in lemma 1 we are allowed to map variables $U_1 \cup U_2 \cup U_3 \cup V_2 \mapsto U_1 \cup U_2 \cup U_3 \cup V_2$ as well as $V_1 \mapsto V_1$. As soon as we map variables from V_1 to any other set of variables, all polynomials would contain variables from V_1 and thus the whole structure of $\mathcal{F}$ would be destroyed. Now we show that using such a transformation Ω of variables, we can uniquely map $\widetilde{S}$ to S' by $\widetilde{S}\Omega = S'$.

$$
\widetilde{S}\Omega := \begin{pmatrix} I & \widetilde{S}^{(1)} & \widetilde{S}^{(2)} & \widetilde{S}^{(3)} & \widetilde{S}^{(4)} \\ 0 & I & \widetilde{S}^{(5)} & \widetilde{S}^{(6)} & \widetilde{S}^{(7)} \\ 0 & 0 & I & \widetilde{S}^{(8)} & \widetilde{S}^{(9)} \\ 0 & \widetilde{S}^{(10)} & \widetilde{S}^{(11)} & I & 0 \\ 0 & \widetilde{S}^{(12)} & \widetilde{S}^{(13)} & \widetilde{S}^{(14)} & I \end{pmatrix} \begin{pmatrix} \Omega^{(1)} & \Omega^{(2)} & \Omega^{(3)} & 0 & \Omega^{(4)} \\ \Omega^{(5)} & \Omega^{(6)} & \Omega^{(7)} & 0 & \Omega^{(8)} \\ \Omega^{(9)} & \Omega^{(10)} & \Omega^{(11)} & 0 & \Omega^{(12)} \\ \Omega^{(13)} & \Omega^{(14)} & \Omega^{(15)} & \Omega^{(16)} & \Omega^{(17)} \\ \Omega^{(18)} & \Omega^{(19)} & \Omega^{(20)} & 0 & \Omega^{(21)} \end{pmatrix} \overset{!}{=} S'
$$

Obviously $\Omega^{(16)} = I$ and thus $\widetilde{S}^{(3)}, \widetilde{S}^{(6)}, \widetilde{S}^{(8)}$ and $\widetilde{S}^{(14)}$ remain unchanged. As $\widetilde{S}$ is regular, all other $\Omega^{(i)}$ are uniquely determined by $\widetilde{S}^{-1}S'$. Showing that T' is a good key is trivial: If we only want $f_{2r+1}, \ldots, f_{3r}$ to contain no V_1 variables, we are allowed to map all polynomials except $f_1, \ldots, f_r$ to one another.   □

Using the good keys of lemma 1 we end up with 405 cubic equations, 2916 quadratic equations and 405 variables. The complexity of solving such a system using F_4 is still 2^{151}. To bring this game to an end, *i.e.* to preserve as less structure as possible and thus reduce the number of variables as much as possible, we only need to assure that f_{30} do not contain the variable v_1. With (2) we now obtain $|(U \cup V_2 \cup V_1 \setminus \{v_1\}) \times \{v_1\}| = 44$ quadratic equations and one cubic equation. Using good keys analogous to lemma 1, we obtain 9 variables t_{27j} for $1 \le j \le 9$ as well as 36 variables s_{i28} for $1 \le i \le 36$. Applying the generic complexity analysis as before still provides the same, and hence infeasible complexity of 2^{151}. Reason: now the number of equations equals the number of variables, which is assumed to have worst-case complexity. To obtain a better attack complexity we somehow have to use the fact that all quadratic equations are bihomogeneous, *i.e.* of the form $\sum_{i=1}^{36} \sum_{j=1}^{9} \alpha_{ij} t_{27j} s_{i28}$ for some $\alpha_{ij} \in \mathbb{F}_q$. In [7] Faugère *et al.* analyzed systems of such a special structure and gave an upper bound on the degree of regularity for F_4. To use their results we first have to guess one variable t_{ij} such that we obtain a system of 44 bihomogeneous equations in 44 variables. According to their results we now obtain a degree of regularity of 9 and a complexity of $2^9 \binom{44+9}{9}^2 \approx 2^{73}$. In general the degree of regularity is r, as we have $r-1$ variables t_{ij} after guessing and thus the complexity of our attack for arbitrary parameters is given by

$$q \binom{2m-1}{r}^2.$$

Once we obtained a single row/column of $\widetilde{S}$ and $\widetilde{T}$, the whole system breaks down as all other elements are now determined through linear equations. To show that this is actually true for all elements of $\widetilde{S}, \widetilde{T}$, let us label every equation obtained by a zero coefficient of $u_i u_j$ in f_k by (u_i, u_j, k) (cf. (2)). Now, (u_i, v_1, k) and (v_j, v_1, k) with $i = 1, \ldots, 27$, $j = 1, \ldots, 18$ and $k = 19, \ldots, 26$ provide linear equations in t_{ij} with $i = 19, \ldots, 26$ and $j = 1, \ldots, 9$. Next we can apply the same approach using good keys as above for v_1 to v_i, $i = 2, \ldots, 9$. As we already know the coefficients t_{ij} of the appropriate good key, all bihomogeneous equations become linear in s_{ij}. Next we can determine the next blocks in T through linear equations only. We repeat the process until all secret coefficients are recovered.

To summarize our new attack, we first used the fact that cross-terms from $(U \cup V_2) \times V_1$ do not exist to obtain quadratic instead of cubic equations in the key recovery attack. Second, we reduced the number of variables through good keys. And third, we used the special bihomogeneous structure of the equations to lower the attack's complexity. In order to protect the scheme against this attack we either have to increase m or r. But as the complexity of the signing algorithm is $3q \binom{r-1+d_{reg}}{r-1}^2$, i.e. in the same order of magnitude of our attack, Enhanced STS cannot be efficient and secure at the same time. In general it do not seem to be a good idea to use an exponential time signing algorithm (cf. section 5).

3   Cryptanalysis of Enhanced STS Variants

Check Equation Enhanced STS. The original Enhanced STS contain m quadratic equations in $2m-r$ variables in the public key and thus have q^{m-r} possible valid signatures to one message. Even if current algorithms cannot take advantage of underdetermined $\mathcal{MQ}$-systems, Tsujii et al. [19] suggested to strength their signature by adding $m - r$ check equations and thus fix one unique signature. From a message recovery point of view, the attacker now would have to solve a $\mathcal{MQ}$-system of $2m - r$ (public key) equations and variables. Before he had to solve a system of m equations and variables after just guessing the additional $m - r$ variables.

However, the check equations do not affect the algebraic key recover attack in section 2. Moreover, if the check equations are not chosen purely random and thus introducing new structure, the attack may even benefit.

Hidden Pair of Bijection. The overall idea is very general. Take a pair F_1, F_2 : $\mathbb{F}_q^m \to \mathbb{F}_q^m$ of bijections with a disjoint set of variables, i.e. $u = (u_1, \ldots, u_m)$ and $v = (v_1, \ldots, v_m)$ and connect them with a function H containing all the cross-terms of u and v. The central polynomial $f^{(k)}$ is given by

$$f^{(k)}(u,v) := F_1(u) + F_2(v) + H(u,v) \text{ for some } H(u,v) := \sum_{j=1}^{m} \sum_{i=1}^{m} \alpha_{ij} u_i v_j.$$

If F_1 and F_2 contain some trapdoor and we assign u or v zero, we can invert the central map. An instantiation of this scheme using the STS trapdoor is depicted in figure 5.

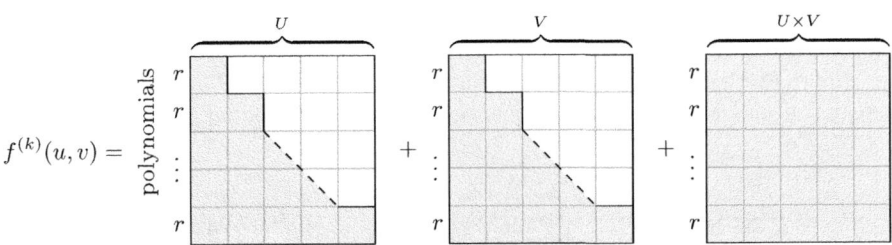

Fig. 5. Secret map $\mathcal{F}$ of Hidden Pair of Bijection using STS trapdoor

The first observation is that due to the cross-terms in H all the secret matrices $\mathfrak{F}^{(i)}$ have full rank $2m$ and thus rank attacks are not trivially applicable. But there is a smart way in applying rank attacks to the scheme. The weak point is the signing algorithm proposed by Tsujii *et al.*, which first chooses u or v to be zero. They claimed that this would not help an attacker, as his chance to guess the right choice is $\frac{1}{2}$. Well, if we collect $4m - 1$ valid signatures $x_1, \ldots, x_{4m-1}$ to arbitrary massages, which are all signed using the same secret S, we can built an efficient distinguisher. We know $X := (x_1^\mathsf{T}, \ldots, x_{2m-1}^\mathsf{T})$ is (up to column permutations) of the following form

$$X = S \cdot \begin{array}{|c|c|} \hline & 0 \\ \hline 0 & \\ \hline \end{array}$$

The probability of matrix X to have rank $2m - 1$ is $(1/2)^{2m-1} 2\binom{2m-1}{m}$ which is sufficiently large—for example choosing $m = 30$ this equals 0.21. Once we found a collection of signatures $x_1, \ldots, x_{2m-1}$, such that $\mathrm{rank}(X) = 2m - 1$ we obtained an efficient distinguisher. If $X || x_j$ for $j \geq 2m$ still has rank $2m - 1$ we add x_j to the set A. If the rank increase by one we add x_j to the set B. As soon as both sets A and B are of cardinality m we easily obtain a transformation $\widetilde{S}$ which separates the U and V space through linear algebra. After fixing one of the both sets of variables we obtain a plain STS scheme and can apply the HighRank or the Key Recovery attack from above.

In order to prevent this attack we would have to assign arbitrary values to u respectively v instead of all zeros. This immediately invalidate the trapdoor and renders the scheme unusable. In every step we would have to solve a quadratic underdetermined system of equation without destroying possible solution through guessing variables. We will discuss this question further in section 5.

4   Cryptanalysis of Enhanced TTS

Enhanced TTS was proposed by Yang and Chen in 2005 [25]. The overall idea of the scheme was to use several layers of UOV trapdoors and to make them as sparse as possible. In contrast to UOV this would prevent the Kipnis and Shamir attack [13] without increasing the number of vinegar variables. In fact, while we have a signature blow up of factor 3 for UOV, enTTS improves this figure to 1.3. As enTTS was designed for high speed implementation it uses as few monomials as possible.

There are two different scalable central maps given in [25], one is called *even* sequence and the other *odd* sequence. The following equations show the even sequence.

$$f^{(i)} = u_i + \sum_{j=1}^{2\ell-5} \gamma_{ij} u_j u_{2\ell-4+(i+j+1 \bmod 2\ell-2)} \qquad \text{for } 2\ell - 4 \le i \le 4\ell - 7,$$

$$f^{(i)} = u_i + \sum_{j=1}^{\ell-4} \gamma_{ij} u_{i+j-(4\ell-6)} u_{i-j-2\ell-1} + \sum_{j=\ell-3}^{2\ell-5} \gamma_{ij} u_{i+j-3\ell+5} u_{i-j+\ell-4}$$
$$\text{for } 4\ell - 6 \le i \le 4\ell - 3,$$

$$f^{(i)} = u_i + \gamma_{i0} u_{i-2\ell+2} u_{i-2\ell-2} + \sum_{j=i+1}^{6\ell-5} \gamma_{i,j-(4\ell-3)} u_{4\ell-3+i-j} u_j$$
$$+ \gamma_{i,i-4\ell+3} u_0 u_i + \sum_{j=4\ell-2}^{i-1} \gamma_{i,j-(4\ell-3)} u_{2(i-j)-(i \bmod 2)} u_j + \gamma_{i,i-4\ell+2} u_0 u_i$$
$$\text{for } 4\ell - 2 \le i \le 6\ell - 5.$$

The number of equations and variables is $m = 4\ell$ and $n = 6\ell - 4$, respectively, for some parameter ℓ. The first observation is that the number of equations obtained by (2) is very large, as only $2\ell - 3$ monomials per equation are non-zero. The second observation is that the linear terms provide an enormous amount of new equations, as their coefficients are not chosen at random but fixed. Considering only the linear parts of the public polynomials $p^{(j)}$ we obtain the following equation analogously to (1)

$$e_{i+2\ell-5} = \widetilde{S} \left(\sum_{j=1}^{m} \widetilde{t}_{ij} (\gamma_1^{(j)}, \dots, \gamma_n^{(j)})^{\mathsf{T}} \right) \qquad \text{for } 1 \le i \le m, \qquad (3)$$

where e_i denote the all-zero vector with a single 1 in the i-th entry and $\gamma_i^{(j)}$ is the coefficient of x_i in $p^{(j)}$. We obtain a total amount of $4\ell(6\ell - 4)$ bihomogeneous equations in the $(4\ell)^2$ variables of $\widetilde{T}$ and in the $(6\ell - 4)^2$ variables of $\widetilde{S}$. But despite of this large amount of equations a theoretical complexity analysis of solving those equations provide infeasible large results, due to the large amount of variables. Note that in practice the solving algorithm may seriously benefit of the equations internal structure. We leave it as an open problem to implement this attack and run experiments to determine the real complexity of attacking enTTS this way.

In the sequel we once again focus on reducing the number of variables. Note that most of the equations (3) vanish as soon as we use equivalent keys. This is also true for a large amount of zero-coefficients in the quadratic part. Thus we generalize the scheme by adding *more* monomials. In particular, we adapt the definition of enTTS as follows: As soon as a monomial $x_i x_j$ with $x_i \in U$ and $x_j \in V$ occurs in the original enTTS polynomial $f^{(k)}$, we just assume that all monomials $x_i x_j$ with $x_i \in U$ and $x_j \in V$ occur as well. This way we easily see that enTTS is a very special case of the Rainbow signature scheme, neglecting the linear parts. We chose the parameter set $(n, m) = (32, 24)$ and thus $\ell = 6$ given in [25], as this provides a security level of 2^{88}. See figure 6 for an illustration.

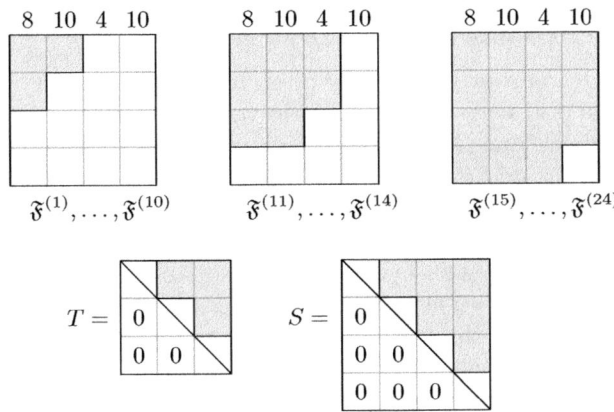

Fig. 6. Secret map $\mathcal{F}$ of TTS $(32, 24)$ and equivalent keys T and S

The attack is similar to the one described in section 2. Suppose we just want do preserve zero coefficients of $x_{32} x_i$ in polynomial $u^\intercal \mathfrak{F}^{(14)} u$. This leads to the good keys given in figure 7 and thus to 31 bihomogeneous equations in 10 variables t_{14i} with $i = 15, \ldots, 24$ and 22 variables s_{j32} with $j = 1, \ldots, 22$. Analogous to section 2 we first have to guess one variable t_{ij}. Solving the remaining system of 31 bihomogeneous equations in 31 variables has complexity $2^8 \binom{31+10}{10}^2 \approx 2^{68}$.

But due to the special structure of enTTS we can do even better. Applying the transformation of variables Ω analogous to lemma 1, we see that the monomial $u_{32} u_{32}$ do not occur in *any* of the secret polynomials. This way we additionally obtain 23 quadratic equations in s_{ij}. The complexity of solving a generic system of $23 + 31$ quadratic and 1 cubic equation in 32 variables is $2^{52.4}$. Note that this complexity is just an upper bound as we assumed generic equations and thus did not use the special structure.

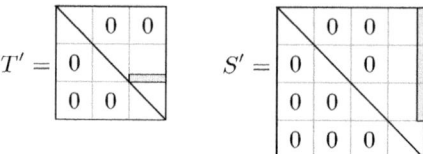

Fig. 7. Good Keys T' and S' for enTTS $(32, 24)$

5   Conclusions or: *Where Do We Take It from Here?*

In summary, we have introduced a new attack that is applicable to both Enhanced STS and Enhanced TTS. It uses equations on cross-terms and the inherent bihomogenious structure of them. In the case of Enhanced STS the question arise if non-linearity could help in any way to improve UOV or Rainbow. Or in other words, is it possible to repair STS at all?

Quick Fix. One answer was already given by Kipnis *et al.* in the paper that proposed UOV [12]. One of their possible variants to repair the *balanced* Oil and Vinegar scheme and thus to avoid the attack of Kipnis and Shamir [13] was called *Oil, Vinegar and Salt* signature scheme. Here the variables are divided into three sets O, V and S. The central map $\mathcal{F}$ is constructed such that there are no monomials $u_i u_j$ with $u_i \in O$ and $u_j \in V \cup S$. After fixing the vinegar variables we obtain a system linear in the O variables and quadratic in the S variables. The best known way to solve such a system is to brute-force the S variables and then solve the remaining linear system. This way we loose a factor of $q^{|S|}$ in terms of efficiency. As it turned out later, a modified version of the Kipnis and Shamir attack actually *can* be applied to the Oil, Vinegar and Salt scheme. Ironically, the factor we gain compared to the original scheme is exactly the factor we loose in terms of efficiency. But as the (positive) effect of non-linearity to the public key size is negligible compared to the (negative) effect to the efficiency of the scheme, the best trade-off is to just skip the salt variables and hence use the original UOV scheme.

The Dilemma. STS can be seen as a layer-based version of Oil, Vinegar and Salt. So we can rephrase the question between UOV and UOV+S in this setting. In particular, we have to ask ourselves if the layered structure of STS allows for a better trade-off between efficiency and security than UOV. Unfortunately, we have to leave the final answer as an open question. However, we incline to the negative. To illustrate this, we want to elaborate some thoughts on this matter. One the one hand, it is not clear even for UOV if the ratio between efficiency and security increases for the layer-based scheme Rainbow. Especially the attack of section 4, which is not applicable to UOV, challenges this hope. On the other hand, the attack of Kipnis and Shamir [13] is exponential and not practical for layer-based schemes like Rainbow. So the question remains, if and how much security we can gain at all by introducing some non-linearity in each layer. Our intuition is that the loss of efficiency is always greater or equal than the gain of security in these cases and hence of no avail in practice. The reason is that on the one hand the signing algorithm becomes exponential instead of polynomial, as soon as we introduce non-linear parts. In comparison, the attack stays exponential in *both* cases, *i.e.* there is no security gap between the legitimate user and the attacker.

A Way Out? The only exception from this rule seem to be Gröbner bases that are used without any additional structure as a trapdoor. Clearly we have to use Vinegar variables in that case, as otherwise MinRank attacks are applicable. But we found no way to fuse this into a working scheme—but got the impression that this is not possible at all. Hence, we leave it as an open problem, how to embed a Gröbner Basis into a scheme using Vinegar variables and to derive a both secure *and* efficient scheme.

Acknowledgments. We want to thank Peter Czypek (Bochum) for fruitful discussions and helpful remarks on Enhanced TTS. Furthermore we thank the reviewers for helpful comments.

The authors were supported by the German Science Foundation (DFG) through an Emmy Noether grant where the second author is principal investigator. All authors were in part supported by the European Commission through the IST Programme under contract *ICT-2007-216676 Ecrypt II*.

References

1. Bardet, M., Faugère, J.-C., Salvy, B.: On the complexity of Gröbner basis computation of semi-regular overdetermined algebraic equations. In: Proceedings of the International Conference on Polynomial System Solving, pp. 71–74 (2004)
2. Bardet, M., Faugère, J.-C., Salvy, B., Yang, B.-Y.: Asymptotic expansion of the degree of regularity for semi-regular systems of equations. In: Gianni, P. (ed.) MEGA 2005, Sardinia, Italy (2005)
3. Bettale, L., Faugère, J.-C., Perret, L.: Hybrid approach for solving multivariate systems over finite fields. Journal of Mathematical Cryptology 3, 177–197 (2009)
4. Billet, O., Gilbert, H.: Cryptanalysis of Rainbow. In: De Prisco, R., Yung, M. (eds.) SCN 2006. LNCS, vol. 4116, pp. 336–347. Springer, Heidelberg (2006)
5. Computational Algebra Group, University of Sydney. The MAGMA Computational Algebra System for Algebra, Number Theory and Geometry, http://magma.maths.usyd.edu.au/magma/
6. Ding, J., Yang, B.-Y., Chen, C.-H.O., Chen, M.-S., Cheng, C.-M.: New Differential-Algebraic Attacks and Reparametrization of Rainbow. In: Bellovin, S.M., Gennaro, R., Keromytis, A.D., Yung, M. (eds.) ACNS 2008. LNCS, vol. 5037, pp. 242–257. Springer, Heidelberg (2008)
7. Faugère, J.-C., Din, M.S.E., Spaenlehauer, P.-J.: Gröbner bases of bihomogeneous ideals generated by polynomials of bidegree (1, 1): Algorithms and Complexity. J. Symb. Comput. 46(4), 406–437 (2011)
8. Faugère, J.-C., Levy-dit-Vehel, F., Perret, L.: Cryptanalysis of MinRank. In: Wagner, D. (ed.) CRYPTO 2008. LNCS, vol. 5157, pp. 280–296. Springer, Heidelberg (2008)

9. Garey, M.R., Johnson, D.S.: Computers and Intractability — A Guide to the Theory of NP-Completeness. W.H. Freeman and Company (1979) ISBN 0-7167-1044-7 or 0-7167-1045-5

10. Gotaishi, M., Tsujii, S.: Hidden Pair of Bijection signature scheme. IACR Cryptology ePrint Archive (2011), http://eprint.iacr.org/2011/353

11. Kasahara, M., Sakai, R.: A construction of public-key cryptosystem based on singular simultaneous equations. In: Symposium on Cryptography and Information Security — SCIS 2004, Sendai, Japan, January 27-30. The Institute of Electronics, Information and Communication Engineers (2004)

12. Kipnis, A., Patarin, J., Goubin, L.: Unbalanced Oil and Vinegar signature schemes — extended version, 17 pages (2003)

13. Kipnis, A., Shamir, A.: Cryptanalysis of the Oil & Vinegar Signature Scheme. In: Krawczyk, H. (ed.) CRYPTO 1998. LNCS, vol. 1462, pp. 257–266. Springer, Heidelberg (1998)

14. Moh, T.: A public key system with signature and master key function. Communications in Algebra 27(5), 2207–2222 (1999), electronic version, http://citeseer/moh99public.html

15. Petzoldt, A., Thomae, E., Bulygin, S., Wolf, C.: Small Public Keys and Fast Verification for Multivariate Quadratic Public Key Systems. In: Preneel, B., Takagi, T. (eds.) CHES 2011. LNCS, vol. 6917, pp. 475–490. Springer, Heidelberg (2011)

16. Shamir, A.: Efficient Signature Schemes Based on Birational Permutations. In: Stinson, D.R. (ed.) CRYPTO 1993. LNCS, vol. 773, pp. 1–12. Springer, Heidelberg (1994)

17. Thomae, E.: A Generalization of the Rainbow Band Separation Attack and its Applications to Multivariate Schemes. IACR Cryptology ePrint Archive (2012)

18. Tsujii, S., Fujioka, A., Hirayama, Y.: Generalization of the public-key cryptosystem based on the difficulty of solving non-linear equations. Transactions of the Institute of Electronics and Communication Engineers of Japan (1989)

19. Tsujii, S., Gotaishi, M.: Enhanced STS using check equation - extended version of the signature scheme proposed in the PQCrypt 2010. IACR Cryptology ePrint Archive (2010), http://eprint.iacr.org/2010/480

20. Tsujii, S., Gotaishi, M., Tadaki, K., Fujita, R.: Proposal of a Signature Scheme Based on STS Trapdoor. In: Sendrier, N. (ed.) PQCrypto 2010. LNCS, vol. 6061, pp. 201–217. Springer, Heidelberg (2010)

21. Tsujii, S., Kurosawa, K., Itho, T., Fujioka, A., Matsumoto, T.: A public-key cryptosystem based on the difficulty of solving a system of non-linear equations. Transactions of the Institute of Electronics and Communication Engineers of Japan (1986)

22. C. Wolf, A. Braeken, and B. Preneel. Efficient cryptanalysis of RSE(2)PKC and RSSE(2)PKC. In Conference on Security in Communication Networks — SCN 2004, volume 3352 of Lecture Notes in Computer Science, pages 294–309. Springer, Sept. 8–10 2004. Extended version: http://eprint.iacr.org/2004/237.

23. Wolf, C., Preneel, B.: Equivalent Keys in HFE, C*, and Variations. In: Dawson, E., Vaudenay, S. (eds.) Mycrypt 2005. LNCS, vol. 3715, pp. 33–49. Springer, Heidelberg (2005), extended version, 15 pages, http://eprint.iacr.org/2004/360/

24. Wolf, C., Preneel, B.: Equivalent keys in multivariate quadratic public key systems. Journal of Mathematical Cryptology 4(4), 375–415 (2011)

25. Yang, B.-Y., Chen, J.-M.: Building Secure Tame-like Multivariate Public-Key Cryptosystems: The New TTS. In: Boyd, C., González Nieto, J.M. (eds.) ACISP 2005. LNCS, vol. 3574, pp. 518–531. Springer, Heidelberg (2005)

A Complementary Analysis of the (s)YZ and DIKE Protocols

Augustin P. Sarr[1] and Philippe Elbaz–Vincent[2]

[1] Université de Strasbourg
aug.sarr@gmail.com
[2] Institut Fourier – CNRS, Université Grenoble 1

Abstract. The Canetti–Krawczyk (CK) model remains widely used for the analysis of key agreement protocols. We recall the CK model, and its variant used for the analysis of the HMQV protocol, the CK_{HMQV} model; we recall also some of the limitations of these models. Next, we show that the (s)YZ protocols do not achieve their claimed CK_{HMQV} security. Furthermore, we show that they do not achieve their claimed computational fairness. Our attack suggests that no two–pass key establishment protocol can achieve this attribute. We show also that the Deniable Internet Key Exchange fails in authentication; this illustrates the inability of capturing some impersonation attacks in the CK model. Besides, we propose a secure, efficient, and deniable protocol, geared to the post peer specified model.

Keywords: authentication, key establishment, computational fairness, deniability, (e)CK models, (s)YZ, DIKE, SMQV-1.

1 Introduction

The design and analysis of key agreement protocols is a notoriously subtle topic; a large part of the proposed designs appears to be flawed. In [1], Bellare and Rogaway proposed a new approach for the analysis of key agreement protocols. Since their work, other models was proposed, including the Canetti–Krawczyk (CK) [3] and the extended Canetti–Krawczyk (eCK) [13] models, which are now considered as advanced security definitions. However, there remains a large class of attacks which are not considered in these security definitions [6,22].

Recently, Yao and Zhao [25] proposed a new family of authenticated key establishment protocols, the (s)YZ protocols, they analyzed in the CK_{HMQV} model (the variant of the CK model used in [11,12] for the analysis of the HMQV protocol). They introduced also a new security notion, *computational unfairness*, which aims to capture the difference that may exist between the computational effort it requires for an honest and a malicious party to complete a session; and showed that the (s)YZ protocols are computationally fair, while (H)MQV is not. Also, in [27], they proposed a new protocol termed Deniable Internet Key Exchange (DIKE), which "adds novelty and new value to the IKE" standard; they showed the DIKE secure in the CK model.

A. Mitrokotsa and S. Vaudenay (Eds.): AFRICACRYPT 2012, LNCS 7374, pp. 203–220, 2012.

In this work, we propose a complementary analysis of the (s)YZ and DIKE protocols; we examine also the computational unfairness security attribute. First, we show that, contrary to the claims of [25], the (s)YZ protocols do not achieve the CK_{HMQV}–security. Second, we show that the (s)ZY protocols do not achieve the computational fairness attribute; further, our attack suggests that no two–pass key establishment protocol can achieve this attribute. Third, we show that the DIKE protocol fails in authentication. Namely, if an attacker learns the ephemeral secret at a session initiator, it can impersonate any party to the initiator; this illustrates also the inability of capturing some impersonation attacks in the CK model.

The remainder of this paper is organized as follows. In section 2, we recall the CK and CK_{HMQV} security models, and some of their limitations. In section 3, we recall the YZ protocols family. In section 4 we discuss the YZ protocols attributes, and propose an attack which invalidates their CK_{HMQV} security, we show also that these protocols do not achieve their claimed computational fairness. In section 5, we recall the DIKE protocol, and propose an attack which shows its failure in authentication, we also present a SMQV variant geared to the post peer specified model. We conclude in section 6.

Notations and terminology: $\mathcal{G}$ denotes a multiplicatively written cyclic group of prime order q generated by G, $|q|$ is the bit length of q; $\mathcal{G}^*$ is the set of non–identity elements in $\mathcal{G}$. For $X \in \mathcal{G}$, the lowercase x denotes the discrete logarithm of X in base G. The identity of a party with public key A is denoted $\hat{A}$; $\hat{A}$ is supposed to contain A, and may be a certificate. If $\hat{A} \neq \hat{B}$, we suppose that no substring of $\hat{A}$ equals $\hat{B}$. H, H_1, and H_K are λ–bit cryptographic hash function, where λ is the length of session keys, and $\bar{H}$ is a l–bit hash function, where $l = (\lfloor \log_2 q \rfloor + 1)/2$. The symbol $\in_R$ stands for "chosen uniformly at random in."

2   The Canetti–Krawczyk Security Model(s)

In the CK model, a protocol is defined as a collection of procedures run by a finite number of parties. Each protocol specifies its processing rules for incoming and outgoing messages. A *two–party key agreement* is a protocol which involves two parties. A *session* is an instance of a protocol run at a party. In a two–party key agreement, each session is activated with a quadruple $(\hat{P}_i, \hat{P}_j, \psi, \varsigma)$, where $\hat{P}_i$ is the session owner, $\hat{P}_j$ is the peer, ψ is the session identifier, and ς is the role of $\hat{P}_i$ in the session. A session identifier is required to be unique at each party involved in the session, i.e., a party never uses the same identifier twice. Two sessions with activation parameters $(\hat{P}_i, \hat{P}_j, \psi, \varsigma)$ and $(\hat{P}_j, \hat{P}_i, \psi', \varsigma')$ are said to be matching if $\psi = \psi'$. Notice that CK matching sessions can have the same role.

The adversary, denoted by $\mathcal{A}$, is a probabilistic polynomial time machine in control of communications between parties; outgoing messages are submitted to $\mathcal{A}$, which decides about their delivery. The adversary decides also about session activations. In addition, it is given the following queries, aiming to model practical information leakages.

- SessionStateReveal($\hat{P}_i, \psi$): when this query is issued on the uncompleted session ψ at $\hat{P}_i$, the adversary obtains the session's ephemeral information. However, the model does not specify the information revealed by this query; it leaves this to be specified by protocol designers.
- SessionKeyReveal($\hat{P}_i, \psi$): with this query, the adversary obtains, the session key derived in the session ψ at $\hat{P}_i$, if the session is completed and unexpired.
- Corrupt($\hat{P}_i$): when this query is issued on a party $\hat{P}_i$, the adversary obtains all the information the party holds, including its static private key and session states. Once the query issued, the attacker (which is in control of communication links) can impersonate the party at will; one then consider the party under the attacker's control. A party against which this query is not issued is said to be *honest*.
- Expire($\hat{P}_i, \psi$): this query models the erasure of a session key and state from the session owner's memory. Notice that a session can be expired while its matching session is unexpired.
- Test($\hat{P}_i, \psi$): when this query is issued on a completed (and unexpired) session ψ at $\hat{P}_i$, a bit γ is chosen at random, and depending on the value of γ, the attacker is provided with either the session key, or a random value chosen under the distribution of session keys. The attacker is allowed to continue its run with regular queries, but not to reveal the test session or its matching session's key or state.

Definition 1 (CK Session Freshness). *A session at a party is said to be* locally exposed *if it was sent a* SessionStateReveal *query, a* SessionKeyReveal *query, or if its owner is corrupted. A session is said to be* exposed *if it or its matching session is locally exposed. An unexposed session is said to be* CK–fresh.

With this session freshness definition, a CK–secure protocol is as follows.

Definition 2 (CK–Security). *A two–party key agreement protocol is said to be* CK–secure *if: (1) when two uncorrupted parties complete matching sessions then, except with negligible probability, they both compute the same session key, and (2) no polynomially bounded adversary can distinguish a CK–fresh session key from a random value (chosen under the distribution of session keys) with probability significantly greater than $1/2$.*

2.1 The CK$_{\text{HMQV}}$ Model

In [12], Krawczyk uses a variant of the CK–model for the analysis of the HMQV protocol. In this variant, termed here CK$_{\text{HMQV}}$, a session is identified with a quadruple $(\hat{P}_i, \hat{P}_j, X, Y)$ where $\hat{P}_i$ is the session owner, $\hat{P}_j$ is the peer, and X and Y are respectively the outgoing and incoming ephemeral public keys. Two sessions with identifiers $(\hat{P}_i, \hat{P}_j, X, Y)$ and $(\hat{P}_j, \hat{P}_i, Y, X)$ are said to be *matching*. In addition, there is no Expire query in the CK$_{\text{HMQV}}$ model (the motivation is that the CK$_{HMQV}$ model does not aim to capture *forward secrecy*[1], but *weak forward secrecy* [11]).

In a separate analysis, Krawczyk [12, sections 6 and 7.4] allows the adversary to query a SessionStateReveal on the test session, or to learn the static private key of the session's owner. Notice that, the purpose of [12], was not to propose a new security model, as it refers to [3] for details [12, p. 9], and considers its session identifiers and matching sessions definitions as consistent with the CK–model [12, p. 10], while the CK and CK$_{HMQV}$ models are formally and practically incomparable [5,6]. Except the differences on (1) session identifiers and matching sessions definition, and (2) the absence of the Expire query in the CK$_{HMQV}$ model, the CK and CK$_{HMQV}$ session freshness and security definitions are the same.

Some Weaknesses in the CK($_{HMQV}$) Models

In this section, we recall some of the reported weaknesses on the CK and CK$_{HMQV}$ security models. The discussion is voluntarily limited to the aspects related to this work. Notice that contrary to [25], and in accordance with [2,4,5,22,6], by CK–model we mean the security model defined in [3], and by CK$_{HMQV}$, the model(s) used in [11] for the analysis of the HMQV protocol.

On the CK Matching Sessions. Besides not modelling *key compromise impersonation resilience,* a main limitation of the CK model is its matching sessions definition. Indeed, it is a requirement of the model that the layer calling a key agreement protocol makes sure that a party never uses the same identifier twice. One may ask how can this be achieved over an unauthenticated network in control of an active adversary. Moreover, in the CK model, session identifiers may be nonces generated by the session initiator and provided to the peer in the first message of the protocol. In this case, when each party stores the previously used identifiers, and verifies at session activation that the identifier was not used before; the requirement that a party never uses the same identifier twice is then achieved. Unfortunately, in such a case, the model fails in capturing some practical impersonation attacks. A kind of impersonation attacks not captured in the CK model, was reported and illustrated in [22, section 2] on the protocol $\mathcal{P}$ from [17].

Limitation of the CK$_{HMQV}$ Session Identifiers. By defining matching sessions using the identities and ephemeral keys of the involved parties, the CK$_{HMQV}$ model, patches the impossibility of capturing, in the CK model, the kind of impersonation attacks reported in [22, section 2]. However, the CK$_{HMQV}$ session identifiers and matching sessions definitions, remain limited. Indeed, as reported in [5,6], protocols such that the way a party involved in a session derives

---

[1] Some authors, [11] for instance, use the term 'perfect forward secrecy', but following [2], we prefer 'forward secrecy' to avoid a confusion with Shannon's 'perfect secrecy'.

the session key is dependent from its role (*initiator* or *responder*) are insecure in the CK_{HMQV} model. The security of such protocols can be invalided by an attacker performing as in Attack 1.

Attack 1. Crossing Attack to invalidate CK_{HMQV} security

---

(1) Activate a session at $\hat{A}$ with peer $\hat{B}$, and intercept $\hat{A}$'s message to $\hat{B}$.
(2) Activate a session at $\hat{B}$ with peer $\hat{A}$, and intercept $\hat{B}$'s message to $\hat{A}$.
(3) Send $\hat{B}$'s message to $\hat{A}$ as a responder in the session initiated by $\hat{A}$.
(4) Send $\hat{A}$'s message to $\hat{B}$ as a responder in the session initiated by $\hat{B}$.

In this attack, the sessions at $\hat{A}$ and $\hat{B}$ are CK_{HMQV} matching; but, when the key derivation is role dependent, they do not yield the same session key. As a result, the first requirement in the CK_{HMQV} security definition is not satisfied. Such attacks invalidate a large class of valuable protocols. Consider, for instance, the HMQV protocol. Recall that in an HMQV execution, the initiator, say $\hat{A}$, chooses and ephemeral key $X = G^x$ ans sends $(\hat{A}, \hat{B}, X)$ to the responder $\hat{B}$; $\hat{B}$ chooses an ephemeral key $Y = G^y$ and sends $(\hat{B}, \hat{A}, Y)$ to $\hat{A}$. Both $\hat{A}$ and $\hat{B}$ compute the dual signature $\sigma = (YB^e)^{x+da} = (XA^d)^{y+eb}$, wherein $d = \bar{H}(X, \hat{B})$ and $e = \bar{H}(Y, \hat{A})$; and the session key $K = H(\sigma)$. One can see, through Attack 1 that the HMQV variant wherein the session key is derived as $H(\sigma, X, Y)$ instead of $K = H(\sigma)$ is formally insecure in the CK_{HMQV} model. The CK_{HMQV} matching sessions definition formally invalidates a large class of valuable designs. In another respect, as the CK_{HMQV} model does not differentiate a session initiator and a responder in key derivation, CK_{HMQV} secure protocols may be vulnerable to some kinds of reflection attacks (see the worm–hole attack on HMQV [7], for instance).

3 The YZ Protocols Family

In [26] Yoa and Zhao introduce a family of authenticated Diffie–Hellman protocols. The building blocks of the protocols, termed *joint proof of knowledge*, can be viewed as variants of the (D)XCR scheme. The general construction of the secret group element, shared between two parties, say $\hat{A}$ and $\hat{B}$, with respective ephemeral keys X and Y is $Z = B^{fa+dx}Y^{ca+ex} = A^{fb+cy}X^{db+ey}$, where c, d, e and f are publicly computable digest values. The main instantiations, the YZ and sYZ protocols, are close enough. An execution of the YZ protocol is as in Protocol 2.

To achieve *reasonable deniability*, the inability of an attacker to compute a session key from ephemeral private keys is sacrificed. Notice also, that the inclusion of the static keys in the messages is superfluous, as in effect $\hat{A}$ and $\hat{B}$ are certificates.

To obtain the *single–hash YZ* (sYZ) variant, it suffices to modify Protocol 2, with the digests d, c and e set to $d = c = 1$ and $e = H_1(\hat{A}, A, \hat{B}, B, X, Y)$.

Protocol 2. The YZ Protocol

I) The initiator $\hat{A}$ does the following:
   (a) Choose $x \in_R [1, q - 1]$ and compute $X = G^x$.
   (b) Send $(\hat{A}, A, X)$ to the peer $\hat{B}$.
II) At receipt of $(\hat{A}, A, X)$, $\hat{B}$ does the following:
   (a) Verify that $X \in \mathcal{G}^*$.
   (b) Choose $y \in_R [1, q - 1]$ and compute $Y = G^y$.
   (c) Send $(\hat{B}, B, Y)$ to $\hat{A}$.
   (d) Compute $c = H_1(\hat{A}, A, Y)$, $d = H_1(\hat{B}, B, X)$, and $e = H_1(Y, X)$.
   (e) Compute $\sigma = A^{cy} X^{db+ey}$ and $K = H(\sigma)$.
III) At receipt of $(\hat{B}, B, Y)$, $\hat{A}$ does the following:
   (a) Verify that $Y \in \mathcal{G}^*$.
   (b) Compute $c = H_1(\hat{A}, A, Y)$, $d = H_1(\hat{B}, B, X)$, and $e = H_1(Y, X)$.
   (c) Compute $\sigma = B^{dx} Y^{ca+ex}$ and $K = H(\sigma)$.
IV) The shared session key is K.

When $c = H_1(\hat{A}, A, \hat{B}, B, Y)$, $d = H_1(\hat{B}, B, \hat{A}, A, X)$, $e = H_1(\hat{A}, A, \hat{B}, B, X, Y)$, and $f = H_1(\hat{A}, A, \hat{B}, B)$, the resulting protocol is termed *robust YZ* (rYZ); and *single hash robust YZ* (srYZ) when $c = d = f = 1$, and $e = H_1(\hat{A}, A, \hat{B}, B, X, Y)$.

In [28], other protocols, inspired by the (H)MQV protocols are proposed, namely the YZ–MQV–$i_{i=1,4}$ protocols, defined with the following digest values.

- YZ–MQV–1: $c = H_1(\hat{A}, A, \hat{B}, B, X, Y)$, $d = H_1(c)$, $e = 1$, and $f = cd$.
- YZ–MQV–2: $d = H_1(\hat{A}, A, \hat{B}, B, X, Y)$, $c = H_1(d)$, $e = cd$, and $f = 1$.
- YZ–MQV–3: $c = H_1(\hat{A}, A, X, pub_1)$, $d = H_1(\hat{B}, B, Y, pub_2)$, $e = 1$, and $f = cd$, wherein pub_1 and pub_2 are public information.
- YZ–MQV–4: $c = H_1(\hat{B}, B, Y, pub_2)$, $d = H_1(\hat{A}, A, X, pub_2)$, $e = cd$, and $f = 1$.

Contrary to the (s)YZ protocols, these protocols do not sacrifice the inability of an attacker to compute a session key from ephemeral private keys, and are not reasonably deniable.

Origins of the YZ–MQV Protocols. In [28, p. 352] one can read that the YZ–MQV–4 protocol is named YZ–MQV in [24] (the prefix in the protocol names have changed from 'YYZ' to 'YZ'), and that the SMQV and FHMQV protocols are originated from [24]. The authors of [28] refer also to the Chinese version of [24]; unfortunately, we do not read Chinese, so we use [24].

The claim that YZ–MQV–4 protocol is named YZ–MQV in [24], and that SMQV and FHMQV are originated from [24] is erroneous. Indeed, there is a fundamental difference between the YZ–MQV–4 protocol and the YZ–MQV protocol, defined in [24, Claim 30] and in [25, p. 49], also drawn in [24, Figure 2]. In the YZ–MQV protocol, the values of c, d, e, and f are defined as $c = H_1(\hat{A}, A, X)$, $d = H_1(\hat{B}, B, Y)$, $e = 1$, and $f = cd$. This protocol increases the HMQV weakness reported in [22], and fixed in the FHMQV and SMQV designs [20,22]. In the YZ–MQV protocol, when an attacker learns an intermediate secret exponent in a session, it can not only *impersonate indefinitely* the session owner to its peer in the leaked session, as in HMQV [22], but to *any party*. The other protocols defined in [24] do not match the YZ–MQV–$i_{i=3,4}$ protocols. One can find definitions parametrized by "public information" $pub_{i,i=1,\cdots,4}$ in [24, claims 24–25] where pub_i is a subset of $\{\hat{A}, A, m_1, \hat{B}, B, m_2\}$, but none of these designs matches YZ–MQV–$i_{i=3,4}$, as m_1, m_2 "denote other messages, other than the DH–components, exchanged in (or related to) the protocol run" [24, p. 18].

Even if FHMQV and SMQV can be instantiated from the YZ–MQV–$i_{i=3,4}$ protocols, which appeared after the FHMQV and SMQV designs was proposed, we cannot see how SMQV and FHMQV can be considered as originated from [24].

4   On the Attributes of the (s)YZ Protocols

In this section, we discuss the main attributes of the (s)YZ protocols. We show that their claimed security and *computational fairness* do not hold.

On the Security of the (s)YZ Protocols

In [26] the (s)YZ protocols are shown secure in the CK_{HMQV} model under the Gap Diffie–Hellman assumption. As in these protocols, the session key derivation is role dependent, matching sessions do not necessarily yield the same key; hence their CK_{HMQV} security arguments are invalid. When an attacker executes Attack 1, the two parties involved in the run, say $\hat{A}$ and $\hat{B}$, both believe being the session initiator, and respectively compute $e_A = H_1(X, Y)$ and $e_B = H_1(Y, X) \neq e_A$ (except with negligible probability). So, they do not derive the same session key, while their sessions are matching. The requirement that if two honest parties complete matching session, they should compute the same session key is not achieved, the (s)YZ protocols do not achieve CK_{HMQV} security.

Notice that, unless changed fundamentally, using the CK session identifiers and matching sessions definition does not patch the security arguments invalidity. And, as in the (s)YZ protocols, session keys can be computed from ephemeral private keys, it is also straightforward to see that these protocols are insecure in the (s)eCK security models.

In [28, Remark 2 and Table 2], the srYZ protocol is presented as seCK–secure. Here also, this is erroneous. As in the srYZ protocol $c = d = f = 1$, and $e = H_1(\hat{A}, A, \hat{B}, B, X, Y)$ [28, p. 351], the shared secret group element in an execution of this protocol is $\sigma = B^{a+x}Y^{a+ex} = A^{b+y}X^{b+ey}$, Attack 3 invalidates the protocol's security in the seCK model. Using x and y, the attacker can compute the same key as $\hat{B}$, for the secret element $\hat{B}$ derives is

$$Z_B = A^{b+y}X'^{b+ey} = A^{b+y}(G^x/A)^{b+ey} = A^{(1-e)y}(BY^e)^x.$$

With Attack 1, we show that the (s)YZ protocols do not achieve CK_{HMQV} security, the protocols are also (s)eCK insecure; and Attack 3 invalidates the srYZ protocol's security in the seCK model.

Attack 3. Attack against srYZ in the seCK model

---

(1) Choose $x \in_R [1, q-1]$, and send $(\hat{A}, A, X' = G^x/A)$ to $\hat{B}$.
(2) Intercept $\hat{B}$'s response to $\hat{A}$ $(\hat{B}, B, Y)$.
(3) Issue an EphemeralKeyReveal query on the session at $\hat{B}$ to learn y.
(4) Use x and y to compute the same session key as $\hat{B}$, and communicate with $\hat{B}$ on behalf of $\hat{A}$.

Computational (Un)fairness

In [26], Yoa and Zhao introduce a new notion, termed *computational unfairness* between an attacker and an honest player. The aim is to capture the ability of an adversary to compute a secret shared with an honest party, while performing much less operations than the honest user does. Such attacks can be used, in turn, to mount effective Denial of Service (DoS) attacks. For concreteness, we recall in Attack 4 the *exponent–dependent attack* (EDA) proposed in [25,26] to show that the (H)MQV protocols are computationally unfair. Recall that besides the differences on the digest values, computed as $d = 2^l + (\tilde{X} \mod 2^l)$ and $e = 2^l + (\tilde{Y} \mod 2^l)$ in MQV, wherein $\tilde{X}$ denotes the integer representation of X, the MQV and HMQV descriptions are identical. (Public key validation was voluntarily omitted in the HMQV design, but in this case, the protocol is already known to be insecure [15,16]).

Attack 4. EDA Attack against MQV

---

(1) Choose $X \in \mathcal{G}$ and compute $d = 2^l + (\tilde{X} \mod 2^l)$.
(2) Compute $A = X^{-d^{-1}} G^t$ for some $t \in [0, q-1]$, and register the static key A on behalf of $\hat{A}$.
(3) Send $(\hat{A}, X)$ to $\hat{B}$.
(4) Intercept $\hat{B}$'s message $(\hat{B}, Y)$.
(5) Compute the secret shared with $\hat{B}$, $\sigma = (YB^e)^{td}$, and derive the same session key as $\hat{B}$.

In Attack 4, as $XA^d = G^{td}$, we have $(XA^d)^{y+eb} = (YB^e)^{td}$, hence the attacker derives the same secret as $\hat{B}$. Recall that in the standardized version of (H)MQV [9], the above attack with $t = 0$ cannot work as the shared secret is tested to be non-identity. With other small values of t the attack can be mounted, as discussed in [25,26].

An attempt to formalize computational fairness attribute is given in [26,25]. A protocol is said to be computationally fair "if for any successfully finished session run by a malicious player (e.g., $\hat{B}$) with an honest player (e.g., $\hat{A}$), the session–key computation involves the same number of (strongly or general) non–malleably independent dominant–operation values for both the honest player and the malicious player" [26, Definition 6.3]. And, [26, Proposition 6.1] claims that the (s)YZ protocol is session key computationally fair under the random oracle model, while (H)MQV is not. The formalization of the attribute is unclear, and it is difficult to see how two–pass protocols can achieve this attribute, as the attacker is allowed to register a static public key of its choice. Consider, for instance, the sYZ protocol; when an attacker registers $A = G$ as static public key, and uses $X = G$ as ephemeral public key, the session key derivation, is "unfair" in the sense that it requires much less operations for the attacker than for an honest party (which chooses its public keys at random).

Attack 5. Computational Unfairness Attack against the sYZ Protocol

(1) Register the static public key $A = G$ to obtain a certificate $\hat{A}$.
(2) Choose $X = G$ as ephemeral public key.
(3) Send $(\hat{A}, A, X)$ to $\hat{B}$
(4) Intercept $\hat{B}$'s response $(\hat{B}, B, Y = g^y)$.
(5) Compute $e = H_1(\hat{A}, A, \hat{B}, B, X, Y)$, the secret $\sigma = BY^{1+e}$, and the session key $K = H(\sigma)$.

Consider Attack 5; as $x = a = 1$, it is clear that the attacker computes the same secret as $\hat{B}$. Moreover, the computational effort it requires to execute Attack 5 against the sYZ protocol, one exponentiation, is much less than what is required to execute the EDA attack against MQV (two exponentiations at least, when the simultaneous exponentiation technique [18, section 14.6.1] is used). Naturally, one can ask how does the (s)YZ protocols achieve computational fairness. Further, as the attacker can register and use the keys of its choice (the keys can be chosen with small exponents for instance), one may ask how computational fairness can be achieved in two–pass key agreement protocols.

Remark 1. The YZ protocols are presented as *optimally efficient* [26,28], meaning that no protocol achieving the same security attributes can be more efficient; but there is no proof of such a claim. The "optimal efficiency" of the (s)YZ protocols is sustained by the ability of a party, say $\hat{B}$, to pre–compute A^{fb+cy}, where A is the initiator's static key. Unfortunately, this argument is not careful enough. In fact, in an execution of a protocol from YZ family, the ability of $\hat{B}$ to pre–compute A^{Fb+Cy} may be limited. The reason is that $\hat{B}$ usually evolves in an open network, often with a large number of potential peers; so knowing in advance the next peer seems difficult. This is particularly true, if $\hat{B}$ is a server with a large number of clients (a bank server, for instance). In this case, pre–computability is highly desirable, but the server cannot guess the next client; as a result, it is difficult to see how the A^{fb+cy}s can be adequately precomputed.

5   The Deniable Internet Key Exchange (DIKE)

In this section, we recall DIKE protocol [27], and analyze its security attributes. Namely, we show that if an attacker learns the ephemeral private key at a session initiator, it can impersonate *any party* to the initiator.

Authentication and deniability are the main motivations of the DIKE protocol; it is also another goal that if an attacker completes a session, which matching session exists, then it knows not only the ephemeral private key corresponding to its outgoing ephemeral public key, but also the static private key corresponding to its alleged outgoing static public key [27, pp. 331, 337]. Notice that it is widely admitted that *an attacker should not be able to impersonate a party, unless it knows the party's static private key.*

An execution of DIKE, with initiator $\hat{A}$ and responder $\hat{B}$, is as in Protocol 6, if any verification fails, the execution aborts. Recall that $\mathcal{G}$ is a multiplicatively written cyclic group of prime order q, with generator G.

Protocol 6. The DIKE Protocol in the main model

  I) At session activation with identifier sid, $\hat{A}$ does the following:
  (a) Choose $x \in_R [1, q-1]$ and compute $X = G^x$.
  (b) Send (sid, X) to the peer.
  II) At receipt of (sid, X), the responder $\hat{B}$ does the following:
  (a) Verify that $X \in \mathcal{G}^*$.
  (b) Choose $y \in_R [1, q-1]$ and compute $Y = G^y$.
  (c) Compute $t_B = H(sid, \hat{B}, Y, X, X^y)$.
  (d) Send $(sid, \hat{B}, Y, t_B)$ to the initiator.
  III) At receipt of $(sid, \hat{B}, Y, t_B)$, $\hat{A}$ does the following:
  (a) Verify that $Y \in \mathcal{G}^*$.
  (b) Verify that $t_B = H(sid, \hat{B}, Y, X, Y^x)$.
  (c) Compute $\tau_A = H(sid, \hat{A}, X, Y, Y^a, Y^x)$.
  (d) Send $(sid, \hat{A}, \tau_A)$ to $\hat{B}$.
  IV) At receipt of $(sid, \hat{A}, \tau_A)$, $\hat{B}$ does the following:
  (a) Verify that $\tau_A = H(sid, \hat{A}, X, Y, A^y, X^y)$.
  (b) Compute $\tau_B = H(sid, \hat{B}, Y, X, X^b, X^y)$.
  (c) Send (sid, τ_B) to $\hat{A}$.
  (d) Compute $K = H_K(X^y, X, Y)$.
  V) At receipt of (sid, τ_B), $\hat{A}$ does the following:
  (a) Verify that $\tau_B = H(sid, \hat{B}, Y, X, B^x, Y^x)$.
  (b) Compute $K = H_K(X^y, X, Y)$.
  VI) The shared session key is K.

For the security arguments of the DIKE protocol, Yao and Zhao introduce a new assumption termed the CKEA assumption. They also introduce a simulation based security definition, which aims to model non–malleability for Diffie–Hellman key agreement protocols in concurrent settings. The DIKE protocol is shown CK secure and tag–based robust non–malleable in the restricted RO model, under the Gap Diffie–Hellman and CKEA assumptions.

Failure in Authentication

Despite its security arguments, and the use of the non–standard CKEA assumption, the DIKE protocol fails in authentication, which is a primary goal in key agreement. "A minimal requirement for a secure key–exchange protocol is that the attacker, not knowing the private key of a party $\hat{A}$, should not be able to impersonate $\hat{A}$" [11, p. 14]. This requirement is also considered as minimal in [8, section 2]. In the DIKE protocol, if an attacker learns the ephemeral private key in a session initiated at $\hat{A}$, it can impersonate *any party* to $\hat{A}$ (recall that the DIKE protocol is defined in the post–specified peer model). The impersonation is described in Attack 7. Notice that ephemeral private key leakage is a realistic assumption, as in many applications the ephemeral pairs (x, G^x) are off–line precomputed and kept in a less protected storage than the long–lived private keys.

Attack 7. Impersonation Attack against DIKE

When the initiator, $\hat{A}$ is activated with a session identifier sid, the attacker does the following:

(1) Intercept $\hat{A}$'s message to the responder (sid, X).
(2) Learn the ephemeral private key in the session at $\hat{A}$.
(3) Choose $y \in_R [1, q-1]$ and compute $Y = G^y$.
(4) Compute $t_B = H(sid, \hat{B}, Y, X, X^y)$.
(5) Send $(sid, \hat{B}, Y, t_B)$ to the initiator.
(6) Intercept $\hat{A}$'s message to $\hat{B}$ $(sid, \hat{A}, \tau_A)$.
(7) Verify that $\tau_A = H(sid, \hat{A}, X, Y, A^y, X^y)$.
(8) Compute $\tau_B = H(sid, \hat{B}, Y, X, B^x, Y^x)$.
(9) Send (sid, τ_B) to $\hat{A}$.
(10) Compute and use $K = H_K(X^y, X, Y)$ to communicate with $\hat{A}$ on behalf of $\hat{B}$.

The session at $\hat{A}$ does not abort, as both t_B and τ_B are valid tags, so $\hat{A}$'s verifications at steps IIIb and Va of Protocol 6 do not fail. It is also clear that (i) the attacker has no knowledge of $\hat{B}$'s static private key, while (ii) it derives the same session key as $\hat{A}$, and (iii) $\hat{A}$ believes its session key shared with $\hat{B}$. This is clearly a *failure in authentication*. This attack illustrates not only an insufficiency in the DIKE design, but also the impossibility of capturing some kind of impersonation attacks in the CK–model. Indeed, in the CK model, in contrary to the (s)eCK models for instance, once the ephemeral information in a session is exposed, the model does not care about the security of the session. As a consequence, the CK model cannot guarantee that an attacker cannot impersonate a party unless it knows its static private key.

Notice also that such an attack cannot hold against the SIGMA protocol [10], as in an execution of SIGMA, a peer has to sign a fresh nonce; this cannot be performed without a knowledge of the static private corresponding to its alleged public key.

The SMQV–1 Protocol

In this section we propose a robust variant of the SMQV protocol [22] geared to the post–specified peer model, to reaffirm the usefulness of the SMQV building blocks. A similar variant can be obtained from the FHMQV protocol [20,21].

The protocol's design follows the same principles than SMQV; in addition, a proof of the ability to compute the shared secret is required from each party, before a session is derived and accepted. The shared secret is a dual signature, from which the session key is computed. In accordance with the IKEv2 design choices [8], the initiator reveals its identity first. Notice also that it is straightforward to modify the protocol to make the responder reveal its identity first. In the design, we do not use the CK session identifiers and matching sessions definitions (owing to their limitations); instead, we use the session identifiers from the combined CK model [17]. Sessions at $\hat{A}$ are activated with parameters $(\hat{A}, \tilde{B})$ or $(\tilde{A}, \hat{B}, in)$ wherein $\tilde{A}$ and $\tilde{B}$ are *destination addresses*, and *in* is an incoming message. An execution of SMQV–1 is as in Protocol 8, wherein **I** and **R** are role indicators (*i*nitiator or *r*esponder). When used in a message, a role indicator denotes the intended peer's role, while in a session identifier, it indicates the session owner's role.

Protocol 8. The SMQV–1 Protocol

I) At session activation with parameter $(\hat{A}, \tilde{B})$, $\hat{A}$ does the following:
  (a) Choose $x \in_R [1, q-1]$ and compute $X = G^x$.
  (b) Send $(\tilde{B}, \hat{A}, \mathbf{R}, X)$ to $\tilde{B}$.
II) At receipt of $(\tilde{B}, \hat{A}, \mathbf{R}, X)$, the responder $\hat{B}$ does the following:
  (a) Verify that $X \in \mathcal{G}^*$.
  (b) Choose $y \in_R [1, q-1]$ and compute $Y = G^y$.
  (c) Compute $d = \bar{H}(X, Y, \hat{A}, \hat{B})$ and $e = \bar{H}(Y, X, \hat{A}, \hat{B})$.
  (d) Compute $s_B = ye + b$ and $\sigma = (X^d A)^{s_B}$.
  (e) Compute $\tau_B = H_1(\hat{A}, \hat{B}, Y, X, \sigma)$.
  (f) Send $(\hat{A}, \hat{B}, \mathbf{I}, X, Y, \tau_B)$ to $\hat{A}$.
III) At receipt of $(\hat{A}, \hat{B}, \mathbf{I}, X, Y, \tau_B)$, $\hat{A}$ does the following:
  (a) Verify that $Y \in \mathcal{G}^*$.
  (b) Compute $d = \bar{H}(X, Y, \hat{A}, \hat{B})$ and $e = \bar{H}(Y, X, \hat{A}, \hat{B})$.
  (c) Compute $s_A = xe + a$ and $\sigma = (Y^b B)^{s_A}$.
  (d) Verify that $\tau_B = H_1(\hat{A}, \hat{B}, Y, X, \sigma)$.
  (e) Compute $\tau_A = H_1(\hat{A}, \hat{B}, X, \sigma, Y)$.
  (f) Send $(\hat{B}, \hat{A}, \mathbf{R}, X, Y, \tau_B, \tau_A)$ to $\hat{B}$.
  (g) Compute $K = H(\sigma, X, Y, \hat{A}, \hat{B})$.
IV) At receipt of $(\hat{B}, \hat{A}, \mathbf{R}, X, Y, \tau_B, \tau_A)$, $\hat{B}$ does the following:
  (a) Verify that $\tau_A = H_1(\hat{A}, \hat{B}, X, \sigma, Y)$.
  (b) Compute $K = H(\sigma, X, Y, \hat{A}, \hat{B})$.
V) The shared session key is K.

In a SMQV–1 execution, both parties confirm their ability to compute the secret group element σ. The inputs in the tags computation are set to $(\hat{A}, \hat{B}, X, \sigma, Y)$ for $\hat{A}$ and $(\hat{A}, \hat{B}, Y, X, \sigma)$ for $\hat{B}$ to avoid reflection attacks. The SMQV–1 protocol is more efficient than the DIKE protocol; when ephemeral keys are off–line pre–computed, and execution of SMQV–1 requires 1.25 times a single exponentiation, when the simultaneous exponentiation technique [18, section 14.6.1] is used. Also, the protocol is not vulnerable to the impersonation attack we propose.

The SMQV–1 protocol is secure in the combined eCK model under the RO model and the GDH assumption, and is deniable, under the RO model and the GDH and KEA assumptions. For lack of space, we do not give here the security arguments; instead, we give in the appendix a proof of a variant of the FXCR–1 scheme, and show that the critics on the SMQV building blocks from [28] missed some points.

6   Conclusion

We discussed some of the weaknesses of the CK and CK_{HMQV} security models. We showed that the (s)YZ protocols do not achieve their claimed CK_{HMQV} security. We also showed that the (s)YZ protocols do not achieve the computational fairness attribute; our attack suggests that no two–pass protocol can achieve this attribute. We showed that the Deniable Internet Key Exchange (DIKE) fails in authentication. Besides this failure, our attack emphasizes the inability of capturing some kind impersonation attacks in the CK model. We proposed a variant of the SMQV protocol, the SMQV–1, geared to the post peer specified model. The SMQV–1 protocol is secure in the combined eCK model and deniable.

In a forthcoming stage, we will be interested in clarifying and illustrating the weaknesses of the (e)CK and CK_{HMQV} models. We will also work on an adaptation of the seCK model to the post peer specified model, and on illustrating the differences between the (e)CK, CK_{HMQV}, and seCK security models.

References

1. Bellare, M., Rogaway, P.: Entity Authentication and Key Distribution. In: Stinson, D.R. (ed.) CRYPTO 1993. LNCS, vol. 773, pp. 232–249. Springer, Heidelberg (1994)
2. Boyd, C., Mathuria, A.: Protocols for Authentication and Key Establishment. Springer (2003)
3. Canetti, R., Krawczyk, H.: Analysis of Key-Exchange Protocols and Their Use for Building Secure Channels. In: Pfitzmann, B. (ed.) EUROCRYPT 2001. LNCS, vol. 2045, pp. 453–474. Springer, Heidelberg (2001)
4. Choo, K.-K.R.: Refuting the Security Claims of Mathuria and Jain (2005) Key Agreement Protocols. International Journal of Network Security 7(1), 15–23 (2005)
5. Cremers C.: Formally and Practically Relating the CK, CK–HMQV, and eCK Security Models for Authenticated Key Exchange. Cryptology ePrint Archive, Report 2009/253 (2009)

6. Cremers, C.: Examining Indistinguishability–Based Security Models for Key Exchange Protocols: The case of CK, CK–HMQV, and eCK. In: Proc. of the 6th ACM Symposium on Information, Computer and Communications Security. ACM (2011)

7. Hao, F.: On Robust Key Agreement Based on Public Key Authentication. In: Sion, R. (ed.) FC 2010. LNCS, vol. 6052, pp. 383–390. Springer, Heidelberg (2010)

8. Harkins D., Kaufman C., Kivinen T., Kent S., Perlman R.: Design Rationale for IKEv2. IPSec Working Group Internet Draft (2002), http://tools.ietf.org/html/draft-ietf-ipsec-ikev2-rationale-00

9. IEEE P1363: Draft Standard for Public Key Cryptography. IEEE (2009)

10. Krawczyk, H.: SIGMA: The 'SIGn-and-MAc' Approach to Authenticated Diffie-Hellman and Its Use in the IKE Protocols. In: Boneh, D. (ed.) CRYPTO 2003. LNCS, vol. 2729, pp. 400–425. Springer, Heidelberg (2003)

11. Krawczyk, H.: HMQV: A High-Performance Secure Diffie-Hellman Protocol. In: Shoup, V. (ed.) CRYPTO 2005. LNCS, vol. 3621, pp. 546–566. Springer, Heidelberg (2005)

12. Krawczyk H.: HMQV: A High Performance Secure Diffie–Hellman Protocol. Cryptology ePrint Archive, Report Report 2005/176 (2005)

13. LaMacchia, B., Lauter, K., Mityagin, A.: Stronger Security of Authenticated Key Exchange. In: Susilo, W., Liu, J.K., Mu, Y. (eds.) ProvSec 2007. LNCS, vol. 4784, pp. 1–16. Springer, Heidelberg (2007)

14. Maurer, U.M., Wolf, S.: Diffie-Hellman Oracles. In: Koblitz, N. (ed.) CRYPTO 1996. LNCS, vol. 1109, pp. 268–282. Springer, Heidelberg (1996)

15. Menezes, A., Ustaoglu, B.: On the Importance of Public-Key Validation in the MQV and HMQV Key Agreement Protocols. In: Barua, R., Lange, T. (eds.) INDOCRYPT 2006. LNCS, vol. 4329, pp. 133–147. Springer, Heidelberg (2006)

16. Menezes, A.: Another Look at HMQV. Journal of Mathematical Cryptology 1, 148–175 (2007)

17. Menezes, A., Ustaoglu, B.: Comparing the Pre– and Post–specified Peer Models for Key Agreement. International Journal of Applied Cryptography 1(3), 236–250 (2009)

18. Menezes, A., van Oorschot, P., Vanstone, S.: Handbook of Applied Cryptography. CRC Press (1996)

19. Pointcheval, D., Stern, J.: Security Arguments for Digital Signatures and Blind Signatures. Journal of Cryptology 13, 361–396 (2000)

20. Sarr, A.P., Elbaz-Vincent, P., Bajard, J.-C.: A Secure and Efficient Authenticated Diffie–Hellman Protocol. In: Martinelli, F., Preneel, B. (eds.) EuroPKI 2009. LNCS, vol. 6391, pp. 83–98. Springer, Heidelberg (2010)

21. Sarr, A.P., Elbaz-Vincent, P., Bajard, J.C.: A Secure and Efficient Authenticated Diffie–Hellman Protocol (extended version). Cryptology ePrint Archive, Report 2009/408 (2009)

22. Sarr, A.P., Elbaz-Vincent, P., Bajard, J.-C.: A New Security Model for Authenticated Key Agreement. In: Garay, J.A., De Prisco, R. (eds.) SCN 2010. LNCS, vol. 6280, pp. 219–234. Springer, Heidelberg (2010)

23. Sarr, A.P., Elbaz-Vincent, P., Bajard, J.C.: A New Security Model for Authenticated Key Agreement (extended version). Cryptology ePrint Archive, Report 2010/237 (2010)

24. Yao, A.C., Zhao, Y.: Method and Structure for Self–Sealed Joint Proof–of–Knowledge and Diffie-Hellman Key-Exchange Protocols. In: PCT 2009 (2009), http://www.wipo.int/patentscope/search/en/detail.jsf;jsessionid=C14F61
855C476745B13CFDB74D848875.wapp2?docId=WO2009056048&recNum=1&tab=
PCTDocuments&maxRec=&office=&prevFilter=&sortOption=&queryString=
(accessed September 26, 2011)
25. Yao, A.C., Zhao, Y.: A New Family of Practical Non-Malleable Protocols. Cryptology ePrint Archive, Report 2011/035 (2011)
26. Yao, A.C., Zhao, Y.: A New Family of Practical Non-Malleable Protocols. CoRR abs/1105.1071 (2011)
27. Yao, A.C., Zhao, Y.: Deniable Internet Key Exchange. In: Zhou, J., Yung, M. (eds.) ACNS 2010. LNCS, vol. 6123, pp. 329–348. Springer, Heidelberg (2010)
28. Yoneyama, K., Zhao, Y.: Taxonomical Security Consideration of Authenticated Key Exchange Resilient to Intermediate Computation Leakage. In: Boyen, X., Chen, X. (eds.) ProvSec 2011. LNCS, vol. 6980, pp. 348–365. Springer, Heidelberg (2011)

About the Critics on SMQV from [28]

In [28], Yoneyama and Zhao propose a taxonomy of authenticated key agreement protocols in regard with their security arguments and assumptions. We have already showed that this taxonomy is partly flawed; the srYZ is classified as seCK–secure, while this is erroneous. Again, their claim that SMQV and FH-MQV are not secure even in the CK_{HMQV} model, and then are insecure in the seCK model, suggests that seCK security should imply CK or CK_{HMQV} security. This requires some clarifications. In [22,23], we claimed that "the seCK model is *practically* stronger than the CK model" and that the "seCK model encompasses the eCK one", meaning that the seCK–model captures more security attributes than the CK–model, and that seCK security formally implies eCK–security.

The security of the SMQV and FHMQV protocols depends on that of the FXCR–1 scheme. Yoneyama and Zhao [28] consider the security of the FXCR–1 scheme in the case the signer is the initiator. Strictly speaking, this defines another scheme, as in the definition of the FXCR–1 scheme, the communications are initiated by the verifier (not the signer); and the signature (Y, X^{s_B}) is provided to the verifier *after* it provides its challenge X. When the interaction order is changed, this defines another scheme (we call FXCR–2), and the proof may become invalid. Here, we show that even in this modified variant of the FXCR–1 scheme, the security remains valid.

Definition 3 (FXCR–2 Signature). *Let $\hat{B}$ be a party with public key $B \in \mathcal{G}^*$, and $\hat{A}$ a verifier; $\hat{B}$'s signature on a message m and challenge X, provided by $\hat{A}$ ($x \in_R [1, q-1]$ is chosen and kept secret by $\hat{A}$), after it receives the ephemeral element Y, is $Sig_{\hat{B}}(m, X) = (Y, X^{s_B})$, where $Y = G^y$, $y \in_R [1, q-1]$ is chosen by $\hat{B}$, and $s_B = ye + b$, wherein $e = \bar{H}(Y, X, m)$. And, $\hat{A}$ accepts the pair (Y, σ_B) as a valid signature if $Y \in \mathcal{G}^*$ and $(Y^e B)^x = \sigma_B$.*

The FXCR–2's security is given in the following proposition.

Proposition 1 (FXCR–2 Security). *Under the CDH assumption in $\mathcal{G}$ and the RO model, there is no adaptive probabilistic polynomial time attacker, which given a public key B, a challenge X_0 $(B, X_0 \in_R \mathcal{G}^*)$, together with a hashing and a FCXR–2 signing oracles, outputs with non–negligible success probability a triple (m_0, Y_0, σ_0) such that: (1) (Y_0, σ_0) is a valid signature with respect to the public key B, and the message–challenge pair (m_0, X_0); and (2) (Y_0, σ_0) was not obtained from the signing oracle with a query on (m_0, X_0).*

Proof. We have to distinguish two classes of attacker. Suppose an attacker, which does the following at some point of its execution:

(1) activate $\hat{B}$ with a message m to obtain Y,

(2) issue digest queries on (Y, Z_i, m), for arbitrary Z_is,

(3) send Z_{i_0} to $\hat{B}$, where Z_{i_0} equals some Z_i,

(4) receive the signature (Y, σ, s_B).

Notice that the attacker is given s_B in addition to the signature σ. In this sequence, as the digest value e has to be set before the incoming ephemeral public key is known, we cannot simulate consistently the disclosure of s_B to the verifier. We summarize the sequence of queries in Seq1 below. Without loss of generality, we omit the possible independent computations the attacker may perform between two consecutive steps of Seq1.

Algorithm 9. Seq1

(1) Activate the signer $\hat{B}$ with a message m to obtain Y.

(2) Issue digest queries on (Y, Z_i, m), for arbitrary $Z_i \in \mathcal{G}^*$.

(3) Send Z_{i_0} to $\hat{B}$, where Z_{i_0} equals some Z_i.

(4) Receive the signature on message m and challenge Z_{i_0} (Y, σ, s_B).

Let $\mathfrak{B}$ be the family of polynomial time attackers which at some point of their run, execute Seq1 (the attackers may execute Seq1 many times).

Let $\mathcal{A} \notin \mathfrak{B}$ be a polynomial time attacker which, given $B, X_0 \in_R \mathcal{G}^*$, succeeds with non–negligible probability in forging a fresh and valid signature, with respect to the public key B and challenge X_0. Let Q_h and Q_s be respectively the number of queries $\mathcal{A}$ asks to the hashing and signing oracles. Using $\mathcal{A}$ we build a polynomial time CDH solver $\mathcal{S}$ which succeeds with non–negligible probability. The solver $\mathcal{S}$ provides $\mathcal{A}$ with random coins, and simulates the digest and signature queries. The interactions between $\mathcal{S}$ and $\mathcal{A}$ are detailed in Figure 10.

Under the RO model, the distribution of the simulated signatures is indistinguishable from that of real signatures generated by $\hat{B}$, except the deviation that occurs when the same Y is chosen twice. Since the number of queries to the oracles is less than $(Q_h + Q_s)$, and Y is chosen uniformly at random in $\mathcal{G}$, this deviation occurs with probability less than $(Q_h + Q_s)/q$, which is negligible. Hence this simulation is perfect, except with negligible probability. Moreover the probability of producing a valid forgery without querying $\bar{H}(Y_0, X_0, m_0)$ is 2^{-l}. Thus under this simulation, $\mathcal{A}$ outputs with non–negligible probability a valid forgery $(Y_0, X_0, m_0, \sigma_0)$; we denote $\bar{H}(Y_0, X_0, m_0)$ by e_0.

Figure 10. CDH solver from $\mathcal{A}$

Run of $\mathcal{A}$:

(a) At $\mathcal{A}$'s digest query on (Y, X, m), $\mathcal{S}$ responds as follows: *(i)* if a value is already assigned to $\bar{H}(Y, X, m)$, $\mathcal{S}$ returns $\bar{H}(Y, X, m)$; *(ii)* otherwise $\mathcal{S}$ responds with $e \in_R \{0, 1\}^l$, and sets $\bar{H}(Y, X, m) = e$.

(b) When $\mathcal{S}$ is activated with a message m, it does the following: (i) Choose $s_B \in_R [1, q-1]$, $e \in_R \{0, 1\}^l$, set $Y = (G^{s_B} B)^{e^{-1}}$ and $\bar{H}(Y, \star, m) = e$. (The inputs yielding to e are set temporarily to $(Y, \star, m)$ and updated once X is known.) If Y was previously chosen as ephemeral key, $\mathcal{S}$ aborts. (ii) Responds with (Y, m).

(c) At $\mathcal{A}$'s signature query on (Y, m, X), $\mathcal{S}$ responds as follows: *(i)* Update $\bar{H}(Y, \star, m) = e$ to $\bar{H}(Y, X, m) = e$. *(ii)* Responds with (Y, X^{s_B}, s_B) (s_B is given in addition to X^{s_B}).

(d) At $\mathcal{A}$'s halt, $\mathcal{S}$ verifies that $\mathcal{A}$'s output $(Y_0, X_0, m_0, \sigma_0)$ (if any) satisfies the following conditions. If one of these conditions is not satisfied $\mathcal{S}$ aborts.
  - $Y_0 \in \mathcal{G}^*$ and $\bar{H}(Y_0, X_0, m_0)$ was queried from $\bar{H}$.
  - The signature (Y_0, σ_0) was not returned by $\hat{B}$ on query (m_0, X_0).

Repeat: $\mathcal{S}$ executes a new run of $\mathcal{A}$, using the same input and coins; and answering to all digest queries before $\bar{H}(Y_0, X_0, m_0)$ with the same values as in the previous run. The new query of $\bar{H}(Y_0, X_0, m_0)$ and subsequent queries to $\bar{H}$ are answered with new random values.

Output: If $\mathcal{A}$ outputs a second signature on $(Y_0, X_0, m_0, \sigma_0')$ satisfying conditions of step d, with a hash value $\bar{H}(Y_0, X_0, m_0)_2 = e_0' \neq e_0 = \bar{H}(Y_0, X_0, m_0)_1$, then $\mathcal{S}$ outputs $\left(\sigma_0^{e_0^{-1}} / \sigma_0'^{e_0'^{-1}}\right)^{(e_0^{-1} - e_0'^{-1})^{-1}}$ as a guess for $CDH(B, X_0)$.

From the forking lemma [19], the repeat experiment outputs with non-negligible probability a valid forgery $(Y_0, X_0, m_0, \sigma_0')$ with a digest e_0', which with probability $1 - 2^{-l}$ is different from e_0. Hence, the computation

$$\left(\sigma_0^{e_0^{-1}} / \sigma_0'^{e_0'^{-1}}\right)^{(e_0^{-1} - e_0'^{-1})^{-1}} = \left(\frac{\left(Y_0 B^{e_0^{-1}}\right)^{x_0}}{\left(Y_0 B^{e_0'^{-1}}\right)^{x_0}}\right)^{(e_0^{-1} - e_0'^{-1})^{-1}} = B^{x_0}$$

gives $CDH(B, X_0)$. Recall that such a polynomial CDH solver, succeeding with non-negligible probability, can be transformed into an efficient CDH solver [14].

For attackers in $\mathfrak{B}$, we do not provide a direct simulation; instead, we show that their success probability is bounded by that of a class of attackers which can be efficiently simulated. Let B be an attacker in $\mathfrak{B}$, and $\mathfrak{d}(|q|)$ and $\mathfrak{m}(|q|)$ (for some polynomials $\mathfrak{d}$ and $\mathfrak{m}$) be respectively upper bounds on the number of Z_i the attacker chooses at step 2 of Seq1, and the number of times B executes Seq1. For simplicity (in the notations), we suppose that whenever B executes Seq1, it chooses $\mathfrak{d}(|q|)$ Z_is at step 2.

For all $\mathcal{B} \in \mathfrak{B}$, let $\mathcal{B}_R$ be an attacker, which receives in addition to $\mathcal{B}$'s input, the resource vector $\mathbf{v} = \left((i_1^0, \cdots, i_m^0), (Z_{11}, \cdots, Z_{1\mathfrak{d}}), \cdots, (Z_{m1}, \cdots, Z_{m\mathfrak{d}}) \right)$, where $Z_{ij} \in_R \mathcal{G}^*$ and $i_i^0 \in_R [1, \mathfrak{d}]$, and performs *exactly* the same way as $\mathcal{B}$, except that whenever $\mathcal{B}$ executes the sequence of queries Seq1 for the l–th time, $\mathcal{B}_R$ executes the modified sequence Seq2, using i_l^0 and $(Z_{l1}, \cdots, Z_{l\mathfrak{d}})$. And, when $\mathcal{B}$ uses, for any other computation Z_i, chosen during the l–th execution Seq1, $\mathcal{B}_R$ uses Z_{li}.

Algorithm 11. Seq2

   (1) Activate the signer $\hat{B}$ with a message m to obtain Y ($\mathcal{B}_R$ uses the same message as $\mathcal{B}$).

   (2) Issue digest queries on (Y, Z_{li}, m), for $Z_{li} \in \{Z_{l1}, \cdots, Z_{l\mathfrak{d}}\}$.

   (3) Send $Z_{i_l^0}$ to $\hat{B}$.

   (4) Receive the signature on message m and challenge $Z_{i_l^0}$ (Y, σ, s_B).

Notice that if $\mathcal{B}$ is polynomial, then so is $\mathcal{B}_R$. Let $\mathbf{V}$ be the set of resource vectors. For $\mathbf{v} \in \mathbf{V}$, we say that $\mathcal{B}_R(\mathbf{v})$ *matches* $\mathcal{B}$, if for all $l \in [1, \mathfrak{m}]$, the l–th time $\mathcal{B}$ executes Seq1, it chooses $\{Z_{l1}, \cdots, Z_{l\mathfrak{d}}\}$ at step 2, and sends $Z_{i_l^0}$ at step 3. It is clear that if $\mathcal{B}_R(\mathbf{v})$ matches $\mathcal{B}$, then the success probability of $\mathcal{B}$ is, $\Pr(\mathsf{Succ}_\mathcal{B}) = \Pr(\mathsf{Succ}_{\mathcal{B}_R(\mathbf{v})})$.

For $\mathcal{B} \in \mathfrak{B}$, we say $\mathbf{v} \in \mathbf{V}$ *possible* if there is non–zero probability that $\mathcal{B}_R(\mathbf{v})$ matches $\mathcal{B}$. Let $Poss(\mathbf{V})$ denote the set of possible resource vectors. For every run of $\mathcal{B}$, there is some $\mathbf{v} \in Poss(\mathbf{V})$ such that $\mathcal{B}_R(\mathbf{v})$ matches $\mathcal{B}$ ($\mathbf{v}$ can be built from the choices of $\mathcal{B}$ in its executions of Seq1), hence

$$\Pr(\mathsf{Succ}_\mathcal{B}) \leqslant \max_{\mathbf{v} \in Poss(\mathbf{V})} \Pr(\mathsf{Succ}_{\mathcal{B}_R(\mathbf{v})}).$$

Now, it suffices to show that for all $\mathcal{B}$ and all $\mathbf{v} \in Poss(\mathbf{V})$, $\Pr(\mathsf{Succ}_{\mathcal{B}_R(\mathbf{v})})$ is negligible. For this purpose, we modify the simulation to take as input $\mathbf{v}$ and respond as follows, when $\mathcal{B}_R(\mathbf{v})$ executes the sequence Seq2 for the l–th time.

  – When $\mathcal{B}_R$ activates the signer $\hat{B}$ with a message m to obtain Y, the simulator $\mathcal{S}$ does the following:

    • Choose $s_B \in_R [1, q-1], e \in_R \{0,1\}^l$, set $Y = (G^{s_B} B^{-1})^{e^{-1}}$ and $e = H_1(Y, Z_{i_l^0}, m)$.

    • Respond with (Y, m).

  – At $\mathcal{B}_R$'s signature query on $(Y, Z_{i_l^0}, m,)$, $\mathcal{S}$ responds with $(Z_{i_l^0}, Z_{i_l^0}^{s_B}, s_B)$.

The simulation remains polynomial–time and consistent for all $\mathbf{v} \in Poss(\mathbf{V})$ and $\mathcal{B}_R$. As $\mathcal{S}$ knows, from the resource vector, what will be the incoming challenge, answers to the queries of Seq2 are consistently simulated. If for some $\mathbf{v}$, $\Pr(\mathsf{Succ}_{\mathcal{B}_R(\mathbf{v})})$ is non–negligible, using the oracle replay technique, we build a CDH solver which succeeds with non–negligible probability. Hence under the CDH assumption, $\Pr(\mathsf{Succ}_{\mathcal{B}_R(\mathbf{v})})$ is negligible, for all $\mathbf{v} \in Poss(\mathbf{V})$. This implies $\Pr(\mathsf{Succ}_\mathcal{B})$ is negligible.

A New Attack on RSA and CRT-RSA

Abderrahmane Nitaj

Laboratoire de Mathématiques Nicolas Oresme
Université de Caen, France
abderrahmane.nitaj@unicaen.fr
http://www.math.unicaen.fr/~nitaj

Abstract. In RSA, the public modulus $N = pq$ is the product of two primes of the same bit-size, the public exponent e and the private exponent d satisfy $ed \equiv 1 \pmod{(p-1)(q-1)}$. In many applications of RSA, d is chosen to be small. This was cryptanalyzed by Wiener in 1990 who showed that RSA is insecure if $d < N^{0.25}$. As an alternative, Quisquater and Couvreur proposed the CRT-RSA scheme in the decryption phase, where $d_p = d \pmod{(p-1)}$ and $d_q = d \pmod{(q-1)}$ are chosen significantly smaller than p and q. In 2006, Bleichenbacher and May presented an attack on CRT-RSA when the CRT-exponents d_p and d_q are both suitably small. In this paper, we show that RSA is insecure if the public exponent e satisfies an equation $ex + y \equiv 0 \pmod{p}$ with $|x||y| < N^{\frac{\sqrt{2}-1}{2}}$ and $ex + y \not\equiv 0 \pmod{N}$. As an application of our new attack, we present the cryptanalysis of CRT-RSA if one of the private exponents, d_p say, satisfies $d_p < \frac{N^{\frac{\sqrt{2}}{4}}}{\sqrt{e}}$. This improves the result of Bleichenbacher and May on CRT-RSA where both d_p and d_q are required to be suitably small.

Keywords: RSA, CRT-RSA, Cryptanalysis, Linear Modular Equation.

1 Introduction

In the RSA cryptosystem, the modulus $N = pq$ is the product of two primes of the same bit-size. The public and private exponents e and d are positive integers satisfying $ed \equiv 1 \pmod{(p-1)(q-1)}$. The encryption and decryption in RSA require taking heavy exponential multiplications modulo a large integer N. To reduce the encryption time, one may be tempted to use a small public exponent e. Unfortunately, it has been proven to be insecure against some small public exponent attacks [8]. Conversely, to reduce the decryption time, one may also be tempted to use a short secret exponent d. However, it is well-known that RSA is vulnerable with a small private exponent. In 1990, Wiener [17] showed that RSA is insecure if $d < N^{0.25}$, which was extended to $d < N^{0.292}$ by Boneh and Durfee [3]. Wiener [17] proposed to use the Chinese Remainder Theorem (CRT) for decryption and Quisquater and Couvreur made this explicit in [14]. In CRT-RSA, the public exponent e and the private CRT-exponents d_p and d_q satisfy $ed_p \equiv 1 \pmod{(p-1)}$ and $ed_q \equiv 1 \pmod{(q-1)}$. One can further reduce the decryption time by carefully choosing d so that both d_p and d_q are

A. Mitrokotsa and S. Vaudenay (Eds.): AFRICACRYPT 2012, LNCS 7374, pp. 221–233, 2012.

small. Combining d_p and d_q, the CRT finds d such that $d \equiv d_p \pmod{(p-1)}$ and $d \equiv d_q \pmod{(q-1)}$. The best known attack on CRT-RSA runs in time complexity $\mathcal{O}\left(\min\left\{\sqrt{d_p}, \sqrt{d_p}\right\}\right)$ which is exponential in the bit-size of d_p or d_q. At Crypto'07, Jochemsz and May [11] proposed the first polynomial time attack on CRT exponents that are smaller than $N^{0.073}$ when p and q are balanced and e is full size, that is $\frac{e}{N} \approx 1$. In the special case when e is much smaller than N, Bleichenbacher and May [1] proposed an attack that is applicable if both d_p and d_q are such that $d_p, d_q < \min\left\{\frac{1}{4}\left(\frac{N}{e}\right)^{\frac{2}{5}}, \frac{1}{3}N^{\frac{1}{4}}\right\}$.

In this paper, we present an attack on RSA and a second attack on CRT-RSA. We consider RSA with a modulus $N = pq$ where p, q are of the same bit-size. We present an attack on RSA if one of the primes, p say, satisfies an equation $ex + y \equiv 0 \pmod{p}$, where the unknown parameters x, y satisfy

$$|x||y| < N^{\frac{\sqrt{2}-1}{2}} \text{ and } ex + y \not\equiv 0 \pmod{N}.$$

Our attack is based on the method of Coppersmith [5] for finding small solutions of modular equations. In particular, we make use of a result from Herrmann and May [9] to solve linear equations modulo divisors. Moreover, we estimate a very conservative lower bound on the number of exponents for which our method works as $N^{\frac{\sqrt{2}}{2}-\varepsilon}$ where $\varepsilon > 0$ is a small constant depending only on N. As an application of this method, we present the cryptanalysis of CRT-RSA with a private decryption exponent d_p satisfying

$$d_p < \frac{N^{\frac{\sqrt{2}}{4}}}{\sqrt{e}}.$$

We notice that for balanced p and q and small e, the attack of Bleichenbacher and May [1] works when both d_p and d_q satisfy $d_p, d_q < \min\left\{\frac{1}{4}\left(\frac{N}{e}\right)^{\frac{2}{5}}, \frac{1}{3}N^{\frac{1}{4}}\right\}$ while in our new attack, only d_p (or d_q) is required to be small.

The rest of this paper is organized as follows. In Section 2, we will state preliminaries on RSA, CRT-RSA, and bivariate linear equations modulo divisors. Section 3 will contain the description of the attack for exponents e satisfying $ex + y \equiv 0 \pmod{p}$ with suitably small parameters x, y and give a lower bound for the number of such exponents. In Section 4, we will present an application of our attack to CRT-RSA with small CRT-exponent d_p when p and q are balanced. In Section 5, we provide some experimental results. Finally, we conclude the paper in Section 6.

2   Preliminaries

2.1   The Original RSA and CRT-RSA

We first review the original RSA [15] and CRT-RSA [14].

The Original RSA. The RSA cryptosystem depends on two large primes p and q used to form the RSA modulus $N = pq$. Let e and d be two integers satisfying $ed \equiv 1 \pmod{\phi(N)}$, where $\phi(N) = (p-1)(q-1)$ is the Euler totient function of N. In general, e is called the public exponent, and d is the secret exponent. To encrypt a plaintext message M, one computes the corresponding ciphertext $C \equiv M^e \pmod{N}$. To decrypt the ciphertext C, the receiver computes simply $M \equiv C^d \pmod{N}$.

CRT-RSA. In CRT-RSA, the public exponent e and the private CRT-exponents d_p and d_q satisfy $ed_p \equiv 1 \pmod{(p-1)}$ and $ed_q \equiv 1 \pmod{(q-1)}$. The CRT-RSA decryption is as follows. Compute $M_p \equiv C^{d_p} \pmod{p}$, $M_q \equiv C^{d_q} \pmod{q}$ and use the Chinese Remainder Theorem (CRT) to find M satisfying $M \equiv M_p \pmod{p}$ and $M \equiv M_q \pmod{q}$.

2.2   Bivariate Linear Equations Modulo Divisors

In our attack we will use a theorem of Herrmann and May [9] to factor an RSA modulus $N = pq$ using a linear equation $f(x, y) = ax + by + c \equiv 0 \pmod{p}$. Their method is based on Coppersmith's technique for finding small roots of polynomial equations [5] and consists in using the LLL algorithm [12] to obtain two polynomials $h_1(x, y)$ and $h_2(x, y)$ sharing the same solution (x_0, y_0), that is $h_1(x_0, y_0) = h_2(x_0, y_0) = 0$. If h_1 and h_2 are algebraically independent, then the resultant of h_1 and h_2 recovers the common root (x_0, y_0). This relies on a heuristic assumption for multivariate polynomials as required by most applications of Coppersmith's algorithm [5].

Assumption 1. *Let $h_1(x, y)$, $h_2(x, y)$ be the polynomials that are found by Coppersmith's method. The resultant computations for the polynomials $h_1(x, y)$, $h_2(x, y)$ yield non-zero polynomials.*

Theorem 1 (Herrmann-May [9]). *Let $\varepsilon > 0$ and let N be a sufficiently large composite integer of unknown factorization with a divisor $p > N^\beta$. Furthermore, let $f(x, y) \in \mathbb{Z}[x, y]$ be a linear polynomial in two variables. Then, one can find all solutions (x_0, y_0) of the equation $f(x, y) \equiv 0 \pmod{p}$ with $|x_0| < N^\gamma$ and $|y_0| < N^\delta$ if*

$$\gamma + \delta \leq 3\beta - 2 + 2(1 - \beta)^{\frac{3}{2}} - \varepsilon.$$

The time complexity of the algorithm is polynomial in $\log N$ and $\frac{1}{\varepsilon}$.

For completeness reasons, let us give a sketch of the proof. First we recall two important results. The first gives a bound on the smallest vectors of an LLL-reduced lattice basis [12].

Theorem 2 (LLL [12]). *Let $\mathcal{L}$ be a lattice with dimension n and determinant $\det(\mathcal{L})$. Let $B = \langle b_1, \dots, b_n \rangle$ be an LLL-reduced basis. Then*

$$\|b_1\| \leq \|b_2\| \leq 2^{\frac{n}{4}} (\det(\mathcal{L}))^{\frac{1}{n-1}}.$$

The next result gives a link between the roots of a polynomial modulo some integer and the roots of the polynomial over the integers. For a multivariate polynomial $f(x_1, \ldots, x_k) = \sum_{i_1, \ldots, i_k} a_{i_1, \ldots, i_k} x^{i_1} \cdots x^{i_k}$, the norm is defined as

$$\|f(x_1, \ldots, x_k)\| = \left(\sum_{i_1, \ldots, i_k} a_{i_1, \ldots, i_k}^2 \right)^{\frac{1}{2}}.$$

Theorem 3 (Howgrave-Graham [10]). *Let* $f(x_1, \ldots, x_k) \in \mathbb{Z}[x_1, \ldots, x_k]$ *be a polynomial with at most* ω *monomials. Suppose that* $f(x_1^{(0)}, \ldots, x_k^{(0)}) \equiv 0$ (mod B) *where* $|x_0^{(0)}| < X_1, \ldots, |x_k^{(0)}| < X_k$ *and* $\|f(X_1 x_1, \ldots, X_k x_k)\| < \frac{B}{\sqrt{\omega}}$. *Then* $f(x_1^{(0)}, \ldots, x_k^{(0)}) = 0$ *holds over the integers.*

We assume that $f(x, y) = x + by + c$ since otherwise we can multiply f by a^{-1} (mod N). To find a solution (x_0, y_0) such that $f(x_0, y_0) \equiv 0$ (mod p), the basic idea consists in finding two polynomials $h_1(x, y)$ and $h_2(x, y)$ such that $h_1(x_0, y_0) = h_1(x_0, y_0) = 0$ holds over the integers. Then the resultant of $h_1(x, y)$ and $h_2(x, y)$ will reveal the root (x_0, y_0). To do so, we generate a collection of polynomials $g_{k,i}(x, y)$ as

$$g_{k,i}(x, y) = y^i \cdot f(x, y)^k \cdot N^{\max\{t-k, 0\}}$$

for $0 \le k \le m$, $0 \le i \le m - k$ and integer parameters t and m with $t < m$ that will be specified later. Observe that for all k and i, we have

$$g_{k,i}(x_0, y_0) = y_0^i \cdot f(x_0, y_0)^k \cdot N^{\max\{t-k, 0\}} \equiv 0 \quad (\text{mod } p^t).$$

We define the following ordering for the polynomials $g_{k,i}$. If $k < l$, then $g_{k,i} < g_{l,j}$. If $k = l$ and $i < j$, then $g_{k,i} < g_{k,j}$. On the other hand, each polynomial $g_{k,i}(x, y)$ is ordered in the monomials $x^i y^k$. The ordering for the monomials $x^i y^k$ is as follows. If $i < j$, then $x^i y^k < x^j y^l$. If $i = j$ and $k < l$, then $x^i y^k < x^i y^l$. Let X and Y be positive integers. Gathering the coefficients of the polynomials $g_{k,i}(Xx, Yy)$, we obtain a matrix as illustrated in Table 1.

Let $\mathcal{L}$ be the lattice of row vectors from the coefficients of the polynomials $g_{k,i}(Xx, Yy)$ in the basis $\langle x^k y^i \rangle_{0 \le k \le m, 0 \le i \le m-k}$. The dimension of $\mathcal{L}$ is

$$n = \sum_{i=0}^{m} (m + 1 - i) = \frac{(m+2)(m+1)}{2}.$$

Table 1. Herrmann-May's matrix of the polynomials $g_{k,i}(Xx, Yy)$ in the basis $\langle x^r y^s \rangle_{0 \le r \le m, 0 \le s \le m-r}$

	1 $\cdots$ y^m	x $\cdots$ xy^{m-1}	$\ldots$ x^t $\cdots$ $x^t y^{m-t}$	$\cdots$ x^m
$g_{0,0}$	N^t			
$\vdots$	$\ddots$			
$g_{0,m}$	$N^t Y^m$			
$g_{1,0}$	$*$ $\cdots$ $*$	$N^{t-1}X$		
$\vdots$	$*$ $\cdots$ $*$	$\ddots$		
$g_{1,m-1}$	$*$ $\cdots$ $*$	$*$ $\ldots$ $N^{t-1}XY^{m-1}$		
$\vdots$	$*$ $\vdots$ $*$	$*$ $\vdots$ $*$	$\ddots$	
$g_{t,0}$	$*$ $\cdots$ $*$	$*$ $\cdots$ $*$	$\ldots$ X^t	
$\vdots$	$\vdots$	$\vdots$	$\vdots$ $\ddots$	
$g_{t,m-t}$	$*$ $\cdots$ $*$	$*$ $\ldots$ $*$	$\ldots$ $*$ $\ldots$ $X^t Y^{m-t}$	
$\vdots$	$*$ $\vdots$ $*$	$*$ $\vdots$ $*$	$\vdots$ $*$ $\vdots$ $*$	$\ddots$
$g_{m,0}$	$*$ $\cdots$ $*$	$*$ $\ldots$ $*$	$\ldots$ $*$ $\ldots$ $*$	$\ldots$ X^m

From the triangular matrix of the lattice, we can easily compute the determinant $\det(\mathcal{L}) = X^{s_x} Y^{s_y} N^{s_N}$ where

$$s_x = \sum_{i=0}^{m} i(m+1-i) = \frac{m(m+1)(m+2)}{6},$$

$$s_y = \sum_{i=0}^{m} \sum_{j=0}^{m-i} j = \frac{m(m+1)(m+2)}{6},$$

$$s_N = \sum_{i=0}^{t} (t-i)(m+1-i) = \frac{t(t+1)(3m+4-t)}{6}.$$

We want to find two polynomials with short coefficients that contain all small roots over the integer. This can be achieved by applying the LLL algorithm [12] to the lattice $\mathcal{L}$. From Theorem 2, we get two polynomials $h_1(x,y)$ and $h_2(x,y)$ satisfying

$$\|h_1(Xx, Yy)\| \le \|h_2(Xx, Yy)\| \le 2^{\frac{n}{4}} (\det(\mathcal{L}))^{\frac{1}{n-1}}.$$

To ensure that (x_0, y_0) is a root of both $h_1(x,y)$ and $h_2(x,y)$ over the integers, we apply Howgrave-Graham's Theorem 3 for $h_1(Xx, Yy)$ and $h_2(Xx, Yy)$ with $B = p^t$ and $\omega = n$. A sufficient condition is that

$$2^{n/4}(\det(\mathcal{L}))^{1/(n-1)} \le \frac{p^t}{\sqrt{n}}. \tag{1}$$

Let $X = N^\gamma$, $Y = N^\delta$ and $p > N^\beta$ with $\beta \geq \frac{1}{2}$. We have $n = \frac{(m+2)(m+1)}{2}$ and $\det(\mathcal{L}) = X^{s_x} Y^{s_y} N^{s_N} = N^{s_x(\gamma+\delta)+s_N}$. Then the condition (1) transforms to

$$2^{\frac{(m+2)(m+1)}{8}} N^{\frac{2(\gamma+\delta)s_x+2s_N}{m(m+3)}} \leq \frac{N^{\beta t}}{\sqrt{\frac{(m+2)(m+1)}{2}}}. \tag{2}$$

Define $\varepsilon_1 > 0$ such that

$$\frac{2^{-\frac{(m+2)(m+1)}{8}}}{\sqrt{\frac{(m+2)(m+1)}{2}}} = N^{-\varepsilon_1}.$$

Then, the condition (2) simplifies to

$$\frac{2(\gamma+\delta)s_x + 2s_N}{m(m+3)} \leq \beta t - \varepsilon_1.$$

Neglecting the ε_1 term and using $s_x = \frac{m(m+1)(m+2)}{6}$ and $s_N = \frac{t(t+1)(3m+4-t)}{6}$, we get

$$\frac{m(m+1)(m+2)}{3}(\gamma+\delta) + \frac{t(t+1)(3m+4-t)}{3} < m(m+3)\beta t.$$

It is shown in [9] that setting $t = \left(1 - \sqrt{1-\beta}\right)m$ leads to the condition

$$\gamma + \delta < 3\beta - 2 + 2(1-\beta)^{\frac{3}{2}} - \varepsilon,$$

with a small constant $\varepsilon > 0$ and that the method's complexity is polynomial in $\log(N)$ and $1/\varepsilon$.

3   A New Class of Weak Public Exponents in RSA

In this section, we analyze the security of the RSA cryptosystem where the public exponent e satisfies an equation $ex + y \equiv 0 \pmod{p}$ with parameters x and y satisfying $ex + y \not\equiv 0 \pmod{N}$ $|x| < N^\gamma$ and $|y| < N^\delta$ with $\gamma + \delta \leq \frac{\sqrt{2}-1}{2}$. We firstly show that such exponents lead to the factorization of the RSA modulus and secondly that a very conservative estimate for the number of such weak exponents is $N^{\frac{\sqrt{2}}{2}-\varepsilon}$ where $\varepsilon > 0$ is arbitrarily small for suitably large N.

Theorem 4. *Let $N = pq$ be an RSA modulus with $q < p < 2q$. Let e be a public exponent satisfying an equation $ex + y \equiv 0 \pmod{p}$ with $|x| < N^\gamma$ and $|y| < N^\delta$. If $ex + y \not\equiv 0 \pmod{N}$ and*

$$\gamma + \delta \leq \frac{\sqrt{2}-1}{2},$$

then, under Assumption 1, N can be factored in polynomial time.

Proof. Let $N = pq$ be an RSA modulus with $q < p < 2q$. Then $N < p^2$ and $\sqrt{N} < p$. Hence $p = N^\beta$ for some $\beta > \frac{1}{2}$. Let e be a public exponent satisfying an equation $ex + y \equiv 0 \pmod{p}$, which is linear in the two variables x and y. Assume that $|x| < N^\gamma$ and $|y| < N^\delta$ with γ and δ satisfying

$$\gamma + \delta \le \frac{\sqrt{2} - 1}{2}.$$

Then applying Theorem 1 with any $\beta > \frac{1}{2}$, we find x and y in polynomial time. Using x and y, we get $ex + y = pz$ for some integer z. Moreover, assume that $ex + y \not\equiv 0 \pmod{N}$. Then $\gcd(z, q) = 1$. Hence

$$\gcd(ex + y, N) = \gcd(pz, N) = p.$$

This terminates the proof.   □

Next, we estimate the number of exponents for which our method works.

Theorem 5. *Let $N = pq$ be an RSA modulus with $q < p < 2q$. The number of exponents $e < N$ satisfying $ex + y \equiv 0 \pmod{p}$ and $ex + y \not\equiv 0 \pmod{N}$ where $\gcd(x, y) = 1$, $|x| < N^\gamma$ and $|y| < N^\delta$, with*

$$\gamma + \delta \le \frac{\sqrt{2} - 1}{2},$$

is at least $N^{\frac{\sqrt{2}}{2} - \varepsilon}$ where ε is a small positive constant.

Proof. Consider the set

$$\mathcal{K} = \{e \ : \ 2 \le e < N, \ e = \alpha p + \left(-yx^{-1} \pmod{p}\right), \text{with } \gcd(x, y) = 1,$$
$$0 \le \alpha < q, \ |x| < N^\gamma, \ |y| < N^{\frac{\sqrt{2}-1}{2} - \gamma} \text{ and } ex + y \not\equiv 0 \pmod{N}\}.$$

Here $\left(-yx^{-1} \pmod{p}\right)$ represents the unique positive integer lying in the interval $(0, p - 1)$. Each exponent $e \in \mathcal{K}$ satisfies $ex + y \equiv 0 \pmod{p}$ where x and y fulfil the condition of Theorem 4. Moreover, $ex + y \not\equiv 0 \pmod{N}$. Hence, we can apply Theorem 4 to find the parameters x and y related to each exponent $e \in \mathcal{K}$. This shows that every exponent $e \in \mathcal{K}$ is vulnerable to the attack.

Next, let $e_1 \in \mathcal{K}$ and $e_2 \in \mathcal{K}$ with

$$e_1 = \alpha_1 p + \left(-y_1 x_1^{-1} \pmod{p}\right), \quad e_2 = \alpha_2 p + \left(-y_2 x_2^{-1} \pmod{p}\right).$$

Suppose $e_1 = e_2$. Then $e_1 \equiv e_2 \pmod{p}$ and $-y_1 x_1^{-1} \equiv -y_2 x_2^{-1} \pmod{p}$. Equivalently, we get $y_1 x_1^{-1} - y_2 x_2^{-1} \equiv 0 \pmod{p}$. Multiplying by $x_1 x_2$ modulo p, we get $y_1 x_2 - y_2 x_1 \equiv 0 \pmod{p}$. On the other hand, for $i = 1, 2$, we have $x_i, y_i \le N^{\frac{\sqrt{2}-1}{2}}$. Hence, since $q < p < 2q$ and $\sqrt{N} < p$, we get

$$|y_1 x_2 - y_2 x_1| \le |y_1 x_2| + |y_2 x_1| \le 2N^{2 \times \frac{\sqrt{2}-1}{2}} = 2N^{\sqrt{2}-1} < N^{\frac{1}{2}} < p.$$

This implies that $y_1x_2 - y_2x_1 = 0$ and since $(x_1, y_1) = 1$ and $(x_2, y_2) = 1$, then $x_1 = x_2$ and $y_1 = y_2$. Hence $e_1 = e_2$ reduces to $\alpha_1 p = \alpha_2 p$ and $\alpha_1 = \alpha_2$. This shows that each exponent $e \in \mathcal{K}$ is defined by a unique tuple (α, x, y). Observe that if e satisfies $ex + y \equiv 0 \pmod{p}$ and $ex + y \equiv 0 \pmod{q}$ with $x < q$, then $ex + y \equiv 0 \pmod{N}$ and $e \equiv -yx^{-1} \pmod{N}$. To find an estimation of $\#\mathcal{K}$, consider the set

$$\mathcal{K}' = \{e \ : \ 2 \le e < N, \ e = \left(-yx^{-1} \pmod{N}\right),$$
$$\text{with } \gcd(x, y) = 1 \,, |x| < N^\gamma, \ |y| < N^{\frac{\sqrt{2}-1}{2}-\gamma}\}.$$

On the other hand, observe that the conditions $|x| < N^\gamma$ and $|y| < N^{\frac{\sqrt{2}-1}{2}-\gamma}$ imply that $|x||y| < N^{\frac{\sqrt{2}-1}{2}}$. Let

$$M = \left\lfloor N^{\frac{\sqrt{2}-1}{2}} \right\rfloor.$$

The number $\#\mathcal{K}$ of exponents $e \in \mathcal{K}$ is such that

$$\#\mathcal{K} \ge \sum_{\alpha=0}^{q-1} \sum_{|x|=1}^{M} \sum_{\substack{|y|=1 \\ (x,y)=1}}^{M/|x|} 1 - \#\mathcal{K}'$$

$$\ge q \sum_{|x|=1}^{M} \sum_{\substack{|y|=1 \\ (x,y)=1}}^{M/|x|} 1 - \sum_{|x|=1}^{M} \sum_{\substack{|y|=1 \\ (x,y)=1}}^{M/|x|} 1$$

$$\ge (q-1) \sum_{|x|=1}^{M} \sum_{\substack{|y|=1 \\ (x,y)=1}}^{M/|x|} 1$$

$$\ge (q-1)M.$$

Since $q - 1 = N^{\frac{1}{2}-\varepsilon_1}$ and $M = N^{\frac{\sqrt{2}-1}{2}-\varepsilon_2}$ for some $\varepsilon_1 > 0$ and $\varepsilon_2 > 0$, then

$$\#\mathcal{K} > N^{\frac{1}{2}-\varepsilon_1} \times N^{\frac{\sqrt{2}-1}{2}-\varepsilon_2} = N^{\frac{\sqrt{2}}{2}-\varepsilon},$$

where $\varepsilon > 0$ is a small constant. This terminates the proof.   □

4   Application to CRT-RSA

In this section, we present a new attack on CRT-RSA. Let $N = pq$ be an RSA modulus. Let e be a public exponent corresponding to the private exponent d. Since the attacks of Wiener [17] and Boneh and Durfee [3], we know that RSA with a small private key d is vulnerable. As an alternative approach, Wiener proposed to use the Chinese Remainder Theorem (CRT) for decryption. Then

Quisquater and Couvreur proposed a decryption scheme in [14]. The scheme uses two private exponents d_p and d_q related to d by

$$d_p \equiv d \pmod{(p-1)}, \qquad d_q \equiv d \pmod{(q-1)}.$$

Many attacks on CRT-RSA show that using small d_p and d_q is also dangerous. The best known result from Jochemsz and May [11] asserts that CRT-RSA is vulnerable if d_p and d_q are smaller than $N^{0.073}$.

Notice that the private exponents d_p and d_q satisfy the equations

$$ed_p \equiv 1 \pmod{(p-1)}, \qquad ed_q \equiv 1 \pmod{(q-1)}.$$

Rewriting the equation $ed_p \equiv 1 \pmod{(p-1)}$ as $ed_p = 1 + k_p(p-1)$ where k_p is a positive integer, we get $ed_p = 1 - k_p + k_p p$, and $ed_p + k_p - 1 \equiv 0 \pmod{p}$. It follows that $(d_p, k_p - 1)$ is a solution of the equation $ex + y \equiv 0 \pmod{p}$ in the variables (x, y). Hence one can apply Theorem 4 which leads to the following result.

Corollary 1. *Let $N = pq$ be an RSA modulus with $q < p < 2q$. Let e be a public exponent satisfying $e < N^{\frac{\sqrt{2}}{2}}$ and $ed_p = 1 + k_p(p-1)$ for some d_p with*

$$d_p < \frac{N^{\frac{\sqrt{2}}{4}}}{\sqrt{e}}.$$

Then, under Assumption 1, N can be factored in polynomial time.

Proof. Starting with the equation $ed_p = 1 + k_p(p-1)$ with $e = N^\alpha$, $d_p = N^\delta$ and $p > N^{\frac{1}{2}}$, we get

$$k_p = \frac{ed_p - 1}{p - 1} < \frac{ed_p}{p - 1} < N^{\alpha + \delta - \frac{1}{2}}. \tag{3}$$

On the other hand, we have $ed_p \equiv 1 - k_p \pmod{p}$ with $d_p < N^\delta$ and

$$|1 - k_p| = k_p - 1 < k_p < N^{\alpha + \delta - \frac{1}{2}}.$$

To apply Theorem 4 with the equation $ex + y \equiv 0 \pmod{p}$ where $x = d_p < N^\delta$ and $y = k_p - 1 < N^{\alpha + \delta - \frac{1}{2}}$, the parameters α and δ must satisfy

$$\delta + \alpha + \delta - \frac{1}{2} \leq \frac{\sqrt{2} - 1}{2}.$$

This leads to $\delta < \frac{1}{2}\left(\frac{\sqrt{2}}{2} - \alpha\right)$ and $d_p < N^\delta < \frac{N^{\frac{\sqrt{2}}{4}}}{\sqrt{e}}$. Observe that $\alpha + 2\delta < \frac{\sqrt{2}}{2}$. Plugging in (3), we get

$$k_p < N^{\alpha + \delta - \frac{1}{2}} < N^{\alpha + 2\delta - \frac{1}{2}} < N^{\frac{\sqrt{2}}{2} - \frac{1}{2}} < q.$$

Hence, the parameters d_p and k_p are such that $ed_p + k_p - 1 = k_p p$ with $k_p \not\equiv 0 \pmod{q}$. Hence $ed_p - 1 + k_p \not\equiv 0 \pmod{N}$ which implies that the method of Theorem 4 will give the factorization of N in polynomial time. □

Notice that our attack on CRT-RSA works for exponents $e < N^{\frac{\sqrt{2}}{2}}$, that is when e is much smaller than N. This corresponds to a variant of RSA-CRT proposed by Galbraith, Heneghan and McKee [6] and to another variant proposed by Sun, Hinek and Wu [16]. We want to point out that our new attack improves Bleichenbacher and May's bound [1] where $d_p < \min\left\{\frac{1}{4}\left(\frac{N}{e}\right)^{\frac{2}{5}}, \frac{1}{3}N^{\frac{1}{4}}\right\}$ and $d_q < \min\left\{\frac{1}{4}\left(\frac{N}{e}\right)^{\frac{2}{5}}, \frac{1}{3}N^{\frac{1}{4}}\right\}$, that is when both d_p and d_q are suitably small. In other terms, our attack extends Bleichenbacher and May's attack in the sense that only d_p (or d_q) is small with $d_p < \frac{N^{\frac{\sqrt{2}}{4}}}{\sqrt{e}}$. On the other hand, the existing results on cryptanalysis of CRT-RSA will directly work on the CRT-RSA variant called Dual CRT-RSA. Consequently, our result improves the latest bounds on dual CRT-RSA obtained by Sarkar and Maitra [13].

Next, we consider an instance related to CRT-RSA when the public exponent e satisfies an equation $ex = y + z(p-1)$ with suitably small parameters x, y and z. We obtain the following result as a corollary of Theorem 4.

Corollary 2. *Let $N = pq$ be an RSA modulus with $q < p < 2q$. Suppose e is a public exponent satisfying $e < N$ and $ex = y + z(p-1)$ with*

$$x|z - y| < N^{\frac{\sqrt{2}-1}{2}} \quad \text{and} \quad \gcd(z, q) = 1.$$

Then, under Assumption 1, N can be factored in polynomial time.

Proof. Rewrite the equation $ex = y + z(p-1)$ as $ex + z - y = pz$. Assume that $\gcd(z, q) = 1$, $x < N^{\gamma}$ and $|z - y| < N^{\delta}$. Then, by Theorem 4, we can find the factorization of N in polynomial time if $\gamma + \delta \leq \frac{\sqrt{2}-1}{2}$, that is

$$x|z - y| < N^{\frac{\sqrt{2}-1}{2}},$$

which terminates the proof.   □

5   Experimental Results

We have implemented the attack described in Section 4 using the algebra system Maple on a Intel(R) Core(TM)2 DUO CPU T5870 @ 2.00GHZ 2.00GHZ, 3.00Go RAM machine. Let us first present a detailed example.

5.1   A Working Example

We choose a 200-bit N which is a product of two 100-bit primes p and q satisfying $q < p < 2q$. We also choose a 100-bit e.

$N = 2746482122383906972393557363644983749146398460239422282612197,$

$e = 1908717316858446782674807627631.$

We suppose that e satisfies $ed_p = 1 + k_p(p-1)$ with $d_p < \frac{N^{\frac{\sqrt{2}}{4}}}{\sqrt{e}}$. We rewrite this equation as $x_0 + ey_0 \equiv 0 \pmod{p}$ where $x_0 = k_p - 1$ and $y_0 = d_p$. Next, consider the polynomial $f(x,y) = x + ey$. We apply the lattice-based method of Herrmann and May with $m = 5$ and $t = 2$ as explained in Subsection 2.2. We find that the polynomials $h_1(x,y)$ and $h_2(x,y)$ share the common factor $407851x - 396114y$. Solving over the integers, this leads to the solution $(x_0, y_0) = (k_p - 1, d_p) = (396114, 407851)$. Hence $d_p = 407851 \approx N^{0.09}$ and $k_p = 396115 \approx N^{0.09}$. Using (k_p, d_p), one can find p, q as

$$p = \gcd(ed_p + k_p - 1, N) = 19652683346958190898115521114253,$$

$$q = \frac{N}{p} = 13975099857338325411423163654649.$$

In connection with CRT-RSA, we observe that the private parameter d_q satisfying $ed_q \equiv 1 \pmod{(q-1)}$ is $d_q = 8224463639986525266657880289903 \approx N^{0.49}$. This is greater than the bound $\min\left\{\frac{1}{4}\left(\frac{N}{e}\right)^{\frac{2}{5}}, \frac{1}{3}N^{\frac{1}{4}}\right\} \approx N^{0.2}$ obtained by Bleichenbacher and May in [1]. This shows that the technique of [1] will not work here.

5.2 Massive Experiments

We generated 1000 RSA moduli $N = pq$ with 512-bit primes. For each modulus N, we generated a 512-bit exponent e such that $d_p < \frac{N^{\frac{\sqrt{2}}{4}}}{\sqrt{e}}$. The implementation was in all cases successful and it needs approximately 8 secondes to find the factors of the RSA modulus.

We also ran our experiments with random 1024-bit moduli $N = pq$ and various size of d_p as follows. We randomly select two distinct 512-bit primes p and q and a positive integer d_p of prescribed size such that $\gcd(d_p, (p-1)(q-1)) = 1$. The exponent e is then calculated as $e \equiv d_p^{-1} \pmod{(p-1)}$. Observe that e is of size approximately $N^{\frac{1}{2}}$, so that the condition connecting e and d_p becomes

Table 2. Experimental results for various size of d_p

Size of d_p	Size of e	Size of d_q	LLL execution time
10	511	510	5.35 sec
20	511	508	6.49 sec
40	511	508	6.49 sec
80	510	511	11.45 sec
90	510	510	11.80 sec
95	512	507	11.51 sec
100	511	511	11.74 sec
105	511	511	12.18 sec
110	502	511	11.06 sec

$$d_p < \frac{N^{\frac{\sqrt{2}}{4}}}{\sqrt{e}} \approx N^{\frac{\sqrt{2}-1}{4}}.$$

Hence, for a 1024-bit modulus N, the CRT-exponent d_p is typically of size at most 110.

In Table 2, we give the details of the computations using the method described in Subsection 2.2 with the lattice parameters $m = 4$ and $t = 2$.

6 Conclusion

In this paper, we presented a new attack on the RSA cryptosystem when the public key (N, e) satisfies an equation $ex + y \equiv 0 \pmod{p}$ with the constraint that $|x||y| < N^{\frac{\sqrt{2}-1}{2}}$. We showed that the number of such exponents with $e < N$ is at least $N^{\frac{\sqrt{2}}{2}-\varepsilon}$. As an application of our new attack, we presented the cryptanalysis of CRT-RSA if the private exponent d_p satisfies $d_p < \frac{N^{\frac{\sqrt{2}}{4}}}{\sqrt{e}}$ when p and q are of the same bit-size and e is much smaller than N. This improves the former result of Bleichenbacher and May for CRT-RSA with small CRT-exponents and balanced primes in the case that the public exponent e is significantly smaller than N.

References

1. Bleichenbacher, D., May, A.: New Attacks on RSA with Small Secret CRT-Exponents. In: Yung, M., Dodis, Y., Kiayias, A., Malkin, T. (eds.) PKC 2006. LNCS, vol. 3958, pp. 1–13. Springer, Heidelberg (2006)
2. Blömer, J., May, A.: A Generalized Wiener Attack on RSA. In: Bao, F., Deng, R., Zhou, J. (eds.) PKC 2004. LNCS, vol. 2947, pp. 1–13. Springer, Heidelberg (2004)
3. Boneh, D., Durfee, G.: Cryptanalysis of RSA with Private Key d Less than $N^{0.292}$. In: Stern, J. (ed.) EUROCRYPT 1999. LNCS, vol. 1592, pp. 1–11. Springer, Heidelberg (1999)
4. Cohen, H.: A Course in Computational Number Theory. Graduate Texts in Mathematics. Springer (1993)
5. Coppersmith, D.: Small solutions to polynomial equations, and low exponent RSA vulnerabilities. Journal of Cryptology 10(4), 233–260 (1997)
6. Galbraith, S.D., Heneghan, C., McKee, J.F.: Tunable Balancing of RSA. In: Boyd, C., González Nieto, J.M. (eds.) ACISP 2005. LNCS, vol. 3574, pp. 280–292. Springer, Heidelberg (2005)
7. Hardy, G.H., Wright, E.M.: An Introduction to the Theory of Numbers. Oxford University Press, London (1965)
8. Hastad, J.: Solving simultaneous modular equations of low degree. SIAM J. of Computing 17, 336–341 (1988)
9. Herrmann, M., May, A.: Solving Linear Equations Modulo Divisors: On Factoring Given Any Bits. In: Pieprzyk, J. (ed.) ASIACRYPT 2008. LNCS, vol. 5350, pp. 406–424. Springer, Heidelberg (2008)

10. Howgrave-Graham, N.: Finding Small Roots of Univariate Modular Equations Revisited. In: Darnell, M.J. (ed.) Cryptography and Coding 1997. LNCS, vol. 1355, pp. 131–142. Springer, Heidelberg (1997)
11. Jochemsz, E., May, A.: A Polynomial Time Attack on RSA with Private CRT-Exponents Smaller Than $N^{0.073}$. In: Menezes, A. (ed.) CRYPTO 2007. LNCS, vol. 4622, pp. 395–411. Springer, Heidelberg (2007)
12. Lenstra, A.K., Lenstra, H.W., Lovász, L.: Factoring polynomials with rational coefficients. Mathematische Annalen 261, 513–534 (1982)
13. Maitra, M., Sarkar, S.: Cryptanalysis of Dual CRT-RSA. In: WCC 2011 - Workshop on Coding and Cryptography, pp. 27–36 (2011)
14. Quisquater, J.J., Couvreur, C.: Fast decipherment algorithm for RSA public key cryptosystem. Electronic Letters 18(21), 905–907 (1982)
15. Rivest, R., Shamir, A., Adleman, L.: A Method for obtaining digital signatures and public-key cryptosystems. Communications of the ACM 21(2), 120–126 (1978)
16. Sun, H.-M., Hinek, M.J., Wu, M.-E.: On the design of rebalanced CRT-RSA. Technical Report CACR 2005-35, University of Waterloo (2005)
17. Wiener, M.: Cryptanalysis of short RSA secret exponents. IEEE Transactions on Information Theory 36, 553–558 (1990)

Shift-Type Homomorphic Encryption and Its Application to Fully Homomorphic Encryption

Frederik Armknecht[1], Stefan Katzenbeisser[2], and Andreas Peter[2]

[1] Theoretical Computer Science and IT Security Group
Universität Mannheim, Germany
armknecht@uni-mannheim.de
[2] Security Engineering Group
Technische Universität Darmstadt and CASED, Germany
{stefan.katzenbeisser,andreas.peter}@cased.de

Abstract. This work addresses the characterization of homomorphic encryption schemes both in terms of security and design. In particular, we are interested in currently existing fully homomorphic encryption (FHE) schemes and their common structures and security. Our main contributions can be summarized as follows:

- We define a certain type of homomorphic encryption that we call *shift-type* and identify it as the basic underlying structure of *all existing* homomorphic encryption schemes. It generalizes the already known notion of shift-type *group* homomorphic encryption.
- We give an IND-CPA characterization of all shift-type homomorphic encryption schemes in terms of an abstract subset membership problem.
- We show that this characterization carries over to all leveled FHE schemes that arise by applying Gentry's bootstrapping technique to shift-type homomorphic encryption schemes. Since this is the common structure of all existing schemes, our result actually characterizes the IND-CPA security of all existing bootstrapping-based leveled FHE.
- We prove that the IND-CPA security of FHE schemes that offer a certain type of circuit privacy (for FHE schemes with a binary plaintext space we require circuit privacy for a single AND-gate and, in fact, all existing binary-plaintext FHE schemes offer this) and are based on Gentry's bootstrapping technique is *equivalent* to the circular security of the underlying bootstrappable scheme.

Keywords: Public-Key Cryptography, Homomorphic Encryption, Semantic Security, Circular Security.

1   Introduction

Homomorphic encryption is one of the central topics in public-key cryptography as it allows for the evaluation of certain circuits over encrypted data without the

A. Mitrokotsa and S. Vaudenay (Eds.): AFRICACRYPT 2012, LNCS 7374, pp. 234–251, 2012.
© Springer-Verlag Berlin Heidelberg 2012

ability to decrypt. Many important applications, such as Outsourcing of Computation [18], Electronic Voting [5, 10, 12, 13], Private Information Retrieval [26], Oblivious Polynomial Evaluation [28], and Multiparty Computation [11] are based on this primitive. In the past decades, a substantial number of homomorphic encryption schemes have been proposed (see survey [17]). The majority of these schemes are *group homomorphic*, i.e., the plaintext and ciphertext spaces are groups and the decryption function is a group homomorphism. In other words, group homomorphic schemes allow the evaluation of circuits, consisting solely of group operations in the plaintext group, over the ciphertexts. Recently, Armknecht et al. [3] gave a comprehensive and complete framework of all currently existing group homomorphic encryption schemes and, in particular, gave characterization both in terms of security and design.

Concerning the construction and characterization of more general homomorphic encryption schemes on the other hand, there is still a lot of work to be done. Much effort has been devoted to the construction of so-called *fully homomorphic encryption* (FHE) schemes [7–9, 15, 19, 21–24, 27, 29, 30], which allow the evaluation of *any* circuit (not just consisting of group operation gates as it is the case for group homomorphic encryption) over the ciphertexts. The first such scheme has been proposed by Gentry [20] which uses a certain technique that subsequently has been the basis of all currently existing FHE schemes. Gentry's technique is called *bootstrapping* and can be summarized in the following 2 steps:

1. Construct a *bootstrappable* homomorphic encryption scheme, i.e., a scheme allowing the evaluation of low-degree polynomials over the ciphertexts and, in particular, the evaluation of its own decryption circuit together with one additional set of gates like AND and NOT.
2. Use the *bootstrapping* technique on this scheme to make it fully homomorphic. This technique refreshes a given ciphertext so that it can further be used for evaluation. Usually, ciphertexts are created by adding noise to a given plaintext and once the noise gets too big, the ciphertexts have to be refreshed to reduce the noise again – this is what bootstrapping achieves.

Essentially, the same bootstrapping technique (with minor differences) can be used to construct so-called *leveled* FHE schemes – a relaxed notion of FHE. Such schemes can evaluate all circuits up to a certain depth.[1]

Concerning security, the resulting FHE schemes can be proven secure in terms of IND-CPA (also known as semantic security) under certain assumptions. For a leveled FHE scheme, IND-CPA security follows from the IND-CPA security of the underlying bootstrappable scheme. For a "pure" FHE scheme, we require the

---

[1] The recent leveled FHE scheme by Brakerski et al. [7] is built without the bootstrapping technique. It is the only scheme known so far that deviates from Gentry's blueprint. We stress that we focus on schemes that follow the bootstrapping approach.

We also want to point out that we are not concerned with the "squashing of the decryption circuit" step that Gentry originally proposed in his blueprint. The schemes [7–9, 21] circumvent this "squashing" step but still rely on bootstrapping which is the technique we focus on in this paper.

underlying bootstrappable scheme to be *circular secure* which roughly means that the scheme remains secure even if the adversary gets to see the bits of the secret key encrypted under the corresponding public key.

1.1 Contribution and Related Work

In this paper, we address the above mentioned topic of characterizing the security and the design of homomorphic encryption schemes in the context of FHE, thereby extending the work of Armknecht et al. [3] on group homomorphic encryption to these more general homomorphic schemes:

1. We identify and formalize the underlying structure of *all existing* homomorphic schemes and call such schemes *shift-type* homomorphic. It is a natural generalization of the shift-type *group* homomorphic schemes introduced in [3].
2. We give an IND-CPA security characterization of all shift-type encryption schemes in terms of an abstract subset membership problem. In comparison to the proof of the IND-CPA security characterization of group homomorphic schemes in [3] that heavily relies on the group homomorphic property, it is interesting to see that our result shows that it is actually the shift-type structure of the encryption algorithm that gives the IND-CPA characterization (and not the homomorphic property of the decryption).
3. We show that this characterization carries over to all leveled FHE schemes that are based on Gentry's bootstrapping technique applied to shift-type homomorphic schemes. Since all existing schemes are shift-type homomorphic, this gives a characterization of all existing bootstrapping-based schemes. Additionally, our result has the nice application that once an FHE scheme is constructed using Gentry's technique, the underlying hardness assumption yielding IND-CPA security immediately comes out of this characterization.
4. We prove that the IND-CPA security of "pure" FHE schemes that are based on Gentry's bootstrapping technique and that are *circuit-private for a certain small set of circuits* (meaning that a ciphertext that is the evaluation of ciphertexts under one of these circuits does not reveal any information about the used circuit, even when the secret key is known) is *equivalent* to the circular security of the underlying bootstrappable scheme. We note that Gentry [19, Theorem 4.3.2] has already proved one of the directions, namely that *if* the underlying bootstrappable scheme is circular secure, *then* the resulting FHE scheme is IND-CPA secure. Interestingly enough, all existing FHE schemes where the plaintext space is $\{0, 1\}$ are circuit-private for this special set of circuits.

   Our characterization result gives another important relation between the notion of circular security and IND-CPA security. Moreover, it shows that when the resulting FHE scheme (using the bootstrapping technique) gives a certain "minimal" circuit privacy, the circular security is not only sufficient but also necessary. Therefore it underlines the importance of Brakerski et al.'s work [9]. Therein, they construct a "somewhat" homomorphic scheme (i.e., a homomorphic encryption scheme for low-degree polynomials only) that is provably circular secure. However, this scheme is not bootstrappable. By using standard techniques, they turn it into a bootstrappable scheme. Unfortunately, the proof of circular security gets lost in this transformation. We note that, even with Brakerski et al.'s result, we still do not know how to prove circular security for given IND-CPA secure bootstrappable encryption schemes. So currently existing FHE schemes still rely on the assumption that the circular security and the IND-CPA security of their underlying bootstrappable schemes are equivalent.

In regard to circular security, there are two other papers important to mention. First, there is the work by Barak et al. [4]. Therein, they show that any FHE scheme that is circular secure is actually *fully* KDM secure (i.e., the adversary gets evaluations of *arbitrary* functions on the private key). Second, the work by Applebaum [2] shows that any *simulatable* fully KDM secure scheme (a notion which is even stronger than fully KDM security) is also fully homomorphic. Furthermore, it shows that the same bootstrapping technique that Gentry uses to build FHE schemes can be used to construct fully KDM secure encryption schemes.

We stress that in contrast to the just mentioned works, we prove that the IND-CPA security of FHE schemes (that arise by using the bootstrapping technique) which give a certain "minimal" circuit privacy, is equivalent to the circular security of the underlying bootstrappable scheme.

To complete the list of related works on FHE, we want to mention an approach by Aguilar Melchor et al. [1], which uses so-called "chained encryption schemes" and differs from the bootstrapping technique. Although it is likely that our results extend to their method, we do not cover this here, since the computational cost of their solution is exponential in the number of multiplications that the scheme should be able to evaluate over the ciphertexts (formally, they do not achieve leveled FHE but only *constant-bounded* FHE).

1.2   Outline

Throughout the paper, we use standard notation and definitions that are summarized in Section 2. Therein, we also formally define public-key homomorphic encryption, recall its standard security notion, and define a class of subset membership problems. In Section 3, we define *shift-type* homomorphic encryption schemes and characterize their security in terms of these subset membership problems. Finally, Section 4 is entirely devoted to FHE. First, we recall Gentry's bootstrapping technique for leveled FHE schemes and show that our security characterization for shift-type homomorphic encryption carries over to such schemes. Second, we prove the equivalence of a "pure" bootstrapping-based FHE scheme being IND-CPA secure and the underlying bootstrappable scheme being circular secure. Third, we give a brief overview on existing FHE schemes and their underlying shift-type structures, while focusing on the scheme by van Dijk et al. [15] for a better conceptual understanding. We conclude in Section 5.

2   Preliminaries

2.1   Notation

We write $x \longleftarrow X$ if X is a random variable or distribution and x is to be chosen randomly from X according to its distribution. In the case where X is solely a set, $x \stackrel{U}{\longleftarrow} X$ denotes that x is chosen uniformly at random from X. For an algorithm $\mathcal{A}$ we write $x \longleftarrow \mathcal{A}(y)$ if $\mathcal{A}$ outputs x on fixed input y according to $\mathcal{A}$'s distribution. If $\mathcal{A}$ has access to an oracle $\mathcal{O}$, we write $\mathcal{A}^{\mathcal{O}}$. Sometimes, we need to specify the randomness of a probabilistic algorithm $\mathcal{A}$ explicitly. To this end, we interpret $\mathcal{A}$ as a deterministic algorithm $\mathcal{A}(y, r)$, which has access to random values r from some randomness space Rnd.

By a *description* of a finite set X we mean an efficient sampling algorithm (according to some distribution) for the set X. If X is a group, a *description* of X additionally includes the neutral element and a set of efficient algorithms that allow us to perform the usual group operation on X and the inversion of group elements. We abuse notation and write X both for the description and for the set itself. If a description of X is given, we denote sampling from X according to the distribution given by the sampling algorithm of the description by $x \longleftarrow X$.

For given probabilistic algorithms $\mathcal{A}$ and Gen that run in time polynomial in a given parameter λ, we describe computational problems P through experiments $\mathbf{Exp}^{\mathrm{P}}_{\mathcal{A},\mathsf{Gen}}(\lambda)$. The output of $\mathbf{Exp}^{\mathrm{P}}_{\mathcal{A},\mathsf{Gen}}(\lambda)$ is always defined to be a single bit. We then say that *problem* P *is hard (relative to* Gen*)* if for all probabilistic polynomial time (PPT) algorithms $\mathcal{A}$ there exists a negligible (in λ) function negl such that

$$\left| \Pr[\mathbf{Exp}^{\mathrm{P}}_{\mathcal{A},\mathsf{Gen}}(\lambda) = 1] - \frac{1}{2} \right| \leq \mathtt{negl}(\lambda).$$

We recall that a public-key encryption scheme $\mathcal{E} = (\mathsf{KeyGen}, \mathsf{Enc}, \mathsf{Dec})$ consists of a PPT key generation algorithm KeyGen which generates a pair $(\mathsf{pk}, \mathsf{sk})$ of corresponding public and private keys, a PPT encryption algorithm Enc and a deterministic PT decryption algorithm Dec with the usual correctness condition. We denote the set of plaintexts by $\mathcal{P}$ and the set of ciphertexts by $\widehat{\mathcal{C}}$.

2.2   Public-Key Homomorphic Encryption Schemes

We briefly recall the notion of public-key *homomorphic encryption* (see [25, Definition 5] or [20, Definition 1]).

Definition 1. *A public-key encryption scheme* $\mathcal{E} = (\mathsf{KeyGen}, \mathsf{Enc}, \mathsf{Dec})$ *is called homomorphic for a set of circuits* $\mathbb{C} = \mathbb{C}[\lambda]$ *(that depends on the security parameter* λ*), if there exists a PPT algorithm* Eval *(that outputs a ciphertext and takes as input public keys* pk *from the output of* KeyGen*, circuits* $C \in \mathbb{C}(\lambda)$ *and ciphertexts* $(c_1, \ldots, c_r)$ *with* $c_i \longleftarrow \mathsf{Enc}_{\mathsf{pk}}(m_i)$ *for some* $m_i \in \mathcal{P}$*,* $i = 1, \ldots, r$*) such that for every output* $(\mathsf{pk}, \mathsf{sk})$ *of* $\mathsf{KeyGen}(\lambda)$ *it holds that (correctness condition)*

$$\mathsf{Dec}_{\mathsf{sk}}(\mathsf{Eval}_{\mathsf{pk}}(C, c_1, \ldots, c_r)) = C(m_1, \ldots, m_r),$$

except with negligible (in λ*) probability over the random coins in* Eval*.*

The minimal security property that we require such schemes to have is *semantic security* (or IND-CPA security), which is defined in exactly the same way as for standard public-key encryption schemes and is captured by the following experiment between a challenger and an adversary $\mathcal{A}$:

Experiment $\mathbf{Exp}^{\text{ind-cpa}}_{\mathcal{A},\text{KeyGen}}(\lambda)$:

1. $(\text{pk}, \text{sk}) \longleftarrow \text{KeyGen}(\lambda)$
2. $(m_0, m_1, s) \longleftarrow \mathcal{A}_1(\text{pk})$ where $m_0, m_1 \in \mathcal{P}$ and s a state of $\mathcal{A}_1$
3. Choose $b \overset{U}{\longleftarrow} \{0, 1\}$ and compute $c \longleftarrow \text{Enc}_{\text{pk}}(m_b)$
4. $d \longleftarrow \mathcal{A}_2(m_0, m_1, s, c)$ where $d \in \{0, 1\}$
5. The output of the experiment is defined to be 1 if $d = b$ and 0 otherwise.

We say that $\mathcal{E}$ is IND-CPA *secure (relative to* KeyGen*)* if the advantage

$$\left| \Pr[\mathbf{Exp}^{\text{ind-cpa}}_{\mathcal{A},\text{KeyGen}}(\lambda) = 1] - \frac{1}{2} \right| \text{ is negligible for all PPT algorithms } \mathcal{A}.$$

2.3   The Subset Membership Problem

The *Subset Membership Problem* (SMP) was introduced by Cramer and Shoup in [14]: Let Gen be a PPT algorithm that takes a security parameter λ as input and outputs descriptions $(\mathcal{S}, \mathcal{N})$ where $\mathcal{N}$ is a non-trivial, proper subset of a finite set $\mathcal{S}$. Consider the following experiment for a given algorithm Gen, algorithm $\mathcal{A}$ and parameter λ:

Experiment $\mathbf{Exp}^{\text{SMP}}_{\mathcal{A},\text{Gen}}(\lambda)$:

1. $(\mathcal{S}, \mathcal{N}) \longleftarrow \text{Gen}(\lambda)$
2. Choose $b \overset{U}{\longleftarrow} \{0, 1\}$. If $b = 1$: $z \longleftarrow \mathcal{S}$. Otherwise: $z \longleftarrow \mathcal{N}$.
3. $d \longleftarrow \mathcal{A}(\mathcal{S}, \mathcal{N}, z)$ where $d \in \{0, 1\}$
4. The output of the experiment is defined to be 1 if $d = b$ and 0 otherwise.

This experiment defines the *Subset Membership Problem* SMP *(relative to* Gen*)* which, informally, states that given $(\mathcal{S}, \mathcal{N}, z)$ where $z \longleftarrow \mathcal{S}$, one has to decide whether $z \in \mathcal{N}$ or not.

3   Shift-Type Homomorphic Encryption

Informally, an encryption scheme is *shift-type homomorphic* if the plaintexts form a non-trivial (say multiplicative) group, encryptions of *known* plaintexts can be transformed (or "shifted") to encryptions of 1, and if the same transformation is applied to a random ciphertext, the resulting ciphertext is still random.

Definition 2. *A public-key encryption scheme* $\mathcal{E} = (\text{KeyGen}, \text{Enc}, \text{Dec})$ *is called* shift-type homomorphic, *if for every output* (pk, sk) *of* $\text{KeyGen}(\lambda)$, *the plaintext space* $\mathcal{P}$ *and the ciphertext space* $\widehat{\mathcal{C}}$ *are (multiplicatively written) non-trivial* *groups*[2] *such that the public key* pk *contains a description of a subset* $\mathcal{N} \subseteq \widehat{\mathcal{C}}$ *and an efficient injective homomorphism* $\varphi : \mathcal{P} \to \widehat{\mathcal{C}}$ *so that for all plaintexts* $m \in \mathcal{P}$,

$$\mathsf{Enc}_{\mathsf{pk}}(m) \ outputs \ \varphi(m) \cdot n,$$

where $n \longleftarrow \mathcal{N}$.

We denote the *set of all encryptions* by

$$\mathcal{C} := \{\mathsf{Enc}_{\mathsf{pk}}(m) \mid m \in \mathcal{P}\} \subseteq \widehat{\mathcal{C}}$$

and sometimes call its elements *fresh* ciphertexts/encryptions. Since φ is a homomorphism, we know that $\mathcal{N}$ is actually a subset of $\mathcal{C}$.

Remark 1. 1. The concept of shift-type homomorphic encryption is very similar to the concept of "adding noise" to the plaintext. Here, we are a bit more general, as we allow homomorphic manipulation of the plaintext prior to adding (or multiplying in our case) noise. The "noise" corresponds to the elements of the subset $\mathcal{N}$.

2. The name "shift-type" is due to the fact that we can "shift" encryptions of known plaintexts to encryptions of arbitrary plaintexts under the same noise: Let $c := \varphi(m) \cdot n$ be an encryption of message $m \in \mathcal{P}$. Then, by computing $c' := \varphi(m' \cdot m^{-1}) \cdot c$ for some arbitrary message $m' \in \mathcal{P}$, we receive an encryption $c' = \varphi(m') \cdot n$ of message m' under the same noise n, by using the homomorphic property of φ.

3. Definition 2 is a natural generalization of the notion of shift-type *group* homomorphic encryption as introduced in [3]. For the latter, the decryption procedure is a group homomorphism and the mapping φ is the encryption algorithm under a fixed randomness.

4. We stress that the shift-type structure of the encryption algorithm is not implied by a group homomorphic encryption scheme (recall that this means that the decryption procedure is a group homomorphism, see [3] for details). Although *all existing* IND-CPA secure homomorphic schemes do have this structure, it is easy to construct a group homomorphic scheme (which is insecure in terms of IND-CPA) that does not: Let $\mathcal{E} = (\mathsf{KeyGen}, \mathsf{Enc}, \mathsf{Dec})$ be an arbitrary IND-CPA secure group homomorphic encryption scheme with randomness space Rnd (e.g., ElGamal's scheme [16]) and let r^* be some fixed value in Rnd. We modify its encryption algorithm as follows and denote it by Enc^*: On input a plaintext m, $\mathsf{Enc}^*(m)$ chooses a random bit $b \in \{0,1\}$ and some random $r \in$ Rnd. If $b = 1$ or $m = 1$, $\mathsf{Enc}^*(m)$ outputs $\mathsf{Enc}(m, r)$. Otherwise, it outputs $\mathsf{Enc}(m, r^*)$.

   It is easy to see that the modified scheme $\mathsf{Enc}^* = (\mathsf{KeyGen}, \mathsf{Enc}^*, \mathsf{Dec})$ is group homomorphic but *not* IND-CPA secure. On the other hand, it is also not shift-type homomorphic. Interestingly enough, it is an open question

---

[2] We assume that descriptions of $\mathcal{P}$ and $\widehat{\mathcal{C}}$ are contained in the public key pk. As described in Section 2.1, sampling from $\mathcal{P}$ (resp. $\widehat{\mathcal{C}}$) using the (corresponding) sampling algorithm of the description is denoted by $m \longleftarrow \mathcal{P}$ (resp. $c \longleftarrow \widehat{\mathcal{C}}$).

whether the shift-type structure is implied by the IND-CPA security of a given group homomorphic encryption scheme – meaning that if the output distribution of the encryption algorithm is computationally distinguishable from the shift-type structure, then the given group homomorphic scheme is insecure in terms of IND-CPA.

Next, we will characterize the IND-CPA security of such schemes. We note that by saying that the Subset Membership Problem (SMP) as defined in Section 2.3 is hard relative to KeyGen for a key generator KeyGen of some shift-type homomorphic encryption scheme, we mean that SMP is hard for $(\mathcal{C}, \mathcal{N})$. For a given shift-type homomorphic encryption scheme, we use the notation

$$\mathcal{C}_m := \{c \in \mathcal{C} \mid \mathsf{Dec}_{\mathsf{sk}}(c) = m\}$$

to denote the set of ciphertexts decrypting to $m \in \mathcal{P}$. In particular, we have $\mathcal{N} = \mathcal{C}_1$ in this notation. We are now in a position to prove a characterization of IND-CPA security of such schemes.

Theorem 1 (IND-CPA Security of Shift-Type Schemes). *For a shift-type homomorphic encryption scheme* $\mathcal{E} = (\mathsf{KeyGen}, \mathsf{Enc}, \mathsf{Dec})$ *we have:*

$$\mathcal{E} \text{ is IND-CPA (rel. to KeyGen)} \iff \text{SMP is hard (rel. to KeyGen)}$$

Proof. "$\Leftarrow$": Assume that $\mathcal{E}$ is not IND-CPA secure, i.e. there exists a PPT algorithm $\mathcal{A}^{\mathrm{cpa}} = (\mathcal{A}_1^{\mathrm{cpa}}, \mathcal{A}_2^{\mathrm{cpa}})$ that breaks the security with non-negligible advantage $f(\lambda)$. We derive a contradiction by constructing a PPT algorithm $\mathcal{A}^{\mathrm{smp}}$ that successfully solves SMP with advantage $\frac{1}{2}f(\lambda)$.

Since SMP and IND-CPA are both considered relative to KeyGen, $\mathcal{A}^{\mathrm{smp}}$ can simply forward the public key pk of the output of KeyGen(λ) to $\mathcal{A}_1^{\mathrm{cpa}}$. Next, $\mathcal{A}_1^{\mathrm{cpa}}$ outputs two messages $m_0, m_1 \in \mathcal{P}$ to $\mathcal{A}^{\mathrm{smp}}$. The SMP challenger chooses a bit $b \xleftarrow{U} \{0, 1\}$ and sends the challenge $c \in \mathcal{C}$ to $\mathcal{A}^{\mathrm{smp}}$, who then chooses a bit $d \xleftarrow{U} \{0, 1\}$ and sends the challenge $c_d := \varphi(m_d) \cdot c$ to $\mathcal{A}_2^{\mathrm{cpa}}$. Now, $\mathcal{A}_2^{\mathrm{cpa}}$ outputs a bit d' and sends it back to $\mathcal{A}^{\mathrm{smp}}$ which sends $b' := d \oplus d'$ to the SMP challenger.

We have the following relations: If $b = 0$, then $c \in \mathcal{N} = \mathcal{C}_1$ and $c_d \in \mathcal{C}_{m_d}$ (a fresh encryption of m_d) by definition. Hence, $\mathcal{A}_2^{\mathrm{cpa}}$ makes the right guess with advantage $f(\lambda)$, i.e., $\Pr[b' = b | b = 0] \geq \frac{1}{2} + f(\lambda)$. If $b = 1$, then $c \in \mathcal{C}$, meaning that it is a fresh encryption (by definition of the set $\mathcal{C}$) of some random message m. But φ is a homomorphism and so c_d is a fresh encryption of (the random message) $m_d \cdot m$. Hence, $\mathcal{A}_2^{\mathrm{cpa}}$ guesses d with no advantage, i.e. $\Pr[b' = b | b = 1] = \frac{1}{2}$. We have shown:

$$\Pr[\mathbf{Exp}_{\mathcal{A}^{\mathrm{smp}}, \mathsf{Gen}}^{\mathsf{SMP}}(\lambda) = 1] = \sum_{\beta \in \{0,1\}} \Pr[b' = b | b = \beta] \cdot \Pr[b = \beta]$$

$$\geq \frac{1}{2} \cdot \left(\frac{1}{2} + f(\lambda) + \frac{1}{2}\right) = \frac{1}{2} + \frac{1}{2}f(\lambda).$$

"$\Rightarrow$": For the converse, we assume that there is a PPT algorithm $\mathcal{A}^{\mathrm{smp}}$ that solves SMP with advantage $f(\lambda)$. Similarly to what we have done above, we construct a PPT algorithm $\mathcal{A}^{\text{cpa}} = (\mathcal{A}_1^{\text{cpa}}, \mathcal{A}_2^{\text{cpa}})$ that successfully breaks the IND-CPA security with advantage $f(\lambda)$.

Again as above, $\mathcal{A}_1^{\text{cpa}}$ forwards the output of $\mathsf{KeyGen}(\lambda)$ to $\mathcal{A}^{\text{smp}}$. Next, $\mathcal{A}_1^{\text{cpa}}$ outputs two random messages $m_0, m_1 \in \mathcal{P}$. The IND-CPA challenger chooses a bit $b \xleftarrow{U} \{0,1\}$ and sends the challenge $c_b \longleftarrow \mathsf{Enc}_{\text{pk}}(m_b)$ to $\mathcal{A}_2^{\text{cpa}}$, who then computes $c := \varphi(m_0^{-1}) \cdot c_b \in \mathcal{C}$ and sends the challenge c to $\mathcal{A}^{\text{smp}}$. Now, $\mathcal{A}^{\text{smp}}$ returns a bit d' to $\mathcal{A}_2^{\text{cpa}}$ that then outputs $b' := d'$ to the IND-CPA challenger.

We have the following relations: If $b = 0$, then $c \in \mathcal{C}_1 = \mathcal{N}$ and $\mathcal{A}^{\text{smp}}$ guesses b with advantage $f(\lambda)$, i.e. $\Pr[b' = b | b = 0] \geq \frac{1}{2} + f(\lambda)$. If $b = 1$, then c is a random element in $\mathcal{C}$ and $\mathcal{A}^{\text{smp}}$ guesses b again with advantage $f(\lambda)$, i.e. $\Pr[b' = b | b = 1] \geq \frac{1}{2} + f(\lambda)$. Therefore, we have shown:

$$\Pr[\mathbf{Exp}_{\mathcal{A}^{\text{cpa}},\text{Gen}}^{\text{ind-cpa}}(\lambda) = 1] = \sum_{\beta \in \{0,1\}} \Pr[b' = b | b = \beta] \cdot \Pr[b = \beta]$$

$$\geq \frac{1}{2} \cdot (1 + 2f(\lambda)) = \frac{1}{2} + f(\lambda).$$

$\square$

4   Fully Homomorphic Encryption (FHE)

An encryption scheme $\mathcal{E} = (\mathsf{KeyGen}, \mathsf{Enc}, \mathsf{Dec}, \mathsf{Eval})$ that is homomorphic for *all* circuits (in terms of Definition 1) is called *fully homomorphic* (FHE = Fully Homomorphic Encryption). To rule out trivial FHE schemes $\mathcal{E}$, e.g., where Eval simply outputs its input circuit C together with its input ciphertexts and Dec takes circuits C as input as well and simply outputs the evaluation of C on the decryptions of the plugged-in ciphertexts, we require the additional property of *compactness* (cf. [19, Definition 2.1.2]). Informally this means that the size of the output of Eval does not depend on the size of the circuit it evaluates.

We recall this notion in the more general context of encryption schemes that are homomorphic for a given set of circuits.

Definition 3. *Let $\mathcal{E} = (\mathsf{KeyGen}, \mathsf{Enc}, \mathsf{Dec}, \mathsf{Eval})$ be an encryption scheme that is homomorphic for a set of circuits $\mathbb{C} = \mathbb{C}[\lambda]$. $\mathcal{E}$ is called compact, if Dec can be expressed as a circuit of size at most $p(\lambda)$ for some polynomial p.*

With this definition in mind, we can formalize the notion of FHE:

Definition 4. *An encryption scheme $\mathcal{E} = (\mathsf{KeyGen}, \mathsf{Enc}, \mathsf{Dec}, \mathsf{Eval})$ that is homomorphic for all circuits and compact is called fully homomorphic.*

We note that *all* currently existing FHE schemes in terms of Definition 4 (namely, [7–9, 15, 19, 21–24, 27, 29, 30]) are variants of a scheme proposed by Gentry [20] and do all have the property that decryption Dec is implemented by a circuit that does only depend on the security parameter λ. To achieve this notion of FHE, all these schemes are based on the so-called *bootstrapping* technique by Gentry [20], which we will recall in the next section.

We stress, however, that there is the relaxed notion of *Leveled FHE* that we want to deal with first. Unlike "pure" FHE schemes (as in Definition 4), such schemes can correctly evaluate circuits up to a certain depth only. We will recall this notion in the next section. For such leveled FHE schemes, we remark that except for the scheme by Brakerski, Gentry, and Vaikuntanathan [7], again all existing schemes are based on Gentry's bootstrapping technique.[3] In this paper, we restrict our attention to (leveled) FHE schemes that are based on Gentry's bootstrapping technique.

Our aim is a characterization of the IND-CPA security of all existing (leveled) FHE schemes that are based on the technique of bootstrapping. To do so, we first give a brief summary on Gentry's bootstrapping approach in the next section and prove an IND-CPA characterization of schemes that can be constructed in this way. We will do this both for leveled FHE schemes, as well as for "pure" FHE schemes. For the latter, we need the FHE schemes to have the additional property of *circuit privacy* that we will recall in Section 4.2. Finally, in Section 4.3 we discuss existing schemes, while focusing on a particular scheme by van Dijk et al. [15] for a better conceptual understanding.

4.1 Gentry's Bootstrapping Technique: Leveled FHE Schemes

In this section, we briefly want to recall Gentry's bootstrapping technique [20] on how to construct FHE schemes. Roughly speaking, Gentry constructs a homomorphic encryption scheme for circuits of any depth from an underlying encryption scheme that is homomorphic for "just a little more than its own decryption circuit". We formalize the term in double quotes momentarily (see also [20, Definition 4]), but first need to do some more definitional work. We will prove later that characterizing the IND-CPA security of the underlying schemes is already enough to characterize the IND-CPA security of resulting schemes that are homomorphic for *all circuits up to a certain depth* (such schemes are also known as *Leveled FHE schemes*).

Definition 5. *Let $\mathcal{E} = (\mathsf{KeyGen}, \mathsf{Enc}, \mathsf{Dec}, \mathsf{Eval})$ be an encryption scheme in which Dec is implemented by a circuit that does only depend on the security parameter λ. For every output $(\mathsf{pk}, \mathsf{sk})$ of $\mathsf{KeyGen}(\lambda)$, we let Γ be a set of gates with inputs and output in plaintext space $\mathcal{P}$ including the identity gate (input and output are the same). For gate $g \in \Gamma$, the g-augmented decryption circuit consists of a g-gate connecting multiple copies of Dec (the number of copies equals the number of inputs to g), where Dec takes the secret key sk and a ciphertext as input formatted as elements of $\mathcal{P}^{\ell(\lambda)}$, where $\ell(\lambda)$ is some polynomial in λ. We denote the set of all g-augmented decryption circuits, $g \in \Gamma$, by $\mathsf{Dec}(\Gamma)$.[4]*

---

[3] Some of the existing schemes, however, deviate from Gentry's original blueprint where one starts with a "somewhat homomorphic scheme", then "squashes" the decryption circuit, and then does the bootstrapping. In the present work, we are not interested in the "squashing" step and will restrict our attention to the bootstrapping step.

[4] Recall that Dec always depends on λ and we sometimes write $\mathsf{Dec}[\lambda]$ to make this dependency obvious.

Recall that from now on, we restrict our attention to encryption schemes in which decryption Dec is implemented by a circuit that does only depend on the security parameter λ. The most important property of an encryption scheme to be of any use in Gentry's approach is that of *bootstrappability*.

Definition 6. *Let $\mathcal{E} = (\mathsf{KeyGen}, \mathsf{Enc}, \mathsf{Dec}, \mathsf{Eval})$ be a homomorphic encryption scheme for a set of circuits $\mathbb{C} = \mathbb{C}[\lambda]$. $\mathcal{E}$ is called* bootstrappable *for a set of gates Γ, if $\mathsf{Dec}[\lambda](\Gamma) \subseteq \mathbb{C}[\lambda]$ for all security parameters λ.*

There are two main results in [20] that are of particular interest to us:

Theorem 2 (see Theorem 3 of [20]). *There is an efficient and explicit transformation that for any given bootstrappable scheme $\mathcal{E}$ for a set of gates Γ and parameter $d = d(\lambda)$ outputs another encryption scheme $\mathcal{E}^{(d)}$ that is*

1. *compact and whose decryption circuit is identical to that of $\mathcal{E}$*
2. *homomorphic for all circuits with gates in Γ of depth at most d.*

Theorem 3 (see Theorem 4 of [20]). *Let $\mathcal{E}$ be a bootstrappable scheme for a set of gates Γ. For all parameters $d = d(\lambda)$, we have that the output $\mathcal{E}^{(d)}$ of the transformation from Theorem 2 applied to $\mathcal{E}$ and d is* IND-CPA *secure if $\mathcal{E}$ is.*

We will now prove that the IND-CPA security of $\mathcal{E}^{(d)}$ is actually *equivalent* to that of $\mathcal{E}$. For this we need to recall a few details in Gentry's transformation of Theorem 2. For all remaining details, we refer to [20]. The particular facts, we will need about $\mathcal{E}^{(d)}$ are the following three (cf. [20]):

1. The plaintext space $\mathcal{P}$ of $\mathcal{E}^{(d)}$ is the same as that of $\mathcal{E}$.
2. The key generation algorithm of $\mathcal{E}^{(d)}$ uses the key generator KeyGen of $\mathcal{E}$ $(d+1)$-times to produce $d+1$ public and secret key pairs $(\mathsf{pk}_i, \mathsf{sk}_i)$, $i = 0, \ldots, d$. Let $\mathsf{sk}_{i1}, \ldots, \mathsf{sk}_{i\ell}$ be the representation of sk_i as elements of $\mathcal{P}$ with $\ell = \ell(\lambda)$ as in Definition 5. The key generator of $\mathcal{E}^{(d)}$ then computes $\overline{\mathsf{sk}}_{ij} \longleftarrow \mathsf{Enc}_{\mathsf{pk}_{i-1}}(\mathsf{sk}_{ij})$ for $i = 1, \ldots, d$ and $j = 1, \ldots, \ell$, and outputs the secret key $\mathsf{sk}^{(d)} := sk_0$, and public key

$$\mathsf{pk}^{(d)} := \left((\mathsf{pk}_i)_{i=1,\ldots,d}, (\overline{\mathsf{sk}}_{ij})_{\substack{i=1,\ldots,d \\ j=1,\ldots,\ell}} \right).$$

3. Encryption of a message $m \in \mathcal{P}$ in $\mathcal{E}^{(d)}$ is done by computing a ciphertext $c \longleftarrow \mathsf{Enc}_{\mathsf{pk}_d}(m)$, i.e., an encryption of m under pk_d by using the encryption algorithm Enc of $\mathcal{E}$.

We are now in a position to prove the IND-CPA characterization.

Theorem 4. *Let $\mathcal{E}$ be a bootstrappable scheme for a set of gates Γ. For parameter $d = d(\lambda)$, let $\mathcal{E}^{(d)}$ denote the output of the transformation from Theorem 2 applied to $\mathcal{E}$ and d. For all parameters d, it holds:*

$$\mathcal{E}^{(d)} \text{ is } \mathsf{IND\text{-}CPA} \text{ secure} \iff \mathcal{E} \text{ is } \mathsf{IND\text{-}CPA} \text{ secure}.$$

Proof. "$\Leftarrow$": This is Theorem 3.

"$\Rightarrow$": If $\mathcal{A}$ is a PPT adversary that successfully breaks the IND-CPA security of $\mathcal{E}$, then $\mathcal{A}$ can also be used to break the IND-CPA security of $\mathcal{E}^{(d)}$. By looking at the facts above, we know that in the IND-CPA security game for $\mathcal{E}^{(d)}$, $\mathcal{A}$ receives the public key pk_d, outputs two messages $m_0, m_1 \in \mathcal{P}$ and gets the ciphertext $c \longleftarrow \mathsf{Enc}_{\mathsf{pk}_d}(m_b)$ as the challenge ciphertext, where $b \xleftarrow{U} \{0,1\}$. Due to the initial assumption on $\mathcal{A}$, $\mathcal{A}$ can guess the bit b with non-negligible advantage. $\square$

Unfortunately, the resulting scheme from Theorem 2 after applying the transformation is not yet an FHE scheme as it is only homomorphic for all circuits with gates in Γ of depth at most d (i.e., it is leveled fully homomorphic). However, in [19], Gentry shows how to modify the previously described technique to get "pure" FHE schemes. We will give an IND-CPA security characterization of such schemes (with a certain additional property) in the next section.

4.2   Gentry's Bootstrapping Technique: FHE Schemes

In [19, Section 4.3], Gentry shows that, by changing the transformation as described in the following and by *assuming* that the underlying bootstrappable scheme is *circular secure* (a notion we will recall momentarily), the resulting scheme is indeed fully homomorphic and IND-CPA secure. We start by explaining the modification of the transformation of Theorem 2, whereas we denote the resulting scheme by $\mathcal{E}^*$:

In the key generation step above (this is step 2 right after Theorem 3), $\mathcal{E}^*$ uses the key generator KeyGen of $\mathcal{E}$ only once (instead of $(d+1)$-times) to compute a key pair $(\mathsf{pk}, \mathsf{sk})$ and outputs the secret key $\mathsf{sk}^* := \mathsf{sk}$ and public key $\mathsf{pk}^* := (\mathsf{pk}, \overline{\mathsf{sk}_1}, \ldots, \overline{\mathsf{sk}_\ell})$ where $\overline{\mathsf{sk}_i} \longleftarrow \mathsf{Enc}_{\mathsf{pk}}(\mathsf{sk}_i)$ and $\mathsf{sk}_1, \ldots, \mathsf{sk}_\ell$ is the representation of sk as elements of $\mathcal{P}$. This is the only modification and the rest works exactly as in the transformation of Theorem 2 (see [19, Section 4.3] for details).

Next, we recall the notion of *circular security* for bootstrappable encryption schemes $\mathcal{E} = (\mathsf{KeyGen}, \mathsf{Enc}, \mathsf{Dec}, \mathsf{Eval})$. Consider the following experiment for a given algorithm $\mathcal{A}$ and parameter λ:

Experiment $\mathbf{Exp}^{\mathrm{circular}}_{\mathcal{A},\mathsf{KeyGen}}(\lambda)$:

1. Compute $(\mathsf{pk}, \mathsf{sk}) \longleftarrow \mathsf{KeyGen}(\lambda)$
2. Choose $b \xleftarrow{U} \{0,1\}$. If $b = 0$, then compute $\overline{\mathsf{sk}_j} \longleftarrow \mathsf{Enc}_{\mathsf{pk}}(\mathsf{sk}_j)$ for all $j = 1, \ldots, \ell$ where $\mathsf{sk}_1, \ldots, \mathsf{sk}_\ell$ is the representation of sk as elements of $\mathcal{P}$ with $\ell = \ell(\lambda)$ as in Definition 5. If $b = 1$, then compute $\overline{\mathsf{sk}_j}$ as encryptions of some fixed element $\mathbf{0} \in \mathcal{P}$, unrelated to pk, for all $j = 1, \ldots, \ell$
3. $d \longleftarrow \mathcal{A}\left(\mathsf{pk}, \overline{\mathsf{sk}_1}, \ldots, \overline{\mathsf{sk}_\ell}\right)$ where $d \in \{0,1\}$
4. The output of the experiment is defined to be 1 if $d = b$ and 0 else.

This experiment defines *circular security* for bootstrappable encryption schemes $\mathcal{E}$. We note that, as we consider bootstrappable schemes, this definition is equivalent to the "standard" definition of circular security [6] as originally introduced (this is shown in [19, Chapter 4]).

Before we can state the main result of this section, we need to recall another notion that is related to FHE, namely that of *circuit privacy*. Informally, this notion says that even if the secret key is known, the output of Eval does not reveal any information about the circuit that it evaluates, except for the output value of that circuit. Formally, this idea is captured in the following definition:

Definition 7. *An FHE scheme $\mathcal{E} = (\mathsf{KeyGen}, \mathsf{Enc}, \mathsf{Dec}, \mathsf{Eval})$ is said to be* (computationally) *circuit-private, if for every keypair* $(\mathsf{pk}, \mathsf{sk}) \longleftarrow \mathsf{KeyGen}(\lambda)$, *any circuit C, and any fixed tuple of fresh encryptions $(c_1, \ldots, c_r)$ with $c_i \longleftarrow \mathsf{Enc}_{\mathsf{pk}}(m_i)$ for plaintexts $m_i \in \mathcal{P}$ and $i = 1, \ldots, r$, the following distributions (over the random coins in Enc and Eval) are* (computationally) *indistinguishable:*

$$\mathsf{Enc}_{\mathsf{pk}}(C(m_1, \ldots, m_r)) \approx_c \mathsf{Eval}_{\mathsf{pk}}(C, c_1, \ldots, c_r).$$

Finally, we can formulate the main result:

Theorem 5. *Let $\mathcal{E} = (\mathsf{KeyGen}, \mathsf{Enc}, \mathsf{Dec}, \mathsf{Eval})$ be a bootstrappable scheme for a universal[5] set of gates Γ. If the resulting scheme $\mathcal{E}^*$ is circuit-private, it holds that*

$$\mathcal{E}^* \text{ is } \mathsf{IND\text{-}CPA} \text{ secure} \iff \mathcal{E} \text{ is circular secure.}$$

Proof (Sketch). "$\Leftarrow$": This is shown in [19, Theorem 4.3.2].
"$\Rightarrow$": We assume that $\mathcal{E}$ is not circular secure, i.e., there exists a PPT algorithm $\mathcal{A}^{\mathrm{circular}}$ that breaks the security of $\mathcal{E}$ with non-negligible advantage $f(\lambda)$. We derive a contradiction by constructing a PPT algorithm $\mathcal{A}^{\mathrm{cpa}} = (\mathcal{A}_1^{\mathrm{cpa}}, \mathcal{A}_2^{\mathrm{cpa}})$ that successfully breaks the IND-CPA security of $\mathcal{E}^*$ with advantage $f(\lambda)$.

First, the adversary $\mathcal{A}_1^{\mathrm{cpa}}$ receives the public key $\mathsf{pk}^* = (\mathsf{pk}, \overline{\mathsf{sk}_1}, \ldots, \overline{\mathsf{sk}_\ell})$ where $\overline{\mathsf{sk}_i} \longleftarrow \mathsf{Enc}_{\mathsf{pk}}(\mathsf{sk}_i)$ and $\mathsf{sk}_1, \ldots, \mathsf{sk}_\ell$ is the representation of the secret key sk as elements of $\mathcal{P}$. Then, $\mathcal{A}_1^{\mathrm{cpa}}$ chooses messages $\mathbf{0} \neq m_0 \in \mathcal{P}$ and $m_1 := \mathbf{0}$ together with circuits C_i such that $C_i(m_0, \mathsf{sk}_i) = \mathsf{sk}_i$ and $C_i(m_1, \mathsf{sk}_i) = m_1$ for all $i = 1, \ldots, \ell$. For instance, if we consider all boolean circuits and assume that $\mathcal{P} = \{0, 1\}$, $\mathcal{A}_1^{\mathrm{cpa}}$ could simply choose $m_0 = 1, m_1 = 0$ and C_i as a single AND-gate for all $i = 1, \ldots, \ell$. Now, the IND-CPA challenger chooses a random bit $b \xleftarrow{U} \{0, 1\}$ and sends the challenge $c \longleftarrow \mathsf{Enc}_{\mathsf{pk}}(m_b)$ to $\mathcal{A}_2^{\mathrm{cpa}}$. Since $\mathcal{E}^*$ is fully homomorphic, $\mathcal{A}_2^{\mathrm{cpa}}$ can compute $\overline{\sigma_i} \longleftarrow \mathsf{Eval}_{\mathsf{pk}}(C_i, c, \overline{\mathsf{sk}_i})$ for all $i = 1, \ldots, \ell$. Due to the correctness condition on $\mathcal{E}^*$, this means for all $i = 1, \ldots, \ell$:

$$\sigma_i := \mathsf{Dec}_{\mathsf{sk}}(\overline{\sigma_i}) = C_i(m_b, \mathsf{sk}_i). \tag{1}$$

Next, $\mathcal{A}_2^{\mathrm{cpa}}$ sends $(\mathsf{pk}, \overline{\sigma_1}, \ldots, \overline{\sigma_\ell})$ to $\mathcal{A}^{\mathrm{circular}}$ that returns a bit $d \in \{0, 1\}$ which in turn is the output b' of $\mathcal{A}_2^{\mathrm{cpa}}$, i.e., $b' = d$.

We have the following relations: If $b = 0$, then $\overline{\sigma_i}$ is computationally indistinguishable (since $\mathcal{E}^*$ was assumed to be circuit-private) from a fresh encryption of sk_i, meaning in particular that $\sigma_i = \mathsf{sk}_i$ for all $i = 1, \ldots, \ell$ due to equation (1). Hence, $\mathcal{A}^{\mathrm{circular}}$ makes the right guess on b with advantage $f(\lambda)$, i.e.,

---

[5] This is a set of gates by which any circuit can be expressed, e.g., a NAND-gate when considering boolean circuits.

$\Pr[b' = b|b = 0] \geq \frac{1}{2} + f(\lambda)$. If $b = 1$, then $\overline{\sigma_i}$ is computationally indistinguishable from a fresh encryption of $\mathbf{0}$, unrelated to pk, for all $i = 1, \ldots, \ell$. Hence, $\mathcal{A}^{\text{circular}}$ again guesses b with advantage $f(\lambda)$, i.e., $\Pr[b' = b|b = 1] \geq \frac{1}{2} + f(\lambda)$. We have shown:

$$\Pr[\mathbf{Exp}^{\text{ind-cpa}}_{\mathcal{A}^{\text{cpa}}, \text{Gen}}(\lambda) = 1] = \sum_{\beta \in \{0,1\}} \Pr[b' = b|b = \beta] \cdot \Pr[b = \beta]$$

$$\geq \frac{1}{2} \cdot (1 + 2f(\lambda)) = \frac{1}{2} + f(\lambda).$$

$\square$

Some remarks on this result are in order:

Remark 2. 1. We would like to stress that Theorem 5 actually holds in a more general context as well. Looking at the proof, one notices that there is no need for $\mathcal{E}^*$ to be circuit-private for all circuits. The circuit privacy is only needed for the special circuits C_i used in the proof. In particular, in the case when only boolean circuits are considered and the plaintext space is $\mathcal{P} = \{0,1\}$, the circuits C_i are all the same, namely an AND-gate. It is easy to see that all existing FHE schemes that work on the plaintext space $\mathcal{P} = \{0,1\}$ are circuit-private for a single AND-gate (see also Section 4.3).

2. In Theorem 1, we showed a characterization of the IND-CPA security of shift-type homomorphic encryption schemes. All currently existing FHE schemes rely on the assumption that the IND-CPA security of the underlying scheme already implies its circular security – meaning that for these schemes the two notions of circular security and IND-CPA security are equivalent. So under this assumption, Theorem 5 together with Theorem 1 yield an IND-CPA characterization of *all existing* circuit-private FHE schemes that are based on Gentry's bootstrapping technique.

3. Theorem 5 together with the first item of this remark tell us that the circular security of the underlyling bootstrappable scheme is not only sufficient but also necessary in order to get an FHE scheme. It therefore underlines the importance of Brakerski et al.'s work [9] which actually has the bigger goal of achieving circular secure bootstrappable encryption, instead of only achieving circular security for somewhat homomorphic encryption schemes (cf. Section 1.1).

4.3 Gentry's Bootstrapping Technique: The Existing Schemes

In total, there currently exist 13 FHE schemes that are all based on Gentry's bootstrapping technique (at least concerning the resulting "pure" FHE schemes), namely [7–9, 15, 19–24, 27, 29, 30]. Their underlying schemes are all shift-type homomorphic. This is due to the fact that the concept of shift-type homomorphic encryption is very similar to that of "adding noise" (see Remark 1), which itself is a concept employed in all existing schemes. For the more recently developed schemes [7–9, 21, 23, 24] the shift-type structure of the encryption algorithm can be immediately seen. A good summary of Gentry's original scheme [20] is given in [30, Section 3.1]. Therein, Gentry's scheme and the variants [19] and [30] are presented in a way such that the shift-type structure is easily seen. Concerning the variants [22, 27, 29], a summary is given in [27, Section 3], again presented in a fashion such that the shift-type structure of the encryption is immediately noticeable.

We will recall (only very briefly due to lack of space) the remaining variant by van Dijk et al. [15] to show that it is shift-type homomorphic. To get rid of a very voluminous and confusing introduction of parameters, we will fix a particular setup of parameters in the key generation phase and note that all of the following can be done in a more general fashion (see [15]). Also, we will focus here on the encryption algorithm only and refer the reader to [15] for details on the remaining algorithms for decryption and evaluation. For the security parameter λ, we fix:

$$\rho := \lambda, \rho' := 2\lambda, \eta \in \rho' \cdot \Theta(\lambda \log^2 \lambda), \gamma \in \omega(\eta^2 \log \lambda) \text{ and } \tau := \gamma + \lambda.$$

The secret key sk of the scheme is $p \xleftarrow{U} (2\mathbb{Z}+1) \cap [2^{\eta-1}, 2^\eta)$ and we define the following efficiently sampleable distribution

$$\mathcal{D}_{\gamma,\rho}(p) := \left\{ x = pq + r \mid q \xleftarrow{U} \mathbb{Z} \cap [0, 2^\gamma/p), r \xleftarrow{U} \mathbb{Z} \cap (-2^\rho, 2^\rho) \right\}.$$

With this notation, we let pk $= (x_0, \dots, x_\tau)$ be the public key with $x_i \xleftarrow{U} \mathcal{D}_{\gamma,\rho}(p)$ for all $i = 0, \dots, \tau$ whereas the x_i's are relabeled such that x_0 is the largest (if x_0 is even or $x_0 \bmod p$ is odd, then restart). The plaintext space is $\{0, 1\}$.

The encryption algorithm takes the public key pk and a plaintext $m \in \{0, 1\}$ as input and outputs a ciphertext $c := [(m + 2r + 2\sum_{i \in S} x_i) \bmod x_0]$ whereas S is a random subset of $\{1, \dots, \tau\}$ and $r \xleftarrow{U} \mathbb{Z} \cap (-2^{\rho'}, 2^{\rho'})$. In the notation of the shift-type homomorphic definition (see Definition 2), we have that $\widehat{\mathcal{C}}$ is the ring $\mathbb{Z}_{x_0}$ and

$$\mathcal{N} = \left\{ 2(r + \sum_{i \in S} x_i) \bmod x_0 \mid r \in \mathbb{Z} \cap (-2^{\rho'}, 2^{\rho'}), S \subseteq \{1, \dots, \tau\} \right\}.$$

The injective homomorphism φ is given by $m \mapsto m \bmod x_0$, which is even a ring homomorphism. Encryption is then given by $\varphi(m) + n$ where $n \in \mathcal{N}$. Concerning the homomorphic property in Definition 2, we need to make more effort:

It is shown in [15, Lemma 3.3] that the scheme is homomorphic for Boolean circuits with the property that for any $\alpha \geq 1$ and any set of integer inputs all less than $2^{\alpha(\rho'+2)}$ in absolute value, it must hold that the output of the *generalized circuit* (same circuit where the ADD- and MULT-gates are applied to integers instead of bits) has absolute value at most $2^{\alpha(\eta-4)}$. Furthermore, it is shown in [15, Lemma 3.5] that if $f(x_1, \dots, x_t)$ is the multivariate polynomial of degree d computed by the generalized circuit of a given boolean circuit C with

t inputs, then the scheme is homomorphic for C if $|\bar{f}| \cdot (2^{\rho'+2})^d \leq 2^{\eta-4}$, where $|\bar{f}|$ is the l_1 norm of the coefficient vector of f. In respect of the homomorphic property of Definition 2, it suffices to show that the scheme is homomorphic for the boolean circuit C_{ADD} that consists of a single ADD-gate only. Clearly, the multivariate polynomial that is computed by the generalized circuit of C_{ADD} is $f(x_1, x_2) = x_1 + x_2$ and has degree $d = 1$ with $|\bar{f}| = 2$. Therefore, the scheme is homomorphic for this circuit if we have

$$2^{\rho'+3} \leq 2^{\eta-4}, \text{ which in turn is fulfilled if } \eta \geq \rho' + 7.$$

This final condition holds as $\eta \in \rho' \cdot \Theta(\lambda \log^2 \lambda)$. In total we have shown that the above scheme indeed is shift-type homomorphic.

5 Conclusion

With the identification of shift-type encryption as the most basic structure that all existing homomorphic encryption schemes have in common, we were able to deduce IND-CPA characterizations of all existing bootstrapping-based leveled FHE schemes. This result supports an easier design of such schemes, since new candidates can immediately be checked for IND-CPA security by looking at the corresponding subset membership problem that comes out of our characterization. In regard to [3], it is interesting to see that all existing group homomorphic encryption schemes and the more general homomorphic schemes (in particular, the existing FHE schemes) share the same shift-type structure. Further research in this direction could implicate that a given homomorphic scheme has to have this shift-type structure in order to be IND-CPA secure. We leave this as an open question.

Our result that the IND-CPA security of bootstrapping-based FHE schemes that offer a "minimal" type of circuit privacy is *equivalent* to the circular security of the underlying bootstrappable scheme shows: If we want to construct such IND-CPA secure FHE schemes, we are bound to the design of circular secure bootstrappable schemes. We hope that this fact stimulates the research community to devote even more effort to proving existing schemes circular secure and/or finding a radically new approach to FHE that is not based on Gentry's bootstrapping technique.

References

1. Melchor, C.A., Gaborit, P., Herranz, J.: Additively Homomorphic Encryption with d-Operand Multiplications. In: Rabin, T. (ed.) CRYPTO 2010. LNCS, vol. 6223, pp. 138–154. Springer, Heidelberg (2010)
2. Applebaum, B.: Key-Dependent Message Security: Generic Amplification and Completeness. In: Paterson, K.G. (ed.) EUROCRYPT 2011. LNCS, vol. 6632, pp. 527–546. Springer, Heidelberg (2011)

3. Armknecht, F., Katzenbeisser, S., Peter, A.: Group homomorphic encryption: Characterizations, impossibility results, and applications. Designs, Codes and Cryptography, 1–24, 10.1007/s10623-011-9601-2, http://dx.doi.org/10.1007/s10623-011-9601-2

4. Barak, B., Haitner, I., Hofheinz, D., Ishai, Y.: Bounded Key-Dependent Message Security. In: Gilbert, H. (ed.) EUROCRYPT 2010. LNCS, vol. 6110, pp. 423–444. Springer, Heidelberg (2010)

5. Benaloh, J.: Verifiable secret-ballot elections. Ph.D. thesis, Yale University (1987)

6. Boneh, D., Halevi, S., Hamburg, M., Ostrovsky, R.: Circular-Secure Encryption from Decision Diffie-Hellman. In: Wagner, D. (ed.) CRYPTO 2008. LNCS, vol. 5157, pp. 108–125. Springer, Heidelberg (2008)

7. Brakerski, Z., Gentry, C., Vaikuntanathan, V.: (leveled) fully homomorphic encryption without bootstrapping. In: ITCS, pp. 309–325. ACM (2012)

8. Brakerski, Z., Vaikuntanathan, V.: Efficient fully homomorphic encryption from (standard) LWE. In: FOCS, pp. 97–106. IEEE (2011)

9. Brakerski, Z., Vaikuntanathan, V.: Fully Homomorphic Encryption from Ring-LWE and Security for Key Dependent Messages. In: Rogaway, P. (ed.) CRYPTO 2011. LNCS, vol. 6841, pp. 505–524. Springer, Heidelberg (2011)

10. Cohen, J.D., Fischer, M.J.: A robust and verifiable cryptographically secure election scheme (extended abstract). In: FOCS, pp. 372–382. IEEE (1985)

11. Cramer, R., Damgård, I., Nielsen, J.B.: Multiparty Computation from Threshold Homomorphic Encryption. In: Pfitzmann, B. (ed.) EUROCRYPT 2001. LNCS, vol. 2045, pp. 280–299. Springer, Heidelberg (2001)

12. Cramer, R., Franklin, M.K., Schoenmakers, B., Yung, M.: Multi-authority Secret-Ballot Elections with Linear Work. In: Maurer, U.M. (ed.) EUROCRYPT 1996. LNCS, vol. 1070, pp. 72–83. Springer, Heidelberg (1996)

13. Cramer, R., Gennaro, R., Schoenmakers, B.: A Secure and Optimally Efficient Multi-authority Election Scheme. In: Fumy, W. (ed.) EUROCRYPT 1997. LNCS, vol. 1233, pp. 103–118. Springer, Heidelberg (1997)

14. Cramer, R., Shoup, V.: Universal Hash Proofs and a Paradigm for Adaptive Chosen Ciphertext Secure Public-Key Encryption. In: Knudsen, L.R. (ed.) EUROCRYPT 2002. LNCS, vol. 2332, pp. 45–64. Springer, Heidelberg (2002)

15. van Dijk, M., Gentry, C., Halevi, S., Vaikuntanathan, V.: Fully Homomorphic Encryption over the Integers. In: Gilbert, H. (ed.) EUROCRYPT 2010. LNCS, vol. 6110, pp. 24–43. Springer, Heidelberg (2010)

16. El Gamal, T.: A Public Key Cryptosystem and a Signature Scheme Based on Discrete Logarithms. In: Blakely, G.R., Chaum, D. (eds.) CRYPTO 1984. LNCS, vol. 196, pp. 10–18. Springer, Heidelberg (1985)

17. Fontaine, C., Galand, F.: A survey of homomorphic encryption for nonspecialists. EURASIP J. Inf. Secur., 15:1–15:15 (January 2007), http://dx.doi.org/10.1155/2007/13801

18. Gennaro, R., Gentry, C., Parno, B.: Non-interactive Verifiable Computing: Outsourcing Computation to Untrusted Workers. In: Rabin, T. (ed.) CRYPTO 2010. LNCS, vol. 6223, pp. 465–482. Springer, Heidelberg (2010)

19. Gentry, C.: A fully homomorphic encryption scheme. Ph.D. thesis, Stanford University (2009)

20. Gentry, C.: Fully homomorphic encryption using ideal lattices. In: STOC, pp. 169–178. ACM (2009)

21. Gentry, C., Halevi, S.: Fully homomorphic encryption without squashing using depth-3 arithmetic circuits. In: FOCS, pp. 107–109. IEEE (2011)

22. Gentry, C., Halevi, S.: Implementing Gentry's Fully-Homomorphic Encryption Scheme. In: Paterson, K.G. (ed.) EUROCRYPT 2011. LNCS, vol. 6632, pp. 129–148. Springer, Heidelberg (2011)
23. Gentry, C., Halevi, S., Smart, N.P.: Fully Homomorphic Encryption with Polylog Overhead. In: Pointcheval, D., Johansson, T. (eds.) EUROCRYPT 2012. LNCS, vol. 7237, pp. 465–482. Springer, Heidelberg (2012)
24. Gentry, C., Halevi, S., Smart, N.P.: Better bootstrapping in fully homomorphic encryption. Cryptology ePrint Archive, Report 2011/680 (2011)
25. Ishai, Y., Paskin, A.: Evaluating Branching Programs on Encrypted Data. In: Vadhan, S.P. (ed.) TCC 2007. LNCS, vol. 4392, pp. 575–594. Springer, Heidelberg (2007)
26. Kushilevitz, E., Ostrovsky, R.: Replication is not needed: Single database, computationally-private information retrieval. In: FOCS, pp. 364–373 (1997)
27. Loftus, J., May, A., Smart, N.P., Vercauteren, F.: On CCA-Secure Somewhat Homomorphic Encryption. In: Miri, A., Vaudenay, S. (eds.) SAC 2011. LNCS, vol. 7118, pp. 55–72. Springer, Heidelberg (2012)
28. Naor, M., Pinkas, B.: Oblivious polynomial evaluation. SIAM J. Comput. 35(5), 1254–1281 (2006)
29. Smart, N.P., Vercauteren, F.: Fully Homomorphic Encryption with Relatively Small Key and Ciphertext Sizes. In: Nguyen, P.Q., Pointcheval, D. (eds.) PKC 2010. LNCS, vol. 6056, pp. 420–443. Springer, Heidelberg (2010)
30. Stehlé, D., Steinfeld, R.: Faster Fully Homomorphic Encryption. In: Abe, M. (ed.) ASIACRYPT 2010. LNCS, vol. 6477, pp. 377–394. Springer, Heidelberg (2010)

The Collision Security of MDC-4

Ewan Fleischmann, Christian Forler, and Stefan Lucks

Bauhaus-University Weimar, Germany
{ewan.fleischmann,christian.forler,stefan.lucks}@uni-weimar.de

Abstract. There are four somewhat classical double length block cipher based compression functions known: MDC-2, MDC-4, ABREAST-DM, and TANDEM-DM. They all have been developed over 20 years ago. In recent years, cryptographic research has put a focus on block cipher based hashing and found collision security results for three of them (MDC-2, ABREAST-DM, TANDEM-DM). In this paper, we add MDC-4, which is part of the IBM CLiC cryptographic module[1], to that list by showing that – 'instantiated' using an ideal block cipher with 128 bit key/plaintext/ciphertext size – no adversary asking less than $2^{74.76}$ queries can find a collision with probability greater than $1/2$. This is the first result on the collision security of the hash function MDC-4.

The compression function MDC-4 is created by interconnecting two MDC-2 compression functions but only hashing one message block with them instead of two. The developers aim for MDC-4 was to offer a higher security margin, when compared to MDC-2, but still being fast enough for practical purposes.

The MDC-2 collision security proof of Steinberger (EUROCRYPT 2007) cannot be directly applied to MDC-4 due to the structural differences. Although sharing many commonalities, our proof for MDC-4 is much shorter and we claim that our presentation is also easier to grasp.

Keywords: MDC-4, cryptographic hash function, block-cipher based, proof of security, double length, ideal cipher model.

1 Introduction

A cryptographic hash function is a function which maps an input of arbitrary length to an output of fixed length. It should satisfy at least collision-, preimage- and second-preimage resistance and is one of the most important primitives in cryptography [24]. In recent years, most of the functions in the widely used MD4-family (*e.g.*, MD4 [30], MD5 [31], RIPEMD [12], SHA-1 [28], SHA-2 [29]) have been successfully attacked in several ways [5, 11, 34, 35] which has stimulated researchers to look for alternatives. Block cipher based constructions seem promising since they are very well known – they even predate the MD4-approach [23]. One can easily create a hash function using, *e.g.*, the Davies-Meyer [36] mode of operation and the Merkle-Damgård transform [4, 25]. Also, many of the

---

[1] FIPS 140-2 Security Policy for IBM CrytoLite in C, October 2003.

A. Mitrokotsa and S. Vaudenay (Eds.): AFRICACRYPT 2012, LNCS 7374, pp. 252–269, 2012.

proposed SHA-3 designs like Skein [7], SHAvite-3 [1], and SIMD [22] use block cipher based instantiations. Another reason for the resurgence of interest in block cipher based hash functions is due to the rise of resource restricted devices such as RFID tags or smart cards. A hardware designer only needs to implement a block cipher in order to obtain an encryption function as well as a hash function. However, due to the short output length of most practical block ciphers, one is mainly interested in sound design principles for *double length* (DL) hash functions. Such double length hash functions use a block cipher with n-bit output as the building block by which it maps possibly long strings to $2n$-bit hash values. DL compression functions can be parted by the type of block cipher they need to operate: The first group, *(group-1)*, uses an internal block cipher with an n-bit plaintext/ciphertext/key, the second group, *(group-2)*, uses a block cipher with an n-bit plaintext/ciphertext and a k-bit key, $k > n$. DL compression functions in the first group are few. Currently, there are only three known candidates in literature: MDC-2, MDC-4 and a most recent variant of MDC-2: MJH [19]. Group-2 examples are ABREAST-DM TANDEM-DM, CYCLIC-DM [17, 10], etc. The security of group-2 functions is relatively well understood.

MDC-4 is an acronym for Modification Detection Code with ratio $1/4$, and was developed at IBM in the late eighties by Meyer and Schilling [26]. The ratio indicates the number of block cipher calls that are required to process a single message block. MDC-4 was originally specified for the 64-bit block cipher DES [27].

Our Contribution. In this paper, we give the first collision security bound for the hash function MDC-4, a block cipher based hash function that has been publicly known for more than 20 years. In our proof, we use many of the techniques that have been applied in the MDC-2 collision security proof [33]. Our proof is in the ideal cipher model, too. However, we consider MDC-4 using an ideal n-bit block cipher accepting n-bit keys. Furthermore, as in [33], we also ignore an additional *bit-fixing* step that was used back than as an additional security measure to avoid some DES specific key issues.

In this paper we show, assuming a hash output length of 256 bits, that any adversary asking less than $2^{74.76}$ queries to the block cipher cannot find a collision for the *hash function* MDC-4 with probability greater than $1/2$. Note that the optimal security bound for collisions for 256 bit hash functions is about 2^{128}. For MDC-2 (ratio $1/2$) and MJH (ratio $1/2$), the trivial collision resistance bound is 2^{64}, since they both internally use a Davies-Meyer compression function. Although MDC-4 also uses Davies-Meyer type functions inside, even such a trivial bound is not so easy to see.

Related Work. For group-2 functions, there has been a lot of research in recent years, *e.g.* [8, 10, 16, 17, 18, 20, 21]. As a result, there are group-2 compression functions known that are 'provably optimal'. This is in stark contrast to the known results for group-1 functions which are summarized in Table 1.

Outline. The paper is organized as follows: Section 2 includes formal notations and definitions. In Section 3 we prove that an adversary asking less than $2^{74.76}$

Table 1. List of known group-1 hash functions, values evaluated for an internal block cipher with 128 bit plaintext/ciphertext/key [Notation: CF = compression function]

Function	Security (Collision)	Attack (Collision)	Attack (Preimage)
MDC-2	$2^{74.91}$ [33]	2^{121} [14]	2^{2n} (time · space) [14, 17]
MDC-4	$2^{74.76}$ (this paper)	2^{96} [15] (only CF)	2^{224} [15]
MJH [19]	$2^{78.33}$	(no results known)	(no results known)

oracle queries has the threshold probability $1/2$ finding a collision for the MDC-4 hash function.

2   Preliminaries

2.1   General Notations

An n-bit block cipher is a keyed family of permutations consisting of two paired algorithms $E : \{0,1\}^n \times \{0,1\}^n \to \{0,1\}^n$ and $E^{-1} : \{0,1\}^n \times \{0,1\}^n \to \{0,1\}^n$ both accepting a key of size n bits and an input block of size n bits for some $n > 0$. Let $\texttt{Block}(n)$ be the set of all n-bit block ciphers. For any $E \in \texttt{Block}(n)$ and any fixed key $K \in \{0,1\}^n$, decryption $E_K^{-1} := E^{-1}(K, \cdot)$ is the inverse function of encryption $E_K := E(K, \cdot)$, so that $E_K^{-1}(E_K(X)) = X$ holds for any input $X \in \{0,1\}^n$. In the ideal cipher model E is modeled as a family of random permutations $\{E_K\}$ whereas the random permutations are chosen independently for each key K [2, 6, 13], $i.e.$, formally E is selected randomly from $\texttt{Block}(n)$. If $Y = E_K(X)$ we call the value $Z = X \oplus Y$ the XOR-output of a query (K, X, Y).

We use the convention to write oracles, that are provided to an algorithm, as superscripts. For example $\mathcal{A}^E$ is an algorithm $\mathcal{A}$ with oracle access to E to which $\mathcal{A}$ can request forward and backward queries. For ease of presentation, we identify the sets $\{0,1\}^{a+b}$ and $\{0,1\}^a \times \{0,1\}^b$. Similarly, for $A \in \{0,1\}^a$ and $B \in \{0,1\}^b$, the concatenation of these bit strings is denoted by $A||B \in \{0,1\}^{a+b} = \{0,1\}^a \times \{0,1\}^b$.

A compression function is a mapping $H : \{0,1\}^m \times \{0,1\}^r \to \{0,1\}^r$ for some $m, r > 0$. A block cipher-based compression function is a mapping $H^E : \{0,1\}^m \times \{0,1\}^r \to \{0,1\}^r$ that, given an r-bit state R and an m-bit message M, computes $H^E(M, R)$ using oracle access to some $E \in \texttt{Block}(n)$.

2.2   The MDC-4 Compression Function

The MDC-4 compression function H^E (cf. Figure 1) takes an n-bit message M, a $2n$-bit state (S, T) and outputs a new $2n$-bit state (U, V) as follows:

1. Compute $O = (O^L||O^R) = E_S(M) \oplus M$,
2. compute $P = (P^L||P^R) = E_T(M) \oplus M$,

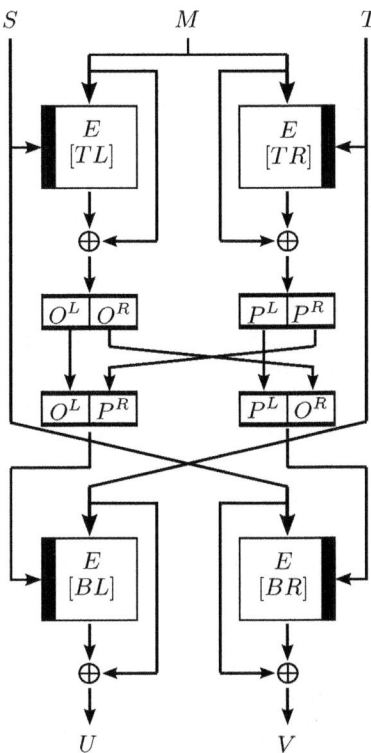

Fig. 1. The double-length compression function H^E where E is an n-bit block cipher. The black bar inside the cipher indicates the key input.

3. compute $U = E_{O^L||P^R}(T) \oplus T$,
4. compute $V = E_{P^L||O^R}(S) \oplus S$,
5. output (U, V).

The superscript L denotes the left $n/2$ bits of an expression, and the superscript R denotes the right $n/2$ bits of an expression.

The original MDC-4 specification [26] swaps the right halves of U and V. But, since we are in the ideal cipher model, this operation does not change the distribution of the output and neither our collision security analysis. So, for ease of presentation, we omitted this additional step.

Our analysis is for the MDC-4 hash function $\mathcal{H}^E$ which is obtained by a simple iteration of the MDC-4 compression function H^E in the obvious manner: Given some $n \cdot \ell$-bit message $(M_1, \ldots, M_\ell)$, $M_j \in \{0, 1\}^n$ for $j = 1, \ldots, \ell$ and an initial value $(S_0, T_0) \in \{0, 1\}^{2n}$ it works by computing $(S_i, H_i) = H^E(M_i, S_{i-1}, T_{i-1})$ for $i = 1, \ldots, \ell$. The hash value is (S_ℓ, T_ℓ).

2.3   Security of the MDC-4 Compression Function and the MDC-4 Hash Function

Generally, insecurity is quantified by the success probability of an optimal resource-bounded adversary. The resource is the number of backward and forward queries to the block cipher E. For a set C, let $Y \xleftarrow{\$} C$ represent random sampling from C under the uniform distribution. For a probabilistic algorithm $\mathcal{D}$, let $Y \xleftarrow{\$} \mathcal{D}$ mean that Y is an output of $\mathcal{D}$ and its distribution is based on the random choices of $\mathcal{D}$.

In our case, an adversary is a computationally unbounded collision-finding algorithm $\mathcal{A}^E$ with access to $E \in \texttt{Block}(n)$. We assume that $\mathcal{A}^E$ is deterministic. The adversary may make a *forward* query $(K, X)_f$ to discover the corresponding value $Y = E_K(X)$, or the adversary may make a *backward* query $(K, Y)_b$, so as to learn the corresponding value $X = E_K^{-1}(Y)$ such that $E_K(X) = Y$. Either way, the result of the query is stored in a triple $(K_i, X_i, Y_i) := (K, X, Y)$ and the *query history* $\mathcal{Q}$ is the tuple $(Q_1, \ldots, Q_q)$ where $Q_i = (K_i, X_i, Y_i)$ and q is the total number of queries made by the adversary.

Without loss of generality, we assume that $\mathcal{A}^E$ asks at most only once on a triplet of a key K_i, a plaintext X_i and a ciphertext Y_i obtained by a query and the corresponding reply.

Collision Resistance of the MDC-4 *compression function.* There is a very simple attack on the compression function which only requires about $2^{n/2}$ invocations of the E oracle: Let the adversary find values $K, K', M, M' \in \{0,1\}^n$ such that $E_K(M) = E_{K'}(M')$. This requires about $2^{n/2}$ E-oracle queries. Then, by

$$H^E(M, K, K) = H^E(M', K', K'),$$

a collision for the full MDC-4 compression function has been found. So our analysis will be for the MDC-4 compression function *in the iteration*. This attack is only possible if the chaining values are equal.

3   Proof of Collision Resistance

3.1   Proof Model

Our analysis is for the MDC-4 hash function $\mathcal{H}^E$ assuming that the initial chaining values are different, *i.e.*, $S_0 \neq T_0$. The goal of the adversary is to output two messages $\mathcal{M}_1 \in \{0,1\}^{n \cdot \ell}$ and $\mathcal{M}_2 \in \{0,1\}^{n \cdot \ell'}$ such that $\mathcal{H}(\mathcal{M}_1) = \mathcal{H}(\mathcal{M}_2)$ for some non-zero integers ℓ, ℓ'.

In our analysis, we dispense the adversary from returning these two messages. Instead we upper bound his success probability by giving the attack to him if

(i) he has found an 'internal' collision, *i.e.*, (M, S, T) such that $(U, V) = H^E(M, S, T)$ with $U = V$ for some $U, V \in \{0,1\}^n$ or

(ii) case (i) is not true but he has either found a collision in the compression function H^E, i.e., (M, S, T) and (M', S', T'), such that $H^E(M, S, T) = H^E(M', S', T')$ with $S \neq T$, $S' \neq T'$, or

(iii) cases (i), (ii) are not true but he has found values (M, S, T) such that $(S_0, T_0) = H^E(M, S, T)$. *Note that this requirement essentially models the preimage resistance of the MDC-4 compression function.*

The proof is simple and straightforward. Assume a collision for $\mathcal{H}^E$ has been found using two not necessarily equal-length messages $\mathcal{M}$ and $\mathcal{M}'$, i.e., $\mathcal{H}^E(\mathcal{M}) = \mathcal{H}^E(\mathcal{M}')$. Also assume that the collision is the earliest possible. Then the adversary has either found (i) or (ii). For case (iii), we also give the attack to the adversary, particularly for reasons already discussed in Section 2.3.

For our analysis, we impose the reasonable condition that the adversary must have made all queries necessary to compute the results. We determine whether the adversary has been successful or not by examining the query history $\mathcal{Q}$. Formally, we say that $\text{COLL}(\mathcal{Q})$ holds if there is such a collision and $\mathcal{Q}$ contains all the queries necessary to compute it.

We now define what we formally mean by a collision of the MDC-4 compression function.

Definition 1. (Collision resistance of the MDC-4 compression function) *Let H^E be a MDC-4 compression function. Fix an adversary $\mathcal{A}$. Then the advantage of $\mathcal{A}$ in finding collisions for H^E is the real number*

$$\mathbf{Adv}_{H^E}^{\text{COLL}}(\mathcal{A}) = \Pr[E \xleftarrow{\$} Block(n); ((M, S, T), (M', S', T')) \xleftarrow{\$} \mathcal{A}^{E, E^{-1}} :$$
$$((M, S, T) \neq (M', S', T')) \wedge H^E(M, S, T) = H^E(M', S', T')].$$

For $q \geq 1$ we write

$$\mathbf{Adv}_{H^E}^{\text{COLL}}(q) = \max_{\mathcal{A}}\{\mathbf{Adv}_{H^E}^{\text{COLL}}(\mathcal{A})\},$$

where the maximum is taken over all adversaries that ask at most q oracle queries, i.e., forward and backward queries to E.

Since our analysis in the next sections is for $\mathcal{H}^E$, we informally say that the probability of a collision of $\mathcal{H}^E$ is upper bounded by using a union bound for the cases (i), (ii) and (iii). This is part of the formalization in Theorem 1.

3.2 Our Results

We now give our main result. Although having a substantial complexity on the first sight in its general form, we can easily evaluate it to numerical terms (cf. Corollary 1).

Theorem 1. *Fix some initial values $S_0, T_0 \in \{0, 1\}^n$ with $S_0 \neq T_0$ and let $\mathcal{H}^E$ be the MDC-4 hash function as given in Section 2.2. Let α, β, γ be constants*

Table 2. Upper bounds on $\mathbf{Adv}^{\mathrm{COLL}}_{\mathcal{H}^E}(q)$ as given by Theorem 1

q	$\mathbf{Adv}^{\mathrm{COLL}}_{\mathcal{H}^E}(q) \leq$	α	β	γ
2^{64}	$7.18 \cdot 10^{-7}$	42	4.0	$2 \cdot 10^6$
$2^{68.26}$	10^{-4}	126	4.0	$6 \cdot 10^6$
$2^{72.19}$	$1/100$	900	4.0	$1.3 \cdot 10^7$
$2^{73.84}$	$1/10$	2600	4.0	$1.4 \cdot 10^7$
$2^{74.40}$	$1/4$	3780	4.0	$1.5 \cdot 10^7$
$2^{74.76}$	$1/2$	4900	4.0	$1.5 \cdot 10^7$

such that $eq2^{n/2}/(2^n - q) \leq \alpha$, $eq/(2^n - q) \leq \beta$ *and let* $\Pr[\mathrm{LUCKY}(\mathcal{Q})]$ *as in Proposition 8. Then*

$$\mathbf{Adv}^{\mathrm{COLL}}_{\mathcal{H}^E}(q) \leq q \left(\frac{\alpha^2 + \gamma}{2^n - q} + \frac{\alpha\beta}{(2^n - q)(2^{n/2} - \alpha)} + \frac{\alpha}{2^n - 2^{n/2}\alpha} + \frac{\beta^2 + 4}{2^n - q} + \frac{\beta}{2^n - q} \right)$$
$$+ 2q \left(\frac{\alpha^4 + \alpha^2 + 3\alpha\gamma + 2\gamma}{N - q} + 6\frac{\alpha^2 + 1}{N^{1/2} - \alpha} \right)$$
$$+ q \left(\frac{\gamma\alpha^2 + \gamma^2}{2^n - q} + \frac{2\alpha}{(2^{n/2} - \alpha)^2} \right) + \Pr[\mathrm{LUCKY}(\mathcal{Q})]. \tag{1}$$

Proof. The proof follows from the following discussion together with Proposition 1 by adding up the individual results from Propositions 2 - 8.   □

As mentioned before, our bound is rather non-transparent, so we discuss it for $n = 128$. We evaluate the equation above such that the adversary's advantage is upper bounded by $1/2$ – thereby maximizing the value of q by numerically optimizing the values of α, β and γ. Our result is the following corollary.

Corollary 1. *No adversary asking less than* $2^{74.76}$ *queries can find a collision for the* MDC-4 *hash function with probability greater than* $1/2$.

An overview of the behavior of our upper bound is given in Table 2. Note that for other values of (α, β, γ) the bound stays *correct* but worsens numerically (as long as the conditions given in Theorem 1 hold).

3.3   Proof Preliminaries

Overview. Our discussion starts with case (ii). We analyze whether the list of oracle queries to E made by the adversary can be used for a collision of the MDC-4 compression function H^E. For a collision, there are eight – not necessarily distinct – block cipher queries necessary (cf. Figure 2).

To upper bound the probability of the adversary obtaining queries that can be used for a collision, we upper bound the probability of the adversary making a

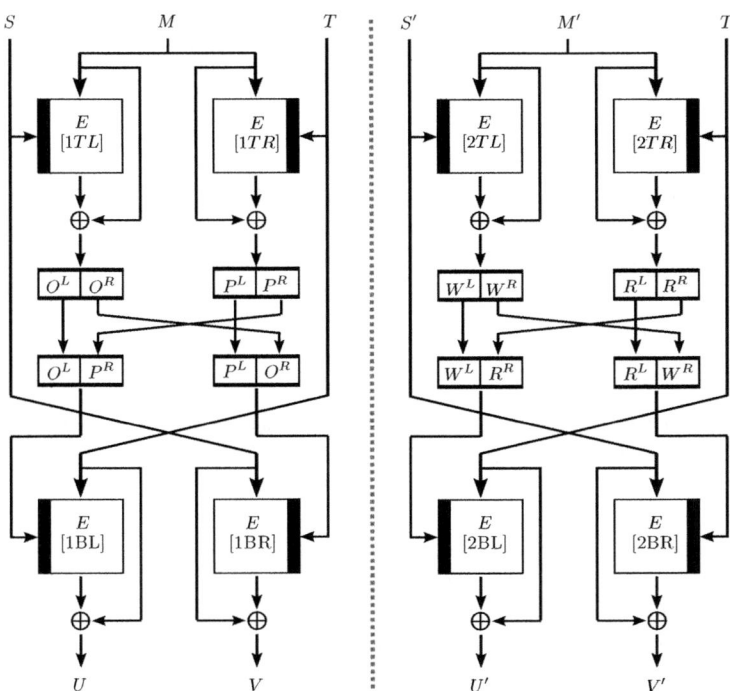

Fig. 2. The double-length MDC-4 compression function H^E, where E is a (n, n)-block cipher. If $(S, M, T) \neq (S', M', T')$ but $(U, V) = (U', V')$ then the adversary has found a collision for H^E. The black beam inside the cipher indicates the key input. For later reference, the different positions a query can be used in are denoted by $1TL, 1TR, \ldots, 2BR$.

final query that can be used as the last query to complete such a collision. Let $\mathcal{Q}_i$ denote the set of the first i queries $(K_1, X_1, Y_1), \ldots, (K_i, X_i, Y_i)$ (either forward or backward) made by the adversary. Furthermore we denote by the term *last query* the latest query made by the adversary. This query has always index i. Therefore, for each i with $1 \leq i \leq q$, we upper bound the success probability of an adversary to use the i-th query to complete the collision.

As the probability depends on the first $i - 1$ queries, we have to put some restrictions on these and also upper bound the probability that these restrictions are not met by an adversary. One example of such a restriction is to assume that, *e.g.*, the adversary has to find too many *collisions* for the underlying component function $E_K(X) \oplus X$.

Thus, our upper bound breaks down into two parts: an upper bound for the probability of an adversary not meeting our restrictions and the probability of an adversary ever making a successful i-th query, conditioned on the fact that the adversary does meet our restrictions and has not been successful by its $(i-1)$-th query. We use some notations that are given in Figure 2, *e.g.*, the statement

1BL $\neq$ 2BL means that the query used in the bottom left of the 'left' side is not the same as the query used in the bottom left of the 'right' side.

3.4   Details

We say $\text{COLL}(\mathcal{Q})$ if the adversary *wins*. Note that winning does not necessarily imply, that the adversary has found a collision. It might be that the adversary got lucky and does not meet our restrictions any more. But in the case of a collision $\text{COLL}(\mathcal{Q})$ always holds.

Proposition 1

$$\text{COLL}(\mathcal{Q}) \implies$$
$$\text{LUCKY}(\mathcal{Q}) \vee \text{INTERNALCOLL}(\mathcal{Q}) \vee \text{COLLTOPROWS}(\mathcal{Q}) \vee$$
$$\text{COLLLEFTCOLUMNS}(\mathcal{Q}) \vee \text{COLLRIGHTCOLUMNS}(\mathcal{Q}) \vee$$
$$\text{COLLBOTHCOLUMNS}(\mathcal{Q}) \vee \text{PREIMAGE}(\mathcal{Q}).$$

We now define the involved predicates of Proposition 1 and then give a proof. The predicates on the 'right' side are made mutually exclusive meaning that if the left side is true it follows that exactly one of the predicates on the right side is true. By upper bounding separately the probabilities of these predicates on the right side it is easy to see that the union bound can be used to upper bound the probability of $\text{COLL}(\mathcal{Q})$ as follows:

$$\Pr[\text{COLL}(\mathcal{Q})] \leq \Pr[\text{LUCKY}(\mathcal{Q})] + \Pr[\text{INTERNALCOLL}(\mathcal{Q})] + \Pr[\text{COLLTOPROWS}(\mathcal{Q})]$$
$$+ \Pr[\text{COLLLEFTCOLUMNS}(\mathcal{Q})] + \Pr[\text{COLLRIGHTCOLUMNS}(\mathcal{Q})]$$
$$+ \Pr[\text{COLLBOTHCOLUMNS}(\mathcal{Q})] + \Pr[\text{PREIMAGE}(\mathcal{Q})].$$

To state the predicate $\text{LUCKY}(\mathcal{Q})$, we give some helper definitions that are also used as restrictions for the other predicates. Let $\texttt{NumEqual}(\mathcal{Q})$ be a function defined on the query set $\mathcal{Q}$, $|\mathcal{Q}| = q$ as follows:

$$\texttt{NumEqual}(\mathcal{Q}) = \max_{Z \in \{0,1\}^n} |\{i : E_{K_i}(X_i) \oplus X_i = Z\}|.$$

It is the maximum size of a set of queries in $\mathcal{Q}$ whose XOR-outputs are all the same. Similarly, we define $\texttt{NumEqualHalf}(\mathcal{Q})$ as the maximum size of a set of queries whose XOR-outputs either share the same left half or the same right half. Let

$$\texttt{NEH-L}(\mathcal{Q}) = \max_{Z \in \{0,1\}^{n/2}} |\{i : (E_{K_i}(X_i) \oplus X_i)^L = Z\}|,$$
$$\texttt{NEH-R}(\mathcal{Q}) = \max_{Z \in \{0,1\}^{n/2}} |\{i : (E_{K_i}(X_i) \oplus X_i)^R = Z\}|,$$

then $\texttt{NumEqualHalf}(\mathcal{Q}) = \max(\texttt{NEH-L}(\mathcal{Q}), \texttt{NEH-R}(\mathcal{Q}))$. Let $\texttt{NumColl}(\mathcal{Q})$ be also defined on a query set $\mathcal{Q}$, $|\mathcal{Q}| = q$, as

$$\texttt{NumColl}(\mathcal{Q}) = |\{(i,j) \in \{1,\ldots,q\}^2 : i \neq j, E_{K_i}(X_i) \oplus X_i = E_{K_j}(X_j) \oplus X_j\}|.$$

It outputs the number of ordered pairs of distinct queries in $\mathcal{Q}$ which have the same XOR-outputs.

We now define the event $\text{LUCKY}(\mathcal{Q})$ as

$$\text{LUCKY}(\mathcal{Q}) = (\texttt{NumEqualHalf}(\mathcal{Q}) > \alpha) \vee (\texttt{NumEqual}(\mathcal{Q}) > \beta) \vee (\texttt{NumColl}(\mathcal{Q}) > \gamma),$$

where α, β and γ are the constants from Theorem 1. These constants are chosen depending on n and q by a simple numerical optimization process such that the upper bound of the advantage of an adversary is minimized for given values of n, q.

We now give the definitions of the other predicates.

FitInternalColl($\mathcal{Q}$). The adversary has found four – not necessarily distinct – queries such that $H^E(M, S, T)$ can be computed and $H^E(M, S, T) = (U, U)$ holds for some arbitrary U with $S \neq T$.

FitCollLeftColumns($\mathcal{Q}$). The adversary has found eight – not necessarily distinct – queries such that $(U, V) = H^E(M, S, T)$ and $(U', V') = H^E(M', S', T')$ can be computed with $U = U'$, 1BL $\neq$ 2BL and 1BR $=$ 2BR.

FitCollRightColumns($\mathcal{Q}$). The adversary has found eight – not necessarily distinct – queries such that $(U, V) = H^E(M, S, T)$ and $(U', V') = H^E (M', S', T')$ can be computed with $V = V'$, 1BR $\neq$ 2BR and 1BL $=$ 2BL.

FitCollTopRows($\mathcal{Q}$). The adversary has found four – not necessarily distinct – queries such that

$$(E_S(M) \oplus M, E_T(M) \oplus M) = (E_{S'}(M') \oplus M', E_{T'}(M') \oplus M')$$

for $S \neq T$, $S' \neq T'$, 1BL $=$ 2BL and 1BR $=$ 2BR.

FitCollBothColumns($\mathcal{Q}$). In this case we assume $\neg\text{FITCOLLLEFTCOLUMNS}(\mathcal{Q})$ and $\neg\text{FITCOLLRIGHTCOLUMNS}(\mathcal{Q})$. The adversary has found eight – not necessarily distinct – queries such that $(U, V) = H^E(M, S, T)$ and $(U', V') = H^E(M', S', T')$ can be computed with $U = U'$, $V = V'$, 1BL $\neq$ 2BL and 1BR $\neq$ 2BR.

FitPreimage($\mathcal{Q}$). This formalizes case (iii). The adversary has found four – not necessarily distinct – queries used in H^E in positions 1TL, 1TR, 1BL, 1BR such that the output of H^E is equal to (S_0, T_0), *i.e.*, the initial chaining values of the MDC-4 hash function.

For practical purposes we derive our predicates as follows.

InternalColl($\mathcal{Q}$) =
    ¬LUCKY($\mathcal{Q}$) ∧ FITINTERNALCOLL($\mathcal{Q}$)
CollLeftColumns($\mathcal{Q}$) =
    ¬(LUCKY($\mathcal{Q}$) ∨ FITINTERNALCOLL($\mathcal{Q}$)) ∧ FITCOLLLEFTCOLUMNS($\mathcal{Q}$)
CollRightColumns($\mathcal{Q}$) =
    ¬(LUCKY($\mathcal{Q}$) ∨ FITINTERNALCOLL($\mathcal{Q}$) ∨ FITCOLLLEFTCOLUMNS($\mathcal{Q}$))
    ∧FITCOLLRIGHTCOLUMNS($\mathcal{Q}$)
CollTopRows($\mathcal{Q}$) =
    ¬(LUCKY($\mathcal{Q}$) ∨ FITINTERNALCOLL($\mathcal{Q}$) ∨ FITCOLLLEFTCOLUMNS($\mathcal{Q}$)
    ∨FITCOLLRIGHTCOLUMNS($\mathcal{Q}$)) ∧ FITCOLLTOPROWS($\mathcal{Q}$)
CollBothColumns($\mathcal{Q}$) =
    ¬(LUCKY($\mathcal{Q}$) ∨ FITINTERNALCOLL($\mathcal{Q}$) ∨ FITCOLLLEFTCOLUMNS($\mathcal{Q}$)
    ∨FITCOLLRIGHTCOLUMNS($\mathcal{Q}$) ∨ FITCOLLTOPROWS($\mathcal{Q}$))
    ∧FITCOLLBOTHCOLUMNS($\mathcal{Q}$)
Preimage($\mathcal{Q}$) =
    ¬(LUCKY($\mathcal{Q}$) ∨ FITINTERNALCOLL($\mathcal{Q}$) ∨ FITCOLLLEFTCOLUMNS($\mathcal{Q}$)
    ∨FITCOLLRIGHTCOLUMNS($\mathcal{Q}$) ∨ FITCOLLTOPROWS($\mathcal{Q}$)
    ∨FITCOLLBOTHCOLUMNS($\mathcal{Q}$)) ∧ FITPREIMAGE($\mathcal{Q}$)

Proof of Proposition 1. Assume that the adversary is not lucky, *i.e.*, ¬LUCKY($\mathcal{Q}$).
Then it is easy to see that

$$\text{FITINTERNALCOLL}(\mathcal{Q}) \lor \text{FITCOLLLEFTCOLUMNS}(\mathcal{Q}) \lor$$
$$\text{FITCOLLRIGHTCOLUMNS}(\mathcal{Q}) \lor \text{FITCOLLTOPROWS}(\mathcal{Q}) \lor$$
$$\text{FITCOLLBOTHCOLUMNS}(\mathcal{Q}) \lor \text{FITPREIMAGE}(\mathcal{Q})$$
$$\implies$$
$$\text{INTERNALCOLL}(\mathcal{Q}) \lor \text{COLLLEFTCOLUMNS}(\mathcal{Q}) \lor \text{COLLRIGHTCOLUMNS}(\mathcal{Q}) \lor$$
$$\text{COLLTOPROWS}(\mathcal{Q}) \lor \text{COLLBOTHCOLUMNS}(\mathcal{Q}) \lor \text{PREIMAGE}(\mathcal{Q})$$

holds. Therefore it is sufficient to show that

$$\text{COLL}(\mathcal{Q}) \implies \text{FITINTERNALCOLL}(\mathcal{Q}) \lor \text{FITCOLLLEFTCOLUMNS}(\mathcal{Q})$$
$$\lor \text{FITCOLLRIGHTCOLUMNS}(\mathcal{Q}) \lor \text{FITCOLLTOPROWS}(\mathcal{Q})$$
$$\lor \text{FITCOLLBOTHCOLUMNS}(\mathcal{Q}) \lor \text{FITPREIMAGE}(\mathcal{Q}).$$

To ensure that the chaining values are always different, we give the attack to the adversary if these values collide, *i.e.*, $U = V$ or $U' = V'$. Note that this is usually not a *real* collision, but we can exclude this case in our analysis. We call this INTERNALCOLL($\mathcal{Q}$). This corresponds to case (i) in Section 3.1.

For the case (ii), we assume that a collision for the MDC-4 compression function H^E can be constructed from the queries in $\mathcal{Q}$. Then there are inputs $\mathcal{M}, \mathcal{M}' \in (\{0,1\}^n)^+$, $\mathcal{M} \neq \mathcal{M}'$ such that $\mathcal{H}(\mathcal{M}) = \mathcal{H}(\mathcal{M}')$. In particular, there are $M, M' \in \{0,1\}^n$ and $(S, T), (S', T') \in \{0,1\}^{2n}$, $(S, T, M) \neq (S', T', M')$, such that $H^E(S, T, M) = H^E(S', T', M')$.

For the following analysis we have ¬INTERNALCOLL($\mathcal{Q}$), *i.e.*, $S \neq T$, $S' \neq T'$. Our case differentiation is based on the disposal of queries in the bottom row.

First assume that 1BL = 2BL and 1BR = 2BR. Then COLLTOPROWS($\mathcal{Q}$). Now assume that 1BL = 2BL and 1BR $\neq$ 2BR. Then COLLRIGHTCOLUMNS($\mathcal{Q}$). Conversely, if 1BL $\neq$ 2BL and 1BR = 2BR, we say COLLLEFTCOLUMNS($\mathcal{Q}$). The only missing case, 1BL $\neq$ 2BL and 1BR $\neq$ 2BR, is denoted by COLLBOTHCOLUMNS($\mathcal{Q}$). PREIMAGE($\mathcal{Q}$) formalizes case (iii) of Section 3.1 and corresponds to FITPREIMAGE($\mathcal{Q}$).   □

General Remarks. The strategy for the other predicates is to upper bound the probability of the last query being successful conditioned on the fact that the adversary has not yet been successful in previous queries. We say that the last query is successful if the output is such that NumEqualHalf($\mathcal{Q}$) $< \alpha$, NumEqual($\mathcal{Q}$) $< \beta$, NumColl($\mathcal{Q}$) $< \gamma$ and that one of the predicates is *true*.

Proposition 2 (InternalColl($\mathcal{Q}$))

$$\Pr[\text{INTERNALCOLL}(\mathcal{Q})] \leq q \left(\frac{\alpha^2 + \gamma}{2^n - q} + \frac{\alpha\beta}{(2^n - q)(2^{n/2} - \alpha)} + \frac{\alpha}{2^n - 2^{n/2}\alpha} \right)$$

Proof The adversary can use the last query Q_i either once or twice. When Q_i is used three times or more then it must occur twice either in the top- or bottom row. But this would imply $S = T$.

In the case that the query is used once it can either be used in the top or bottom row. Due to the symmetric structure of MDC-4, we can assume WLOG that the last query Q_i is either used in position TL or BL^2. The success probability is analyzed in Lemma 1.

In the case that Q_i is used twice, it must be used once in the top and once in the bottom row. We again assume that the last query is WLOG used in TL and BL or TL and BR. The success probability is analyzed in Lemma 2.   □

Lemma 1. *Let $S \neq T$ and $\mathcal{Q}_{i-1}$ the query list not containing the last query Q_i. Assume that Q_i is used once in the MDC-4 compression function H^E. Then*

$$\Pr[(U, U) = H^E(S, T, M)] \leq q \left(\frac{\alpha^2 + \gamma}{2^n - q} \right).$$

Proof

Case 1: Assume first that $Q_i = (K_i^L \| K_i^R, X_i, Y_i)$ is used in position BL. It follows that K_i^L must be equal to the XOR-output Z_{TL}^L of the query in TL. It follows that there are at most α different candidates for the query in TL in the query history $\mathcal{Q}_{i-i}$. Similarly, because K_i^R must be equal to the right half of the XOR-output of TR, Z_{TR}^R, there are at most α candidates for that can be used in TR. For the query in BR, there are at most α^2 possible key inputs, the ciphertext input of BR is determined by the query used in TL. So the probability that there is a query in $\mathcal{Q}_i$ such that $U = V$ is upper bounded by $\alpha^2/(2^n - q)$. For q queries, the total chance of success is $\leq q\alpha^2/(2^n - q)$.

---

[2] In this case we only consider the 'left' side of Figure 2 and denote 1TL by TL, 1TR by TR, 1BL by BL and 1BR by BR.

Case 2: Now assume that Q_i is used in position TL. Since $S \neq T$ it follows that BL $\neq$ BR. So there are at most γ ordered pairs of queries that can be used in BL and BR such that their XOR-output collides. Fixing one of these, it fully determines the XOR-output TL. So, for q queries, Q_i has at most a chance of $q\gamma/(2^n - q)$.   □

Lemma 2. *Let $S \neq T$ and Q_{i-1} the query list not containing the last query Q_i. Assume that Q_i is used twice in the MDC-4 compression function H^E. Then*

$$\Pr[(U, U) = H^E(S, T, M)] \leq q \left(\frac{\alpha\beta}{(2^n - q)(2^{n/2} - \alpha)} + \frac{\alpha}{2^n - 2^{n/2}\alpha} \right).$$

Proof. By symmetry arguments, we assume WLOG that the last query Q_i is used in position TL. Since $S \neq T$, the last query can only appear a second time in position BL, or BR but not in TR.

Case 1: Assume Q_i is used in position TL and BL. This query can be used in these positions if the randomly determined left-side XOR-output Z_i^L is equal to the left-side of the key K_i^L. This event is called P_K and its probability of success can be upper bounded for Q_i by $\Pr[P_K] \leq \alpha/(2^{n/2} - \alpha)$. We now upper bound the number of queries that can be used in BR conditioned on the fact that P_K is successful. There are at most α queries that can be used in TR, since now the key input of BL is fixed. As the ciphertext input of BR is now also fixed by TL, there are at most β possibilities for BR. So the chance of success for the i-th query in this case is $\leq \frac{\beta}{2^n - q} \cdot \Pr[P_K]$. So for q queries the bound becomes $\frac{q\alpha\beta}{(2^n - q)(2^{n/2} - \alpha)}$.

Case 2: Assume Q_i is used in position TL and BR. Then, $K_i = X_i$. The query Q_i can be used in these two positions at the same time if the randomly determined right-half XOR-output Z_i^R is equal to the right-half of the key, $K_i^R = X_i^R$. This event is called O_K and its probability of success can be upper bounded for Q_i by $\Pr[O_K] \leq \frac{1}{2^{n/2}}$.

   We now upper bound the number of queries that can be used in TR conditioned on the fact the O_K is successful. There are at most α queries that can be used in TR such that $Z_{TR}^L = K_i^L$ holds. Hence, there are at most α queries that can be used in BL. We denote the chance that $Z_{BL}^L = Z_i^L$ for the i-the query as $\Pr[Z_i^L]$. This event can thus be upper bounded by $\frac{\alpha}{2^{n/2} - \alpha} \cdot \Pr[O_K] \leq \frac{\alpha}{2^n - 2^{n/2}\alpha}$. For q queries we can upper bound this case by $\frac{q\alpha}{2^n - 2^{n/2}\alpha}$.   □

Proposition 3 (CollTopRows($\mathcal{Q}$))

$$\Pr[\text{COLLTOPROWS}(\mathcal{Q})] \leq \frac{q\beta}{2^n - q}$$

Proof. In this case we consider a collision in the top row, with 1BL = 2BL and 1BR = 2BR. This implies $S = S'$ and $T' = T$. Furthermore it implies $M \neq M'$, because otherwise we would have 1TL = 2TL and 1TR = 2TR. Regarding to this constraints we have to upper bound the probability that the i-th query can be used such that

$$(E_S(M) \oplus M, E_T(M) \oplus M) = (E_{S'}(M') \oplus M', E_{T'}(M') \oplus M').$$

Note, that no internal collision has happened before, *i.e.*, $\neg$INTERNALCOLL$(\mathcal{Q})$, and therefore the chaining values are *always* different. First assume that the last query is used twice or more. In order to find a collision in the top-row, the last query must be used in the top-row or otherwise the success probability is zero. The last query cannot be used in 1TL and 2TL or else 1TL $=$ 2TR and $M = M'$ would follow. The last query also cannot be used in 1TL and 2TR or else $S = T' = S' = T$ would follow.

Now assume that Q_i is used once, WLOG in 1TL. Then there are at most β pairs of queries for 1TR, 2TR that form a collision. So there are at most β queries that can be used in 2TL that may form a collision with the XOR-output of the last query used in 1TL. The success probability for q queries can therefore be upper bounded by $q\beta/(2^n - q)$. □

Proposition 4 (CollLeftColumns($\mathcal{Q}$))

$$\Pr[\text{COLLLEFTCOLUMNS}(\mathcal{Q})] \le q\left(\frac{\alpha^2(\alpha^2 + 2\gamma + 1) + \alpha\gamma + \alpha}{2^n - q} + \frac{\alpha^3 + 2\alpha^2 + \alpha}{(2^{n/2} - \alpha)^2}\right)$$

The proof can be found in the full version of this paper [9, Appendix B].

Proposition 5 (CollRightColumns($\mathcal{Q}$))

$$\Pr[\text{COLLRIGHTCOLUMNS}(\mathcal{Q})] \le q\left(\frac{\alpha^2(\alpha^2 + 2\gamma + 1) + \alpha\gamma + \alpha}{2^n - q} + \frac{\alpha^3 + 2\alpha^2 + 1}{(2^{n/2} - \alpha)^2}\right)$$

Proof. Due to the symmetric structure of MDC-4 this proof is essentially the same as for proposition 4. □

Proposition 6 (CollBothColumns($\mathcal{Q}$))

$$\Pr[\text{COLLBOTHCOLUMNS}(\mathcal{Q})] \le q\left(\frac{\gamma\alpha^2 + \gamma^2}{2^n - q} + \frac{2\alpha}{(2^{n/2} - \alpha)^2}\right)$$

The proof of Proposition 6 is given in Appendix A.

Proposition 7 (Preimage($\mathcal{Q}$))

$$\Pr[\text{PREIMAGE}(\mathcal{Q})] \le \frac{q(4 + \beta^2)}{2^n - q}$$

Proof. The adversary can use the last query either once or twice. If it is used twice, it is used at least once in the bottom row.

Case 1: Assume first, that the last query is used once and that it is used in the top row. Assume WLOG that it is used in 1TL. Since there are at most β queries that can be used in 1BL and also at most β queries for 1BR, the success probability is upper bounded for q queries by $q\beta^2/(2^n - q)$.

Now assume that the last query is used once and that it is used in the bottom row. Whether it is used in 1BL or 1BR, the success probability in each case for one query is $\leq 1/(2^n - q)$.

So the total success probability for q queries for this case is upper bounded by $q(2 + \beta^2)/(2^n - q)$.

Case 2: Now, assume that the last query is used twice. So it is used exactly once in the bottom row and the analysis of Case 1 (bottom row) gives an upper bound of $2q/(2^n - q)$.   □

Proposition 8 (Lucky($\mathcal{Q}$)). *Let $n, q \in \mathbb{N}$, $n \geq q$. Let α, β, and γ be as in Theorem 1 with $eq2^{n/2}/(2^n - q) \leq \alpha$ and $eq/(2^n - q) \leq \beta$. Set $\tau = \frac{\alpha(2^n - q)}{q2^{n/2}}$ and $\nu = \frac{\beta(2^n - q)}{q}$. Then*

$$\Pr[\text{LUCKY}(\mathcal{Q})] \leq \frac{q^2}{\gamma(2^n - q)} + 2q2^{n/2}e^{q2^{n/2}\tau(1 - \ln \tau)/(2^n - q)} + q2^n e^{q2^n \nu(1 - \ln \nu)/(2^n - q)}.$$

A proof can be found in [32, Appendix B].

4   Conclusion

We have derived the first collision security bound for MDC-4, a double length block cipher based compression function which takes 4 calls to hashing a message block using a (n, n) block-cipher. Although MDC-4 is structurally quite different from MDC-2, it is somewhat surprising that the result given by Steinberger for MDC-2 ($2^{74.91}$) and our result for MDC-4 ($2^{74.76}$) are numerically quite similar – although we have applied much more economical proof techniques. This leads to open questions we have not been able to find satisfying answers for as, *e.g., why are these results so similar?* One possible answer is, that MDC-2 and MDC-4 are security-wise very similar. This would lead to the conclusion that MDC-4 is totally dominated by MDC-2. Another answer might be that the limitations are due to the applied techniques in the proofs. Then it would be interesting and important to find new proof methods that help overcome these.

References

[1] Biham, E., Dunkelman, O.: The SHAvite-3 Hash Function. Submission to NIST, Round 2 (2009)
[2] Black, J., Rogaway, P., Shrimpton, T.: Black-Box Analysis of the Block-Cipher-Based Hash-Function Constructions from PGV. In: Yung, M. (ed.) CRYPTO 2002. LNCS, vol. 2442, pp. 320–335. Springer, Heidelberg (2002)
[3] Brassard, G. (ed.): CRYPTO 1989. LNCS, vol. 435. Springer, Heidelberg (1990)
[4] Damgård, I.: A Design Principle for Hash Functions. In: Brassard [3], pp. 416–427

[5] den Boer, B., Bosselaers, A.: Collisions for the Compression Function of MD-5. In: Helleseth, T. (ed.) EUROCRYPT 1993. LNCS, vol. 765, pp. 293–304. Springer, Heidelberg (1994)

[6] Even, S., Mansour, Y.: A Construction of a Cipher From a Single Pseudorandom Permutation. In: Imai, H., Rivest, R.L., Matsumoto, T. (eds.) ASIACRYPT 1991. LNCS, vol. 739, pp. 210–224. Springer, Heidelberg (1993)

[7] Ferguson, N., Lucks, S., Schneier, B., Whiting, D., Bellare, M., Kohno, T., Callas, J., Walker, J.: The Skein Hash Function Family. Submission to NIST, Round 2 (2009)

[8] Fleischmann, E., Forler, C., Gorski, M., Lucks, S.: Collision Resistant Double-Length Hashing. In: Heng, S.-H., Kurosawa, K. (eds.) ProvSec 2010. LNCS, vol. 6402, pp. 102–118. Springer, Heidelberg (2010)

[9] Fleischmann, E., Forler, C., Lucks, S., Wenzel, J.: The collision security of mdc-4. Cryptology ePrint Archive, Report 2012/096 (2012), http://eprint.iacr.org/

[10] Fleischmann, E., Gorski, M., Lucks, S.: Security of Cyclic Double Block Length Hash Functions. In: Parker, M.G. (ed.) Cryptography and Coding 2009. LNCS, vol. 5921, pp. 153–175. Springer, Heidelberg (2009)

[11] Dobbertin, H.: The status of MD5 after a recent attack (1996)

[12] Dobbertin, H., Bosselaers, A., Preneel, B.: RIPEMD (RACE integrity primitives evaluation message digest) (1996)

[13] Kilian, J., Rogaway, P.: How to Protect DES against Exhaustive Key Search. In: Koblitz, N. (ed.) CRYPTO 1996. LNCS, vol. 1109, pp. 252–267. Springer, Heidelberg (1996)

[14] Knudsen, L.R., Mendel, F., Rechberger, C., Thomsen, S.S.: Cryptanalysis of MDC-2. In: Joux, A. (ed.) EUROCRYPT 2009. LNCS, vol. 5479, pp. 106–120. Springer, Heidelberg (2009)

[15] Knudsen, L.R., Preneel, B.: Fast and Secure Hashing Based on Codes. In: Kaliski Jr., B.S. (ed.) CRYPTO 1997. LNCS, vol. 1294, pp. 485–498. Springer, Heidelberg (1997)

[16] Krause, M., Armknecht, F., Fleischmann, E.: Preimage Resistance Beyond the Birthday Bound: Double-Length Hashing Revisited. Cryptology ePrint Archive, Report 2010/519 (2010), http://eprint.iacr.org/

[17] Lai, X., Massey, J.L.: Hash Functions Based on Block Ciphers. In: Rueppel, R.A. (ed.) EUROCRYPT 1992. LNCS, vol. 658, pp. 55–70. Springer, Heidelberg (1993)

[18] Lee, J., Kwon, D.: The security of abreast-dm in the ideal cipher model. Cryptology ePrint Archive, Report 2009/225 (2009), http://eprint.iacr.org/

[19] Lee, J., Stam, M.: MJH: A Faster Alternative to MDC-2. In: Kiayias, A. (ed.) CT-RSA 2011. LNCS, vol. 6558, pp. 213–236. Springer, Heidelberg (2011)

[20] Lee, J., Stam, M., Steinberger, J.: The collision security of tandem-dm in the ideal cipher model. Cryptology ePrint Archive, Report 2010/409 (2010), http://eprint.iacr.org/

[21] Lee, J., Stam, M., Steinberger, J.: The preimage security of double-block-length compression functions. Cryptology ePrint Archive, Report 2011/210 (2011), http://eprint.iacr.org/

[22] Leurent, G., Bouillaguet, C., Fouque, P.-A.: SIMD Is a Message Digest. Submission to NIST, Round 2 (2009)

[23] Rabin, M.: Digitalized Signatures. In: DeMillo, R., Dobkin, D., Jones, A., Lipton, R. (eds.) Foundations of Secure Computation, pp. 155–168. Academic Press (1978)

[24] Menezes, A., van Oorschot, P.C., Vanstone, S.A.: Handbook of Applied Cryptography. CRC Press (1996)

[25] Merkle, R.C.: One Way Hash Functions and DES. In: Brassard [3], pp. 428–446
[26] Meyer, C.H., Schilling, M.: Secure program load with manipulation detection code. In: SECURICOM 1988, France, Paris, pp. 111–130 (1988)
[27] National Bureau of Standards. FIPS Publication 46-1: Data Encryption Standard (January 1988)
[28] NIST National Institute of Standards and Technology. FIPS 180-1: Secure Hash Standard (April 1995), http://csrc.nist.gov
[29] NIST National Institute of Standards and Technology. FIPS 180-2: Secure Hash Standard (April 1995), http://csrc.nist.gov
[30] Rivest, R.L.: The MD4 Message Digest Algorithm. In: Menezes, A., Vanstone, S.A. (eds.) CRYPTO 1990. LNCS, vol. 537, pp. 303–311. Springer, Heidelberg (1991)
[31] Rivest, R.L.: RFC 1321: The MD5 Message-Digest Algorithm. Internet Activities Board (April 1992)
[32] Steinberger, J.P.: The Collision Intractability of MDC-2 in the Ideal Cipher Model. Cryptology ePrint Archive, Report 2006/294 (2006), http://eprint.iacr.org/
[33] Steinberger, J.P.: The Collision Intractability of MDC-2 in the Ideal-Cipher Model. In: Naor, M. (ed.) EUROCRYPT 2007. LNCS, vol. 4515, pp. 34–51. Springer, Heidelberg (2007)
[34] Wang, X., Lai, X., Feng, D., Chen, H., Yu, X.: Cryptanalysis of the Hash Functions MD4 and RIPEMD. In: Cramer, R. (ed.) EUROCRYPT 2005. LNCS, vol. 3494, pp. 1–18. Springer, Heidelberg (2005)
[35] Wang, X., Yin, Y.L., Yu, H.: Finding Collisions in the Full SHA-1. In: Shoup, V. (ed.) CRYPTO 2005. LNCS, vol. 3621, pp. 17–36. Springer, Heidelberg (2005)
[36] Winternitz, R.S.: A Secure One-Way Hash Function Built from DES. In: IEEE Symposium on Security and Privacy, pp. 88–90 (1984)

A   Proof of Proposition 6

In case 1, we discuss the implication if the last query is only used once, the cases 2-4 give bounds if the last query is used at least twice.

Case 1: The last query is used exactly once. We can WLOG assume the it is either used in 1TL or 1BL.

Subcase 1.1: The last query is used in position 1BL. Since 1BR = 2BR, there are at most γ pairs of queries in the query history that can be used for position 1BR, 2BR. Now, for any one query 2BR, there are at most α matching queries in position 2TL and at most α matching queries in 2TR. Since the queries in 2TL and 2TR uniquely determine the query 2BL, there are at most $\gamma\alpha^2$ queries that can be used for 2BL. Therefore the last query has a chance of being successful of $\leq \gamma\alpha^2/(2^n - q)$. For q queries, the total chance of success in this case is $\leq q\gamma\alpha^2/(2^n - q)$.

Subcase 1.2: The last query is used in position 1TL. There are at most γ possible pairs of queries that can be used for 1BL and 2BL and there are at most γ possible queries that can be used for 1BR and 2BR. We now upper bound the probability that the last query can be used in 1TL assuming a collision. There are at most γ^2 pairs of queries that can be used for 1BL and 1BR. Therefore the success probability of the last query can be upper bounded by $\leq \gamma^2/(2^n - q)$ and for q queries by $q\gamma^2/(2^n - q)$.

Case 2: The last query is only used in the bottom row. Then it is used exactly twice, WLOG in positions 1BL and 2BR. This would imply $U = V'$ which then – in the case of success – implies INTERNALCOLL($\mathcal{Q}$).

Case 3: The last query is only used in the top row. We can WLOG assume it is used in 1TL. We can use the same reasoning as in Subcase 1.2 and therefore extend Subcase 1.2 to also handle this slightly more general situation here.

Case 4: The last query is used at least once in the bottom row and at least once in the top row. We can WLOG assume that it is used in position 1TL. Using the same argument as for Case 2, the last query must then appear exactly once in the bottom row. The following four subcases discuss the implications of the last query being also used in 1BL, 1BR, 2BL and 2BR. Note that the adversary may use it also a second time – apart from 1TL– in the top row but this does not change our bounds.

> **Subcase 4.1:** The last query is also used in 1BL. The left half of the XOR-output of 1TL has a chance of being equal to its key input (*i.e.*, the key input of 1BL) of $\leq 1/(2^{n/2} - \alpha)$. The following analysis is now based on the fact the the left half of the XOR-output has matched the left half of the key input. Since we now also know the left half of the XOR-output of 2BL, there are at most α queries that can be used in 2BL. The chance that the right half of the XOR-output of 2BL matches the right half of the XOR-output of 1BL is therefore $\leq \alpha/(2^{n/2} - \alpha)$. So for q queries the total chance of success is $\leq q\alpha/(2^{n/2} - \alpha)^2$.

> **Subcase 4.2:** The last query is also used in 1BR. The same arguing as for Subcase 4.1 can be used (apart from exchanging 'left' and 'right') and the bound for q queries is again $\leq \alpha/(2^{n/2} - \alpha)^2$.

> **Subcase 4.3** The last query is also used in position 2BL. There are at most γ possible pairs of query in the query history that can be used for the pair 1BR, 2BR that form a collision. The probability that the right half of the XOR-output of 1TL matches the right half of its key input (*i.e.*, for the last query being also used in 1BR) is $\leq 1/(2^{n/2} - \alpha)$. Conditioned on the fact that the right half of the XOR-output is now fixed there are at most α queries that can be used in 1BL such that the XOR-outputs of 1BL and 2BL collides. The probability that the left half of the XOR-output of 1TL is equal to the left half of the key of 1BL is therefore $\leq \alpha/(2^{n/2} - \alpha)$ and the total chance of success for q queries is $\leq q\alpha/(2^{n/2} - \alpha)^2$.

> **Subcase 4.4** The last query is also used in 2BR. The same arguing as for Subcase 4.3 can be used (apart from exchanging 'left' and 'right') and the bound for q queries is again $\leq q\alpha/(2^{n/2} - \alpha)^2$. $\qquad\square$

SPN-Hash: Improving the Provable Resistance against Differential Collision Attacks[*]

Jiali Choy[1], Huihui Yap[1], Khoongming Khoo[1], Jian Guo[2],
Thomas Peyrin[3,**], Axel Poschmann[3,***], and Chik How Tan[4]

[1] DSO National Laboratories, 20 Science Park Drive, Singapore 118230
{cjiali,yhuihui,kkhoongm}@dso.org.sg
[2] Institute for Infocomm Research, A*STAR, Singapore
ntu.guo@gmail.com
[3] SPMS, Nanyang Technological University, Singapore
{thomas.peyrin,aposchmann}@ntu.edu.sg
[4] Temasek Laboratories, National University of Singapore
tsltch@nus.edu.sg

Abstract. Collision resistance is a fundamental property required for cryptographic hash functions. One way to ensure collision resistance is to use hash functions based on public key cryptography (PKC) which reduces collision resistance to a hard mathematical problem, but such primitives are usually slow. A more practical approach is to use symmetric-key design techniques which lead to faster schemes, but collision resistance can only be heuristically inferred from the best probability of a single differential characteristic path. We propose a new hash function design with variable hash output sizes of 128, 256, and 512 bits, that reduces this gap. Due to its inherent Substitution-Permutation Network (SPN) structure and JH mode of operation, we are able to compute its differential collision probability using the concept of differentials. Namely, for each possible input differences, we take into account all the differential paths leading to a collision and this enables us to prove that our hash function is secure against a differential collision attack using a single input difference. None of the SHA-3 finalists could prove such a resistance. At the same time, our hash function design is secure against pre-image, second pre-image and rebound attacks, and is faster than PKC-based hashes. Part of our design includes a generalization of the optimal diffusion used in the classical wide-trail SPN construction from Daemen and Rijmen, which leads to near-optimal differential bounds when applied to non-square byte arrays. We also found a novel way to use parallel copies of a serial matrix over the finite field $GF(2^4)$, so as to create lightweight and secure byte-based diffusion for our design. Overall, we obtain hash functions that are fast in software, very lightweight in hardware (about 4625 GE for the 256-bit

---

[*] The full version of this paper can be found on the eprint archive at http://eprint.iacr.org.

[**] This author is supported by the Lee Kuan Yew Postdoctoral Fellowship 2011 and the Singapore National Research Foundation Fellowship 2012.

[***] This author was supported in part by Singapore National Research Foundation under Research Grant NRF-CRP2-2007-03.

A. Mitrokotsa and S. Vaudenay (Eds.): AFRICACRYPT 2012, LNCS 7374, pp. 270–286, 2012.
© Springer-Verlag Berlin Heidelberg 2012

hash output) and that provide much stronger security proofs regarding collision resistance than any of the SHA-3 finalists.

Keywords: SPN, wide-trail strategy, Hash Functions, collision resistance.

1 Introduction

For current hash function designs, there are mainly two approaches to obtain provable security. The first approach is to prove collision and/or preimage resistance in relation to *hard* problems. For instance, Contini et al.'s very smooth hash (VSH) [13] is a number-theoretic hash for which finding a collision can be proven to be equivalent to solving the VSSH problem of the same order of magnitude as integer factorization. Concerning preimage, an example is MQ-HASH [8] for which finding a preimage is proven to be as hard as solving a multivariate system of equations. For the SHA-3 candidate FSB [1], finding collisions or preimages imply solving syndrome decoding. The second approach is more practical and less rigorous, and aims at proving a good differential probability bound for a single characteristic path. However, collision resistance is only heuristically inferred from this bound.

The first approach accomplishes more than a proof of resistance to differential cryptanalyis. However, hash function schemes based on this design strategy often suffer significantly in terms of speed and performance. On the other hand, schemes using the second approach enjoy faster speeds but suffer from incomplete proof of collision resistance. In this paper, we seek to reduce the gap between these two approaches by providing a more powerful proof for collision resistance while maintaining similar speed as compared to the symmetric-key design hashes.

Here, we recall that a *differential characteristic* over a composed mapping consists of a sequence of difference patterns such that the output difference from one round corresponds to the input difference in the next round. On the other hand, a *differential* is the set of all differential characteristics with the same first-round input and last-round output differences. Most hash function designs only aim at showing that any single differential characteristic has sufficiently low probability and heuristically infer collision resistance from this. Examples of hash functions which adopt this approach include hashes such as WHIRLPOOL [21] and some SHA-3 finalists like GRØSTL [17] and JH [28]. In addition, this differential characteristic bound is hard to determine for Addition-Rotation-XOR (ARX) designs such as BLAKE [3] and SKEIN [16]. Therefore, the next step in collision resistance proof, as already done by the second-round SHA-3 candidate ECHO [5], is to give a bound on the best differential probability instead of only the best differential characteristic probability. However, note that this security argument only takes into account attackers that limit themselves to a fixed colliding differential (i.e. with a fixed output difference of the internal permutation), while many exist.

Our proposal for a new hash function design is able to achieve a stronger differential collision resistance proof. For example, for our proposed 512-bit hash, we prove that the differential probability of 4 rounds of its internal permutation function, which has a 1024-bit state size, is upper bounded by 2^{-816}. We sum this upper bound over **all output differences that lead to a collision** (2^{512} candidates) in order to find that the differential collision probability of our proposed hash is then upper bounded by $2^{-304} < 2^{-256}$ after the final truncation. In contrast, for the SHA-3 semi-finalist ECHO [5], the maximal expected differential probability for four rounds of their 2048-bit AES extension, ECHO.AES, is 1.055×2^{-452}, but summing over all possible colliding output difference masks (at least 2^{1536} candidates) completely prevents such a collision-resistance argument. For SHA-3 finalist, GRØSTL, it is easy to compute the internal collision probability of its compression function f. However, its output transformation, involving a permutation P followed by a truncation, makes such a derivation much less straightforward for the external collision probability of the full GRØSTL hash function.

In addition, we have to consider that for some hash function constructions, it is necessary to prove low related-key differential probability instead of just low fixed-key differential probability. For example, consider the Davies-Meyer compression function instantiated with AES. The main AES cipher has very low differential characteristic probability which is bounded by 2^{-150} for every four rounds. However, in the Davies-Meyer mode, each input message block to the hash corresponds to the cipher key of the AES-based compression function. This makes the compression function vulnerable to the multicollision attack by Biryukov et al. [9], because AES does not have good resistance against related-key differential attack.

1.1   Our Contributions

In this paper, we propose a new hash function design, SPN-Hash, with variable output sizes of 128, 256, and 512 bits. It is specially constructed to circumvent the weaknesses in the proofs of differential collision resistance as well as to resist common attacks against hash functions.

Concerning the internal permutations, we use the Substitution-Permutation Network (SPN) structure as the building block for SPN-Hash to ensure that the maximum probability taken over all differentials (not only differential characteristics) will be low enough. In [23], Park et al. presented an upper bound for the maximum differential probability for two rounds of an SPN structure, where the linear transformation can have any value as its branch number. This bound is found to be low for SPN structures. For instance, the maximum differential probability for four rounds of AES is bounded by 1.144×2^{-111}. Based on Park's result, we deduce an upper bound for the differential collision probability of SPN-Hash. We use this bound to show that our hash functions are secure against a differential collision attack. Furthermore for our internal permutations, we need to consider non-square byte-arrays of size $m \times n$ where $m \neq n$. The designers of AES [15] gave a construction for $m \times n$ arrays where $m < n$ using optimal diffusion maps, but the differential bound is the same as that of an $m \times m$ array, which is sub-optimal for mn-byte block size. By their method, a 256-bit permutation would be constructed by a 4×8 byte-array that has the same differential bound 1.144×2^{-111} as a 4×4 byte-array. This is not close enough to $2^{-blocksize} = 2^{-256}$ for our security proof. **We generalize the optimal diffusion map of [15] to construct $m \times n$ byte-arrays where $m > n$, which can achieve near optimal differential bound close to $2^{-blocksize}$.**

We also analyzed the security of our internal permutations against the latest rebound-like attacks [25]. More precisely, we present distinguishing attacks on three versions of the internal permutation P for 8 out of 10 rounds. For the 256-bit permutation P, the 8-round attack requires time 2^{56} and memory 2^{16}. For the 512-bit permutation P, the 8-round attack requires time 2^{48} and memory 2^8, while for the 1024-bit permutation P, the 8-round attack requires time 2^{88} and memory 2^{16}.

Concerning the operating mode, we use the JH mode of operation [28], a variant of the Sponge construction [6]. In this design, assuming a block size of $2x$ bits, each x-bit input message block is XORed with the first half of the state. A permutation function P is applied, and the same message block is XORed with the second half of P's output. For this construction, the message blocks are mapped directly into the main permutation block structure instead of via a key schedule. **This eliminates the need to consider related-key differentials when analyzing protection against collision attacks.** Furthermore, the JH mode of operation is able to provide second preimage resistance of up to 2^x bits for an x-bit hash as compared to only $2^{x/2}$ for the Sponge construction with the same capacity.

To summarize, our SPN-Hash functions use AES-based internal permutations with fixed-key and a generalized optimal diffusion to ensure low and provable maximum differential probability. Then our JH-based operating mode allows us to apply directly our security reasoning and obtain a bound on the maximum probability of an attacker looking for collisions using a fixed input difference. To the best of our knowledge, **this is the only known function so far that provides such a security argument.**

The performances of SPN-Hash are good since the internal permutation is very similar to the one used in the SHA-3 finalist GRØSTL. We propose a **novel construction to use parallel copies of the PHOTON 8×8 serialized MDS matrix over $GF(2^4)$ from [18], to create a secure and very lightweight byte-based diffusion for our design in hardware.**[1] Moreover, the area of SPN-Hash is also lowered by the relatively small internal memory required by the JH mode of operation. Hardware implementations require 4625 GE for 256-bit hash output, while current best results for the SHA-3 competition finalists require 10000 GE or more. Overall, **our proposal achieves both excellent software speed and compact lightweight implementations.**

---

[1] Note that the approach of [18] to do an exhaustive search for serialized MDS matrix over $GF(2^8)$ by MAGMA is only feasible for $n \times n$ matrix up to size $n = 6$. Therefore we need our current approach to construct serailized 8×8 matrix over $GF(2^8)$.

Our paper is organized as follows: We state some necessary preliminaries concerning differential cryptanalysis in Section 2. Then we describe our proposed SPN-Hash design and give instantiations of 128-, 256-, and 512-bit SPN-Hash in Section 3 before proceeding to a summary of our security analysis results against differential collision, preimage, second preimage, and rebound attacks in Section 4. Lastly in Section 5, we show some performance comparisons.

2   Preliminaries

Substitution Permutation Network. One round of an SPN structure consists of three layers: key addition, substitution, and linear transformation. In the key addition layer, a round subkey is XORed with the input state. The substitution layer is made up of small non-linear substitutions called S-boxes implemented in parallel. The linear transformation layer is used to provide a good spreading effect of the cryptographic characteristics in the substitution layer. As such, the SPN structure has good confusion and diffusion properties [26]. One round of the SPN structure is shown in Figure 1 in Appendix A.

Maximum Differential Probability of an S-Box. In this paper, we follow the standard definitions related to differential cryptanalysis, such as those in [15]. We take all S-boxes to be bijections from $GF(2^s)$ to itself. Consider an SPN structure with an st-bit round function. Let each S-box S_i be an s-bit to s-bit bijective function $S_i : GF(2^s) \rightarrow GF(2^s)$, $(1 \leq i \leq t)$. So the S-box layer consists of t s-bit S-boxes in parallel.

Definition 1. *For any given $\Delta x, \Delta y \in GF(2^s)$, the differential probability of each S_i is defined as*

$$DP^{S_i}(\Delta x, \Delta y) = \frac{\#\{x \in GF(2^s) \mid S_i(x) \oplus S_i(x \oplus \Delta x) = \Delta y\}}{2^s},$$

where we consider Δx to be the input difference and Δy the output difference.

Definition 2. *The maximal differential probability of S_i is defined as*

$$DP((S_i)_{max}) = \underset{\Delta x \neq 0, \Delta y}{max} DP^{S_i}(\Delta x, \Delta y).$$

Definition 3. *The maximal value of $DP((S_i)_{max})$ for $1 \leq i \leq t$ is defined as*

$$p = \underset{1 \leq i \leq t}{max} (DP(S_i)_{max}).$$

An S-Box S_i is strong against differential cryptanalysis if $DP((S_i)_{max})$ is low enough, while a substitution layer is strong if p is low enough.

A *differentially active* S-box is an S-box having a non-zero input difference. A differentially active S-box always has a non-zero output difference and vice versa. In order to evaluate security against differential cryptanalysis, other than the differential probabilities of the S-box or S-box layer, one also has to consider the number of active S-boxes whose value is determined by the linear transformation layer.

Substitution-Diffusion-Substitution Function. In order to ease the analysis of the SPN structure, we define an SDS (Substitution-Diffusion-Substitution) function as shown in Figure 2. Let the linear transformation layer of the SDS function be defined by L, its input difference by $\Delta x = x \oplus x^*$, its output difference by $\Delta y = y \oplus y^* = L(x) \oplus L(x^*)$. If L is linear, we have $\Delta y = L(\Delta x)$. The number of differentially active S-boxes on the input/output of the SDS function is given by the branch number of the linear transformation layer.

Definition 4. *The* branch number *of a linear transformation layer L is defined as*

$$\beta_d = \min_{v \neq 0}\{wt(v) + wt(L(v))\},$$

where the $wt(x)$ is the number of non-zero s-bit characters in x.

If we want to find the number of active S-boxes in two consective rounds of the SPN structure, we only need to consider the SDS function. β_d gives a lower bound on the number of active S-boxes in two consecutive rounds of a differential characteristic approximation.

Definition 5. *A linear transformation layer on t elements is* maximal distance separable (MDS) *if $\beta_d = t + 1$.*

Maximum differential Probability of an SPN. The differential probability, which is the sum of all differential characteristic probabilities with the same input and output difference, gives a more accurate estimate of resistance against differential cryptanalysis (than that of a single characteristic path). In [23], Park et al. proved an upper bound for the maximum differential probability for 2 rounds of the SPN structure.

Theorem 1. *[23, Theorem 1] Let L be the linear transformation of an SPN structure and β_d be the branch number of L from the viewpoint of differential cryptanalysis. Then the maximum differential probability for 2 rounds of the SPN structure is bounded by*

$$\max\left\{\max_{1 \leq i \leq t}\max_{1 \leq u \leq 2^s-1}\sum_{j=1}^{2^s-1}\{DP^{S_i}(u,j)\}^{\beta_d}, \max_{1 \leq i \leq t}\max_{1 \leq u \leq 2^s-1}\sum_{j=1}^{2^s-1}\{DP^{S_i}(j,u)\}^{\beta_d}\right\}.$$

As a consequence, we get the following theorem.

Theorem 2. *[23, Corollary 1] Let L be the linear transformation of an SPN structure and β_d be the branch number of L from the viewpoint of differential cryptanalysis. Then the maximum differential probability for 2 rounds of the SPN structure is bounded by p^{β_d-1}, where p is the maximal value of $DP((S_i)_{max})$ for $1 \leq i \leq t$.*

3   The SPN-Hash Functions

In this section we describe our proposed hash function design, SPN-Hash , with variable hash output sizes of 128, 256, and 512 bits. We adopt the JH mode of operation [28], a variant of the Sponge construction [6], operating on a state of $b = r + c$ bits. b is called the width, r the rate, and c the capacity. Our design is a simple iterated construction based on a fixed-length unkeyed permutation P, where $r = c$. The internal state of P can be represented by an $n \times m$ matrix of 8-bit cells, where n is the number of bytes in a bundle, and m is the number of bundles. Thus, P operates on a width of $b = 8nm$ bits, the rate and capacity are $4nm$-bit each, and the output is a $4nm$-bit hash value.

Firstly, the input message x of length N bits is padded and divided into blocks of $r = 4nm$ bits each. The padding function produces the padded message, x', of length a multiple of $4nm$. It follows "Padding Method 2" in [22, Algorithm 9.30]: first append the bit '1' to x, followed by a sequence of $z = (-N - 2nm - 1 \mod 4nm)$ '0' bits. Finally, append the $2nm$-bit representation of $l = (N + z + 2nm + 1)/4nm$. The integer l represents the number of message blocks in the padded message x'. The maximum message length for $4nm$-bit SPN-Hash is thus set as $4nm \cdot (2^{2nm} - 1) - 2nm - 1$.

Then, all the bits of the state are initialized to the value of an Initialization Vector (IV). The IV of $4nm$-bit SPN-Hash is taken to be the $8nm$-bit binary representation of $4nm$. That is, in big-endian notation, the IVs are 0x00...0080 for 128-bit SPN-Hash , 0x00...0100 for 256-bit SPN-Hash, and 0x00...0200 for 512-bit SPN-Hash .

For each padded message block, the JH mode of operation iteratively XORs the incoming $4nm$-bit input message block M_i into the left half of the state, applies the permutation $P : GF(2)^{8nm} \to GF(2)^{8nm}$ to the internal state and XORs M_i into its right half. After all the message blocks have been processed, the right half of the last internal state value is the final message digest and therefore our construction produces a $4nm$-bit hash. It is summarized as follows:

$$Padded\ Input = M_0, M_1, \ldots, M_{N-1}$$
$$(H_{0,L}, H_{0,R}) = IV$$
For $i = 0$ to $N - 1$:
$$(H_{i+1,L}, H_{i+1,R}) = P((M_i \oplus H_{i,L}, H_{i,R})) \oplus (0, M_i)$$
$$Hash = H_{N,R}$$

where $M_i \in GF(2)^{4nm}, (H_{i,L}, H_{i,R}) \in GF(2)^{8nm}$ and N is the total number of padded message blocks. A diagram of our JH mode of operation is shown in Figure 3 in Appendix A.

Using appropriate parameters m and n such that m is even and m divides n, we will be able to construct a wide range of hash functions of different output sizes:

128-bit SPN-Hash : $m = 4, n = 8$
256-bit SPN-Hash : $m = 8, n = 8$
512-bit SPN-Hash : $m = 8, n = 16$

3.1   The Internal Permutation P

The $8nm$-bit permutation P iterates a round function for 10 rounds. Its internal state can be represented by an $n \times m$ matrix of 8-bit cells, where n is the number of bytes in a bundle, and m is the number of bundles. Here, each column can be viewed as a bundle consisting of n bytes. In each round, there is a substitution layer, followed by an MDS layer, a generalized optimal diffusion layer, and lastly, an XOR with a round constant. Thus, the linear transformation layer of the SPN structure introduced in Section 2 is actually a composition of the MDS layer and the generalized optimal diffusion layer while the "round keys" of the SPN structure are taken to be the round dependant constants. A diagram of the permutation function P is shown in Figure 4 in Appendix A.

The Substitution Layer σ. takes in a $8nm$-bit input and splits it into nm bytes. It then applies the AES 8-bit S-box [15] to each of these bytes in parallel. This is chosen due to its low maximum differential and linear approximation probabilities of 2^{-6}, which strengthens resistance against differential and linear attacks. In hardware, it is possible to achieve a very compact implementation of the AES S-box using "tower-field" arithmetic, as proposed in [12]. In software, one could use the Intel AES-NI instruction set [14] for efficient implementation.

The MDS Layer θ. combines consecutive n bytes into bundles and applies on each of these m bundles an MDS transformation described in Section 3.3.

The Generalized Optimal Diffusion Layer π. is a permutation of bytes that achieves good spreading effect. It is an instantiation of the generalized optimal diffusion which we define in Section 3.2. We write this layer π as $(\pi_1, \pi_2, \ldots, \pi_n)$, where $0 \le \pi_i \le m - 1$. This notation indicates that row i is rotated by π_i positions to the left:

128-bit SPN-Hash: $\pi = (0, 0, 1, 1, 2, 2, 3, 3)$
256-bit SPN-Hash: $\pi = (0, 1, 2, 3, 4, 5, 6, 7)$
512-bit SPN-Hash: $\pi = (0, 0, 1, 1, 2, 2, 3, 3, 4, 4, 5, 5, 6, 6, 7, 7)$

These byte permutations are indeed generalized optimal diffusions since exactly n/m bytes from each column is sent to each of the m columns.

The Round Constant $RCon_i$. that is XOR-ed with the state is different for every round i. This is to defend against slide attacks [10,11] and to prevent fixed points present over reduced rounds from being propagated to the entire permutation P. Each $RCon_i$ can be viewed as an $n \times m$ matrix A, where $A_{x,y}$ ($0 \le x < n$, $0 \le y < m$) denotes the entry in row x and column y. Then for $RCon_i$ used in round i,

$$A_{x,y} = \begin{cases} y \oplus i & \text{if } x = 0 \\ 0 & \text{otherwise,} \end{cases}$$

where i is the round number viewed as an 8-bit value. These values of round constants are chosen as they are light in hardware.

3.2 Generalized Optimal Diffusion

Definition 6. Generalized Optimal Diffusion: *Let m divide n. We consider a concatenation of n bytes as a* bundle *and we consider a concatenation of m bundles as a* block. *A linear transform, π, mapping a block of m bundles to m bundles is called a (m, n)-*generalized optimal diffusion *if for each input bundle of a block, n/m bytes of that input bundle is mapped to each of the m output bundles.*

Our (m, n)-generalized optimal diffusion is a generalization of the optimal diffusion layer used in the wide-trail strategy of Rijmen and Daemen [15]. The latter corresponds to the case $m = n$ and the ShiftRows function in AES is a particular instantiation of it. For our hash function design, m must be even and m must divide n.

The following two results compute the maximum differential probability of SPN-Hash. Their proofs can be found in Appendix ??.

Theorem 3. *Let $\theta : [GF(2^8)^n]^m \rightarrow [GF(2^8)^n]^m$ be an MDS layer formed by concatenating m $n \times n$ MDS transforms over $GF(2^8)$. Let $\pi : [GF(2^8)^n]^m \rightarrow [GF(2^8)^n]^m$ be a (m, n)-generalized optimal diffusion mapping m bundles to m bundles. Then $\pi \circ \theta \circ \pi$ is a $m \times m$ MDS transform over $GF(2^{8n})$.*

Theorem 4. *The probability of any non-zero input-output differential for the internal permutation P described in Section 3.1 is upper bounded by*

$$\left(126 \times (2^{-7})^{n+1} + (2^{-6})^{n+1}\right)^m.$$

3.3 MDS Layer

The MDS layer provides an independent linear mixing of each column. In the following, we describe the mixing function of each column and show that it is indeed an MDS transform.

128- and 256-bit SPN-Hash. In [18], the authors proposed a method for generating the 8×8 MDS transform over $GF(2^4)$ in a serial way that is very compact. However, it is difficult to find an 8×8 serialized MDS matrix over $GF(2^8)$ using the exhaustive search method of [18]. Thus, we show here a way to construct such a matrix using two parallel copies of the PHOTON 8×8 serialized MDS matrix[2] over $GF(2^4)$ [18, Appendix C]. This method of construction, similar to

---

[2] We use PHOTON 's serialized matrix as we verified that it has the lowest binary weight over $GF(2^4)$.

the one used for the MDS layer of ECHO [5], produces an MDS transform that is very lightweight as compared to, for example, the 8×8 matrices[3] over $GF(2^8)$ used in WHIRLPOOL [4] or GRØSTL [17].

In what follows, we describe this MDS transform for 128- and 256-bit SPN-Hash. Label the 8 bytes in each column as $a_1, a_2, \ldots, a_8$. We may write each byte as a concatenation of two 4-bit values, $a_i = a_i^L \parallel a_i^R$. Let $a^L = (a_1^L, a_2^L, \ldots, a_8^L)$ and $a^R = (a_1^R, a_2^R, \ldots, a_8^R)$. Let Q be the 8×8 MDS matrix over $GF(2^4)$ used in the PHOTON [18, Appendix C] hash function, i.e.

$$Q = (A_{256})^8 = \begin{pmatrix} 0 & 1 & 0 & 0 & 0 & 0 & 0 & 0 \\ 0 & 0 & 1 & 0 & 0 & 0 & 0 & 0 \\ 0 & 0 & 0 & 1 & 0 & 0 & 0 & 0 \\ 0 & 0 & 0 & 0 & 1 & 0 & 0 & 0 \\ 0 & 0 & 0 & 0 & 0 & 1 & 0 & 0 \\ 0 & 0 & 0 & 0 & 0 & 0 & 1 & 0 \\ 0 & 0 & 0 & 0 & 0 & 0 & 0 & 1 \\ 2 & 4 & 2 & 11 & 2 & 8 & 5 & 6 \end{pmatrix}^8 = \begin{pmatrix} 2 & 4 & 2 & 11 & 2 & 8 & 5 & 6 \\ 12 & 9 & 8 & 13 & 7 & 7 & 5 & 2 \\ 4 & 4 & 13 & 13 & 9 & 4 & 13 & 9 \\ 1 & 6 & 5 & 1 & 12 & 13 & 15 & 14 \\ 15 & 12 & 9 & 13 & 14 & 5 & 14 & 13 \\ 9 & 14 & 5 & 15 & 4 & 12 & 9 & 6 \\ 12 & 2 & 2 & 10 & 3 & 1 & 1 & 14 \\ 15 & 1 & 13 & 10 & 5 & 10 & 2 & 3 \end{pmatrix}$$

The matrix Q is chosen as it can be implemented with a very low area footprint in hardware. This is due to the shifting property of A which simply updates the last cell of the column vector with a linear combination of all the vector components, and then rotates the vector by one position towards the top. The MDS layer is thus composed of 8 applications of A to the input column vector. This allows reuse of existing memory without need for temporary storage or additional control logic. Furthermore, the hash function using Q can be implemented efficiently in software using precomputed tables that combine the S-box and matrix coefficients.

We compute $b^L = Q \cdot a^L = (b_1^L, b_2^L, \ldots, b_8^L)$ and $b^R = Q \cdot a^R = (b_1^R, b_2^R, \ldots, b_8^R)$. For field multiplication over $GF(2^4)$, the irreducible polynomial $x^4 + x + 1$ is chosen with compactness as the main criterion. Then the output of the local diffusion layer is taken to be $(b_1, b_2, \ldots, b_8)$, where each b_i is a concatenation of the two 4-bit values, $b_i = b_i^L \parallel b_i^R$.

It can be shown that this transform is indeed MDS over $GF(2^8)$. Suppose the input a is non-zero. Then at least one of a^L or a^R is non-zero. Without loss of generality, suppose a^L is non-zero. Since Q is MDS, this means that the number of non-zero 4-bit values in (a^L, b^L) is at least 9. Hence, the number of non-zero bytes in (a, b) is at least 9.

512-Bit SPN-Hash. The choice of matrix for the 16×16 MDS is left open to the reader. One possibility is to use the matrix proposed by Nakahara et al. in [20]. Note that Nakahara et al.'s matrix may not be lightweight due to its large size necessitating a large number of primitive operations. However, this is not an issue since it is unlikely that a 512-bit hash function will be used for lightweight purposes.

---

[3] A comparison of their hardware estimations can be found in Section 5.2.

4   Security Analysis of SPN-Hash

In this section, we give a summary of our security analysis results against various attacks [4].

4.1   Differential Collision Attack

We analyzed the security of SPN-Hash against differential collision attacks. While some hash functions such as ECHO [5] do provide upper bounds on the maximum differential probability for a certain number of rounds, in actual fact, one has to *sum the maximum differential probability bound over all the possible colliding output differences* for a sharper estimation of the collision resistance of a hash function. To the best of our knowledge, no known hash function has yet provided such a collision resistance proof.

Let $\Delta Input$ denote the input differential and $\Delta Output$ be the output differential of the 4 last rounds of the SPN-Hash internal permutation. A collision for the hash function can occur either by an internal collision (a collision on the full $8nm$-bit internal state) or by an external collision during the last iteration (a collision on the right side of the $8nm$-bit internal state, the left side being truncated before outputing the hash value).

In the case of an external collision, this corresponds to P having an output differential of the form $(\Delta x, \Delta M) \in GF(2)^{4nm} \times GF(2)^{4nm}$, where XOR with the message difference ΔM in the right half will give a zero difference. Then we can show that $Pr(External\ Collision) < 2^{4nm} \times \left[(2^{-6n})(2^{-n} + 2^{-6}) \right]^m < 2^{-2nm}$, where the complexity of a generic birthday attack is $2^{4nm/2} = 2^{2nm}$.

In the case of an internal collision on the $8nm$-bit permutation P, since there is no truncation, the differential probability is given by $Pr(\Delta Input \xrightarrow{4R} (0, \Delta M_i))$ for all possible message differences ΔM_i. By Theorem 4 and in the same way as the computation above, we can show that this is lower than 2^{-2nm}, the complexity of a generic birthday attack for the hash function.

Applying these bounds, we can conclude that the differential collision probabilities of 128-bit, 256-bit, and 512-bit SPN-Hash are upper bounded by $2^{-86.73} < 2^{-64}$, $2^{-173} < 2^{-128}$, and $2^{-303.99} < 2^{-256}$ respectively. This means that a differential collision attack will not perform better than a generic birthday attack.

In summary, we are able to show that SPN-Hash can provide good maximum differential probability upper bounds for 4 rounds of its internal permutation and that its operating mode allows us to go further to prove that the sum of all colliding differential probabilities is still much lower than what an attacker would get with a generic birthday collision attack.

4.2   (Second)-Preimage Attack

In the JH mode of operation, there is an XOR of the message in the right half at the end of the permutation to make the meet-in-the-middle (MITM)

---

[4] A full description of the security analysis can be found on the eprint archive at http://eprint.iacr.org.

attacks, originally applicable to the Sponge construction, invalid. This MITM attack on the Sponge construction can easily be modified into a second pre-image attack, which is also defeated by the feedforward XOR in the JH mode of operation.

The preimage attack against the JH-512 hash function by Bhattacharyya et al. [7] has time and memory complexity 2^{507}, which remains a theoretical result because the complexity is of the same magnitude as brute force search. Moreover, a generic time-memory trade-off (TMTO) attack will perform much better with 2^{512} pre-computation complexity, 2^{507} memory, and 2^{10} time complexity.

4.3   Rebound Attack - Distinguishing Attack on Permutation P

We analyzed the security of our internal permutations against the latest rebound-like attack [25] which uses the non-full-active Super S-box cryptanalysis technique. More precisely, we present distinguishing attacks on three versions of the internal permutation P for 8 out of 10 rounds. For the 256-bit permutation P, the 8-round attack requires time 2^{56} and memory 2^{16}. For the 512-bit permutation P, the 8-round attack requires time 2^{48} and memory 2^{8}, while for the 1024-bit permutation P, the 8-round attack requires time 2^{88} and memory 2^{16}. In comparison, the complexity of attacking an ideal permutation is 2^{64}, 2^{96} and 2^{256} for 256-bit, 512-bit, and 1024-bit permutations P respectively.

To the best of our knowledge, the differential paths presented are among the longest paths with the least complexities. Since P comprises ten round functions, the distinguishing attacks do not threaten the security of the hash function.

4.4   Exploiting the MDS Layer Structure for 128- and 256-bit SPN-Hash

Since the MDS layer is built by applying a diffusion matrix over $GF(2^4)$ two times independently, an attacker could try to exploit this special structure in a truncated differential attack by forcing the differences at some stage to remain on the left or on the right side of the bytes processed. This observation was used in the first attacks [24] on the ECHO hash function.

However, we believe such a strategy would very likely fail because this right/left property would be destroyed by the application of the AES S-box. Alternatively, forcing this property to be maintained for each active byte through the S-box layer would imply a big cost for the attacker, bigger than the gain from the truncated differential transitions. This has been confirmed by experiments, as there is no strong bias through the AES S-box in order to reach an all-right or an all-left difference (forward or backward). In the case of ECHO this is not true since the 128-bit ECHO S-box is implemented by two AES rounds, for which forcing good truncated differential paths at no cost is easy.

5   Implementation

5.1   Software Performance

Due to its similarity with GRØSTL concerning the construction of the internal permutation, it is interesting to analyze SPN–Hash's software speed in the light of this SHA-3 candidate. The internal permutation of 256-bit SPN–Hash is comparable with GRØSTL-256 since their (individual) internal permutation are of the same size, and their amount of message bits per call to the internal permutation is the same (256-bit SPN–Hash compression function processes 256 bits message in 10 round operations, compared to 512-bit message in 20 very similar round operations by GRØSTL-256). The round function of these two hash functions should take about similar amount of time due to: 1) The equal number of substitution operations using the same AES sbox; 2) The speed of MDS multiplication is independent of the MDS coefficients in most table-based implementations; 3) The ShiftByte in GRØSTL is done together with step 2 in table-based implementations; 4) The round constants are a bit simpler than those in GRØSTL; and 5) There are three times $\oplus$ for 512 bits in GRØSTL and twice 256-bit $\oplus$ in 256-bit SPN hash. We did a simple and unoptimized implementation based on table lookups, which turns to be 34 cycles per byte on a Intel(R) Xeon(R) CPU E5640 clocked at 2.67GHz. We believe that there remains an important room for improvements by implementing SPN–Hash with optimized assembly instructions. Similar comparison argument applies when one considers implementations with the AES new instruction set, while GRØSTL-256 runs at 12 cycles per byte with internal parallelization of the two permutations P and Q, we expect SPN–Hash-256 to run at 12 to 24 cycles per byte mostly due to the fact that similiar parallelization is not possible. Note that the 128-bit SPN–Hash shall run as fast as the 256-bit version, since its compression function takes half the message bits, and uses roughly half the amount of operations. Test vectors are provided in Appendix Table 2.

5.2   Hardware Performance

We have implemented 128-bit and 256-bit SPN hash in VHDL and used *Synopsys DesignCompiler A-2007.12-SP1* to synthesize it to the *Virtual Silicon* (VST) standard cell library *UMCL18G212T3*, which is based on the *UMC L180 0.18μm 1P6M* logic process with a typical voltage of 1.8 V. We used *Synopsys Power Compiler* version *A-2007.12-SP1* to estimate the power consumption of our ASIC implementations. For synthesis and for power estimation we advised the compiler to keep the hierarchy and use a clock frequency of 100 KHz.

Table 1 in Appendix A compares our implementations of SPN hash with the remaining five SHA-3 candidates with regards to area, latency and a FOM proposed by [2]. In order to have a fair comparison, we only include figures for fully-autonomous low-area ASIC implementations and omit figures for implementations that are optimized for high throughput. Among the SHA-3 candidates BLAKE, GRØSTL, and SKEIN, 256-bit SPN–Hash is by far the most compact proposal. Though it has only the second highest FOM, our estimates for a 64-bit datapath implementation indicate that it can achieve the highest FOM, while still being 35% smaller than the most compact SHA-3 candidate.

References

1. Augot, D., Finiasz, M., Gaborit, P., Manuel, S., Sendrier, N.: SHA-3 Proposal: FSB. Submission to NIST (2008)
2. Aumasson, J.-P., Henzen, L., Meier, W., Naya-Plasencia, M.: QUARK: A Lightweight Hash. In: Mangard, S., Standaert, F.-X. (eds.) CHES 2010. LNCS, vol. 6225, pp. 1–15. Springer, Heidelberg (2010), http://131002.net/quark/
3. Aumasson, J.-P., Henzen, L., Meier, W., Phan, R.C.-W.: SHA-3 Proposal BLAKE. Candidate to the NIST Hash Competition (2008), http://131002.net/blake/
4. Barreto, P., Rijmen, V.: The Whirlpool Hashing Function, http://www.larc.usp.br/~pbarreto/WhirlpoolPage.html
5. Benadjila, R., Billet, O., Gilbert, H., Macario-Rat, G., Peyrin, T., Robshaw, M., Seurin, Y.: SHA-3 Proposal: ECHO. Submission to NIST (2009) (updated)
6. Bertoni, G., Daemen, J., Peeters, M., Van Assche, G.: Sponge Functions. In: ECRYPT Hash Workshop (2007)
7. Bhattacharyya, R., Mandal, A., Nandi, M.: Security Analysis of the Mode of JH Hash Function. In: Hong, S., Iwata, T. (eds.) FSE 2010. LNCS, vol. 6147, pp. 168–191. Springer, Heidelberg (2010)
8. Billet, O., Robshaw, M.J.B., Peyrin, T.: On Building Hash Functions from Multivariate Quadratic Equations. In: Pieprzyk, J., Ghodosi, H., Dawson, E. (eds.) ACISP 2007. LNCS, vol. 4586, pp. 82–95. Springer, Heidelberg (2007)
9. Biryukov, A., Khovratovich, D., Nikolić, I.: Distinguisher and Related-Key Attack on the Full AES-256. In: Halevi, S. (ed.) CRYPTO 2009. LNCS, vol. 5677, pp. 231–249. Springer, Heidelberg (2009)
10. Biryukov, A., Wagner, D.: Slide Attacks. In: Knudsen, L.R. (ed.) FSE 1999. LNCS, vol. 1636, pp. 245–259. Springer, Heidelberg (1999)
11. Biryukov, A., Wagner, D.: Advanced Slide Attacks. In: Preneel, B. (ed.) EUROCRYPT 2000. LNCS, vol. 1807, pp. 589–606. Springer, Heidelberg (2000)
12. Canright, D.: A Very Compact S-Box for AES. In: Rao, J.R., Sunar, B. (eds.) CHES 2005. LNCS, vol. 3659, pp. 441–455. Springer, Heidelberg (2005); The HDL specification is available at the author's official webpage http://faculty.nps.edu/drcanrig/pub/index.html
13. Contini, S., Lenstra, A.K., Steinfeld, R.: VSH, an Efficient and Provable Collision-Resistant Hash Function. In: Vaudenay, S. (ed.) EUROCRYPT 2006. LNCS, vol. 4004, pp. 165–182. Springer, Heidelberg (2006)
14. Intel Corporation. Advanced Encryption Standard (AES) Instruction Set (October 30, 2008), http://softwarecommunity.intel.com/articles/eng/3788.htm
15. Daemen, J., Rijmen, V.: The Design of Rijndael: AES - The Advanced Encryption Standard. Springer (2002)
16. Ferguson, N., Lucks, S., Schneier, B., Whiting, D., Bellare, M., Kohno, T., Callas, J., Walker, J.: The Skein Hash Function Family. Submission to NIST, Round 2 (2009)
17. Gauravaram, P., Knudsen, L.R., Matusiewicz, K., Mendel, F., Rechberger, C., Schlaffer, M., Thomsen, S.S.: Grøstl addendum. Submission to NIST (2009) (updated)

18. Guo, J., Peyrin, T., Poschmann, A.: The PHOTON Family of Lightweight Hash Functions. In: Rogaway, P. (ed.) CRYPTO 2011. LNCS, vol. 6841, pp. 222–239. Springer, Heidelberg (2011)
19. Henzen, L., Aumasson, J.-P., Meier, W., Phan, R.C.W.: VLSI Characterization of the Cryptographic Hash Function BLAKE. IEEE Transactions on Very Large Scale Integration (VLSI) Systems (99), 1–9
20. Nakahara Jr., J., Abrahão, É.: A New Involutary MDS Matrix for AES. International Journal of Network Security 9(2), 109–116 (2009)
21. Lamberger, M., Mendel, F., Rechberger, C., Rijmen, V., Schläffer, M.: Rebound Distinguishers: Results on the Full Whirlpool Compression Function. In: Matsui, M. (ed.) ASIACRYPT 2009. LNCS, vol. 5912, pp. 126–143. Springer, Heidelberg (2009)
22. Menezes, A.J., van Oorschot, P.C., Vanstone, S.A.: Handbook of Applied Cryptography. CRC Press (1996)
23. Park, S., Sung, S.H., Lee, S., Lim, J.: Improving the Upper Bound on the Maximum Differential and the Maximum Linear Hull Probability for SPN Structures and AES. In: Johansson, T. (ed.) FSE 2003. LNCS, vol. 2887, pp. 247–260. Springer, Heidelberg (2003)
24. Peyrin, T.: Improved Differential Attacks for ECHO and Grøstl. In: Rabin, T. (ed.) CRYPTO 2010. LNCS, vol. 6223, pp. 370–392. Springer, Heidelberg (2010)
25. Sasaki, Y., Li, Y., Wang, L., Sakiyama, K., Ohta, K.: Non-full-active Super-Sbox Analysis: Applications to ECHO and Grøstl. In: Abe, M. (ed.) ASIACRYPT 2010. LNCS, vol. 6477, pp. 38–55. Springer, Heidelberg (2010)
26. Shannon, C.: Communication Theory of Secrecy System. Bell System Technical Journal 28, 656–715 (1949)
27. Tillich, S., Feldhofer, M., Issovits, W., Kern, T., Kureck, H., Mühlberghuber, M., Neubauer, G., Reiter, A., Köfler, A., Mayrhofer, M.: Compact Hardware Implementations of the SHA-3 Candidates Arirang, Blake, Grøstl, and Skein. IACR ePrint archive, Report 2009/349 (2009)
28. Wu, H.J.: The Hash Function JH. Submission to NIST (September 2009) (updated), http://ehash.iaik.tugraz.at/uploads/1/1d/Jh20090915.pdf

A   Tables and Figures

Table 1. Comparison of Low-Area Hardware implementations of SPN hash and a selection of SHA-3 finalists

Digest size	Alg.	Ref.	Msg. size	Technology	Area [GE]	Latency [clk]	T'put@100KHz [kbps]	FOM [nbps/GE²]
128	SPN-Hash-128		256	UMC 0.18	2 777	710	36.1	2 338
	SPN-Hash-128		256	*estimate*	4 600	230	55.7	2 627
256	SPN-Hash-256		512	UMC 0.18	4 625	1 430	35.8	837
	SPN-Hash-256		512	*estimate*	8 500	230	111.3	1 541
	BLAKE-32	[19]	512	UMC 0.18	13 575	816	62.8	340
	GRØSTL-224/256	[27]	512	AMS 0.35	14 622	196	261.2	1 222
	SKEIN-256-256	[27]	256	AMS 0.35	12 890	1 034	24.8	149

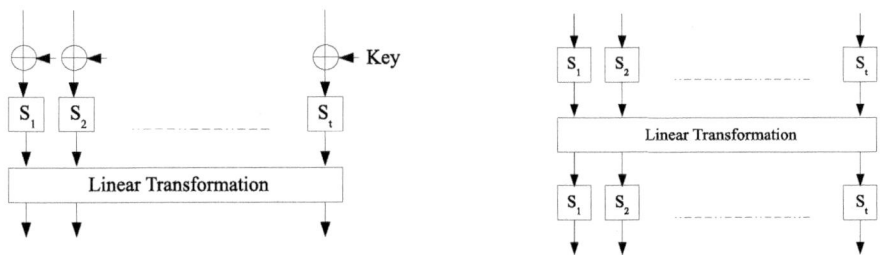

Fig. 1. One round of a SPN structure   **Fig. 2.** The SDS function

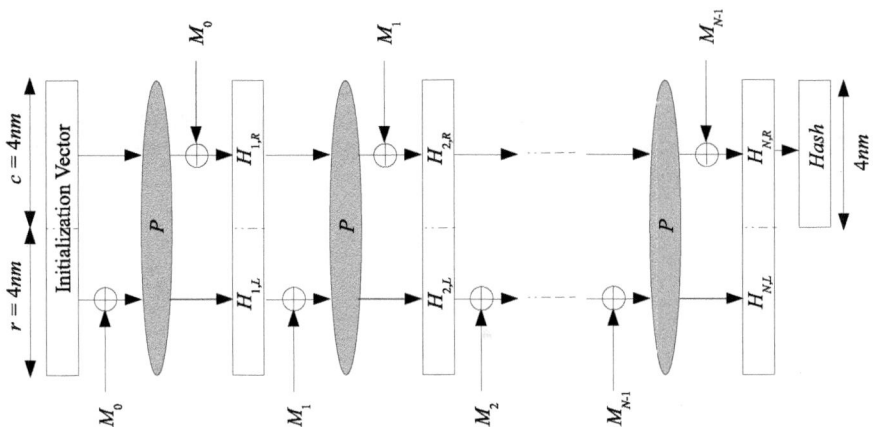

Fig. 3. The JH mode of operation

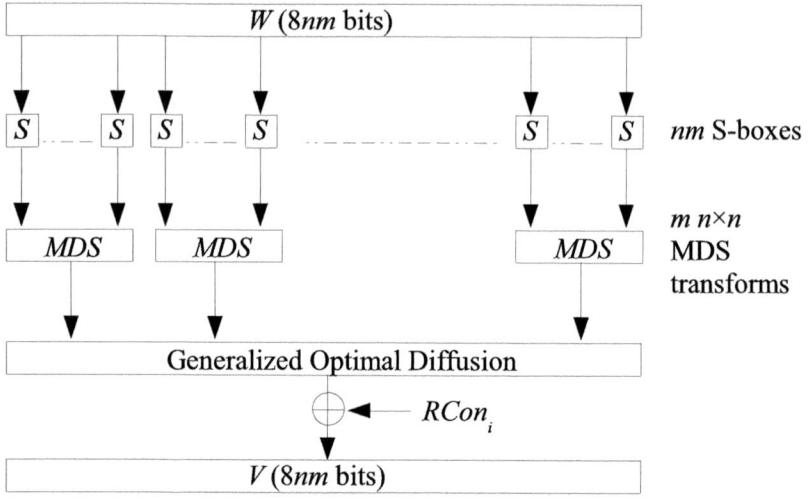

Fig. 4. The round function in permutation P

B   Test Vector

We hash the message "SPN-Hash: Improving the Provable Resistance Against Differential Collision Attacks" with three variants of the SPN-Hash family, and the following are digests generated by our reference implementation.

Table 2. Test vectors for three variants of SPN-Hash family

SPN-Hash-128	2b021df78220afd2a41fa3592dc7d284
SPN-Hash-256	eabd18110d48e81d0663a7034b265462bf93f8019ca292e58ec1d830f90d67c5
SPN-Hash-512	f3e4a3dcc44acb2cf4d6f5f67bd8ce50ef030f55e0189a322136b5fc46af3cf5 e071f1ee9bf1851bbd854540da1ccc496d679b43090f8e24f486d6866092ac02

Security Analysis and Comparison of the SHA-3 Finalists BLAKE, Grøstl, JH, Keccak, and Skein

Elena Andreeva, Bart Mennink, Bart Preneel, and Marjan Škrobot

Dept. Electrical Engineering, ESAT/COSIC and IBBT
Katholieke Universiteit Leuven, Belgium
{elena.andreeva,bart.mennink,bart.preneel}@esat.kuleuven.be,
marjanskrobot@yahoo.com

Abstract. In 2007, the US National Institute for Standards and Technology announced a call for the design of a new cryptographic hash algorithm in response to the vulnerabilities identified in widely employed hash functions, such as MD5 and SHA-1. NIST received many submissions, 51 of which got accepted to the first round. At present, 5 candidates are left in the third round of the competition. At NIST's second SHA-3 Candidate Conference 2010, Andreeva et al. provided a provable security classification of the second round SHA-3 candidates in the ideal model. In this work, we revisit this classification for the five SHA-3 finalists. We evaluate recent provable security results on the candidates, and resolve remaining open problems for Grøstl, JH, and Skein.

1 Introduction

Hash functions are a building block for numerous cryptographic applications. In 2004 a series of attacks by Wang et al. [41,42] showed security vulnerabilities in the design of the widely adopted hash function SHA-1. In response, the US National Institute for Standards and Technology (NIST) recommended the replacement of SHA-1 by the SHA-2 hash function family and announced a call for the design of a new SHA-3 hash algorithm [34]. The call prescribes that SHA-3 must allow for message digests of length $224, 256, 384$ and 512 bits, it should be efficient, and most importantly it should provide an adequate level of security. Five candidates have reached the third and final round of the competition: BLAKE [6], Grøstl [25], JH [43], Keccak [9], and Skein [22]. These candidates are under active evaluation by the cryptographic community. As a result of comparative analysis, several classifications of the SHA-3 candidates, mostly concentrated on hardware performance, appeared in the literature [23,27,40]. At NIST's second SHA-3 Candidate Conference 2010, Andreeva et al. [4,5] provided a classification based on the specified by NIST security criteria. Below we recall the security requirements by NIST in their call for the SHA-3 hash function.

NIST Security Requirements. The future SHA-3 hash function is required to satisfy the following security requirements [34]: (i) at least one variant of the hash function must securely support HMAC and randomized hashing. Next, for

A. Mitrokotsa and S. Vaudenay (Eds.): AFRICACRYPT 2012, LNCS 7374, pp. 287–305, 2012.

all n-bit digest values, the hash function must provide (ii) preimage resistance of approximately n bits, (iii) second preimage resistance of approximately $n - L$ bits, where the first preimage is of length at most 2^L blocks, (iv) collision resistance of approximately $n/2$ bits, and (v) it must be resistant to the length-extension attack. Finally, (vi) for any $m \leq n$, the hash function specified by taking a fixed subset of m bits of the function's output is required to satisfy properties (ii)-(v) with n replaced by m.

Our Contributions. We revisit the provable security classification of Andreeva et al. [4,5], focussing on the five remaining SHA-3 finalists. More concretely, we reconsider the preimage, second preimage and collision resistance (security requirements (ii)-(iv)) for the $n = 256$ and $n = 512$ variants of the five candidates. We also include their indifferentiability security results. The security analysis in this work is realized in the ideal model, where one or more of the underlying integral building blocks (e.g., the underlying block cipher or permutation(s)) are assumed to be ideal, i.e. random primitives.

In our updated security classification of the SHA-3 finalists, we include the recent full security analysis of BLAKE by Andreeva et al. and Chang et al. [2,18], and the collision security result of JH by Lee and Hong [29]. Despite these recent advances, there still remain open questions in the earlier security analysis and classification of [4,5]. The main contribution of this work is to address these questions. More concretely, we do so by either providing new security results or improving some of the existing security bounds. We list our findings for the relevant hash functions below and refer to Table 1 for the summary of all results.

- Grøstl. We analyze Grøstl with respect to its second preimage security due to the lack of an optimal security result as indicated in [4,5]. While optimal collision and preimage security are achieved following a property-preservation argument, this is not true for the second preimage security. Another way (than property-preservation) to derive security bounds for hash function properties is via an indifferentiability result (Thm. 2 in [4,5]). Following this approach, an approximately 128-bit and 256-bit second preimage resistance bound is obtained, where the output size of the Grøstl hash function is 256 or 512 bits, respectively. This result is unfortunately not optimal. In this work we take a different approach to improve these bounds, and we provide a direct second preimage security proof for the Grøstl hash function. Our proof indicates that Grøstl, in addition to collision and preimage security, is also optimally $((256 - L)$-bit and $(512 - L)$-bit, respectively) second preimage secure, where 2^L is the length of the first preimage in blocks;
- JH. The existing bounds on JH for second and preimage security are derived via the indifferentiability result of [13] and are not optimal; approximately 170-bit security for both the 256 and 512 variants. To improve these results, we follow the direct approach and derive bounds for both security properties in the ideal permutation model. As a result we achieve optimal 256-bit security for the 256 variant of the hash function. The new bound for the 512 variant is still not optimal (as is the existing bound), but improved to 256-bit

Table 1. Preimage, second preimage, collision, and indifferentiability security results of the SHA-3 finalists in bits. Here, l and m denote the chaining value and the message input sizes, respectively. Regarding second preimage resistance, the first preimage is of length 2^L blocks. The ideality assumptions are "E ideal" for BLAKE and Skein, "P, Q ideal" for Grøstl, and "P ideal" for JH and Keccak. The results in **bold** are presented in this work. A more detailed summary can be found in the full version of this paper.

	l	m	pre	sec	coll	indiff		l	m	pre	sec	coll	indiff
BLAKE-256	256	512	256	256	128	128	BLAKE-512	512	1024	512	512	256	256
Grøstl-256	512	512	256	**256−L**	128	128	Grøstl-512	1024	1024	512	**512−L**	256	256
JH-256	1024	512	**256**	**256**	128	256	JH-512	1024	512	**256**	**256**	256	256
Keccak-256	1600	1088	256	256	128	256	Keccak-512	1600	576	512	512	256	512
Skein-256	512	512	256	**256**	128	256	Skein-512	512	512	512	**512**	256	256
NIST's requirements [34]			256	256−L	128	—	NIST's requirements [34]			512	512−L	256	—

security. Using different proof techniques, it may be possible to improve the (second) preimage bound for JH-512, yet we note that by a preimage attack of [13] the maximum amount of security is upper bounded by 507-bit;[1]

- Skein. By the implications of the existing indifferentiability results of Skein we can directly conclude an optimal 256-bit second preimage security for the 256 version of the hash function. This is however not true for the 512 version, which offers only 256-bit security following the indifferentiability argument. We, thus, analyze the generic second preimage security of Skein in the ideal block cipher model and obtain optimal bounds for both its versions, confirming the second preimage result for the 256 version and optimally improving the bound for the 512 version.

The results of Table 1 show that all candidates, with the exception of the (second) preimage security of JH-512, achieve optimal collision, second and preimage security for both their 256 and 512 variants. The optimal results refer to the general iterative structure of all the algorithms. The analysis in all cases is performed in the ideal setting. But more importantly, we claim that the provided comparison is sufficiently fair due to the fact that the ideality assumption is hypothesized on basic underlying primitives, such as block ciphers and permutations, as opposed to higher level compression function building blocks.

On the other hand, while optimality results hold for the five the hash function finalists, the security of their compression functions again in the ideal model differs. The security here varies from trivially insecure compression functions for JH and Keccak to optimally secure ones for BLAKE, Grøstl and Skein. We want to note that the latter remark does not reflect any security criteria indicated in the security requirements of NIST. In addition to the classical notions of collision, second and preimage security, we also investigate the notion of indifferentiability [31]. Indifferentiability encompasses structural attacks, such as the length

---

[1] In independent concurrent research, Moody et al. [33] have reconsidered the indifferentiability bound on JH and improved it to 256-bit security, therewith confirming our findings on the (second) preimage resistance of JH.

extension attack in single round interactive protocols [36], and is therefore an important security criteria satisfied by all five candidates. We include the indifferentiability notion not only because it is relevant by itself, but it is also an important tool to derive further security results. JH and Skein offer 256-bit indifferentiability security for both their variants, and BLAKE and Grøstl offer 128-bit and 256-bit security for their respective 256 and 512 variants. Keccak provides higher indifferentiability guarantees: 256-bit and 512-bit, respectively, and that is achieved by increasing the iterated state size to 1600 bits as compared to sizes from 256 bits to 1024 bits for the other hash function candidates.

Outline. Section 2 briefly covers the notation, and the basic principles of hash function design. In Sects. 3-7, we consider the five SHA-3 finalists from a provable security point of view. We give a high level algorithmic description of each hash function, and discuss the existing and new security results. We conclude the paper with Sect. 8 and give some final remarks on the security comparison.

2   Preliminaries

For $n \in \mathbb{N}$, we denote by $\mathbb{Z}_2^n$ the set of bit strings of length n, and by $(\mathbb{Z}_2^n)^*$ the set of strings of length a positive multiple of n bits. We denote by $\mathbb{Z}_2^*$ the set of bit strings of arbitrary length. For two bit strings x, y, $x\|y$ denotes their concatenation and $x \oplus y$ their bitwise XOR. For $m, n \in \mathbb{N}$ we denote by $\langle m \rangle_n$ the encoding of m as an n-bit string. The function $\mathrm{chop}_n(x)$ takes the n leftmost bits of a bit string x. We denote by $\mathrm{Func}(m, n)$ the set of all functions $f : \mathbb{Z}_2^m \to \mathbb{Z}_2^n$. A random oracle [8] is a function which provides a random output for each new query. A random m-to-n-bit function is a function sampled uniformly at random from $\mathrm{Func}(m, n)$.

Throughout, we use a unified notation for all candidates. The value n denotes the output size of the hash function, l the size of the chaining value, and m the number of message bits compressed in one iteration of the compression function. A padded message is always parsed as a sequence of $k \geq 1$ message blocks of length m bits: $(M_1, \ldots, M_k)$.

2.1   Preimage, Second Preimage and Collision Security

In our analysis we model the adversary $\mathcal{A}$ as a probabilistic algorithm with oracle access to a randomly sampled primitive $\mathcal{P} \xleftarrow{\$} \mathrm{Prims}$. The set Prims depends on the hash function to be analyzed. We consider information-theoretic adversaries only. This type of adversary has unbounded computational power, and its complexity is measured by the number of queries made to his oracle. The adversary can make queries to $\mathcal{P}$, which are stored in a query history $\mathcal{Q}$ as indexed elements. In the remainder, we assume that $\mathcal{Q}$ always contains the queries required for the attack and that the adversary never makes queries to which it knows the answer in advance.

Let $F : \mathbb{Z}_2^p \to \mathbb{Z}_2^n$ for $p \geq n$ be a compressing function instantiated with a randomly chosen primitive $\mathcal{P} \xleftarrow{\$} \mathrm{Prims}$. Throughout, F will either denote the compression function f or the hash function $\mathcal{H}$ specification of one of the SHA-3 finalists. For the preimage and second preimage security analysis in this work, we consider the notions of everywhere preimage and second preimage resistance [37], which guarantees security on every range (resp. domain) point.

Definition 1. *Let $p, n \in \mathbb{N}$ with $p \geq n$ and let $F : \mathbb{Z}_2^p \to \mathbb{Z}_2^n$ be a compressing function using primitive $\mathcal{P} \in \mathrm{Prims}$. The advantage of an everywhere preimage finding adversary $\mathcal{A}$ is defined as*

$$Adv_F^{\mathrm{epre}}(\mathcal{A}) = \max_{y \in \mathbb{Z}_2^n} Pr\left(\mathcal{P} \xleftarrow{\$} \mathrm{Prims}, \ z \leftarrow \mathcal{A}^{\mathcal{P}}(y) \ : \ F(z) = y \right).$$

We define by $Adv_F^{\mathrm{epre}}(q)$ the maximum advantage of any adversary making q queries to its oracles.

Definition 2. *Let $p, n \in \mathbb{N}$ with $p \geq n$ and let $F : \mathbb{Z}_2^p \to \mathbb{Z}_2^n$ be a compressing function using primitive $\mathcal{P} \in \mathrm{Prims}$. Let $\lambda \leq p$. The advantage of an everywhere second preimage finding adversary $\mathcal{A}$ is defined as*

$$Adv_F^{\mathrm{esec}[\lambda]}(\mathcal{A}) = \max_{z' \in \mathbb{Z}_2^\lambda} Pr\left(\mathcal{P} \xleftarrow{\$} \mathrm{Prims}, \ z \leftarrow \mathcal{A}^{\mathcal{P}}(z') \ : \ z \neq z' \wedge F(z) = F(z') \right).$$

We define by $Adv_F^{\mathrm{esec}[\lambda]}(q)$ the maximum advantage of any adversary making q queries to its oracles.

If F is a compression function, we require $\lambda = p$. Note that, while the length of the first preimage is of 2^L blocks following NIST's security requirements, here we bound the length by λ bits. This translates to $2^L \approx \lambda/m$, where m is the size of the message block.

We define the collision security of F as follows.

Definition 3. *Let $p, n \in \mathbb{N}$ with $p \geq n$ and let $F : \mathbb{Z}_2^p \to \mathbb{Z}_2^n$ be a compressing function using primitive $\mathcal{P} \in \mathrm{Prims}$. Fix a constant $h_0 \in \mathbb{Z}_2^n$. The advantage of a collision finding adversary $\mathcal{A}$ is defined as*

$$Adv_F^{\mathrm{col}}(\mathcal{A}) = Pr\left(\mathcal{P} \xleftarrow{\$} \mathrm{Prims}, \ z, z' \leftarrow \mathcal{A}^{\mathcal{P}} \ : \ z \neq z' \wedge F(z) \in \{F(z'), h_0\} \right).$$

We define by $Adv_F^{\mathrm{col}}(q)$ the maximum advantage of any adversary making q queries to its oracles.

If a compressing function F outputs a bit string of length n, one expects to find collisions with high probability after approximately $2^{n/2}$ queries (due to the birthday attack). Similarly, (second) preimages can be found with high probability after approximately 2^n queries[2]. Moreover, finding second preimages is provably harder than finding collisions [37].

---

[2] Kelsey and Schneier [26] describe a second preimage attack on the Merkle-Damgård hash function that requires at most approximately 2^{n-L} queries, where the first preimage is of length at most 2^L blocks. This attack does, however, not apply to all SHA-3 candidates. In particular, the wide-pipe SHA-3 candidates ($l \gg n$) remain mostly unaffected due to their increased internal state (see the remark on Thm. 3).

2.2   Indifferentiability

The indifferentiability framework introduced by Maurer et al. [31] is an extension of the classical notion of indistinguishability; it ensures that a hash function has no structural defects. We denote the indifferentiability security of a hash function $\mathcal{H}$ by $\mathbf{Adv}_{\mathcal{H}}^{\mathrm{pro}}$, maximized over all distinguishers making at most q queries of maximal length $K \geq 0$ message blocks to their oracles. We refer to Coron et al. [19] for a formal definition. An indifferentiability bound guarantees security of the hash function against specific attacks. Although recent results by Ristenpart et al. [36] show that indifferentiability does not capture all properties of a random oracle, indifferentiability still remains the best way to rule out structural attacks for a large class of hash function applications.

It has been demonstrated in [4,5] that

$$\mathbf{Adv}_{\mathcal{H}}^{\mathrm{atk}} \leq \mathbf{Pr}_{RO}^{\mathrm{atk}} + \mathbf{Adv}_{\mathcal{H}}^{\mathrm{pro}} \tag{1}$$

for any security notion atk, where $\mathbf{Pr}_{RO}^{\mathrm{atk}}$ denotes the success probability of a generic attack against $\mathcal{H}$ under atk and RO is an ideal function with the same domain and range space as $\mathcal{H}$.

2.3   Hash Function Design Strategies

In order to allow the hashing of arbitrarily long strings, all SHA-3 candidates employ a specific mode of operation. Central to all designs is the *iterated hash function principle* [28]: on input of an initialization vector IV and a message M, the iterated hash function $\mathcal{H}^f$ based on the compression function f, applies a padding mechanism pad to M resulting in $(M_1, \ldots, M_k)$, and outputs h_k where $h_0 = $ IV and $h_i = f(h_{i-1}, M_i)$ for $i = 1, \ldots, k$. This principle is also called the plain Merkle-Damgård (MD) design [20,32]. Each of the five remaining candidates is based on this design, possibly followed by a final transformation (FT), and/or a chop-function[3].

The padding function pad : $\mathbb{Z}_2^* \rightarrow (\mathbb{Z}_2^m)^*$ is an injective mapping that transforms a message of arbitrary length to a message of length a multiple of m bits (the number of message bits compressed in one compression function iteration). The padding rule is called *suffix-free* (resp. *prefix-free*) if for any distinct M, M' there exists no bit string X such that pad$(M') = X\|$pad(M) (resp. pad$(M') = $ pad$(M)\|X$). The MD design (possibly with final transformation or chop-function) using suffix-free padding preserves collision resistance [4,5]. The MD design with prefix-free padding, based on ideal compression function, is proven to be indifferentiable from a random oracle [19]. Furthermore, everywhere preimage resistance is preserved by the MD design. All candidates have a sufficiently strong padding rule (see Fig. 1). Additionally, for BLAKE and Skein, the message blocks are compressed along with specific counters or tweaks.

---

[3] The chop-function is not considered to be (a part of) a final transformation. It refers to the chopping off or discarding a specified number of bits from the output.

HAIFA Design. A concrete design based on the MD principle is the HAIFA construction by Biham and Dunkelman [14]. In HAIFA the message is padded in a specific way so as to solve some deficiencies of the original MD construction: in the iteration, each message block is accompanied with a fixed (optional) salt of s bits and a (mandatory) counter C_i of t bits. The counter C_i keeps track of the number of message bits hashed so far, and equals 0 by definition if the i-th block does not contain any message bits. Due to the properties of this counter the HAIFA padding rule is suffix- and prefix-free, and consequently the construction preserves collision resistance and the indifferentiability results of Coron et al. [19] carry over. For the HAIFA design, these indifferentiability results are improved by Bhattacharyya et al. in [12]. Furthermore, the HAIFA construction is proven optimally secure against second preimage attacks if the underlying compression function is assumed to behave ideal [17].

Wide-Pipe Design. In the wide-pipe design [30], the iterated state size is significantly larger than the final hash output: at the end of the iteration, a fraction of the output of a construction is discarded. As proved in [19], the MD construction with a distinct final transformation and/or chopping at the end is indifferentiable from a random oracle.

Sponge Functions. The sponge hash function design is a particular design by Bertoni et al. [11]. It has been generalized by Andreeva et al. [1]. Two SHA-3 finalists are known to be sponge(-like) functions, JH and Keccak.

3   BLAKE

The **BLAKE** hash function [6] is a HAIFA construction. The message blocks are accompanied with a HAIFA-counter, and the function employs a suffix- and prefix-free padding rule. The underlying compression function f is based on a block cipher $E : \mathbb{Z}_2^{2l} \times \mathbb{Z}_2^m \to \mathbb{Z}_2^{2l}$. It moreover employs an injective linear function L, and a linear function L' that XORs the first and second halves of the input. The BLAKE hash function design is given in Fig. 1.

As the mode of operation of BLAKE is based on the HAIFA structure, all security properties regarding this type (cf. Sect. 2.3) hold [14], provided the compression function is assumed to be ideal. However, as independently shown by Andreeva et al. [2] and Chang et al. [18], the BLAKE compression function shows non-random behavior: it is differentiable from a random compression function in about $2^{n/4}$ queries, making the above-mentioned security properties invalid. This attack has invalidated the results on BLAKE reported in the second round SHA-3 classification of [4,5].

The security results have been reconfirmed by Andreeva et al. [2] in the ideal cipher model. Firstly, the authors prove optimal security bounds on the compression function, $\mathbf{Adv}_f^{\mathrm{epre}} = \Theta(q/2^n)$ and $\mathbf{Adv}_f^{\mathrm{col}} = \Theta(q^2/2^n)$. In the ideal model, everywhere second preimage resistance of the compression function can be proven similar as the preimage resistance, up to a constant (the security analysis differs only in that we give the adversary one query for free). The BLAKE

BLAKE:

$(n, l, m, s, t) \in \{(256, 256, 512, 128, 64),$
$\qquad\qquad (512, 512, 1024, 256, 128)\}$
$E : \mathbb{Z}_2^{2l} \times \mathbb{Z}_2^m \to \mathbb{Z}_2^{2l}$ block cipher
$L : \mathbb{Z}_2^{l+s+t} \to \mathbb{Z}_2^{2l}, L' : \mathbb{Z}_2^{2l} \to \mathbb{Z}_2^l$ (cf. Sect. 3)
$f(h, M, S, C) =$
$\qquad L'(E_M(L(h, S, C))) \oplus h \oplus (S\|S)\}$

$\text{BLAKE}(M) = h_k$, where:
$(M_1, \ldots, M_k) \leftarrow \text{pad}_b(M); h_0 \leftarrow \text{IV}$
$S \in \mathbb{Z}_2^s; (C_i)_{i=1}^k$ HAIFA-counter
$h_i \leftarrow f(h_{i-1}, M_i, S, C_i)$ for $i = 1, \ldots, k$

Grøstl:

$(n, l, m) \in \{(256, 512, 512), (512, 1024, 1024)\}$
$P, Q : \mathbb{Z}_2^l \to \mathbb{Z}_2^l$ permutations
$f(h, M) = P(h \oplus M) \oplus Q(M) \oplus h$
$g(h) = P(h) \oplus h$

$\text{Grøstl}(M) = h$, where:
$(M_1, \ldots, M_k) \leftarrow \text{pad}_g(M); h_0 \leftarrow \text{IV}$
$h_i \leftarrow f(h_{i-1}, M_i)$ for $i = 1, \ldots, k$
$h \leftarrow \text{chop}_n(g(h_k))$

JH:

$(n, l, m) \in \{(256, 1024, 512), (512, 1024, 512)\}$
$P : \mathbb{Z}_2^l \to \mathbb{Z}_2^l$ permutation
$f(h, M) = P(h \oplus (0^{l-m}\|M)) \oplus (M\|0^{l-m})$

$\text{JH}(M) = h$, where:
$(M_1, \ldots, M_k) \leftarrow \text{pad}_j(M); h_0 \leftarrow \text{IV}$
$h_i \leftarrow f(h_{i-1}, M_i)$ for $i = 1, \ldots, k$
$h \leftarrow \text{chop}_n(h_k)$

Keccak:

$(n, l, m) \in \{(256, 1600, 1088), (512, 1600, 576)\}$
$P : \mathbb{Z}_2^l \to \mathbb{Z}_2^l$ permutation
$f(h, M) = P(h \oplus (M\|0^{l-m}))$

$\text{Keccak}(M) = h$, where:
$(M_1, \ldots, M_k) \leftarrow \text{pad}_k(M); h_0 \leftarrow \text{IV}$
$h_i \leftarrow f(h_{i-1}, M_i)$ for $i = 1, \ldots, k$
$h \leftarrow \text{chop}_n(h_k)$

Skein:

$(n, l, m) \in \{(256, 512, 512), (512, 512, 512)\}$
$E : \mathbb{Z}_2^m \times \mathbb{Z}_2^{128} \times \mathbb{Z}_2^l \to \mathbb{Z}_2^m$ tweakable block cipher
$f(h, T, M) = E_{h,T}(M) \oplus M$

$\text{Skein}(M) = h$, where:
$(M_1, \ldots, M_k) \leftarrow \text{pad}_s(M); h_0 \leftarrow \text{IV}$
$(T_i)_{i=1}^k$ round-specific tweaks
$h_i \leftarrow f(h_{i-1}, T_i, M_i)$ for $i = 1, \ldots, k$
$h \leftarrow \text{chop}_n(h_k)$

Padding functions:

$\text{pad}_b(M) = M\|10^{-|M|-t-2 \bmod m}1\| \langle |M| \rangle_t$
$\text{pad}_g(M) = M\|10^{-|M|-65 \bmod l}\| \left\langle \left\lceil \frac{|M|+65}{l} \right\rceil \right\rangle_{64}$
$\text{pad}_j(M) = M\|10^{383+(-|M| \bmod m)}\| \langle |M| \rangle_{128}$
$\text{pad}_k(M) = M\|10^{-|M|-2 \bmod m}1$
$\text{pad}_s(M) = M'\|0^{(-|M'| \bmod m)+m},$

$\quad$ where $M' = \begin{cases} M \text{ if } |M| \equiv 0 \bmod 8, \\ M\|10^{-|M|-1 \bmod 8} \text{ otherwise.} \end{cases}$

Fig. 1. Descriptions of the SHA-3 finalists. Here, h denotes state values, M denotes message blocks, S denotes a (fixed) salt, C denotes a counter and T denotes a tweak.

mode of operation preserves collision resistance and everywhere preimage resistance due to which we obtain $\mathbf{Adv}_{\mathcal{H}}^{\text{col}} = \Theta(q^2/2^n)$ and $\mathbf{Adv}_{\mathcal{H}}^{\text{epre}} = \Theta(q/2^n)$. The hash function is moreover proven optimally second preimage resistance in the ideal cipher model by Andreeva et al. [2], which gives $\mathbf{Adv}_{\mathcal{H}}^{\text{esec}[\lambda]} = \Theta(q/2^n)$. Finally, the BLAKE hash function is reproven indifferentiable from a random oracle up to bound $\Theta((Kq)^2/2^n)$, this time under the assumption that the underlying block cipher is assumed to be ideal [2,18].

4   Grøstl

The **Grøstl** hash function [25] is a chop-MD construction, with a final transformation before chopping. The hash function employs a suffix-free padding rule. The underlying compression function f is based on two permutations $P, Q : \mathbb{Z}_2^l \to \mathbb{Z}_2^l$. The final transformation g is defined as $g(h) = P(h) \oplus h$. The Grøstl hash function design is given in Fig. 1.

The compression function of Grøstl is permutation based, and the generic attacks of [38,39] apply. Furthermore, the preimage resistance of the compression function is analyzed in [24], and an upper bound for collision resistance can be obtained easily. As a consequence, we obtain tight security bounds on the compression function, $\mathbf{Adv}_f^{\text{epre}} = \Theta(q^2/2^l)$ and $\mathbf{Adv}_f^{\text{col}} = \Theta(q^4/2^l)$. In the ideal model, everywhere second preimage resistance of the compression function can be proven similar as the preimage resistance, up to a constant (the security analysis differs only in that we give the adversary one query for free). The Grøstl mode of operation preserves collision resistance and everywhere preimage resistance due to which we obtain $\mathbf{Adv}_{\mathcal{H}}^{\text{col}} = \Theta(q^2/2^n)$ and $\mathbf{Adv}_{\mathcal{H}}^{\text{epre}} = \Theta(q/2^n)$. Finally, it is proven indifferentiable from a random oracle up to bound $O((Kq)^4/2^l)$ if the underlying permutations are ideal [3].

As an addition to above results, in this work we consider second preimage resistance of the Grøstl hash function. We prove that optimal second preimage resistance (up to a constant) is achieved for all versions.

Theorem 1. *Let* $n \in \mathbb{N}$, *and* $\lambda \geq 0$. *The advantage of any adversary* $\mathcal{A}$ *in finding a second preimage for the* Grøstl *hash function* $\mathcal{H}$ *after* $q < 2^{l-1}$ *queries can be upper bounded by*

$$\mathbf{Adv}_{\mathcal{H}}^{\text{esec}[\lambda]}(q) \leq \frac{((\lambda + 65)/m + 2)q(q-1)}{2^l} + \frac{2q}{2^n}.$$

Proof. Let $M' \in \mathbb{Z}_2^\lambda$ be any target preimage. Denote by $h'_0, \dots, h'_{k'}$ the state values corresponding to the evaluation of $\mathcal{H}(M')$, and let $h = \text{chop}_n(P(h'_{k'}) \oplus h'_{k'})$.

We consider any adversary $\mathcal{A}$ making q queries to its underlying permutations P and Q. Associated to these queries, we introduce an initially empty graph G that indicates compression function calls for Grøstl that can be derived from these queries. Note that any P-query (x_P, y_P) and any Q-query (x_Q, y_Q) correspond to exactly one compression function call, namely $x_P \oplus x_Q \to x_P \oplus y_P \oplus x_Q \oplus y_Q$ where the message input is x_Q. In order to find a second preimage, the adversary

(1) either needs to end up with a graph that contains a path (labeled differently from the first preimage) from IV to any node of $\{h'_0, \dots, h'_{k'}\}$,
(2) or he needs to find a P-query (x_P, y_P) with $x_P \neq h'_{k'}$ such that $\text{chop}_n(x_P \oplus y_P) = h$ and G contains a path from IV to x_P.

A proof of this claim can be found in [2,17]. To achieve the first goal, the adversary needs to find a preimage for the Grøstl compression function, for any image in $\{h'_0, \dots, h'_{k'}\}$. To achieve the second goal, the adversary needs to find a preimage for the final transformation of the Grøstl compression function. For $i = 1, \dots, q$, we consider the probability of the i-th query to render success. We distinguish between the two success cases.

Case (1). Without loss of generality the i-th query is a forward query x_P to P, let y_P be the oracle answer drawn uniformly at random from a set of size at least $2^l - q$. Let (x_Q, y_Q) be any Q-query in the query history. The query results in a compression function call $x_P \oplus x_Q \to x_P \oplus y_P \oplus x_Q \oplus y_Q$. This value hits any of $\{h'_0, \dots, h'_{k'}\}$ with probability at most $\frac{k'+1}{2^l-q}$. Considering any of the at most

$i-1$ possible Q-queries, case (1) is achieved with probability at most $\frac{(k'+1)(i-1)}{2^l-q}$. The same bound is found for queries to Q and for inverse queries.

Case (2). Case (2) can only be achieved in a query to P. Without loss of generality, the i-th query is a forward query x_P, let y_P be the oracle answer drawn uniformly at random from a set of size at least $2^l - q$. This value satisfies $\mathsf{chop}_n(x_P \oplus y_P) = h$ with probability at most $\frac{2^{l-n}}{2^l-q}$.

By the union bound, we obtain the following bound on the second preimage resistance of Grøstl:

$$\mathbf{Adv}_{\mathcal{H}}^{\mathrm{esec}[\lambda]}(q) \le \sum_{i=1}^{q} \left(\frac{(k'+1)(i-1)}{2^l - q} + \frac{2^{l-n}}{2^l - q} \right) \le \frac{(k'+1)q(q-1)}{2(2^l - q)} + \frac{q2^{l-n}}{2^l - q}.$$

As for $q < 2^{l-1}$ we have $\frac{1}{2^l-q} \le \frac{2}{2^l}$ and $k' \le (\lambda + 65)/m + 1$, we obtain our result.   □

Given that for Grøstl we have $l = 2n$, for $q < 2^n$ the result of Thm. 1 directly implies a $\Theta(\lambda/m \cdot q/2^n)$ bound on the second preimage resistance.

5   JH

The **JH** hash function [43] is a sponge-like function, but can also be considered as a parazoa function [1] or a chop-MD construction. The hash function employs a suffix-free padding rule. The compression function f is based on a permutation $\mathbb{Z}_2^l \to \mathbb{Z}_2^l$. The JH hash function design is given in Fig. 1. Note that the parameters of JH satisfy $l = 2m$.

The compression function of JH is based on one permutation, and collisions and preimages for the compression function can be found in one query to the permutation [15]. The JH hash function is proven optimally collision resistant [29], and we obtain $\mathbf{Adv}_{\mathcal{H}}^{\mathrm{col}} = \Theta(q^2/2^n)$. Furthermore, it is proven indifferentiable from a random oracle up to bound $O\left(\frac{q^3}{2^{l-m}} + \frac{Kq^3}{2^{l-n}} \right)$ if the underlying permutation is assumed to be ideal [13]. As explained in [4,5], using (1) this indifferentiability bound additionally renders an improved upper bound $O\left(\frac{q}{2^n} + \frac{q^3}{2^{l-m}} \right)$ on the preimage and second preimage resistance.

We note, however, that these bounds on the preimage and second preimage resistance of JH are non-optimal for both variants. We improve these bounds in Thms. 2 and 3. Although the new bounds are still not better than the trivial bound for $n = 512$ (as was the previous bound), they are now optimal (up to a constant) for the 256 variant. In independent concurrent research Moody et al. [33] improved the indifferentiability bound on JH to $O((Kq)^2/2^{l-m})$, therewith confirming our findings on the (second) preimage resistance of JH.

In the proofs of Thms. 2 and 3 we will use the chop-function for both the left and right side of x. Therefore, we introduce the functions $\mathsf{left}_n(x)$ and $\mathsf{right}_n(x)$ that take the n leftmost and rightmost bits of x, respectively.

Theorem 2. *Let $n \in \mathbb{N}$. The advantage of any adversary $\mathcal{A}$ in finding a preimage for the JH hash function $\mathcal{H}$ after $q < 2^{l-1}$ queries can be upper bounded by*

$$\mathbf{Adv}_{\mathcal{H}}^{\mathrm{epre}}(q) \leq \frac{4q^2}{2^{l-m}} + \frac{2q}{2^n}.$$

Proof. Let $h \in \mathbb{Z}_2^n$ be any point to be inverted (cf. Def. 1). IV denotes the initialization vector of size l bits. We consider any adversary $\mathcal{A}$ making q queries to its underlying permutation P. Associated to these queries, we introduce an initially empty graph G that indicates compression function calls for JH that can be derived from these queries. We denote G_i as the graph after the i-th query $(i = 0, \ldots, q)$. Each query adds 2^m edges to the graph, and G_i thus contains $i2^m$ edges. In order to find a preimage, the adversary must necessarily end up with a graph that contains a path from node IV to any node in $H := \{h \| h' \mid h' \in \mathbb{Z}_2^{l-n}\}$. We denote by winA_i the event that after the i-th query this property is satisfied.

We denote by G_i^{out}, resp. G_i^{in}, the set of nodes in G_i with an outgoing, resp. incoming, edge. We denote by τ_i^{IV} the subgraph of G_i consisting of all nodes and edges reachable from IV. Similarly, τ_i^H denotes the subgraph of G_i consisting of all nodes and edges from which any node in H can be reached. Next to event winA_i, we say the adversary also wins if either of the following events occurs for any $i = 1, \ldots, q$:

winB_i : τ_i^{IV} contains two nodes v, v' with $\mathrm{left}_{l-m}(v) = \mathrm{left}_{l-m}(v')$,

winC_i : $\tau_i^H \backslash H$ contains two nodes v, v' with $\mathrm{right}_{l-m}(v) = \mathrm{right}_{l-m}(v')$.

We denote by $\mathrm{win}_i = \mathrm{winA}_i \vee \mathrm{winB}_i \vee \mathrm{winC}_i$ the event that after the i-th query the adversary has won. We have

$$\mathbf{Adv}_{\mathcal{H}}^{\mathrm{epre}}(q) \leq \mathbf{Pr}\left(\mathrm{winA}_q\right) \leq \mathbf{Pr}\left(\mathrm{win}_q\right) = \sum_{i=1}^{q} \mathbf{Pr}\left(\mathrm{win}_i \wedge \neg\mathrm{win}_{i-1}\right). \qquad (2)$$

For $i = 1, \ldots, q$, we consider the probability of the i-th query to render success. We distinguish between forward and inverse queries.

Forward Query. Suppose the adversary makes a forward query x_i to receive a random y_i. By $\neg\mathrm{winB}_{i-1}$, there is at most one $v \in \tau_{i-1}^{\mathrm{IV}}$ such that $\mathrm{left}_{l-m}(v) = \mathrm{left}_{l-m}(x_i)$. Denote $M = \mathrm{right}_{l-m}(v) \oplus \mathrm{right}_{l-m}(x_i)$; this query will add only the edge $v \rightarrow y_i \oplus (M \| 0^{l-m}) =: w$ to the tree. We define the following events.

badA_i : $\mathrm{right}_{l-m}(y_i) \in \{\mathrm{right}_{l-m}(w) \mid w \in \tau_{i-1}^H\}$,

badB_i : $\mathrm{left}_{l-m}(w) \in \{\mathrm{left}_{l-m}(v) \mid v \in \tau_{i-1}^{\mathrm{IV}}\}$,

badC_i : $w \in G_i^{\mathrm{out}}$,

badD_i : $\mathrm{left}_n(w) = h$.

Here, badA_i covers the event that τ_{i-1}^H is extended. Event badB_i covers the case that the updated τ_i^{IV} contains two nodes with the same left half (note that this would directly make winB_i satisfied). The case badC_i covers the event that the newly added edge to τ_i^{IV} hits any node with outgoing edge, and badD_i covers the event that the newly added edge to the tree would hit h (in both cases a valid preimage path may have been established). Denote $\mathsf{bad}_i = \mathsf{badA}_i \vee \mathsf{badB}_i \vee \mathsf{badC}_i \vee \mathsf{badD}_i$.

By basic probability theory, we have in case of forward queries

$$\mathbf{Pr}\left(\mathsf{win}_i \wedge \neg\mathsf{win}_{i-1}\right) \le \mathbf{Pr}\left(\mathsf{win}_i \wedge \neg\mathsf{win}_{i-1} \wedge \neg\mathsf{bad}_i\right) + \mathbf{Pr}\left(\mathsf{bad}_i \wedge \neg\mathsf{win}_{i-1}\right).$$

We consider the first probability. Assume $\neg\mathsf{win}_{i-1} \wedge \neg\mathsf{bad}_i$. Recall, by $\neg\mathsf{winB}_{i-1}$, $v \to w$ is the only edge added to τ_{i-1}^{IV}. Now, we have $\neg\mathsf{winA}_i$ by $\neg\mathsf{winA}_{i-1}$ and as by $\neg\mathsf{badC}_i \wedge \neg\mathsf{badD}_i$ this new edge does not connect τ_i^{IV} with H. Case $\neg\mathsf{winB}_i$ follows from $\neg\mathsf{winB}_{i-1} \wedge \neg\mathsf{badB}_i$. Finally, by $\neg\mathsf{badA}_i$, the tree τ_{i-1}^H is not extended, and hence $\neg\mathsf{winC}_i$ follows from $\neg\mathsf{winC}_{i-1}$. Thus, the first probability equals 0 and for forward queries we have $\mathbf{Pr}\left(\mathsf{win}_i \wedge \neg\mathsf{win}_{i-1}\right) \le \mathbf{Pr}\left(\mathsf{bad}_i \wedge \neg\mathsf{win}_{i-1}\right)$. This probability will be analyzed later.

Inverse Query. Suppose the adversary makes an inverse query y_i to receive a random x_i. By $\neg\mathsf{winC}_{i-1}$, there is at most one $v \in \tau_{i-1}^H$ such that $\mathsf{right}_{l-m}(v) = \mathsf{right}_{l-m}(y_i)$. Denote $M = \mathsf{left}_{l-m}(v) \oplus \mathsf{left}_{l-m}(y_i)$; this query will add only the edge $w := x_i \oplus (0^{l-m}\|M) \to v$ to the tree. We define the following events.

$$\mathsf{badA}_i' : \quad \mathsf{left}_{l-m}(x_i) \in \{\mathsf{left}_{l-m}(v) \mid v \in \tau_{i-1}^{\mathsf{IV}}\},$$
$$\mathsf{badB}_i' : \quad \mathsf{right}_{l-m}(v) \in \{\mathsf{right}_{l-m}(w) \mid w \in \tau_{i-1}^H\},$$
$$\mathsf{badC}_i' : \quad v \in G_i^{\mathsf{in}},$$
$$\mathsf{badD}_i' : \quad v = \mathsf{IV}.$$

Here, badA_i' covers the event that τ_{i-1}^{IV} is extended. Event badB_i' covers the case that the updated τ_i^H contains two nodes with the same right half (note that this would directly make winC_i satisfied). The case badC_i' covers the event that the newly added edge to τ_i^H hits any node with incoming edge, and badD_i' covers the event that the newly added edge to the tree would hit IV (in both cases a valid preimage path may have been established). Denote $\mathsf{bad}_i' = \mathsf{badA}_i' \vee \mathsf{badB}_i' \vee \mathsf{badC}_i' \vee \mathsf{badD}_i'$.

By basic probability theory, we have in case of inverse queries

$$\mathbf{Pr}\left(\mathsf{win}_i \wedge \neg\mathsf{win}_{i-1}\right) \le \mathbf{Pr}\left(\mathsf{win}_i \wedge \neg\mathsf{win}_{i-1} \wedge \neg\mathsf{bad}_i'\right) + \mathbf{Pr}\left(\mathsf{bad}_i' \wedge \neg\mathsf{win}_{i-1}\right).$$

We consider the first probability. Assume $\neg\mathsf{win}_{i-1} \wedge \neg\mathsf{bad}_i'$. Recall, by $\neg\mathsf{winC}_{i-1}$, $v \to w$ is the only edge added to τ_{i-1}^H. Now, we have $\neg\mathsf{winA}_i$ by $\neg\mathsf{winA}_{i-1}$ and as by $\neg\mathsf{badC}_i' \wedge \neg\mathsf{badD}_i'$ this new edge does not connect IV with τ_i^H. By $\neg\mathsf{badA}_i'$, the tree τ_{i-1}^{IV} is not extended, and hence $\neg\mathsf{winB}_i$ follows from $\neg\mathsf{winB}_{i-1}$. Finally, case $\neg\mathsf{winC}_i$ follows from $\neg\mathsf{winC}_{i-1} \wedge \neg\mathsf{badB}_i'$. Thus, the first probability equals 0 and for inverse queries we have $\mathbf{Pr}\left(\mathsf{win}_i \wedge \neg\mathsf{win}_{i-1}\right) \le \mathbf{Pr}\left(\mathsf{bad}_i' \wedge \neg\mathsf{win}_{i-1}\right)$. This probability will be analyzed later.

As each query is either a forward or an inverse query, we obtain for $i = 1, \ldots, q$:

$$\mathbf{Pr}\left(\mathsf{win}_i \wedge \neg\mathsf{win}_{i-1}\right) \leq \max\{\mathbf{Pr}\left(\mathsf{bad}_i \mid \neg\mathsf{win}_{i-1}; \text{ forward query}\right),$$

$$\mathbf{Pr}\left(\mathsf{bad}'_i \mid \neg\mathsf{win}_{i-1}; \text{ inverse query}\right)\}. \qquad (3)$$

As explained above, provided $\neg\mathsf{win}_{i-1}$, the i-th query adds at most one node to τ^{IV}_{i-1} and at most one node to τ^H_{i-1}, regardless whether it is a forward or inverse query. This particularly means that $|\tau^{\mathsf{IV}}_{i-1}| \leq i$ and $|\tau^H_{i-1}| \leq i - 1$. Additionally, $|G^{\mathrm{out}}_i|, |G^{\mathrm{in}}_i| \leq i2^m$. It is now straightforward to analyze the success probabilities of $\mathsf{bad}_i, \mathsf{bad}'_i$ to occur. As the answer from P is drawn uniformly at random from a set of size at least $2^l - q$, we obtain from (3):

$$\mathbf{Pr}\left(\mathsf{win}_i \wedge \neg\mathsf{win}_{i-1}\right) \leq \frac{(2i-1)2^m}{2^l - q} + \frac{i2^m}{2^l - q} + \frac{2^{l-n}}{2^l - q}. \qquad (4)$$

This combines with (2) to

$$\mathbf{Adv}^{\mathrm{epre}}_{\mathcal{H}}(q) \leq \sum_{i=1}^{q}\left(\frac{(3i-1)2^m}{2^l - q} + \frac{2^{l-n}}{2^l - q}\right) \leq \frac{2q^2 2^m}{2^l - q} + \frac{q2^{l-n}}{2^l - q},$$

The result is now obtained as for $q < 2^{l-1}$ we have $\frac{1}{2^l - q} \leq \frac{2}{2^l}$. □

The proof of second preimage resistance of JH is similar. Note that the attack by Kelsey and Schneier [26] only impacts JH in the internal state, which is reflected by the second part of the bound. In accordance with NIST's security requirements, we can assume $q < 2^{n-L}$, or in particular that $\lambda/m \cdot q \lesssim 2^n$ (see the remark below Def. 2). Consequently, the second term of the second preimage bound is negligible.

Theorem 3. *Let $n \in \mathbb{N}$, and $\lambda \geq 0$. The advantage of any adversary $\mathcal{A}$ in finding a second preimage for the JH hash function $\mathcal{H}$ after $q < 2^{l-1}$ queries can be upper bounded by*

$$\boldsymbol{Adv}^{\mathrm{esec}[\lambda]}_{\mathcal{H}}(q) \leq \frac{4q^2}{2^{l-m}} + \frac{2(\lambda/m + 2)q}{2^l} + \frac{2q}{2^n}.$$

Proof. The proof follows the same argument as the proof of Thm. 2; we only highlight the differences. Let $M' \in \mathbb{Z}^\lambda_2$ be any target preimage. Denote by $h'_0, \ldots, h'_{k'}$ the state values corresponding to the evaluation of $\mathcal{H}(M')$, and set $\mathsf{left}_n(h'_{k'}) = h$. Now, the adversary necessarily needs to end up with a graph that contains a path from IV to any node in $\{h'_0, \ldots, h'_{k'}\} \cup \{h\|h' \mid h' \in \mathbb{Z}^{l-n}_2\}$.

This path must be labeled by a message different from M'. The analysis of Thm. 2 carries over, with the minor difference that badC_i and badC'_i are replaced by

$$\mathsf{badC}_i : \quad w \in G^{\mathrm{out}}_i \cup \{h'_0, \ldots, h'_{k'-1}\}, \quad \mathsf{badC}'_i : \quad v \in G^{\mathrm{in}}_i \cup \{h'_1, \ldots, h'_{k'}\}.$$

Similar as before, we obtain

$$\mathbf{Adv}^{\mathrm{esec}[\lambda]}_{\mathcal{H}}(q) \leq \sum_{i=1}^{q}\left(\frac{(3i-1)2^m + k'}{2^l - q} + \frac{2^{l-n}}{2^l - q}\right) \leq \frac{2q^2 2^m}{2^l - q} + \frac{k'q}{2^l - q} + \frac{q2^{l-n}}{2^l - q}.$$

The result is now obtained from the fact that $k' \leq \lambda/m + 2$. □

6   Keccak

The **Keccak** hash function [9] is a sponge function, but can also be considered as a parazoa function [1] or a chop-MD construction. The compression function f is based on a permutation $\mathbb{Z}_2^l \to \mathbb{Z}_2^l$. The hash function output is obtained by chopping off $l - n$ bits of the state[4]. Notice that the parameters of Keccak satisfy $l = 2n + m$. The Keccak hash function design is given in Fig. 1.

The compression function of Keccak is based on one permutation, and collisions and preimages for the compression function can be found in one query to the permutation [15]. The Keccak hash function is proven indifferentiable from a random oracle up to bound $\Theta((Kq)^2/2^{l-m})$ if the underlying permutation is assumed to be ideal [10]. Using (1), this indifferentiability bound renders an optimal collision resistance bound for Keccak, $\mathbf{Adv}_{\mathcal{H}}^{\mathrm{col}} = \Theta(q^2/2^n)$, as well as optimal preimage second preimage resistance bounds $\Theta(q/2^n)$.

7   Skein

The **Skein** hash function [22] is a chop-MD construction. The message blocks are accompanied with a round-specific tweak, and the function employs a suffix- and prefix-free padding rule. The compression function f is based on a tweakable block cipher $E : \mathbb{Z}_2^m \times \mathbb{Z}_2^{128} \times \mathbb{Z}_2^l \to \mathbb{Z}_2^m$. The Skein hash function design is given in Fig. 1.

The compression function of Skein is the PGV1, or Matyas-Meyer-Oseas, compression function [35], with a difference that a tweak is involved. As claimed in [7], the results of [16] carry over, giving optimal preimage and collision security bounds on the compression function, $\mathbf{Adv}_f^{\mathrm{epre}} = \Theta(q/2^l)$ and $\mathbf{Adv}_f^{\mathrm{col}} = \Theta(q^2/2^l)$. In the ideal model, everywhere second preimage resistance of the compression function can be proven similar as the preimage resistance, up to a constant (the security analysis differs only in that we give the adversary one query for free). The Skein mode of operation preserves collision resistance and everywhere preimage resistance due to which we obtain $\mathbf{Adv}_{\mathcal{H}}^{\mathrm{col}} = \Theta(q^2/2^n)$ and $\mathbf{Adv}_{\mathcal{H}}^{\mathrm{epre}} = \Theta(q/2^n)$. Furthermore, the Skein hash function is proven indifferentiable from a random oracle up to bound $O((Kq)^2/2^l)$ if the underlying tweakable block cipher is assumed to be ideal [7]. This proof is based on the preimage awareness approach [21]. Using (1), this indifferentiability bound additionally renders an improved upper bound $O\left(\frac{q}{2^n} + \frac{q^2}{2^l}\right)$ on the second preimage resistance.

The second preimage bound for Skein is optimal for the $n = 256$ variant, but meets the trivial bound for the $n = 512$ variant. Therefore, we reconsider second preimage resistance of the Skein hash function. We prove that optimal second preimage resistance (up to a constant) is achieved for all versions.

---

[4] We notice that sponge function designs are more general [11], but for Keccak this description suffices.

Theorem 4. *Let $n \in \mathbb{N}$, and $\lambda \geq 0$. The advantage of any adversary $\mathcal{A}$ in finding a second preimage for the Skein hash function $\mathcal{H}$ after $q < 2^{l-1}$ queries can be upper bounded by*

$$\mathbf{Adv}_{\mathcal{H}}^{\text{esec}[\lambda]}(q) \leq \frac{2q}{2^l} + \frac{2q}{2^n}.$$

Proof. The proof follows a similar reasoning as the proof of Thm. 1, and we only highlight the differences. Let $M' \in \mathbb{Z}_2^{\lambda}$ be any target preimage. Denote by $h_0', \ldots, h_{k'}'$ the state values corresponding to the evaluation of $\mathcal{H}(M')$, and let $h = \text{chop}_n(h_{k'}')$.

We consider any adversary $\mathcal{A}$ making q queries to its underlying block cipher E. Associated to these queries, we introduce an initially empty graph G that indicates compression function calls for Skein that can be derived from these queries. Note that any query tuple $(M, T, h) \to C$ corresponds to exactly one compression function call, namely $h \to C \oplus M$ where the message input is M and where T is a tweak value. These tweaks are round-specific (see Fig. 1). In order to find a second preimage, the adversary needs to end up with a graph that contains a path (labeled different from the first preimage) from IV to any node of $\{h_0', \ldots, h_{k'}'\} \cup \{h\|h' \mid h' \in \mathbb{Z}_2^{l-n}\}$, where the associated tweaks need to be compliant with the hash function evaluation corresponding to the path. A proof of this claim can be found in [2,17]. To achieve the first goal, the adversary needs to find a preimage for the Skein compression function, for any image in $H_1 := \{h_0', \ldots, h_{k'}'\}$ or $H_2 := \{h\|h' \mid h' \in \mathbb{Z}_2^{l-n}\}$ (where the tweak is compliant). For $i = 1, \ldots, q$, we consider the probability of the i-th query to render success. We distinguish between the two sets H_1, H_2. Without loss of generality, let the i-th query be a forward query M, T, h, and let C be the oracle answer drawn uniformly at random from a set of size at least $2^l - q$. The same bounds are found for inverse queries.

Set H_1. As the tweaks need to be compliant, depending on T there is at most one value $h \in H_1$ for which a collision $h = C \oplus M$ may result in a valid second preimage. The i-th query thus renders a collision with H_1 probability at most $\frac{1}{2^l - q}$.

Set H_2. A collision with any element from H_2 may result in a valid preimage. $C \oplus M$ collides with any element from H_2 with probability at most $\frac{2^{l-n}}{2^l - q}$.

By the union bound, we obtain the following bound on the second preimage resistance of Skein:

$$\mathbf{Adv}_{\mathcal{H}}^{\text{esec}[\lambda]}(q) \leq \sum_{i=1}^{q} \left(\frac{1}{2^l - q} + \frac{2^{l-n}}{2^l - q} \right) \leq \frac{q}{2^l - q} + \frac{q 2^{l-n}}{2^l - q}.$$

The result is now obtained as for $q < 2^{l-1}$ we have $\frac{1}{2^l - q} \leq \frac{2}{2^l}$. $\square$

8 Conclusions

In this work we revisited the previous summary of [4,5] with respect to the five finalist SHA-3 hash functions. More concretely, we updated existing results with the new results in the area in Table 1, part of which are freshly proved in this paper. A more detailed summary can be found in the full version of this paper. A main improvement of this work is that all results in our analysis hold for ideal primitives of comparable size; either ideal ciphers or permutations. Secondly, most "security gaps" (with respect to preimage, second preimage, and collision resistance) remaining from [4,5] are closed. One of the few open problems left in the ideal model is achieving an optimal (second) preimage bound of the 512 variant of the JH hash function.

We note that our security analysis needs to be read with care and for this purpose we provide the following discussion:

- Ideal primitives do not exist and the ideal model proofs are only an indication for security. In particular, none of the candidates' underlying block cipher or permutation is ideal. However, due to the lack of security proofs in the standard model (other than preserving collision security of the compression function in MD based designs), assuming ideality of these underlying primitives gives significantly more confidence in the security of the higher level hash function structure than any ad-hoc analysis or no proof at all;
- While assuming ideality of sizable underlying building blocks like permutations and block ciphers allows for a fair security comparison of the candidates on one hand, it disregards internal differences between the idealized primitives on the other. Such specific design details can distort the security results for the distinct hash functions when concrete attacks exploiting the internal primitive weaknesses are applied.

Acknowledgments. This work has been funded in part by the IAP Program P6/26 BCRYPT of the Belgian State (Belgian Science Policy), and in part by the European Commission through the ICT program under contract ICT-2007-216676 ECRYPT II. The second author is supported by a Ph.D. Fellowship from the Institute for the Promotion of Innovation through Science and Technology in Flanders (IWT-Vlaanderen).

References

1. Andreeva, E., Mennink, B., Preneel, B.: The parazoa family: Generalizing the sponge hash functions. Int. J. Inf. Sec. 11(3), 149–165 (2012), doi:10.1007/s10207-012-0157-6
2. Andreeva, E., Luykx, A., Mennink, B.: Provable security of BLAKE with non-ideal compression function. Cryptology ePrint Archive, Report 2011/620 (2011)
3. Andreeva, E., Mennink, B., Preneel, B.: On the Indifferentiability of the Grøstl Hash Function. In: Garay, J.A., De Prisco, R. (eds.) SCN 2010. LNCS, vol. 6280, pp. 88–105. Springer, Heidelberg (2010)

4. Andreeva, E., Mennink, B., Preneel, B.: Security Reductions of the Second Round SHA-3 Candidates. In: Burmester, M., Tsudik, G., Magliveras, S., Ilić, I. (eds.) ISC 2010. LNCS, vol. 6531, pp. 39–53. Springer, Heidelberg (2011)
5. Andreeva, E., Mennink, B., Preneel, B.: Security reductions of the SHA-3 candidates (2010). In: NIST's 2nd SHA-3 Candidate Conference 2010 (2010)
6. Aumasson, J., Henzen, L., Meier, W., Phan, R.: SHA-3 proposal BLAKE. Submission to NIST's SHA-3 Competition (2010)
7. Bellare, M., Kohno, T., Lucks, S., Ferguson, N., Schneier, B., Whiting, D., Callas, J., Walker, J.: Provable security support for the Skein hash family (2009)
8. Bellare, M., Rogaway, P.: Random oracles are practical: A paradigm for designing efficient protocols. In: ACM Conference on Computer and Communications Security, pp. 62–73. ACM, New York (1993)
9. Bertoni, G., Daemen, J., Peeters, M., Assche, G.: The KECCAK sponge function family. Submission to NIST's SHA-3 Competition (2011)
10. Bertoni, G., Daemen, J., Peeters, M., Van Assche, G.: On the Indifferentiability of the Sponge Construction. In: Smart, N.P. (ed.) EUROCRYPT 2008. LNCS, vol. 4965, pp. 181–197. Springer, Heidelberg (2008)
11. Bertoni, G., Daemen, J., Peeters, M., Van Assche, G.: Sponge functions. In: ECRYPT Hash Workshop 2007 (2007)
12. Bhattacharyya, R., Mandal, A., Nandi, M.: Indifferentiability Characterization of Hash Functions and Optimal Bounds of Popular Domain Extensions. In: Roy, B., Sendrier, N. (eds.) INDOCRYPT 2009. LNCS, vol. 5922, pp. 199–218. Springer, Heidelberg (2009)
13. Bhattacharyya, R., Mandal, A., Nandi, M.: Security Analysis of the Mode of JH Hash Function. In: Hong, S., Iwata, T. (eds.) FSE 2010. LNCS, vol. 6147, pp. 168–191. Springer, Heidelberg (2010)
14. Biham, E., Dunkelman, O.: A framework for iterative hash functions – HAIFA. Cryptology ePrint Archive, Report 2007/278 (2007)
15. Black, J., Cochran, M., Shrimpton, T.: On the Impossibility of Highly-Efficient Blockcipher-Based Hash Functions. In: Cramer, R. (ed.) EUROCRYPT 2005. LNCS, vol. 3494, pp. 526–541. Springer, Heidelberg (2005)
16. Black, J., Rogaway, P., Shrimpton, T.: Black-Box Analysis of the Block-Cipher-Based Hash-Function Constructions from PGV. In: Yung, M. (ed.) CRYPTO 2002. LNCS, vol. 2442, pp. 320–335. Springer, Heidelberg (2002)
17. Bouillaguet, C., Fouque, P.: Practical hash functions constructions resistant to generic second preimage attacks beyond the birthday bound. Submitted to Information Processing Letters (2010)
18. Chang, D., Nandi, M., Yung, M.: Indifferentiability of the hash algorithm BLAKE. Cryptology ePrint Archive, Report 2011/623 (2011)
19. Coron, J.-S., Dodis, Y., Malinaud, C., Puniya, P.: Merkle-Damgård Revisited: How to Construct a Hash Function. In: Shoup, V. (ed.) CRYPTO 2005. LNCS, vol. 3621, pp. 430–448. Springer, Heidelberg (2005)
20. Damgård, I.B.: A Design Principle for Hash Functions. In: Brassard, G. (ed.) CRYPTO 1989. LNCS, vol. 435, pp. 416–427. Springer, Heidelberg (1990)
21. Dodis, Y., Ristenpart, T., Shrimpton, T.: Salvaging Merkle-Damgård for Practical Applications. In: Joux, A. (ed.) EUROCRYPT 2009. LNCS, vol. 5479, pp. 371–388. Springer, Heidelberg (2009)
22. Ferguson, N., Lucks, S., Schneier, B., Whiting, D., Bellare, M., Kohno, T., Callas, J., Walker, J.: The Skein Hash Function Family. Submission to NIST's SHA-3 Competition (2010)

23. Fleischmann, E., Forler, C., Gorski, M.: Classification of the SHA-3 candidates. Cryptology ePrint Archive, Report 2008/511 (2008)

24. Fouque, P.-A., Stern, J., Zimmer, S.: Cryptanalysis of Tweaked Versions of SMASH and Reparation. In: Avanzi, R.M., Keliher, L., Sica, F. (eds.) SAC 2008. LNCS, vol. 5381, pp. 136–150. Springer, Heidelberg (2009)

25. Gauravaram, P., Knudsen, L., Matusiewicz, K., Mendel, F., Rechberger, C., Schläffer, M., Thomsen, S.: Grøstl – a SHA-3 candidate. Submission to NIST's SHA-3 Competition (2011)

26. Kelsey, J., Schneier, B.: Second Preimages on n-Bit Hash Functions for Much Less than 2^n Work. In: Cramer, R. (ed.) EUROCRYPT 2005. LNCS, vol. 3494, pp. 474–490. Springer, Heidelberg (2005)

27. Kobayashi, K., Ikegami, J., Matsuo, S., Sakiyama, K., Ohta, K.: Evaluation of hardware performance for the SHA-3 candidates using SASEBO-GII. Cryptology ePrint Archive, Report 2010/010 (2010)

28. Lai, X., Massey, J.L.: Hash Functions Based on Block Ciphers. In: Rueppel, R.A. (ed.) EUROCRYPT 1992. LNCS, vol. 658, pp. 55–70. Springer, Heidelberg (1993)

29. Lee, J., Hong, D.: Collision resistance of the JH hash function. Cryptology ePrint Archive, Report 2011/019 (2011)

30. Lucks, S.: A Failure-Friendly Design Principle for Hash Functions. In: Roy, B. (ed.) ASIACRYPT 2005. LNCS, vol. 3788, pp. 474–494. Springer, Heidelberg (2005)

31. Maurer, U., Renner, R., Holenstein, C.: Indifferentiability, Impossibility Results on Reductions, and Applications to the Random Oracle Methodology. In: Naor, M. (ed.) TCC 2004. LNCS, vol. 2951, pp. 21–39. Springer, Heidelberg (2004)

32. Merkle, R.C.: One Way Hash Functions and DES. In: Brassard, G. (ed.) CRYPTO 1989. LNCS, vol. 435, pp. 428–446. Springer, Heidelberg (1990)

33. Moody, D., Paul, S., Smith-Tone, D.: Improved indifferentiability security bound for the JH mode. In: NIST's 3rd SHA-3 Candidate Conference 2012 (2012)

34. National Institute for Standards and Technology. Announcing Request for Candidate Algorithm Nominations for a New Cryptographic Hash Algorithm (SHA-3) Family (November 2007)

35. Preneel, B., Govaerts, R., Vandewalle, J.: Hash Functions Based on Block Ciphers: A Synthetic Approach. In: Stinson, D.R. (ed.) CRYPTO 1993. LNCS, vol. 773, pp. 368–378. Springer, Heidelberg (1994)

36. Ristenpart, T., Shacham, H., Shrimpton, T.: Careful with Composition: Limitations of the Indifferentiability Framework. In: Paterson, K.G. (ed.) EUROCRYPT 2011. LNCS, vol. 6632, pp. 487–506. Springer, Heidelberg (2011)

37. Rogaway, P., Shrimpton, T.: Cryptographic Hash-Function Basics: Definitions, Implications, and Separations for Preimage Resistance, Second-Preimage Resistance, and Collision Resistance. In: Roy, B., Meier, W. (eds.) FSE 2004. LNCS, vol. 3017, pp. 371–388. Springer, Heidelberg (2004)

38. Rogaway, P., Steinberger, J.: Security/Efficiency Tradeoffs for Permutation-Based Hashing. In: Smart, N.P. (ed.) EUROCRYPT 2008. LNCS, vol. 4965, pp. 220–236. Springer, Heidelberg (2008)

39. Stam, M.: Beyond Uniformity: Better Security/Efficiency Tradeoffs for Compression Functions. In: Wagner, D. (ed.) CRYPTO 2008. LNCS, vol. 5157, pp. 397–412. Springer, Heidelberg (2008)

40. Tillich, S., Feldhofer, M., Kirschbaum, M., Plos, T., Schmidt, J.M., Szekely, A.: High-speed hardware implementations of BLAKE, Blue Midnight Wish, Cube-Hash, ECHO, Fugue, Grøstl, Hamsi, JH, Keccak, Luffa, Shabal, SHAvite-3, SIMD, and Skein. Cryptology ePrint Archive, Report 2009/510 (2009)

41. Wang, X., Yin, Y.L., Yu, H.: Finding Collisions in the Full SHA-1. In: Shoup, V. (ed.) CRYPTO 2005. LNCS, vol. 3621, pp. 17–36. Springer, Heidelberg (2005)
42. Wang, X., Yu, H.: How to Break MD5 and Other Hash Functions. In: Cramer, R. (ed.) EUROCRYPT 2005. LNCS, vol. 3494, pp. 19–35. Springer, Heidelberg (2005)
43. Wu, H.: The Hash Function JH. Submission to NIST's SHA-3 Competition (2011)

The GLUON Family: A Lightweight Hash Function Family Based on FCSRs[*]

Thierry P. Berger[1], Joffrey D'Hayer[2], Kevin Marquet[2],
Marine Minier[2], and Gaël Thomas[1]

[1] XLIM (UMR CNRS 7252), Université de Limoges
123 avenue Albert Thomas, 87060 Limoges Cedex, France
{firstname.lastname}@unilim.fr
[2] Université de Lyon, INRIA
INSA-Lyon, CITI, F-69621, Villeurbanne, France
{firstname.lastname}@insa-lyon.fr

Abstract. Since the beginning of the SHA3 competition, the cryptographic community has seen the emergence of a new kind of primitives: the lightweight cryptographic hash functions. At the time writing this article, two representatives of this category have been published: QUARK [7] and PHOTON [18] designed to match RFID constraints.

In this paper, we propose a third representative of this category which is called GLUON. It is based on the sponge construction model [11] as QUARK and PHOTON and inspired by two stream ciphers F-FCSR-v3 [4] and X-FCSR-v2 [10]. From the generic definition of our lightweight hash function, we derive three different instances according to the required security level that must be reached.

For example, our lightest instance (GLUON-128/8) dedicated to 64-bit security level fits in 2071 gate-equivalents which stays competitive when compared with the parallel implementation of U-QUARK. The software performances are good for GLUON-224/32, our heaviest instance.

Keywords: lightweight hash function, FCSRs, sponge functions.

Introduction

The last five years have seen the emergence of new challenging tasks that consist in designing lightweight primitives dedicated to very constrained environments such as sensors or RFID tags. Among those proposals, many block ciphers such as PRESENT [13], HIGH [20], mCrypton [23] or KATAN & KTANTAN [15] have been specially designed to fit with a very compact hardware implementation.

The same kind of works concerning lightweight hash functions has just been initiated with two existing standalone proposals: QUARK [7] and PHOTON [18] both based on sponge constructions [11]. The need for such proposals comes first from the embedded system community (RFID and sensor) and second from

---

[*] This work was partially supported by the French National Agency of Research: ANR-11-INS-011.

A. Mitrokotsa and S. Vaudenay (Eds.): AFRICACRYPT 2012, LNCS 7374, pp. 306–323, 2012.

the lack of lightweight SHA3 finalists [26]. Indeed, all the SHA3 finalists require more than 12000 GE for a 128-bit security level. Some previous proposals such as SQUASH [29] or ARMADILLO [8] have been done but show their respective weaknesses [28,1]. The first step in the design of lightweight hash functions dates from the use of the block cipher PRESENT in the Davies-Meyer mode of operation. However, and as already noticed in [7,18], sponge constructions allow a better ratio between internal state size and security level, better than for traditional modes of operations even if hashing small messages is not really efficient due to the squeezing step.

Following the recent proposals for lightweight hash functions taking their name from small particles[1], we propose a new lightweight hash function family called GLUON based on a sponge construction. This new family is based on a particular Feedback with Carry Shift Register (FCSR), elementary building block well studied during the last two decades. Even if the hardware size of such a primitive is a little bit heavier than the basic building blocks used in QUARK and PHOTON, we think that the well-known design principles of FCSRs could be considered as a strength of our proposed design. Moreover, the software performances of our design are also good.

This paper is organized as follows: in Section 1, we recall the definitions of sponge constructions and of word ring FCSRs. In Section 2, we describe the underlying function that composes the sponge construction based on a word ring FCSR. In Section 3, we give some insights about our chosen design whereas in Section 4 we sum up all the security observations we made concerning the f function. In Section 5, we provide performance results for hardware and software implementations. Finally, Section 6 concludes this paper.

1 Background

1.1 Sponge Constructions

Sponge constructions have been proposed by Bertoni et al. in [11] as a new way of building hash functions from a fixed function or a fixed permutation. A sponge construction as defined in Fig. 1 has a *rate* r which corresponds with the block length, a *capacity* cp and an *output length* N. The *width* of its internal state b is defined as $r + cp$ that must be greater than N. Of course, we could set $N = cp$ for non null r.

Given an initial state, the sponge construction processes a message M of length in words of size r bits $|M|$ as follows:

1. **Initialization:** The message is padded by appending a '1' bit and sufficiently many zeros to reach a length multiple of r.
2. **Absorbing phase:** The r-bit message blocks are xored into r bits of the state interleaved with applications of the function f.
3. **Squeezing phase:** Some r bits of the state are returned as output, interleaved with applications of the function f, until N bits are returned.

---

[1] See: http://www.131002.net/data/talks/quarks_rump.pdf

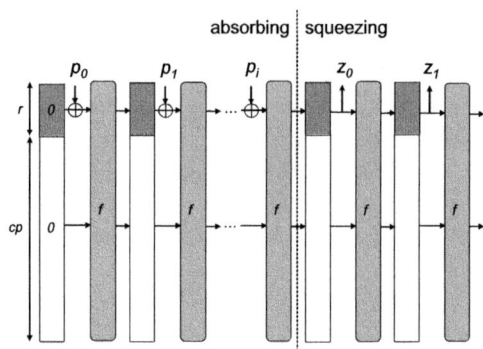

Fig. 1. The sponge construction

1.2 FCSR Automata in Word Ring Representation

Roughly speaking, a FCSR as defined in [17,22] consists of a binary main register and of a carry register but contrary to LFSRs the performed operations are no more xors over $\mathbb{F}_2$ but additions with carry in the set of 2-adic integers $\mathbb{Z}_2$ (i.e. the set of power series: $\sum_{i=0}^{\infty} s_i 2^i$, $s_i \in \{0,1\}$). Each cell of the main register produces a sequence $S = (s_n)_{n \in \mathbb{N}}$ that is eventually periodic if and only if there exist two numbers p and q in $\mathbb{Z}$, q odd, such that $s = \sum_{i=0}^{\infty} s_i 2^i = p/q$. This sequence is strictly periodic if and only if $pq \leq 0$ and $|p| \leq |q|$. The period of S is the order of 2 modulo q, i.e., the smallest integer P such that $2^P \equiv 1 \pmod{q}$. The period satisfies $P \leq |q| - 1$. If q is prime and if $P = |q| - 1$, the sequence S is called an ℓ-sequence. ℓ-sequences have many proved properties that could be compared to the ones of m-sequences: known period, good statistical properties, fast generation, etc.

F. Arnault et al. have studied in [4] and in [10] efficient hardware and software FCSRs using matrix representations. They give the following definition:

Definition 1. *A (diversified or ring) FCSR is an automaton composed of a main shift register of n binary cells $m = (m_0, \ldots, m_{n-1})$, and a carry register of n integer cells $c = (c_0, \ldots, c_{n-1})$. It is updated using the following relations:*

$$\begin{cases} m(t+1) = Tm(t) + c(t) \mod 2 \\ c(t+1) = Tm(t) + c(t) \ \div 2 \end{cases} \tag{1}$$

where T is a $n \times n$ matrix with coefficients 0 or 1 in $\mathbb{Z}$, called transition matrix. Note that $\div 2$ is the traditional expression: $X \div 2 = \frac{X - (X \mod 2)}{2}$.

They also prove the following property:

Theorem 1 ([4] Theorem 1). *The series $M_i(t)$ observed in the cells of the main register are 2-adic expansion of p_i/q with $p_i \in \mathbb{Z}$ and with $q = \det(I - 2T)$.*

The T transition matrix completely defines the ring FCSR as shown in Theorem 1. Moreover and as shown in [4], ring FCSRs have better hardware implementations than classical Galois or Fibonacci FCSRs. Moreover, the diffusion speed (which is faster than in Galois/Fibonacci FCSRs) is related to the diameter d of the transition graph. This diameter is the maximal distance between two cells of the main register. In other words, d is the distance after which each cell of the main register has been influenced by all the other cells. It corresponds to the minimal number of clocks required to have each cell of the main register influenced by all the other cells. d should be small for better diffusion. Thus, in the case of a ring FCSR, the diffusion of differences is also improved because these diffusions could be also computed as the diameter d of the graph associated to the transition matrix T. Typically this value is close to $n/4$ for a ring FCSR instead of n in the Galois or Fibonacci cases.

In [10], Berger et al. describe word ring FCSRs that are efficient both in hardware and in software. Those FCSRs are completely determined by the choice of the matrix T. Contrary to ring FCSRs, word ring FCSRs act on words of size r bits depending on the targeted architecture. Classically, r could be equal to 8, 16, 32 or 64 bits. Then, in the generic description of a word ring FCSR, the associated matrix T is defined on r-bit words. The main register of this kind of FCSR could thus be represented as w r-bit words $m_0, \cdots, m_{w-1}$ with feedback words $c_0, \cdots, c_{w-1}$. The deduced T matrix is of size $w \times w$. For example, the following T matrix represents a word ring FCSR acting on $r = 8$ bits words:

$$
T = \begin{pmatrix}
0 & I & 0 & SL^3 & 0 \\
0 & 0 & I & 0 & SR^2 \\
0 & 0 & SL^1 & I & 0 \\
SR^3 & 0 & 0 & 0 & I \\
I & 0 & 0 & 0 & 0
\end{pmatrix}
$$

where I is the $r \times r$ identity matrix, the SL^a operation is the left shift at 8-bit level by a bits, SR^b is the right shift operation at 8-bit level by b bits (two other operations could also be used: RL^d, the rotation on the left by d bits and RR^e, the rotation on the right by e bits).

This matrix defines the associated word ring FCSR described in Figure 2 with $n = 40$ and $r = 8$.

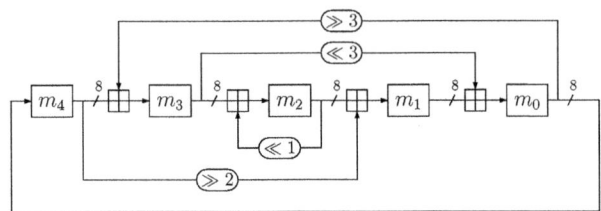

Fig. 2. A FCSR with efficient software design. The pluses in the boxes represent eight parallel binary adders with carry.

The corresponding q value could be directly computed using the formula given in Theorem 1 and is equal to -1497813390989. This number is prime and has a maximal order. Thus the corresponding FCSR produces ℓ-sequences, and is not only efficient in software due to the word oriented structure, it is also efficient in hardware (here only 23 binary additions are required) because the intrinsic word ring nature of this FCSR representation limits the number of required gates. Moreover, the diameter of the associated graph is equal for this example to 15 ($d = 15$) which means that a complete diffusion of all the cells is achieved after $d + 4 = 19$ clocks.

2   Description of the GLUON Hash Family

The GLUON family is based on a sponge construction where the f function calls a filtered FCSR. The filtered FCSR is directly inspired by the F-FCSR-v3 hardware stream cipher [4] and by the X-FCSR-v2 software stream cipher [10]. All the proposed instances of the GLUON family varies according to the version but all versions are based on "ring-word FCSRs" to be efficient not only in hardware but also in software. The general structure of the GLUON family is described on Fig. 3. The elementary building blocks are the following ones:

- The content of the word ring FCSR of size w words of r bits is denoted $m(t) = (m_0(t), \cdots, m_{w-1}(t))$ for the main register where w is the length in words of the considered FCSR and $c(t) = (c_0(t), \cdots, c_{w-1}(t))$ for the carry register with a active memories (i.e. a internal feedbacks). The FCSR is defined by its associated matrix T as seen in the previous section.
- A filter FI is also defined to filter the content of the main register $m(t)$. It is xor-linear to break the 2-adic structure of the automaton. As done in [4], it consists in xoring together some shifted version of the words of the main register that have active carries. More precisely, let $\mathcal{F} = \{m_{f_0}, \cdots, m_{f_{\ell-1}}\}$ be the set of all the words m_i that have a feedback. Then, r bits of output are: $FI(m) = \bigoplus_{j=0}^{\ell-1} (m_{f_j})_{<<<k_j}$ with k_j a value in the set $[-r/2, r/2]$. This linear filter is only used at the end of the computation of the function to extract the output from the state of the FCSR.

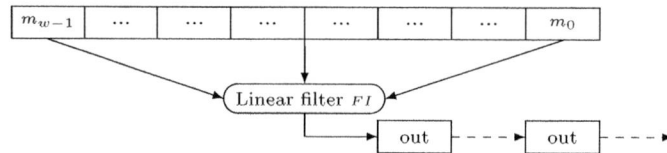

Fig. 3. General view of the f function of the GLUON family

The size of the input/output of f is $b = (w - 1) \times r$ (instead of $w \times r$ as expected because a particular word (the word $w - 1$) of the main register is not used as input of the function).

2.1   Details of the f Function

f processes a b-bit input in three steps:

Initialization: For an input $s = (s_0, \cdots, s_{b-1})$, f initializes its internal state as follows:
- The $w - 1$ first words of m are initialized with the $(w - 1) \times r$ input bits.
- The last word of m is initialized with the all-one string of length r.
- The carry register c is initialized with the all-zero string.

State Update: From the internal state $(m(t), c(t))$, the FCSR is clocked $d + 4$ times using its internal transition function:

$$m(t + 1) = Tm(t) + c(t) \mod 2$$
$$c(t + 1) = Tm(t) + c(t) \div 2$$

Computation of the Output: The FCSR is then clocked $w - 1$ times. At each iteration, a r-bit word is extracted with the linear filter F in order to obtain the $(w - 1) \times r$ bits of output.

2.2   The Sponge Construction Deduced from the f Function

The rate of the associated sponge construction is r, its capacity is $cp = (w-2) \times r$. The size of f is $b = r + cp$. Let us now analyze in a few words how this f function fits in the sponge model. The external part of the f function is composed of the first r-bit word of the input whereas the internal part consists of the following $(w - 2)$ r-bit words of the input. In other words, during the absorbing steps, at each call of f, a message word p_i of length r bits is xored with the first r-bit word of the FCSR main register. Then, this first r-bit word is output when the squeezing step begins.

2.3   Proposed Instances

As done for QUARK and PHOTON, we propose 3 different instances of our GLUON family functions that we will denote GLUON-N/r (the same that for QUARK). From the sizes parameters, we use the same algorithm than the one proposed in [10] to compute the different T matrices: we randomly pick matrices T such as $\log_2(q) \geq n$, $q = \det(I - 2T)$ is prime, the order of 2 modulo q is equal to $|q| - 1$ and is maximal to ensure that the outputs are composed of ℓ-sequences. Moreover, q has been chosen such that the diameter d is sufficiently small to ensure a quick diffusion and with a number of carries close to $wr/2$. The filters are randomly chosen but guaranteeing that all the picked words have a carry.

- *64-bit security level:* $r = 8$, $cp = 128$, $b = 136$, $N = 128$ leading to a FCSR composed of 18 8-bit words and with about 70 carries. The complete description of the Matrix T and of the filter FI is given in Appendix A.

- *80-bit security level:* $r = 16$, $cp = 160$, $b = 176$, $N = 160$ leading to a FCSR composed of 12 16-bit words and with about 90 carries. The complete description of the Matrix T and of the filter FI is given in Appendix B.
- *112-bit security level:* $r = 32$, $cp = 224$, $b = 256$, $N = 224$ leading to a FCSR composed of 9 32-bit words and with about 130 carries. The complete description of the Matrix T and of the filter FI is given in Appendix C.

As done for PHOTON, we could also add some other instances with as possible output sizes 80 and 256. In those cases, the corresponding r values are respectively 8 and 32.

3   Design Rationale

3.1   Flat Sponge Claim

Sponge construction is a recent model for iterated hash functions and random number generation developed in [11] and in [12]. The general security claim is done in the indifferentiability framework introduced by Maurer, Renner and Holenstein [24]. In [11], the authors prove that the success probability of differentiating a sponge construction calling a random permutation or transformation from a random oracle is upper bounded by $1 - \exp(-Q^2 2^{-(cp+1)})$ with Q the number of calls to f or its inverse when possible.

From this particular bound, the authors of [11] deduce a simplification of the proof model which considers from the previous result only the worst-case success probability. This simplification called the *flat sponge claim* makes the security of a concrete function seen as a random sponge depend on the capacity of the random sponge. More precisely, the collision resistance of a sponge construction under the flat sponge claim is $2^{\min(cp,N)/2}$, the (second) preimage resistance is $2^{\min(cp/2,N)}$.

Thus, we design our function using this flat sponge argument which allows to minimize the internal state (looking at the indifferentiability in the random oracle model) of the used function when compared with other traditional hash constructions such as the Merkle-Damgård one for example. In fact, sponge constructions lead to achieve the highest security level that could be obtained for a hash construction.

3.2   Choice of the f Function

As already mentioned for the hash function QUARK [7], the design choice of f comes from this simple idea: from a stream cipher with an internal state of size n, one can construct a function from $\{0,1\}^b$ into itself as follows:

- The b-bit input is padded to an initial state of size n bits,
- The stream cipher is initialized as usual,
- The first b output bits compose the output of the f function.

Under the hypothesis that the stream-cipher is "perfect", the f function looks like a random function. In other words, finding a bias in the function f is equivalent to find a weakness of the stream-cipher.

F-FCSR-v3 and X-FCSR-v2. We have based our f design on a mix between two FCSR based stream ciphers which are F-FCSR-v3 [4] and X-FCSR-v2 [10]. The first one is dedicated to hardware and uses a linear filter as done here whereas the second one introduces the word ring oriented structure of a FCSR which is efficient both in hardware and in software. This kind of automata is the building block of our f design.

Since the first proposal of a stream cipher based on a FCSR in 2005 in [2], the security of such designs has been carefully studied through the eStream call for stream ciphers [27]. One of the first proposals called F-FCSR-v2 based on a Galois FCSR was however successfully attacked by M. Hell and T. Johansson in 2008 in [19]. This attack exploits a particular dependence between the feedback bit and all the carry bits. This attack is also efficient against the first version of X-FCSR (X-FCSR-v1) as shown in [30]. Those particular attacks led to the modification of the original proposals into the new versions F-FCSR-v3 and X-FCSR-v2 based on new matrix representations of the FCSR leading to discard the two previous attacks as detailed in Section 4. Since their publications, two years ago, no attack has been exhibited against the two new stream ciphers which are based on strong security arguments. This leads to have a relative level of confidence concerning those two particular primitives, particularly if we look at the absence of existing distinguishers against the building blocks.

Moreover, those designs are simple and relatively efficient both in software and hardware. Thus, these simple arguments concerning the efficiency of F-FCSR-v3 and of X-FCSR-v2 and the security level claimed lead to naturally consider them as possible instance for a compression function in the sponge model.

Quality of the f Function. The good statistical properties (period, balanced sequences and so on) of the underlying building blocks come from the 2-adic properties and are equivalent over $\mathbb{Z}_2$ to the ones of LFSRs over $\mathbb{F}_2$. We will see now how the design choices made here are efficient to prevent classical attacks.

First, the number of clocks in f is $d + 4$ to ensure a complete diffusion of the message block into all the words of the FCSR. Even if a difference is introduced in the message block, this difference will influence all the output blocks. This is due to the diameter definition which clearly improves the diffusion speed in a word ring representation. In other words, the diffusion is complete after $d + 4$ clocks.

Let us consider a FCSR with connection integer q which produces ℓ-sequences, i.e. such that the order of 2 modulo q is $P = |q| - 1$. After a few iterations from an initial state, the automaton is in a periodic sequence of states of length P. The average number of required iterations to be in such a state is experimentally less than $log_2(n)$, where n is the size of the main register (see [5] for more details). Thus, during the application of f such states are always reached because for all our cases $log_2(n) < d$. Those particular periodic states are all on a (the) main cycle of size P, generally the number of periodic state is close to 2^n (equal to 2^{wr} in our design). This leads to consider a function f which is really close to a permutation from $\{0, 1\}^b$ into itself because the surjective part of the construction is really limited once the function f acts on the main cycle. In other words, we exploit here the fact that the transition function of a FCSR becomes a permutation on its periodic states.

So, our f function could be considered as an application from $\{0,1\}^b$ into the set of periodic states, i.e. into a set of size 2^n that has a behavior close to a permutation leading to a very low collision probability. Indeed, each possible input value conducts to a particular part of the main cycle. The entering function is thus a quasi-permutation on its cycles with a very small loss of entropy. As soon as the main cycle is reached, f does not anymore lose entropy even after several iterations. The entropy lost that could be considered here comes from the extraction step. Thus, in summary, the design of f prevents any entropy loss and the behavior of f is close to the behavior of a random function. To corroborate what we say, we have tested the linear, differential and algebraic properties (using cube testers for this last category) of the GLUON functions considering r input and output bits. Those tests have shown that those functions have the same behavior as random functions.

However, the generic word ring FCSR structure brings with it a particular problem: there are on the graph representation of the FCSR two particular fixed points which are the all-zero point and the all-one point. Thus, to prevent attacks producing collisions on two different messages M and M' which differ on a certain number of all-zero blocks at the beginning (i.e. $M = 0||0||m_0$ and $M' = 0||m_0$ for example which lead to the same output results), we introduce the all-one bit constant in a word of the main register to avoid the all-zero point. The all-one point is discarded by the initialization of the carry register to the all-zero word at each f application. These two states can never be reached by design.

4   Security Analysis

As for QUARK and PHOTON, we follow the *hermetic sponge strategy*, which consists in adopting the sponge construction and building an underlying function f that should not have any structural distinguishers. The indifferentiability proof of the sponge construction shows that any non-generic attack on a GLUON hash function implies a distinguisher for its function f (but the inverse is not necessarily true). This reduces the security of the hash function to the security of f. As already explained in Section 3.1, the indifferentiability proof of the sponge construction ensures an expected complexity against any differentiating attack such as collision or (second) preimage attacks. Thus, as GLUON follows the hermetic sponge strategy, we directly apply those results and analyze, in this section, the f function.

Collision Attack and Preimage Attack. If one tries to inverse the f function from the outputs, he will face a combinatorial explosion, for a given m_{k+1} bit value of the main register, the values c_k and m_k producing m_{k+1} are not unique because contrary to the Galois or Fibonacci FCSRs, zeroing the content of the carry register no more guarantees to be on the main cycle of the FCSR (see [5] for more details). Whereas in this case, the knowledge of a part of the carry register and of the main register guarantees the possible inversion of those values, this is no more the case for a word ring FCSR (see [4] for more details). One point of the state graph could have two preimages. So, the inversion of the f function could not be easily done. Thus, due to the combinatorial explosion, the (second) preimage search has a complexity of 2^{3w*r}, the combined size of the two registers.

The complexity of the collision search for the f function could be directly deduced also from the previous remark noticing that the direct collisions search is to find p and p' such that $p \equiv p' \mod q$. So if we write again this equation at binary level for the contents of the main register and of the carry register, we are facing an instance of the subset sum problem, with a complexity equals to $2^{w*r/2}$ (if the carries are zeroes) or $2^{3w*r/2}$ (in the general case).

Cube Attacks and Cube Testers. Recently, a new kind of attacks called "Cube attacks" has appeared (the most recent reference in this area is [6]). Those attacks could be efficient as soon as "Cube testers" show their efficiency in simplifying a part of the ANF of a function. Thus, those attacks could be applied against functions which have particular weaknesses in their algebraic structure. As shown in [9] for the case of a Galois FCSR, such a particular structure (with a low degree component) does not exist in a Galois FCSR. This is the same thing for a word ring FCSR and thus for the f function chosen here. Indeed, for example with a Galois FCSR of size 16 after 7 clocks, the number of monomials in the output algebraic equations is 125420 with a degree of at least 10 considering only the variables of the main register as unknowns. The number of monomials of the obtained system becomes huge with a high degree as mentioned in [9] as soon as at least 10 clocks are performed. We thus conjecture that it discards the potential use of cube testers and renders cube attacks harmless as soon as at least 10 clocks are performed.

Linear and Differential Attacks. Linear attacks have been performed against Galois FCSRs using a method called LFSRization by Hell and Johansson in [19] and against Fibonacci FCSRs by Fischer et al. in [16]. The first attack relies on the existence of correlations between the carries and the feedback values. More precisely, the probability that the feedback bit is equal to 0 during t consecutive clocks is 2^{-t} for a Galois FCSR allowing with this probability to linearize the FCSR (i.e. if the feedbacks are forced to 0 during t clocks the behavior of the FCSR becomes linear). With a word ring FCSR, this probability becomes 2^{-tu} where u is the number of bits of the main register controlling a feedback. Thus, for example, with a word ring FCSR of size 128 bits with around 70 feedbacks, this leads to a probability of 2^{-70} to control at the null value the feedback bits during one clock. The attack presented in [16] is also discarded because it only concerns stream ciphers where the underlying building block is a Fibonacci FCSR which is not the case here.

Differential attacks stay a very powerful tool to find inner collisions in compression functions as shown with MD5 and SHA-1 [31]. The main idea relies on the non-ideal behavior of difference propagations through the compression function. The resistance of F-FCSR stream ciphers against differential attacks have been proven after some changes in F-FCSR-H v2 due to a slow diffusion of differences presented in [21]. More precisely, in [21], the authors show that a difference introduced in some cells of the FCSR automaton remains localized as long as this difference does not reach the feedback end of the register. From this remark, they deduce an attack on the IV process of F-FCSR-H v1. Thus, in [3], the designers prevent this attack from happening by redesigning the IV setup and increasing the number of initial clocks to be sure that a sufficient diffusion of differences occurs. In the new ring and word ring design, the diffusion criterion given by the diameter d allows to determine the minimal value from which a sufficient diffusion level occurs. Therefore, the number of clocks of the f function is $d + 4$: we are sure that a minimal diffusion (in general and for differences in particular) is reached. In [21], the authors especially focus on one bit differences due to the structure of the FCSR, this is the same case for a word ring FCSR, the word structure being just a representation. So, after d clocks and for the best differential case, a one bit difference becomes a two bits difference, after $d + 1$ clocks, this difference is spread on average into many cells becoming in average at least a four bits difference at different places and so on. So, we conjecture that the number of clocks equal to $d + 4$ is sufficient to correctly spread on average differences in several cells.

Slide Distinguishers. As mentioned in Section 3.2, slide distinguishers could be built on the two particular fix points of the graph of a FCSR which are the all-zero point transformed into itself and the all-one point also transformed into itself. The all-one point could not be reached for f when used inside the sponge construction due to the way the sponge construction builds its internal states. However, the all-zero point could be reached for f if a particular initial value is not given to a particular word of the main register of the FCSR. This is why, to discard slide distinguishers that make use of block messages equal to zero, a particular word of the main register is initialized to the all-one point.

In conclusion, we could say that since the beginning of FCSR study in the cryptographic context 6 years ago, all the original awkwardnesses leading to conventional attacks or to more tricky attacks have been discarded along the design process. This is why, we think that cryptanalyzing ring FCSRs passes through creating new attacks exploiting really original sorts of relations that are no more linear, differential or algebraic.

5   Performances

This section details our experimental results. We describe the tools used and compare our results with the existing works. We also provide in Appendix D the test vectors for the three GLUON instances.

5.1   Hardware Performances

This section reports our hardware implementation of the GLUON instances. For simulation, we used the *ModelSim PE* simulator [25], version *10,0a*. For synthesis, we used the ASIC synthetisor *Cadence RTL* version *RC10.1.101* (32-bits version) [14]. Our implementation consists into two components: the function f and a register R used to store the intermediate results.

We now detail the optimizations made for GLUON and discuss our implementation choices.

Loading the FCSR in Parallel. There are two ways to load data into the main register of a ring FCSR. All parts (*i.e.* $m_0..m_i$) can be loaded in parallel by inserting multiplexers before each m_i. This solution allows fast execution as the entire main register is loaded in one step. The other solution is to load the main register serially. Such a solution is usual for the classical representations of an FCSR, *i.e.* Galois or Fibonacci. The data is injected by one side of the register (m_{N-1}). A word m_i reaches its correct position after i-th steps of the FCSR. However, all the feedbacks of the FCSR must be inactivated using multiplexers. For the Galois or the Fibonacci representation a single multiplexer is enough. For a ring-FCSR, more multiplexers are needed: one per feedback. As a consequence, the cost of a parallel solution is very close to the cost of the serial one. We keep the parallel version.

Storage. The different GLUON instances require to store the output of the filter at different times. These values are stored directly in the register R to save memory.

Optimization of the Adders. Adders are used in the FCSR. In our design, adders are implemented as in [4], that is to say: $c = (a.b) \oplus (a \oplus b).c$ and $s = (a \oplus b) \oplus c$ where . denotes the binary AND. The synthesizer optimizes the design by factorizing the common sub-expression $a \oplus b$. An interesting solution to implement adders is the one used in PRESENT [13], but we did not implement adders this way because it is too costly in our case.

Table 1. Performances of GLUON with previous works

| Hash function | Security | | Block | Area | Lat. | Thr. |
	Pre.	Coll.	[bits]	[GE]	[cycles]	kbps
GLUON-64	128	64	8	2071	66	12.12
GLUON-80	160	80	16	2799.3	50	32
GLUON-112	224	112	32	4724	55	58.18
U-QUARK×8	128	64	8	2392	68	11.76
D-QUARK×8	160	80	16	2819	88	18.18
S-QUARK×16	224	112	32	4640	64	50.00
PHOTON-80	160	80	16	1168	132	12.15

Results. Results are reported in Table 1. As we can see, our proposals compete well in terms of area with QUARK proposals: they are 13.4% smaller for the 64-bit version and similar for the 80-bit and 112-bit versions. However, it seems that the greater the size is, the greater the gap between our results and those of QUARK. The throughput is similar for the 64-bit version, worst for the 80-bits version and better for the last one. Compared to PHOTON (we only give the results for 80 bits as it is the provided version for which can compare), the area is clearly not in our favor but our throughput is better.

We did not include power consumption because the power consumption strongly depends on the technology used and cannot be compared between different technologies in a fair manner. In addition, simulated power results strongly depend on the simulation method used, and the effort spent.

5.2   Software Performances

This section reports our software implementations. Table 2 gives the software performances we obtained on the variants detailed in Section 2.3. The processor used for the benchmarks is an Intel Core 2 Duo clocked at 2.66 GHz. Note that our implementation is not optimized for a particular processor, *e.g.* it is not optimized for running on a 64-bit processor. Results are good and better than the QUARK versions we benchmarked on the same machine. As expected, PHOTON is better (we only give performance comparison for the 80 bits version as it is the only provided version with which we can compare with).

Table 2. Software performances in cycles per byte of the GLUON variants for long messages, compared to QUARK versions and PHOTON when possible

GLUON-64	17319
U-QUARK	43373

GLUON-80	8523
D-QUARK	35103
PHOTON-80	1243

GLUON-112	1951
S-QUARK	25142

6   Conclusion

After the lightweight hash proposals QUARK and PHOTON, the family of lightweight particles expands with the GLUON family and three particular instances GLUON-128/8, GLUON-160/16 and GLUON-224/32. Even if the software and hardware performances of GLUON are worst than the ones of PHOTON, they are comparable when targeting hardware to the parallelized versions of QUARK. We think that our design is relevant and of real interest because the basic building blocks have been well-studied since twenty years.

We do not develop here (as done for PHOTON) the case where the squeezing step is reduced and produces more output blocks at each step. An initial study concerning this aspect shows that we could transform GLUON-128/8 into a more challenging version fitting with the requirements of such a modified version.

The idea is to directly output, during the squeezing step, one 8-bit word at each clock without waiting for $d + 4$ clocks and without changing the input of the f function at each f call. Of course, due to its simplicity, this version is more risky but the reached security level could be compared to the one of F-FCSR-v3.

References

1. Abdelraheem, M.A., Blondeau, C., Naya-Plasencia, M., Videau, M., Zenner, E.: Cryptanalysis of armadillo2. Cryptology ePrint Archive, Report 2011/160 (2011), http://eprint.iacr.org/
2. Arnault, F., Berger, T.P.: F-FCSR: Design of a New Class of Stream Ciphers. In: Gilbert, H., Handschuh, H. (eds.) FSE 2005. LNCS, vol. 3557, pp. 83–97. Springer, Heidelberg (2005)
3. Arnault, F., Berger, T.P., Lauradoux, C.: Update on F-FCSR Stream Cipher. ECRYPT - Network of Excellence in Cryptology, Call for stream Cipher Primitives - Phase 2 (2006), http://www.ecrypt.eu.org/stream/
4. Arnault, F., Berger, T., Lauradoux, C., Minier, M., Pousse, B.: A New Approach for FCSRs. In: Jacobson Jr., M.J., Rijmen, V., Safavi-Naini, R. (eds.) SAC 2009. LNCS, vol. 5867, pp. 433–448. Springer, Heidelberg (2009)
5. Arnault, F., Berger, T.P., Minier, M.: Some Results on FCSR Automata With Applications to the Security of FCSR-Based Pseudorandom Generators. IEEE Transactions on Information Theory 54(2), 836–840 (2008)
6. Aumasson, J.-P., Dinur, I., Meier, W., Shamir, A.: Cube Testers and Key Recovery Attacks on Reduced-Round MD6 and Trivium. In: Dunkelman, O. (ed.) FSE 2009. LNCS, vol. 5665, pp. 1–22. Springer, Heidelberg (2009)
7. Aumasson, J.-P., Henzen, L., Meier, W., Naya-Plasencia, M.: QUARK: A Lightweight Hash. In: Mangard, S., Standaert, F.-X. (eds.) CHES 2010. LNCS, vol. 6225, pp. 1–15. Springer, Heidelberg (2010)
8. Badel, S., Dağtekin, N., Nakahara Jr., J., Ouafi, K., Reffé, N., Sepehrdad, P., Sušil, P., Vaudenay, S.: ARMADILLO: A Multi-purpose Cryptographic Primitive Dedicated to Hardware. In: Mangard, S., Standaert, F.-X. (eds.) CHES 2010. LNCS, vol. 6225, pp. 398–412. Springer, Heidelberg (2010)
9. Berger, T.P., Minier, M.: Two Algebraic Attacks Against the F-FCSRs Using the IV Mode. In: Maitra, S., Veni Madhavan, C.E., Venkatesan, R. (eds.) INDOCRYPT 2005. LNCS, vol. 3797, pp. 143–154. Springer, Heidelberg (2005)
10. Berger, T.P., Minier, M., Pousse, B.: Software Oriented Stream Ciphers Based upon FCSRs in Diversified Mode. In: Roy, B., Sendrier, N. (eds.) INDOCRYPT 2009. LNCS, vol. 5922, pp. 119–135. Springer, Heidelberg (2009)
11. Bertoni, G., Daemen, J., Peeters, M., Van Assche, G.: On the Indifferentiability of the Sponge Construction. In: Smart, N.P. (ed.) EUROCRYPT 2008. LNCS, vol. 4965, pp. 181–197. Springer, Heidelberg (2008)
12. Bertoni, G., Daemen, J., Peeters, M., Van Assche, G.: Sponge-Based Pseudo-Random Number Generators. In: Mangard, S., Standaert, F.-X. (eds.) CHES 2010. LNCS, vol. 6225, pp. 33–47. Springer, Heidelberg (2010)
13. Bogdanov, A., Knudsen, L.R., Leander, G., Paar, C., Poschmann, A., Robshaw, M.J.B., Seurin, Y., Vikkelsoe, C.: PRESENT: An Ultra-Lightweight Block Cipher. In: Paillier, P., Verbauwhede, I. (eds.) CHES 2007. LNCS, vol. 4727, pp. 450–466. Springer, Heidelberg (2007)
14. Cadence. Encounter rtl compiler, http://www.cadence.com/products/ld/rtl_compiler

15. De Cannière, C., Dunkelman, O., Knežević, M.: KATAN and KTANTAN — A Family of Small and Efficient Hardware-Oriented Block Ciphers. In: Clavier, C., Gaj, K. (eds.) CHES 2009. LNCS, vol. 5747, pp. 272–288. Springer, Heidelberg (2009)

16. Fischer, S., Meier, W., Stegemann, D.: Equivalent Representations of the F-FCSR Keystream Generator. In: ECRYPT Network of Excellence - SASC Workshop, pp. 87–94 (2008), http://www.ecrypt.eu.org/stvl/sasc2008/

17. Goresky, M., Klapper, A.: Periodicity and Distribution Properties of Combined FCSR Sequences. In: Gong, G., Helleseth, T., Song, H.-Y., Yang, K. (eds.) SETA 2006. LNCS, vol. 4086, pp. 334–341. Springer, Heidelberg (2006)

18. Guo, J., Peyrin, T., Poschmann, A.: The Photon Family of Lightweight Hash Functions. In: Rogaway, P. (ed.) CRYPTO 2011. LNCS, vol. 6841, pp. 222–239. Springer, Heidelberg (2011)

19. Hell, M., Johansson, T.: Breaking the F-FCSR-H Stream Cipher in Real Time. In: Pieprzyk, J. (ed.) ASIACRYPT 2008. LNCS, vol. 5350, pp. 557–569. Springer, Heidelberg (2008)

20. Hong, D., Sung, J., Hong, S., Lim, J., Lee, S., Koo, B.-S., Lee, C., Chang, D., Lee, J., Jeong, K., Kim, H., Kim, J., Chee, S.: HIGHT: A New Block Cipher Suitable for Low-Resource Device. In: Goubin, L., Matsui, M. (eds.) CHES 2006. LNCS, vol. 4249, pp. 46–59. Springer, Heidelberg (2006)

21. Jaulmes, É., Muller, F.: Cryptanalysis of the F-FCSR Stream Cipher Family. In: Preneel, B., Tavares, S. (eds.) SAC 2005. LNCS, vol. 3897, pp. 20–35. Springer, Heidelberg (2006)

22. Klapper, A., Goresky, M.: 2-adic Shift Registers. In: Anderson, R. (ed.) FSE 1993. LNCS, vol. 809, pp. 174–178. Springer, Heidelberg (1994)

23. Lim, C.H., Korkishko, T.: mCrypton – A Lightweight Block Cipher for Security of Low-Cost RFID Tags and Sensors. In: Song, J.-S., Kwon, T., Yung, M. (eds.) WISA 2005. LNCS, vol. 3786, pp. 243–258. Springer, Heidelberg (2006)

24. Maurer, U.M., Renner, R., Holenstein, C.: Indifferentiability, Impossibility Results on Reductions, and Applications to the Random Oracle Methodology. In: Naor, M. (ed.) TCC 2004. LNCS, vol. 2951, pp. 21–39. Springer, Heidelberg (2004)

25. ModelSim. Modelsim pe - simulation and debug, http://model.com/content/modelsim-pe-simulation-and-debug

26. National Institute of Standards and Technology. Announcing Request for Candidate Algorithm Nominations for a NewCryptographic Hash Algorithm (SHA-3) Family. Federal Register 27(212), 62212–62220 (2007), http://csrc.nist.gov/groups/ST/hash/documents/FR_Notice_Nov07.pdf (October 17, 2008)

27. Network of Excellence in Cryptology ECRYPT. Call for stream cipher primitives, http://www.ecrypt.eu.org/stream/

28. Ouafi, K., Vaudenay, S.: Smashing SQUASH-0. In: Joux, A. (ed.) EUROCRYPT 2009. LNCS, vol. 5479, pp. 300–312. Springer, Heidelberg (2009)

29. Shamir, A.: SQUASH – A New MAC with Provable Security Properties for Highly Constrained Devices Such as RFID Tags. In: Nyberg, K. (ed.) FSE 2008. LNCS, vol. 5086, pp. 144–157. Springer, Heidelberg (2008)

30. Stankovski, P., Hell, M., Johansson, T.: An Efficient State Recovery Attack on X-FCSR-256. In: Dunkelman, O. (ed.) FSE 2009. LNCS, vol. 5665, pp. 23–37. Springer, Heidelberg (2009)

31. Wang, X., Yu, H.: How to Break MD5 and Other Hash Functions. In: Cramer, R. (ed.) EUROCRYPT 2005. LNCS, vol. 3494, pp. 19–35. Springer, Heidelberg (2005)

A   Matrix T and FI Function for the 64-Bit Security Level GLUON Version

We first define the two operations Shift Left SL and Shift Right SR in big endian notation for an n bits word $a = (a_0, \cdots, a_{n-1})$ as follows:

- Shift Left: $SL(a) = (0, a_0, \cdots a_{n-2})$ which is a Shift Right operation in little endian notation.
- Shift Right: $SR(a) = (a_1, \cdots a_{n-1}, 0)$ which is a Shift Left operation in little endian notation.

Matrix T: Parameters: $w = 18$ blocks of $r = 8$ bits. The value of q is equal to:

$$-27013336179990468777742546164977981767038829$$

$$
T =
\begin{pmatrix}
0 & I & 0 & 0 & 0 & 0 & 0 & 0 & 0 & 0 & 0 & 0 & 0 & 0 & 0 & I & 0 & 0 \\
0 & 0 & I & 0 & 0 & 0 & 0 & 0 & 0 & 0 & 0 & 0 & 0 & 0 & 0 & 0 & 0 & 0 \\
0 & 0 & 0 & I & 0 & 0 & 0 & I & 0 & 0 & 0 & 0 & 0 & 0 & 0 & 0 & 0 & 0 \\
0 & 0 & SR^5 & 0 & I & 0 & 0 & 0 & 0 & 0 & 0 & 0 & 0 & 0 & 0 & 0 & 0 & 0 \\
0 & 0 & 0 & 0 & 0 & I & 0 & 0 & 0 & 0 & 0 & 0 & 0 & 0 & 0 & 0 & 0 & 0 \\
0 & 0 & 0 & 0 & 0 & 0 & I & 0 & 0 & 0 & 0 & 0 & I & 0 & 0 & 0 & 0 & 0 \\
0 & 0 & 0 & 0 & 0 & 0 & 0 & I & 0 & 0 & 0 & 0 & 0 & 0 & 0 & 0 & SL^3 & 0 \\
0 & 0 & 0 & 0 & 0 & 0 & 0 & 0 & I & 0 & 0 & 0 & 0 & 0 & 0 & 0 & 0 & 0 \\
0 & 0 & 0 & 0 & 0 & 0 & 0 & 0 & 0 & I & 0 & I & 0 & 0 & 0 & 0 & 0 & 0 \\
0 & 0 & 0 & 0 & 0 & 0 & 0 & 0 & 0 & 0 & I & 0 & 0 & 0 & 0 & 0 & 0 & 0 \\
0 & 0 & 0 & 0 & 0 & 0 & 0 & 0 & 0 & 0 & 0 & I & 0 & 0 & 0 & 0 & 0 & SR^5 \\
0 & 0 & 0 & 0 & 0 & 0 & 0 & 0 & 0 & 0 & 0 & 0 & I & 0 & 0 & 0 & 0 & 0 \\
0 & 0 & 0 & 0 & 0 & I & 0 & 0 & 0 & 0 & 0 & 0 & 0 & I & 0 & 0 & 0 & 0 \\
0 & 0 & 0 & 0 & 0 & 0 & 0 & 0 & SL^1 & 0 & 0 & 0 & 0 & I & 0 & 0 & 0 & 0 \\
0 & 0 & I & 0 & 0 & 0 & 0 & 0 & 0 & 0 & 0 & 0 & 0 & 0 & I & 0 & 0 & 0 \\
0 & 0 & 0 & 0 & 0 & 0 & 0 & 0 & 0 & 0 & 0 & 0 & 0 & 0 & 0 & 0 & I & 0 \\
0 & 0 & 0 & SR^3 & 0 & 0 & 0 & 0 & 0 & 0 & 0 & 0 & 0 & 0 & 0 & 0 & 0 & I \\
I & 0 & 0 & 0 & 0 & 0 & 0 & 0 & 0 & 0 & 0 & 0 & 0 & 0 & SL^6 & 0 & 0 & 0 \\
\end{pmatrix}
$$

$$m(t) = (m_0(t), \cdots, m_{17}(t))^T \text{ and } m(t+1) = Tm(t)$$

8-bit words with carries: m_0, m_2, m_3, m_5, m_6, m_8, m_{11}, m_{12}, m_{13}, m_{14}, m_{16}, m_{17}. The diameter d is equal to 29.

Filter FI:

$$
\begin{aligned}
FI(m(t)) = {} & (m_0(t) \oplus (m_2(t)_{>>>4})) \oplus (m_3(t)_{>>>5}) \oplus (m_5(t)_{>>>3}) \oplus \\
& (m_6(t)_{<<<1}) \oplus (m_8(t)_{>>>2}) \oplus (m_{11}(t)_{<<<4}) \oplus (m_{12}(t)_{>>>1}) \oplus \\
& (m_{13}(t)_{>>>5}) \oplus (m_{14}(t)_{>>>3}) \oplus (m_{16}(t)_{>>>1}) \oplus (m_{17}(t)_{<<<2})
\end{aligned}
$$

B   Matrix T and FI Function for the 80-Bit Security Level GLUON Version

Matrix T: Parameters: $w = 12$ blocks of $r = 16$ bits. The value of q is equal to:

$$-59843125551244501341385076303169721098141944604920486685101$$

$$T = \begin{pmatrix}
0 & I & 0 & 0 & SL^{12} & 0 & 0 & 0 & 0 & 0 & 0 & 0 \\
0 & 0 & I & 0 & 0 & 0 & 0 & 0 & 0 & 0 & 0 & 0 \\
0 & 0 & 0 & I & 0 & 0 & 0 & 0 & 0 & SL^3 & 0 & 0 \\
0 & SL & 0 & 0 & I & 0 & 0 & 0 & 0 & 0 & 0 & 0 \\
0 & 0 & 0 & 0 & 0 & I & SL^2 & 0 & 0 & 0 & 0 & 0 \\
0 & I & 0 & 0 & 0 & 0 & I & 0 & 0 & 0 & 0 & 0 \\
I & 0 & 0 & 0 & 0 & 0 & 0 & I & SL^{12} & 0 & 0 & 0 \\
SL^3 & 0 & 0 & 0 & 0 & 0 & 0 & 0 & I & 0 & 0 & 0 \\
0 & 0 & 0 & 0 & 0 & 0 & 0 & SL^2 & 0 & I & 0 & 0 \\
0 & 0 & SR^3 & 0 & 0 & 0 & 0 & 0 & 0 & 0 & I & 0 \\
0 & 0 & 0 & 0 & 0 & 0 & 0 & 0 & 0 & 0 & 0 & I \\
I & 0 & 0 & 0 & 0 & 0 & 0 & 0 & 0 & 0 & 0 & 0
\end{pmatrix}$$

16-bit words with carries: m_0, m_2, m_3, m_4, m_6, m_7, m_8, m_9. The diameter d is equal to 58.

Filter FI:

$$\begin{aligned}
F(m) = (m_0(t) \oplus (m_2(t)_{>>>3})) \qquad &\oplus \\
(m_3(t)_{>>>7}) \oplus (m_4(t)_{>>>2}) &\oplus \\
(m_6(t)_{>>>2}) \oplus (m_7(t)_{>>>4}) &\oplus \\
(m_8(t)_{<<<1}) \oplus (m_9(t)_{>>>2})&
\end{aligned}$$

C   Matrix T and FI Function for the 112-Bit Security Level GLUON Version

Matrix T: Parameters: $w = 9$ blocks of $r = 32$ bits. The value of q is equal to:

$$-4228841923935277938113658149538688438595997356223832672089412465139266477362728972043613$$

$$
T = \begin{pmatrix}
SR^{12} & I & 0 & 0 & 0 & 0 & 0 & 0 & 0 \\
0 & 0 & I & 0 & 0 & 0 & 0 & 0 & 0 \\
0 & 0 & 0 & I & 0 & 0 & 0 & 0 & 0 \\
0 & 0 & 0 & 0 & I & 0 & SR^{7} & 0 & 0 \\
0 & 0 & 0 & 0 & 0 & I & 0 & 0 & 0 \\
0 & 0 & 0 & 0 & 0 & 0 & I & SR^{9} & 0 \\
0 & 0 & 0 & SL^{7} & 0 & 0 & 0 & I & 0 \\
0 & 0 & 0 & 0 & 0 & 0 & 0 & 0 & I \\
I & 0 & SL^{6} & 0 & 0 & 0 & 0 & 0 & 0
\end{pmatrix}
$$

32-bit words with carries: m_0, m_3, m_5, m_6, m_8. The diameter d is equal to 42.

Filter FI:

$$
\begin{aligned}
F(m) = {} & (m_0(t) \oplus (m_3(t)_{>>>15})) && \oplus \\
& (m_5(t)_{>>>3} \oplus (m_6(t)_{<<<5})) \oplus m_8(t)_{>>>13}
\end{aligned}
$$

D   Test Vectors

We provide the following test vectors given in little endian and in hexaximal for the three GLUON instances:

- For GLUON-64:

```
input_message = a5a6a7a8a9aaabacadaeafb0b1b2b3b4b5b6
hash = 06a93c1fca21875a1ccd6c2bdcfafa972
```

- For GLUON-80:

```
input_message = a5a6a7a8a9aaabacadaeafb0
hash = 047a6630739e7c5cbb9ce735c0f9a89a
```

- For GLUON-112:

```
input_message = a5a6a7a8a9aaabacad
hash = 0adb1f3f38b769719c0e62868
```

SHA-3 on ARM11 Processors

Peter Schwabe[1], Bo-Yin Yang[1], and Shang-Yi Yang[2,⋆]

[1] Institute of Information Science and Research Center for Information Technology
Innovation
Academia Sinica,
128 Section 2 Academia Road, Taipei 115-29, Taiwan
peter@cryptojedi.org, by@crypto.tw
[2] Department of Electrical Engineering
National Taiwan University
1, Section 4, Roosevelt Road, Taipei 10617, Taiwan
ilway25@crypto.tw

Abstract. This paper presents high-speed assembly implementations of
the 256-bit-output versions of all five SHA-3 finalists and of SHA-256 for
the ARM11 family of processors. We report new speed records for all of
the six implemented functions. For example our implementation of the
round-3 version of JH-256 is 35% faster than the fastest implementation
of the round-2 version of JH-256 in eBASH. Scaled with the number of
rounds this is more than a 45% improvement. We also improve upon previous assembly implementations for 32-bit ARM processors. For example
the implementation of Grøstl-256 described in this paper is about 20%
faster than the arm32 implementation in eBASH.

Keywords: SHA-3, ARM processors, software implementation.

1 Introduction

In 2007 the National Institute for Standards and Technology (NIST) issued a
public call for submissions to a hash function competition (SHA-3 competition)
[18]. This call received 64 submissions by October 2008, 51 of which entered
round 1 of the competition. These 51 candidates have since been analyzed by
the international cryptologic research community. Based on this analysis, NIST
selected 14 candidates in July 2009 for round 2, and 5 finalists out of these 14
in December 2010.

In 2012, NIST will announce the winner of the competition, which will be
standardized as SHA-3. The security of the 5 SHA-3 finalists has been carefully

⋆ This work was supported by the National Science Council, National Taiwan
University and Intel Corporation under Grant NSC99-2911-I-002-001 and 99-
2218-E-001-007, and by the Academia Sinica Career Award. Part of the work
was done while the first author was employed by National Taiwan University.
Part of the work was done during a research retreat co-sponsored by NIST
grant 60NANB10D004 and NSF grant 1018836. Permanent ID of this document:
fd40a1bbff5e17e661dfed3102dbf1fa. Date: April 22, 2012.

A. Mitrokotsa and S. Vaudenay (Eds.): AFRICACRYPT 2012, LNCS 7374, pp. 324–341, 2012.
© Springer-Verlag Berlin Heidelberg 2012

analyzed in the last 3 years and no attacks against NIST's main requirements have been found in any of the candidates. The only attack against a full version of one of the finalists is the distinguisher for JH presented by Naya-Plasencia, Toz, and Varıcı in [17]. One of the main criteria for NIST's decision is therefore going to be performance of the finalists in hardware and software. Consequently much effort had been dedicated to optimizing software implementations of the SHA-3 finalists by many groups for a variety of platforms. Benchmarks of these software implementations are collected by the eBASH benchmarking project led by Bernstein and Lange [10].

It is notable that most of the aforementioned optimizations in software implementations target high-end 64-bit processors by Intel and AMD. In many cases, they make significant use of the x86 sophisticated vector instructions. Although the number of processors in embedded devices, smartphones and other "small computers" is much larger than the number of high-end Intel and AMD desktop and server processors, the number of optimized implementations of the SHA-3 finalists targeting such small computers is comparatively small.

This paper describes assembly implementations of all SHA-3 finalists for the ARM11 family of processors. These implementations set new speed records for all of the SHA-3 finalists; for comparison we also implemented SHA-256 for the ARM11. ARM11 processors can be found in many smartphones by Apple, Samsung, HTC, Nokia and others. They can also be found in embedded devices, cars and other small devices. According to [3,1,2] ARM ships more than half a billion ARM11 CPUs each year, many of them are used in environments that need fast cryptography, including hash functions.

Aside from new speed records on a particular processor that help evaluate the performance of the SHA-3 finalists, we may draw two perhaps surprising conclusions from our results: First one would expect that compilers are able to transform C implementations of the SHA-3 finalists into high-performance code for this relatively simple 32-bit RISC architecture. However, in some cases we were able to improve upon the fastest C implementations included in eBASH by more than a factor of 2. This shows the importance of platform-specific optimization on the assembly level. Second some of the finalists are designed to achieve high performance on 64-bit processors or for implementations that use 128-bit or 256-bit vector instructions. This paper shows the consequences of such design decisions for performance on a simple 32-bit platform that does not support vector instructions.

We submitted the software described in this paper to the eBASH benchmarking project for public benchmarking. All benchmarks reported in this paper are from the SUPERCOP benchmarking suite. We put all software described in this paper into the public domain to maximize reusability.

Notation. We use $\oplus$ for a bitwise *xor*, $\vee$ for bitwise *or* and $\wedge$ for bitwise *and*.

2   The ARM11 Processor Family

The ARM11 family of microprocessors has been introduced by ARM in 2002 and is the only implementation of the ARMv6 architecture. The most widely used processor of this family is the ARM1136, others are the ARM1156 and the ARM1176. We developed and benchmarked the software described in this paper on an ARM1136 processor, more specifically on a Samsung GT i7500 Galaxy smartphone containing a Qualcomm MSM7200A chip released in 2007. The characteristics of ARM11 processors are described in detail in the ARM11 technical reference manuals [6,4,5,7,8]. In the following we give a summary of the features that are most relevant to the implementations described in this paper.

ARM11 processors have a 32-bit instruction set and 16 architectural 32-bit integer registers. One register is used as stack pointer, one as program counter, so 14 registers are freely usable. Instructions are issued in order, one instruction per cycle. The arithmetic instructions relevant to the implementations described in this paper have a latency of 1 cycle, the result of an instruction can thus be used as input to the next instruction without latency penalty. Access to memory is cached with cache sizes between 4 KB and 64 KB. Loads from cache have a latency of 3 cycles.

The instruction set is a standard RISC load-store instruction set except for two features: free shifts and rotates and loads and stores of more than 32 bits.

Free Shifts and Rotates. All arithmetic instructions have three operands, the output does not necessarily overwrite one of the inputs. Additionally, the second input operand can be shifted or rotated by arbitrary distances provided as immediate value or through a register. These shifts or rotates as part of arithmetic instructions do not decrease throughput or increase latency of the instruction, they are essentially for free. However, the shifted or rotated input value is required one stage earlier in the pipeline than a non-shifted input. Therefore, using the output of one instruction as shifted or rotated input to the next instruction imposes a penalty of one cycle.

Load and Store Double and Multiple. The ARMv6 instruction set contains load and store instructions that move more than 32 bits between memory and registers. More specifically, the strd instruction stores 64 bits from two consecutive registers (e.g., r0 and r1) to a 64-bit memory location, the ldrd instruction loads 64 bits from memory into two consecutive registers. Some additional restrictions apply for these 64-bit load and store instructions:

- The first register argument has to be an even register (r0, r2, r4, ...),
- the instructions do not support all addressing modes that their 32-bit counterparts support, in particular they do not support shifted register offsets (documentation is very misleading here; for example, [6, Section 16.11] says that performance of ldrd and strd depends on the shift distance of the register offset), and
- they take one memory cycle only if the memory location is 8-byte aligned, otherwise they take 2 memory cycles.

For details also see [6, Section 16.11]. The ARMv6 architecture also supports loads and stores of more than 64 bits in one instruction (ldm and stm instructions). Addressing modes are even more limited than for strd and ldrd. They need as many memory cycles as a corresponding sequence of 64-bit loads or stores and thus yield better performance only in very special cases that we were not able to exploit in our implementations.

Accessing the Cycle Counter. Access to the 32-bit cycle counter is only possible from kernel mode, for example using the following code:

```
unsigned int c;
asm volatile("mrc p15, 0, %0, c15, c12, 1" : "=r"(c));
```

In a posting to the eBATS mailing list ebats@list.cr.yp.to from August 12, 2010, Bernstein publicized code for a kernel module that gives access to the cycle counter on ARM11 devices through the Linux device file /dev/cpucycles4ns. The SUPERCOP benchmarking suite [10] supports cycle counts through this device file; we use SUPERCOP for all benchmarks.

3   Blake

The full specification of Blake is given in [9]. We only briefly recall the structure of the computationally most expensive part, the compression function. The inputs to the Blake-256 compression function are a chaining value of 8 32-bit words $h_0, \ldots, h_7$, a message block of 16 32-bit words $m_0, \ldots, m_{15}$, a salt of 4 32-bit words $s_0, \ldots, s_3$. and counter consisting of 2 32-bit words t_0, t_1 The output is a new chaining value consisting of 8 32-bit words. The compression consists of 3 main steps:

- An initialization expands the 14 words of chaining value, salt and counter to a 16-word state $(v_0, \ldots, v_{15})$.
- The 16-word state is transformed through 14 rounds. Each round consists of 8 evaluations of a function G, which modifies 4 words of the state in place and takes as additional inputs 2 words of the message block and two out of a set of 16 constants $c_0, \ldots, c_{15}$ The total of $14 \cdot 8 = 112$ evaluations of G are the main computation of the Blake-256 hash function. Each evaluation of G requires 6 32-bit word additions, 6 32-bit xor operations, and 4 rotations of 32-bit words by 16,12,8, and 7 bits, respectively. The 8 evaluations of G can be seen as 2 blocks of 4 evaluations each; evaluations of G in each of the two blocks are independent and can be swapped or interleaved.
- The finalization uses 24 32-bit xor operations to map $h_0, \ldots, h_7, s_0, \ldots, s_3$, $v_0, \ldots, v_{15}$ to a new chaining value $h'_0, \ldots, h'_7$.

3.1   Implementation Details

The 6 additions and 6 xors in each evaluation of G add up to a total of $112 \cdot 12 = 1344$ arithmetic instructions throughout the 14-round main loop. This corresponds to a $1344/64 = 21$ cycles lower bound for Blake-256. This lower bound is ignoring costs for loads of message words, costs for loads of constants, spills of state words, as the 16 state words do not fit into the usable 14 registers, and overhead from the initialization and finalization phase. Furthermore it assumes that all rotations can be carried out for free in the second argument of additions or xors.

To obtain the speed of 33.93 cycles per byte for long messages we applied two optimization techniques. First we manage to merge (almost) all rotations with arithmetic instructions and second we carefully reschedule code to reduce the number of spills.

Removing Rotations. As explained in Section 2, the second argument of arithmetic instructions can be shifted or rotated arbitrarily. This shift or rotation does not cost any additional cycles, if the shifted value is not the output of the directly preceding instruction. In other words, the combination of an arithmetic operation $\odot$ with a rotation by n of the form

$$a \leftarrow b \odot (c \ggg n)$$

costs the same as $\odot$ without the rotation (but imposes an additional scheduling constraint). The 4 rotations used inside the function G are not of this form, they rotate the result of an arithmetic instruction instead of one of the inputs:

$$a \leftarrow (b \odot c) \ggg n).$$

This can easily be decomposed into two instructions

$$a \leftarrow (b \odot c), \text{ and}$$
$$a \leftarrow a \ggg n.$$

Our implementation instead only computes the first of the two instructions and rotates a by n the next time a is used as input. We consistently apply this technique to all variables. This means that we keep track of the implicit rotation distances for each variable and apply this rotation whenever the variable is used as an input. Very soon this will lead to the case that both inputs to an arithmetic instruction need to be rotated, i.e.,

$$a \leftarrow (b \ggg n_1) \odot (c \ggg n_2).$$

In this case we compute

$$a \leftarrow b \odot (c \ggg (n_2 - n_1))$$

and set the implicit rotation distance of a to n_1. Note at this point that all rotation distances are constants; the value $n_2 - n_1$ is computed at compile time.

In principle we can merge all rotations with arithmetic instructions in this way; the only restriction is that implicit rotation distances of variables must be invariant across different iterations of loops. We fully unrolled the 14 rounds of the Blake-256 compression function, so we only need to make the implicit rotations distances explicit by actual rotations at the very end of the loop. Out of the 16 state words, 12 end up with a implicit rotation distance of 0, so we only need 4 dedicated rotation instructions for the whole compression function.

Reducing Spills. The 16 32-bit words $v_0, \ldots, v_{15}$, the 16 constants $c_0, \ldots, c_{15}$, and the 16 32-bit message words clearly do not fit into the 14 usable 32-bit registers. Even worse, not even the 16 state words can be kept in registers, the compression function thus requires loads and stores. To keep the number of loads and stores low we do the following:

- Before entering the compression loop we put the 16 constants on the stack so that they can be accessed through the stack pointer. We could also access them through offsets to the program counter, but our code is too long to access constants from any position in the code through the allowed 8-bit offset.
- In each iteration of the compression loop we place the 16 message words on the stack. This saves one register containing the pointer to the message block, furthermore we can easily convert from big-endian to little-endian encoding by loading message blocks in big-endian mode once and storing them in little endian mode on the stack.
- We partition the set of state words into low words $v_0, \ldots, v_7$ and high words $v_8, \ldots, v_{15}$, we keep the low state words in registers throughout the whole computation. Each evaluation of G transforms 2 low state words and 2 high state words, so we can compute G with 12 arithmetic instructions, 2 loads of high words, 2 stores of high words, 2 loads of message words, and 2 loads of constants – a total of 20 instructions.
- We replace the two loads of high 32-bit words by one 64-bit load, this reduces the number of instructions per evaluation of G to 19. For this to work we need to make sure that previous stores of these two words store them to consecutive memory locations.
- We reorder evaluations of G in a way that allows us to reuse the output high state words as input to the next evaluation where possible.

In total the 112 evaluations of G take 2044 instructions, 18.25 instructions per evaluation of G. These instructions are carefully scheduled to hide all latencies and thus contribute $2044/64 = 31.94$ cycles/byte to the total cost.

4 Grøstl

We only recall the computationally intensive part of Grøstl-256, the compression function. The full specification of Grøstl is given in [16]. The compression function maps a 512-bit state h_{i-1} and a 512-bit message block m_i to a 512-bit state h_i. This compression uses two 512-bit permutations P and Q and computes

$$h_i = P(h_{i-1} \oplus m_i) \oplus Q(m_i) \oplus h_{i-1}.$$

The design of the permutations P and Q is inspired by AES, the main change is the size of the state which for Grøstl is an 8×8 byte matrix instead of the 4×4

matrix for AES. This change allows to make more efficient use of 64-bit architectures. The permutations P and Q are very similar, both transform the state in 10 rounds each round consists of the operations ADDROUNDCONSTANT, SUB-BYTES, SHIFTBYTES, and MIXBYTES. The SUBBYTES and the MIXBYTES operations are the same for P and Q; SUBBYTES is the byte substitution also used in AES. The ADDROUNDCONSTANTS and SHIFTBYTES operations are slightly different in P and Q; this requires separate implementations of P and Q but has no effect on the implementation techniques. Everything explained in the following is valid for both P and Q.

4.1   Implementation Details

The designers of Grøstl recommend in [16, Section 8.1.3] to use a lookup-table based implementation for 32-bit processors that do not support 128-bit vector instructions. The idea is to compute the SUBBYTES, SHIFTBYTES, and MIXBYTES operations columnwise, where the computation of each column consists of

- 8 table lookups of 64-bit values from 8 tables $T_0, \ldots, T_7$ of size 2 KB each, each lookup indexed by one byte of the state, and
- 7 64-bit xors of these 8 values to obtain the new the 64-bit column.

This is the same idea as the lookup-table-based approach for AES described in [14, Section 5.2].

For a 32-bit implementation all operations on 64-bit values need to be split into 2 operations on 32-bit values; a small benefit is that the total size of the tables can be halved because entries in tables $T_1, \ldots, T_7$ are simply rotations of values in table T_0. ARM addressing modes do not allow to load from a base address (pointer to the tables) plus a shifted offset register value. Each of these column computations thus requires 8 byte extractions (for example single-byte loads), 8 additions of the table pointer to a (shifted) byte offset, 16 32-bit loads, 14 xors, and 2 32-bit stores of the computed new state column. These final stores are required because the complete state does not fit into registers and allows to perform byte extraction through single-byte loads. This total of 48 instructions, performed 8 times per round, over 10 rounds in both P and Q yields a lower bound of $(48 \cdot 8 \cdot 10 \cdot 2)/64 = 120$ cycles per byte, ignoring the cost of ADDROUNDCONSTANTS.

This approach is what the `arm32` assembly implementation for 32-bit ARM processors by Wieser (included in SUPERCOP since version 20110914) does. With about 140 cycles/byte it comes remarkably close to the lower bound if we consider cost for ADDROUNDCONSTANTS and loop overhead.

At a speed of about 110 cycles per byte for long messages, our implementation improves upon this implementation by more than 20%. The main reason is that it makes use of 64-bit table lookups.

64-Bit Lookups. Instead of performing the table lookups with 32-bit loads we use the `ldrd` instruction to perform 64-bit lookups. As the result of such a lookup is returned in two 32-bit registers, we do not need larger tables; "rotation by 32" is free, the tables only need 8 KB of storage. With this improvement the computation of one column only requires 8 byte lookups, 8 additions of the table base pointer to the shifted byte offsets, 8 64-bit lookups, 14 xors, and 1 64-bit store. These 39 instructions yield a lower bound of $(39 \cdot 8 \cdot 10 \cdot 2)/64 = 97.5$ cycles per byte, again ignoring the cost of the ADDROUNDCONSTANTS operation and loop overhead.

Interleaved Tables. If the 4 lookup tables of size 2 KB each were laid out in memory one after the other, we would need to either keep 4 table addresses in memory or add constant offsets of 2048, 4096 or 6192 to 75% of the lookup addresses. The ARM addressing modes for the ldrd instruction support adding constant offsets to a base address, but these offsets must not be larger than 8 bytes (signed). We circumvent this problem by interleaving 64-bit entries of the 4 tables in memory, two consecutive 64-bit entries of the same table thus start at addresses that are 32 bytes apart. The bytes extracted from the state thus need to be shifted by 5 instead of 2 to serve as lookup offsets.

5   JH

The JH construction may be considered a modified sponge. The full specification of JH-256 is given in [19]. The central part of the JH hash function is the compression function. This compression function transforms a 1024-bit state and a 512-bit input block into a 1024-bit state as follows:

- Xor the input block into the first half of the state,
- apply a permutation, constructed as a block cipher E_8 with a fixed key (expanded to hash-function round constants), and
- xor the input block into the second half of the state.

The speed-critical part of this compression is the application of E_8 which consists of 42 rounds of a substitution-permutation network designed for efficient bitsliced implementations using 128-bit or 256-bit vector registers. In bitsliced implementation using 128-bit vector registers the state is decomposed into 8 128-bit vectors. Each round operates on these 128-bit vectors of the state and 2 128-bit round constants. One round consists of the following operations:

- 2 applications of the Sbox operation, an in-place transformation of 4 state vectors involving 1 round constant (see Listing 1),
- 1 application of the L operation, an in-place transformation of 8 state vectors (see Listing 1), and
- swapping of adjacent bit blocks in 4 of the state vectors. The size of these bit blocks is $2^{(i \bmod 7)}$ in round i, i.e., in rounds 0, 7, 14, 21, 28, and 35 swap adjacent bits; in rounds 1, 8, 15, 22, 29, and 36 swap adjacent blocks of 2 bits; in rounds 2, 9, 16, 23, 30, and 37 swap adjacent blocks of 4 bits; and so on; and in rounds 6, 13, 20, 27, 34, and 41 swap adjacent blocks of 64 bits.

Listing 1. The Sbox and the L operations of the JH compression function

```
#define Sbox(v0,v1,v2,v3,rcst)       \    #define L(v0,v1,v2,v3,v4,v5,v6,v7) \
  v3  = ~(v3);                       \      (v4) ^= (v1);                    \
  v0 ^= ((~(v2)) & (rcst));          \      (v5) ^= (v2);                    \
  tmp0 = (rcst) ^ ((v0) & (v1));     \      (v6) ^= (v0) ^ (v3);             \
  v0 ^= ((v2) & (v3));               \      (v7) ^= (v0);                    \
  v3 ^= ((~(v1)) & (v2));            \      (v0) ^= (v5);                    \
  v1 ^= ((v0) & (v2));               \      (v1) ^= (v6);                    \
  v2 ^= ((v0) & (~(v3)));            \      (v2) ^= (v4) ^ (v7);             \
  v0 ^= ((v1) | (v3));               \      (v3) ^= (v4);
  v3 ^= ((v1) & (v2));               \
  v1 ^= (tmp0 & (v0));               \
  v2 ^= tmp0;
```

5.1   Implementation Details

For the ARM11, each operation on 128-bit vectors needs to be decomposed into 4 operations on 32-bit values. The 19 bit-logical operations in the Sbox operation (ignoring negations) and the 10 bit-logical operations in the L operation thus yield a lower bound on JH performance of $42 \cdot 4 \cdot (2 \cdot 19 + 10) = 8064$ cycles per block or 126 cycles per byte. This ignores costs for loads and stores, loop overhead and costs of the bit-block swapping. We now describe the optimization techniques that we applied to obtain the performance of 156.43 cycles per byte for long messages.

Partial Unrolling. Fully unrolling the compression function would result in code larger than 32 KB, more than the instruction cache on by far most ARM11 processors. Instead we unroll 7 rounds, a choice that comes from the block sizes in the swapping step. This way we keep the size of the compression function comfortably below 8 KB. Instead of using a round counter in a register we place a sentinel value at the end of the round-constant table and exit the loop when this sentinel value is read.

Loop Reordering. As we decomposed 128-bit vectors into 4 32-bit values, the compression function has two loops, one loop over the 42 rounds, another one over the 4 vector chunks. If we ignored the bit-block swapping step at the end of each round these loops could permute, but in the last two out of 7 rounds (bit block sizes of 32 and 64) registers at different positions in the vector communicate. The obvious way of ordering the loops is thus an outside (partially unrolled) loop of the rounds and then a loop of length 4 (unrolled) inside each round. Each of these iterations of the inside loop operates on different 8 32-bit state values, so with the 14 available registers this solution requires 32 load and 32 store operations per round.

However, by swapping the order of the two loops in the first 5 rounds of a 7-round block, these 32 load-save pairs can avoided. Only the last two rounds of a 7-round block require frequent loads and stores. We then reverse the processing order in the last round of a 7-round block, saving a further 4 stores and 4 loads between this round and the previous round, as well as this round and the next block.

For the state we use a memory layout that allows us to perform all loads and stores of the state in 64-bit, halving the number of load-store operations. This layout also allows us to use 64-bit loads and stores in the xor sequences at the beginning and the end of the compression function.

Optimized Sbox Operation. The ARMv6 instruction set allows to combine a logical and with a negation of one of the arguments (`bic` instruction). Most negations inside the Sbox operation are exactly of this type but the negation in the first line (cmp. Listing 1) can not easily be eliminated. However, in 2/7 of all uses of Sbox the negated value is the output of a swap operation. In these cases the negation can be combined with a logical and in the swap operation (see below).

Efficient Bit-Block Swapping. The swapping of 16-bit blocks is a rotation that is free if we merge it with subsequent uses of the value in arithmetic instructions. Swapping 8-bit blocks can be done in just one instruction using the `rev16` instruction. Swapping of adjacent bit blocks of size 1, 2, and 4 is not that straightforward but can still make use of free shifts. For example swapping adjacent bits in a register x uses a mask $m = \mathtt{0xaaaaaaaa}$ in another register and three instructions as follows:

$$t \leftarrow m \wedge (x \ll 1)$$
$$x \leftarrow m \wedge x$$
$$x \leftarrow t \oplus (x \gg 1)$$

Note that in one out of four swaps, the `bic` instruction (which negates the shifted second operand) is substituted for the logical and to save the negation at the beginning of the Sbox operation (see above).

6   Keccak

The KECCAK hash function uses a sponge construction. The message is absorbed into a 1600-bit state in r-bit blocks, for KECCAK with 256-bit output the SHA-3 submission specifies $r = 1088$ [12, Section 2]. Each absorption of an r-bit block consists of two steps:

- Xor the message block with the first r bits of the state, and
- transform the state through the 1600-bit permutation KECCAK-f[1600].

After all blocks of the (padded) message have been absorbed, the hash value is extracted from the state in a squeeze operation. The speed-critical part of hashing long messages is the absorption and in particular the KECCAK-f[1600] transformation. A full specification of KECCAK is given in [11] and in [12].

The KECCAK-f[1600] transformation considers the state a $5 \times 5 \times 8$ byte cuboid or a 5×5 matrix of 64-bit lanes. The transformation is performed in 24 rounds, each round consists of the following steps:

- xor the 5 lanes of each column to obtain values $b_0, \ldots, b_4$,
- compute 5 values $c_0, \ldots, c_4$, each as the xor of one of the b_i with another of the b_i rotated by 1,
- compute the updated state columnwise, for each column
  - pick up 5 state lanes diagonally,
  - xor each of these state lanes with a different c_i (one lane of the whole state is additionally xored with a round constant),
  - rotate each of these lanes by a different fixed distance,
  - compute each lane of the updated column by negating one of the lanes, computing the logical and with another lane and then xoring the result to a third lane.

6.1 Implementation Details

For 32-bit architectures without vector registers the designers of KECCAK suggest the technique of bit interleaving [13, Sections 1.4 and 2.2]. The idea is to collect all bits on even positions of a 64-bit lane in one 32-bit register and all bits at odd positions in another 32-bit register. This requires interleaving every 64-bit chunk of the message, but allows to perform all rotations as rotations of 32-bit words which is particularly efficient for the ARM11 as such rotations are essentially free.

All logical operations on 64-bit lanes need to be carried out as two 32-bit operations. Computation of $b_0, \ldots, b_4$ thus takes 40 xors, computation of $c_0, \ldots, c_4$ takes another 10 xors. The computation of each column requires 10 xors with a constant, and 10 xors and 10 ands (with negation) of 32-bit half-lanes. A lower bound on the number of cycles for all 24 rounds (ignoring rotations and negations) can thus be derived as $24 \cdot (40 + 10 + 5 \cdot (10 + 10 + 10)) = 4800$, this corresponds to $4800/136 = 35.294$ cycles per byte, an additional cost of about 4 cycles per byte is required for the interleaving of the 64-bit message chunks.

The KECCAK designers recommend the `simple32bi` implementation as starting point for implementations targeting 32-bit architectures. This implementation is included in SUPERCOP, it uses the interleaving technique and provides best performance on an ARM11 of all KECCAK implementations benchmarked in eBACS; the `armasm` implementation by van Keer fails the tests of the SUPERCOP benchmarking suite.

Our assembly implementation requires 71.73 cycles per byte for long messages, 17.5% faster than the simple32bi implementation but quite a bit slower than the lower bound derived above. The main reason that neither the `simple32bi` nor our implementation get closer to the lower bound is the overhead from frequent loads and stores of parts of the large state. There are mainly two reasons why our implementation outperforms previous implementations: we manage to reduce the number of load and store instructions and we merge more rotations with arithmetic instructions.

Reducing the Number of Loads and Stores. Updating the state columnwise as described above uses 5 blocks of operations on 64-bit lanes or 10 blocks of computations on 32-bit half-lanes. A straight-forward implementation loads 5 half-lanes per block, then loads 5 32-bit c_i values, performs arithmetic instructions and then uses 5 store instructions to update the column half-lanes. With all rotations merged into arithmetic instructions each block only uses 15 arithmetic instructions, loads and stores thus contribute a 50% overhead.

With an appropriate memory layout of the state we reduce the number of store instructions to 3 by using 2 64-bit stores. Furthermore, we reorganize the 10 blocks of computations such that c_i in registers can be reused across blocks as much as possible. The initial computation of $b_0, \ldots, b_4$ (in 10 32-bit words) uses 64-bit loads of the state.

Removing Rotations. We use the same techniques as for Blake to merge almost all rotations with arithmetic instructions. Unrolling all 24 rounds would result in excessively large code. Instead, we perform the first round, then a loop of length 11 around 2 rounds and then the final round. All rounds but the last produce shifted state half-lanes, the shift distances are the same for all rounds. All rounds but the first perform shifts of state half-lanes whenever they are used as input to an arithmetic instruction. In order to keep shift distances invariant over iterations of the loop we need to perform 10 dedicated shifts in the computation of $b_0, \ldots, b_4$.

7   Skein

The idea of Skein is to build a hash function out of the tweakable block cipher Threefish. The full specification of Skein is given in [15]. We only briefly review the Threefish block cipher, the most important component of Skein. Threefish as used in Skein uses a 512-bit state that is transformed in 72 rounds. Each round consists of 4 so-called MIX operations. After every 4 rounds the 64-bit words of the state are permuted and a key (round constant) is injected. An additional round constant is injected before the first round. The key injection loads 8 out of 9 64-bit extended-key words, it loads 2 out of 3 64-words of extended tweak value, adds each of the 8 extended-key words to one of the state words, adds each of the 2 tweak values to one of the state words, and in i-th key injection adds i to one of the state words.

7.1   Implementation Details

Each MIX operation takes 2 64-bit integers x and y as inputs. It computes 2 64-bit output integers u and v as

$$u = (x + y) \bmod 2^{64}, \text{ and } v = u \oplus (y \ggg R),$$

where R is a round-dependent constant. On the 32-bit ARMv6 architecture we need to split each 64-bit word into two 32-bit chunks. With $x = (x_0, x_1)$ and $y = (y_0, y_1)$ we can compute $u = (u_0, u_1)$ with one addition and one addition with carry. Xoring u with the shifted y can be done in 4 instructions as follows:

$$t \leftarrow u_1 \oplus (y_0 \gg (32 - R))$$
$$v_0 \leftarrow u_0 \oplus (y_0 \ll R)$$
$$v_0 \leftarrow v_0 \oplus (y_1 \gg (32 - R))$$
$$v_1 \leftarrow t \oplus (y_1 \ll R).$$

From 72 rounds with 4 mix operations each we get 1728 instructions per block. From 19 key injections we would expect another $19 \cdot 11$ 64-bit additions, i.e. $19 \cdot 22 = 418$ instructions; this would together yield a lower bound from pure arithmetic instructions of $(1728 + 418)/64 = 33.53$ cycles per byte.

Since the 14 general-purpose registers cannot hold all the state words, the most important optimization required to come close to this bound is minimizing the number of loads and stores of the state words. We do this by rearranging the execution sequence to keep as many state words in memory as long as possible. This task is aided by a self-written program that traces the use of state words. Furthermore, we show how key injection can be done with less than 11 additions and less than 10 64-bit loads.

Rearranging the Execution Sequence. Before entering the key injection, there are four rounds, each of which consists of four MIX operations followed by a permutation. Instead of performing MIX and permutation in order, we mix the "permuted" state. This way, we can interleave the MIX functions of all these four rounds to achieve a much small number of loads and stores.

Consider for example the first 4 rounds. Let s_0 to s_7 be the state words. The original sequence of MIX operations is the following:

Round 1: $\mathrm{MIX}(s_0, s_1)$, $\mathrm{MIX}(s_2, s_3)$, $\mathrm{MIX}(s_4, s_5)$, $\mathrm{MIX}(s_6, s_7)$
Round 2: $\mathrm{MIX}(s_2, s_1)$, $\mathrm{MIX}(s_4, s_7)$, $\mathrm{MIX}(s_6, s_5)$, $\mathrm{MIX}(s_0, s_3)$
Round 3: $\mathrm{MIX}(s_4, s_1)$, $\mathrm{MIX}(s_6, s_3)$, $\mathrm{MIX}(s_0, s_5)$, $\mathrm{MIX}(s_2, s_7)$
Round 4: $\mathrm{MIX}(s_6, s_1)$, $\mathrm{MIX}(s_0, s_7)$, $\mathrm{MIX}(s_2, s_5)$, $\mathrm{MIX}(s_4, s_3)$.

Performing the mix operations in this order would cause a lot of overhead from loading and storing state words. For example s_0 is used in the first MIX operation, then all other state words are used before s_0 is used again, this means that s_0 needs to be spilled. Similar statements hold for the other state values.

To keep as many state words in registers as long as possible, we reorder the MIX sequence as follows:

$\mathrm{MIX}(s_0, s_1)$, $\mathrm{MIX}(s_2, s_3)$, $\mathrm{MIX}(s_2, s_1)$, $\mathrm{MIX}(s_0, s_3)$
$\mathrm{MIX}(s_4, s_5)$, $\mathrm{MIX}(s_6, s_7)$, $\mathrm{MIX}(s_6, s_5)$, $\mathrm{MIX}(s_4, s_7)$
$\mathrm{MIX}(s_4, s_1)$, $\mathrm{MIX}(s_6, s_3)$, $\mathrm{MIX}(s_6, s_1)$, $\mathrm{MIX}(s_4, s_3)$
$\mathrm{MIX}(s_0, s_5)$, $\mathrm{MIX}(s_2, s_7)$, $\mathrm{MIX}(s_2, s_5)$, $\mathrm{MIX}(s_0, s_7)$.

This order of MIX operations allows us to load and store state words only every four MIX functions. Furthermore, we interleave each round-constant injection with the preceding MIX operations to eliminate some loads and stores.

Precomputing Parts of the Key Injection. In the key injection, two of the 64-bit state words, s_5 and s_6, are modified by adding a 64-bit word of the extended key k and a 64-bit word of the extended tweak value t. In the i-th key injection this is done as

$$s_5 \leftarrow s_5 + k_{(i+5) \bmod 9} + t_{i \bmod 3},$$

$$s_6 \leftarrow s_6 + k_{(i+6) \bmod 9} + t_{(i+1) \bmod 3},$$

where the additions are all modulo 2^{64}. In the intuitive implementation this takes 4 loads of 64-bit words and 4 64-bit additions, a total of $4 + 2 \cdot 4 = 12$ instructions.

In our implementation, we see that regarding to all possible values of i, there are only nine possibilities for $k_{(i+5) \bmod 9} + t_{i \bmod 3}$ and $k_{(i+6) \bmod 9} + t_{(i+1) \bmod 3}$, namely $\{k_0, k_3, k_6\} + t_1$, $\{k_1, k_4, k_7\} + t_2$ and $\{k_2, k_5, k_8\} + t_0$. We precompute these 9 values as $kt_{0,1}$, $kt_{3,1}$, $kt_{6,1}$, $kt_{1,2}$, $kt_{4,2}$, $kt_{7,2}$, etc. and perform only two 64-bit loads and two 64-bit additions, which saves 6 instructions per key schedule or about $(19 \cdot 6)/64 = 1.78$ cycles per byte.

8 SHA-256

For reference we also optimized SHA-256 in assembly. Unlike all SHA-3 candidates, the 256-bit state of SHA-256 fits into the available registers. Furthermore, the design favors 32-bit architectures such as the ARMv6 and can make efficient use of the free rotations. For example a transformation like

$$(x \ggg a) \oplus (x \ggg b) \oplus (x \ggg c)$$

with constants a, b, and c can turn into

$$(x \oplus (x \ggg (b - a)) \oplus (x \ggg (c - a))) \ggg a$$

and thus make use of the same techniques we used for Blake to eliminate dedicated rotations. Another optimization consists in writing

$$\mathrm{Maj}(b, c, d) = (b \wedge c) \oplus (c \wedge d) \oplus (b \wedge d) = (b \wedge c) \vee (d \wedge (b \vee c)),$$

and caching the value of $b \wedge c$ and $b \vee c$ until they can be reused when calculating $\mathrm{Maj}(a, b, c) = (b \wedge c) \vee (a \wedge (b \vee c))$. It is thus not surprising to see that SHA-256 outperforms all SHA-3 candidates on this platform.

9 Results and Comparison

This section presents performance results of our implementations and a comparison with the previously fastest implementation in eBASH (SUPERCOP version 20110914). All numbers in Tables 1–6 are cycles per byte as reported by the SUPERCOP benchmarking suite. For the benchmarks we removed several compiler options from SUPERCOP that are irrelevant for ARM11 (such as -m64 or -mcpu=ultrasparc). We also added compiler options, specifically we added

Table 1. Results for Blake-256: cycles/byte for different message lengths

# bytes		long	4096	1536	576	64	8
this paper[a]	25%-quartile	33.13	34.95	36.62	40.95	94.88	509.00
	median	33.93	34.97	36.68	41.04	95.00	521.50
	75%-quartile	34.29	35.11	36.94	41.48	98.19	546.00
sphlib (ver. 3.0)[b]	25%-quartile	45.93	47.49	49.48	54.82	123.06	614.00
	median	46.29	47.49	49.48	55.09	123.06	614.50
	75%-quartile	46.81	47.74	49.52	55.97	123.13	719.16

[a] Compiled with gcc -funroll-loops -fno-schedule-insns -O2
-fomit-frame-pointer
[b] Compiled with gcc -mcpu=arm1136j-s -Os -fomit-frame-pointer
-fno-schedule-insns

Table 2. Results for Grøstl-256: cycles/byte for different message lengths

# bytes		long	4096	1536	576	64	8
this paper[a]	25%-quartile	108.92	113.17	118.26	131.87	301.88	1551.00
	median	110.16	113.24	118.44	131.95	301.94	1559.50
	75%-quartile	112.32	114.28	120.38	132.47	304.63	1604.13
arm32[b]	25%-quartile	139.79	143.48	149.52	165.86	374.63	1882.00
	median	140.17	143.62	149.65	165.86	374.63	1882.00
	75%-quartile	141.61	144.34	152.00	168.01	377.80	1998.38

[a] Compiled with gcc -funroll-loops -fno-schedule-insns -O2
-fomit-frame-pointer
[b] Compiled with gcc -mcpu=arm1020t -O -fomit-frame-pointer

the flag -no-schedule-insns to various previously contained combinations of compiler flags. This flag is crucial for best performance of many C implementations; we also informed the eBACS editors about this observation, the changes are included in SUPERCOP since version 20111120. SUPERCOP in version 20110914 did not contain any implementation of the round-3 version of JH-256. We compare our results with the benchmarks of the round-2 version, note that this version is only using 35.5 rounds instead of the 42 of our implementation.

For the display of benchmarks we follow eBACS [10]. Specifically, for each message length we report the median of 45 measurements and the 25% and 75% quartiles. The value for "long" messages is extrapolated from measurements of 4096-byte messages and 2048-byte messages.

All measurements were performed on a Samsung GT I7500 Galaxy smartphone with a 528-MHz ARM1136 processor inside a Qualcomm MSM7200A chip. All code was compiled with gcc 4.4.5.

Other Related Work. The tables only compare with the fastest implementation in eBASH as of SUPERCOP version 20110914; there are many more slower

Table 3. Results for JH-256: cycles/byte for different message lengths

# bytes		long	4096	1536	576	64	8
this paper[a]	25%-quartile	155.95	159.09	163.73	176.26	337.43	2733.50
	median	156.43	159.17	163.76	176.43	339.00	2746.00
	75%-quartile	157.68	159.78	163.95	179.02	341.59	2773.50
bitslice_opt32[b,c]	25%quartile	244.91	250.37	257.26	276.41	519.83	4155.88
	median	247.16	250.89	257.60	276.74	523.06	4195.00
	75%quartile	259.55	256.98	259.02	277.17	529.19	4232.50

[a] Compiled with gcc -funroll-loops -O3 -fomit-frame-pointer
[b] Compiled with gcc -funroll-loops -fno-schedule-insns -O2 -fomit-frame-pointer
[c] Round-2 version with only 35.5 instead of 42 rounds

Table 4. Results for Keccak: cycles/byte for different message lengths

# bytes		long	4096	1536	576	64	8
this paper[a]	25%-quartile	71.13	74.31	77.46	87.80	180.59	1438.00
	median	71.73	74.45	77.50	87.91	182.22	1447.00
	75%-quartile	73.24	75.18	77.78	88.79	185.20	1486.38
simple32bi[b]	25%-quartile	86.72	90.22	93.89	106.33	216.06	1723.00
	median	86.95	90.28	93.92	106.54	217.75	1731.00
	75%-quartile	88.41	90.99	94.51	106.80	218.81	1752.50

[a] Compiled with gcc -funroll-loops -O3 -fomit-frame-pointer
[b] Compiled with gcc -mcpu=arm1136jf-s -O3 -fomit-frame-pointer
-fno-schedule-insns

Table 5. Results for Skein-256: cycles/byte for different message lengths

# bytes		long	4096	1536	576	64	8
this paper[a]	25%-quartile	41.94	43.13	44.91	49.64	108.48	867.88
	median	42.10	43.16	45.04	49.67	108.73	874.13
	75%-quartile	43.66	43.93	45.83	50.05	113.11	893.50
sphlib-small	25%-quartile	94.15	96.32	99.39	107.58	209.11	1688.00
(ver. 3.0)[b]	median	94.57	96.40	99.41	107.65	210.64	1688.88
	75%-quartile	97.51	97.83	99.63	108.79	211.30	1698.50

[a] Compiled with gcc -funroll-loops -march=iwmmxt -O2
-fomit-frame-pointer
[b] Compiled with gcc -mcpu=arm1136jf-s -O3 -fomit-frame-pointer
-fno-schedule-insns

implementations for all candidates submitted to eBASH that can be used on ARM11 CPUs. An assembly implementation of Skein supporting different output and state sizes targeting the ARM Cortex-A8 family of CPUs by Hitland

Table 6. Results for SHA-256: cycles/byte for different message lengths

# bytes		long	4096	1536	576	64	8
this paper[a]	25%-quartile	26.57	27.48	28.95	32.48	78.20	454.50
	median	26.68	27.52	29.02	32.64	79.55	461.00
	75%-quartile	26.93	27.59	29.06	32.72	80.98	493.88
sphlib (ver. 3.0)[b]	25%-quartile	39.14	40.19	41.86	46.33	103.31	522.50
	median	39.19	40.19	41.86	46.33	103.31	522.50
	75%-quartile	39.31	40.25	41.86	46.34	103.38	535.50

[a] Compiled with gcc -mcpu=arm1136j-s -O3 -fomit-frame-pointer
[b] Compiled with gcc -mcpu=arm1136jf-s -O2 -fomit-frame-pointer
-fno-schedule-insns

can be found on https://github.com/unbounded/skein-arm. We ran the benchmarking tool shipped with this implementation on the same platform we used for eBASH benchmarks. For Skein with a 512-bit state size and 256-bit output size the tool reports a median of 48.78 cycles per byte, only slightly slower than our implementation.

Acknowledgments. We thank the CyanogenMod and GAOSP teams for their work on alternative firmware for Android smartphones. Their work made it possible to install Debian GNU/Linux in a chroot environment on a Samsung GT i7500 Galaxy phone and use it as development and benchmarking platform. We thank Dan Bernstein for his help and advice. Furthermore, we thank all the authors of SHA-3-candidate implementations who published their software and included it in eBASH.

References

1. ARM Holdings plc reports results for the third quarter and nine months ended (September 30, 2010),
http://www.arm.com/about/newsroom/arm-holdings-plc-reports-results-for
-the-third-quarter-and-nine-months-ended-30-september-2010.php
2. ARM Holdings plc reports results for the third quarter and nine months ended (September 30, 2011),
http://www.arm.com/about/newsroom/arm-holdings-plc-reports-results-for
-the-third-quarter-and-nine-months-ended-30-september-2011.php
3. Processors – ARM (2012), http://arm.com/products/processors/index.php
4. ARM Limited. ARM1156T2-S Technical Reference Manual, Revision: r0p4 (2007),
http://infocenter.arm.com/help/topic/com.arm.doc.ddi0338g/DDI0338G_
arm1156t2s_r0p4_trm.pdf
5. ARM Limited. ARM1156T2F-S TechnicalReference Manual, Revision: r0p4 (2007),
http://infocenter.arm.com/help/topic/com.arm.doc.ddi0290g/DDI0290G_
arm1156t2fs_r0p4_trm.pdf

6. ARM Limited. ARM1136JF-S and ARM1136J-S Technical Reference Manual, Revision: r1p5 (2009), http://infocenter.arm.com/help/topic/com.arm.doc.ddi0211k/DDI0211K_arm1136_r1p5_trm.pdf
7. ARM Limited. ARM1176JZ-S Technical Reference Manual, Revision: r0p7 (2009), http://infocenter.arm.com/help/topic/com.arm.doc.ddi0333h/DDI0333H_arm1176jzs_r0p7_trm.pdf
8. ARM Limited. ARM1176JZF-S Technical Reference Manual, Revision: r0p7 (2009), http://infocenter.arm.com/help/topic/com.arm.doc.ddi0301h/DDI0301H_arm1176jzfs_r0p7_trm.pdf
9. Aumasson, J.-P., Henzen, L., Meier, W., Phan, R.C.-W.: SHA-3 proposal BLAKE (version 1.3). Revised Submission to NIST (2010), http://131002.net/blake/blake.pdf
10. Bernstein, D.J., Lange, T.: eBACS: ECRYPT benchmarking of cryptographic systems, http://bench.cr.yp.to
11. Bertoni, G., Daemen, J., Peeters, M., Van Assche, G.: The Keccak reference, version 3.0 (2011), http://keccak.noekeon.org/Keccak-reference-3.0.pdf
12. Bertoni, G., Daemen, J., Peeters, M., Van Assche, G.: The Keccak SHA-3 submission (version 3). Revised Submission to NIST (2011), http://keccak.noekeon.org/Keccak-submission-3.pdf
13. Bertoni, G., Daemen, J., Peeters, M., Van Assche, G., Van Keer, R.: Keccak implementation overview, version 3.0 (2011), http://keccak.noekeon.org/Keccak-implementation-3.0.pdf
14. Daemen, J., Rijmen, V.: AES proposal: Rijndael, version 2 (1999), http://csrc.nist.gov/archive/aes/rijndael/Rijndael-ammended.pdf
15. Ferguson, N., Lucks, S., Schneier, B., Whiting, D., Bellare, M., Kohno, T., Callas, J., Walker, J.: The Skein hash function family, version 1.3. Revised Submission to NIST (2008), http://www.skein-hash.info/sites/default/files/skein1.3.pdf
16. Gauravaram, P., Knudsen, L.R., Matusiewicz, K., Mendel, F., Rechberger, C., Schläffer, M., Thomsen, S.S.: Grøstl a SHA-3 candidate (version 2.0). Revised Submission to NIST (2011), http://www.groestl.info/Groestl.pdf
17. Naya-Plasencia, M., Toz, D., Varici, K.: Rebound Attack on JH42. In: Lee, D.H., Wang, X. (eds.) ASIACRYPT 2011. LNCS, vol. 7073, pp. 252–269. Springer, Heidelberg (2011), http://homes.esat.kuleuven.be/ kvarici/Papers/Rebound_Attack_on_JH42.pdf
18. Announcing request for candidate algorithm nominations for a new cryptographic hash algorithm (SHA-3) family. Federal Register 72(212), 62212–62220 (2007), http://csrc.nist.gov/groups/ST/hash/documents/FR_Notice_Nov07.pdf
19. Wu, H.: The hash function JH (updated version from January 16, 2011). Revised submission to NIST (2011), http://www3.ntu.edu.sg/home/wuhj/research/jh/jh_round3.pdf

Improved Fixed-Base Comb Method
for Fast Scalar Multiplication

Nashwa A.F. Mohamed[1], Mohsin H.A. Hashim[1], and Michael Hutter[2]

[1] Faculty of Mathematical Sciences, University of Khartoum,
P.O. Box 321, Khartoum, Sudan
{nafarah,mhashim}@uofk.edu, nashwaabbas@gmail.com
[2] TU Graz, Institute for Applied Information Processing and Communications
Inffeldgasse 16a, 8010 Graz, Austria
michael.hutter@iaik.tugraz.at

Abstract. Computing elliptic-curve scalar multiplication is the most time consuming operation in any elliptic-curve cryptosystem. In the last decades, it has been shown that pre-computations of elliptic-curve points improve the performance of scalar multiplication especially in cases where the elliptic-curve point P is fixed. In this paper, we present an improved fixed-base comb method for scalar multiplication. In contrast to existing comb methods such as proposed by Lim and Lee or Tsaur and Chou, we make use of a width-ω non-adjacent form representation and restrict the number of rows of the comb to be greater or equal ω. The proposed method shows a significant reduction in the number of required elliptic-curve point addition operation. The computational complexity is reduced by 33 to 38% compared to Tsaur and Chou method even for devices that have limited resources. Furthermore, we propose a constant-time variation of the method to thwart simple-power analysis attacks.

Keywords: Elliptic-curve cryptosystem, scalar multiplication, Lim-Lee method, Tsaur-Chou method, non-adjacent form, width-ω NAF.

1 Introduction

In 1985, N. Koblitz [13] and V. Miller [19] introduced elliptic curves for their use in cryptography. The difficulty of solving the elliptic curve discrete logarithm problem is mathematically hard so that Elliptic Curve Cryptography (ECC) can be efficiently applied in modern cryptosystems. Among the most time consuming operation of ECC is the scalar multiplication. A secret scalar k is multiplied with a point P on an elliptic curve $E(\mathbb{F}_q)$ resulting in the point $Q \in E(\mathbb{F}_q)$. Over the last years, there have been many publications that propose new methods to efficiently calculate $Q = kP$, e.g., [5] or [8].

When the elliptic-curve point P is fixed, suggestion to pre-compute some data that depend only on P was first made by Brickell, Gordon, McCurley, and Wilson (BGMW) in 1992 [4]. They observed that if the multiplier k is expressed in a

A. Mitrokotsa and S. Vaudenay (Eds.): AFRICACRYPT 2012, LNCS 7374, pp. 342–359, 2012.
© Springer-Verlag Berlin Heidelberg 2012

base b, more time may be saved by adding together powers with like coefficients first.

Another improvement was proposed by Lim and Lee [16] in 1994. They proposed a more flexible pre-computation technique for speeding up the computation of exponentiation. Later in 2005, Tsaur and Chou [28] proposed a new fixed-base comb method by applying a NAF representation of the scalar k and Sakai and Sakurai [23] method for direct doubling.

In this paper, we propose an efficient method for scalar multiplication by combining the ideas of Lim-Lee [16] and Tsaur-Chou [28]. Our method makes use of a fixed-base comb technique and represents the scalar k in a width-ω NAF representation. Furthermore, we restrict the number of rows of the comb to be greater or equal ω. As a result, our proposed method provides a significant reduction in the number of required elliptic-curve point addition operation. In practice, a speed improvement by 33 to 38 % is achieved.

The rest of this paper is organized as follows. In Section 2, we give an introduction to elliptic curves and review some of existing scalar-multiplication methods. In Section 3, we review the methods of Lim-Lee and Tsaur-Chou. In Section 4, we propose efficient method for speeding up elliptic curve scalar multiplication. In Section 5, we show that our proposed method can accelerate simultaneous scalar multiplication. In Section 6, we discuss the resistance against side-channel attacks. In Section 7, we give results of our method compared with Tsaur and Chou method. In Section 8 we draw conclusions. Finally, in the appendix, we give an example to illustrate our method.

2   Preliminaries

This section introduces some elementary background on elliptic curves. We refer the reader to [5], [9], and [25] for further details.

An elliptic curve E over a finite field $\mathbb{F}_q$ of characteristic $\neq 2, 3$ can be given by the short Weierstrass equation

$$E : y^2 = x^3 + ax + b$$

where $a, b \in \mathbb{F}_q$, for which $4a^3 + 27b^2 \neq 0$. Elliptic-curve points $E(\mathbb{F}_q)$ are defined to be

$$E(\mathbb{F}_q) = \{(x, y) \in \mathbb{F}_q \times \mathbb{F}_q : y^2 = x^3 + ax + b\} \cup O$$

where O is the point at infinity. $E(\mathbb{F}_q)$ forms an additively abelian group with the point at infinity O which serves as the identity element. Adding two points in $E(\mathbb{F}_q)$ is defined by the *chord-and-tangent* rule.

The most time consuming operation in elliptic curve cryptography is the scalar multiplication, i.e., $Q = kP$, where P and Q are points on the curve E and k is a scalar such that $0 \leq k < ord_E(P)$. The Elliptic Curve Discrete Logarithm Problem (ECDLP) is to find the scalar k given points P and Q.

Since scalar multiplication largely determines the execution time of ECC-based protocols, it is attractive to provide efficient methods that reduce the computational complexity by applying different multiplication techniques. There are many proposals given in literature which provide improvements for different kind of scenarios: (1) both the scalar and the base point are unknown, (2) the scalar is fixed, and (3) the base point is fixed [5,9]. In the following sections, we will describe generic methods and methods where the base point is fixed. For methods where the scalar is fixed, addition chains can be used to improve the performance of scalar multiplication. We refer the reader to [5,9] for more details.

2.1   Generic Methods

One of the most easiest way to perform a scalar multiplication where both the scalar and the base point are unknown is the binary method (or often referred as *double-and-add*). A point doubling operation is performed at every loop iteration whereas point addition is only performed if the scalar bit value k_i is 1, where $i \in [0, l-1]$ denotes the bit index of the scalar k with size l. It therefore achieves a density of approximately $1/2$ which results in a computational complexity of $\frac{l}{2}A + lD$, where A and D represent the costs for addition and doubling, respectively. Note that the binary method does not need any pre-computations but does not provide resistance against timing [14] or Simple Power Analysis [15] attacks.

Windowing Techniques. A generalization of the binary method has been proposed by Brauer [3] in 1939 (also often referred as 2^r-ary or *window* method). The idea is to slice the representation of the scalar k into pieces and to process ω digits at a time. For this, k is represented in a base 2^ω where $\omega > 1$. The method scans the bits either from left-to-right or from right-to-left (like for the binary method). Note that windowing techniques require extra memory but they significantly improve the speed of scalar multiplication.

An efficient variant of the 2^r-ary method is the *sliding window* method introduced by Thurber [27] in 1973. By pre-computing iP for $i \in \{1, 3, 5, 7, ..., 2^\omega - 1\}$, one can move a width-$\omega$ window across the scalar k and search for the first non-zero bit. After finding the bit, the window is placed such that the value of the window is odd.

Non-Adjacent Form (NAF) Representations. The density of the prior described methods can be further reduced by using a signed-digit representation. The advantage of this representation is that the cost of computing the inverse of elliptic-curve points, e.g., $-P$, comes almost for free. Booth [1] proposed in 1951 to expand the coefficients in the representation of the scalar k to $\{0, \pm 1\}$. However, the disadvantage of his proposal has been that the representation is not unique. Thus, Reitwiesner [22] proposed to apply a Non-Adjacent Form (NAF) representation in 1960. A NAF of a positive integer k is an expression $k = \sum_{i=0}^{l-1} k_i 2^i$ where $k_i \in \{0, \pm 1\}$, $k_{l-1} \neq 0$, and no two consecutive digits k_i are nonzero. The length of the NAF is l. It is a canonical representation with the fewest number of non-zero digits for a given scalar k. The expected number of

---

Algorithm 1. Width-ω NAF method for a positive integer k

Require: Window width w and a positive integer k.
Ensure: Width-ω NAF(k).
  1: $i = 0$.
  2: **While** $k > 0$ **do**
  3:   **If** k is odd **then**
  4:     $b \equiv k \bmod 2^\omega$.
  5:     **If** $b \geq 2^{\omega-1}$ **then**
  6:       $b = b - 2^\omega$;
  7:       $k = k - b$.
  8:   **Else** $b = 0$.
  9:   $k_i = b$; $i = i + 1$; $k = k/2$.
 10: **Return** $(k_{i-1}, k_{i-2}, ..., k_1, k_0)$.

---

non-zero bits in a NAF is $l/3$ as shown by Morain and Olivos[21]. The runtime complexity of a binary NAF method is therefore approximately $\frac{l}{3}A + lD$ (cf. [2] and [21]).

A generalization of NAF is the width-ω NAF, proposed by Solinas[26] in 2000. For the width-ω NAF, the scalar k is represented by

$$k = \sum_{i=0}^{l-1} k_i 2^i \qquad (1)$$

where each nonzero coefficient k_i is odd, $|k_i| < 2^{\omega-1}$, $k_{l-1} \neq 0$, and at most one of any ω consecutive digits is nonzero. Algorithm 1 can be used to obtain the width-ω NAF of a positive integer k and is denoted by $\mathrm{NAF}_\omega(k)$.

In order to perform the scalar multiplication using width-ω NAF, the points $P, 3P, ..., (2^{\omega-1} - 1)P$ are pre-computed and the scalar multiplication is performed in the evaluation phase as shown in Algorithm 2. The average density of non-zero bits among all width-ω NAFs is asymptotically $1/(1 + \omega)$[21]. The expected runtime of Algorithm 2 is therefore

---

Algorithm 2. Width-ω NAF method for scalar multiplication

Require: Window width-ω, positive integer k and $P \in E(\mathbb{F}_q)$.
Ensure: $Q = kP$.
  1: Use Algorithm 1 to compute $\mathrm{NAF}_\omega(k) = \sum_{i=0}^{l-1} k_i 2^i$.
  2: Compute $P_i = iP$ for all $i \in \{1, 3, 5, 7, ..., 2^{\omega-1} - 1\}$.
  3: $Q = O$.
  4: **For** $i = l - 1$ **downto** 0 **do**
  5:   $Q = 2Q$.
  6:   **If** $k_i \neq 0$ **then**
  7:     **If** $k_i > 0$ **then** $Q = Q + P_{k_i}$.
  8:     **Else** $Q = Q - P_{k_i}$.
  9: **Return** (Q).

$$[1D + [2^{\omega-2} - 1]A] + [\frac{l}{\omega + 1}A + lD]. \tag{2}$$

Note that most of the described methods above do not *per se* provide resistance against side-channel attacks [15,18]. The methods have to provide at least a constant runtime and (even better) a regular structure to resist against most of these attacks, for example, as provided by the Montgomery powering ladder [12,20]. There, a point addition and doubling is performed in every loop iteration achieving a density of 1 $(lA + lD)$.

2.2   Fixed Base-Point Methods

When the base point P is fixed, the efficiency of scalar multiplication can be improved by pre-computations. The idea is to pre-compute every multiple $2^i P$ where $0 < i < l$. If theoretically all $2^i P$ points are pre-computed, the complexity of scalar multiplication is reduced to only $\frac{1}{2}A$ (without the need of any doublings).

Similar to generic methods, fixed base-point methods can be mainly separated into windowing, NAF windowing, and fixed-base comb techniques. One of the first who proposed a fixed-base windowing technique has been due to Brickell, Gordon, McCurley, and Wilson (BGMW) [4]. They proposed to split the scalar k into d slices, where $d = \lceil l/\omega \rceil$. The runtime complexity is then reduced to $(2^\omega + d - 3)A$. Similarly, a NAF windowing technique can be applied which further reduces the complexity to approximately $(\frac{2^{\omega+1}}{3} + d - 2)A$, where $d = \lceil (l+1)/\omega \rceil$.

In the following, we will introduce two common techniques proposed by Lim and Lee [16] as well as Tsaur and Chou [28]. Both methods are based on a fixed-base comb technique. Afterwards, we will present our proposed method that makes use of both ideas to reduce the complexity.

3   Fixed-Base Comb Methods

The main idea of fixed-base comb methods is to represent the scalar k as a binary matrix of h rows and v columns. The matrix is then processed column-wise from right-to-left or from left-to-right.

3.1   Lim and Lee Method

In 1994, Lim and Lee [16] introduced a comb technique that divides the scalar k into h blocks K_i from right-to-left, for $0 \le i \le h - 1$, of equal size $a = \lceil \frac{l}{h} \rceil$ (we pad zeros if necessary). Then, subdivide each block K_i from up-to-down into v subblocks $k_{i,j}$ of equal size $b = \lceil \frac{a}{v} \rceil$, where $0 \le j \le v - 1$. We can rewrite the h blocks of k in terms of a binary matrix, i.e.,

$$k = \begin{bmatrix} K_0 \\ \vdots \\ K_i \\ \vdots \\ K_{h-1} \end{bmatrix} = \begin{bmatrix} k_{0,v-1} & \cdots & k_{0,j} & \cdots & k_{0,0} \\ \vdots & & \vdots & & \vdots \\ k_{i,v-1} & \cdots & k_{i,j} & \cdots & k_{i,0} \\ \vdots & & \vdots & & \vdots \\ k_{h-1,v-1} & \cdots & k_{h-1,j} & \cdots & k_{h-1,0} \end{bmatrix} = \sum_{j=0}^{v-1}\sum_{i=0}^{h-1} k_{i,j} 2^{jb} 2^{ia}.$$

Let $P_0 = P$ and $P_i = 2^a P_{i-1} = 2^{ia} P$ for $0 < i < h$. Then, we can rewrite kP as

$$kP = \sum_{j=0}^{v-1}\sum_{i=0}^{h-1} k_{i,j} 2^{jb} 2^{ia} P$$

$$= \sum_{j=0}^{v-1}\sum_{i=0}^{h-1} k_{i,j} 2^{jb} P_i. \tag{3}$$

Since K_i is of size a, we can let $K_i = e_{i,a-1}...e_{i,1}e_{i,0}$ be the binary representation of K_i for all $0 \le i < h$, and hence $k_{i,j} = e_{i,jb+b-1}...e_{i,jb+1}e_{i,jb}$ is the binary representation of $k_{i,j}$, therefore

$$kP = \sum_{t=0}^{b-1} 2^t \left(\sum_{j=0}^{v-1}\sum_{i=0}^{h-1} e_{i,jb+t} 2^{jb} P_i \right). \tag{4}$$

Suppose that the following values are pre-computed and stored for all $1 \le s < 2^h$ and $1 \le j \le v - 1$,

$$G[0][s] = e_{h-1}P_{h-1} + e_{h-2}P_{h-2} + ... + e_0 P_0,$$
$$G[j][s] = 2^b(G[j-1][s]) = 2^{jb} G[0][s],$$

where the index s is equal to the decimal value of $e_{h-1}...e_1 e_0$. Therefore, we can rewrite kP as follows

$$kP = \sum_{t=0}^{b-1} 2^t \left(\sum_{j=0}^{v-1} G[j][I_{j,t}] \right) \tag{5}$$

where $I_{j,t}$ is the decimal value of $e_{h-1,jb+t}...e_{0,jb+t}$.

Now we can use the left-to-right binary method to compute kP using these pre-computed values. The number of elliptic-curve operations in the worst case is $a + b - 2$, and since $I_{j,t}$ is of size h, we may assume that the probability of $I_{j,t}$ being zero is $\frac{1}{2^h}$ and $I_{j,t}$ occurs a times, thus the expected number of elliptic-curve operations is reduced to $(1 - \frac{1}{2^h})a + b - 2$.

3.2   Tsaur and Chou Method

In 2005, Tsaur and Chou [28] proposed a new fixed-base comb method by applying a NAF representation of the scalar k. Furthermore, they divided k into $h \times v$ blocks from up-to-down and then from right-to-left. Moreover, they used a special doubling operation proposed by Sakai and Sakurai [23] which increases the performance in addition.

Let k be an l-bit scalar represented in NAF. First, we divide k from up-to-down into a blocks of equal size $h = \lceil \frac{l}{a} \rceil$. Thus we can write k as follows

$$k = c_{a-1}c_{a-2}...c_1c_0 = \sum_{l=0}^{a-1} c_l 2^{lh}, \tag{6}$$

Then, from right-to-left we divide the $h \times a$ blocks into $h \times v$ blocks, each of size $b = \lceil \frac{a}{v} \rceil$.

Let $P_0 = P$ and $P_j = 2^{hb}P_{j-1} = 2^{jhb}P$ for $0 < j < v$. Therefore, we can rewrite kP as follows

$$kP = c_{a-1}c_{a-2}...c_1c_0 P = \sum_{l=0}^{a-1} c_l 2^{lh} P = \sum_{t=0}^{b-1} 2^{th} (\sum_{j=0}^{v-1} c_{jb+t} 2^{jhb} P), \tag{7}$$

where $c_{jb+t} = e_{h-1,jb+t}...e_{1,jb+t}e_{0,jb+t}$ is the NAF representation. Suppose that the following values are pre-computed and stored for all $1 \le s \le \sum_{i=1}^{\lceil \frac{h}{2} \rceil} 2^{h-2i+1}$ and $0 \le j \le v - 1$

$$G[0][s] = e_{h-1}2^{h-1}P + e_{h-2}2^{h-2}P + ... + e_0 P,$$
$$G[j][s] = 2^{hb}(G[j-1][i]) = 2^{jhb}G[0][s],$$

where the index s is equal to the decimal value of $e_{h-1}...e_1 e_0$. Therefore, we can rewrite kP as follows

$$kP = \sum_{t=0}^{b-1} 2^{th} (\sum_{j=0}^{v-1} G[j][I_{j,t}]), \tag{8}$$

where $I_{j,t}$ is the decimal number of $e_{h-1,jb+t}...e_{1,jb+t}e_{0,jb+t}$.

We know that NAF is always sparse, hence the probability of $I_{j,t}$ being zero is $\frac{1}{2^h}$ and $I_{j,t}$ occurs a times, thus the number of elliptic-curve operations in the worst case is $(1 - \frac{1}{2^h})a + b - 2$. And the expected number of elliptic-curve operations required is $(1 - (\frac{2}{3})^h)a + b - 2$ on average.

Direct Doubling Method. When the multiplier k is a power of 2, Sakai and Sakurai [23] introduced an efficient method to compute $kP = 2^r P(r \ge 1)$ on elliptic curves over $\mathbb{F}_p$. Given a point $P = (x_1, y_1) \in \mathbb{F}_p$, their method compute $2^r P$ directly. Algorithm 3 from [23] illustrates their method.

Algorithm 3. Sakai-Sakurai method for direct doubling

Require: A positive integer r such that $k = 2^r$ and $P \in E(\mathbb{F}_q)$.
Ensure: $k = 2^r P$
1: $A_1 = x_1$, $B_1 = 3x_1^2 + a$ and $C_1 = -y_1$.
2: **For** $i = 2$ **to** r.
3: $\quad A_i = B_{i-1}^2 - 8A_{i-1}C_{i-1}^2$.
4: $\quad B_i = 3A_i^2 + 16^{i-1}a(\prod_{j=1}^{i-1} C_j)^4$.
5: $\quad C_i = -8C_{i-1}^4 - B_{i-1}(A_i - 4A_{i-1}C_{i-1}^2)$.
6: Compute $D_r = 12A_r C_r^2 - B_r^2$.
7: Compute $x_{2^r} = \frac{B_r^2 - 8A_r C_r^2}{(2^r \prod_{i=1}^r C_i)^2}$.
8: Compute $y_{2^r} = \frac{8C_r^4 - B_r D_r}{(2^r \prod_{i=1}^r C_i)^3}$.
9: **Return** x_{2^r} and y_{2^r}.

In Table 1, we give a comparison of required numbers of multiplication (M), squaring (S), and inversion (I) required to performed the scalar multiplication $k = 2^r P$ between direct doubling method and separate r doubling.

Table 1. Complexity Comparison

Method	S	M	I
Direct Doubling	$4r + 1$	$4r + 1$	1
Separate r Doubling	$2r$	$2r$	r

4   Our Proposed Method

We propose a new method for elliptic-curve scalar multiplication based on the methods of Lim-Lee [16] and Tsaur-Chou [28]. In our method, the scalar k is represented in width-ω NAF. Furthermore, it is divided into $\omega \times v$ blocks from up-to-down and then from right-to-left as in the method of Tsaur-Chou. In order to illustrate our method, let k be represented in width-ω NAF with size l. First, we divide k into $a = \lceil \frac{l}{\omega} \rceil$ blocks of equal size ω (we pad the last block with $a\omega - l$ zeros if necessary), therefore, we can write k as follows

$$k = K_{a-1}K_{a-2}...K_1K_0 = \sum_{d=0}^{a-1} K_d 2^{d\omega}, \tag{9}$$

where $0 \le d < a$.

Then, each block K_d is a column of ω bits (K_0 represents the first ω bits, K_1 the second ω bits, ... , and K_{a-1} the last ω bits), i.e.,

$$k = \begin{bmatrix} K_{a-1}...K_d...K_0 \end{bmatrix} = \begin{bmatrix} k_{a-1,(a-1)\omega} & \cdots & k_{d,d\omega} & \cdots & k_{0,0} \\ \vdots & & \vdots & & \vdots \\ k_{a-1,(a-1)\omega+i} & \cdots & k_{d,d\omega+i} & \cdots & k_{0,i} \\ \vdots & & \vdots & & \vdots \\ k_{a-1,(a-1)\omega+(\omega-1)} & \cdots & k_{d,d\omega+(\omega-1)} & \cdots & k_{0,\omega-1} \end{bmatrix}.$$

Note that, for each element $k_{d,d\omega+i}$ in the matrix the first subscript d indicates the column, whereas the second subscript $d\omega + i$ indicates the exact bit index from width-ω NAF(k). To simplify the notation in the following we write $k_{d,d\omega+i}$ as $k_{d,i}$.

From right-to-left we divide the $\omega \times a$ blocks into $\omega \times v$ blocks, each of size $b = \lceil \frac{a}{v} \rceil$, i.e.,

$$k = \begin{bmatrix} K_{a-1}...K_{a-b} & \cdots & K_{jb+b-1}...K_{jb} & \cdots & K_{b-1}...K_0 \end{bmatrix}$$

$$= \begin{bmatrix} k_{a-1,0}...k_{a-b,0} & \cdots & k_{jb+b-1,0}...k_{jb,0} & \cdots & k_{b-1,0}...k_{0,0} \\ \vdots & & \vdots & & \vdots \\ k_{a-1,i}...k_{a-b,i} & \cdots & k_{jb+b-1,i}...k_{jb,i} & \cdots & k_{b-1,i}...k_{0,i} \\ \vdots & & \vdots & & \vdots \\ k_{a-1,\omega-1}...k_{a-b,\omega-1} & \cdots & k_{jb+b-1,\omega-1}...k_{jb,\omega-1} & \cdots & k_{b-1,\omega-1}...k_{0,\omega-1} \end{bmatrix}.$$

$$kP = K_{a-1}K_{a-2}...K_1K_0P = \sum_{j=0}^{v-1}\sum_{t=0}^{b-1}(K_{jb+t}2^{t\omega})2^{jb\omega}P = \sum_{t=0}^{b-1}2^{t\omega}\sum_{j=0}^{v-1}K_{jb+t}2^{jb\omega}P,$$

where $K_{jb+t} = k_{jb+t,\omega-1}...k_{jb+t,0}$ is in width-ω NAF representation. The maximum value of K_{jb+t} is $(2^{\omega-1}-1)2^{\omega-1}$.

Suppose that the following values are all pre-computed and stored for all $s \in \{1, 2, 2^2, 2^3, ..., 2^{\omega-1}\}, 0 < j \le v-1$ and $d \in \{1, 3, ..., 2^{\omega-1}-1\}$

$$G[0][sd] = e_{\omega-1}2^{\omega-1}P + e_{\omega-2}2^{\omega-2}P + ... + e_0P = sdP,$$
$$G[j][sd] = 2^{\omega b}(G[j-1][sd])$$
$$= 2^{j\omega b}G[0][sd] = 2^{j\omega b}sdP,$$

where the index sd is equal to the decimal value of $(e_{\omega-1}...e_1e_0)$. Therefore, we can rewrite kP as follows

$$kP = \sum_{t=0}^{b-1}2^{t\omega}(\sum_{j=0}^{v-1}G[j][I_{j,t}]) \tag{10}$$

where $I_{j,t}$ is the decimal value of $k_{jb+t,\omega-1}...k_{jb+t,0}$. Algorithm 4 can be used to compute kP using the proposed method.

Algorithm 4. Proposed width-ω NAF method for scalar multiplication

---

Require: Positive integers ω, v, $k = (k_{l-1}, ..., k_1, k_0)_{NAF_\omega}$ and $P \in E(\mathbb{F}_q)$.
Ensure: $Q = kP$.

1:   $a = \lceil \frac{l}{\omega} \rceil$ and $b = \lceil \frac{a}{v} \rceil$.
2:   Compute $G[0][sd]$ and $G[j][sd]$ for all $s \in \{1, 2, 2^2, 2^3, ..., 2^{\omega-1}\}, 0 < j \leq v - 1$ and
    $d \in \{1, 3, 5, ..., 2^{w-1} - 1\}$.
3:   $Q = O$.
4:   **For** $t = b - 1$ **downto** 0 **do**
5:     **If** $\omega = 1$ **then**
6:       $Q = 2Q$.
7:     **Else**
8:       Use Algorithm 3 to compute $Q = 2^\omega Q$.
9:     **For** $j = v - 1$ **downto** 0 **do**
10:      $I_{j,t} = (k_{jb+t,\omega-1}...k_{jb+t,0})_{NAF_\omega}$.
11:      **If** $I_{j,t} > 0$ **then**
12:        $Q = Q + G[j][I_{j,t}]$.
13:      **Else if** $I_{j,t} < 0$
14:        $Q = Q - G[j][-I_{j,t}]$.
15: **Return** (Q).

From [21], we know that the average density of non-zero digits among all width-ω NAF of length l is approximately $1/(\omega + 1)$, therefore, we can assume that the probability of $I_{j,t}$ being zero on average is $(\omega/(\omega + 1))^\omega$, hence the average cost of our proposed method is

$$(1 - (\frac{\omega}{\omega+1})^\omega)a + b - 2. \tag{11}$$

On the other hand, the density of non-zero digits among all width-ω NAF of length l in the worst case is $1/\omega$, therefore, we can assume that the probability of $I_{j,t}$ being zero is at most $((\omega-1)/\omega)^\omega$, hence the cost of our proposed method in the worst case is

$$(1 - (\frac{\omega-1}{\omega})^\omega)a + b - 2. \tag{12}$$

5   Simultaneous Scalar Multiplication

In elliptic curve cryptosystems, like in ECDSA, we need to perform the computation of multiple scalar multiplication, i.e., the computation of $kP + rQ$, where $P, Q \in E(\mathbb{F}_q)$ are two elliptic-curve points and k, r are two large integers such that, $0 \leq k < ord_E(P)$ and $0 \leq r < ord_E(Q)$. The direct way is to perform two single scalar multiplications kP, rQ and then one point addition, but, since scalar multiplication is the most time consuming operation in ECC, it is advisable to perform two scalar multiplications simultaneously. There are many proposals given in literature to perform multiple scalar multiplications, we refer the reader to [5,9] for further details.

Our proposed method in Section 4 can be used to accelerate the computation of simultaneous scalar multiplication. In order to illustrate that, assume that we want to compute $kP + rQ$, let k and r be represented in width-w NAF be l-bit multipliers, then k and r can be represented as follows

$$k = K_{a-1}...K_0 = \sum_{d=0}^{a-1} K_d 2^{d\omega} \quad \text{and} \quad r = R_{a-1}...R_0 = \sum_{d=0}^{a-1} R_d 2^{d\omega}. \tag{13}$$

Let $P_0 = P, Q_0 = Q, P_j = 2^{\omega b} P_{j-1} = 2^{j\omega b} P$, and $Q_j = 2^{\omega b} Q_{j-1} = 2^{j\omega b} Q$ for $0 < j < v$. Therefore, as in Section 4 we can write kP and rQ as follows

$$kP = \sum_{t=0}^{b-1} 2^{t\omega} \sum_{j=0}^{v-1} K_{jb+t} 2^{jb\omega} P \quad \text{and} \quad rQ = \sum_{t=0}^{b-1} 2^{t\omega} \sum_{j=0}^{v-1} R_{jb+t} 2^{jb\omega} Q, \tag{14}$$

where $K_{jb+t} = k_{jb+t,\omega-1}...k_{jb+t,0}$ and $R_{jb+t} = r_{jb+t,\omega-1}...r_{jb+t,0}$ are in width-w NAF representations.

Therefore we can write $kP + rQ$ as follows

$$kP + rQ = \sum_{t=0}^{b-1} 2^{t\omega} \sum_{j=0}^{v-1} (K_{jb+t} 2^{jb\omega} P + R_{jb+t} 2^{jb\omega} Q), \tag{15}$$

Suppose that the following values are pre-computed and stored for all $s \in \{1, 2, 2^2, 2^3, ..., 2^{w-1}\}, 0 < j \leq v - 1$ and $d \in \{1, 3, ..., 2^{w-1} - 1\}$

$$G_p[0][sd] = e_{\omega-1} 2^{\omega-1} P + e_{\omega-2} 2^{\omega-2} P + ... + e_0 P = sdP,$$
$$G_p[j][sd] = 2^{\omega b} (G_p[j-1][sd])$$
$$\qquad = 2^{j\omega b} G_p[0][sd] = 2^{j\omega b} sdP$$
$$G_q[0][sd] = e_{\omega-1} 2^{\omega-1} Q + e_{\omega-2} 2^{\omega-2} Q + ... + e_0 Q = sdQ,$$
$$G_q[j][sd] = 2^{\omega b} (G_q[j-1][sd])$$
$$\qquad = 2^{j\omega b} G_q[0][sd] = 2^{j\omega b} sdQ,$$

where the index sd is equal to the decimal value of $(e_{\omega-1}...e_1 e_0)$. Therefore, we can rewrite $kP + rQ$ as follows

$$kP + rQ = \sum_{t=0}^{b-1} 2^{t\omega} \sum_{j=0}^{v-1} (G_p[j][M_{j,t}] + G_q[j][N_{j,t}]), \tag{16}$$

where $M_{j,t}$ is the decimal value of $k_{jb+t,\omega-1}...k_{jb+t,0}$ $(0 \leq t < b)$, and $N_{j,t}$ is the decimal value of $r_{jb+t,\omega-1}...r_{jb+t,0}$ $(0 \leq t < b)$. Algorithm 5 can be used to compute kP using the proposed method.

The expected runtime of Algorithm 5 is

$$2(1 - (\frac{\omega}{\omega + 1})^\omega)a + b - 2. \tag{17}$$

Algorithm 5. Proposed width-ω NAF method for multiple scalar multiplication

Require: Positive integers ω, v, $P, Q \in E(\mathbb{F}_q)$, $k = (k_{l-1}, ..., k_1, k_0)_{NAF_\omega}$,
  $r = (r_{l-1}, ..., r_1, r_0)_{NAF_\omega}$.
Ensure: $kP + rQ$.
1: $a = \lceil \frac{l}{\omega} \rceil$ and $b = \lceil \frac{a}{v} \rceil$.
2: Compute $G_p[0][sd]$ and $G_p[j][sd]$ for all $s \in \{1, 2, 2^2, 2^3, ..., 2^{\omega-1}\}, 0 < j \leq v - 1$
  and $d \in \{1, 3, 5, ..., 2^{w-1} - 1\}$.
3: Compute $G_q[0][sd]$ and $G_q[j][sd]$ for all $s \in \{1, 2, 2^2, 2^3, ..., 2^{\omega-1}\}, 0 < j \leq v - 1$
  and $d \in \{1, 3, 5, ..., 2^{w-1} - 1\}$.
4: $R = O$.
5: **For** $t = b - 1$ **downto** 0 **do**
6:   **If** $\omega = 1$ **then**
7:     $R = 2R$.
8:   **Else**
9:     Use Algorithm 3 to compute $R = 2^\omega R$.
10:   **For** $j = v - 1$ **downto** 0 **do**
11:     $M_{j,t} = (k_{jb+t,\omega-1}...k_{jb+t,0})_{NAF_\omega}$.
12:     **If** $M_{j,t} > 0$ **then**
13:       $R = R + G_p[j][M_{j,t}]$.
14:     **Else if** $M_{j,t} < 0$
15:       $R = R - G_p[j][-M_{j,t}]$.
16:   **For** $j = v - 1$ **downto** 0 **do**
17:     $N_{j,t} = (r_{jb+t,\omega-1}...r_{jb+t,0})_{NAF_\omega}$.
18:     **If** $N_{j,t} > 0$ **then**
19:       $R = R + G_q[j][N_{j,t}]$.
20:     **Else if** $N_{j,t} < 0$
21:       $R = R - G_q[j][-N_{j,t}]$.
22: **Return** (R).

6   Resistance to Side Channel Attacks

The method of Lim-Lee, Tsaur-Chou, and our proposed method are *per se* not
resistant to side-channel attacks. Side-Channel Analysis (SCA) attacks have been
first introduced by Kocher et al. [14,15,18] in 1996. By monitoring physical characteristics of a given implementation, e.g., the power consumption or the timing
behavior, an attacker is able to extract secret information such as the ephemeral
key or private key in asymmetric-key cryptography. One simple countermeasure
to prevent an attacker from being able to recover the bit values of the scalar
k by timing attacks and Simple Power Analysis (SPA) [14], is to execute the
same code independently of the value of the scalar k, i.e., to make the algorithm
have constant runtime. By having a look at the given fixed-base comb methods
of Lim-Lee, Tsaur-Chou, and our proposed method, it shows that the scalar is
leaking by implementations because the runtime of the algorithms depends on
the number of non-zero digits of the secret scalar, cf. [24]. Therefore, one can
(regularly) add the point at infinity O when $I_{j,t}$ is equal to zero and even add O
to the pre-computed values. In this case, a point addition is executed in every
loop iteration and a constant runtime is obtained with complexity of $a + b - 2$.

Table 2. Number of non-zero columns for different block sizes h of Tsaur-Chou and our proposed method for a 160-bit scalar multiplication

h	Tsaur-Chou worst	Tsaur-Chou average	Proposed worst	Proposed average
2	61	45	61	45
3	48	38	38	32
4	39	33	29	25
5	32	29	23	20
6	27	25	18	17
7	23	22	16	14
8	21	21	14	13
9	18	18	12	12
10	17	17	12	11
11	15	15	10	10
12	14	14	10	9
13	13	13	9	9
14	12	12	8	8
15	11	11	8	7

A more sophisticated approach is to guarantee that all values of $I_{j,t}$ are non-zero, as for example proposed by Hedabou et al. [10,11] or Feng et al. [7]. Another solution would be to use highly regular (exponent-recoding) techniques such as proposed by Joye and Tunstall [17]. In order to provide resistance against Differential Power Analysis (DPA), we also recommend to include randomization techniques as proposed by Coron [6].

7   Discussion and Results

In Table 3, we give a runtime-complexity comparison of Tsaur-Chou and our proposed method. We compare the runtime in terms of worst-runtime cost, average-runtime cost, and memory-storage cost. By having a look at the table, one can notice that when $h = \omega = 2$, our proposed method and Tsaur-Chou method are identical. When $h = \omega = 3$, the worst cost of our proposed method is equal to the average cost of Tsaur-Chou method. Furthermore, when $h = \omega > 3$, the worst cost of our proposed method is less than the average cost of Tsaur-Chou method. For fixed values of h and v, the term $b - 2$ is fixed for both methods for fixed key-bit size of the scalar in average cost and worst cost.

Table 3. Runtime complexity of Tsaur-Chou and our proposed method

Method	Worst cost	Average cost	Storage cost
Tsaur-Chou [28]	$(1 - (\frac{1}{2})^h)a + b - 2$	$(1 - (\frac{2}{3})^h)a + b - 2$	$\sum_{i=1}^{\lceil \frac{h}{2} \rceil} 2^{h-2i+1}v$
Proposed	$(1 - (\frac{\omega-1}{\omega})^\omega)a + b - 2$	$(1 - (\frac{\omega}{\omega+1})^\omega)a + b - 2$	$\omega 2^{\omega-2}v$

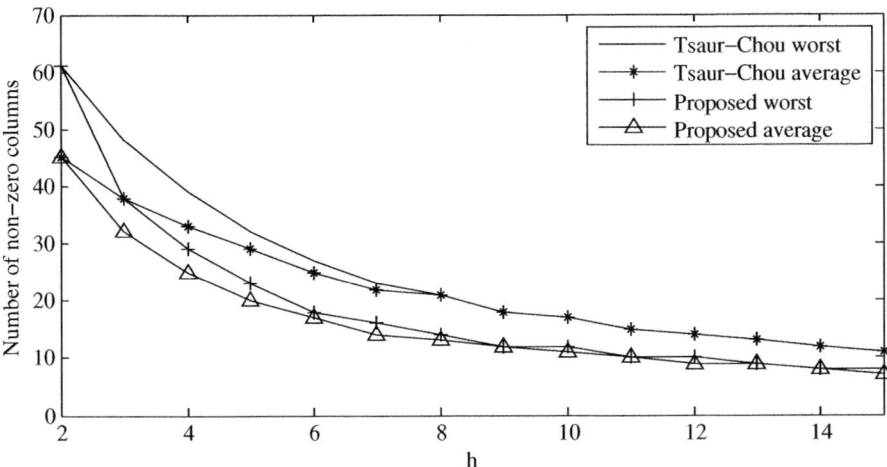

Fig. 1. Comparison of Tsaur-Chou [28] and our proposed method for a 160-bit scalar multiplication

In Table 2 and Figure 1, we analyze the number of non-zero columns for Tsaur-Chou and our proposed method. Values are given for different block sizes h and a 160-bit scalar multiplication. For our method and in order to simplify the comparison, we have chosen $h = \omega$. It shows that our method performs best in both the average-cost and the worst-cost scenario. In particular, by evaluating the performance for all possible block sizes $2 \leq h \leq 15$, we obtain an improvement by 33 to 38 % (for the worst and average case).

For a fixed value of h, we noticed that the number of pre-computations (storage cost) is increased in our proposed method. In devices with limited resources (memory), in most cases we found a suitable choice of h, the window size ω and v, which makes our method best. In order to illustrate this, we assume that the scalar has a bit size of 160 bits. First, we will fix the window size ω to be equal h and then, depending on the available memory, we choose h and v. For example, if storage is available for 5 elements and if we apply the Tsaur-Chou method, we have two choices: (1) $h = 2$ and $v = 2$ (the cost[1] is 84), or (2) $h = 3$ and $v = 1$ (the cost is 90). Now, using our proposed method, we have only one choice, i.e., $h = 2$ and $v = 2$ (the cost is 84). This coincides with what we previously noted.

If storage is available for 18 elements and if we use the Tsaur-Chou method, one can choose between three choices: (1) $h = 2$ and $v = 9$ (the cost is 52), (2) $h = 3$ and $v = 3$ (the cost is 49), or (3) $h = 4$ and $v = 1$ (the cost is 72). For our proposed method, there are only two choices, i.e., (1) $h = 2$ and $v = 9$ (the cost is 52) or (2) $h = 3$ and $v = 3$ (the cost is 48). Thus, we will choose $h = 3$ and $v = 3$ which has a minimum cost of 48. In Table 4, we give the suitable choices of h and v when the available storage vary from 2 to 50 elements.

---

[1] The cost is measured in terms of number of elliptic-curve point addition operations.

Table 4. Runtime complexity of Tsaur-Chou and our proposed method for different available storage elements (2-50) and suitable choices of h and v for 160-bit key size

Available storage elements	Tsaur-Chou method				Proposed method			
	h	v	costs	AUS^a	h	v	costs	AUS^a
2-3	2	1	124	2	2	1	124	2
4-5	2	2	84	4	2	2	84	4
6-7	2	3	70	6	2	3	70	6
8-9	2	4	64	8	2	4	64	8
10-11	2	5	60	10	2	5	60	10
12-13	2	6	57	12	2	6	57	12
					3	2	57	12
14	2	7	55	14	2	7	55	14
15	3	3	54	15	2	7	55	14
16-17	2	8	54	16	2	8	54	16
18-19	2	9	52	18	3	3	48	18
20-23	3	4	50	20	3	3	48	18
24	3	4	50	20	3	4	44	24
25-29	3	5	47	25	3	4	44	24
30-34	3	6	45	30	3	5	41	30
35	3	7	44	35	3	5	41	30
36-39	3	7	44	35	3	6	39	36
40-41	4	4	42	40	3	6	39	36
42-47	4	4	42	40	3	7	38	42
45	3	9	42	45				
48-49	4	4	42	40	3	8	37	48
50	4	5	40	50	3	8	37	48

^{a} The term AUS is referred to the number of elements actually used to store.

8   Conclusion

In this paper, we proposed an efficient method for scalar multiplication by combining the ideas of Lim-Lee [16] and Tsaur-Chou [28]. Our proposed method makes a significant reduction in terms of number of elliptic-curve point addition operations. By comparing our method with previous work, it shows that when $h = \omega = 2$ our proposed method and Tsaur-Chou method are identical, when $h = \omega = 3$ the worst cost of our proposed method is equal to the average cost of Tsaur-Chou method, and when $h = \omega > 3$ the worst cost of our proposed method is less than the average cost of Tsaur-Chou method.

Also we showed that our proposed method can be used for speeding up simultaneous scalar multiplication of elliptic curves which is interesting, for example, in many digital signature verification algorithms.

For pre-computations, if storage space is disregarded, our proposed method is the best choice and we can define $h \geq \omega$, otherwise $\omega = h$. There is always a suitable choice for h and v which make our method best. In Table 4, we gave the suitable choices of h and v when the available storage vary from 2 to 50 elements.

Acknowledgements. This work has been supported by the Faculty of Mathematical Sciences of the University of Khartoum (Sudan) and the European Commission through the ICT program under contract ICTSEC- 2009-5-258754 (Tamper Resistant Sensor Node - TAMPRES).

References

1. Booth, A.D.: A signed binary multiplication technique. Q. J. Mech. Applied Math., 236–240 (1951)
2. Bosma, W.: Signed bits and fast exponentiation. Jornal de Théorie des Nombers de Bordeaux 13, 27–41 (2001)
3. Brauer, A.: On addition chains. Bull. Amer. Math. Soc. 45, 736–739 (1939)
4. Brickell, E.F., Gordon, D.M., McCurley, K.S., Wilson, D.B.: Fast Exponentiation with Precomputation (Extended Abstract). In: Rueppel, R.A. (ed.) EUROCRYPT 1992. LNCS, vol. 658, pp. 200–207. Springer, Heidelberg (1993)
5. Cohen, H., Frey, G., Avanzi, R., Doche, C., Lange, T., Nguyen, K., Vercauteren, F.: Handbook of elliptic and hyperelliptic curve cryptography. Taylor and Francis Group, LLC (2006)
6. Coron, J.-S.: Resistance against Differential Power Analysis for Elliptic Curve Cryptosystems. In: Koç, Ç.K., Paar, C. (eds.) CHES 1999. LNCS, vol. 1717, pp. 292–302. Springer, Heidelberg (1999)
7. Feng, M., Zhu, B.B., Xu, M., Li, S.: Efficient comb elliptic curve multiplication methods resistant to power analysis. IACR Cryptology ePrint Archive, 2005:222 (2005)
8. Gordan, D.M.: A survey of fast exponentiation methods. Journal of Algorithms 27, 129–146 (1998)
9. Hankerson, D., Menezes, A., Vanstone, S.: Guide to elliptic curve cryptography. Springer, New York (2004)
10. Hedabou, M., Pinel, P., Bénéteau, L.: A comb method to render ecc resistant against side channel attacks. Paper submitted only to the Cryptology ePrint Archive. hedabou@insa-toulouse.fr 12754 (received, December 2, 2004)
11. Hedabou, M., Pinel, P., Bénéteau, L.: Countermeasures for Preventing Comb Method Against SCA Attacks. In: Deng, R.H., Bao, F., Pang, H., Zhou, J. (eds.) ISPEC 2005. LNCS, vol. 3439, pp. 85–96. Springer, Heidelberg (2005)
12. Joye, M., Yen, S.-M.: The Montgomery Powering Ladder. In: Kaliski Jr., B.S., Koç, Ç.K., Paar, C. (eds.) CHES 2002. LNCS, vol. 2523, pp. 291–302. Springer, Heidelberg (2003)
13. Koblitz, N.: Elliptic curve cryptosystems. Mathematics of Computation 48, 203–220 (1987)
14. Kocher, P.C.: Timing Attacks on Implementations of Diffie-Hellman, RSA, DSS, and Other Systems. In: Koblitz, N. (ed.) CRYPTO 1996. LNCS, vol. 1109, pp. 104–113. Springer, Heidelberg (1996)
15. Kocher, P.C., Jaffe, J., Jun, B.: Differential Power Analysis. In: Wiener, M. (ed.) CRYPTO 1999. LNCS, vol. 1666, pp. 388–397. Springer, Heidelberg (1999)

16. Lim, C.H., Lee, P.J.: More Flexible Exponentiation with Precomputation. In: Desmedt, Y.G. (ed.) CRYPTO 1994. LNCS, vol. 839, pp. 95–107. Springer, Heidelberg (1994)
17. Joye, M., Tunstall, M.: Exponent Recoding and Regular Exponentiation Algorithms. In: Preneel, B. (ed.) AFRICACRYPT 2009. LNCS, vol. 5580, pp. 334–349. Springer, Heidelberg (2009)
18. Mangard, S., Oswald, E., Popp, T.: Power Analysis Attacks – Revealing the Secrets of Smart Cards. Springer (2007) ISBN 978-0-387-30857-9
19. Miller, V.S.: Use of Elliptic Curves in Cryptography. In: Williams, H.C. (ed.) CRYPTO 1985. LNCS, vol. 218, pp. 417–426. Springer, Heidelberg (1986)
20. Montgomery, P.L.: Speeding the pollard and elliptic curve methods of factorization. Mathematics of Computation 48, 243–264 (1987)
21. Morain, F., Olivos, J.: Speeding up the computations on an elliptic curve using addition-subtraction chains. Theor. Inform. Appli. 24, 531–543 (1989)
22. Reitwiesner, G.W.: Binary arithmetic. Advances in Computers 1, 231–308 (1960)
23. Sakai, Y., Sakurai, K.: Speeding up elliptic scalar multiplication using multidoubling. IEICE Transactions Fundamentals E85-A(5), 1075–1083 (2002)
24. Sakai, Y., Sakurai, K.: A New Attack with Side Channel Leakage During Exponent Recoding Computations. In: Joye, M., Quisquater, J.-J. (eds.) CHES 2004. LNCS, vol. 3156, pp. 298–311. Springer, Heidelberg (2004)
25. Silverman, J.H.: The arithmetic of elliptic curves, vol. 106. Springer, Berlin (1986)
26. Solinas, J.A.: Effiecient arithmetic on koblitz curves. Designs, Codes and Cryptography 19, 195–249 (2000)
27. Thurber, E.G.: On addition chains $l(mn) \leq l(n) - b$ and lower bounds for $c(r)$. Duke Mathematical Journal 40, 907–913 (1973)
28. Tsaur, W.-J., Chou, C.-H.: Efficient algorithm for speeding up the computations of elliptic curve cryptosystem. Applied Mathematics and Computation 168, 1045–1064 (2005)

A   Example

In order to illustrate our method, we select at random a positive integer $k = 1065142573068$ and choose $\omega = 3$. First, we represent k in width-3 NAF,

$$k = (010000\bar{1}00000000000\bar{1}00\bar{1}00100\bar{1}00300000000300).$$

Then, we divide from up-to-down to $a = \lceil \frac{41}{3} \rceil = 14$ blocks of size 3, such that

$$k = \begin{bmatrix} 0\,0\,0\,0\,0\,0\,0\,0\,0\,0\,0\,0\,0\,0 \\ 1\,0\,0\,0\,0\,0\,0\,0\,0\,0\,0\,0\,0\,0 \\ 0\,0\,\bar{1}\,0\,0\,0\,\bar{1}\,\bar{1}\,1\,\bar{1}\,3\,0\,0\,3 \end{bmatrix}. \tag{18}$$

Then, from right-to-left we divide the 3×14 blocks to 3×7 blocks, each of size $b = \lceil \frac{14}{7} \rceil = 2$, such that

$$k = \begin{bmatrix} 00\ 00\ 00\ 00\ 00\ 00\ 00 \\ 10\ 00\ 00\ 00\ 00\ 00\ 00 \\ 00\ \bar{1}0\ 00\ \bar{1}\bar{1}\ 1\bar{1}\ 30\ 03 \end{bmatrix}. \tag{19}$$

Next, we compute and store the following values. For pre-computed values $G[0][sd]$, where $s \in \{1, 2, 4\}$ and $d \in \{1, 3\}$:

$$G[0][1] = P, G[0][2] = 2P, G[0][4] = 4P, G[0][3] = 3P, G[0][6] = 6P, G[0][12] = 12P.$$

For pre-computed values $G[j][sd]$, where $s \in \{1, 2, 4\}, d \in \{1, 3\}$ and $0 \le j \le 6$:

$$G[j][1] = 2^{6j}P, G[j][2] = 2^{6j}(2P), G[j][4] = 2^{6j}(4P),$$
$$G[j][3] = 2^{6j}(3P), G[j][6] = 2^{6j}(6P), G[j][12] = 2^{6j}(12P).$$

Next, compute $I_{j,t} = (e_{2,2j+t}e_{1,2j+t}e_{0,2j+t})_2$ for all $0 \le t \le 1$ and $0 \le j \le 6$ as follows:

$$I_{0,0} = (e_{2,0}e_{1,0}e_{0,0})_{NAF_3} = (300)_{NAF_3} = 12,$$
$$I_{1,0} = (e_{2,2}e_{1,2}e_{0,2})_{NAF_3} = 0,$$
$$I_{2,0} = (e_{2,4}e_{1,4}e_{0,4})_{NAF_3} = (\bar{1}00)_{NAF_3} = -4,$$
$$I_{3,0} = (e_{2,6}e_{1,6}e_{0,6})_{NAF_3} = (\bar{1}00)_{NAF_3} = -4,$$
$$I_{4,0} = (e_{2,8}e_{1,8}e_{0,8})_{NAF_3} = 0,$$
$$I_{5,0} = (e_{2,10}e_{1,10}e_{0,10})_{NAF_3} = 0,$$
$$I_{6,0} = (e_{2,12}e_{1,12}e_{0,12})_{NAF_3} = 0,$$
$$I_{0,1} = (e_{2,1}e_{1,1}e_{0,1})_{NAF_3} = 0,$$
$$I_{1,1} = (e_{2,3}e_{1,3}e_{0,3})_{NAF_3} = (300)_{NAF_3} = 12,$$
$$I_{2,1} = (e_{2,5}e_{1,5}e_{0,5})_{NAF_3} = (100)_{NAF_3} = 4,$$
$$I_{3,1} = (e_{2,7}e_{1,7}e_{0,7})_{NAF_3} = (\bar{1}00)_{NAF_3} = -4,$$
$$I_{4,1} = (e_{2,9}e_{1,9}e_{0,9})_{NAF_3} = 0,$$
$$I_{5,1} = (e_{2,11}e_{1,11}e_{0,11})_{NAF_3} = (\bar{1}00)_{NAF_3} = -4,$$
$$I_{6,1} = (e_{2,13}e_{1,13}e_{0,13})_{NAF_3} = (010)_{NAF_3} = 2.$$

Finally, we can compute kP by using above values as follows:

$$kP = G[0][12] + G[1][0] - G[2][4] - G[3][4] + G[4][0] + G[5][0] + G[6][0] +$$
$$2^3(G[0][0] + G[1][12] + G[2][4] - G[3][4] + G[4][0] - G[5][4] + G[6][2]).$$

Optimal First-Order Masking
with Linear and Non-linear Bijections

Houssem Maghrebi[1], Claude Carlet[2],
Sylvain Guilley[1,3], and Jean-Luc Danger[1,3]

[1] TELECOM-ParisTech, Crypto Group,
37/39 rue Dareau, 75 634 Paris Cedex 13, France
[2] LAGA, UMR 7539, CNRS, Department of Mathematics,
University of Paris XIII and University of Paris VIII,
2 rue de la liberté, 93 526 Saint-Denis Cedex, France
[3] Secure-IC S.A.S., 80 avenue des Buttes de Coësmes,
35 700 Rennes, France

Abstract. Hardware devices can be protected against side-channel attacks by introducing one random mask per sensitive variable. The computation throughout is unaltered if the shares (masked variable and mask) are processed concomitantly, in two distinct registers. Nonetheless, this setup can be attacked by a zero-offset second-order CPA attack. The countermeasure can be improved by manipulating the mask through a bijection F, aimed at reducing the dependency between the shares. Thus dth-order zero-offset attacks, that consist in applying CPA on the dth power of the centered side-channel traces, can be thwarted for $d \geq 2$ at no extra cost. We denote by n the size in bits of the shares and call F the transformation function, that is a bijection of $\mathbb{F}_2^n$. In this paper, we explore the functions F that thwart zero-offset HO-CPA of maximal order d. We mathematically demonstrate that optimal choices for F relate to optimal binary codes (in the sense of communication theory). First, we exhibit optimal linear F functions. Second, we note that for values of n for which non-linear codes exist with better parameters than linear ones. These results are exemplified in the case $n = 8$, the optimal F can be identified:it is derived from the optimal rate $1/2$ binary code of size $2n$, namely the Nordstrom-Robinson $(16, 256, 6)$ code. This example provides explicitly with the optimal protection that limits to one mask of byte-oriented algorithms such as AES or AES-based SHA-3 candidates. It protects against all zero-offset HO-CPA attacks of order $d \leq 5$. Eventually, the countermeasure is shown to be resilient to imperfect leakage models.

Keywords: First-order masking countermeasure (CM), high-order correlation power analysis (HO-CPA), zero-offset HO-CPA, linear and non-linear codes.

1 Introduction

Hardware implementations of block-oriented cryptographic functions are vulnerable to side-channel attacks. Yet their lack of algebraic structure makes them

A. Mitrokotsa and S. Vaudenay (Eds.): AFRICACRYPT 2012, LNCS 7374, pp. 360–377, 2012.

hard to protect efficiently. Boolean masking is one answer to secure them, because it can be adapted to any function implemented. Early masking schemes involved only one mask per data to protect [26]. Nonetheless, straightforward implementations of this "first-order" countermeasure (CM) happened to be vulnerable to zero-offset "second-order" attacks [29,17]. We call a "first-order" CM an implementation where one single mask protects the sensitive data. Zero-offset attacks use one sample of side-channel trace, and are thus monovariate. They apply when the masked variable and the mask are consumed simultaneously by the implementation, which is commonplace in hardware. Indeed, this architectural strategy allows to keep the throughput unchanged. Zero-offset second-order attacks consider not the plain observations themselves, but their variance instead. The variance of the leakage function, that involves its squaring (second-order moment), does depend strongly on the sensitive data, which allows for an attack. Consequently, a branch of the research on masking CMs has evolved towards masking schemes with multiple masks. Besides, another improvement direction consists in the adaptation of the first-order CMs to resist attacks that use high-order moments of one single side-channel observation (commonly referred to as zero-offset HO-CPA, of order $d > 1$). Such result can be obtained by transforming the mask before it is latched in register [7]. Concretely, a bijection F is applied to the mask, in a view to reduce its dependency with the masked data. The goal of this article is to find bijections F that protect against zero-offset attacks of order d as high as possible.

The rest of the paper is structured as follows. In Sec. 2, the first-order masking scheme that involves the bijection F is described, and its leakage is explained under the Hamming distance model. In Sec. 3, the best zero-offset HO-CPA is derived for all orders d; also, a necessary and sufficient condition on F for the CM to resist all zero-offset HO-CPA of orders $1, 2, \cdots, d$ is formulated. Based on this formal statement of the problem, optimal solutions for F are researched and given in Sec. 4. The characterization of some optimal bijections F is conducted in Sec. 5, where both a security analysis against zero-offset HO-CPA and a leakage analysis with an information theoretic metric are conducted. This analysis is carried out both with a perfect and an imperfect leakage model. The conclusions are in Sec. 6. The article is self-contained without those appendices; however, they bring interesting insights to support the article's body.

2   Studied Implementation and Its Leakage

The sensitive variable is noted x and the mask m. The two shares manipulated in a Boolean first-order CM are $(x \oplus m, m)$. In the CM we study, a bijection F is applied on the mask share. Thus, the shares are now $(x \oplus m, F(m))$. The schematic of this scheme is illustrated in Fig. 1. The variables x and x' are the two consecutive values of the sensitive variable. Similarly, m and m' are the two consecutive values of the mask. This figure highlights two registers, able to hold each one n-bit word. The left register hosts the masked data, $x \oplus m$, whereas the register on the right holds $F(m)$, the mask m passed through the bijection F.

In this article, we are concerned with the leakage from those two registers only. Indeed, they are undoubtedly the resource that leaks the most. Also, the rest of the logic can be advantageously hidden in tables, thereby limiting their side-channel leakage [22]. It is referred to as "tabulated round logic" in Fig. 1. This figure provides with an abstract description of the round, since it usually splits nicely into independent datapaths of smaller bitwidth. Typically, an AES can be pipelined to manipulate only bytes. However, in practice, article [16] (resp. [20]) shows how to handle AES substitution box with 4 bit (resp. 2 bit) non-linear data transformations.

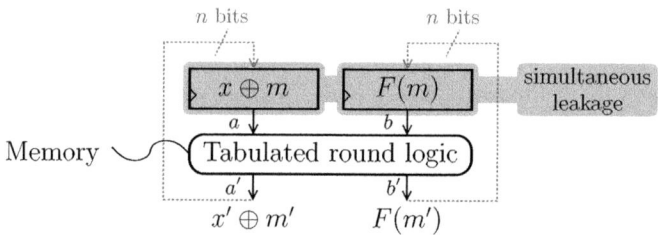

Fig. 1. Setup of the first-order masking countermeasure with bijection F

The computation of the bijection F shall not leak. Actually, F can be merged into memories, hence being totally dissolved. Therefore, the two shares $(x \oplus m, F(m))$ remain manipulated concomitantly only once, namely at the clock rising edge. For the sake of illustration, we provide with a typical functionality of this combinational logic hidden in memory. If we denote by C the round function and by R the mask refresh function, then the table implements:

- $a' = C(a \oplus F^{-1}(b)) \oplus R(F^{-1}(b))$ and
- $b' = F(R(F^{-1}(b)))$.

The detail of the tabulated round logic is represented in Fig. 2.

In the context of a side-channel attack against a block cipher, either the first round or the last round is targeted. Thus either the input x (plaintext) or the output x' (ciphertext) is known by the attacker. We make the assumption that the device leaks in the Hamming distance model. This model is realistic and customarily assumed in the literature related to side-channel analysis [2,25]. Therefore, the sensitive variable to protect is $x \oplus x'$, noted z. The leakage of the studied hardware (Fig. 1) is thus:

$$\mathsf{HD}(x \oplus m, x' \oplus m') + \mathsf{HD}(F(m), F(m'))$$
$$= \mathsf{HW}(z \oplus m \oplus m') + \mathsf{HW}(F(m) \oplus F(m')) \ . \tag{1}$$

In this equation, the Hamming distance operator HD and the Hamming weight operator HW are defined as $\mathsf{HD}(a,b) = \mathsf{HW}(a \oplus b) \doteq \sum_{i=1}^{n}(a \oplus b)_i$. F is a constant bijection that will contribute to increase the security of the CM. In addition, F is a public information, that we assume known by an attacker.

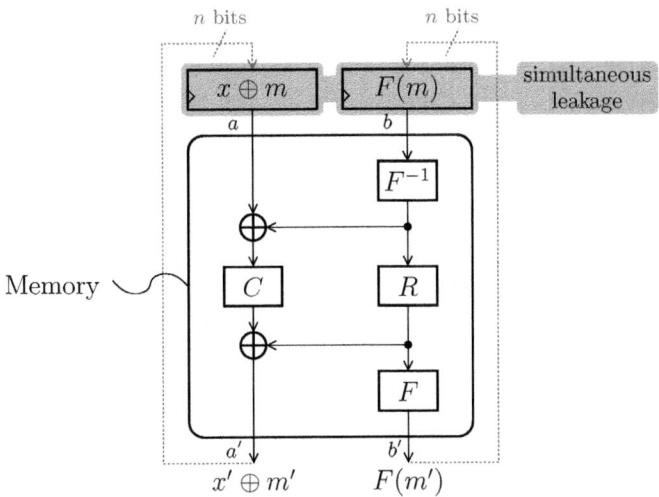

Fig. 2. Detail of the function implemented in the tabulated round logic shown in Fig. 1

3 Optimal Function in Zero-Offset dth-Order CPA

3.1 Optimal Function f_{opt} Definition

Prouff *et al.* have shown in [19] that an attacker can optimize a CPA [2] against a device leaking L by computing the correlation between the random variables L and $f_{\mathrm{opt}}(Z)$, where Z is the sensitive variable. The function $f_{\mathrm{opt}}(\cdot)$ is called the "optimal function", and is defined as $f_{\mathrm{opt}}(z) = \mathbb{E}[L - \mathbb{E}[L] \mid Z = z]$. In this definition, the capital letters denote random variables, and $\mathbb{E}$ is the expectation operator. If $z \mapsto f_{\mathrm{opt}}(z)$ is constant (*i.e.* $f_{\mathrm{opt}}(Z)$ is deterministic), then [19] shows that the correlation coefficient of the attack is null, which means that the attack fails.

This result can be applied on the studied leakage function of Eqn. (1), without F (*i.e.* with F equal to the identity function Id). The leakage function therefore simplifies in $\mathsf{HW}(Z \oplus M'') + \mathsf{HW}(M'')$, where $M'' \doteq M \oplus M'$ is a uniformly distributed random variable in $\mathbb{F}_2^n$.

- In a zero-offset first-order attack, the attacker uses $f_{\mathrm{opt}}(Z) = \mathbb{E}[\mathsf{HW}(Z \oplus M'') + \mathsf{HW}(M'') - n \mid Z] = 0$, which is deterministic,
- whereas in a zero-offset second-order attack, the attacker uses $f_{\mathrm{opt}}(Z) = \mathbb{E}[(\mathsf{HW}(Z \oplus M'') + \mathsf{HW}(M'') - n)^2 \mid Z] = n - \mathsf{HW}(Z)$, which depends on Z. This result is easily obtained by developing the square. The only non-trivial term in this computation is $\mathbb{E}[\mathsf{HW}(z \oplus M'') \times \mathsf{HW}(M'')]$, which is proved to be equal to $\frac{n^2+n}{4} - \frac{1}{2}\mathsf{HW}(z)$ in [19, Eqn. (19)].

In summary, without F, a first-order attack is thwarted, but a second-order zero-offset attack will succeed. In the sequel, when mentioning HO-CPA attacks, we implicitly mean "zero-offset HO-CPA", *i.e.* a mono-variate attack that uses a high-order moment of the traces instead of the raw traces. Nonetheless, as explained in [29], this second-order attack requires more traces than a first-order attack on an unprotected version that do not use any mask. Indeed, the noise is squared and thus its effect is exacerbated. More generally, the higher the order d of a HO-CPA attack, the greater the impact of the noise. Thus, attacks are still possible for small d, but get more and more difficult when d increases. Therefore, our objective is to improve the masking CM so that the zero-offset HO-CPA fails for orders $[\![1, d]\!]$, with d being as high as possible. This translates in terms of $f_{\mathrm{opt}}(Z)$ by having $\mathbb{E}[(\mathsf{HW}(Z \oplus M \oplus M') + \mathsf{HW}(F(M) \oplus F(M')) - n)^d \mid Z]$ deterministic (*i.e.* independent of random variable Z) for the highest possible values of the integer d. Thus, when developing the sum raised at the power d, we are led to study terms of this form:

$$\mathsf{Term}[p, q](f_{\mathrm{opt}})(z) \doteq \mathbb{E}[\mathsf{HW}^p[z \oplus M \oplus M'] \times \mathsf{HW}^q[F(M) \oplus F(M')]$$
$$= \mathbb{E}[\mathsf{HW}^p[z \oplus M''] \times \mathsf{HW}^q[F(M) \oplus F(M \oplus M'')] , \quad (2)$$

where p and q are two positive integers. If either p or q is null, then trivially, $\mathsf{Term}[p, q](f_{\mathrm{opt}})$ is constant. We are thus interested more specifically in p and q values that are strictly positive. We note that in order to resist d-th order zero-offset HO-CPA, $\mathsf{Term}[p, q](f_{\mathrm{opt}})(z)$ must not depend on z for all p and q that satisfy $p + q \leq d$.

3.2   Condition on F for the Resistance against 2nd-Order CPA

To resist zero-offset second-order CPA, the term in Eqn. (2) must be constant for $p + q \leq 2$. As just mentioned, the cases $(p, q) = (2, 0)$ and $(0, 2)$ are trivial. This subsection thus focuses on the case where $p = q = 1$.

The term $F(m) \oplus F(m \oplus m'')$ is also known as the value at m of the derivative of F in the direction m'', and noted $D_{m''}F(m)$. This notion is for instance defined in the Definition 8.2 in §8.2.2 of [5]. It can be observed that Eqn. (2) also writes as a convolution product: $\mathsf{Term}[p, q](f_{\mathrm{opt}})(z) = \frac{1}{2^n} \left(\mathsf{HW} \otimes \mathbb{E}[\mathsf{HW}(D_{(\cdot)}F(M))]\right)(z)$. An appealing property of the Walsh-Hadamard transform is that it turns a convolution into a product. So, we have:

$$f_{\mathrm{opt}}(z) = \mathrm{cst} \iff \widehat{f_{\mathrm{opt}}}(a) \propto \delta(a) \quad \begin{array}{l} // \text{ where } \propto \text{ means "is proportional to"} \\ // \text{ and } \delta(\cdot) \text{ is the Kronecker symbol.} \end{array}$$
$$\iff \widehat{\mathsf{HW}}(a) \times \mathbb{E}[\widehat{\mathsf{HW} \circ D_{(\cdot)}F(M)}](a) = \left(n \times 2^{n-1}\right)^2 \times \delta(a)$$
$$\iff \forall a \neq 0, \widehat{\mathsf{HW}}(a) = 0 \quad \text{or} \quad \mathbb{E}[\widehat{\mathsf{HW} \circ D_{(\cdot)}F(M)}](a) = 0. \quad (3)$$

To prove the second line, we note that on the one hand: $\widehat{\mathsf{HW}}(0) = \sum_z \mathsf{HW}(z) \cdot (-1)^{0 \cdot z} = \frac{n}{2} 2^n$ and on the other hand:

$$\mathbb{E}[\mathsf{HW} \circ \widehat{D_{(\cdot)}F(M)}](0)$$
$$= \sum_z \mathbb{E}[\mathsf{HW}(D_z F(M))(-1)^{0 \cdot z}]$$
$$= \mathbb{E}[\sum_z \mathsf{HW}(F(M) \oplus F(M \oplus z))]$$
$$= \mathbb{E}[\sum_{z'} \mathsf{HW}(z')] \quad // \text{ Because } \forall m, z \mapsto F(m) \oplus F(m \oplus z) \text{ is bijective}$$
$$= \mathbb{E}[\tfrac{n}{2} 2^n] = \tfrac{n}{2} 2^n \ .$$

Now, if we denote by e_i the lines of the identity matrix I_n of size $n \times n$,

$$\widehat{\mathsf{HW}}(a) = \sum_z \frac{1}{2} \sum_{i=1}^{n} (1 - (-1)^{z_i}) (-1)^{a \cdot z}$$
$$= n \cdot 2^{n-1} \delta(a) - \tfrac{1}{2} \sum_z \sum_{i=1}^{n} (-1)^{(a \oplus e_i) \cdot z}$$
$$= \begin{cases} n \cdot 2^{n-1} & \text{if } a = 0, \\ -2^{n-1} & \text{if } \exists i \in [\![1, n]\!], \text{ such that } a = e_i, \\ 0 & \text{otherwise.} \end{cases} \tag{4}$$

Thus, the problem comes down to finding a function F such that:
$\mathbb{E}[\mathsf{HW} \circ \widehat{D_{(\cdot)}F(M)}](a) = 0$ for all $a = e_i$. This condition rewrites:

$$\forall a = e_i, \quad \sum_{z,m} \mathsf{HW}(F(m) \oplus F(m \oplus z))(-1)^{a \cdot z} = 0 \ . \tag{5}$$

Let $a \neq 0$. Then:

$$\sum_{z,m} \mathsf{HW}(F(m) \oplus F(m \oplus z))(-1)^{a \cdot z}$$
$$= \sum_{z,m} \tfrac{1}{2} \sum_{i=1}^{n} \left(1 - (-1)^{F_i(m) \oplus F_i(m \oplus z)}\right) (-1)^{a \cdot z}$$
$$= \overline{n 2^{2n-1} \delta(a)} - \tfrac{1}{2} \sum_{i=1}^{n} \sum_{z,m} (-1)^{F_i(m) \oplus F_i(m \oplus z) \oplus a \cdot z}$$
$$= -\tfrac{1}{2} \sum_{i=1}^{n} \sum_m (-1)^{F_i(m)} \sum_z (-1)^{a \cdot z \oplus F_i(m \oplus z)}$$
$$= -\tfrac{1}{2} \sum_{i=1}^{n} \sum_m (-1)^{F_i(m)} \sum_z (-1)^{a \cdot (z \oplus m) \oplus F_i(z)} \quad // z \leftarrow z \oplus m$$
$$= -\tfrac{1}{2} \sum_{i=1}^{n} \sum_m (-1)^{a \cdot m \oplus F_i(m)} \sum_z (-1)^{a \cdot z \oplus F_i(z)}$$
$$= -\tfrac{1}{2} \sum_{i=1}^{n} \left(\sum_m (-1)^{a \cdot m \oplus F_i(m)}\right)^2$$
$$= -\tfrac{1}{2} \sum_{i=1}^{n} \left(\widehat{(-1)^{F_i}}(a)\right)^2 \ .$$

Thus, this quantity is null if and only if $\forall i \in [\![1, n]\!]$, $\widehat{(-1)^{F_i}}(a) = 0$. Thus, if we generalize the Walsh-Hadamard transform on vectorial Boolean functions (by applying the transformation component-wise), and use the notation f_χ for the sign function of f (also component-wise), then Eqn. (5) is equivalent to: $\forall a = e_i$, $\widehat{F_\chi}(a) = 0$. Now, as F is balanced (since bijective), this equality also holds for $a = 0$. This means that every coordinate of F is 1-resilient. Constructions exist, as explained in [4, Sec. 8.7].

In the next subsection, we use P-resilient functions F: by definition, they are functions that are balanced when up to P input bits are fixed.

3.3   Condition on F for the Resistance against dth-Order CPA

A generalization of the previous result for arbitrary $p, q \in \mathbb{N}^* \doteq \mathbb{N}\backslash\{0\}$ is presented in this section. We have the following theorem:

Theorem 1. *Let P and Q be two positive integers, and F a bijection of $\mathbb{F}_2^n$. Eqn. (2) is constant for all $p \in [\![0, P]\!]$ and $q \in [\![0, Q]\!]$ if and only if:*

$$\forall a, b \in \mathbb{F}_2^n, 0 < \mathsf{HW}(a) \le P, 0 \le \mathsf{HW}(b) \le Q, \quad \widehat{(b \cdot F)}_\chi(a) = 0 \ . \tag{6}$$

An (n, m)-function is defined as a vectorial Boolean function from $\mathbb{F}_2^n$ to $\mathbb{F}_2^m$.

Proposition 1. *The condition expressed in Eqn. (6) of theorem 1 can be reformulated as follows. Every restriction of the bijective (n, n)-function F to Q components is an (n, Q)-function that is P-resilient.*

4   Existence of Bijections Meeting Eqn. (6)

In this section, we find bijections that meet Eqn. (6).

The condition expressed in Eqn. (6) for theorem 1 rewrites: $\forall b \in \mathbb{F}_2^{n*} \doteq \mathbb{F}_2^n\backslash\{0\}$ and $\forall a \in \mathbb{F}_2^n$, if $\mathsf{HW}(a) \le d - \mathsf{HW}(b)$ then $\widehat{(b \cdot F)}_\chi(a) = 0$.

4.1   Optimal Linear Bijections

F can be chosen linear. All linear (n, n)-functions write $F(x) = (x \cdot v_1, \cdots, x \cdot v_n)$, where v_i are elements of $\mathbb{F}_2^n$. F is bijective if and only if $(v_1, \cdots, v_n)$ is a basis of $\mathbb{F}_2^n$. We have:

$$\begin{aligned}
\widehat{(b \cdot F)}_\chi(a) = 0 &\iff \textstyle\sum_x (-1)^{b \cdot F(x) \oplus x \cdot a} = 0 \\
&\iff \textstyle\sum_x (-1)^{\oplus_{i=1}^n b_i (x \cdot v_i) \oplus x \cdot a} = 0 \\
&\iff \textstyle\sum_x (-1)^{x \cdot \oplus_{i=1}^n (b_i v_i) \oplus x \cdot a} = 0 \\
&\iff \textstyle\bigoplus_{i=1}^n b_i v_i \ne a \ .
\end{aligned}$$

As this is true for all a such that $\mathsf{HW}(a) \le d - \mathsf{HW}(b)$, we have the necessary and sufficient condition:

$$\forall b \ne 0, \quad \mathsf{HW}(\textstyle\bigoplus_{i=1}^n b_i v_i) > d - \mathsf{HW}(b) \ . \tag{7}$$

We notice that the set of ordered pairs $\{(b, \bigoplus_{i=1}^n b_i v_i), b \in \mathbb{F}_2^n\}$ forms a vector subspace of $\mathbb{F}_2^{2n}$. Therefore, it defines a $[2n, n, \delta]$ binary linear code, where δ is its minimum distance. Because of Eqn. (7), the necessary and sufficient condition becomes $\delta > d$. Reciprocally, a $[2n, n, \delta]$ binary linear code (modulo a permutation of its coordinates) can be spawned by a generator matrix $(I_n \ \ G)$, where G is an $n \times n$ matrix. This representation is the systematic form of the code.

Table 1. Minimal distance of some binary optimal linear rate $1/2$ codes

Sboxes of algorithm	DES	n/a	n/a	n/a	AES
$2n$	8	10	12	14	16
$\delta_{\max}(n)$	4	4	4	4	5

Now, $[2n, n, \delta]$ binary linear codes have been well studied. They are also referred to as $1/2$-rate codes in the literature. Their greatest minimal distance $\delta_{\max}(n)$ is known (refer for instance to [12]); corresponding codes are called "optimal". For some practical values of n, they are recalled in Tab. 1.

Thus, the best achievable d using a linear bijection F is $\delta_{\max}(n) - 1$. In particular, this result proves that with linear F, it is possible to protect:

- DES against all zero-offset HO-CPA of order $d \leq 3$, and
- AES against all zero-offset HO-CPA of order $d \leq 4$.

4.2 Optimal Non-linear Bijections

Under some circumstances, a non-linear bijection F allows to reach better performances. The condition on F given by (Eqn. (6)) is satisfied for every P and every Q such that $P + Q = d$ if and only if the Boolean function equal to the indicator of the graph $\{(x, F(x)); x \in \mathbb{F}_2^n\}$ of F is d-th order correlation immune (see definition in [3]). Given any (n, n)-function F, let $C = \{(x, F(x)), x \in \mathbb{F}_2^n\}$. The weight enumerator $W_C(X, Y)$ and distance enumerator $D_C(X, Y)$ of this code are:

- $W_C(X, Y) = \sum_{x \in \mathbb{F}_2^n} X^{2n - \mathrm{HW}(x, F(x))} Y^{\mathrm{HW}(x, F(x))}$ and
- $D_C(X, Y) = \frac{1}{|C|} \sum_{x, y \in \mathbb{F}_2^n} X^{2n - \mathrm{HW}(x \oplus y, F(x) \oplus F(y))} Y^{\mathrm{HW}(x \oplus y, F(x) \oplus F(y))}$.

We have $W_C(X + Y, X - Y) = \sum_{a, b \in \mathbb{F}_2^n} \left(\sum_{x \in \mathbb{F}_2^n} (-1)^{b \cdot F(x) + a \cdot x} \right) X^{2n - \mathrm{HW}(a, b)} Y^{\mathrm{HW}(a, b)}$

and $D_C(X + Y, X - Y) = \frac{1}{|C|} \sum_{a, b \in \mathbb{F}_2^n} \left(\sum_{x \in \mathbb{F}_2^n} (-1)^{b \cdot F(x) \oplus a \cdot x} \right)^2 X^{2n - \mathrm{HW}(a, b)} Y^{\mathrm{HW}(a, b)}$.

Hence $d + 1$ is exactly the minimum value of the nonzero exponents of Y with nonzero coefficients in $D_C(X + Y, X - Y)$, called the dual distance of C in the sense of Delsarte [8,13].

There is no non-linear code for $n = 4$ that has a better dual distance than linear codes of the same length and size, but there are some for $n = 8$. A non-linear optimal code for $n = 8$ is the Nordstrom-Robinson $(16, 256, 6)$ code (see more in [6]). With these parameters, this code coincides with Preparata and Kerdock codes [23] and has same minimum distance and dual distance. Some codewords, as obtained from Golay code in standard form [10], are listed in Tab. 2.

It happens that the code cannot be trivially split into two halves that each fill exactly $\mathbb{F}_2^n$. Indeed, if the codewords are partitioned with bits $[\![15, 8]\!]$ on the one hand, and bits $[\![7, 0]\!]$ on the other,

Table 2. Some codewords of the Nordstrom-Robinson $(16, 256, 6)$ code

Bit index	15	14	13	12	11	10	9	8	7	6	5	4	3	2	1	0
Codeword $x = 0$	0	0	0	0	0	0	0	0	0	0	0	0	0	0	0	0
Codeword $x = 1$	1	1	0	0	1	1	0	0	1	1	0	0	1	1	0	0
Codeword $x = 2$	1	0	1	0	1	0	1	0	1	0	1	0	1	0	1	0
Codeword $x = 3$	1	1	1	1	1	1	1	1	1	1	1	1	1	1	1	1
Codeword $x = 4$	0	1	1	0	0	1	1	0	0	1	1	0	0	1	1	0
Codeword $x = 5$	0	0	1	1	0	0	1	1	0	0	1	1	0	0	1	1
Codeword $x = 6$	0	1	0	1	0	1	0	1	0	1	0	1	0	1	0	1
Codeword $x = 7$	1	1	1	1	1	1	1	1	0	0	0	0	0	0	0	0
Codeword $x = 8$	1	1	1	1	0	0	0	0	1	1	1	1	0	0	0	0
$\vdots$	$\vdots$	$\vdots$	$\vdots$	$\vdots$	$\vdots$	$\vdots$	$\vdots$	$\vdots$	$\vdots$	$\vdots$	$\vdots$	$\vdots$	$\vdots$	$\vdots$	$\vdots$	$\vdots$
Codeword $x = 254$	1	0	1	1	0	0	1	0	1	0	0	0	0	0	0	1
Codeword $x = 255$	0	1	0	0	0	0	1	0	0	1	1	1	0	0	0	1

– then 11111111 is present (at least) twice in the first half (from the high byte of codewords $x = 3$ and $x = 7$),
– and 00000000 is present (at least) twice in the second half (from the low byte of codewords $x = 0$ and $x = 7$).

We tested all the $\binom{16}{8}$ partitionings. For 2760 of them, the code can be cut in two bijections F_{high} and F_{low} of $\mathbb{F}_2^8$. This means that if we note $x \in \mathbb{F}_2^8$ the codewords index in Tab. 2, the Nordstrom-Robinson $(16, 256, 6)$ code writes as $F_{\text{high}}(x) \,\|\, F_{\text{low}}(x)$. The codewords can be reordered according to the first column, so that the code rewrites $x \,\|\, F_{\text{low}}(F_{\text{high}}^{-1}(x))$ [6]. So the bijection F can be chosen equal to $F = F_{\text{low}} \circ F_{\text{high}}^{-1}$. For example, when F_{high} consists in bits $[\![15, 9]\!] \cup \{7\}$ of the code (and F_{low} in bits $\{8\} \cup [\![6, 0]\!]$), F takes the values tabulated as follows: $\{F(x), x \in \mathbb{F}_2^8\} = \{$0x00, 0xb3, 0xe5, 0x6a, 0x2f, 0xc6, 0x5c, 0x89, 0x79, 0xac, 0x36, 0xdf, 0x9a, 0x15, 0x43, 0xf0, 0xcb, 0x1e, 0xb8, 0x51, 0x72, 0xfd, 0x97, 0x24, 0xd4, 0x67, 0x0d, 0x82, 0xa1, 0x48, 0xee, 0x3b, 0x9d, 0x74, 0xd2, 0x07, 0xe8, 0x5b, 0x31, 0xbe, 0x4e, 0xc1, 0xab, 0x18, 0xf7, 0x22, 0x84, 0x6d, 0xa6, 0x29, 0x7f, 0xcc, 0x45, 0x90, 0x0a, 0xe3, 0x13, 0xfa, 0x60, 0xb5, 0x3c, 0x8f, 0xd9, 0x56, 0x57, 0xd8, 0x8e, 0x3d, 0xb4, 0x61, 0xfb, 0x12, 0xe2, 0x0b, 0x91, 0x44, 0xcd, 0x7e, 0x28, 0xa7, 0x6c, 0x85, 0x23, 0xf6, 0x19, 0xaa, 0xc0, 0x4f, 0xbf, 0x30, 0x5a, 0xe9, 0x06, 0xd3, 0x75, 0x9c, 0x3a, 0xef, 0x49, 0xa0, 0x83, 0x0c, 0x66, 0xd5, 0x25, 0x96, 0xfc, 0x73, 0x50, 0xb9, 0x1f, 0xca, 0xf1, 0x42, 0x14, 0x9b, 0xde, 0x37, 0xad, 0x78, 0x88, 0x5d, 0xc7, 0x2e, 0x6b, 0xe4, 0xb2, 0x01, 0xfe, 0x4d, 0x1b, 0x94, 0xd1, 0x38, 0xa2, 0x77, 0x87, 0x52, 0xc8, 0x21, 0x64, 0xeb, 0xbd, 0x0e, 0x35, 0xe0, 0x46, 0xaf, 0x8c, 0x03, 0x69, 0xda, 0x2a, 0x99, 0xf3, 0x7c, 0x5f, 0xb6, 0x10, 0xc5, 0x63, 0x8a, 0x2c, 0xf9, 0x16, 0xa5, 0xcf, 0x40, 0xb0, 0x3f, 0x55, 0xe6, 0x09, 0xdc, 0x7a, 0x93, 0x58, 0xd7, 0x81, 0x32, 0xbb, 0x6e, 0xf4, 0x1d, 0xed, 0x04, 0x9e, 0x4b, 0xc2, 0x71, 0x27, 0xa8, 0xa9, 0x26, 0x70, 0xc3, 0x4a, 0x9f, 0x05, 0xec, 0x1c, 0xf5, 0x6f, 0xba, 0x33, 0x80, 0xd6, 0x59, 0x92, 0x7b, 0xdd, 0x08, 0xe7, 0x54, 0x3e, 0xb1, 0x41, 0xce,

0xa4, 0x17, 0xf8, 0x2d, 0x8b, 0x62, 0xc4, 0x11, 0xb7, 0x5e, 0x7d, 0xf2, 0x98, 0x2b, 0xdb, 0x68, 0x02, 0x8d, 0xae, 0x47, 0xe1, 0x34, 0x0f, 0xbc, 0xea, 0x65, 0x20, 0xc9, 0x53, 0x86, 0x76, 0xa3, 0x39, 0xd0, 0x95, 0x1a, 0x4c, 0xff}.

Thus byte-oriented cryptographic implementations can be protected with this code against all zero-offset HO-CPA of order $d \leq 5$.

5 Security and Leakage Evaluations of the Optimal Linear and Non-linear Bijections

As argued in [24], the robustness evaluation of a CM encompasses two dimensions: its resistance to specific attacks, and its amount of leakage irrespective of any attack strategy. Indeed, a CM could resist some attacks, but still be vulnerable to others. For instance, in our study, we have focused on zero-offset HO-CPA, but we have disregarded other attacks, such as mutual information analysis (MIA [1]) or attacks based on generic side-channel distinguishers [28]. Therefore, in addition to a security evaluation conducted in Sec. 5.1, we will also estimate the leakage of the CM in Sec. 5.2.

5.1 Verification of the Security for $n = 8$

In this section, we illustrate the efficiency of the identified bijection from an zero-offset HO-CPA point of view. We focus more specifically on the $n = 8$ bit case, because of its applicability to AES. We compute the values of $f_{opt}(z)$ for the centered leakage raised at power $1 \leq d \leq 6$ for four linear bijections (noted $F1$, $F2$, $F3$ and $F4$) and the non-linear bijection given in Sec. 4.2 (noted $F5$). The linear functions are defined from their matrix:

- $G1$ is the identity I_8, *i.e.* the Boolean masking function without F;
- $G2$ is a matrix that allows second-order resistance and is found without method;
- $G3$ is the circulant matrix involved in the AES block cipher;
- $G4$ is non-systematic half of the $[16, 8, 5]$ code matrix.

The $G2$, $G3$ and $G4$ matrices are:

$$G2 = \begin{pmatrix} 0&0&0&0&0&1&1&1 \\ 0&0&0&1&1&0&1&1 \\ 1&0&1&0&0&0&1&1 \\ 0&0&1&1&1&0&0&0 \\ 1&1&1&0&0&0&0&0 \\ 1&1&1&1&1&1&1&1 \\ 1&0&1&0&1&1&0&0 \\ 0&1&0&1&0&1&1&0 \end{pmatrix}, G3 = \begin{pmatrix} 1&0&0&0&1&1&1&1 \\ 1&1&0&0&0&1&1&1 \\ 1&1&1&0&0&0&1&1 \\ 1&1&1&1&0&0&0&1 \\ 1&1&1&1&1&0&0&0 \\ 0&1&1&1&1&1&0&0 \\ 0&0&1&1&1&1&1&0 \\ 0&0&0&1&1&1&1&1 \end{pmatrix}, G4 = \begin{pmatrix} 1&0&0&1&1&1&1&0 \\ 0&1&0&0&1&1&1&1 \\ 1&1&0&0&1&1&0&0 \\ 0&1&1&0&0&1&1&0 \\ 0&0&1&1&0&0&1&1 \\ 1&1&1&1&0&0&1&0 \\ 0&1&1&1&1&0&0&1 \\ 1&1&0&1&0&1&1&1 \end{pmatrix}.$$

It can be checked that they are invertible. Namely, their inverses are:

$$G2^{-1} = \begin{pmatrix} 0&1&1&1&0&0&0&0 \\ 1&1&1&0&0&1&0&0 \\ 1&0&0&1&1&1&0&0 \\ 0&0&1&0&1&1&1&0 \\ 1&0&1&0&0&0&1&0 \\ 0&1&0&0&1&1&0&0 \\ 1&0&0&0&0&1&1&1 \\ 0&1&0&0&1&0&1&1 \end{pmatrix}, G3^{-1} = \begin{pmatrix} 0&0&1&0&0&1&0&1 \\ 1&0&0&1&0&0&1&0 \\ 0&1&0&0&1&0&0&1 \\ 1&0&1&0&0&1&0&0 \\ 0&1&0&1&0&0&1&0 \\ 0&0&1&0&1&0&0&1 \\ 1&0&0&1&0&1&0&0 \\ 0&1&0&0&1&0&1&0 \end{pmatrix}, G4^{-1} = \begin{pmatrix} 1&1&1&0&1&0&1&1 \\ 1&0&0&1&1&1&1&0 \\ 0&1&0&0&1&1&1&1 \\ 1&1&0&0&1&1&0&0 \\ 0&1&1&0&0&1&1&0 \\ 0&0&1&1&0&0&1&1 \\ 1&1&1&1&0&0&1&0 \\ 0&1&1&1&1&0&0&1 \end{pmatrix}.$$

Table 3, in Appendix A, reports some values of the optimal functions. The lines represented in gray are those for which the $f_{\text{opt}}(z)$ are the same for all the values of the sensitive variable $z \in \mathbb{F}_2^n$. For the sake of clarity, we represent only $n+1$ values of z, *i.e.* one per value of $\text{HW}(z)$. But we are aware that unlike in the case where $F = \text{Id}$, the optimal functions are not invariant in the bits reordering of x. If the line d is represented in gray, then a d-th order zero-offset HO-CPA cannot succeed. The table shows that amongst the linear functions, $F4 : x \mapsto G4 \times x$ is indeed the best, since it protects against zero-offset HO-CPA of orders 1, 2, 3 and 4. It can also be seen that the non-linear function $F5$ further protects against 5-th order zero-offset HO-CPA, as announced in Sec. 4.2.

5.2 Verification of the Leakage of the Identified Bijections

As a complement to the security analysis carried out in Sec. 5.1, the leakage of the CM using the bijections $F1$, $F2$, $F3$, $F4$ and $F5$ is computed. It consists in the mutual information metric (MIM), defined as $I[\text{HW}(Z \oplus M'') + \text{HW}(F(M) \oplus F(M \oplus M'')) - n + N; Z]$. The random variable N is an additive noise, that follows a normal law of variance σ^2. The result of the MIM computation is shown in Fig. 3.

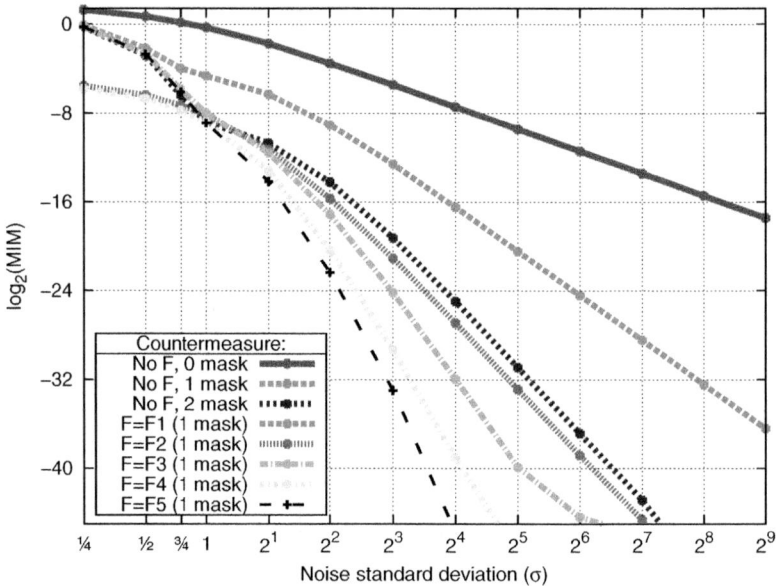

Fig. 3. Mutual information of the leakage with the sensitive variable Z for $n = 8$ bit

It appears that the leakage agrees with the strength of the CM against HO-CPA: the greater the order of resistance against HO-CPA, the smaller the mutual information, at least for a reasonably large noise $\sigma \geq 1$. This simulated characterization validates (in the particular scheme of Fig. 2) the relevance of choosing F based on a HO-CPA criterion.

Furthermore, Fig. 3 represents the leakage of a similar CM, where more than two shares would be used. More precisely, the shares would be the triple $(x \oplus m_1 \oplus m_2, m_1, m_2)$, where the masks m_i are not transformed by bijections. This CM is obviously more costly than our proposal of keeping one single mask, but passed through F. We notice that all the proposed bijections (suboptimal $F2$ and $F3$, optimal linear $F4$ and optimal non-linear $F5$) perform better, in that they leak less irrespective of σ.

5.3   Results in Imperfect Models

Masking schemes randomize more or less properly the leakage. In the straightforward example studied in this paper (Eqn. (1) with $F = \mathsf{Id}$), when the sensitive variable z has all its bits equal to '1' (*i.e.* $Z = \mathtt{0xff}$), then the mask has no effect whatsoever on the leakage. Indeed, this is due to a well-known property of the Hamming weight function: $\forall M'' \in \mathbb{F}_2^n, \mathsf{HW}(\mathtt{0xff} \oplus M'') + \mathsf{HW}(M'') = \mathsf{HW}(\overline{M''}) + \mathsf{HW}(M'') = n$. To avoid this situation, the proposed CM based on the bijection F consists in tuning the leakage, so that the masks indeed dispatch randomly the leakage for most (if not all [15]) values of the sensitive data. The working factor of is improvement is the introduction of a specially crafted Boolean function F aiming at weakening the link between the data to protect and the leakage function.

This technique has been shown to be very effective in the previous sections. Now, the analysis assumed a perfect leakage model. But the Hamming distance leakage model is in practice an idealization of the reality. Indeed, the assumption that all the bits leak identically, and without interfering, does not hold in real hardware [27]. Also, it has been shown that with specific side-channel capturing systems the attacker can distort the measurement. For instance, in [18], the authors show that with a home-made magnetic coil probing the circuit at a crucial location, the rising edges can be forced to dissipate 17% more than the falling edges.

Therefore, we study how the CM is resilient to imperfections of the leakage model. To do so, we define a general model that depends on random variables. The variability is quantified in units of the side-channel dissipation of a bit-flip. The model is affected by small imperfections (due to process variation, or small cross-coupling) when the variability is about 10%. We also consider the 20% case, that would reflect a distortion of the leakage due to measurements in weird conditions. Eventually, the cases of a 50% and of a 100% deviation indicate that the designer has few or no a priori knowledge about the device leakage's model.

More precisely, the leakage model is written as a multivariate polynomial in $\mathbb{R}[X_1, \cdots, X_n, X_1', \cdots, X_n']$ of degree less or equal to $\tau \in [\![1, 2n]\!]$, where $X = (X_{i \in [\![1,n]\!]})$ and $X' = (X'_{i \in [\![1,n]\!]})$ are the initial and final values of the sensitive variable. It takes the following form:

$$L \doteq P(X_1, \cdots, X_n, X_1', \cdots, X_n') = \sum_{\substack{(u,v) \in \mathbb{F}_2^n \times \mathbb{F}_2^n, \\ \mathsf{HW}(u) + \mathsf{HW}(v) \leq \tau}} A_{(u,v)} \cdot \prod_{i=1}^n X_i^{u_i} X_i'^{v_i}, \qquad (8)$$

where the $A_{(u,v)}$ are real coefficients. This leakage formulation is similar to that of the high-order stochastic model [21]. For example, it is shown in [19, Eqn. (3)] that $P(X_1, \cdots, X_n, X_1', \cdots, X_n')$ is equal to $\mathsf{HW}(X \oplus X')$ when the coefficients $A_{(u,v)} \doteq a_{(u,v)}^{\mathrm{HD}}$ satisfy:

$$
a_{(u,v)}^{\mathrm{HD}} = \begin{cases} +1 & \text{if } \mathsf{HW}(u) + \mathsf{HW}(v) = 1\,, \\ -2 & \text{if } \mathsf{HW}(u) = 1 \text{ and } v = u\,, \\ 0 & \text{otherwise}\,. \end{cases} \tag{9}
$$

In the following experiments, we compute the mutual information between L and $Z = X \oplus X'$ when $\tau \leq 2$ and when the coefficients $A_{(u,v)}$ deviate randomly from those of (9) or are completely random (*i.e.* deviate from a "NULL" model). More precisely, the coefficients $A_{(u,v)}$ are respectively drawn at random from one of these laws:

$$
\begin{aligned}
A_{(u,v)}^{\mathrm{HD}} &\sim a_{(u,v)}^{\mathrm{HD}} + \mathcal{U}\!\left(\left[-\tfrac{\delta}{2}, +\tfrac{\delta}{2}\right]\right)\,, \\
A_{(u,v)}^{\mathrm{NULL}} &\sim 0 \quad + \mathcal{U}\!\left(\left[-\tfrac{\delta}{2}, +\tfrac{\delta}{2}\right]\right)\,.
\end{aligned} \tag{10}
$$

The randomness lays in the uniform law $\mathcal{U}\!\left(\left[-\tfrac{\delta}{2}, +\tfrac{\delta}{2}\right]\right)$, that we parametrize by the deviation $\delta \in \{0.1, 0.2, 0.5, 1.0\}$. The mutual information $\mathsf{I}[L; Z]$ is computed ten times for ten different randomized models. Four bit variables (case useful for DES) are considered, because the computation time for the MI would have been too long for $n = 8$. The study is conducted on three bijections:

$F1'$: the identity (Id), that acts as a reference,
$F2'$: one bijection that cancels the first-order leakage but not the second-order,
$F3'$: another that cancels both first- and second-orders.

They are linear, *i.e.* write $Fi'(x) = Gi' \times x$, where the generating matrix Gi' are given below:

$$
G1' = I_4 = \begin{pmatrix} 1\,0\,0\,0 \\ 0\,1\,0\,0 \\ 0\,0\,1\,0 \\ 0\,0\,0\,1 \end{pmatrix}, \quad G2' = \begin{pmatrix} 0\,0\,1\,1 \\ 0\,1\,0\,1 \\ 1\,1\,1\,0 \\ 1\,0\,0\,1 \end{pmatrix}, \quad G3' = \overline{I_4} = \begin{pmatrix} 0\,1\,1\,1 \\ 1\,0\,1\,1 \\ 1\,1\,0\,1 \\ 1\,1\,1\,0 \end{pmatrix}.
$$

In this section, we use bijections Fi' from $\mathbb{F}_2^4$ to $\mathbb{F}_2^4$, noted with a prime, to mark the difference with the bijections $Fi : \mathbb{F}_2^8 \to \mathbb{F}_2^8$ that were studied in Sec. 5.1 and 5.2. The simulation results are provided in the extended version [14]. it can be seen that despite the HD model degradation, the leakage of the CM:

 – remains ordered ($F3'$ leaks less than $F2'$, and $F2'$ in turn leaks less than $F1'$),
 – and remains low, irrespective of δ.

The average leakage is unchanged, and the leakage values are simply getting slightly scattered. The reason for this resilience comes from the rationale of the CM: the masked value and the mask are decorrelated as much as possible. The dispatching is guided by a randomized pigeon-hole of the values in the image of the leakage function. The CM thus looses efficiency only in the case where two different values of leakage become similar due to the imperfection. This can happen for some variables, but it is very unlikely that it occurs coherently for all variables at the same time. Rather, given the way the imperfect model is built (Eqn. (10)), it is almost as likely that two classes get nearer or further away. This explains why, in average, the leakage is not affected: the model noise acts as a random walk, that has an impact on the variance but not on the average. Of course, some samples (with a degraded model) will be weaker than the others (because the variance of the MIA increases with the variance[1] $\delta^2/12$ of the model).

It is interesting to contrast the leakage squeezing with the first-order leak-free CM presented in [15]. This CM aims at leaking no information when the HD leakage model is perfect. A study for model imperfection has also been conducted (see [14]). It appears that this CM is much less robust to deviation from the ideal model. Indeed, the working factor of the CM is to have one share leak nothing. But as soon as there is some imperfection, the very principle of the CM is violated, and it starts to function less well. Concretely the leaked information increases with the model variance, up to a point where the CM is less efficient than the straightforward first-order Boolean masking (starting from $\delta > 50\%$).

For the sake of comparison, we also computed the same curves when the unnoised model is a constant one (called "NULL" model in Eqn. (10)) [14]. The reference leakage (when $\delta = 0$) is null; consequently only the noisy curves are shown. It is noticeable that despite this "NULL" leakage model is random, the different CMs have clearly distinguishable efficiencies. This had already been noticed by Doget et al. in [9]. In particular, it appears that our CM continues to work ($F3$ leaks less than $F2$, that leaks less than $F1$), at least for large enough noise standard deviations σ. At the opposite, the leak-free CM is not resilient to this random model: it leaks more than the straightforward masking (i.e. with $F1$). Eventually, the impact of the leakage degree τ can be studied. Results are computed for τ in $\{1, 2, 3\}$. In all the cases, τ does not impact the general conclusions.

Regarding the deviation from the HD model, the greater the multivariate degree τ, the more possible deviations from the genuine ideal model. Indeed, the number of random terms in Eqn. (8) is increasing with τ (and is equal to $\sum_{t=0}^{\tau} \binom{2n}{t}$). This explains the greatest variability in the mutual information results. In the meantime, the argumentation for the robustness of the CM against the model deviation still holds, which explains why the average leakage is unchanged. In the Null model, the greater τ, the less singularities in the leakage. This explains why the mutual information curves get smoother despite the additional noise. But with the greater τ, the more leaking sources (because the more non-zero terms in the polynomial), which explains why the leaked mutual information increases in average with τ.

---

[1] The variance of a uniform law of amplitude δ is indeed equal to $\mathsf{Var}\left(\mathcal{U}([-\delta/2, +\delta/2])\right) = \frac{1}{\delta} \int_{-\delta/2}^{+\delta/2} (u - 0)^2 \, du = \left[\frac{u^3}{3\delta}\right]_{u=-\delta/2}^{u=+\delta/2} = \frac{\delta^2}{12}$.

6   Conclusions

Masking is a CM against side-channel attacks that consists in injecting some randomness in the execution of a computation. The sensitive value is split in several shares; altogether, they allow to reconstruct the sensitive data by an adequate combination [11]. In this article, we focus on a Boolean masking CM that uses two shares, computed concomitantly. Zero-offset HO-CPA attacks can defeat this CM. They consist in computing a correlation with the centered side-channel traces, raised at the power $d \in \mathbb{N}^*$. We show that by storing $F(m)$ (the image of m by a bijection F) instead of m in the mask register, the highest order d of a successful zero-offset attack can be increased significantly. Typically, when the data to protect are bytes, the state-of-the-art implementations with one mask could be attacked with HO-CPA of order $d = 2$. We show how to find optimal linear F, that protects against zero-offset HO-CPA of orders 1, 2, 3 and 4. We also show that optimal non-linear functions F protect against zero-offset HO-CPA of orders 1, 2, 3, 4 and 5. This security increase also translates into a leakage reduction. An information-theoretic study reveals that the mutual information between the leakage and the sensitive variable is lower than the same metric computed on a similar CM without F but that uses two masks (instead of one).

Acknowledgments. The authors are grateful to Sébastien Briais (Secure-IC S.A.S.) and M. Abdelaziz Elaabid (Paris 8 University) for insightful discussions.

References

1. Batina, L., Gierlichs, B., Prouff, E., Rivain, M., Standaert, F.-X., Veyrat-Charvillon, N.: Mutual Information Analysis: a Comprehensive Study. J. Cryptology 24(2), 269–291 (2011)
2. Brier, E., Clavier, C., Olivier, F.: Correlation Power Analysis with a Leakage Model. In: Joye, M., Quisquater, J.-J. (eds.) CHES 2004. LNCS, vol. 3156, pp. 16–29. Springer, Heidelberg (2004)
3. Camion, P., Carlet, C., Charpin, P., Sendrier, N.: On Correlation-Immune Functions. In: Feigenbaum, J. (ed.) CRYPTO 1991. LNCS, vol. 576, pp. 86–100. Springer, Heidelberg (1992)
4. Carlet, C.: Boolean Functions for Cryptography and Error Correcting Codes. Chapter of the Monography Boolean Models and Methods in Mathematics, Computer Science, and Engineering, pp. 257–397. Cambridge University Press (2010), Preliminary version,
   http://www.math.univ-paris13.fr/~carlet/chap-fcts-Bool-corr.pdf
5. Carlet, C.: Vectorial Boolean Functions for Cryptography. Crama, Y., Hammer, P. (eds.) Chapter of the Monography Boolean Models and Methods in Mathematics, Computer Science, and Engineering, pp. 398–469. Cambridge University Press, Cambridge (2010), Preliminary version,
   http://www.math.univ-paris13.fr/~carlet/pubs.html
6. Carlet, C., Gaborit, P., Kim, J.-L., Solé, P.: A new class of codes for Boolean masking of cryptographic computations, October 6 (2011),
   http://arxiv.org/abs/1110.1193

7. Danger, J.-L., Guilley, S.: Cryptography Circuit Protected Against Observation Attacks, in Particular of a High Order, September 23, International patent, published as FR2941342 (A1), WO2010084106 (A1) & (A9), EP2380306 (A1), CA2749961, A1 (2010)
8. Delsarte, P.: An algebraic approach to the association schemes of coding theory. PhD thesis, Université Catholique de Louvain, Belgium (1973)
9. Doget, J., Prouff, E., Rivain, M., Standaert, F.-X.: Univariate side channel attacks and leakage modeling. J. Cryptographic Engineering 1(2), 123–144 (2011)
10. David Forney Jr., G., Sloane, N.J.A., Trott, M.D.: The Nordstrom-Robinson Code is the Binary Image of the Octacode. In: Calderbank Amer, R., Forney Jr., G.D., Moayeri, N. (eds.) Coding and Quantization: DIMACS/IEEE Workshop, October 19-21. Math. Soc., pp. 19–26 (1992)
11. Goubin, L., Patarin, J.: DES and Differential Power Analysis. In: Koç, Ç.K., Paar, C. (eds.) CHES 1999. LNCS, vol. 1717, pp. 158–172. Springer, Heidelberg (1999)
12. Aaron Gulliver, T., Östergård, P.R.J.: Binary optimal linear rate 1/2 codes. Discrete Mathematics 283(1-3), 255–261 (2004)
13. Jessie MacWilliams, F., Sloane, N.J.A.: The Theory of Error-Correcting Codes. Elsevier, Amsterdam (1977) ISBN: 978-0-444-85193-2
14. Maghrebi, H., Carlet, C., Guilley, S., Danger, J.-L.: Optimal first-order masking with linear and non-linear bijections. Cryptology ePrint Archive, Report 2012/175, April 6 (2012), http://eprint.iacr.org/2012/175/
15. Maghrebi, H., Prouff, E., Guilley, S., Danger, J.-L.: A First-Order Leak-Free Masking Countermeasure. In: Dunkelman, O. (ed.) CT-RSA 2012. LNCS, vol. 7178, pp. 156–170. Springer, Heidelberg (2012), doi:10.1007/978-3-642-27954-6_10
16. Mathew, S.K., Sheikh, F., Kounavis, M., Gueron, S., Agarwal, A., Hsu, S.K., Kaul, H., Anders, M.A., Krishnamurthy, R.K.: 53 Gbps Native $GF(2^4)^2$ Composite-Field AES-Encrypt/Decrypt Accelerator for Content-Protection in 45 nm High-Performance Microprocessors. IEEE Journal of Solid-State Circuits 46(4), 767–776 (2011)
17. Peeters, E., Standaert, F.-X., Donckers, N., Quisquater, J.-J.: Improved Higher-Order Side-Channel Attacks with FPGA Experiments. In: Rao, J.R., Sunar, B. (eds.) CHES 2005. LNCS, vol. 3659, pp. 309–323. Springer, Heidelberg (2005)
18. Peeters, É., Standaert, F.-X., Quisquater, J.-J.: Power and electromagnetic analysis: Improved model, consequences and comparisons. Integration, The VLSI Journal, Special Issue on Embedded Cryptographic Hardware 40, 52–60 (2005), doi:10.1016/j.vlsi.2005.12.013
19. Prouff, E., Rivain, M., Bevan, R.: Statistical Analysis of Second Order Differential Power Analysis. IEEE Trans. Computers 58(6), 799–811 (2009)
20. Satoh, A., Morioka, S., Takano, K., Munetoh, S.: A Compact Rijndael Hardware Architecture with S-Box Optimization. In: Boyd, C. (ed.) ASIACRYPT 2001. LNCS, vol. 2248, pp. 239–254. Springer, Heidelberg (2001)
21. Schindler, W., Lemke, K., Paar, C.: A Stochastic Model for Differential Side Channel Cryptanalysis. In: Rao, J.R., Sunar, B. (eds.) CHES 2005. LNCS, vol. 3659, pp. 30–46. Springer, Heidelberg (2005)
22. Shah, S., Velegalati, R., Kaps, J.-P., Hwang, D.: Investigation of DPA Resistance of Block RAMs in Cryptographic Implementations on FPGAs. In: Prasanna, V.K., Becker, J., Cumplido, R. (eds.) ReConFig, pp. 274–279. IEEE Computer Society (2010)
23. Snover, S.L.: The uniqueness of the Nordstrom-Robinson and the Golay binary codes. PhD thesis, Department of Mathematics, Michigan State University, USA (1973)

24. Standaert, F.-X., Malkin, T.G., Yung, M.: A Unified Framework for the Analysis of Side-Channel Key Recovery Attacks. In: Joux, A. (ed.) EUROCRYPT 2009. LNCS, vol. 5479, pp. 443–461. Springer, Heidelberg (2009)
25. Standaert, F.-X., Peeters, É., Rouvroy, G., Quisquater, J.-J.: An Overview of Power Analysis Attacks Against Field Programmable Gate Arrays. Proceedings of the IEEE 94(2), 383–394 (2006) (invited paper)
26. Standaert, F.-X., Rouvroy, G., Quisquater, J.-J.: FPGA Implementations of the DES and Triple-DES Masked Against Power Analysis Attacks. In: FPL, Madrid, Spain. IEEE (August 2006)
27. Veyrat-Charvillon, N., Standaert, F.-X.: Mutual Information Analysis: How, When and Why? In: Clavier, C., Gaj, K. (eds.) CHES 2009. LNCS, vol. 5747, pp. 429–443. Springer, Heidelberg (2009)
28. Veyrat-Charvillon, N., Standaert, F.-X.: Generic Side-Channel Distinguishers: Improvements and Limitations. In: Rogaway, P. (ed.) CRYPTO 2011. LNCS, vol. 6841, pp. 354–372. Springer, Heidelberg (2011)
29. Waddle, J., Wagner, D.: Towards Efficient Second-Order Power Analysis. In: Joye, M., Quisquater, J.-J. (eds.) CHES 2004. LNCS, vol. 3156, pp. 1–15. Springer, Heidelberg (2004)

A   Computation of the Optimal Function $z \mapsto f_{\mathrm{opt}}(z)$ for Some Bijections F

Some $f_{\mathrm{opt}}(z)$ have been computed in Tab. 3 for centered traces raised at power $d \in [\![1, 6]\!]$, for some representative bijections, including the optimal linear ($F4$) and non-linear ($F5$) ones. The last column shows the optimal correlation coefficient ρ_{opt} that an attacker can expect (See definition in [19, Eqn. (15)]). It can be seen that the first nonzero ρ_{opt} approximately decreases with the CM strength: it is about 25% for $F1$, about 4% for $F2$ and $F3$, and about 2% for $F4$ and $F5$.

Table 3. Computation of $f_{opt}(z)$ for centered traces raised at several powers d, and optimal correlation coefficient ρ_{opt}

z	$f_{opt}(z)$									ρ_{opt}
	0x00	0x01	0x03	0x07	0x0f	0x1f	0x3f	0x7f	0xff	
Bijection $F = F1$ (reference $F1 : x \mapsto I_8 \times x = x$)										
$d=1$	0	0	0	0	0	0	0	0	0	0.000000
$d=2$	8	7	6	5	4	3	2	1	0	0.258199
$d=3$	0	0	0	0	0	0	0	0	0	0.000000
$d=4$	176	133	96	65	40	21	8	1	0	0.235341
$d=5$	0	0	0	0	0	0	0	0	0	0.000000
$d=6$	5888	3787	2256	1205	544	183	32	1	0	0.197908
Bijection $F = F2$ (linear $F2 : x \mapsto G2 \times x$)										
$d=1$	0	0	0	0	0	0	0	0	0	0.000000
$d=2$	4	4	4	4	4	4	4	4	4	0.000000
$d=3$	−1.5	−1.5	−1.5	−1.5	0	0	0	0	1.5	0.036509
$d=4$	49	49	49	49	49	46	49	46	46	0.015548
$d=5$	−120	−75	−37.5	−30	7.5	22.5	15	22.5	67.5	0.051072
$d=6$	1399	1061	949	971.5	971.5	821.5	971.5	821.5	979	0.027247
Bijection $F = F3$ (linear $F3 : x \mapsto G3 \times x$)										
$d=1$	0	0	0	0	0	0	0	0	0	0.000000
$d=2$	4	4	4	4	4	4	4	4	4	0.000000
$d=3$	0	0	0	0	0	0	0	0	0	0.000000
$d=4$	70	61	52	43	40	37	40	43	46	0.043976
$d=5$	0	0	0	0	0	0	0	0	0	0.000000
$d=6$	2584	1684	1144	694	544	484	544	694	664	0.067175
Bijection $F = F4$ (linear $F4 : x \mapsto G4 \times x$)										
$d=1$	0	0	0	0	0	0	0	0	0	0.000000
$d=2$	4	4	4	4	4	4	4	4	4	0.000000
$d=3$	0	0	0	0	0	0	0	0	0	0.000000
$d=4$	46	46	46	46	46	46	46	46	46	0.000000
$d=5$	−90	−37.5	−15	15	7.5	−22.5	7.5	7.5	0	0.023231
$d=6$	1339	956.5	799	799	866.5	821.5	776.5	821.5	844	0.016173
Bijection $F = F5$ (non-linear F tabulated in Sec. 4.2)										
$d=1$	0	0	0	0	0	0	0	0	0	0.000000
$d=2$	4	4	4	4	4	4	4	4	4	0.000000
$d=3$	0	0	0	0	0	0	0	0	0	0.000000
$d=4$	46	46	46	46	46	46	46	46	46	0.000000
$d=5$	0	0	0	0	0	0	0	0	0	0.000000
$d=6$	2104	1159	844	799	664	799	844	1159	844	0.023258

Size-Hiding in Private Set Intersection:
Existential Results and Constructions

Paolo D'Arco[1], María Isabel González Vasco[2],
Angel L. Pérez del Pozo[2], and Claudio Soriente[3]

[1] Dipartimento di Informatica, Universitá di Salerno,
84084 Fisciano (SA), Italy
paodar@dia.unisa.it
[2] Dpto. de Matemática Aplicada, Univ. Rey Juan Carlos,
c/ Tulipán, s/n, 28933 Madrid, Spain
{mariaisabel.vasco,angel.perez}@urjc.es
[3] Institute of Information Security, ETH Zurich
claudio.soriente@inf.ethz.ch

Abstract. In this paper we focus our attention on private set intersection. We show impossibility and existential results, and we provide some explicit constructions. More precisely, we start by looking at the case in which *both* parties, client and server, in securely computing the intersection, would like to hide the sizes of their sets of secrets, and we show that:

- It is impossible to realize an unconditionally secure size-hiding set intersection protocol.
- In a model where a TTP provides set up information to the two parties and disappears, unconditionally secure size-hiding set intersection is possible.
- There exist computationally secure size-hiding set intersection protocols.

Then, we provide some explicit constructions for *one-sided* protocols, where only the client *gets* the intersection and *hides* the size of her set of secrets. In the model with the TTP, we design two protocols which are computationally secure under standard assumptions, and two very efficient protocols which are secure in the random oracle model. We close the paper with some remarks and by pointing out several interesting open problems.

1 Introduction

The Private Set Intersection (PSI) problem revolves around two parties, each holding a set of inputs drawn from a ground set, that wish to jointly compute the intersection of their sets, without leaking *any* additional information [14]. In particular, cryptographic solutions to PSI allow interaction between a server S and client C, with respective private input sets $C = \{c_1, \ldots, c_v\}$, $S = \{s_1, \ldots, s_w\}$, both drawn from a ground set U. At the end of the interaction, C learns $S \cap C$ and $|S|$, while S learns nothing beyond $|C|$. Real-life applications of PSI include the Department of Homeland Security that wishes to check its list of terrorists against the passenger list of a flight operated by a foreign air carrier, federal tax authority wishing to check if any suspect tax evader has foreign bank account and other folklore case scenarios [8].

A. Mitrokotsa and S. Vaudenay (Eds.): AFRICACRYPT 2012, LNCS 7374, pp. 378–394, 2012.

Related work. Freedman et al. [14] introduced the first PSI protocol based on oblivious polynomial evaluation (OPE). The key intuition is that elements in the client's private set can be represented as roots of a polynomial, i.e., $P(x) = \prod_{i=1}^{v}(x - c_i) = \sum_{i=1}^{v} a_i x^i$. Hence, leveraging any additively homomorphic encryption scheme (e.g., [21]) the encrypted polynomial is obliviously evaluated by S on each element of its data set. In particular, S computes $\{u_j\}_{j=1,\ldots,w} = \{E(r_j P(s_j) + s_j)\}_{j=1,\ldots,w}$ where $E()$ is the encryption function of the additively homomorphic encryption scheme and r_j is chosen at random. Clearly, if $s_j \in S \cap C$, then C learns s_j upon decryption of the corresponding ciphertext (i.e., u_j); otherwise C learns a random value. OPE-based PSI protocols have been extended in [19,9,10] to support multiple parties and other set operations (e.g., union, element reduction, etc.).

Hazay et al. [16] proposed Oblivious Pseudo-Random Function (OPRF) [13] as an alternative primitive to achieve PSI. In [16], given a secret index k to a pseudorandom function family, S evaluates $\{u_j\}_{j=1,\ldots,w} = \{f_k(s_j)\}_{j=1,\ldots,w}$ and sends it to C. Later, C and S engage in v executions of the OPRF protocol where C is the receiver with private input C and S is the sender with private input k. As a result, C learns $\{f_k(c_i)\}_{i=1,\ldots,v}$ such that $c_i \in S \cap C$ if and only if $f_k(c_i) \in \{u_j\}_{j=1,\ldots,w}$.

Given $\mathcal{U}$ as the ground set where elements of C and S are drawn (i.e., $C, S \subseteq \mathcal{U}$), none of the above techniques prevents a client to run a PSI protocol on private input $C \equiv \mathcal{U}$ in order to learn the elements in S. To this end, Camenisch et al. extended PSI to *Certified Sets* [5], where a Trusted Third Party (TTP) ensures that private inputs are valid and binds them to each participant.

All of the above techniques reveal the size of the participants' sets. That is, C (resp. S) learns $|S|$ (resp. $|C|$), even if $S \cap C \equiv \emptyset$. To protect the size of private input sets, Ateniese et al. [1] proposed a so-called Size-Hiding PSI (SHI-PSI) protocol where C can privately learn $S \cap C$ without leaking the size of C. Their scheme is based on RSA accumulators and the property that the RSA function is an unpredictable function. The authors proved its security against honest but curious adversaries in the Random Oracle Model (ROM).

Contributions. This paper builds on top of [1] and explores PSI protocols where parties hide the size of their private sets, under different security models. We start looking at *unconditionally secure* SHI-PSI where *both* parties hide the size of their sets. In this context, we show that SHI-PSI protocols where both the client and the server hide the size of their sets are not achievable, while this is possible for the authorized flavor of PSI, namely APSI.

Then we move to computational security and show that there exist an APSI protocol where both parties hide the size of their sets. Finally, we provide some explicit constructions for *one-sided* protocols, where only the client hides the size of her set. More precisely, leveraging a TTP that authorized private inputs, we design two protocols which are computationally secure under standard assumptions, and two very efficient protocols which are secure in the random oracle model. The following table summarizes our findings.

Result	Model	Size-Hiding	Assumption	Efficiency	Rounds
Impossible	C/S	Two-side	None	×	×
Prot. Fig. 1	C/S with TTP	Two-side	None	NO	2
Prot. Fig. 2	C/S	Two-side	Standard Model	NO	2
Prot. Fig. 3	C/S	Two-side*	Standard Model	YES	2
Prot. Fig. 4	C/S with TTP	One-side	Standard Model	YES	1
Prot. Fig. 5	C/S with TTP	One-side	Standard Model	YES	2
Prot. Fig. 6	C/S with TTP	One-side	ROM	YES	3
Prot. Fig. 7	C/S with TTP	One-side	ROM	YES	1

* an upper bound on the sizes of both sets (client's and server's) is needed

2 Preliminaries: Definitions and Tools

In this section we provide definitions and tools used in the rest of the paper.

2.1 Definitions

We refer to the formalization used in [1]. However, we slightly refine the definitions in order to deal with both computationally and unconditionally secure protocols, and to introduce the size-hiding constraint on both client and server side. Moreover, we will also consider the setting in which a trusted third party interacts with the parties in a setup phase and then disappears.

Definition 1. *A party is referred to as honest-but-curious, HBC for short, if it correctly follows the steps of the protocol but eventually tries to get extra-knowledge from the transcript of the execution.*

A two-side size-hiding private set intersection protocol, can be defined as:

Definition 2. *A* TS-SHI-PSI *is a scheme involving two parties, C and S, with two components, $Setup$ and $Interaction$, where*

- *$Setup$ is an algorithm that selects all global parameters*
- *$Interaction$ is a protocol between S and C on respective input sets $S=\{s_1,\ldots,s_w\}$ and $C = \{c_1,\ldots,c_v\}$, which are subsets of a ground set $\mathcal{U} = \{u_1,\ldots,u_{|\mathcal{U}|}\}$,*

satisfying correctness, client privacy and server privacy.

Correctness is formalized by:

Definition 3. *A* TS-SHI-PSI *is correct if, when both parties are HBC, at the end of Interaction, run on inputs S and C, with overwhelming probability S outputs $\perp$ and C outputs $S \cap C$ or $\perp$ if the intersection is empty.*

Notice that, compared to the definition of correctness provided in [1], we do not require that $|\mathcal{S}|$ is part of the client's output. Note that in Section 5 in which we will consider protocols hiding only the size of the client's set, we will stick to the definition of correctness from [1] and require C to output $\mathcal{S} \cap C$ and $|\mathcal{S}|$ or just $|\mathcal{S}|$ if the intersection is empty.

Concerning client privacy, since the server does not get any output from the protocol, it is enough to require that the server, from the interaction, does not distinguish between cases in which the client has different input sets.

Definition 4. *Let $Views_S(C, \mathcal{S})$ be a random variable representing S's view during the execution of Interaction with inputs C and $\mathcal{S}$. A TS-SHI-PSI guarantees client privacy if, for every S^* that plays the role of S, for every set $\mathcal{S}$, and for any two possible client input sets C_0, C_1 it holds that:*

$$Views_{S^*}(C_0, \mathcal{S}) \equiv Views_{S^*}(C_1, \mathcal{S}).$$

Notice that in the above definition, when considering the unconditional setting, the parties S, C and S^* are unbounded and indistinguishable means that the two views are *perfectly indistinguishable*, i.e., they are identically distributed. On the other hand, in the computational setting, S, C and S^* are PPT machines and, hence, indistinguishable means that the two views are *computationally indistinguishable*.

Server privacy needs a bit more: the client gets the output of the protocol, and by using his input and the output, by analysing the transcript of the execution, could get extra-knowledge about the server's secrets. Neverthless, if the transcript can be simulated by using only input and output, then server privacy is achieved.

Definition 5. *Let $View_C(C, \mathcal{S})$ be a random variable representing C's view during the execution of Interaction with inputs C and $\mathcal{S}$. Then, the TS-SHI-PSI scheme guarantees server privacy if there exists an algorithm C^* such that*

$$\{C^*(C, \mathcal{S} \cap C)\}_{(C, \mathcal{S})} \equiv \{View_C(C, \mathcal{S})\}_{(C, \mathcal{S})}.$$

As before, in the unconditional setting the parties are unbounded and the transcript produced by C^* and the real view need to be identically distributed. On the other hand, in the computationally secure setting, the parties are PPT machines and the transcript produced by C^* and the real view are required to be computationally indistinguishable.

We will also consider a model where a trusted third party (TTP, for short) interacts with client and server during a setup phase and disappears. The TTP might provide secret information to the parties, as well as it may act as a certification authority for the sets of secrets held by the parties. The model we consider is essentially the model considered by Rivest [23]. Let us remark that the use of a TTP is limited to a setup phase which can actually take place well in advance of the actual protocol execution; in many real-life scenarios such an authority is probably essential to prevent clients from using fabricated inputs to learn information on the set held by the server. We introduce the presence of the TTP by modifying Definition 2 as follows:

Definition 6. *A* TS-SHI-PSI-TTP *is a scheme involving a TTP and two parties, C and S, with four components, Setup, SetupC, SetupS, and Interaction, where*

- *Setup is an algorithm that selects all global parameters*
- *SetupC is a protocol between TTP and C on input TTP secret data and $C = \{c_1, \ldots, c_v\}$*
- *SetupS is a protocol between TTP and S on input TTP secret data and $S = \{s_1, \ldots, s_w\}$*
- *Interaction is a protocol between S and C on respective input sets $S = \{s_1, \ldots, s_w\}$ and $C = \{c_1, \ldots, c_v\}$. The outputs that S and C get from SetupS and SetupC respectively are also used as inputs for this protocol.*

satisfying correctness, client privacy and server privacy.

Roughly speaking, TS-SHI-PSI-TTP is a TS-SHI-PSI where, during the setup phase, client and server, one after the other, interact with the TTP and get some private information which could be used later on when they interact between each other. We remark that in this paper we will always consider HBC parties, even though the above Definitions 4 and 5 are written without that restriction.

2.2 Tools

Homomorphic Encryption. An encryption scheme is *additively homomorphic* if, for any two encryptions $E(m_1)$ and $E(m_2)$ of any two messages m_1 and m_2, it holds that $E(m_1) \cdot E(m_2) = E(m_1 + m_2)$, where $\cdot$ is the group operation on ciphertexts. By repeated application of the property, for any integer c, it follows that $E(m_1)^c = E(cm_1)$. Paillier's cryptosystem [21] is a semantically secure public-key cryptosystem which exhibits such properties. It is easy to check that the following claim, already used in previous works, holds: given encryptions $E(a_0), \ldots, E(a_k)$ of the coefficients $a_0, \ldots, a_k$ of a polynomial P of degree k, and knowledge of a plaintext value y, it is possible to compute $E(P(y))$, i.e., an encryption of $P(y)$.

Oblivious Transfer. An oblivious transfer protocol is a two-party protocol. A sender has two secrets, s_0 and s_1, while a receiver is interested in one of them. Her choice is represented by a bit σ. After running the protocol the receiver gets s_σ and nothing else, while the sender does not learn which secret the receiver has recovered. Introduced by Rabin [22], and later on redefined in different equivalent ways, it is a key-tool in secure two-party and multy-party computation. We will denote this primitive as $OT(s_0, s_1, \sigma)$.

3 Two-Side Size-Hiding: The Unconditional Case

We now focus on the unconditionally secure setting and we show, first, that it is impossible to provide an unconditionally secure set intersection protocol where both parties hide the sizes of their sets of secrets. Further, we prove the existence of such a protocol if a set up phase involving a trusted third party is performed.

3.1   Impossibility in the Plain Model

The impossibility result for the unconditional secure setting follows by putting together some known results. Note that an unconditionally secure set intersection protocol where both parties hide the sizes of their sets of secrets exists *only if* an unconditionally secure set intersection protocol (without the privacy-preserving requirement on the sizes of the sets) exists. Then, by ruling out the possibility of the latter, we rule out the possibility of the former. To this aim, notice that, in [14], the authors described a *reduction from* OT *to* PSI (therein referred to as PM). Then, due to the results of Impagliazzo and Rudich [18], they concluded that there is no black-box reduction of set intersection from one-way functions. On the other hand, it is also very well known (see [4], page 22, for a clear description) that *unconditionally secure oblivious transfer is impossible*. Hence, due to the former reduction, it follows that unconditionally secure TS-SHI-PSI is impossible, and we get our claim. Details can be found in the full version. In conclusion, we show that:

Theorem 1. *Unconditionally secure TS-SHI-PSI schemes do not exist.*

	Common input: $\mathcal{U}$	
C	TTP	S
On input: $\mathcal{C}$	On input: $f, g : \mathcal{P}(\mathcal{U}) \longrightarrow \{0,1\}^{|\mathcal{U}|}$	On input: $\mathcal{S}$

$$\xrightarrow{\ \mathcal{C}\ }$$
$$\xleftarrow{\ R,\mathcal{L}\ } \quad R = f(\mathcal{C})$$
$$\mathcal{L} = \{(g(D), D) \ : \ D \subseteq \mathcal{C}\}$$
$$\mathcal{T} = \{(f(E), g(E \cap \mathcal{S})) \ : \ E \subseteq \mathcal{U}\} \xleftarrow{\ \mathcal{S}\ }$$
$$\xrightarrow{\ \mathcal{T}\ }$$

$$\xrightarrow{\ R\ }$$
$$\xleftarrow{\ R'\ } \qquad \text{Search } (R, R') \in \mathcal{T}$$

Search $(R', D) \in \mathcal{L}$
Output D

Fig. 1. Unconditionally secure protocol in the model with a TTP and unbounded parties

3.2   Feasibility in the Model with a Setup by a TTP

The presence of a TTP, which sets up the system and disappears, makes unconditionally secure size-hiding set intersection possible. Parties are unbounded. We prove the following result:

Theorem 2. *Unconditionally secure TS-SHI-PSI-TTP schemes do exist.*

Essentially, the idea of the protocol which proves our claim is the following. The TTP chooses two random bijections $f, g : \mathcal{P}(\mathcal{U}) \longrightarrow \{0,1\}^{|\mathcal{U}|}$. It interacts with the client and, once received the client's set of secrets, the TTP sends her an *identifier*, computed by using the first random function, and a list of *sub-identifiers*, one for each possible subset of the client' set of secrets, computed through the second random function. On the other hand, when the TTP interacts with the server and receives her set of secrets, it constructs a two-column table: in the first column there is, for each possible subset E of the ground set, an identifier of E, computed with the first random function; the second column has an identifier, computed with the second random function, of the *intersection* $E \cap S$ of the subset E and the server's set of secrets S. The table is given to the server. The protocol between client and server is a simple two-round protocol: the client sends her set identifier; the server looks up in the table the row with the received identifier, and sends her back the identifier of the second column. Finally, the client looks up in the list of sub-identifiers and determines the intersection with the server. Details are given in Fig. 1

It is easy to check that the protocol is correct. Similarly, it is also easy to check that the server privacy is unconditionally guaranteed: from the interaction the client only gets an identifier which determines a subset of her set of secrets. On the other hand, the client privacy needs a more accurate analysis. First of all, notice that the server does not get any information about the correspondence value-subset, since the construction of the table is completely blind to her. Moreover, notice that, *independently of the client set of secrets*, the table the server gets has in the second column exactly $2^{|S|}$ different random values, that is, the number of all possible subsets of S. Each of these values appears exactly the same number of times, namely $2^{|\mathcal{U}|-|S|}$. This follows from the fact that, for every $F \subseteq S$,

$$\#\{E \subseteq \mathcal{U} : S \cap E = F\} = \#\{F \cup E' : E' \subseteq \mathcal{U} \setminus S\} = 2^{|\mathcal{U}|-|S|}$$

Hence, a request from a client only allows the server to learn the two values $(f(\mathcal{C}), g(\mathcal{C} \cap S))$ which do not leak any information about the client' set of secrets nor its size.

4   Two-Side Size-Hiding: The Computationally Secure Case

In this section we show that in the computational case, without a TTP, two-side size-hiding private set intersection is possible. The first construction is an existential argument and has an interesting implication. The second one can be useful in practice if the sizes of the sets of secrets are reasonable small and an upper bound is known a-priori.

4.1   An AND-Based TS-SHI-PSI Protocol

A private $AND(a, b)$ protocol is a two-party protocol, run by A and B, at the end of which the players get the logical AND of their bits and nothing else (i.e., a private protocol for computing $a \cdot b$). It can be realized by using an $OT(b_0, b_1, s)$ protocol. Indeed it is enough to invoke the instance $OT(0, a, b)$, since the bit b_s that the receiver gets in an $OT(b_0, b_1, s)$ can be expressed as $b_s = (1 \oplus s)b_0 \oplus sb_1$. The key-idea underlying the protocol is that, if the set of secrets of C and S are represented by means of two *characteristic vectors* I_C and I_S of elements of $\mathcal{U}$ then, by running an $AND(I_{c_i}, I_{s_i})$ protocol for each bit of the vectors, C and S get the intersection and nothing else. Indeed, each $AND(I_{c_i}, I_{s_i}) = 1$ means that they share the i-th element of the ground set $\mathcal{U}$. Details are in Fig. 2.

Let n be a security parameter and let $\mathcal{U} = \{u_1, \ldots, u_{|\mathcal{U}|}\}$ be a ground set of size $poly(n)$. Assume that C (resp. S) can be encoded in a characteristic vector I_C (resp. I_S), such that $I_C[j] = 1$ (resp. $I_S[j] = 1$) iff the $j - th$ element of $\mathcal{U}$ is in C (resp. S).

Common input: $\mathcal{U} = \{u_1, \ldots, u_{|\mathcal{U}|}\}$

C
On input: $C = \{c_1, \ldots, c_v\}$

S
On input: $S = \{s_1, \ldots, s_w\}$

Encode C in $I_C = [I_{c_1}, \ldots, I_{c_{|\mathcal{U}|}}]$

Encode S in $I_S = [I_{s_1}, \ldots, I_{s_{|\mathcal{U}|}}]$

Run $|\mathcal{U}|$ parallel instances
$C \equiv Receiver - S \equiv Sender$
$AND(I_{c_1}, I_{s_1}), \ldots, AND(I_{c_{|\mathcal{U}|}}, I_{s_{|\mathcal{U}|}})$

For $1 \le j \le |\mathcal{U}|$
     If $AND(I_j, I_j) = 1$
         Output u_j

Fig. 2. A computationally secure size-hiding set intersection protocol

It is easy to check that the protocol is correct. Moreover, it is secure as long as the AND protocol is secure. If we realize the AND protocol by using the OT construction proposed in [11] based on the existence of trapdoor permutations, since the executions are run by using independent randomness, we could use, for each execution, the simulators for the OT protocol. Thus, it is possible to show that the server cannot distinguish which set of secrets the client is using, and that there exists a simulator which, by using input and output of the client, provides transcripts which are indistinguishable from the real ones. Therefore, Definitions 4 and 5 are satisfied. More precisely, we prove the following result (details[1] and the proof can be found in the full version):

Theorem 3. *The protocol given in Fig. 2, when instantiated with the OT protocol of [11], realizes a computationally secure TS-SHI-PSI scheme.*

Remark. Notice that, since OT reduces to PSI but, as the protocol of Fig. 2 shows, *also* PSI reduces to OT, it follows that OT and PSI are *equivalent*. Note that the fact PSI reduces to OT can also be argued from the general statement that two-party computation can be reduced to OT (e.g., see [17]).

---

[1] Due to lack of space we provide a simplified (and somehow approximated) description. See [15] for a rigorous treatment of the protocol and the security analysis in the honest but curious model.

4.2   Threshold-Based Protocol

Assuming some a-priori information on the sizes of both sets $\mathcal{C}$ and $\mathcal{S}$ is known, more efficient protocols may be achieved. Here we assume that a known value M upper bounds the sizes of both client and server's sets. Indeed, the smaller M is with respect to $|\mathcal{U}|$, the greater the interest of this construction (actually, we need M of polynomial size but $|\mathcal{U}|$ may as well be exponential).

In a Setup phase, C generates public parameters ($params$) and a key pair (sk, pk) for Paillier encryption. Let Enc and Dec be the encryption and decryption algorithms, respectively. C makes sure that the message space $\mathbb{Z}_n$, is exponentially larger than $|\mathcal{U}|$. Further, she fixes an encoding of $\mathcal{U}$ into $\mathbb{Z}_n \setminus \{0\}$, denoted by $Encoding$. For the sake of readability, in Fig. 3, elements of C and S are assumed to belong to $\mathbb{Z}_n \setminus \{0\}$. We will denote by π a random permutation of M elements.

Common input: $\mathcal{U} = \{u_1, \ldots, u_{|\mathcal{U}|}\}$,
$params, pk, Encoding$

C
On input: $sk, \mathcal{C} = \{c_1, \ldots, c_v\}$

S
On input: $\mathcal{S} = \{s_1, \ldots, s_w\}$

Compute

$P(x) = x^{M-v} \sum_{j=1}^{v} (x - c_j)$

$P(x) = \sum_{j=0}^{M} a_j x^j$

$\xrightarrow{\{\mathsf{Enc}(a_i)\}_{i=0}^{M}}$

For $1 \leq i \leq w$
$\quad r_i \leftarrow_\$ \mathbb{Z}_{n^2}$
$\quad e_i = \mathsf{Enc}(r_i \cdot P(s_i) + s_i)$
For $w + 1 \leq i \leq M$
$\quad e_i \leftarrow_\$ \mathbb{Z}_{n^2}$

$\xleftarrow{\pi(e_1, \ldots, e_M)}$

For $1 \leq j \leq v$
$\quad$ If $(\exists\, j\ : \mathsf{Dec}(e_i) = c_j \wedge c_j \in \mathcal{C})$
$\quad\quad$ Output c_j

Fig. 3. Polynomial-based construction for $|\mathcal{C}|, |\mathcal{S}| \leq M$

Our protocol is depicted in Fig. 3, and it is actually a twist on the polynomial construction from [14], which main tool is a semantically secure (additively) homomorphic encryption scheme. As the authors of [14], we suggest to use Paillier encryption to this aim; further refinements of the protocol may of course be advisable if another encryption scheme is chosen. In the sequel, we set the notation $I := |\mathcal{C} \cap \mathcal{S}|$ and $L := w - I$.

Correctness. It is easy to see that the proposed protocol is correct, as the client's output is constructed by comparing her set $\mathcal{C}$ with the one consisting of $\mathcal{S} \cap \mathcal{C}$ plus the decryption of $M - I$ uniform random values from $\mathbb{Z}_{n^2}$. Namely, this sequence will consist of random values from $\mathbb{Z}_n$ which is exponentially larger than $\mathcal{U}$. As a result, the probability that they actually encode an element in $\mathcal{U}$ (disrupting thus the computation of the intersection) is negligible.[2]

Client Privacy. Due to the semantic security of Enc the distribution of $\{\mathsf{Enc}(a_0), \ldots, \mathsf{Enc}(a_M)\}$ is indistinguishable of that induced by selecting $M + 1$ elements independently and uniformly at random from $\mathbb{Z}_{n^2}$.

Server Privacy. In order to argue the existence of a pptm algorithm C^* which is able to simulate the clients view on input $\mathcal{C}$ and $\mathcal{C} \cap \mathcal{S}$, we modify C's view replacing the true input values from the server, constructed as encryptions involving values $s \in \mathcal{S} \setminus \mathcal{C}$ with encryptions of elements chosen uniformly and independently at random from $\mathbb{Z}_n \setminus \{0\}$. Consider thus the true distribution $\mathcal{D}_0 := \{\rho_0, \ldots, \rho_M, \mathsf{Enc}(r_{s_1} P(s_1) + s_1), \ldots, \mathsf{Enc}(r_{s_w} P(s_w) + s_w), \xi_1, \ldots, \xi_{M-w}\}$ where for $i = 0 \ldots M$ each ρ_i denotes the random value involved in the Paillier encryption yielding $\mathsf{Enc}(a_i)$, namely, they are values chosen uniformly and independently at random from $\mathbb{Z}_n^*$, and $\{\mathsf{Enc}(r_{s_1} P(s_1) + s_1), \ldots, \mathsf{Enc}(r_{s_w} P(s_w) + s_w), \xi_1, \ldots, \xi_{M-w}\}$ are constructed as in Fig. 3 (w.l.o.g., we assume this sequence is not randomly permuted before output, and, moreover, that $\mathcal{S} \cap \mathcal{C} = \{s_1, \ldots, s_I\}$).
Further, consider the distribution $\mathcal{D}_L = \{\rho_0, \ldots, \rho_M, \mathsf{Enc}(r_{s_1} P(s_1) + s_1), \ldots, \mathsf{Enc}(r_{s_I} P(s_I) + s_I), \nu_1, \ldots, \nu_L, \xi_1, \ldots, \xi_{M-w}\}$ where $\nu_1, \ldots, \nu_L$ are elements chosen independently and uniformly at random from $\mathbb{Z}_{n^2}$.

Again from the semantic security of Enc it follows that this two distributions are computationally indistinguishable.

Efficiency. Having Paillier encryption in mind, we have designed the polynomial P in Step 2. of Round 1 (see Fig. 3), maximizing the number of its coefficients which are equal to zero (as encryptions of 0 with Paillier are cheap). That is the reason for excluding 0 from the domain when defining the encoding of $\mathcal{U}$ into $\mathbb{Z}_n$. Different refinements of this step may suit better if another encryption scheme is used, always ensuring that the resulting polynomial has no roots that may correspond to an encoding of an element outside $\mathcal{C}$ and yet in $\mathcal{U}$.

5   One-Side Size-Hiding Set Intersection Protocols

In this section, we follow the spirit of [1] and try to provide *one-side* private set intersection protocols, i.e., protocols in which the client actually learns $|\mathcal{S}|$ from the interaction, while keeping $|\mathcal{C}|$ secret. We will thus, in the sequel, follow the definitions of correctness, client privacy and server privacy from [1].[3]

---

[2] We leverage the fact that Paillier encryption actually defines a trapdoor permutation from $\mathbb{Z}_n \times \mathbb{Z}_n^*$ into $\mathbb{Z}_{n^2}$. There is actually a negligible "loss" here, as we exclude 0 as a legitimate ciphertext.

[3] Correctness is defined including $|\mathcal{S}|$ as part of the client's output, the definition of client privacy coincides with the one we have given here for two-sided protocols, while server's privacy ensures the client's view is polynomial-time simulatable on input $\mathcal{C}, \mathcal{S} \cap \mathcal{C}$ and $|\mathcal{S}|$ (the latter definition does not coincide with the one from [1], but $|\mathcal{S}|$ is needed in the simulation included in their proof).

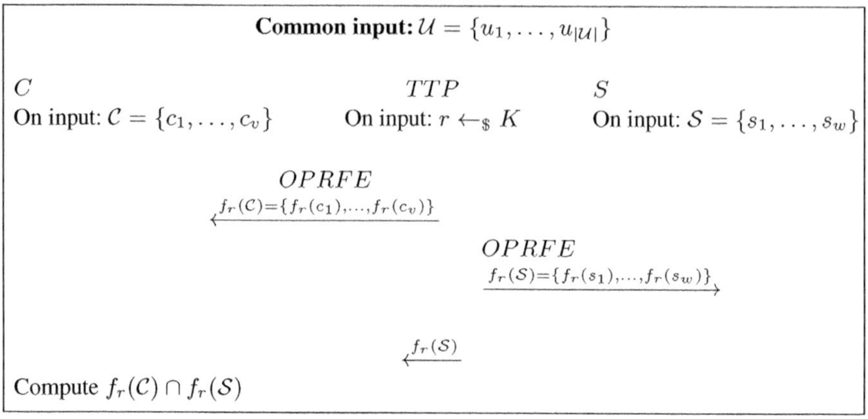

Common input: $\mathcal{U} = \{u_1, \ldots, u_{|\mathcal{U}|}\}$

C	TTP	S
On input: $\mathcal{C} = \{c_1, \ldots, c_v\}$	On input: $r \leftarrow_\$ K$	On input: $\mathcal{S} = \{s_1, \ldots, s_w\}$

$OPRFE$
$$\overleftarrow{\quad f_r(\mathcal{C})=\{f_r(c_1),\ldots,f_r(c_v)\} \quad}$$

$OPRFE$
$$\overrightarrow{\quad f_r(\mathcal{S})=\{f_r(s_1),\ldots,f_r(s_w)\} \quad}$$

$$\overleftarrow{\quad f_r(\mathcal{S}) \quad}$$

Compute $f_r(\mathcal{C}) \cap f_r(\mathcal{S})$

Fig. 4. One-Side protocol based on OPRFE

5.1 Pseudorandom Function Evaluation Based Protocols

This protocol requires a setup phase where a TTP obliviously evaluates a function (secretly chosen from a pseudorandom family) on the participants' inputs. This protocol follows the ideas in [16] but with the function evaluation delegated to the TTP, and is described in Fig. 4. Here we will make use of a pseudorandom function family $\{f_r\}_{r \in K}$ (with key set K) which can be evaluated in an oblivious way, that is, the TTP (holding the key r) learns nothing and a participant with input x learns $f_r(x)$.

Correctness. As f_r is a pseudorandom function, there is only negligible probability that two different values from $\mathcal{U}$ are mapped to the same image, which is the only case in which C's computation of the intersection would not output $\mathcal{S} \cap \mathcal{C}$.

Client Privacy. Straightforward: the client sends nothing to the server.

Server Privacy. This follows from the the pseudorandomness property of the function family $\{f_r\}_{r \in K}$. At this, a pptm algorithm C^* can simulate the client's view on input $\mathcal{C}, \mathcal{C} \cap \mathcal{S}$, and $|\mathcal{S}|$, by constructing a sequence $\{R_1^*, \ldots, R_w^*\}$ so that, for each $u_i \in \mathcal{C} \cap \mathcal{S}$, a corresponding R_i^* is defined as $f_r(u_i)$, while the rest are values chosen independently and uniformly at random in G.

Indeed, doing without the oblivious evaluation part, the protocol from Fig. 4 can be made substantially more efficient; as a trade off, more trust on the TTP is required, as the sets $\mathcal{C}$ and $\mathcal{S}$ are completely revealed to her. It is worth mentioning that this modification is not possible in the protocols from [16] because client's privacy would be immediately lost.

In order to implement these two protocols, the efficient proposal of a pseudorandom function family from [20] can be used. Therefore, we will additionally need an encoding of the ground set $\mathcal{U}$ into the set $\{0,1\}^n$ for big enough n. Furthermore, the protocol proposed in [13] can be used to evaluate f_r in an oblivious way, suitable for protocol in Fig. 4.

5.2 RSA-Based Protocol

Figure 5 shows an RSA based protocol along the lines of [1], but proven secure in the standard model. Once again, our construction makes use of a TTP which can go offline after the Setup phase. Loosely speaking, the TTP certifies to S and C their input elements by means of values in a set V, computed in a two-step process. Such a process associates unpredictable *intermediate* values, exactly RSA signatures, to the input elements and, then, it uses a strongly universal hash function to get *final* values, which are unrelated among each other and close to uniformly distributed over V. For details on strongly universal hash functions we refer to [3,24].

More precisely, in the Setup phase of the protocol, TTP executes an RSA key generation algorithm and keeps (N, e, d) private. We assume that elements of the ground set $\mathcal{U}$ are encoded as elements of $\mathbb{Z}_N^* \setminus \{1\}$. Further, TTP fixes a group $\mathbb{G}$ of prime order p (for p the smallest prime larger than N) and g a generator of $\mathbb{G}$. Finally, it selects and keeps private a strongly universal hash function $H : \mathbb{Z}_N^* \mapsto \mathbb{Z}_p$ from a given family, by selecting uniformly at random $a, b \in Z_p$ and setting $H_{a,b}(x) := ax + b \mod p$.

In the last round of the protocol, π denotes a permutation of w elements chosen u.a.r. by the server. An analogous choice is made in the schemes in subsections 5.3 and 5.4.

Before moving to the proof, let us recall the following:

Definition 7. *A family* $\mathcal{H} = \{h_s : \{0,1\}^\ell \to \{0,1\}^m\}$ *of hash functions is called* ϵ-*almost strongly universal if and only if:*

1. $\forall a \in \{0,1\}^\ell, \forall b \in \{0,1\}^m$, *it holds that* $Pr_{s \in S}[h_s(a) = b] = 2^{-m}$
2. $\forall a_1 \neq a_2 \in \{0,1\}^\ell, \forall b_1, b_2 \in \{0,1\}^m$, *it holds that* $Pr_{s \in S}[h_s(a_2) = b_2 | h_s(a_1) = b_1] \leq \epsilon$.

Notice that, the first condition states that any input a is mapped to any hashed value b with probability $\frac{1}{2^m}$. A 2^{-m}-almost strongly universal hash function family $\mathcal{H}$ is called a strongly universal hash function family.

The function $H_{a,b}$ is used for two reasons: first, RSA signatures are malleable, e.g., from c_1^d and c_2^d it is immediate to compute the signature $(c_1 c_2)^d$ for the product $c_1 c_2$. Moreover, we do not have any idea about the distribution of the secrets $c_1, \ldots, c_v$ and $s_1, \ldots, s_w$. Since RSA is a permutation, then it preserves the input distribution. By postprocessing the signatures we get randomized values through the hash function which are unrelated and more or less uniformly distributed.

Correctness. Comes from the fact that, as H is a bijection, two different elements of the universe will never end up getting the same encoding from the TTP; as a result, the check up from the Client at the last step of the protocol will exactly result in the intersection.

Client Privacy. As X is the only public output of C, it suffices to argue that it is indistinguishable from a random group element from G. That is so, as G is cyclic of primer order and thus g^{PCH} generates G.

Server Privacy (Sketch). We again make use of the hybrid argument from [1], and gradually modify the client's view replacing values "outside" of $\mathcal{S} \cap \mathcal{C}$ with elements chosen

Common input: $\mathcal{U} = \{u_1, \ldots, u_{|\mathcal{U}|}\}, G, g, p$

C	TTP	S
On input: $\mathcal{C} = \{c_1, \ldots, c_v\}$	On input: $r \leftarrow_\$ K$	On input: $\mathcal{S} = \{s_1, \ldots, s_w\}$

$$\xrightarrow{\quad \mathcal{C} = \{c_1, \ldots, c_v\} \quad}$$
$$\xleftarrow{\quad \hat{c}_1, \ldots, \hat{c}_v \quad} \qquad \xleftarrow{\quad \mathcal{S} = \{s_1, \ldots, s_w\} \quad}$$
$$\hat{c}_i = H_{a,b}(c_i^d) \qquad\qquad \xrightarrow{\quad \hat{s}_1, \ldots, \hat{s}_w \quad}$$
$$\hat{s}_i = H_{a,b}(s_i^d)$$

$R_C \leftarrow_\$ \mathbb{Z}_p$

$PCH = \prod_{i=1}^{v} \hat{c}_i$

$$\xrightarrow{\quad X = g^{R_C \cdot PCH} \quad} \qquad\qquad R_S \leftarrow_\$ \mathbb{Z}_p$$
$$\text{For } 1 \le i \le w$$
$$\xleftarrow{\quad g^{R_S}, \pi(Y_1, \ldots, Y_w) \quad} \qquad Y_i = (X^{R_S})^{\frac{1}{\hat{s}_i}}$$

For $1 \le i \le v$
  $PCH_i = \prod_{j=1, j \ne i}^{v} \hat{c}_j$
  $Z_i = (g^{R_S})^{R_C \cdot PCH_i}$
  If $Z_i \in \{Y_1, \ldots, Y_w\}$
    Output c_i

Fig. 5. RSA based protocol

uniformly and independently at random from G. Let $\mathcal{I} = \mathcal{S} \cap \mathcal{C}$ and $|\mathcal{I}| = t$ and consider distributions $D_1 = \{R_C, g^{R_S}, Y_1, \ldots, Y_w\}$ and $D_{w-t} = \{R_C, g^{R_S}, Y_1, \ldots, Y_t, R_1, \ldots, R_{w-t}\}$.

We assume w.l.o.g. that the elements from the intersection i.e., $Y_1, \ldots, Y_t$, come at the beginning in D_{w-t}, and they are constructed from the simulator exactly as in the real protocol; while $R_1, \ldots, R_{w-t}$ are generated as follows: the simulator chooses $r_1, \ldots, r_{w-t}$ uniformly at random from $\mathbb{Z}_p$ and, for $i = 1, \ldots, w - t$, sets the value $R_i = ((g^{R_S})^{R_C PCH})^{\frac{1}{r_i}}$.

The difference between two distributions $\mathcal{D}_i$ and $\mathcal{D}_{i+1}$, for $i = 1, \ldots, w - t - 1$, is the replacement of the i-th element; hence, a distinguisher between them should be able to distinguish an element of the form $(X^{R_S})^{\frac{1}{\hat{s}_j}} = ((g^{R_C PCH})^{R_S})^{\frac{1}{\hat{s}_j}}$ from the element $R_j = ((g^{R_S})^{R_C PCH})^{\frac{1}{r_j}}$, constructed by the simulator. However, due to the first property of a strongly universal hash function, the value $\hat{s}_j$ is associated to the input value s_j with probability $1/p$. Similarly, r_j is chosen uniformly at random, i.e., with probability $1/p$. Therefore, both $(X^{R_S})^{\frac{1}{\hat{s}_j}}$ and R_j are *uniformly distributed* over G. Hence, no PPT distinguisher can distinguish between them.

5.3 Three-Round ROM Based Protocol

This protocol is inspired by [5]. The TTP choses a full-domain hash function (see [2]) $H(\cdot)$, sets up a group $\mathbb{G}$ of prime order q and randomly picks $\gamma \in \mathbb{Z}_q$ as her secret key. Elements of the ground set are encoded as integers in $\mathbb{Z}_q$. Element $x \in \mathbb{Z}_q$ is certified

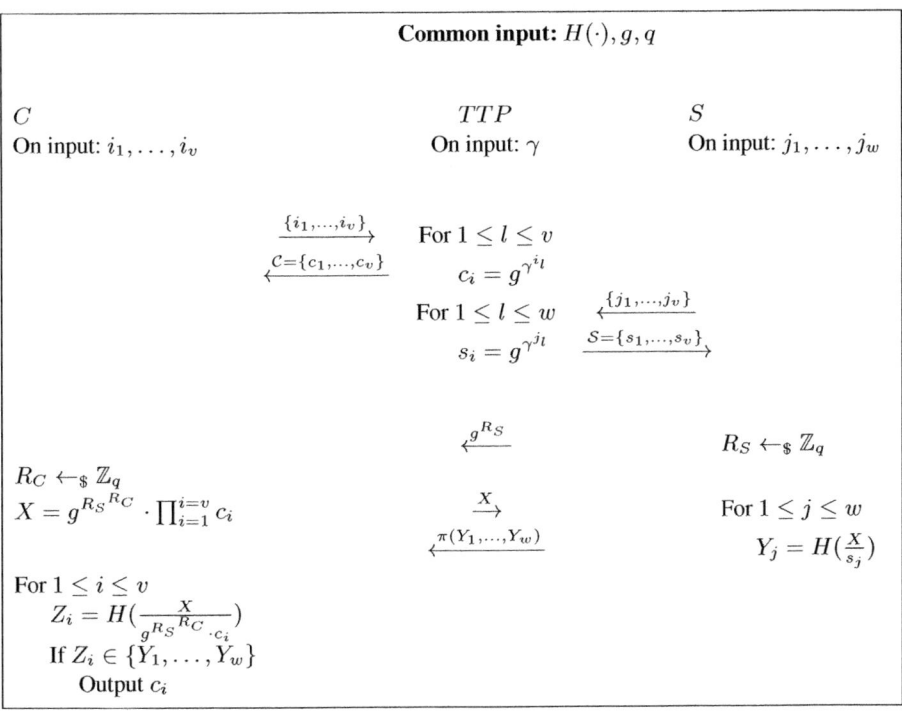

Fig. 6. Three-round Multiplicative protocol

as g^{γ^x}. Let $i_1, \ldots, i_v$ and $j_1, \ldots, j_w$ be the set of (non-certified) elements held by C and S, respectively. The protocol is depicted in Fig. 6. Both C and S get their elements certified by the TTP; S also uses a random permutation π. Later they interact so that C outputs $C \cap S$ and $|S|$.

Client Privacy. During the protocol execution, C sends X to the server. Since R_C is chosen uniformly at random from $\mathbb{Z}_q$, and since G is a cyclic group of prime order q, then X is uniformly distributed element over G.

Server Privacy (Sketch). We use the same argument used before, that is, the simulator reproduces the client view from his input and the output of the protocol, by replacing values "outside" of $S \cap C$ with elements *chosen uniformly and independently at random*. Let $\mathcal{I} = S \cap C$ and $|\mathcal{I}| = t$ and consider the distributions $D_I = \{(R_C, T) : R_C \leftarrow_\$ \mathbb{Z}_q, T = (H(\frac{X}{s_1}), \ldots, H(\frac{X}{s_w}))\}$ and $D_{w-t} = \{(R_C, T) : R_C \leftarrow_\$ \mathbb{Z}_q, T = (H(\frac{X}{s_1}), \ldots, H(\frac{X}{s_t}), r_{t+1}, \ldots, r_w)\}$, where $s_1, \ldots, s_w \in \mathcal{I}$ and $r_{t+1}, \ldots, r_w$ are values chosen uniformly at random. Since $H(\cdot)$ is a random oracle, there exists no distinguisher which is able to take apart D_I from D_{w-t}.

5.4   One-Round ROM Based Protocol

Fig. 7 shows a very efficient protocol that allows for OS-SHI-PSI in the ROM. The TTP uses an RSA signature scheme $Sign(\cdot)$ to certify elements; the secret signing key is sk.

Client Privacy. During the protocol C does not provide any input so its privacy is trivially preserved.

Server Privacy (Sketch). Since hash functions are modeled as a random oracle, the simulator reproduces the client view from his input and the output of the protocol, by replacing values "outside" of $S \cap C$ with elements *chosen uniformly and independently at random*. As before, we argue no distinguisher D can tell apart a real transcript from a simulated one.

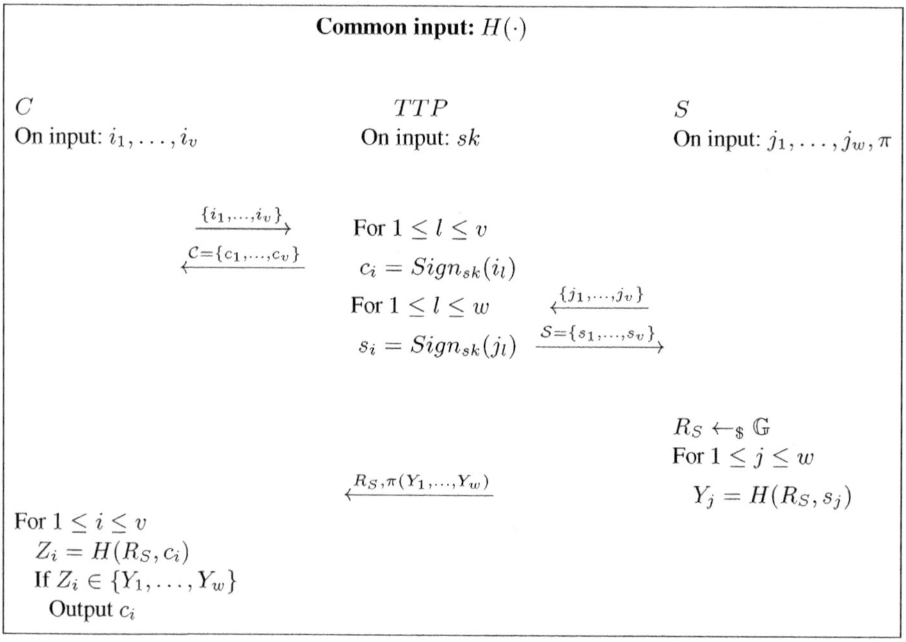

Common input: $H(\cdot)$

C TTP S

On input: $i_1, \ldots, i_v$ On input: sk On input: $j_1, \ldots, j_w, \pi$

$\xrightarrow{\{i_1,\ldots,i_v\}}$ For $1 \le l \le v$

$\xleftarrow{C=\{c_1,\ldots,c_v\}}$ $c_i = Sign_{sk}(i_l)$

For $1 \le l \le w$ $\xleftarrow{\{j_1,\ldots,j_v\}}$

$s_i = Sign_{sk}(j_l)$ $\xrightarrow{S=\{s_1,\ldots,s_v\}}$

$R_S \leftarrow_{\$} \mathbb{G}$

For $1 \le j \le w$

$\xleftarrow{R_S, \pi(Y_1,\ldots,Y_w)}$ $Y_j = H(R_S, s_j)$

For $1 \le i \le v$

    $Z_i = H(R_S, c_i)$

    If $Z_i \in \{Y_1, \ldots, Y_w\}$

       Output c_i

Fig. 7. One-round ROM based protocol

6   Open Problems

Several interesting open problems are left: concerning two-side size-hiding private set intersection, it would be nice to get an *efficient* unconditionally secure protocol in the model with a TTP and a computationally secure protocol which does not consider the whole ground set (or an impossibility result in that respect). Moreover, it is of interest to study the same problem in the malicious setting and to consider the extension of the problem to n parties.

Acknowledgements. The first three authors were partially supported by the Spanish "Ministerio de Economía y Competitividad" through the project grant MTM-2012-15167.

References

1. Ateniese, G., De Cristofaro, E., Tsudik, G.: (If) Size Matters: Size-Hiding Private Set Intersection. In: Catalano, D., Fazio, N., Gennaro, R., Nicolosi, A. (eds.) PKC 2011. LNCS, vol. 6571, pp. 156–173. Springer, Heidelberg (2011)
2. Bellare, M., Rogaway, P.: The Exact Security of Digital Signatures - How to Sign with RSA and Rabin. In: Maurer, U.M. (ed.) EUROCRYPT 1996. LNCS, vol. 1070, pp. 399–416. Springer, Heidelberg (1996)
3. Carter, J.L., Wegman, M.N.: Universal classes of hash functions. Journal of Computer and System Sciences 18, 143–154 (1979)
4. Cramer, R.: Introduction to Secure Computation. In: Damgård, I.B. (ed.) Lectures on Data Security. LNCS, vol. 1561, pp. 16–62. Springer, Heidelberg (1999)
5. Camenisch, J., Kohlweiss, M., Soriente, C.: An Accumulator Based on Bilinear Maps and Efficient Revocation for Anonymous Credentials. In: Jarecki, S., Tsudik, G. (eds.) PKC 2009. LNCS, vol. 5443, pp. 481–500. Springer, Heidelberg (2009)
6. Camenisch, J., Lysyanskaya, A.: A Signature Scheme with Efficient Protocols. In: Cimato, S., Galdi, C., Persiano, G. (eds.) SCN 2002. LNCS, vol. 2576, pp. 268–289. Springer, Heidelberg (2003)
7. Camenisch, J., Zaverucha, G.M.: Private Intersection of Certified Sets. In: Dingledine, R., Golle, P. (eds.) FC 2009. LNCS, vol. 5628, pp. 108–127. Springer, Heidelberg (2009)
8. De Cristofaro, E., Tsudik, G.: Practical Private Set Intersection Protocols with Linear Complexity. In: Sion, R. (ed.) FC 2010. LNCS, vol. 6052, pp. 143–159. Springer, Heidelberg (2010)
9. Dachman-Soled, D., Malkin, T., Raykova, M., Yung, M.: Efficient Robust Private Set Intersection. In: Abdalla, M., Pointcheval, D., Fouque, P.-A., Vergnaud, D. (eds.) ACNS 2009. LNCS, vol. 5536, pp. 125–142. Springer, Heidelberg (2009)
10. Dachman-Soled, D., Malkin, T., Raykova, M., Yung, M.: Secure Efficient Multiparty Computing of Multivariate Polynomials and Applications. In: Lopez, J., Tsudik, G. (eds.) ACNS 2011. LNCS, vol. 6715, pp. 130–146. Springer, Heidelberg (2011)
11. Even, S., Goldreich, O., Lempel, A.: A Randomized Protocol for Signing Contracts. Communications of the ACM 28(6), 637–647 (1985)
12. Frikken, K.: Privacy-Preserving Set Union. In: Katz, J., Yung, M. (eds.) ACNS 2007. LNCS, vol. 4521, pp. 237–252. Springer, Heidelberg (2007)
13. Freedman, M.J., Ishai, Y., Pinkas, B., Reingold, O.: Keyword Search and Oblivious Pseudorandom Functions. In: Kilian, J. (ed.) TCC 2005. LNCS, vol. 3378, pp. 303–324. Springer, Heidelberg (2005)
14. Freedman, M.J., Nissim, K., Pinkas, B.: Efficient Private Matching and Set Intersection. In: Cachin, C., Camenisch, J.L. (eds.) EUROCRYPT 2004. LNCS, vol. 3027, pp. 1–19. Springer, Heidelberg (2004)
15. Goldreich, O.: Foundations of Cryptography - Volume II Basic Applications. Cambridge Press (2004)
16. Hazay, C., Lindell, Y.: Efficient Protocols for Set Intersection and Pattern Matching with Security Against Malicious and Covert Adversaries. In: Canetti, R. (ed.) TCC 2008. LNCS, vol. 4948, pp. 155–175. Springer, Heidelberg (2008)

17. Ishai, Y., Prabhakaran, M., Sahai, A.: Founding Cryptography on Oblivious Transfer – Efficiently. In: Wagner, D. (ed.) CRYPTO 2008. LNCS, vol. 5157, pp. 572–591. Springer, Heidelberg (2008)
18. Impagliazzo, R., Rudich, S.: Limits on the provable consequences of one-way permutations. In: Proc. of the 21st Annual ACM Symposium on Theory of Computing, Seattle, Washington, pp. 44–61 (May 1989)
19. Kissner, L., Song, D.: Privacy-Preserving Set Operations. In: Shoup, V. (ed.) CRYPTO 2005. LNCS, vol. 3621, pp. 241–257. Springer, Heidelberg (2005)
20. Naor, M., Reingold, O.: Number-theoretic constructions of efficient pseudo-random functions. Journal of the ACM 51(2), 231–262 (2004)
21. Paillier, P.: Public-Key Cryptosystems Based on Composite Degree Residuosity Classes. In: Stern, J. (ed.) EUROCRYPT 1999. LNCS, vol. 1592, pp. 223–239. Springer, Heidelberg (1999)
22. Rabin, M.: How to exchange secrets by oblivious transfer, Technical Report TR-81, Aiken Computation Laboratory, Harvard University (1981)
23. Rivest, R.: Unconditionally Secure Commitment and Oblivious Transfer Schemes Using Private Channels and a Trusted Initializer (August 11, 1999) (unpublished manuscript), http://people.csail.mit.edu/rivest/publications.html
24. Stinson, D.R.: Universal hash families and the leftover hash lemma, and applications to cryptography and computing. J. Combin. Math. Combin. Comput. 42, 3–31 (2002)

Round-Optimal Black-Box Statistically Binding Selective-Opening Secure Commitments

David Xiao[*]

LIAFA, CNRS, Université Paris 7
dxiao@liafa.univ-paris-diderot.fr

Abstract. Assuming t-round statistically hiding commitments in the stand-alone model, we build a $(t + 2)$-round statistically binding commitment secure against selective opening attacks under parallel composition. In particular, assuming collision-resistant hash functions, we build such commitments in 4 rounds.

Keywords: Commitments, selective opening attacks.

1 Introduction

Selective opening attacks against commitment schemes occur when the commitment scheme is repeated in parallel and an adversary can choose depending on the commit-phase transcript to see the values and openings to some subset of the committed bits. Commitments are secure under such attacks if one can prove that the remaining, unopened commitments stay secret. Related notions such as chameleon blobs, equivocal commitments, and trapdoor commitments have been widely studied in the literature [BCC88, BCY89, Fis01, Bea96, DCIO98, DCO99]. The notion of selective opening security that we study here was defined by [DNRS03]. One of the primary motivations of studying such commitment schemes is their application to parallel composition of zero knowledge: when used as the commitment scheme in, say, the zero knowledge protocol of [GMW86], that protocol remains zero knowledge under parallel composition (which is not known to be the case when using a commitment scheme without selective opening attack security).

[BHY09, Xia11] studied the optimal round complexity for commitments secure against selective opening attacks. [Xia11] claimed round-optimal constructions under parallel composition, but it was subsequently shown in [ORSV11] that there were flaws in the argument of [Xia11]. In particular, [ORSV11] gave a 3-round construction in the case of computationally binding (and statistically hiding) commitments secure against selective opening attacks. The (corrected) lower bound of [Xia11] states that this is optimal (for black-box simulation).

[ORSV11] leave open the question of round-optimal black-box constructions of *statistically binding commitments* secure against selective opening attacks. The statistically binding commitment of [Xia11] is 5 rounds, but in light of the flaw discovered by [ORSV11], the lower bound is 4 rounds.

[*] Partially supported by the French ANR Defis program under contract ANR-08-EMER-012 (QRAC project).

A. Mitrokotsa and S. Vaudenay (Eds.): AFRICACRYPT 2012, LNCS 7374, pp. 395–411, 2012.

Our contribution: in this paper we construct a $(t+2)$-round scheme that is secure under parallel composition assuming the existence of t-round stand-alone statistical hiding commitments (SHC). In particular, 2-round SHC can be built from collision-resistant hash functions [DPP93, DPP98, HM96], which gives an optimal 4-round construction of statistically binding selective-opening attack secure commitments.

Our analysis introduces a novel simulation strategy that generalizes the Goldreich-Kahan simulation strategy for constant-round zero knowledge [GK90]. At a high level, our strategy differs from the Goldreich-Kahan simulation strategy because it allows the simulator to continue even if the receiver aborts individual sessions, and it guarantees that the simulator's output distribution will be indistinguishable from the distribution in an interaction with the honest sender even when taking into account the aborted sessions. In contrast, the Goldreich-Kahan simulation strategy completely aborts if any individual session is aborted.

2   Preliminaries

We adopt the following standard notation: for a distribution $\mathcal{D}$ and a variable x, $x \leftarrow_{\textrm{R}} \mathcal{D}$ denotes that x is sampled according to D. For distributions $\mathcal{D}_0, \mathcal{D}_1$, we let $\Delta(\mathcal{D}_0, \mathcal{D}_1)$ denote their statistical distance. We say that a function $\varepsilon(n)$ is negligible if $\varepsilon(n) \leq n^{-\omega(1)}$. For a bit b, $\bar{b}$ denotes the complement of b. We frequently use underlined variables to represent vectors, *e.g.* $\underline{b} \in \{0,1\}^k$ and $b_i \in \{0,1\}$ for every $i \in [k]$.

A *commitment protocol* is given by a pair of interactive algorithms Send and Rec. Both algorithms take an input indicating the phase (either *com* or *decom*) and a security parameter 1^n, which we often omit. Send takes a one-bit input and both algorithms may be randomized.

Commit phase: Generate a transcript $\tau \leftarrow_{\textrm{R}} \langle \textsf{Rec}(com), \textsf{Send}(com, b) \rangle$. Send also generates an internal state variable σ.

Decommit phase: Generate $(v, b') \leftarrow_{\textrm{R}} \langle \textsf{Rec}(decom, \tau), \textsf{Send}(decom, b, \sigma) \rangle$, where v is the receiver's view (including the entire transcript and its random coins) and $b' \in \{0, 1, \perp\}$, where $\perp$ denotes that the receiver rejects the sender's opening.

We will often omit the phase variable (*i.e.* either *com, decom*) and the state variable σ when it is convenient and their values are implicitly defined by the context. In this paper the round complexity refers only to the number of rounds in the commit phase, and we work only with commitments with non-interactive openings (*i.e.* the opening consists of a single message from sender to receiver).

We will study commitments under parallel composition, *i.e.* the commitment is executed many times simultaneously and, for each i, the i'th step of the commitment is finished in all sessions before the $i + 1$'th step begins in any session.

Definition 1 (Binding). *Define* $\textsf{Adv}_{bind}$ *to be the supremum over all possible strategies* $\textsf{Send}^*$ *(computationally unbounded) that the probability of the following experiment succeeds:*

1. *Generate* $\tau \leftarrow_R \langle \mathsf{Rec}(com), \mathsf{Send}^*(com) \rangle$ *along with sender state* σ.
2. *Generate* $(v_0, b_0) \leftarrow_R \langle \mathsf{Rec}(decom, \tau), \mathsf{Send}^*(decom, 0, \sigma) \rangle$ *and*
   $(v_1, b_1) \leftarrow_R \langle \mathsf{Rec}(decom, \tau), \mathsf{Send}^*(decom, 1, \sigma) \rangle$.
3. *The experiment is a success if* $b_0 = 0$ *and* $b_1 = 1$.

We say that $(\mathsf{Rec}, \mathsf{Send})$ is statistically binding if Adv_{bind} is negligible. We say it is perfectly binding if $\mathsf{Adv}_{bind} = 0$. We say it is computationally binding if the Adv_{bind} is negligible when the supremum is taken over polynomial-size Send^*.

The binding property is preserved under parallel composition.

Definition 2 (Statistically hiding (stand-alone)). *A commitment* $\mathsf{Send}, \mathsf{Rec}$ *is (stand-alone) statistically hiding (i.e. it is a SHC) if for all (possibly unbounded)* Rec^*, *it holds that* $\Delta(\mathcal{D}_0, \mathcal{D}_1)$ *is negligible, where* $b \in \{0, 1\}$ *and* $\mathcal{D}_b$ *denotes the distribution of* $\tau \leftarrow_R \langle \mathsf{Rec}^*(com), \mathsf{Send}(com, b) \rangle$ *along with the private coins of* Rec^*.

Definition 3 (Hiding under selective opening attacks). *A commitment is secure against selective opening attacks with black-box simulation if for all* $k = \mathrm{poly}(n)$, *there is an efficient simulator* Sim_k *such that the following holds. Define* Adv_{hide} *to be the supremum over all polynomial-size cheating receiver strategies* Rec^*, *all polynomial-size distinguisher circuits* D, *all inputs* $\underline{b}$, *of the difference between the probability that* D *outputs* 1 *in the following two experiments (in the following,* $I \subseteq [k]$ *and* $\underline{b}_I$ *denotes the vector containing* b_i *for* $i \in I$, *and likewise for* $\underline{\tau}_I, \underline{sigma}_I$):

1. *Let* $\underline{\mathsf{Send}}$ *denote* k *parallel instances of the sender algorithm,* $\mathsf{Send}_1, \ldots, \mathsf{Send}_k$.
   (a) *Generate* $\tau_i \leftarrow_R \langle \mathsf{Rec}^*(com), \underline{\mathsf{Send}}(com, b_i) \rangle$ *along with sender state* σ_i *for all* $i \in [k]$.
   (b) Rec^* *outputs a set* $I \subseteq [k]$.
   (c) *Generate* $(v, \underline{b}_I) \leftarrow_R \langle \mathsf{Rec}^*(decom, \underline{\tau}_I), \underline{\mathsf{Send}}(decom, \underline{b}_I, \underline{\sigma}_I) \rangle$.
   (d) *Output* $D(v, \underline{b}_I)$.
2. Sim_k *samples random coins for* Rec^* *and fixes them; in the following* Sim_k *queries* Rec^* *for this fixed choice of coins.*
   (a) *Generate* $I \leftarrow_R \mathsf{Sim}_k^{\mathsf{Rec}^*}(com)$.
   (b) *Generate* $v \leftarrow_R \mathsf{Sim}_k^{\mathsf{Rec}^*}(decom, I, \underline{b}_I)$.
   (c) *Output* $D(v, \underline{b}_I)$.

Security against selective opening attacks holds if Adv_{hide} *is negligible.*

This definition is stronger than necessary for many applications (where security is only needed with respect to certain message distributions and certain families of valid subsets to be opened). However since we only study constructions in this paper, working with this definition is stronger than working with weaker definitions.

3 Construction

Let $\mathsf{Send}_{\mathsf{SH}}, \mathsf{Rec}_{\mathsf{SH}}$ be the sender and receiver algorithms for a t-round statistically hiding bit commitment. A construction for $t = 2$ exists based on collision-resistant hash functions [DPP93, DPP98, HM96]. Let $\mathsf{Send}_{\mathsf{NI}}, \mathsf{Rec}_{\mathsf{NI}}$ be the sender and receiver

---

Send's input: $b \in \{0, 1\}$.

Commitment phase

1. Rec samples $\beta \leftarrow_R \{0, 1\}^n$ and commits to each bit in parallel using $(\text{Send}_{\text{SH}}, \text{Rec}_{\text{SH}})$ (namely, Rec plays the role of Send_{SH} and Send plays the role of Rec_{SH}). Let c_i denote the transcript of the commitment to β_i. If any c_i is not well-formed, the protocol aborts.

2. Define $M(b, \eta) = \begin{pmatrix} b & \eta \oplus b \\ b & \eta \oplus \bar{b} \end{pmatrix}$

   For each $i = 1, \ldots, n$ in parallel, Send samples $\eta_i \leftarrow_R \{0, 1\}$. In parallel, Send uses Send_{NI} to generate a commitment to all bits of $M(b, \eta_i)$. Call this commitment d_i. Send sends d_i to Rec. If any d_i is not well-formed, Rec aborts.

3. For each $i \in [n]$ in parallel, Rec generates an opening ϕ_i to c_i and sends it to Send. Send calculates $\beta_i = \text{Rec}_{\text{SH}}(decom, c_i, \phi_i)$. If any $\beta_i = \bot$, Send aborts.

Opening phase

1. Send sends b to Rec, and for each $i \in [n]$, Send opens the bits in d_i that correspond to the row in $M(b, \eta_i)$ that equals $(b, \beta_i \oplus b)$.

2. For each $i = 1, \ldots, n$, Rec computes the two bits in the row opened by Send, call these (x_i^0, x_i^1). Rec checks that $x_i^0 = b$ and $x_i^1 = b \oplus \beta_i$. If the check fails, then Rec rejects and outputs $\bot$, otherwise Rec outputs b.

Algorithm 1. *4-round statistically binding and selective opening attack secure commitment*

---

algorithms for a non-interactive perfectly binding commitment (*e.g.* based on one-way permutations). Our commitment is given in Algorithm 1. The following two lemmas prove the security of the commitment.

Lemma 1. *Algorithm 1 is statistically binding.*

Lemma 2. *The simulator given in Algorithm 2 proves that Algorithm 1 is secure against selective opening attacks.*

Proof (of Lemma 1). Fix any Send^* a (possibly cheating and computationally unbounded) sender strategy. Let $(\underline{c}, \underline{d}, \underline{\phi}) \leftarrow_R \langle \text{Rec}(\beta), \text{Send}^* \rangle$ be the commit-phase transcript: $\underline{c}$ denotes the n parallel SHC to β sent by Rec, $\underline{d}$ denotes the n non-interactive commitments to matrices $m_1, \ldots, m_n$ sent by Send^* in response to $\underline{c}$, and $\underline{\phi}$ denotes Rec's opening of $\underline{c}$. Note that given $\underline{d}$, $\underline{m} = (m_1, \ldots, m_n)$ are well-defined because the non-interactive commitment is perfectly binding.

We say that a matrix m_i *matches* a bit β_i if it holds that the bits in the first column are different and the XOR of the two bits in each row equals β_i. Formally, this holds if $m_i^{0,0} \neq m_i^{1,0}$ and also $m_i^{j,0} = m_i^{j,1} \oplus \beta_i$ for all $j \in \{0, 1\}$. We say that $\underline{m}$ matches $\underline{\beta}$ if for all $i \in [n]$ it holds that m_i matches β_i.

Claim. Let $(\underline{c}, \underline{d}, \underline{\phi})$ denote a valid commit-phase transcript. Let β be the opening of $\underline{c}$ using $\underline{\phi}$, and let $\underline{m}$ be the opening of $\underline{d}$. Given this commit-phase transcript, Send^* can successfully break binding iff $\underline{m}$ matches $\underline{\beta}$.

Proof. Suppose $\underline{m}$ matches $\underline{\beta}$, then for each $i \in [n]$ there exists a row in m_i that equals $(0, \beta_i)$ and a row that equals $(1, \overline{\beta_i})$. Therefore, it is possible for Send^* to generate an opening to the row that equals $(b, b \oplus \beta_i)$ for all $b \in \{0, 1\}$.

Suppose that Send^* can open to both values of $b \in \{0, 1\}$. This means it can open each d_i to $(b, b \oplus \beta_i)$ for both $b \in \{0, 1\}$. Since $\mathsf{Send}_{\mathsf{NI}}$ is perfectly binding, therefore it must be that $\underline{m}$ matches $\underline{\beta}$. ∎

A standard argument says that soundness holds because the initial commitment to $\underline{\beta}$ by Rec does not contain any information about $\underline{\beta}$, therefore it is impossible for Send^* to commit to $\underline{m}$ that will match $\underline{\beta}$.

For the sake of completeness, we give a formal proof: by the statistical hiding property of the initial commitment, we have that for any $\underline{\beta}$, it holds that $(\underline{c}, \underline{d}) \leftarrow_{\mathsf{R}} \langle \mathsf{Rec}(\underline{\beta}), \mathsf{Send}^* \rangle$ and $(\underline{c}, \underline{d}) \leftarrow_{\mathsf{R}} \langle \mathsf{Rec}(0^n), \mathsf{Send}^* \rangle$ are $n^{-\omega(1)}$-close in statistical distance. Therefore we may write:

$$
\begin{aligned}
\mathsf{Adv}_{\mathsf{bind}} &\leq \Pr_{\substack{\underline{\beta} \leftarrow_{\mathsf{R}} \{0,1\}^n \\ (\underline{c}, \underline{d}, \underline{\phi}) \leftarrow_{\mathsf{R}} \langle \mathsf{Rec}(\underline{\beta}), \mathsf{Send}^* \rangle}} [\underline{d} \text{ opens to } \underline{m} \text{ matching } \underline{\beta}] \\
&= \sum_{\underline{\beta} \in \{0,1\}^n} 2^{-n} \Pr_{(\underline{c}, \underline{d}, \underline{\phi}) \leftarrow_{\mathsf{R}} \langle \mathsf{Rec}(\underline{\beta}), \mathsf{Send}^* \rangle} [\underline{d} \text{ opens to } \underline{m} \text{ matching } \underline{\beta}] \\
&\leq 2^{-n} \sum_{\underline{\beta} \in \{0,1\}^n} \Pr_{(\underline{c}, \underline{d}, \underline{\phi}) \leftarrow_{\mathsf{R}} \langle \mathsf{Rec}(0^n), \mathsf{Send}^* \rangle} [\underline{d} \text{ opens to } \underline{m} \text{ matching } \underline{\beta}] + n^{-\omega(1)} \\
&\leq 2^{-n} + n^{-\omega(1)}
\end{aligned}
$$

where the last inequality holds because if $\underline{m}$ matches one $\underline{\beta}$, it cannot match any $\underline{\beta}' \neq \underline{\beta}$, and so the sum of the probabilities is bounded by 1. This means that Send^* has a negligible probability of breaking binding. ∎

4   Analyzing the Simulator

Proof (of Lemma 2). We use "initial commitment" to denote the SHC used by the receiver in the first step of the protocol. We use "final commitment" to denote the overall selective-opening attack secure commitment we are trying to simulate. As is typical with black-box simulation strategies, this simulator tries to rewind Rec^* to discover the values in the initial commitment, and then use those values to construct a final commitment that can be opened to both 0 and 1. One subtlety where care is need is the possibility of individual sessions aborting. We observe that, for each session j that successfully completes the initial commitment, the simulator needs to successfully discover the committed β^j just once (the receiver cannot change it, otherwise this would contradict the binding property of the initial commitment). Once β^j is discovered, the simulator can always successfully open the final commitment to both 0 and 1 in session j.

The idea is to successively increase the number of sessions where the simulator knows $\underline{\beta}^j$, so that eventually Rec^* will be non-aborting only in sessions where the simulator can open to any value and therefore the simulation can be successfully terminated. Care must be taken that one does not bias the distribution of non-aborting sessions in the final transcript. The intuition is the following strategy: suppose at some point we know that how to reveal arbitrary values for some set of sessions X. The next time the simulator queries the receiver, if the set S of non-aborting sessions returned satisfies $S \subseteq X$ then the simulator can successfully open any subset of S that the receiver requests and so we can terminate the simulation. Otherwise, $S \not\subseteq X$ and so we have increased the number of sessions where we know $\underline{\beta^j}$, and so in future samples we have a better chance of being able to open all the non-aborting sessions to both 0 and 1. However, in order not to bias the distribution of opened sessions, in future iterations, if the simulator receives a response from the receiver whose non-aborting sessions are contained in X, we ignore it and resample. The actual simulator follows this intuition, although there are details about how exactly to query the receiver that need to be taken care of.

As in the case of constant-round zero knowledge, one point we must be careful about is that the simulator must run in expected polynomial time. This is done by using the Goldreich-Kahan strategy of estimating the success probability of queries, and then setting a timeout based on this estimate. In the case of Goldreich-Kahan "success" means obtaining a response without aborting sessions, while in our case success means that the set of non-aborting sessions lies inside X but not inside Y, where $Y \subsetneq X$ are subsets that evolve during the course of simulation.

4.1 General Observations

The simulator is given in Algorithm 2. In the following we omit k from the notation and write simply Sim. We can divide the simulator algorithm into two parts: the initial commitment where the receiver commits to some β^j (consisting of all the steps up to Step 3), and the remainder. We will frequently analyze the simulator for a fixed value of Rec*'s random coins and a fixed initial commitment transcript, since this part is executed exactly once and is distributed identically to the honest interaction.

Fix any choice of Rec*'s random coins and the initial commitment transcript, which in turn fixes some $\Sigma \subseteq [k]$ of non-aborting sessions so far. This defines a distribution $\mathcal{D}_{\text{dummy}}$ as follows: construct dummy commitments $\underline{d^j}$ for $j \in \Sigma$ as in Step 6a and send these to Rec*, and let s denote the receiver's response. Let $S = S(s)$ denote the set of sessions where s contains a non-aborting response (*i.e.* in those sessions, Rec* produces a valid opening of the initial commitment). Let $\mathcal{D}_{\text{dummy}}$ denote the distribution over S thus sampled.

For $X \subseteq \Sigma$, let q_X denote

$$q_X = \Pr_{S \leftarrow_R \mathcal{D}_{\text{dummy}}} [S \not\subseteq X] \tag{4.1}$$

Observe that $q_\varnothing$ is the probability that Rec*'s response contains at least one non-aborting session.

For $Y \subsetneq X \subseteq \Sigma$, define:

$$q_{X|Y} = \Pr_{S \leftarrow_R \mathcal{D}_{\text{dummy}}} [S \not\subseteq X \mid S \not\subseteq Y] \tag{4.2}$$

Given oracle access to a cheating k-fold receiver Rec^*:

1. Initialize $X, Y = \varnothing$. Initialize variables $\underline{\beta}^1, \ldots, \underline{\beta}^k$ to empty. Initialize a counter t to 0 and a timeout T to 0.
2. Sample random coins for Rec^* and fix them. Sample coins for the honest sender and execute the initial commitment with Rec^*. Write Rec^*'s random coins and the initial commitment phase transcript to the output.
3. Let $\Sigma \subseteq [k]$ denote the set of sessions in which Rec^* does not abort in the initial commitment. In the following, only continue interaction in Σ.
4. In the following, if Rec^* ever outputs an invalid opening of a commitment in session j, the simulator interprets this as the receiver aborting in session j. The simulator also checks the values of all the valid openings, and if Rec^* ever opens the same commitment to two distinct values then the simulator outputs "binding broken" and halts.
5. Define $F(\gamma, \beta) = \begin{pmatrix} \gamma & \beta \oplus \gamma \\ \overline{\gamma} & \beta \oplus \overline{\gamma} \end{pmatrix}$.
6. *First loop:* Repeat the following:
   (a) *Dummy commitments:* For each $j \in \Sigma, i \in [n]$, sample $\gamma_i^j \leftarrow_{\mathsf{R}} \{0,1\}, \nu_i^j \leftarrow_{\mathsf{R}} \{0,1\}$ and generate commitments to $F(\gamma_i^j, \nu_i^j)$. Call these commitments $\underline{d}^j = (d_1^j, \ldots, d_n^j)$. Send $\underline{d}^j$ to Rec^*.
   (b) Read Rec^*'s response, call this s. Let $S \subseteq \Sigma$ be the set of non-aborting sessions in s. Do the following:
       i. If $S = X = Y = \varnothing$ (this can only occur in the first iteration), write the $\underline{d}^j$ and s to the output and halt.
       ii. If $S \subseteq Y$, continue the loop.
       iii. If $S \not\subseteq Y$ and $S \subseteq X$ then break the loop.
       iv. If $S \not\subseteq X$ then set $Y \leftarrow X, X \leftarrow X \cup S$, and for all $j \in S \setminus X$, set β^j to be the value that was opened by Rec^*. Continue the loop.
7. *Calculate timeout:* Repeat the following trial until $(nk)^2$ successes occur: for each $j \in \Sigma$, generate $\underline{d}^j$ by the method in Step 6a, and let S' denote the set of sessions in Rec^*'s response that are not aborted; the trial is a success if $S' \not\subseteq Y$ and $S' \subseteq X$. Let ℓ denote the number of repetitions that were used to obtain $(nk)^2$ successes. Set $T = \min(\frac{\ell}{nk}, nk2^{nk})$ and set $t = 0$.
8. *Second loop:* Repeat the following while $t \leq T$
   (a) For $j \in \Sigma$, construct and send $\underline{d}^j$ to the receiver, defined as:
       i. For each $j \in \Sigma \setminus X$, let $\underline{d}^j$ be generated by the method in Step 6a.
       ii. For $j \in X$ and for each $i \in [n]$, sample $\gamma_i^j \leftarrow_{\mathsf{R}} \{0,1\}$ and construct d_i^j to be a commitment to $F(\gamma_i^j, \beta_i^j)$.
   (b) Let s be Rec^*'s response and S the set of non-aborted sessions in s.
       i. If $S \subseteq Y$ or $S \not\subseteq X$ then increment t and continue the loop.
       ii. Otherwise, it must be that $S \not\subseteq Y$ and $S \subseteq X$. Write all the $\underline{d}^j$ and s to the output. Complete the simulation as follows:
           A. Ask Rec^* for a set I to be opened. If Rec^* aborts, then the simulator halts. Otherwise, Rec^* picks a subset $I \in \mathcal{I}, I \subseteq S$ to be revealed and the simulator asks for the values $\{b_j\}_{j \in I}$. Write I to the output.
           B. For each $j \in I$, each $i \in [n]$, the simulator outputs b_j and an opening to the row in $F(\gamma_i^j, \beta_i^j)$ that equals $(b_j, \beta_i^j \oplus b_j)$.
           C. Halt.
9. We exceeded the timeout, so output "timeout".

Algorithm 2. *Simulator* Sim_k *for Algorithm 1*

Input: black-box access to a distribution $\mathcal{D}$ over $[k]$.

1. Initialize $X = Y = \varnothing$.
2. Repeat the following:
   (a) Sample $S \leftarrow_R \mathcal{D}$. If $S = X = Y = \varnothing$, output S and halt.
   (b) If $S \subseteq Y$, continue the loop.
   (c) If $S \not\subseteq Y$ and $S \subseteq X$, output S.
   (d) If $S \not\subseteq X$, then we have seen some new elements $(S \setminus X)$. Set $Y \leftarrow X$ and $X \leftarrow X \cup S$ and continue the loop.

Algorithm 3. *Abstraction of simulator*

Remark 1. For any $Y \subsetneq X$, it holds that $q_X = q_{X|Y} \cdot q_Y$, and so $q_X = q_{X|\varnothing} \cdot q_\varnothing$.

An abstraction of the simulator. The simulator basically solves the following problem: we are given black-box access to a distribution $\mathcal{D}$ over subsets of $[k]$. Each time we obtain a sample $S \leftarrow_R \mathcal{D}$, we say that we have "seen" all the elements $j \in S$. The goal is to output some $S' \subseteq [k]$ such that S' is distributed identically to $\mathcal{D}$, and each element of S' was already seen during the execution of the algorithm. (In our simulator, having seen some $j \in S$ means we have the opening for β^j and so can equivocate in the j'th session. We also have to do some additional work (Steps 7 and 8 in Algorithm 2) because we want to output a complete transcript, not just S.)

In the setting of this abstract problem, the strategy of our simulator is given in Algorithm 3.

The intuition why Algorithm 3 (and hence our simulator) produces a set that is distributed according to $\mathcal{D}$ is the following claim: for any $V \subsetneq U \subseteq \Sigma$, if we run Algorithm 3 with $X = U, Y = V$ (rather than $X = Y = \varnothing$), then it outputs a random $S \leftarrow_R \mathcal{D}$ conditioned on $S \not\subseteq V$. The reasoning is as follows.

- With probability $1 - q_{U|V}$ we get a sample distributed according to $S \leftarrow_R \mathcal{D}$ conditioned on $S \subseteq U$ and $S \not\subseteq V$, and this is our output.
- With probability $q_{U|V}$ we get $S \not\subseteq U$ and so we see some new elements, and we update X, Y. In this case we can use induction to show that, since the new value Y is U, the final output will be distributed according to $S \leftarrow_R \mathcal{D}$ conditioned on $S \not\subseteq U$.

Combining the two, the overall distribution is correct. (This intuition is formalized later in Lemma 10.)

In the following we will analyze the simulator directly (*i.e.* with all the details pertaining to outputting a transcript and not just the set of non-aborting sessions), but it helps to keep this abstraction in mind for intuition.

4.2 Running Time

We first show that the expected running time of the simulator in Algorithm 2 is polynomial. Clearly the steps before Step 6 are efficient, so fix any choice of random coins for Rec* and any initial commitment transcript and let Σ be the set of non-aborting sessions so far. We count the number of steps starting at Step 6 and afterwards.

We will count the number of iterations in each of the loops, and multiply this by the number of steps each iteration takes. Therefore, let $c_{\text{iteration}}$ denote the maximum amount of time it takes in one iteration of any of the loops: it upper bounds the time to construct $\underline{d}^j$, send them to Rec*, and calculate S the set of sessions where Rec*'s responses are non-aborting and do not break binding, and compare S to Y and X, and possibly updating Y, X. It holds that $c_{\text{iteration}} = \text{poly}(n, k)$.

Let Σ^* denote $\cup_{S \subseteq \text{supp}(\mathcal{D}_{\text{dummy}})} S$. Suppose at some point in its execution, the simulator sets $X = U$ and $Y = V$ for some $V \subsetneq U \subseteq \Sigma^*$. Let $c_{U,V}$ denote the total expected number of steps the simulator takes after having set $X = U, Y = V$.

Lemma 3. *For all $V \subsetneq U \subseteq \Sigma^*$, let $v = |V|$, then it holds that $c_{U,V} \leq (k-v)((nk)^2 + 4nk)c_{\text{iteration}}/q_V$.*

Proof. We prove the lemma by induction.

Base case. Consider the base case where $U = \Sigma^*$ (and $V \subsetneq \Sigma^*$ is arbitrary). The simulator repeatedly samples S until it obtains $S \not\subseteq V$. It takes $1/q_V$ executions of the loop at Step 6 on average to sample $S \not\subseteq V$. Each such execution takes $c_{\text{iteration}}$ steps, so this part contributes a total of $c_{\text{iteration}}/q_V$ on average.

Since $U = \Sigma^*$, therefore for any $S \not\subseteq V$ that is sampled, $S \subseteq \Sigma^*$ and so the simulator goes to Step 7. We count the number of iterations needed to calculate the timeout: a success in each trial means sampling $S' \not\subseteq V$, and so on average it takes $1/q_V$ samples to get one success, and $(nk)^2/q_V$ to get $(nk)^2$ successes. Each sample takes $c_{\text{iteration}}$ steps, so overall we execute on average $(nk)^2 c_{\text{iteration}}/q_V$ steps.

Next, the simulator goes to the loop at Step 8. Here it executes at most T iterations. There are two cases: either $T \leq 2nk/q_V$ or $T > 2nk/q_V$. The number of iterations in the first case is at most $2nk/q_V$. By a standard Chernoff bound, the probability that the second case occurs is at most 2^{-nk}, and in this case we can apply the bound $T \leq nk2^{nk}$. Therefore the expected contribution of this loop is at most $2nkc_{\text{iteration}}/q_V + c_{\text{iteration}}nk \leq (4nk - 1)c_{\text{iteration}}/q_V$.

Summing up, we get that $c_{\Sigma^*,V} \leq ((nk)^2 + 4nk)c_{\text{iteration}}/q_V \leq (k - v)((nk)^2 + 4nk)c_{\text{iteration}}/q_V$.

Inductive case. Suppose $U \neq \Sigma^*$. Suppose the lemma holds for all U', V' where $|U'| > |U|$.

It takes on average $1/q_V$ samples to obtain $S \not\subseteq V$. Each sample takes $c_{\text{iteration}}$ so this contributes $c_{\text{iteration}}/q_V$.

For the set $S \not\subseteq V$ that is sampled, there are two cases:

1. With conditional probability $1 - q_{U|V}$, we obtain $S \subseteq U$. Let us write $p_{U,V} = 1 - q_{U|V}$. In this case we calculate the timeout (Step 7). Calculating the timeout takes on average $1/(q_V p_{U,V})$ samples to obtain a success, and each sample requires $c_{\text{iteration}}$ steps, so overall this contributes on average $p_{U,V} \cdot (nk)^2 \cdot c_{\text{iteration}}/(q_V \cdot p_{U,V}) = (nk)^2 c_{\text{iteration}}/q_V$ steps.

   Next the simulator enters the loop at Step 8. This loop runs at most T times. As with the base case, there are two cases: either $T \leq 2nk/(q_V p_{U,V})$ or $T >$

$2nk/(q_V p_{U,V})$. As before, we may argue that in the first case T contributes at most $2nk/(q_V p_{U,V})$ and the expected contribution of the second case is at most nk, so overall the contribution is $p_{U,V} \cdot c_{\text{iteration}}(2nk/(q_V p_{U,V}) + nk) \le (4nk - 1)c_{\text{iteration}}/q_V$.

2. The other case is when $S \not\subseteq U$. Such an S is sampled with conditional probability $q_{U|V}$. In this case we update the variables so that $X = U \cup S$ and $Y = U$, as well as updating the values of the β^j. From this point on, the remaining number of steps spent in the loop is given by $c_{U\cup S, U}$. Since $S \not\subseteq U$, therefore $|U \cup S| > |U|$ and $|U| \ge v + 1$, and we can apply the inductive hypothesis. That is, for any such S, the inductive hypothesis states that

$$c_{U \cup S, U} \le (k - v - 1)((nk)^2 + 4nk)c_{\text{iteration}}/q_U$$

Therefore, by applying Remark 1, this contributes $q_{U|V} \cdot (k - v - 1)((nk)^2 + 4nk)c_{\text{iteration}}/q_U = (k - v - 1)((nk)^2 + 4nk)c_{\text{iteration}}/q_V$.

Taking the sum of all the terms we have $c_{U,V} \le (k - v)((nk)^2 + 4nk)/q_V$. ∎

Finally, we observe that the expected running time C of the simulator is bounded by:

$$
\begin{aligned}
C &= \text{poly}(n, k) + q_\varnothing \cdot \mathbb{E}_S[c_{S,\varnothing} \mid S \ne \varnothing] \\
&\le \text{poly}(n, k) + q_\varnothing \cdot \mathbb{E}_S[k((nk)^2 + 4nk)c_{\text{iteration}}/q_\varnothing \mid S \ne \varnothing] \\
&\le \text{poly}(n, k)
\end{aligned}
$$

The first $\text{poly}(n, k)$ comes from the steps before Step 6 and the contribution from when the very first iteration of the first loop samples $S = \varnothing$. The second term is the contribution from when $S \ne \varnothing$. ∎

4.3 Indistinguishability

Next we prove that the output of the simulator is computationally indistinguishable from the honest interaction. To do this we use a sequence of hybrid simulators, which unlike the simulator know the input $\underline{b}$ during the entire simulation.

$\text{HSim}(\underline{b})^{\text{Rec}^*}$ which is identical to Sim except it knows the input $\underline{b}$ beforehand and it has the following modifications:

1. In Step 6a, Step 7, and Step 8a, to construct $\underline{d}^j$ for $j \in \Sigma$ do the following: for each $i \in [n]$, sample $\eta_i^j \leftarrow_{\text{R}} \{0, 1\}$ and construct d_i^j to be a commitment to $M(b_j, \eta_i^j)$ (recall that M was defined in Algorithm 1).
2. In Step 8(b)iiB, for each $j \in \Sigma$, open the row in d_i^j that equals $(b_j, \beta_i^j \oplus b_j)$.

Namely, it constructs all the commitments honestly, which it can do because it knows $\underline{b}$. Observe that the simulator can still successfully open its final commitments because they are generated honestly (without relying on learning the β^j sent in the initial commitment by Rec^*).

We define a second hybrid BSim that is identical to HSim except it does not check whether or not the openings given by Rec^* are consistent (i.e. whether binding is ever broken). However BSim still calculates and enforces the timeout.

We define a third hybrid TSim that is identical to BSim except it does not check the timeout condition. (Namely, TSim is like HSim except it enforces neither the timeout nor the binding broken conditions.)

Lemma 4. $\mathsf{HSim}^{\mathsf{Rec}^*}(\underline{b})$ and $\mathsf{BSim}^{\mathsf{Rec}^*}(\underline{b})$ both run in expected polynomial time.

Proof. The proof of the expected polynomial running time of Sim applies to each of these simulators as well: it only used the fact that with high probability the timeout calculation is accurate, and then afterwards bounds the running time by using the timeout.

Namely, one can apply the entire proof with the sole modification being the definition of the $q_X, q_{X|Y}$ (Equation 4.1, Equation 4.2), which, instead of using $\mathcal{D}_{\mathsf{dummy}}$, are now defined with respect to the following distribution $\mathcal{D}_{\underline{b}}$:

Definition 4. *Fix a transcript of the initial commitment. Let $S \leftarrow_R \mathcal{D}_{\underline{b}}$ be defined as follows: construct $\underline{d}^j$ commitments to b_j for $j \in \Sigma$ as an honest sender would and send them to* Rec^*. *Let S be the sessions in* Rec^**'s response that are non-aborting.*

Since the actual steps in each iteration of the loops at Step 6a, Step 7, and Step 8 (which are the only differences between Sim and HSim) never really entered into the proof, one can apply the rest of the proof for Sim to HSim.

Since the proof never used the fact that Sim sometimes outputs "binding broken", and since outputting "binding broken" can only reduce the running time, this same argument also extends to BSim. ∎

Let $(\mathsf{Sim}^{\mathsf{Rec}^*} \mid \underline{b})$ denote the distribution of the output of the simulator, where the "conditioned on $\underline{b}$" notation emphasizes the fact that the simulator does not see $\underline{b}$ until it requests some subset I to be opened, and even then it only sees $\underline{b}_I$. The following four lemmas show that, by using these hybrids, it holds that $(\mathsf{Sim}^{\mathsf{Rec}^*} \mid \underline{b})$ and $\langle \mathsf{Send}, \mathsf{Rec}^* \rangle(\underline{b})$ are computationally indistinguishable.

Lemma 5. *For all sufficiently large n, k and all $\underline{b} \in \{0, 1\}^k$, the two distributions $(\mathsf{Sim}^{\mathsf{Rec}^*} \mid \underline{b})$ and $\mathsf{HSim}^{\mathsf{Rec}^*}(\underline{b})$ are computationally indistinguishable.*

Lemma 6. *For all sufficiently large n, k and all $\underline{b} \in \{0, 1\}^k$, the two distributions $\mathsf{HSim}^{\mathsf{Rec}^*}(\underline{b})$ and $\mathsf{BSim}^{\mathsf{Rec}^*}(\underline{b})$ have negligible statistical distance.*

Lemma 7. *For all n, k and all $\underline{b} \in \{0, 1\}^k$, the two distributions $\mathsf{BSim}^{\mathsf{Rec}^*}(\underline{b})$ and $\mathsf{TSim}^{\mathsf{Rec}^*}(\underline{b})$ have negligible statistical distance.*

Lemma 8. *For all n, k and all $\underline{b} \in \{0, 1\}^k$, the two distributions $\mathsf{TSim}^{\mathsf{Rec}^*}(\underline{b})$ and $\langle \mathsf{Send}, \mathsf{Rec}^* \rangle(\underline{b})$ are identical.*

We now turn to proving these lemmas.

Proof (of Lemma 5, Sim and HSim are computationally indistinguishable.). Suppose there exists an efficient distinguisher D, a polynomial $P(n)$ and infinitely many $n, k = \mathsf{poly}(n), \underline{b} \in \{0, 1\}^k$ such that D distinguishes $(\mathsf{Sim}^{\mathsf{Rec}^*} \mid \underline{b})$ from $\mathsf{HSim}^{\mathsf{Rec}^*}(\underline{b})$ with advantage $1/P(n)$. We build a distinguisher that breaks hiding for $(\mathsf{Send}_{\mathsf{NI}}, \mathsf{Rec}_{\mathsf{NI}})$.

Let C denote the maximum of the expected running times of $\mathsf{HSim}^{\mathsf{Rec}^*}(\underline{b})$ and $(\mathsf{Sim}^{\mathsf{Rec}^*} \mid \underline{b})$ and the running time of the distinguisher D. Construct the following algorithm E, which is supposed to distinguish oracle $\mathcal{O}_1$ from $\mathcal{O}_2$ taking input $b \in \{0,1\}, \beta \in \{0,1\}$ and behaving as follows:

1. $\mathcal{O}_1(b, \beta)$ outputs a commitment using $\mathsf{Send}_{\mathsf{NI}}$ to $(b, \beta \oplus \bar{b})$.
2. $\mathcal{O}_2(b, \beta)$ outputs a commitment using $\mathsf{Send}_{\mathsf{NI}}$ to $(\bar{b}, \beta \oplus \bar{b})$.

As advice E receives an input $(n, k, \underline{b})$ where D achieves advantage $1/P(n)$.

E executes $\mathsf{Sim}^{\mathsf{Rec}^*}$ (*i.e.* Algorithm 2) except for the following modifications. For each $j \in X$,

1. In Step 6a and Step 7, for each $j \in \Sigma, i \in [n]$, construct d_i^j as follows: E samples $\nu_i^j \leftarrow_{\mathsf{R}} \{0,1\}$ and calculates by itself commitments under $\mathsf{Send}_{\mathsf{NI}}$ to the bits $(b_j, \nu_i^j \oplus b_j)$, call these $d_{i,0}^j$. It calls $\mathcal{O}(b_j, \nu_i^j)$ to get a commitment to two more bits, call these $d_{i,1}^j$. E creates d_i^j by setting with probability $1/2$ the commitments $d_{i,0}^j$ as the top row and $d_{i,1}^j$ as the bottom row, and with probability $1/2$ the other way around.
2. In Step 8a, for each $j \in \Sigma, i \in [n]$, generate d_i^j as follows: E calculates by itself commitments under $\mathsf{Send}_{\mathsf{NI}}$ to the bits $(b_j, \beta_i^j \oplus b_j)$, call these $d_{i,0}^j$. It calls $\mathcal{O}(b_j, \beta_i^j)$ to get a commitment to two more bits, call these $d_{i,1}^j$. E creates d_i^j by setting with probability $1/2$ the commitments $d_{i,0}^j$ as the top row and $d_{i,1}^j$ as the bottom row, and with probability $1/2$ the other way around.
3. In Step 8(b)iiB, opens the row in d_i^j where it inserted $d_{i,0}^j$.

Finally, E applies the distinguisher D to the output transcript and outputs the same thing as D. Let $E^{\mathcal{O}}(\underline{b})$ denote E run with oracle $\mathcal{O}$ and input $\underline{b}$.

Claim. $\Pr[E^{\mathcal{O}_2}(\underline{b}) = 1] = \Pr[D(\mathsf{Sim}^{\mathsf{Rec}^*} \mid \underline{b}) = 1]$.

Proof. The only place where E differs from Sim is in how it constructs $\underline{d}^j$.

Let us look at Step 6a, the case of the other steps is identical (for Step 8a, replace ν_i^j by β_i^j). For each $j \in X, i \in [n]$, observe that d_i^j constructed according to E using $\mathcal{O}_2$ gives a commitment to a matrix where one randomly chosen row equals $(b_j, \nu_i^j \oplus b_j)$ and the other row equals $(\bar{b}_j, \nu_i^j \oplus \bar{b}_j)$. This is the same as a commitment to $F(\gamma, \nu_i^j)$ for $\gamma \leftarrow_{\mathsf{R}} \{0,1\}$, which is how Sim constructs d_i^j. Since the openings to the non-interactive commitments are deterministic given fixed d_i^j, this means that the distribution of output of $E^{\mathcal{O}_2}(\underline{b})$ is identical to the distribution of $(\mathsf{Sim}^{\mathsf{Rec}^*} \mid \underline{b})$.   ∎

Claim. $\Pr[E^{\mathcal{O}_1}(\underline{b}) = 1] = \Pr[D(\mathsf{HSim}^{\mathsf{Rec}^*}(\underline{b})) = 1]$

Proof. Again it suffices to look only at the loop at Step 6a. For each $j \in X, i \in [n]$, observe that d_i^j constructed according to E using $\mathcal{O}_1$ gives a commitment to a matrix where one randomly chosen row equals $(b_j, \nu_i^j \oplus b_j)$ and the other row equals $(b_j, \nu_i^j \oplus \bar{b}_j)$. This is the same as a commitment to $M(b_j, \eta)$ for $\eta \leftarrow_{\mathsf{R}} \{0,1\}$, which is how HSim constructs d_i^j. Since the opening to the non-interactive commitments are deterministic given fixed d_i^j, this means that the distribution of output of $E^{\mathcal{O}_1}(\underline{b})$ is identical to the distribution of $\mathsf{HSim}^{\mathsf{Rec}^*}(\underline{b})$.   ∎

These two claims imply that $E^{(\cdot)}(\underline{b})$ distinguishes between $\mathcal{O}_1$ and $\mathcal{O}_2$ with advantage $1/P(n)$. Furthermore, the expected running time of E is bounded by $2C$. Let us truncate its running time to $6P(n)C$, then the distinguishing advantage remains at least $1/(3P(n))$. Furthermore, the fact that HSim and Sim are expected polynomial time means that $6P(n)C$ is polynomial. By a standard hybrid argument, this can be transformed into an efficient distinguisher for a single call to $\mathcal{O}_1$ vs $\mathcal{O}_2$. By another standard argument, this can be transformed into an efficient distinguisher breaking the hiding property of the commitment. ∎

Proof (of Lemma 6, HSim and BSim are statistically close.). By definition, HSim and BSim are identical except in the case that HSim outputs "binding broken". This can only happen with negligible probability: otherwise using a standard argument, *e.g.* given in Goldreich-Kahan, if C bounds the expected running time of $\mathsf{HSim}^{\mathsf{Rec}^*}(\underline{b})$ and $\mathsf{HSim}^{\mathsf{Rec}^*}(\underline{b})$ outputs "binding broken" with non-negligible $1/P(n)$, then by truncating the execution of HSim at $2P(n)C$ we get an algorithm that outputs "binding broken" with non-negligible probability $\frac{1}{2P(n)}$. By Lemma 4 $C = \mathrm{poly}(n,k)$ and so this algorithm is efficient. This can then be used to break the binding of the commitment used by the receiver, which contradicts the computational binding property of the commitment. ∎

Proof (of Lemma 7, BSim and TSim are statistically close.).

By definition, BSim and TSim are identical except in the case that BSim times out. We calculate this probability. For the following, fix any choice of $\underline{b}$, Rec^*'s random coins, and initial commitment from Rec^*.

Let $B_{U,V}$ denote the event that BSim breaks from the first loop with $X = U, Y = V$. Since a timeout can only occur when $B_{U,V}$ occurs with $U \neq \varnothing$, we observe that:

$$\Pr_{\mathsf{BSim}}[\mathsf{BSim}\text{ times out}] = \sum_{V \subsetneq U \subseteq \Sigma} \Pr_{\mathsf{BSim}}[\mathsf{BSim}\text{ times out} \wedge B_{U,V}] \qquad (4.3)$$

Since there are less than 2^{2k} choices for U, V, it suffices to show that each term of the summation is bounded by $2^{-\Omega(nk)}$. To do this, we relate $\Pr[B_{U,V}]$ to the following quantity:

$$\delta_{U,V} = \Pr_{S \leftarrow_{\mathrm{R}} \mathcal{D}_{\underline{b}}}[S \subseteq U \wedge S \not\subseteq V] \qquad (4.4)$$

where $\mathcal{D}_{\underline{b}}$ is as defined in Definition 4. We claim that

Lemma 9. $\Pr_{\mathsf{BSim}}[B_{U,V}] \leq \delta_{U,V}$

Let us apply this lemma to complete the proof of the lemma; we will prove the lemma later. By the lemma, all terms in Equation 4.3 satisfy either $\Pr[B_{U,V}] \leq 2^{-nk}$ or $\delta_{U,V} > 2^{-nk}$. The second case is the only interesting one, so fix such U, V. It suffices to show that $\Pr[\mathsf{BSim}\text{ times out} \mid B_{U,V}] \leq 2^{-\Omega(nk)}$.

Let T denote the timeout calculated in the simulation. Since each trial in the timeout calculation is a success with probability $\delta_{U,V}$, the expected number of trials necessary to obtain $(nk)^2$ successes is $\frac{(nk)^2}{\delta_{U,V}}$. Therefore by a standard Chernoff bound, the probability that $T < \frac{nk}{2\delta_{U,V}}$ is at most 2^{-nk}. (Here the assumption that $\delta_{U,V} > 2^{-nk}$ is important, since by definition T is limited to be at most $nk2^{nk}$.)

Conditioned on $T \geq \frac{nk}{2\delta_{U,V}}$, the probability of timeout is at most $(1 - \delta_{U,V})^T \leq 2^{-nk/2}$. In total therefore $\Pr[\text{BSim times out} \mid B_{U,V}] \leq 2^{-nk} + 2^{-nk/2} < 2^{-nk/3}$. Therefore, every term in Equation 4.3 is bounded by $2^{-\Omega(nk)}$ and since there are less than 2^{2k} terms in total, the total probability of timeout is negligible. ∎

We now prove Lemma 9.

Proof (of Lemma 9). Let $\overline{\alpha}$ denote a vector of Send_{NI} commitments $(\underline{d}^j)_{j \in \Sigma}$. Let z denote a pair containing a vector of queries $\overline{\alpha}$ and a response s from Rec^*. For a fixing of $z = (\overline{\alpha}, s)$, let Z denote the set of non-aborting sessions in s.

For any z, let A_z denote the event that the simulator breaks from the first loop where, in the iteration that causes the loop to break, the query to Rec^* are the queries in z and the response received is the response in z. By definition, it holds that

$$\Pr_{\text{BSim}}[B_{U,V}] \leq \sum_{z \mid Z \not\subseteq V, Z \subseteq U} \Pr_{\text{BSim}}[A_z] \tag{4.5}$$

The following says that $\Pr_{\text{BSim}}[A_z] = \Pr[(\overline{\alpha}, s) = z]$, where $\overline{\alpha}$ are constructed as honest commitments to $\underline{b}$ and s is Rec^*'s response (*i.e.* the same probability space as $\mathcal{D}_{\underline{b}}$). This implies that the RHS of Equation 4.5 is equal to $\delta_{U,V}$ and Lemma 9 follows.

Claim. For all z where $Z \neq \varnothing$, $\Pr_{\text{BSim}}[A_z] = \Pr[(\overline{\alpha}, s) = z]$.

Proof. Let $\Sigma^* = \bigcup_{S \subseteq \text{supp}(\mathcal{D}_{\underline{b}})} S$. If $Z \not\subseteq \Sigma^*$ then $\Pr[A_z] = \Pr[(\overline{\alpha}, s) = z] = 0$ and we are done, so suppose that $Z \subseteq \Sigma^*$. For any $V \subsetneq U \subseteq \Sigma^*$, let $\rho_{U,V,z}$ denote the probability A_z occurs, conditioned on BSim ever executing the first loop (Step 6) with $X = U, Y = V$ (but not necessarily breaking from the first loop with $X = U, Y = V$). We prove that

$$\rho_{U,V,z} = \Pr[(\overline{\alpha}, s) = z \mid S \not\subseteq V] \tag{4.6}$$

where S is the set of non-aborting sessions of the response contained in s. This would imply the claim, since for any z with non-empty Z, we have

$$\Pr_{\text{BSim}}[A_z] = \Pr[S \neq \varnothing] \cdot \mathbb{E}_S[\rho_{S,\varnothing,z} \mid S \neq \varnothing] = \Pr[(\overline{\alpha}, s) = z]$$

since it must be that the first iteration of the loop sampled $S \neq \varnothing$ and then conditioned on this the probability of sampling z is given by $\rho_{S,\varnothing,z}$. (This corresponds to our earlier intuition that the abstract sampling algorithm of Algorithm 3 samples the correct distribution.)

We prove Equation 4.6. If $Z \subseteq V$ then both sides of Equation 4.6 are 0. So suppose that $Z \not\subseteq V$. There are two cases:

1. Suppose that $Z \subseteq U$. Let us look at the very first sample $(\overline{\alpha}, s)$ satisfying $S \not\subseteq V$ that is obtained after the simulator sets $X = U, Y = V$. If $(\overline{\alpha}, s) \neq z$ then either BSim breaks the loop with this different query/response, or else Y is updated to be $U \cup S$ and in the subsequent iterations of the loop, Z is contained in the updated Y, and so z can no longer possibly be sampled.

   Therefore, the only contribution to the probability of z being sampled is when this first sample $(\overline{\alpha}, s) = z$. This occurs with probability $\Pr[(\overline{\alpha}, s) = z \mid S \not\subseteq V]$. In particular, this shows that Equation 4.6 holds for any $V \subsetneq \Sigma^*$ when $U = \Sigma^*$.

2. Suppose that $Z \not\subseteq U$. Since the first point establishes Equation 4.6 when $U = \Sigma^*$, we may use induction and assume that it holds for all $\rho_{U',U,z}$ where $|U'| > |U|$. Since $Z \not\subseteq U$, it follows that A_z only occurs if BSim does not break the loop while $X = U$. Therefore, $\rho_{U,V,z}$ equals:

$$\sum_{W \not\subseteq U} \Pr[S = W \mid S \not\subseteq V] \cdot \rho_{U \cup W, U, z}$$

$$= \Pr[(\overline{\alpha}, s) = z \mid S \not\subseteq U] \sum_{W \not\subseteq U} \Pr[S = W \mid S \not\subseteq V]$$

$$= \Pr[(\overline{\alpha}, s) = z \mid S \not\subseteq U] \Pr[S \not\subseteq U \mid S \not\subseteq V]$$

$$= \Pr[(\overline{\alpha}, s) = z \mid S \not\subseteq V]$$

where in the last step we use the fact that $Z \not\subseteq U$ and that for events A, B, C such that A implies B implies C, it holds that $\Pr[A \mid B] \Pr[B \mid C] = \Pr[A \mid C]$. ∎

Proof (of Lemma 8, TSim and $\langle$Send, Rec$^*\rangle$ are identical.).

By definition, the output of TSim and an honest interaction are identical up to the end of the initial commitment, so fix any random coins of Rec* and fix any initial commitment transcript. As in Lemma 9, let z be any tuple of queries to and responses of Rec* to open its initial commitments, *i.e.* z is of the form $(\overline{\alpha}, s)$. Let Z denote the set of non-aborting sessions in s.

If $Z = \varnothing$, then it is clear that the probability that TSim outputs z is identical to the probability of z being output in an honest transcript, since this can only be output in the first iteration of the first loop in TSim and by definition this is identical to an honest interaction.

So consider z such that $Z \neq \varnothing$. As in the proof of Lemma 9, let A_z denote the probability that the TSim breaks from the first loop and the last query to and response received from Rec* before breaking being given by the tuple z. TSim and BSim are completely identical in the first loop, so we can apply Equation 4.3 to show that $\Pr_{\mathsf{TSim}}[A_z] = \Pr[(\overline{\alpha}, s) = z]$.

Let A'_z denote the event that TSim outputs z as the query/response in the step corresponding to Step 8(b)ii.

Lemma 10. *For all z containing at least one non-aborting session, it holds that* $\Pr_{\mathsf{TSim}}[A'_z] = \Pr_{\mathsf{TSim}}[A_z]$.

This combined with Equation 4.3 imply that $\Pr_{\mathsf{TSim}}[A'_z] = \Pr[(\overline{\alpha}, s) = z]$.

If A'_z occurs then z is written to the output. From the definition of the TSim, conditioned on outputting z, the rest of the output, namely the choice of I and opening, are identical to the honest interaction conditioned on outputting z. Since the probability of outputting z is identical, this proves that $\mathsf{TSim}^{\mathsf{Rec}^*}(\underline{b})$ and $\langle$Send, Rec$^*\rangle(\underline{b})$ are identical.

It remains to prove Lemma 10.

Proof (of Lemma 10). If A_z occurs, then it must be that TSim breaks out of the first loop for some U, V satisfying $Z \not\subseteq V$ and $Z \subseteq U$. This is exactly the event $B_{U,V}$

as defined in Lemma 9. Likewise, if A'_z occurs then $B_{U,V}$ must occur for some $Z \not\subseteq V, Z \subseteq U$. Therefore it suffices to show that for all U, V such that $Z \not\subseteq V, Z \subseteq U$ and $\Pr[B_{U,V}] > 0$, it holds that

$$\Pr_{\mathsf{TSim}}[A'_z \mid B_{U,V}] = \Pr_{\mathsf{TSim}}[A_z \mid B_{U,V}] \qquad (4.7)$$

since we could apply this as follows to deduce Lemma 10:

$$\Pr[A_z] = \sum_{U,V \mid Z \not\subseteq V, Z \subseteq U} \Pr[A_z \wedge B_{U,V}] = \sum_{U,V \mid Z \not\subseteq V, Z \subseteq U} \Pr[A'_z \wedge B_{U,V}] = \Pr[A'_z]$$

We now prove Equation 4.7. The LHS is equal to $\Pr[(\overline{\alpha}, s) = z \mid S \not\subseteq V, S \subseteq U]$ because by definition of TSim, it generates $\overline{\alpha}$ as honest commitments to $\underline{b}$ and gets a response s satisfying $S \not\subseteq V$ and $S \subseteq U$ (notice this requires the fact that there is no timeout or binding broken condition).

To evaluate the RHS, let $E_{U,V}$ denote the event of TSim ever executing the first loop with $X = U, Y = V$. By definition if $B_{U,V}$ occurs then so does $E_{U,V}$. Therefore we may develop:

$$\Pr_{\mathsf{TSim}}[A_z \mid B_{U,V}] = \frac{\Pr_{\mathsf{TSim}}[A_z \wedge B_{U,V}]}{\Pr_{\mathsf{TSim}}[B_{U,V}]}$$

$$= \frac{\Pr_{\mathsf{TSim}}[A_z \wedge B_{U,V} \mid E_{U,V}]}{\Pr_{\mathsf{TSim}}[B_{U,V} \mid E_{U,V}]}$$

In the last line, we can simplify the numerator to $\Pr[A_z \mid E_{U,V}]$, because conditioned on $E_{U,V}$, A_z implies $B_{U,V}$. Since $Z \subseteq U$, it also holds that $\Pr[A_z \mid E_{U,V}] = \Pr[(\overline{\alpha}, s) = z \mid S \not\subseteq V]$. The denominator in the last line equals $\Pr[S \subseteq U \mid S \not\subseteq V]$.

Therefore we have that

$$\Pr_{\mathsf{TSim}}[A_z \mid B_{U,V}] = \frac{\Pr[(\overline{\alpha}, s) = z \mid S \not\subseteq V]}{\Pr[S \subseteq U \mid S \not\subseteq V]}$$

Using the fact that $(\overline{\alpha}, s) = z$ implies that $S = Z \subseteq U$, we can simplify the fraction to $\Pr[(\overline{\alpha}, s) = z \mid S \not\subseteq V, S \subseteq U]$. This proves Equation 4.7 for all U, V satisfying $Z \not\subseteq V, Z \subseteq U$. ∎

5   Conclusion

Combined with [ORSV11, Xia11], we now have a fairly comprehensive view of commitments with selective opening attack security (under parallel composition): for statistically hiding commitments there exist 3-round protocols and these are optimal for black-box simulation [ORSV11, Xia11], and for statistically-binding commitments there exist 4-round protocols and these are optimal for black-box simulation [ORSV11, Xia11]. Interestingly, the situation is the reverse of stand-alone commitments, where we know non-interactive statistically-binding commitments yet the minimal complexity of statistically hiding commitments is two rounds (without setup assumptions).

[ORSV11] showed that their statistically-hiding commitment is not only secure under parallel composition but also under "concurrent-with-barrier" composition: the commit-phase may occur with arbitrary scheduling of the messages, but the reveal phase happens at the same time across all sessions. An interesting open question is to show whether this is possible for statistically-binding commitments.

References

Bea96.   Beaver, D.: Adaptive zero knowledge and computational equivocation (extended abstract). In: STOC 1996: Proceedings of the Twenty-Eighth Annual ACM Symposium on Theory of Computing, pp. 629–638. ACM, New York (1996)

BHY09.   Bellare, M., Hofheinz, D., Yilek, S.: Possibility and Impossibility Results for Encryption and Commitment Secure under Selective Opening. In: Joux, A. (ed.) EUROCRYPT 2009. LNCS, vol. 5479, pp. 1–35. Springer, Heidelberg (2009)

BCC88.   Brassard, G., Chaum, D., Crépeau, C.: Minimum Disclosure Proofs of Knowledge. J. of Comp. and Sys. Sci. 37(2), 156–189 (1988)

BCY89.   Brassard, G., Crépeau, C., Yung, M.: Everything in NP Can Be Argued in *Perfect* Zero-Knowledge in a *Bounded* Number of Rounds. In: Quisquater, J.-J., Vandewalle, J. (eds.) EUROCRYPT 1989. LNCS, vol. 434, pp. 192–195. Springer, Heidelberg (1990)

DPP93.   Damgård, I.B., Pedersen, T.P., Pfitzmann, B.: On the Existence of Statistically Hiding Bit Commitment Schemes and Fail-Stop Sigantures. In: Stinson, D.R. (ed.) CRYPTO 1993. LNCS, vol. 773, pp. 250–265. Springer, Heidelberg (1994)

DPP98.   Damgård, I.B., Pedersen, T.P., Pfitzmann, B.: Statistical Secrecy and Multibit Commitments. IEEE Transactions on Information Theory 44(3), 1143–1151 (1998)

DCIO98. Di Crescenzo, G., Ishai, Y., Ostrovsky, R.: Non-interactive and non-malleable commitment. In: STOC 1998: Proceedings of the Thirtieth Annual ACM Symposium on Theory of Computing, pp. 141–150. ACM, New York (1998)

DCO99.   Di Crescenzo, G., Ostrovsky, R.: On Concurrent Zero-Knowledge with Pre-processing (Extended Abstract). In: Wiener, M. (ed.) CRYPTO 1999. LNCS, vol. 1666, pp. 485–502. Springer, Heidelberg (1999)

DNRS03. Dwork, C., Naor, M., Reingold, O., Stockmeyer, L.: Magic Functions: In Memoriam: Bernard M. Dwork 1923-1998. J. ACM 50(6), 852–921 (2003)

Fis01.   Fischlin, M.: Trapdoor Commitment Schemes and Their Applications. Ph.D. Thesis (Doktorarbeit), Department of Mathematics, Goethe-University, Frankfurt, Germany (2001)

GK90.   Goldreich, O., Krawczyk, H.: On the Composition of Zero-Knowledge Proof Systems. SIAM J. of Com. 25(1), 169–192 (1996); preliminary version appeared in ICALP 1990

GMW86.   Goldreich, O., Micali, S., Wigderson, A.: Proofs that Yield Nothing But Their Validity or All Languages in NP Have Zero-Knowledge Proof Systems. Journal of the ACM 38(3), 691–729 (1991); preliminary version in FOCS 1986

HM96.   Halevi, S., Micali, S.: Practical and Provably-Secure Commitment Schemes from Collision-Free Hashing. In: Koblitz, N. (ed.) CRYPTO 1996. LNCS, vol. 1109, pp. 201–215. Springer, Heidelberg (1996)

ORSV11. Ostrovsky, R., Rao, V., Scafuro, A., Visconti, I.: Revisiting Lower and Upper Bounds for Selective Decommitments. Cryptology ePrint Archive, Report 2011/536 (2011), http://eprint.iacr.org/

Xia11.   Xiao, D.: (Nearly) Round-Optimal Black-Box Constructions of Commitments Secure against Selective Opening Attacks. In: Ishai, Y. (ed.) TCC 2011. LNCS, vol. 6597, pp. 541–558. Springer, Heidelberg (2011)

Stream Ciphers, a Perspective

Willi Meier

FHNW Windisch, Switzerland
willi.meier@fhnw.ch

Abstract. Synchronous stream ciphers are commonly used in applications with high throughput requirements or on hardware devices with restricted resources. Well known stream ciphers are A5/1, used in GSM, RC4, used in SSL, or E0 as specified in Bluetooth, but also some block cipher modes of operation. A review of the development of stream ciphers is given which starts with classical designs and is directed to modern dedicated stream ciphers as in the European NoE eSTREAM project. The history of stream ciphers is rich in new proposals followed by devastating breaks, e.g., by statistical or algebraic attacks. Differential cryptanalysis is probably the most popular tool for chosen plaintext attacks on block ciphers. It also applies to the initialization step in stream ciphers, but here, high order differential attacks are shown to be surprisingly successful, namely on constructions based on linear and nonlinear feedback shift registers. The process of designing and cryptanalyzing stream ciphers has not only resulted in a number of building blocks for stream ciphers: Similar components turn out to be useful as well in the design of lightweight block ciphers, hash functions and in algorithms for authenticated encryption.

Keywords: Stream Ciphers, Symmetric Cryptography, Design, Cryptanalysis.

A. Mitrokotsa and S. Vaudenay (Eds.): AFRICACRYPT 2012, LNCS 7374, p. 412, 2012.
© Springer-Verlag Berlin Heidelberg 2012

Black-Box Reductions and Separations
in Cryptography

Marc Fischlin

Darmstadt University of Technology, Germany
marc.fischlin@cryptoplexity.de
www.cryptoplexity.de

Abstract. Cryptographic constructions of one primitive or protocol from another one usually come with a reductionist security proof, in the sense that the reduction turns any adversary breaking the derived scheme into a successful adversary against the underlying scheme. Very often the reduction is black-box in the sense that it only looks at the input/output behavior of the adversary and of the underlying primitive. Here we survey the power and the limitations of such black-box reductions, and take a closer look at the recent method of meta-reductions.

1 Introduction

Since the beginning of modern cryptography in the 70's the design methodology for cryptographic protocols has shifted from ad-hoc constructions and "security by obscurity" techniques to well-founded approaches. This transition shows in the agreed-upon methodology to provide clean attack models and security goals of a protocol, and to give a rigorous proof that the protocol meets these goals. Here, the term "proof" should be understood from a reductionist viewpoint, saying that any successful adversary breaking a cryptographic scheme would entail the efficient break of a presumably hard primitive.

Today a special type of proof, called *black-box reduction*, is pervasive in cryptography and provides a very powerful tool to analyze protocols. Roughly, a reduction is black-box if it does not use any internals of the adversary beyond the input and output behavior, and analogously if nothing about the structure of the underlying primitive except for its basic properties is exploited (such reductions are called fully black-box [33]). It turns out that a vast number of cryptographic primitives such as one-way functions, pseudorandom generators [22], and pseudorandom functions [20] can all be derived from each other in a black-box way. Starting with a result by Impagliazzo and Rudich [27], though, for some important problems it has been proven that black-box reductions cannot exist. These negative results are summarized under the name *black-box separations*.

In this paper we survey the three main techniques for black-box separation results, namely, the relativization technique [27], the two-oracle technique [24], and the increasingly more popular meta-reduction technique [5]. We start with an overview about black-box constructions and, after having reviewed the three

A. Mitrokotsa and S. Vaudenay (Eds.): AFRICACRYPT 2012, LNCS 7374, pp. 413–422, 2012.

separation techniques, we also briefly discuss *non*-black-box constructions to indicate potential limitations and bypasses of black-box separation results.

2   Black-Box Constructions

In this section we look at the positive cases of constructions which are black-box and the equivalence class of symmetric-key primitives, called Minicrypt [25].

2.1   One-Way Functions Are Necessary

Most of today's cryptography is impossible without assuming the existence of (cryptographic) one-way functions. Of course, we can symmetrically encrypt messages securely with the One-Time Pad encryption, but as shown by Shannon [38] this basically requires the key to be of equal length as the message. If, on the other hand, one tries to securely encrypt messages which are larger than the key, then this immediately implies the existence of one-way functions, as formally shown by Impagliazzo and Luby [26]. In this paper, Impagliazzo and Luby also show further primitives to imply one-way functions, like bit commitments, (private-key) identification, and coin-flipping over phone.

It should be mentioned that all these implications are constructive in the sense that one can build a concrete one-way function f given the primitive in question, even given the primitive as a black-box only. For instance, for a semantically-secure symmetric encryption scheme Enc which allows to encrypt messages of twice the length as the key, the one-way function is given by $f(k, m) = \text{Enc}(k, m) \| m$. Furthermore, the reduction from the one-wayness to the security of the underlying primitive treats both the adversary and the primitive as black-boxes, such that the overall constructions are also called fully black-box [33].

The implications also mean that most cryptographic primitives are not known to exist for sure. That is, the existence of (cryptographic) one-way functions implies (worst-case) one-way functions and thus $\mathcal{P} \neq \mathcal{NP}$. In other words, $\mathcal{P} \neq \mathcal{NP}$ is necessary for numerous cryptographic tasks. It is, however, currently not known if it is also sufficient [1,3].

2.2   One-Way Functions Are Sufficient for Minicrypt

In a sense, one-way functions appear to be "very low" in the hierarchy of assumptions. They are not only necessary for most cryptographic tasks, but they also suffice to build a lot of cryptographic primitives. In a series of papers it has been shown that one-way functions imply pseudorandom generators [22], that such pseudorandom generators imply pseudorandom functions [20], and that pseudorandom functions imply pseudorandom permutations [28]. Once one has the powerful pseudorandom functions then other primitives like message authentication codes (MACs), private-key encryption, and private-key identification are derived easily. All these constructions and reductions are of the fully black-box type.

Impagliazzo [25] calls the world in which we have cryptographic one-way functions, but no public-key cryptography, "Minicrypt"; as opposed to "Cryptomania" in which we have all the power of public-key encryption. In Minicrypt, we can still do a remarkably number of cryptographic tasks like sending messages securely to parties which we have met before; only secure communication with strangers in impossible then. Somewhat unexpected, another very interesting primitive which can also be built from one-way functions and thus lies in Minicrypt, are secure digital signature schemes. This has been shown in a sequence of papers [30,34], again in the fully black-box sense. The noteworthy property here is that, structurally, digital signatures are of course related to public-key primitives; existentially, though, they belong to the family of symmetric-key primitives.

3   Black-Box Separations

In this section we review the three main techniques for black-box separations ans the questions which primitives lie (presumably) outside of Minicrypt.

3.1   Relativizing Reductions: Separating Key Agreement from One-Way Functions

In their seminal paper, Impagliazzo and Rudich [27] show that one cannot base (even weakly) secure key agreement on one-way functions. More precisely, they first use a (random) permutation oracle to implement a one-way permutation. This oracle can later be derandomized and one "good" oracle Π can be found by standard counting arguments and the Borel-Cantelli lemma (see [27] for details). In the next step they show that relative to the random permutation oracle, no key agreement protocol can be secure. (A simplified version of this fact for the case of perfect completeness can be found in [6].) Put differently, there cannot exist *relativizing* constructions of key agreement from one-way permutations, i.e., where the security of the construction remains intact in the presence of an arbitrary oracle.

As pointed out by [27,39,33] relativing reductions where the relativizing oracle allows for an embedding of an $\mathcal{NP}$-complete oracle —or more generally, any $\mathcal{PSPACE}$-complete oracle, such that any "standard" cryptography besides the one-way permutation can be broken— can be shown to rule out so-called $\forall\exists$ semi-black-box reductions [33]. Roughly, these are efficient reductions which turn efficient successful adversaries (both with access to the oracle) for one scheme into an adversary for the other one. Since such reductions only use the underlying primitive as a black-box, separations on this level are "somewhat less black-box" than in the case of fully black-box reductions, strengthening the separation result.

Relativizing separations can be found in [27,39,19,14,23]. In particular, Rudich [35] used this technique to separate k-round key agreement from any $(k + 1)$-round key agreement, implying an infinite hierarchy of primitive classes.

3.2 Fully Black-Box Reductions: The Two-Oracle Technique by Hsiao and Reyzin

Since relativizing reductions (with embedding) are equivalent to $\forall \exists$ semi-black-box reductions [33] showing impossibility results is much more challenging than for the fully black-box case. Hence, Hsiao and Reyzin [24] introduced the idea of moving from relativizing reductions to fully black-box reductions, and use a so-called two-oracle technique. The idea is roughly to have an oracle Ω which is used to implement the primitive Q we would like to have, say, a one-way function or permutation. The second oracle Π is used to break the primitive P which we are trying to build out of the one given through Ω. For a separation it then suffices to show that one can implement Q from Ω (ignoring Π), such that that for all algorithms $\mathcal{R}$ there exists some adversary $\mathcal{A}$ such that $\mathcal{A}^{\Pi}$ breaks P, but $\mathcal{R}^{\mathcal{A}^{\Pi,\Omega},\Omega}$ cannot break Q. Note that in the latter case $\mathcal{R}$ only has access to Π through the black-box access to $\mathcal{A}$, although most proofs later use a universal $\mathcal{A}$ which basically merely runs Π, such that this essentially boils down to show that $\mathcal{R}^{\Pi,\Omega}$ should not be able to break Q.

Because the two-oracle technique allows for easier separations it became quite popular and has been applied more often in recent papers. Examples include [24,10,4,15,13].

3.3 The Meta-reduction Technique

Recently, a new kind of black-box separation technique has gained significant attention, called *meta-reductions* [5].[1] Roughly, a meta-reduction is a "reduction against the reduction". The situation is depicted in Figure 1: The reduction $\mathcal{R}$ is given black-box access to an adversary $\mathcal{A}$, which supposedly attacks a scheme $\mathcal{S}$, but where $\mathcal{S}$ is now simulated by the reduction. The reduction itself is supposed to break a so-called cryptographic game C with the help of $\mathcal{A}$. This game usually models any falsifiable assumption [29], including assumptions like computing discrete logarithms or inverting the RSA function. We note that, in order to avoid trivial reductions like to the security of the scheme itself, the game C often consists of less rounds than the interactive phase of the scheme.

The meta-reduction now simulates the adversarial part in order to turn $\mathcal{R}$ in a black-box manner into an efficient and successful algorithm $\mathcal{M}^{\mathcal{R}}$ against C directly, without reference to an allegedly successful adversary $\mathcal{A}$. Note that this clearly requires the existence of a successful adversary $\mathcal{A}$ against $\mathcal{S}$ in the first place, or else the reduction $\mathcal{R}$ would not need to break C at all. Usually, one can build such an (inefficient) adversary by exhaustive search and then make sure

---

[1] Albeit the idea appears in [5] it seems as if the term meta-reduction has only been mentioned later in [7] and [31].

that $\mathcal{M}$ replaces $\mathcal{A}$ efficiently. Similarly to the case of zero-knowledge, where the efficient simulator can mimic the behavior of the all-powerful prover, the meta-reduction's advantage over the adversary here is that it can rewind the reduction (or potentially take advantage of its code or behavior). Overall, if the meta-reduction is sufficiently close to $\mathcal{A}$ from $\mathcal{R}$'s perspective, it follows that the probability for $\mathcal{M}^{\mathcal{R}}$ breaking C is close to the one of $\mathcal{R}^{\mathcal{A}}$.

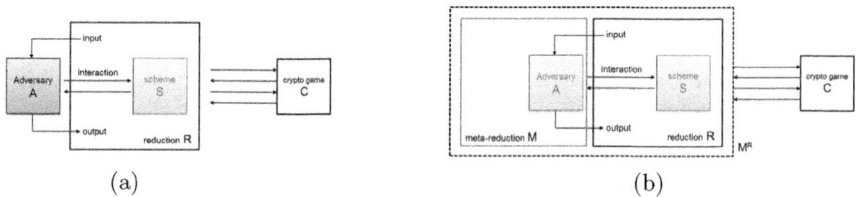

(a)   (b)

Fig. 1. (a) shows the reduction $\mathcal{R}$ turning a successful adversary $\mathcal{A}$ against scheme $\mathcal{S}$ into a successful attacker $\mathcal{R}^{\mathcal{A}}$ against a cryptographic game C, by simulating the scheme $\mathcal{S}$; (b) shows the meta-reduction $\mathcal{M}$ simulating the adversary $\mathcal{A}$ and turning $\mathcal{R}$ into a successful algorithm $\mathcal{M}^{\mathcal{R}}$ against C directly

The advantage of meta-reductions over the other separation types is that this technique usually only makes black-box use of the adversary, but works with arbitrary primitives. The technique therefore applies to cases where one, say, seeks to show that certain constructions cannot be based on the RSA assumption. As such, this separation technique is in between the cases of fully black-box reductions and of ($\forall\exists$)semi-black-box reductions. On the other hand, it seems that the method is mainly suitable for interactive protocols in which the scheme can be queried first, before the adversary is required to produce an output. Examples include unforgeability of signature schemes under chosen-message attacks or chosen-ciphertext security for encryption schemes.

In summary, the meta-reduction technique usually consist of the following three steps:

1. Design an all-powerful adversary $\mathcal{A}$ which breaks the scheme.
   For example, in the signature case let $\mathcal{A}$ first compute a secret key sk^* from pk, then let it query the signature oracle to collect signatures (note that this step is only necessary to build the meta-reduction), and finally let $\mathcal{A}$ compute a forgery.
2. Replace the (inefficient) adversary by the efficient meta-reduction.
   This is usually done by carefully rewinding the reduction at appropriate places in the query phase. To prevent the reduction from making further queries the rewinding is usually done when the reduction does not make queries to the game C. This may also require further conditions on the reduction to prevent the nested-rewinding problem (the reduction seeking to reset the adversary while the meta-reduction aims to reset the reduction). This problem may yield an exponential blow-up and is known from the area of zero-knowledge [11].

3. Show that the meta-reduction's behavior is sufficiently close to the one of the all-powerful adversary.

   This step is usually the most challenging step as the meta-reduction's output is somewhat closer entangled with the reduction's state than the adversary's behavior, due to the rewinding.

With these steps it follows that $\mathcal{M}^{\mathcal{R}}$ breaks the game C with probability close to the reduction $\mathcal{R}^{\mathcal{A}}$ (given adversary $\mathcal{A}$).

Meta-reductions have been successfully applied in a number of cases since [5], such as [8,7,31,16,32,18,9,37]. It is clear that the exact use of meta-reductions differ, e.g., some results also impose restrictions on the primitives and work for black-box groups only.

4   Non-black-Box Constructions

In this section we mention some non-black-box constructions resp. reductions. Both examples stem form the area of zero-knowledge proofs but the issue is in principle not restricted to this area.

4.1   Karp Reductions Are Non-black-Box

The first examples touches the issue of Karp reductions between problems. Recall that a Karp reduction from one language A to another language B is a deterministic polynomial-time algorithm k such that $x \in A \iff \mathsf{k}(x) \in B$. If such an algorithm exist then we write $A \leq_p B$, intuitively meaning that the problem B is at least as hard as A (in the sense that any decision algorithm for B would immediately yield a decider for A). Cook and Levin have shown that the satisfiability is complete for $\mathcal{NP}$, i.e., any other problem $A \in \mathcal{NP}$ reduces to the satisfiability problem. This reduction, however, makes use of the (Turing machine) code of the algorithm M_A deciding A by representing its computation state as a boolean formula. In other words, the Karp reduction of A to the satisfiability problem requires access to the code for deciding A.

The code-dependence is exactly where the black-box property for cryptographic purposes may break down. Given an arbitrary one-way function f and, say, proving in zero-knowledge that one knows a pre-image to some y under f, one would reduce this problem to some $\mathcal{NP}$-complete language L for which such a proof is known via a Karp reduction, and to run the zero-knowledge protocol for L.[2] However, the reduction from f to L would then require knowledge of the code of f and does not apply to black-box constructions for f. Note that it may still be possible to find direct zero-knowledge proofs for specific one-way functions, like the Schnorr proof for discrete logarithms [36], or find

---

[2] Speaking of zero-knowledge proofs of *knowledge* in our example, one would need to ensure that the Karp reduction is such that a witness extracted from the proof for L also allows to recover a pre-image for f; this is usually the case and such reductions are sometimes called Levin reductions.

other alternatives to the Karp reduction to L. We finally note that Brakerski et al. [6] recently introduced special zero-knowledge oracles to argue about separations in the presence of such proofs.

4.2 Barak's Non-black-Box Zero-Knowledge Proofs

The second example is based on a non-black-box use of the adversary. Barak [2] designs a zero-knowledge proof based on *non-black-box* use of the adversary which overcomes previous black-box impossibility results. Neglecting many technical subtleties, the protocol to prove $x \in L$ is as follows. The protocol first runs an initialization phase whose only purpose is to give the zero-knowledge simulator some freedom. In this phase, the prover commits to the all-zero string π and the verifier send a random string r. Now the prover and the verifier engage in a witness-indistinguishable protocol [12] that $x \in L$ or that the commitment π describes a program that predicts the verifier's string r.

A malicious prover cannot take advantage of the initialization phase — predicting r remains infeasible— and thus really needs to prove $x \in L$ in the second step. A zero-knowledge simulator against a malicious verifier, on the other hand, can simply use the non-black-box access to the verifier's code and commit to the verifier's program on behalf of the prover. By the hiding property of the commitment scheme this is indistinguishable from a commitment to zeros. It is clear that this code π predicts r correctly, such that the simulator can use π as the witness in the second part of the proof to faithfully simulate these steps, even without knowing a witness to $x \in L$ or by using the usual rewinding techniques. The zero-knowledge property follows from the hiding of the commitment and the witness indistinguishability of the second part.

5 Conclusion

Black-box separations (of any kind) are today thought of as good indications that one cannot derive one primitive out of the other. But they can also been viewed as a shortcoming of the proof technique itself. A few non-black-box constructions do exist, and one option to circumvent black-box separations may be to use more non-black-box techniques. For example, Harnik and Naor [21] showed that, using a complexity-theoretic assumption, one can build (in a non-black-box way) collision-resistant hash functions out of one-way functions, allowing to bypass Simon's black-box separation result for this case [39]. Unfortunately, Fortnow and Santhanam [17] later showed that the assumption is unlikely to hold, or else the polynomial hierarchy collapses. Still, it remains open to explore the limitations of black-box separations via non-black-box techniques, or to strengthen the separation results along the line of Brakerski et al. [6].

Acknowledgments. I would like to thank Paul Baecher and Christina Brzuska for discussions about black-box reductions, and the Africacrypt program committee and its chair, Serge Vaudenay, for inviting me to present the topic.

References

1. Akavia, A., Goldreich, O., Goldwasser, S., Moshkovitz, D.: On basing one-way functions on NP-hardness. In: Kleinberg, J.M. (ed.) 38th ACM STOC, May 21-23, pp. 701–710. ACM Press, Seattle (2006)
2. Barak, B.: How to go beyond the black-box simulation barrier. In: 42nd FOCS, October 14-17, pp. 106–115. IEEE Computer Society Press, Las Vegas (2001)
3. Bogdanov, A., Trevisan, L.: On worst-case to average-case reductions for np problems. SIAM J. Comput. 36(4), 1119–1159 (2006)
4. Boldyreva, A., Cash, D., Fischlin, M., Warinschi, B.: Foundations of Non-malleable Hash and One-Way Functions. In: Matsui, M. (ed.) ASIACRYPT 2009. LNCS, vol. 5912, pp. 524–541. Springer, Heidelberg (2009)
5. Boneh, D., Venkatesan, R.: Breaking RSA May Not Be Equivalent to Factoring. In: Nyberg, K. (ed.) EUROCRYPT 1998. LNCS, vol. 1403, pp. 59–71. Springer, Heidelberg (1998)
6. Brakerski, Z., Katz, J., Segev, G., Yerukhimovich, A.: Limits on the Power of Zero-Knowledge Proofs in Cryptographic Constructions. In: Ishai, Y. (ed.) TCC 2011. LNCS, vol. 6597, pp. 559–578. Springer, Heidelberg (2011)
7. Brown, D.R.L.: Breaking rsa may be as difficult as factoring. IACR Cryptology ePrint Archive (2005), http://eprint.iacr.org/2005/380
8. Coron, J.-S.: Security Proof for Partial-Domain Hash Signature Schemes. In: Yung, M. (ed.) CRYPTO 2002. LNCS, vol. 2442, pp. 613–626. Springer, Heidelberg (2002)
9. Dodis, Y., Haitner, I., Tentes, A.: On the Instantiability of Hash-and-Sign RSA Signatures. In: Cramer, R. (ed.) TCC 2012. LNCS, vol. 7194, pp. 112–132. Springer, Heidelberg (2012)
10. Dodis, Y., Oliveira, R., Pietrzak, K.: On the Generic Insecurity of the Full Domain Hash. In: Shoup, V. (ed.) CRYPTO 2005. LNCS, vol. 3621, pp. 449–466. Springer, Heidelberg (2005)
11. Dwork, C., Naor, M., Sahai, A.: Concurrent zero-knowledge. J. ACM 51(6), 851–898 (2004)
12. Feige, U., Shamir, A.: Witness indistinguishable and witness hiding protocols. In: STOC, pp. 416–426. ACM (1990)
13. Fiore, D., Schröder, D.: Uniqueness Is a Different Story: Impossibility of Verifiable Random Functions from Trapdoor Permutations. In: Cramer, R. (ed.) TCC 2012. LNCS, vol. 7194, pp. 636–653. Springer, Heidelberg (2012)
14. Fischlin, M.: On the Impossibility of Constructing Non-interactive Statistically-Secret Protocols from Any Trapdoor One-Way Function. In: Preneel, B. (ed.) CT-RSA 2002. LNCS, vol. 2271, pp. 79–95. Springer, Heidelberg (2002)
15. Fischlin, M., Lehmann, A., Ristenpart, T., Shrimpton, T., Stam, M., Tessaro, S.: Random Oracles with(out) Programmability. In: Abe, M. (ed.) ASIACRYPT 2010. LNCS, vol. 6477, pp. 303–320. Springer, Heidelberg (2010)
16. Fischlin, M., Schröder, D.: On the Impossibility of Three-Move Blind Signature Schemes. In: Gilbert, H. (ed.) EUROCRYPT 2010. LNCS, vol. 6110, pp. 197–215. Springer, Heidelberg (2010)

17. Fortnow, L., Santhanam, R.: Infeasibility of instance compression and succinct PCPs for NP. In: Ladner, R.E., Dwork, C. (eds.) 40th ACM STOC, May 17-20, pp. 133–142. ACM Press, Victoria (2008)

18. Gentry, C., Wichs, D.: Separating succinct non-interactive arguments from all falsifiable assumptions. In: Fortnow, L., Vadhan, S.P. (eds.) 43rd ACM STOC, June 6-8, pp. 99–108. ACM Press, San Jose (2011)

19. Gertner, Y., Kannan, S., Malkin, T., Reingold, O., Viswanathan, M.: The relationship between public key encryption and oblivious transfer. In: 41st FOCS, November 12-14, pp. 325–335. IEEE Computer Society Press, Redondo Beach (2000)

20. Goldreich, O., Goldwasser, S., Micali, S.: How to construct random functions. Journal of the ACM 33, 792–807 (1986)

21. Harnik, D., Naor, M.: On the compressibility of NP instances and cryptographic applications. In: 47th FOCS, October 21-24, pp. 719–728. IEEE Computer Society Press, Berkeley (2006)

22. Håstad, J., Impagliazzo, R., Levin, L.A., Luby, M.: A pseudorandom generator from any one-way function. SIAM Journal on Computing 28(4), 1364–1396 (1999)

23. Hofheinz, D.: Possibility and impossibility results for selective decommitments. Journal of Cryptology 24(3), 470–516 (2011)

24. Hsiao, C.-Y., Reyzin, L.: Finding Collisions on a Public Road, or Do Secure Hash Functions Need Secret Coins? In: Franklin, M. (ed.) CRYPTO 2004. LNCS, vol. 3152, pp. 92–105. Springer, Heidelberg (2004)

25. Impagliazzo, R.: A personal view of average-case complexity. In: Structure in Complexity Theory Conference, pp. 134–147 (1995)

26. Impagliazzo, R., Luby, M.: One-way functions are essential for complexity-based cryptography. In: 30th FOCS, October 30-November 1, pp. 230–235. IEEE Computer Society Press, Research Triangle Park (1989)

27. Impagliazzo, R., Rudich, S.: Limits on the provable consequences of one-way permutations. In: 21st ACM STOC, May 15-17, pp. 44–61. ACM Press, Seattle (1989)

28. Luby, M., Rackoff, C.: How to construct pseudorandom permutations from pseudorandom functions. SIAM Journal on Computing 17(2) (1988)

29. Naor, M.: On Cryptographic Assumptions and Challenges. In: Boneh, D. (ed.) CRYPTO 2003. LNCS, vol. 2729, pp. 96–109. Springer, Heidelberg (2003)

30. Naor, M., Yung, M.: Universal one-way hash functions and their cryptographic applications. In: 21st ACM STOC, May 15-17, pp. 33–43. ACM Press, Seattle (1989)

31. Paillier, P., Vergnaud, D.: Discrete-Log-Based Signatures May Not Be Equivalent to Discrete Log. In: Roy, B. (ed.) ASIACRYPT 2005. LNCS, vol. 3788, pp. 1–20. Springer, Heidelberg (2005)

32. Pass, R.: Limits of provable security from standard assumptions. In: Fortnow, L., Vadhan, S.P. (eds.) 43rd ACM STOC, June 6-8, pp. 109–118. ACM Press, San Jose (2011)

33. Reingold, O., Trevisan, L., Vadhan, S.P.: Notions of Reducibility between Cryptographic Primitives. In: Naor, M. (ed.) TCC 2004. LNCS, vol. 2951, pp. 1–20. Springer, Heidelberg (2004)

34. Rompel, J.: One-way functions are necessary and sufficient for secure signatures. In: 22nd ACM STOC, May 14-16, pp. 387–394. ACM Press, Baltimore (1990)

35. Rudich, S.: The Use of Interaction in Public Cryptosystems (Extended Abstract). In: Feigenbaum, J. (ed.) CRYPTO 1991. LNCS, vol. 576, pp. 242–251. Springer, Heidelberg (1992)

36. Schnorr, C.P.: Efficient signature generation by smart cards. Journal of Cryptology 4(3), 161–174 (1991)

37. Seurin, Y.: On the Exact Security of Schnorr-Type Signatures in the Random Oracle Model. In: Pointcheval, D., Johansson, T. (eds.) EUROCRYPT 2012. LNCS, vol. 7237, pp. 554–571. Springer, Heidelberg (2012)
38. Shannon, C.E.: Communication theory of secrecy systems. Bell Systems Technical Journal 28(4), 656–715 (1949)
39. Simon, D.R.: Findings Collisions on a One-Way Street: Can Secure Hash Functions Be Based on General Assumptions? In: Nyberg, K. (ed.) EUROCRYPT 1998. LNCS, vol. 1403, pp. 334–345. Springer, Heidelberg (1998)

Author Index